English Legal System

ENGLISH LEGAL SYSTEM

FOURTH EDITION

Steve Wilson | Helen Rutherford | Tony Storey

Natalie Wortley | Birju Kotecha

OXFORD
UNIVERSITY PRESS

OXFORD
UNIVERSITY PRESS

Great Clarendon Street, Oxford, OX2 6DP,
United Kingdom

Oxford University Press is a department of the University of Oxford. It furthers the University's objective of excellence in research, scholarship, and education by publishing worldwide. Oxford is a registered trade mark of Oxford University Press in the UK and in certain other countries

First Edition 2014
Second Edition 2016
Third Edition 2018

Impression: 1

Published in the United States of America by Oxford University Press
198 Madison Avenue, New York, NY 10016, United States of America

British Library Cataloguing in Publication Data
Data available

Library of Congress Control Number: 2020932233
ISBN 978-0-19-885380-0

Printed in Great Britain by
Bell & Bain Ltd., Glasgow

Preface

The English legal system is arguably the most challenging subject a first-year law student will encounter. A brief survey of a book on the subject reveals that it encompasses the nature of law, the sources of law, the institutions and personnel of the law, and the civil and criminal justice systems. In studying the English legal system you will be expected not only to find and interpret source materials, but to demonstrate an understanding of diverse topics including, for example, judges as law-makers, the role of the jury, access to justice, and the operation of the courts. You must also learn to analyse and evaluate institutions such as Parliament as a law-making body and the function of the courts. The volume and diversity of material to be studied can begin to feel overwhelming, particularly when considered alongside the constant changes being made to many aspects of the English legal system. Do not fear—this book is designed to help you find your way through the mass of material available.

Our aim in writing this book is to help you to focus on the essential points you need to understand to navigate the English legal system. Its purpose is to provide an explanation of essential information concerning the English legal system and then to guide you to the significant debates which underpin the system. The text is not intended to be an exhaustive account of the law; rather, it is intended to introduce important concepts, principles, themes, and issues, and to suggest further sources for you to explore. Primary sources of information (i.e. legislation and case law) are highlighted in the text and you are encouraged to consult the original sources to develop your skills in research and interpretation. It is essential to keep abreast of fast-moving developments as the English legal system enters a period of some uncertainty and change, particularly in relation to our relationship with the European Union. This fourth edition of the book includes important changes that have been made to the law but also highlights areas of likely change in the future The law has been stated as it currently stands but an indication is also given of laws yet to come into force.

The features in the book aid a structured approach to the study of the English legal system. Each chapter begins with a Talking Point, which poses some questions for you to consider at the outset and to keep in mind as you read further. The aims of chapters are clearly signposted at the beginning and the significant points summarised at the end of each chapter. Understanding of material may be tested by Thinking Points in the text and then extended by the Critical Debate features. We have included reading lists to encourage and support you to continue your independent research. The lists outline the significance of the reading identified. The book is complemented by online resources which will be used to inform you of important changes and developments in the law. The online resources include multiple-choice questions at the end of each substantive section, enabling you to test your knowledge and understanding of the content of the chapter.

This book will also aid the development of study skills in this subject area. Unlike substantive areas of law, which tend to be based upon the study of legislation and case law and take, in large part, a problem-based approach, the English Legal System module tends to take an evaluative and discussion-based approach. Chapter 1 gives advice, for example, on how to prepare for tutorials and how to write essays. Sample examination and coursework questions and answers are also to be found at the end of chapters. This feature gives guidance on answer structure, how to choose relevant content, and how to relate such material to the requirements of the question.

The authors would like to acknowledge the work done on earlier incarnations of this book by Michael Stockdale, Rebecca Mitchell, and Steve Wilson. Thanks also go to the following for their much appreciated comments and advice: Nicola Kotecha, Richard Glancey, Nicola Hyam, Chris Rogers, and Leslie Rutherford. Thanks also go to the anonymous reviewers, both academics and students, for their helpful and insightful comments and encouraging words. Finally, our thanks go to Carlotta Fanton for her help, guidance, and patience in managing the project and keeping us on track.

New to the edition

- Updated talking points
- End-of-section test questions
- Update on reform to legal aid
- Update on plans for reform to legal education and training for lawyers
- European Union (Withdrawal) Act 2018
- Update on the use of stop and search powers by the police
- Changes to the law governing police bail
- Coverage of disclosure issues in criminal cases
- Updates in the case law including *R v Secretary of State for Work and Pensions* [2019] UKSC 52; *Lee v Ashers Baking Company Ltd* [2018] UKSC 49; and *In the Matter of an Application by the Northern Ireland Human Rights Commission for Judicial Review (Northern Ireland)* [2018] UKSC 27.

Guide to the features in *English Legal System*

Learning objectives

By the end of this chapter you should be able to:

- outline the characteristics of law;
- identify the main sources of law and explain the different processes of law-making;
- understand the various meanings of the term common law;

Learning objectives

Each chapter begins with a bulleted outline of the main concepts and ideas you will encounter. These provide a helpful signpost to what you can expect to learn from the chapter.

Talking point

An issue often reported in the newspapers is that of parents taking their c
of school during term-time to go on holiday. In *Isle of Wight Council v*
UKSC 28, Mr Platt had sought permission from the head-teacher to take h
out of school during term time. His request was refused. Despite the refus
took his daughter out of school and went on holiday, with the result that h
missed seven school days. In consequence, the local authority issued a fi

Talking points

Each chapter continues with an outline of a particularly interesting or controversial matter in the subject to capture your interest and to provide a real-world context for the overview which follows.

Thinking point
The right to a jury trial

Trial in the Crown Court is more time-consuming and costly than trial in the magistrates' co
However, a defendant is entitled to be tried by a jury at the Crown Court. To what extent d
think that offences should be more readily tried at the magistrates' court (or that more offe
should be reclassified as summary only)? Would such an approach be defensible and to wl
extent would the interference with the defendant's right to be tried by a jury be justified?

Thinking points

Throughout each chapter there are numerous thinking points which ask you to pause and consider questions around whether the legal system is effective and where reforms are proposed or needed.

Critical debate

The concept of the rule of law is frequently mentioned by parliamentarians, lawyers, and
political commentators. It is a difficult concept to define precisely. The late Tom Bingham
(a former Lord Chief Justice), in his book *The Rule of Law*, provided the following descripti

> [A]ll persons and authorities within the state, whether public or private, should be bou
> by and entitled to the benefits of laws publicly made, taking effect (generally) in the fut
> and publicly administered in the courts.

One of the principles which is to be derived from this description is, in the words of
Bingham, that 'the law must be accessible and so far as possible intelligible, clear and

Critical debates

Each chapter has its own critical debate, where you are asked to consider a controversial or thought-provoking topic and encouraged to develop your own views on it.

A court of first instance A case will commence in a court of first instance (that is, a court of trial). This jurisdiction is also termed original jurisdiction. Decisions of courts may be challenged on appeal and erroneous decisions corrected. Courts hearing appeals are said to have appellate jurisdiction.

jurisdiction, for example, in terms of money or supervisory jurisdiction over the inferior court appeals from decisions in those lower courts. In Acts 1873–1875, the Senior Courts Act 1981, anc 2005 all variously and rather confusingly confirm roles and powers of the various courts. Generally UK are understood to be the Supreme Court (pr of the House of Lords), the Court of Appeal, High and Employment Appeal Tribunal; the inferior cou the County Court and other ***first instance*** tribuna

Definitions

Key terms are clearly and concisely explained in definition boxes.

The Parliament Act procedure allows for a bill to be p the monarch without the consent of the House of Lo allowing for a bill to be passed by the House of Lords of the House of Commons.

Key points

Key points are highlighted to draw your attention to the essential matters in each chapter.

See further 8.1.1, 'The Lord Chancellor'.

and there was therefore a risk that power could be abu

The office of the Lord Chancellor was altered by th 2005. The creation of the Judicial Appointments Comm curtailed the Lord Chancellor's role in relation to the Lord Chancellor no longer acts as speaker for the Ho Justice is now the Head of the Judiciary and the Lord C a judge.

The holder of the office of Lord Chancellor is also (and oversees the Ministry of Justice). One of their func defend and maintain the independence of the courts. the Lord Chancellor be a lawyer and several previous o

Cross-references

Frequent cross-referencing between chapters highlights where topics overlap.

Summary

- Defining law is problematic but it is important to recognise the vari law.
- The term 'common law' has various meanings which depend upon which the term is used.
- The role of the judges is to interpret statutes and to develop the cor through the rules of judicial precedent.
- Law made by Parliament, on the one hand, and by judges, on the ot

Chapter summaries

The central points and concepts covered are distilled into a summary at the end of each chapter.

Questions

1 Explain public legislation, private legislation, and hybrid legislation.
2 Explain the differences between government bills and private mem
3 What are the conditions that must be satisfied before a public bill money bill) can be passed under the terms of the Parliament Act pr
4 Explain the differences between the affirmative laying procedure a tive laying procedure for statutory instruments.
5 Give three justifications for the existence of secondary legislation.

End-of-chapter questions

The self-test questions at the end of each chapter encourage you to test your understanding of the topic as a whole, helping to develop your analytical skills.

 Sample question and outline answer

Question

The changes to the composition of the House of Lords that have take the past sixty years mean that the procedure for passing legislation u Parliament Act 1911 (as amended) is no longer justified. Explain the le cedure under the Parliament Act 1911 (as amended) and consider wh justified in the twenty-first century.

Sample questions and outline answers

At the end of each chapter is a sample question which is accompanied by an outline answer. This provides an example of how this topic might be assessed and gives you an insight into how to approach your answer using the information provided in the chapter you have just read.

 Further reading

- ***Brazier, R.*** *'Royal Assent to Legislation'* (2013) 129 LQR 184

  Provides 'a comprehensive analysis of the mechanics of royal assent to leg United Kingdom'.
- ***Lord Burns***, *'Report of the Lord Speaker's Committee on the Size of t* **.parliament.uk/documents/lords-committees/size-of-house/si: report.pdf**
- ***Gover, D.*** and ***Kenny, M.*** *'Finding the Good in EVEL: An Evaluation c*

Further reading

Selected further reading is included at the end of each chapter to provide a reliable platform for further study.

 Example

The following is an example of a bill becoming an Act: the Racial and Religious Hatred Act

The Racial and Religious Hatred Bill, a government bill, was designed to extend the rac hatred offences in the Public Order Act 1986 to cover stirring up hatred against persor religious grounds. There was a variety of offences under the 1986 Act, each offence re ing that words, behaviour, written material, recordings, or programmes must be threa ing, abusive, or insulting and intended or likely to stir up *racial hatred*. Under the new b these offences would be amended so that each would apply to the stirring up of either *or religious* hatred, 'religious hatred' being defined as hatred against a group of person

Examples

Everyday examples of the practical application of systems and procedures are given in each chapter.

This book's online resources

www.oup.com/he/wilson-rutherford4e

Self-test questions

All chapters are accompanied by automatically marked self-test questions to check understanding of key sections and monitor progress.

End-of-chapter questions

All chapters are accompanied by end-of-chapter, multiple-choice questions to test the application of knowledge.

Videos

Additional video material brings topics to life.

Web links

A library of web links is available to aid reading around the topics.

Further guidance

A guide to reading cases and additional advice on legal research are available to help build these key legal skills.

Outline contents

Detailed contents

2 An overview of the English legal system

3 Legislation and the law-making process

4 The interpretation of statutes

7 Human rights in the United Kingdom

8 The judiciary

10 The jury

13 The criminal process: pre-trial and trial

14 Sentencing

15 The civil process

16 Alternative dispute resolution

Table of cases

Table of legislation

Table of statutes

Table of European legislation

Treaties

Directives

Regulations

Table of International Conventions

Table of statutory instruments

Chapter 1

Studying the English legal system

Talking point

The foreword to a government report entitled *When Laws Become Too Complex* states:

> The volume of legislation, its piecemeal structure, its level of detail and frequent amendments, and the interaction with common law and European law, mean that even professional users can find law complex, hard to understand and difficult to comply with.

A legal system must consist of laws that are clear and accessible to everyone and not just lawyers. Without clarity and accessibility, citizens will not know the extent of their rights and duties. This is important because rights need to be protected and duties (i.e. obligations) need to be fulfilled. However, there can often be disputes about whether those rights have been properly protected or whether those duties have been met. These might arise because the law is not clear and there is disagreement about how the law should apply. In the English legal system, it is the courts that help to resolve disputes. The courts are essential because they determine what the law is and then apply the law in order to resolve the dispute.

The ambition to have a clear and accessible legal system can be a little difficult to achieve in practice. As you will no doubt discover, the law can be quite complicated and unpredictable but thankfully, this book will help you take the first steps towards making sense of the English legal system. The book will provide you with an essential foundation that will support your learning of other areas of law too. Many fundamental questions are addressed here. To offer only a sample, consider any views you may already have on the following questions.

- What is law?
- How is law made and how can it be changed or developed?
- How are the courts organised and how are decisions made by judges in those courts?
- What are the roles and responsibilities of different types of judges and lawyers?
- What is the legal process that takes place when an individual is arrested by the police or an individual wants to sue another person for compensation?

This book will help you answer these questions and many more too. In the process, we hope the book will stimulate your curiosity and ultimately leave you considerably more informed about the English legal system.

Introduction

The subject 'English Legal System' has always occupied an awkward position on undergraduate degree courses. The content of a module entitled 'English Legal System' depends very much upon your university course. Indeed, the course might not even be referred to by that name, instead being called 'Legal Process', 'Legal Institutions', or 'Legal System and Method'. The content of syllabuses will be varied, and different approaches may be taken. On one level, there is a focus on the making of law and on institutions such as Parliament or the Judiciary; on another level, there is attention paid to the court process, how it is accessed, and final outcomes such as sentencing or other forms of dispute resolution.

One feature which is common to the teaching of the English Legal System, however, is that it is almost always, and for good reason, taught at a very early stage. Students need to know about the operation of laws and the legal system as a whole to make sense of the substantive subjects, such as Criminal Law, Contract, and Tort. A first-year student has, therefore, the initial task of learning about the personnel, principles, and institutions of the English legal system. Once this knowledge has been acquired, you can then undertake the more challenging task of criticising and evaluating the legal system.

See 2.4 'Criminal law and civil law—terminology, differences, and themes'.

You will find that studying the English legal system is dynamic; it is subject to considerable change and development. For example, the passing of the Legal Aid, Sentencing and Punishment of Offenders Act 2012 represented a major change to the funding of civil legal services, the consequences of which will take a number of years to be fully evaluated. The criminal justice system is notoriously dynamic: the past decade has seen Parliament pass a significant amount of legislation that concerns crime, policing, and justice matters, with examples including the Anti-social Behaviour, Crime and Policing Act 2014, the Criminal Justice and Courts Act 2015, and the Serious Crime Act 2015. Going back a little further, there were some fundamental changes to the English legal system brought about by the Constitutional Reform Act 2005, which saw the introduction of the Supreme Court in 2009 as a replacement for the Appellate Committee of the House of Lords, and by the Tribunals, Courts and Enforcement Act 2007, which established a new simplified structure for tribunals. It is important to be aware of the fast-moving changes and developments to the English legal system and the reasons why such changes are debated and contemplated. We would advise you to stay ahead of the debate, keep up to date with government policy on the law and legal system, and frequently monitor developments in Parliament. There are various reliable websites you can use but we would recommend reading a quality daily newspaper. In addition, there are various popular podcasts on the law such as BBC Radio 4's 'Law in Action' and 'Unreliable Evidence'.

Critical debate

The pace of technological change and the introduction of advanced communication tools, particularly in the last thirty years, have raised the possibility of improving the use of online technology in the legal system. The legal system has often been criticised for sticking too closely to tradition, and being overly reliant on in-person hearings and paper procedures. The system is frequently said to be too slow and too expensive, resulting in people being denied access to justice. The pace of change has been slow, but in the past five years, the use of online processes has slowly become established. These include being allowed to plead guilty online to minor traffic offences, for example, or to appeal social security payments that have been refused, to enable one to seek a divorce, and even to apply for probate so that you can manage a deceased person's estate.

Her Majesty's Courts and Tribunals Service (HMCTS) is currently working on a range of ambitious reforms to develop and improve the use of IT systems. These are due to be implemented over the next three to five years. The aim of the reforms is to deliver justice more efficiently and effectively in both civil claims and criminal prosecutions. One key reform that has attracted attention has been the opportunity to determine cases online, including the use of 'virtual hearings' that will rely on telephone and video conferencing. One such proposal along these lines is online dispute resolution (ODR), so that, for example, cases involving low-value claims (for compensation) would be decided online rather than being dealt with in a courtroom. Such a process would involve an online submission portal where documents and evidence could be submitted, an evaluation and facilitation service that would help to evaluate and resolve the case at the earliest possible stage, and, if that should fail, an 'online judge' to determine the dispute. The use of information technology is not without its dangers, with some pointing out that it will not be transparent and that ultimately it might not offer the proper quality of justice required, instead being justice 'on the cheap'. However the reforms unfold, there is no doubt that the English legal system will be going through a dynamic period of modernisation and reform over the next ten years.

What do you think the role of information technology should be in the legal system? What are the advantages and disadvantages of online dispute resolution? Do you think there should be limits to online dispute resolution in civil and/or criminal cases?

For a selection of reading see the following;

1. The reports of the Online Dispute Resolution Advisory Group of the Civil Justice Council at **www.judiciary.gov.uk/reviews/online-dispute-resolution**.
2. Joshua Rozenberg QC, *The Online Court: will IT work?* at **https://long-reads.thelegaleducationfoundation.org/**.
3. Public Law Project Research Paper, *The Digitalisation of Tribunals: what we know and what we need to know* at **https://publiclawproject.org.uk/wp-content/uploads/2018/04/The-Digitalisation-of-Tribunals-for-website.pdf**.

1.1 Studying law in higher education

Many of you will have studied A-Levels or other equivalent qualifications at colleges and sixth forms before arriving at university. The jump to degree or Higher Education study may not be that obvious but there are very important differences.

The first important point is that at degree level the emphasis is placed upon the process of study. It is as much about *how* you learn as it is about *what* you learn. What this refers to is the process of independent thinking and *research*, and this includes locating and reading source materials with precision and skill. Your previous studies may have consisted of a teacher-led collection of information and its interpretation. However, once at university the emphasis is placed upon *you* to become, eventually, an active, critical, and independent learner. After all, once you are in the workplace, the answers will rarely be given to you. At university, one of the aims is to enable you to discover the answer yourself and for you to eventually come to informed views and judgments. This will not happen overnight, but over the course of the degree you will become better at acquiring knowledge, distilling the most essential points, and using this for particular academic purposes. You will eventually become self-sufficient. Thus, some of your lectures may be used to direct you towards particular source materials. Alternatively, the lecturer may only focus on a particular issue, assuming that you will explore the background information for yourself when you leave the lecture theatre. This is the reason why students are often said to be *reading* a subject at university, be it History, Economics, or Law. This describes the university's expectation that students will, under the direction of their lecturers and tutors, read independently. This reading will include the essential sources and the necessary background research to help students fully understand the law, how it applies, and its consequences.

A second point to appreciate is that the reading will be directed to various sources, but most significantly to the primary sources of law: legislation and judgments of reported cases. This material is the same as that used by judges and lawyers. It is essential in the early days of study that you recognise that there is a hierarchy of materials that you need to be able to find, read, and use. You may previously have worked from worksheets, pre-prepared notes, or textbooks; however throughout your course you will be expected to consult primary legal materials. This is not to say that secondary sources, such as textbooks or journal articles, have no role to play—they do. They are often used as a guide to finding, reading, and understanding the primary sources of law. In particular, those textbooks, and especially journal articles, are very valuable in themselves and can help you to critically comment, analyse, and evaluate the law, allowing you to explore its flaws and weaknesses. Do take the opportunity to attend your induction sessions that focus on legal research. These sessions will help you understand and locate sources, whether they are in hard copy or can be found online, such as those found in legal databases like LexisLibrary or Westlaw.

See 1.2.3, 'Reading' for a discussion of primary and secondary sources.

Studying law requires the use and development of a range of skills. Your teaching staff will help develop and nurture those skills but the real progress will be down to you, the student. Put the necessary work and preparation into your studies and you will ultimately reap the rewards of your labour. You will learn more and develop stronger skills at a faster pace. You should try to get the most out of your lectures, seminars, or tutorials. Contribute to class discussion. Ask questions in class. Don't be afraid to voice opinions, even if you are unsure or afraid you may be corrected. Studying for a degree is often the final educational stage before you enter the world of work. If your lecturers and tutors did most of the research and work for you, you wouldn't be getting the most from your degree. There may be a transitional period at the beginning but you will eventually adjust. Make the most of it, embrace the challenge . . . and don't forget to enjoy it too.

1.2 **Advice on studying the English legal system**

The English legal system is usually a core first-year subject on a law degree. There may be some variation and the material may differ from syllabus to syllabus. For example, some modules on the English legal system may seek to emphasise the operation of law in a political and social context; others may emphasise the law itself and its technical application and interpretation. That said, a typical English Legal System syllabus will broadly cover the following themes:

- **Legal method.** This includes an analysis of the sources of law and how law is created, developed, and applied. Legal method encompasses essential topics such as statutory interpretation and the doctrine of judicial precedent.
- **The institutions of the English legal system.** This will involve an analysis and evaluation of institutions, such as Parliament's role as a law-making body, the government, and the jurisdiction and structure of the courts.
- **The personnel of the law.** This involves a consideration of the roles and responsibilities of some essential persons in the legal system including solicitors, barristers, judges, juries, and the law enforcement agencies such as the police.

The module covers a wide range of topics but it is designed so that you can fully understand how various components, bodies, and 'players' fit into the system. These topics are often the building blocks for your understanding so that you eventually learn how the various jigsaw pieces fit together and ultimately how the law is understood and implemented. Occasionally, the topics in isolation may appear a little 'dry'. However, they are helping you to build critical skills such as 'analysis' when you consider the contested interpretation of words in legislation, or 'evaluation' when you weigh up benefits and limits of trial by jury, or 'justification' when you reason why a judge can avoid being bound by a previous rule when deciding upon a particular case.

1.2.1 Aims and outcomes

It is always useful to know and understand what your English Legal System module is trying to achieve. A small amount of time spent reading the aims and outcomes of the module will give you an insight into what is expected of you by the end of the module. Use the aims and outcomes as a checklist to monitor your development on the module. Also be aware that it is the aims and outcomes that are ultimately tested in the assessment process. Bearing this in mind will aid your preparation for the assessment.

1.2.2 Syllabus

Equally, a perusal of the syllabus will give further guidance. This might be given to you in the form of a lecture and seminar plan and/or in the form of a series of topics. Identifying the syllabus content of the English Legal System module is important so that you can see where the greatest emphasis is being placed. This will also help you to make the best use of secondary sources such as textbooks.

For an explanation of the significance of Explanatory Notes, see 4.4.2.

1.2.3 Reading

You should acquaint yourself with the range and types of materials you will have access to on your course. These materials will be found in the library or online, most frequently through the use of online databases. In terms of what you read, reading this textbook carefully is an excellent starting point but, as with other textbooks, this is not sufficient. Reliance on a textbook alone will not help you to fully develop your understanding of the English legal system.

You will be expected to and should be reading a range of materials. Most importantly, these materials will include **primary sources**: these contain the law itself and are authoritative. The most important examples of primary sources include legislation such as Acts of Parliament and 'case law', i.e. the judgments of reported cases. Reading and applying primary sources is one of the most important skills you will develop on a law course. A popular alternative term for primary sources is 'authorities'. Your reading materials will also include **secondary sources**: these are discussions and opinions of the law. Often they will simply describe the law. Secondary sources include academic textbooks (including this one!), encyclopaedias, reviews, articles, and other commentaries on, or about, the law. These will often be written by authors who will be free to venture an opinion on the law, for example to highlight its weaknesses or limitations. They are secondary because they do not have the same authoritative status as primary sources. However, they are incredibly useful if you want to simply digest the law for background research, or equally, if you want to focus in on a particular legal problem or dilemma. They can often be more accessible than a very long Act of Parliament and will almost always offer an overview of the topic and are an excellent starting point for further research.

Of course, it is impossible to ignore that most students will commence legal research by use of a search engine on the internet. There is a wealth of invaluable information on the internet, with the official websites being particularly useful. These include, for instance, **www.parliament.uk** or **www.lawsociety.org.uk**. There are many other secondary sources of information on the internet (e.g. blogs, summaries, etc.) but a word of warning is needed. Some material on the internet will not have been thoroughly checked, updated, or reviewed. It may even have been written by someone with a very sketchy understanding of the law. Please treat internet sources with considerable caution and undertake all the required checks to determine the authenticity and accuracy of the content. These online sources will generally not reflect the depth and quality of research required at this level of study, especially if you do not use other academic sources too.

To summarise, some of the main materials you will be directed to and will need to be familiar with include;

1. *Legislation*. An invaluable website is **www.legislation.gov.uk**. This site is the official database of all published legislation in its primary form and you can also find supporting materials, such as Explanatory Notes. Otherwise you will find Acts of Parliament on legal databases too (see later in the chapter).
2. *Case Law*. You will want to consider the judgments of the cases that have been reported. These will often explain the factual background of the case, the relevant and applicable law, and how the law applies to those facts. A range of law reports records

the decisions of the courts but you can find cases of the UK Supreme Court on its own excellent website **https://www.supremecourt.uk/**. You may be able to retrieve case reports in hard copy from your library but you will need to become conversant with legal databases such as 'LexisLibrary', 'Westlaw', and 'Lawtel'. Please attend any relevant induction session on these databases because they are probably the most important and efficient research tool you will use throughout your course.

See Chapter 5, 'The doctrine of judicial precedent'.

3. *Journal articles*. Your law library will house a series of journals such as *Law Quarterly Review* (LQR), *Modern Law Review* (MLR), *Cambridge Law Journal* (CLJ), and the *Oxford Journal of Legal Studies* (OJLS). These contain, for example, articles where academics (such as those that are teaching you) critically explore various issues raised by the law, often in some detail. These issues may include the impact of recent legislation or decisions made by the courts or may offer a range of new perspectives on the law. Reading relevant journal articles on particular topics can really develop your understanding and critical thinking skills, as well as demonstrate the depth of your research. This may well boost the mark that your essays or examination answers attract.

Visit the online resources to watch a video on primary and secondary legal sources

1.3 Lectures

On any module, lectures may be used to serve a variety of purposes. The lecture may be used to explain how to undertake analysis of a particular issue or problem; it may concentrate on a small point of law or on a difficult legal topic, or it may be used to give an explanation of trends or themes across the law. It is important for you to determine what it is that the lecturer is seeking to achieve; put another way, you need to be aware of what outcome the lecture is intended to serve. This may be made plain by the lecturer or it may be that this is something you have to deduce for yourself from the content of the lecture and where it fits in the course as a whole. Some students believe that lectures are there solely to provide a set of notes which, when learned, will be the basis for examination success. The lecturer will soon warn you about any such assumptions. No lecturer would seek to provide an exhaustive set of notes that you would merely need to learn and nothing more. The purpose of the lecture is to explain key concepts, ideas, and themes that enable you to understand the fundamentals. It is a starting point and not the end of your effort in fully understanding the law. The lecturer may often direct you to further primary and secondary sources to read. A lecturer may also provoke debate and present different points of view or critical perspectives to help you analyse and evaluate the law. In all, the lecture is intended to inspire further independent effort, learning, research, and reflection.

1.3.1 Note taking

If you are attending a lecture you should be taking notes either on paper or typed on your laptop or tablet. You should actively look for the structure of the lecture, including the key areas to be covered. This might be made clear in the introductory comments made by the lecturer or in PowerPoint slides that are being used, for example in the form of a lecture overview or a set of objectives or outcomes. This structure can then form the skeleton for your notes, which can be usefully organised with subheadings. Under these subheadings, key points and important sources should be written (or typed). These notes are the key starting point for your post-lecture study.

Do not attempt to capture every word uttered by the lecturer. Lecturers will often repeat themselves in summarising what has been explained, or explain the same point in several ways. The main purpose of note taking is to write the *essential* points or principles that are being emphasised and that are necessary for you to follow the logic of the law (as developed in legislation and/or cases), or the train of thought/thinking that your lecturer is trying to convey.

A word of warning—it is essential to check your notes. Cases or statutes may be misspelt or the names of concepts phonetically reproduced in notes. Should such errors find their way into essays or exam answers it becomes immediately apparent to the marker that a student has done little beyond reading the notes made in a lecture.

To save time you may wish to develop a system of abbreviations. For example, court could be abbreviated to c/t, Parliament to Parl't, Senior Courts Act 1981 to SCA 1981, Court of Appeal to CA, and so on. You may also want to use diagrams, tables, or other symbols such as arrows. Discover and find a method that works for you. Note taking is not easy and it is a skill that you will develop on your degree.

It may be that lectures are recorded at your university and made available to you online. This is useful if you want to listen to an explanation again or check a source, or if, due to illness for example, attendance was not possible. However, recorded lectures should not be seen as a substitute for attendance. Being at a lecture is part of a structured approach to academic study. You have the opportunity to interact and ask questions. There is no substitute for being there in person. Besides, the technology might occasionally fail!

In summary, it is important to appreciate what it is that the lecture seeks to achieve and what your expectations of a lecture should be. The lecture is there to guide you as to the significant issues and/or arguments on a particular topic, to point you in the direction of relevant source materials, and to expose you to the methods of the law. At the end of a lecture there may be time for questions to be answered, but if not, a note should be kept and any queries followed up in general reading or in a tutorial or seminar. The lecture is not designed to give you a complete set of notes or to exhaustively consider all the points on a particular subject. The lecture is the starting point of the learning process and not the end.

1.3.2 After the lecture

After the lecture you should consolidate your notes. This means that you take steps to ensure that the notes you have taken are accurate and that you understand (and can read!) the contents. Such a process is likely to fix the material in your mind and promote long-term retention. Reading a textbook at this point alongside your notes will help you to retain and develop your understanding. Further, you should compile a list of sources that you need to read and then go and locate them.

Precisely *how best* to read those cases, legislation, journal articles etc. will be a skill you will continue to fine-tune throughout your degree. There is no substitute for reading something cover to cover, but more often you will either be directed or discover independently that only parts of the source will be relevant for your purposes. Or that some parts can be selectively scanned, and other parts read with enhanced care and attention. You will want to highlight key sections, passages, and quotes. Sometimes it is useful to read the introduction followed by the conclusion to allow you to appreciate the author's key argument or simply the general direction of the arguments. Often it is helpful to annotate these paragraphs with some key words that will help you find and summarise the point you want to recall. Alternatively, you may want to write a summary of the source in your own words. Reading primary and secondary sources effectively is an essential part of academic study, and effort spent in the first year developing this skill will offer long-term rewards.

1.4 Preparing for seminars

Lectures and seminars (called tutorials in some universities) serve different, but complementary, purposes. Lectures provide foundational knowledge and give overall direction and guidance. Seminars provide an opportunity for a more focused and detailed exploration of the law. These sessions are interactive, allow students to ask questions and offer comments and opinions, and are intended to fully explore and embed your understanding of the law. There may be times when you are placed in groups and are expected to work on activities such as preparing feedback or presenting findings. Some students find group work challenging but it is important that everyone contributes and that there is good open communication between you all. You will have to work with people who will not necessarily be your best friends but that adjustment is something that working professionals make all the time. Besides, working with your friends carries its own potential risks and won't necessarily lead to the best work.

Misunderstandings or confusion about complex points may be corrected at a seminar, or alternatively, your understanding of an area or point may be confirmed. Seminars may be based on the content of a lecture and there will often be a series of tasks or activities such as questions to answer, or devising essay plans, or preparing presentations. Ultimately, all seminars are intended to inspire confidence and stimulate and push the depth and quality of your knowledge and understanding, as well as skills such as critical analysis.

However, in order to maximise the benefit from the seminar you need to undertake all the necessary reading and preparation; failure to undertake the reading means that you will find it difficult, if not impossible, to take part in the seminar discussions. The benefit you will gain will be limited. Your work after the lecture will have started the preparation for the seminar but you should come to the seminar with fully prepared answers to the questions/activities (unless told otherwise). There is a further reason for the importance of preparation. Your preparation, understanding, and contribution(s) will benefit your fellow students and theirs will benefit you. Seminars work best when everyone has attempted the preparation and has a good grasp of the material. If you have attempted the preparation but have found it difficult then you should feel free to ask your tutor either in the seminar or outside at a later time. They are there to help. The most important lesson is that the seminar is not intended for you to collect answers but, rather, for you to offer them and explore how they apply. In summary, attendance at the seminar is absolutely essential but it is not enough: you must be fully prepared.

For instance, you may be asked a range of questions in seminars. These may be closed questions (e.g. 'How can the Court of Appeal overrule its own past precedent?' or 'What does s.3 of the Human Rights Act 1998 state?'); you may also be given essay questions for you to write a plan. This will be excellent practice if your assessment involves writing an essay too. The following essay question might be an example you are asked to consider:

 **Example**

The creation of the Judicial Appointments Commission (JAC) in April 2006 was a positive development. However, the judiciary stubbornly lacks the required diversity to ensure that it is adequately representative of people in wider society. It is clear therefore that the Judicial Appointments Commission does not have the authority or powers to boost the diversity of the judiciary.

Critically discuss.

You may wish to return to this section once you have read the section on written assignments. However, to offer some general advice for the time being, first, you need to identify the requirements of the question, and second, think about writing a plan or outline to your answer. Your essay should have a beginning, middle, and end. However, before you consider writing your plan it is worthwhile considering some general questions that apply to any essay question. These questions may reflect the progress of your essay. It is generally worthwhile considering the following issues.

- What is the problem and/or how and why did the problem arise?
- Why is the problem significant (e.g. in terms of democracy, fairness, and/or justice)?
- How was, or is, the problem being dealt with?
- Is the solution adequate and/or to what extent has it worked?
- If it has not worked, where are the weaknesses and are there any potential solutions?

The fourth and fifth questions above will be particularly significant in your answer. This will be where your essay engages in critical analysis (taking a critical approach and breaking the topic up into its various components), arguments, and discussion. In addressing these questions you should be able to marshal evidence to support your arguments in relation to, say, the weaknesses in the law and/or policies or objectives that underpin the law. The evidence can include developments in legislation or in the case law, or opinion expressed by academic authors (e.g. arguments found in journals), but also various other forms of evidence that support what you are saying (e.g. statistics, popular perceptions etc.).

To see how this approach might apply to the example above, we can take each of the questions in turn and consider your specific essay plan on the JAC and judicial diversity. In brief, your essay might include the following:

(a) The criticism/perception of the judiciary that too many of its members come from a narrow social background (e.g. white, middle-class, from an elite/private school background, and still male-dominated) and that therefore they do not proportionately mirror the gender, class, and ethnic diversity of society. It would be helpful to break down specific features of the criticism/problem;

(b) The significance of diversity in terms of democracy and fairness of decision-making (e.g. to avoid judges that are of a particular political persuasion, or are more likely to be punitive in their sentences/favour the prosecution), to promote meritocracy and enable those from all backgrounds to access the professions;

(c) An overview of the system for the appointment of judges prior to the creation of the JAC, including identifying previous problems such as a lack of transparency in the appointments process. Then, turning to consider the establishment of the JAC by the Constitutional Reform Act 2005. This should include a discussion of its role, powers, and composition;

(d) A discussion as to how far the creation of the JAC has been effective. To what extent are the authority or powers of the JAC limited? Has it worked? Is the system more transparent? Can it be shown that the diversity has improved since the establishment of the JAC? Has the rate of progress been sufficient?

(e) If you determine that the JAC has not been working well, discuss what more can and should it do. What reforms are necessary?

Hopefully you can appreciate how asking these general questions can provide you with the foundation for an essay plan. Next, we turn to look at the question of assessment.

Visit the online resources for further guidance on legal research.

1.5 Assessment

You will, unavoidably, be concerned by how your English Legal System module is to be assessed. There may be an end-of-year coursework assignment, such as a written essay, or there may be an end-of-semester/year examination, or a combination of the two. Although these are the most commonly used assessments, increasingly, many courses now conduct assessments by oral presentation, either delivered individually or in groups. You will have learned in your previous studies about *how* to answer assessment questions. We would strongly encourage you not to be *too* obsessed by this concern. It should never influence you so heavily from an early stage that you are only concerned by the assessment. If you take this approach the quality of your learning will be limited and in fact a little too shallow. Enjoy the module and the course. Get the most from it. If you work hard throughout the module, then the assessment should not concern you as much: you will already be in the best position to pass the assessment with flying colours.

1.5.1 Assessment criteria

The piece of work set should indicate the criteria against which your assignment is to be assessed. Such criteria may include the ability to research and awareness of sources; analysis; relevance of subject matter; clarity of expression; accuracy; presentation; and appropriate citation of authority, referencing, and inclusion of a bibliography. Use these criteria as a checklist so as to ensure that you have done all the things expected of you by the examiner. Your university tutors will explain and elaborate on any specific criteria and demonstrate how and what you can do to ensure that your work has the best chance of attracting the most credit.

1.5.2 Written assignments

This is the most common form of assessment adopted in many English Legal System modules. Before you begin, ensure that you know the requirements of the assignment, for example the word limit, including whether footnotes and bibliography are included in the word count, the hand-in date, and any express formatting requirements for the submission (e.g. the referencing guide, the font, margins, and spacing). You should not be making mistakes and thus losing potential marks or credit for any of these things.

Follow the requirements carefully. For example, do not exceed the word limit; at some universities, exceeding the word limit will result in automatic failure. In any event, even if there is some leeway in the word count, you must always ensure that you do not write more than the expected word limit. Being concise and demonstrating brevity is a skill you should be aiming for as a future lawyer. Please review any guidance in the assessment regulations of your university or the assignment instructions.

The expectation is that you will research and write the essay by yourself and your tutor will not be prepared to discuss your own specific assignment with you (although we are sure plenty of very useful general advice will be given). Certainly, no tutor will comment upon drafts of your answer. This is another reason for taking all the opportunities throughout your module, such as attending lectures, preparing and participating in seminars, and submitting non-assessed work for ongoing feedback on your understanding or writing.

There are some useful general pieces of advice to consider in preparing, planning, and then writing your essay. First, the starting point is to determine precisely what it is that you have been asked to complete. Many English Legal System assignments are in the form of essays so pay particularly close attention to the question. Often, those essay questions will ask you to do something very precise. Those are known as command words. You will come across command words in many different contexts. Table 1.1 lists some of the more descriptive command words that you may come across, while Table 1.2 goes on to list the more challenging critical ones.

Probably the most frequently used command words for written assessment essays will be *analyse*, *discuss*, or *evaluate*. However, even when you are asked one of these question you might deem it necessary in your response to describe, outline, or define something first.

This takes us to the second piece of advice: the importance of a clear structure to your answer. This is about coherently and logically organizing your material. The purpose of a written answer is to show that you understand an area of law as it applies to the question. In writing your answer you should list the issues raised by the question and then select material relevant to those issues. The process of selecting material is important as this, in part, demonstrates to the examiner that you understand what the question is about and what material is relevant. The question is not usually an invitation to simply describe everything that you know about a topic area; material must be selected by you and its link to the question made plain.

The third and final piece of advice is that the essay question is inviting you to sustain an argument or position. Think about how lawyers advocate their views in court. Legal writing is similar, in that the best essays will have a clear line of argument that can be readily spotted from a very early stage in the essay. The best essays will not be too 'even-handed', for example simply providing a series of pros and cons and then coming to a conclusion. This will take time to develop but eventually it will come. Finally, of course, you must justify your arguments with references to primary and secondary sources that demonstrate your grasp of the material and that you

Table 1.1 Descriptive command words

Command Word	Meaning
Clarify	Provide clarification. This means making a topic less confusing and easier to follow and understand, for example by explaining it in more straightforward terms.
Compare	Identify the similarities between two or more subjects of discussion. You can go further by trying to understand the roots of the similarities, their extent, and their significance. You may even consider whether those similarities are desirable and why/why not.
Contrast	Identify the differences between two or more subjects. Much of what is said for 'compare' applies here but the focus is on differences (or dissimilarities). Identify the features and consider what sets them apart, to what degree, and are they different and why? You may even consider whether those differences are desirable and why/why not.
Define	You must outline the precise meaning of the subject of the question. If the definition you provide is a contested one then make sure you discuss or explore this as it will demonstrate your mastery of the concept and debate at large.
Demonstrate	Display or show. The key to tackling 'demonstrate' questions is to use examples, evidence, and logical arguments to support a proposition.
Describe	Provide clear and effective observations about the main characteristics of a subject. Try not to offer criticisms or opinions at this stage because that might confuse the reader, especially if you have not laid out what the core features of the topic are.
Elaborate	Offer more explanation and detail to a description and/or to a topic that can develop the reader's understanding of the area.
Explain	Similar to 'clarify', you are essentially detailing your understanding of a particular area. You may think it necessary to fully define something as part of your explanation. Otherwise, it may be useful to think of 'who', 'what', 'where', 'when', and 'why.'
Explore	Adopt a questioning approach and consider various perspectives before coming to a clearer line of argument. Try to adopt the right tone with the appropriate degree of nuance.
Identify	Concisely point out the main concepts, ideas, or features in a topic.
Illustrate	Use various examples. These examples should demonstrate your knowledge and understanding of a topic and thus assist with any explanation. Examples can come in the form of tables, figures, and statistics but also excerpts from primary sources (e.g. judicial quotations) or arguments in secondary sources (e.g. academic opinion).
Outline	Outlining involves a concise and organised description of the main points or features of a particular topic or debate. It should not stray into minor and unnecessary detail or a lengthy and thorough explanation.
Summarise	A summary is a concise and condensed run-through of the key points. The best summaries are focused and punchy and convey only what is necessary to reinforce the key issues.

Table 1.2 Critical command words

Command Word	Meaning
Analyse	Break an issue apart into its various elements. Then look critically and in depth at each element, looking at their relationship, their effect, their meaning, their weaknesses etc. The best analysis will include evidence (e.g. reference to primary and secondary sources) to support your argument(s). If there are any limitations to your argument, you can highlight them but don't be afraid to explain why they are less persuasive, and why you still maintain your view.
Assess	Consider or make an informed judgment about the value, strengths, or weaknesses of an argument, claim or topic. You should weigh up all views but you must give some priority to your own thoughts or views and their significance. Again, this must be supported by evidence (primary and secondary sources). Similar to analysis, if there are any limitations to your argument, you can highlight them but don't be afraid to explain why they are less persuasive, and why you still maintain your view.
(Critically) Discuss	These questions typically require an all-round in-depth answer that takes into account all aspects of the debate concerning a research topic or argument. Most importantly, 'discuss' question often have to incorporate other elements in this table, e.g. to briefly assess or evaluate features as part of your discussion. Again, you must use evidence to make a case for or against a research topic/argument. Remember to clearly state your position based on all the evidence you present.
(Critically) Evaluate	This is about weighing up and getting the measure of a topic in light of its pros and cons. You are being asked to give your verdict as to what extent a statement, argument, or finding is true or accurate, and/or the extent to which you agree. You should consider and analyse evidence from a range of sources which both agree with and contradict an argument. Your response should be critical and assertive and you should take on and challenge counter-arguments to your view and explain why your view is more persuasive and why. Come to a final conclusion and justify how you have made your choice.
Examine	Similar to analysis, an examination requires you to establish the key facts, issues, or points concerning a topic by looking at them in close detail. You must adopt a critical approach. It may be useful to consider the context of a topic too.
Justify	Explain the basis of your argument by presenting evidence that informs your position. You need to present your evidence in a convincing way and demonstrate good reasons for adopting your position. You may want to consider arguments that are contrary to your position and seek to explain why they are unsatisfactory or hold less weight. This will tend to make your own view or opinion more critical and convincing.

(continued)

Table 1.2 (continued)

Command Word	Meaning
Review	A critical discussion that will involve some description or summarising but may require an analysis/examination too. For instance, after describing or summarising the state of the law, you will need to develop arguments or challenge the evidence that the law rests on.
To what extent or to what degree . . .	This asks how far you agree with a proposition put forward in the question. This requires an assessment or evaluation of the topic, and especially of the evidence used to present the argument or position you are being asked to respond to. You will need to conclude with a direct view and explain throughout why you are taking that position.

have really read those sources carefully. For instance, you might decide to selectively highlight a quote or argument from a judgment or a case, or an academic author's opinion that you need to explain, explore, or even criticise.

1.5.3 Writing an assignment

Consider the following, reasonably typical, essay question (note you may want to come back to this question after you have completed your learning on statutory interpretation).

Example

In the interpretation of legislation, the role of judges is to give effect to the intention of Parliament. This process is not without its difficulties.

Discuss.

It is entirely up to you how to plan and prepare for an essay. Different students will have different approaches. However, I would urge you to consider the general questions in 1.4 above as that will be a useful starting point. Alternatively, you may simply want to list a series of points and issues that are going to be relevant to the question. Once you have selected your material, you should be thinking about the structure and how to organise it within the word limits you have been given.

As we have already mentioned, essays need to have a beginning, middle, and end. They should have a clear introduction that sets the scene and background, interprets the question, and then signals the structure to be followed in the middle of the essay. Some introductions also hint at the line of argument the essay is going to take. The essay should also have a clear conclusion that reinforces the key argument powerfully. Importantly, a conclusion should not introduce new material; a conclusion draws from material already discussed in the body of the text. Of course it is in the middle where the main discussion is going to be and this should reflect your knowledge, understanding, research, and the arguments that address the question. You should ideally be selective and demonstrate *depth* in your understanding, rather than trying to cover too much and thus only give issues a very sweeping descriptive treatment. The depth of your understanding can be demonstrated by referring to both primary sources (e.g. quotes from judges in particular cases, or legislation) and secondary sources, such as academic opinion. Those will be used to clarify and support your own argument.

You will have to make the necessary judgments about what you want to focus on and what you want to merely reference briefly or even omit entirely, because you feel it does not serve or add to your key argument.

Many students prefer to write the introduction and conclusion at the end after you are satisfied with the middle section. However, as with most things, it is entirely a question for you and your personal writing preference. You will no doubt need to spend time editing, re-drafting, and re-writing various sections of your essay, probably several times. Often, it is in the work you do after your first draft that makes your argument clearer and the writing sharper. You may want to make further editing changes so that your writing has variety and rhythm. Vary the lengths of your sentences; some long and some short. Your work will be more persuasive for doing so. As a result, do not leave writing the essay until the last minute and you should ideally complete your first draft several days before the deadline. Having a break for a few days before you review and re-draft will be very useful as you will be able to identify areas for improvement.

When you have completed your learning on statutory interpretation (see Chapter 4) you can return to this question. However, to help, the following three paragraphs contain some points and observations that will help you plan the middle section of your answer.

The central issue in the question concerns the role of judges in the process of statutory interpretation. The constitutional position is that Parliament makes law and the judges interpret and apply the law. However, therein lies a key problem—the question of interpretation and applying the law is made difficult because the intention of Parliament must be clear and identifiable in the language used in the legislation. The case law reveals that language in a statute is often contested, vague, or unclear and it is hard to identify Parliament's intent in adopting those words. How do the judges overcome this challenge and what are the difficulties? You will be in a better position to critically evaluate the process of interpretation by firstly explaining the relevant rules of statutory interpretation and the uncertainties those rules attract.

See 4.3, 'The approach to statutory interpretation'.

Traditionally, to ascertain the intention of Parliament, the courts have employed the *literal*, *golden*, and *mischief* rules. You will need to explain these rules, with examples (e.g. cases), and you may find it useful to assess the intrinsic and extrinsic aids to construction (e.g. use of the debates in Parliament, as found in Hansard). The recent case law indicates that the courts favour a purposive construction of legislation—see for example *R (on the application of Black) (Appellant) v Secretary of State for Justice (Respondent)* [2017] UKSC 81. The purposive approach needs to be explained and any difficulties associated with the approach identified. Additionally, you can make the point that where there are human rights consequences in a case because a right under the European Convention on Human Rights is engaged, then, by s.3 of the Human Rights Act 1998, the courts are under a duty to read and give effect to primary legislation in a way which is compatible with the Convention rights 'in so far as it is possible to do so'. The difficulties encountered in interpreting and applying s.3 may also be explored. So, to summarise the main headlines, your middle section may consider:

- the relationship between Parliament and the courts and the search for the intention of Parliament;
- the rules and process of statutory interpretation and the difficulties with the approaches, including the purposive approach and the challenges of using the aids to construction;
- Section 3 of the Human Rights Act 1998 and its consequences for the interpretation of legislation.

1.5.4 **Referencing**

An important part of scholarship is appropriate and effective referencing. The idea behind referencing is that the reader is able easily to locate the sources upon which you rely. Referencing also ensures that credit is given to the originator of the work; without referencing, the ideas of another person may appear to be those of the assignment writer. Failure to acknowledge the work of another through an appropriate reference may infringe your university's plagiarism regulations. It is important that you give credit to ideas, terms, and language that you have taken from other sources.

There are various ways in which references may be presented. In the first instance, establish whether your law school specifies a particular referencing system; if so, use it. Otherwise, the one that is most likely to be adopted by law schools is the system in the Oxford University Standard for Citation of Legal Authorities (OSCOLA). This system relies on the inclusion of footnotes. You will need to practise using OSCOLA and ensure that your references are in the correct format, whether they are cases, legislation, book chapters, academic books, official reports, or other online sources such as blogs or media articles. The important point is to include all information necessary for the marker to find the source and to be consistent in the presentation of such information. One word of advice: do your references as you go along and when you are writing your draft. If you leave it to the end, referencing can be very time-consuming and, worse still, you may not be able to recall or find a specific reference, for example to an article and/or even the precise page number.

1.5.5 Finally . . .

Before submitting your assignment, check for obvious mistakes of presentation, grammar, punctuation, and typography.

1.5.6 What to do after the return of your assignment

While an assignment may count towards your final mark for this module, it should also be viewed as a learning experience. There is an important feedback opportunity to be taken. Feedback may be given orally in a lecture, in written form dealing with general issues, and/or in specific comments on your assignment. Reflect on the comments and seek to discover where extra marks were lost and where they might have been gained. It may be useful to precisely identify any weaknesses in your understanding of the question set, the relevant law, or the problem may just have been your essay technique. Should you be unclear on any of these matters, make an appointment to see your tutor for further guidance.

1.6 Advice on oral presentations

Presenting in public is an essential skill for many careers. It is particularly important if you are pursuing a legal career, whether that be as a barrister or as a solicitor. In fact, there are not many workplace environments where you won't be asked to present in front of people at some time or another. Presentation skills are vital. Many of you will have had some practice at presenting before coming to university. Most people find that presentations tend to induce nerves but this is one of those skills where the more opportunity you take to present, the more likely you are to get better at delivering them. It is a cliché, but practice really does make perfect (or at least very good).

This is not the right place to give you exhaustive advice on how to present. However, I would offer the following, fairly basic, rules of thumb. First, the key to a successful presentation is structure. Think about what you have been asked to present and break it down into different components. Then consider the most logical order of those components (e.g. the background or context of the problem would tend to go first, and then your key findings and final conclusion would be at the end). To help the audience, convey the structure of your presentation at the outset. This is sometimes known as 'signalling' or 'signposting' and it will help your audience know what is going to come and when.

Secondly, a key aspect of effective presentation is timing and managing the pace of your presentation: deliver too fast and you will lose your audience; too slow, and their attention will wander. For most people, a good piece of advice is that, if you feel you are talking too slowly then it is usually the correct pace. You will also have to judge the pace of your presentation in terms of the overall time that you have been given to present. There is nothing worse than a presentation that goes on and on past the allocated time. Again, you will lose the audience and you may even be cut off and asked to finish early before you have had the chance to fully convey the most important aspect of your presentation. Always practise the timing and pace of your presentation. If you have too much information, ask yourself: What are the most important aspects of my talk? What do I really need to get across that is the most interesting and illuminating? What do my audience *really* need to know? Is there anything that I can safely assume the audience already know? Answering these questions will help you manage the amount you convey. Sometimes less is more (but not too little!).

Thirdly, it is best to deliver the material as if you are talking naturally, rather than reading a prepared speech. This is difficult if you are not confident of remembering your material but you will improve with practice. It is possible to use cue cards for the main points you wish to make and hold these in your hand as an aide-memoire. By not over-relying on scripted notes you can maintain eye contact, which makes your presentation more interesting and engaging for your audience and allows you to gauge whether your explanation is being understood. Don't be afraid to alter your vocal pitch and change your tone to emphasise the most important statements or points.

Fourthly, by all means use visual aids, flipchart paper, and PowerPoint slides but be careful that you use them effectively. Be imaginative with your visuals or slides (e.g. use pictures, diagrams, statistics, etc.). Do not include too much text and only put the essential information or points on display in a size that is readable for someone sitting at the back of the room. Please talk around and elaborate on your points, including any pictures. There is nothing worse than simply reading from the presentation without any development or background information.

Finally, do try to enjoy it. Relax and invite some interaction with the audience by posing or inviting questions. Above all, you will improve with practice so if a presentation could have gone better, don't get too downhearted. Reflect on any mistakes and take steps to improve for the next time. Always be willing to speak up and participate.

1.7 **Examinations**

There is not much to say about exams. We will all have taken them in one form or another. However, to remind you, examinations are an opportunity to demonstrate what you know, but also, more importantly, what you understand. Admittedly, getting to grips with the content of the module is one thing but ensuring you give yourself the best opportunity to demonstrate the depth of your understanding might require something more. Knowledge is a prerequisite for examination success but it is not the only element, and often developing a strategy and appropriate technique is incredibly important. You will discover and practise this with advice from your tutors. The examiner is looking for an ability to address the precise question and an answer that demonstrates a detailed understanding of the relevant area of law.

Your examination may take the form of a closed-book or open-book examination. The difference is that in a closed-book examination no materials, such as notes and textbooks, are allowed in the exam room, whereas an open-book examination allows materials to be taken into the examination. Often a closed-book exam may permit you to enter the examination hall only with a statute book. The type of exam will determine your approach to preparing for the examination. Remember the examiner will know what realistically can be expected of you in the exam, in the time that you have been given.

1.7.1 Preparing for examinations

An obvious key to examination success in law is that you must know the relevant law. You must have a reasonable memory and hopefully the process of learning will help you to improve yours. Unless you possess a photographic memory, there is no avoiding the effort and labour that is required to recall such material from the back of your mind to the very front (of course, the approach for open-book exams may be a little different). The process will be made considerably easier if you adopt good working practices throughout your study of the English Legal System module. This will include excellent attendance, complete preparation for seminars, and other regular tasks such as carrying out post-lecture consolidation of your notes and/or spending some time each week or every fortnight refreshing your knowledge.

Nonetheless, it is probably unavoidable that, in the weeks leading up to the examinations, you will have to immerse yourself in the revision process and spend a significant amount of time making new notes, diagrams, and mind-maps or simply re-reading your notes to ensure that you have instant recall of the concepts and detail in the examination room. Even if you are taking an open-book exam, this is not an excuse for a revision-free run-up to the exam. The examiner's expectations may well be different, and straightforward knowledge will be assumed. You will therefore have to be able to locate material speedily otherwise you may lose valuable time. The best advice is that you should really prepare for an open-book examination in very similar ways to one that is closed. If you have already mastered most of the law, you will find completing the exam much easier as you will be less reliant on any book you have with you.

Try to be systematic in your revision by drawing up a revision schedule. This will help with organisation and time-management. An important part of preparing for examinations is practising answering questions, particularly under exam conditions. Locate past exam papers for your module and ask your tutor for feedback on your attempts to answer the questions. This will not only reinforce your knowledge of subject areas, but also help develop your examination technique.

Otherwise, although it sounds obvious, there are a couple of simple things that you should do to help reduce any nerves you may have about the examination.

- First, ensure that you know where the examination is to be held; if you are unfamiliar with the location, visit it before the date of the examination.

- Secondly, although you will already be aware of this, double-check requirements of the examination; for example, open-book, closed or statute-book only; how many questions must be attempted; what is the duration of the examination; how much time you might spend per question; and whether there is a compulsory question or a free choice of questions to answer.

Finally, many students seek to 'question spot', that is, to predict the topics that will appear on the exam and focus their revision on those areas accordingly, often to the exclusion of any other revision on other topics. This is partly human nature perhaps. My advice would be to avoid this at all costs; however, if you do decide to gamble, then you should proceed with utmost caution.

The emphasis in your lectures and seminars will be a useful guide to examinable topics. It would be an unusual approach to examine topics that have not been substantively taught or addressed. Past exam papers may be useful as an indication but you may want to double-check the emphasis placed on the module in previous years to give some indication of likely question areas. Do remember, though, that the emphasis of the module might have been different in previous years.

Some topics are highly likely to be examined because they go to the core of the English legal system. For instance, it would be improbable that no question on statutory interpretation or on the doctrine of judicial precedent would feature in an exam. If you are going to question spot, then be careful not to take chances that would damage your grade. If you are required to answer four questions, then studying only four topics would be very risky as not all of the areas may feature in the examination paper and, even if the four areas do appear, they might not be in a question form that you can answer. In consequence, if you do tailor your revision accordingly, build in a margin for the 'unexpected'. However, once again, my advice is to avoid this altogether.

1.7.2 **The examination**

Relax and manage your nerves. Don't be concerned by what others are doing. If someone is writing furiously next to you and you are still reading the question, don't be put off. Keep an eye on the clock. Otherwise, effective preparation is the best recipe for success. In the examination, make sure that you concentrate your efforts on writing the requisite number of answers. You must use the time available effectively. Practising writing essays under exam conditions prior to the exam should have alerted you to how much writing is possible within the allotted time. Obviously, effective time management will avoid the trap of failing to attempt all the questions required by the instructions. Success or failure in an exam may rest on a last answer. You must ensure that you attempt all the questions, because even writing very little for one question will still influence the final mark. Should you be running out of time then, as a last resort, at least indicate your understanding of the final question by making brief notes or bullet points. The marker is likely to look at your notes and give you a mark that, in part, predicts what you may have gone on to discuss in your full answer. You will not achieve anything like full marks but you may do enough to make a significant difference to your final result.

Another aspect of time management is directing your efforts according to the weighting of marks within the exam paper and/or within questions. Don't spend longer on those parts of the exam that are worth less in terms of the overall mark. Should the exam paper contain a compulsory question, this may carry, say, 40 per cent of the marks, in which case you should use 40 per cent of the allotted time in producing an answer. Equally, if a question is in two parts and the marks are split between part (a) 60 per cent and part (b) 40 per cent, obviously a larger proportion of time should be spent on part (a).

1.7.3 Post-examination

Once you have finished your examination, try to forget about it. The exam is over and done with. There is nothing you can do now but await the results. Unless this is your last examination, do not be tempted to hold a lengthy analysis of the exam with your friends and fellow students. There is nothing to be gained from this process; indeed, the opposite is true. In general, students are not in the best position to assess their performance in the heat of the examination room and such discussion may unnerve and divert focus and energy from other forthcoming exams. In my experience, as long as they have put the required work in, students tend to think they have done far worse than they actually have in reality.

Once you have received your results, whether you have passed or failed, there will always be something to learn about your performance. You should receive some form of feedback on your paper; it is important to reflect on the good points of your examination performance and also where you could improve. The likelihood is that you will already know where you might have gone wrong. General feedback on the content of answers may be given to you in written form or otherwise be available electronically and your exam paper may be returned to you. Whatever form the feedback takes, seek to learn from it and to carry this guidance forward into the next year of study. If you feel anything is unclear, make an appointment to see your module tutor, who will be able to look at your examination and provide specific advice on how to improve the next time.

Further reading

- ***Finch. E. and Fafinski. S.*** *Legal Skills*, 7th edn, Oxford University Press (2019)

  This is a popular and comprehensive textbook. It is a go-to guide that contains excellent discussions of the academic and practical skills that you will be developing throughout your course. There is a detailed discussion of the sources of law and on developing your research skills in locating, reading, and using primary and secondary sources. There is also a thorough overview of key legal skills, as well as advice on referencing and how to avoid plagiarism. Finally, the book contains useful advice on presentation, mooting, and negotiation skills that most of you will have the opportunity to practise throughout your degree.

- ***Moore, I. and Newberry-Jones, C.*** *The Successful Law Student: An Insider's Guide to Studying Law*, Oxford University Press (2018)

  This book presents itself as the ultimate guide for all prospective and current law students. It is a book with a difference. It is packed with advice and insight but from current and past law students (rather than academics) and draws extensively on real-life examples. It caters for a diverse range of students studying all types of law degree or course. It has dedicated sections on how to learn and think like a lawyer, and on completing assignments successfully, including how to understand and act on feedback. There is also information on striving for success outside the classroom, be it in undertaking extra-curricular activities or in your pursuit of a successful career once you have completed your course.

- ***Strong, S.I.*** *How to Write Law Essays and Exams*, 5th edn, Oxford University Press (2018)

  Designed for students at all levels, this is a very accessible and useful textbook packed with advice on how to develop your skills in analysing and answering essay and exam questions. The book focuses on problem questions, but the advice and strategies offered are useful for essay questions too, whether you are to answer them in coursework assignments in your own time, or within a timed examination. There is plenty of advice on how to use authorities to support arguments in your answer (a key expectation) as well more general help on legal writing and revision techniques.

Online resources

You should now attempt the supporting self-test questions and end-of-chapter questions available at: **www.oup.com/he/wilson-rutherford4e**

Chapter 2

An overview of the English legal system

Learning objectives

By the end of this chapter you should be able to:

- outline the characteristics of law;
- identify the main sources of law and explain the different processes of law-making;
- understand the various meanings of the term common law;
- describe the basic structure, composition, and jurisdiction of the courts;
- explain the impact of the UK's membership of the European Union (EU) and the European Convention on Human Rights (ECHR);
- recall the key features of various legal bodies and the main groups of legal personnel.

Talking point

Law serves many purposes. At its most basic, it seeks to regulate behaviour, to avoid conflict, and to mediate disputes. Should disputes arise then the law must seek to resolve them and then provide an appropriate remedy to the side that has succeeded. The law, however, cannot be static and there must be ways for laws to be changed. For instance, as society develops, the law may have to change to deal with the social, technological, political, and environmental change. From these, the law has often had to keep pace with rapid technological developments. There is considerable evidence of these developments but two examples illustrate the point. The first example is the development of methods of communication, such as the mobile phone and the growth of social media; the second is the creation of automated vehicles, such as driverless cars. If we take the latter, then currently an individual (an in-car user) operates the technology and can optionally resume normal driving control. However, driverless cars raise immediate questions about legal responsibilities and potential liabilities in, say, the case of a collision; for example, who is to blame—the driver or the manufacturer of the vehicle/technology?

There are many further questions about how law should respond to the eventual introduction of 'driverless' technology on the roads. The new Automated and Electric Vehicle Act 2018 only addresses a small part of the picture. At the time of writing the Law Commission is pursuing a project until 2021 that examines the legal framework required to regulate the use of driverless cars while also protecting other road users, including pedestrians, from any possible risks. (See **https://www.lawcom.gov.uk/project/automated-vehicles/**.)

Reflect on the following questions:

- To what degree do you think the criminal law or the law on negligence will need to change to accommodate the liability of in-car users and/or the manufacturers of driverless cars?
- How do you think, in light of driverless technology, the law on being qualified to drive, or the requirement that drivers purchase insurance, or even the law on cybersecurity will need to be updated?
- Finally, can you think of other emerging technological developments in society that will require a significant legal change or response? What do you think the aims of the law will, or should, be in response to the development?

Introduction

The study of the English legal system involves two different but related processes. First, as a law student, you must acquire and understand a large body of knowledge about the sources of English law, the institutions, and various key legal personnel in the system. This knowledge will provide you with the 'basic tools' or building blocks to understand how the legal system operates. Second, this knowledge is required before you can engage in any meaningful critical analysis or evaluation of the law and its institutions; it is one thing to know what the system is and looks like, but it is quite another to evaluate the system and consider whether it is, for example, fair, consistent, or offers sufficient legal certainty.

This chapter provides an overview of some fundamental concepts, terminology, and institutions in the English legal system. Its aim is to sketch the landscape of the English legal system. The concepts and ideas will be new to you but many of these will underpin your understanding of how law works and operates in practice. Much of the chapter's content is outlined in further detail in later chapters and so the coverage here takes a broad-brush approach. Please feel free to follow up the references and links to later sections in the book and, of course, do carry out any further reading and research if you want to develop a more thorough grasp of the material.

2.1 **What is law?**

When one thinks of law, most people tend to refer to a body or system of rules. These rules aim to regulate individual behaviour; what people can and cannot do, and what they ought or ought not to do. Various sets of laws will operate in particular environments or situations, for example, employment, immigration, or commercial law. The law is enforced by the courts holding people liable either by the criminal law (and therefore attracting some form of punishment, e.g. a prison sentence) or by civil law (and therefore usually obliging them to pay compensation or some other remedy) to demonstrate that they acted unlawfully.

You will learn that part of understanding the law is determining whether a particular law or rule applies. A frequent starting point is how the law defines particular concepts or persons, for example, who is an employee, what is a public place, or what is a business?

See Chapter 7, 'Human rights in the United Kingdom', and the difficulties caused by the meaning of 'public authority' under the Human Rights Act 1998.

Many of the disputes that come before the courts require definitions of terms to be determined and resolved. For instance, in 2018, the Court of Appeal in *Uber BV and Others v Aslam and Others* [2018] EWCA Civ 2748 had to determine whether Uber taxi drivers were 'workers' and would therefore be entitled to holiday pay, the minimum wage and other protections. Uber argued the drivers were not 'workers' because Uber simply offered the appropriate booking and payment service and the drivers did not work for them, but instead were effectively self-employed as they independently contracted with the passengers they picked up. The Court disagreed. In the Court's judgment, the drivers *were* workers because, amongst other reasons, Uber exerted sufficient control over the drivers. They concluded there was no real (independent) contract between a given driver and a passenger because the driver has no notice of the passenger's destination until after an agreement to pick them up is made. The relevant contract was with Uber, which accepts a passenger's request before relaying it to a driver who decides to fulfil the request. Under the law, this made the Uber drivers 'workers'.

These debates about definitions can be illustrated with an earlier example. Under s.6 of the Caravan Sites Act 1968 (a provision that is now repealed), a duty was placed on county councils to provide gypsies with adequate accommodation. Immediately, it must be determined who falls within the term 'gypsies'. In its ordinary meaning, 'gypsies' refers to the Romani people who originally came from North India. However, s.16 defined 'gypsies' as 'persons of nomadic habit of life, whatever their race or origin'. The definition in the 1968 Act thus raises a further definitional issue: what is 'nomadic'. The word 'nomadic' originally referred to tribes moving from place to place to find pastures for the purposes of grazing livestock. How would this interpretation apply to certain modern travellers groups, whether Romany Gypsy or other groups such as Irish Travellers? Must they be moving from place to place for an economic purpose, i.e. to make a livelihood, or merely be travelling for any purpose as part of their habitual way of life?

The Court of Appeal in *Regina v South Hams District Council and Another, ex parte Gibb* [1994] 3 WLR 1151 pondered such questions. Lord Millett also wrote about this a few years later in an excellent article, 'Construing Statutes' (1999) 20 Stat LR 107. The Court eventually decided that it was a judgment for the local authorities, who ought to take into account the connections between members of the present group and other groups that had visited the site, the pattern of journeys made by the group, and the purpose of the travel including for any relevant work-related purposes. The Court stated that persons or individuals who move from place to place merely when they simply fancy, and without any connection between that movement and their livelihood, would fall outside the statutory definition.

The most important point in this discussion is to recognise that law is often concerned with contested definitions. There are various meanings that may be given to particular words. In a statute, Parliament may leave a word undefined or provide a definition which may be narrower or broader than the meaning of the word in its everyday usage. It is for lawyers to interpret words and, if such words are not clear, then to argue the point before a court. The meaning of many of the terms to be considered in this chapter depends upon the context in which the term is used. For example, see the variable meaning of the term 'common law' later at 2.2.

See generally Chapter 4, 'The interpretation of statutes'.

Before continuing it would be useful to highlight a few common features that are often presumed when one speaks of the law. The features frequently presumed with law are:

- A consensus for recognising what the law is and what it looks like, as opposed to the rules of a sporting game or contest, or a moral set of rules that depend on individual conscience;
- A common understanding of the area or location where a particular set of law applies, such as in a state or other defined geographical area (this is known as jurisdiction);
- A general assumption that the content of the law consists of various rules, obligations, duties, requirements, and principles.

2.1.1 **Recognised as being law**

The law of England and Wales primarily comes from two sources: Parliament and the courts. These two institutions form two important separate organs of the state. Traditionally, Parliament is the law-maker and so long as a bill is passed by the two chambers in Parliament, the House of Commons and the House of Lords, and later receives royal assent by the Queen, the resulting Act of Parliament is recognised as law (See Chapter 3, 'Legislation and the law-making process'.) The traditional constitutional role of the courts is to apply and interpret the law in the cases that are in front of them. This is one key part of the 'separation of powers': law-makers should not apply the law to disputes that ultimately lead to the law being enforced, and the converse: those that are applying and helping to enforce the law should not create or make the law. This is intended to preserve independence, impartiality, and avoid power being too concentrated in one body or institution.

However, not every law is found in an Act of Parliament. The courts do make and develop the 'common law'—the law as determined over centuries by judges in the cases—see 2.2. This law develops in a system of precedent with a principle declared in a senior Court, such as the UK Supreme Court, binding more junior courts in an established hierarchy. Both Parliament-made and judge-made law have authoritative legal status but with the ascendancy of Parliament, particularly from the sixteenth century, it is the elected Parliament's will, as expressed in Acts of Parliament, that carries the greater authority of the two.

Beyond these two sources of law many observers have debated the role of morality in our legal system. The relationship between morality and the law is complex; the former may be the foundation of the latter and they may often coincide with one another. However, that is not always the case. Using morality as a guide to what the law should be is not without its dangers. The difficulty, of course, lies in defining what is moral. Religion may give guidance, but not all members of a society will necessarily agree on what is, or what is not, immoral. Attempts have been made to identify criteria against which to judge whether conduct should attract legal intervention. For example, John Stuart Mill stated in *On Liberty*: 'The only purpose for which power can be rightfully exercised over any member of a civilised community against his will is to prevent harm to others. His own good, either physical or moral, is not a sufficient warrant.' This quote is often summarised as the 'harm' principle. Of course even this principle raises questions about what constitutes harm and who falls within the category of 'others'.

Putting those uncertainties aside for one moment, perhaps one of the most infamous judgments that appears to offend Mill's harm principle is that of the majority in the case of *R v Brown* [1994] 1 AC 212. You will no doubt come across this judgment in your studies at some point but take a look at the case and in particular the judgments of Lord Templeman and Lord Jauncey. When you have read them, briefly reflect on how and why you think the judgment can be described as 'illiberal'? Do you agree?

Of course, morality may underpin law; for example, the law of contract may be seen as based upon the moral principle that a person should fulfil their agreed promises. Theft is of course both immoral and illegal, and is a criminal offence under the Theft Act 1968. However, not every immoral act will constitute a criminal offence or a civil wrong. For example, prostitution may be considered immoral but being a prostitute is not a crime in itself; however, many activities associated with prostitution are criminal, such as soliciting. Similarly many people would think committing adultery and being unfaithful to your married partner is immoral but it is not made illegal (in the United Kingdom at least). Therefore, morality is not the guiding principle for recognising law. On this view morality does not, therefore, determine what is to be considered law. For theorists of the law, this is sometimes called a positivist approach.

However, it should be noted that another group of legal scholars tie themselves to something called a natural law tradition. This tradition argues for a closer relationship between law and morality. These natural lawyers argue that a law-making process which fails to recognise a moral dimension to law is fundamentally flawed. In a lecture, Lord Steyn identified the tyrannies of Nazi Germany, apartheid in South Africa, and Chile under General Pinochet as demonstrating 'that majority rule by itself, and legality on its own, are insufficient to guarantee a civil and just society. Even totalitarian states mostly act according to the laws of their countries.' Put another way, he argues that the existence of properly made laws that discriminate, persecute, and oppress people should not truly be recognised as lawful and certainly not a society abiding by the rule of law. Further discussion of the positivist/natural law debate is beyond the space permitted here. You can learn and critically explore these complex debates, amongst many others, in a module on legal theory ('jurisprudence')

For present purposes, and taking a more positivist approach, the best approach to understanding the law of the English Legal System is to consider whether it originates in one of two main sources, 1) an Act of Parliament or 2) a principle declared in a Court decision that can subsequently bind other Courts (unless later overruled). It is worth highlighting another concept that is also frequently mentioned.

2.1.2 **Jurisdiction**

Laws apply to a defined geographical area and this usually corresponds to the territorial limits of a state. This is sometimes referred to as jurisdiction (the extent or degree of legal authority). The UK, comprising England, Wales, Scotland, and Northern Ireland, is a sovereign state. However, in the UK there is not a single legal system. English law and the English legal system apply in England and Wales. However, many aspects of the law and legal system of Scotland are markedly different from those of England and Wales; and perhaps to a lesser extent, the same is true of Northern Ireland. Indeed, Scotland has a distinct and separate criminal law, and areas of civil law, such as contract and tort, are also very different from those laws applying in England and Wales. Laws made by judges in England and Wales are only applicable within England and Wales, unless the UK Supreme Court hears a final appeal in the case of Northern Ireland, or a final civil appeal with respect to Scotland. An Act of Parliament will apply to the whole of the UK unless the Act indicates otherwise. Some statutes may be arranged in parts, with one part applying to England and Wales, another part applying to Scotland, and yet another applying to Northern Ireland.

Generally, when interpreting statutes the courts presume that an Act of Parliament only applies to the UK, unless the extraterritorial operation of the Act is expressly or impliedly indicated. It is possible for Parliament to pass laws which apply to acts committed outside the UK. For example, under the War Crimes Act 1991, the courts of the UK are able to try any person (including non-UK citizens) alleged to have committed serious offences of war crimes in German-held territory during the Second World War. To offer another example, the courts in England and Wales (but not Scotland due to their special criminal justice system) can try a case of murder alleged to have been committed by a British national wherever in the world that may be (s.9 of the Offences against the Person Act 1861). Although note that in this latter case another state, for example, the state on whose territory the crime was committed, will want to assert its own jurisdiction over the matter and will usually take priority.

2.1.3 **The commencement of Acts of Parliament**

An Act of Parliament comes into force on the day on which the Act receives royal assent (see s.4 of the Interpretation Act 1978), unless the Act provides otherwise. If an Act is not to come into force on the day of royal assent then it is necessary to look at the Commencement section of the Act, which will specify when the Act is to come into force. This may be done by: (a) stipulating a date when the Act becomes operative; or (b) stating that an Act is to be brought into force, or parts of it are to be brought into force by later statutory instrument to be made by a minister.

See Chapter 3, 'Legislation and the law-making process'.

In summary then, in most cases an Act will only have future or prospective effect in terms of legislating for conduct, behaviour, standards, or whatever the Act provides for. This is not to say that Parliament cannot pass an Act which has retrospective effect, i.e. applying to past conduct; Parliament may do so if such an intention is made clear in an Act of Parliament. However, retrospective effect is considered to be objectionable and against the notion of the rule of law. This is because what was once lawful is now unlawful, but people at the earlier time were unaware that their behaviour would (subsequently) be declared unlawful. In other words, people would be penalised when they thought they were acting perfectly fairly and legitimately. Retrospective laws tend to have considerable negative consequences for the rights, entitlement, or benefits people may have acquired previously. When the courts interpret Acts of Parliament, then, in the absence of a clear intention to the contrary, they will interpret a statute as having no retrospective effect. In any event, the possible retrospective effect of the criminal law is heavily restricted by Article 7 of the European Convention on Human Rights (ECHR).

See Chapter 7, 'Human rights in the United Kingdom'.

 **Critical debate**

The concept of the rule of law is frequently mentioned by parliamentarians, lawyers, and political commentators. It is a difficult concept to define precisely. The late Tom Bingham (a former Lord Chief Justice), in his book *The Rule of Law*, provided the following description:

> [A]ll persons and authorities within the state, whether public or private, should be bound by and entitled to the benefits of laws publicly made, taking effect (generally) in the future and publicly administered in the courts.

One of the principles which is to be derived from this description is, in the words of Bingham, that 'the law must be accessible and so far as possible intelligible, clear and predictable'. Does English law wholly comply with this principle and to what degree is it desirable? What changes, in law, society, or popular culture could be made to ensure further compliance with the principle? Please do take a look at Lord Bingham's concise book which is in the further reading list at the end of the chapter.

2.1.4 Criminal offences and civil wrongs

Glanville Williams, in *Learning the Law*, said:

> [T]he distinction between a crime and civil wrong cannot be stated as depending upon *what is done*, because what is done may be the same in each case. The true distinction resides, therefore, not in the nature of the wrongful act but in the legal *consequences that may follow it.*

 **Example**

If a person punches another then the legal consequences that may follow are twofold: first, the crime of common assault (technically a battery) may have been committed; secondly, the tort of battery may have been committed. In this way one act may lead to two separate legal consequences, these being a criminal prosecution in the criminal courts and punishment of the defendant if convicted, and civil proceedings in the civil courts against the same defendant where the injured party may receive compensation.

The quote above highlights the common overlap between criminal and civil wrongs. Of course, in other cases the difference will be more self-evident. A contractual dispute between, say, a supplier and a manufacturer who alleges that the supplier has breached their contract by supplying goods that were not of satisfactory quality would be a civil matter. To determine whether the supplier breached the contract would therefore require a civil court to hear and then decide the case. However, if the supplier were to have damaged and set alight the manufacturer's headquarters in revenge for the manufacturer taking legal action, then this may well be a criminal wrong (criminal damage and/or the offence of arson).

It is important to note that the criminal law and civil law serve different purposes. The criminal law provides a system for the punishment of wrongdoers by the state and on behalf of society and/or the wider community. It covers the range of crimes, including those involving the unlawful interference with personal integrity (murder, rape, assaults etc.) and those that violate property rights (theft, burglary, fraud etc.). Crimes are alleged to have been committed not only against the complainant (or if proved as alleged, the 'victim') but against society at large. Therefore the criminal law serves a general 'public interest' purpose to maintain social order by deterring criminal behaviour which is capable of creating social instability. The main aim is thus to take the individual victim's desire for some form of retribution and formally channel this desire, alongside that of society, into a process that prosecutes and punishes the wrongdoer (defendant). If the defendant is convicted, then the final question will be how best to punish and deter the defendant (and others in society) as well as protect the public. It may be that the sentence is a fine, a term of imprisonment, or various other community and rehabilitation orders imposed to enable the defendant to re-integrate into society.

The civil law aims at regulating fairly the various interactions between ordinary members of society. These interactions are almost infinite; whether between a customer and a retailer, a manufacturer and a consumer, a doctor and a patient, a will-maker and those who stand to inherit under the will, a landlord and a tenant, a school and a pupil, and so on. The civil law helps in the resolution of such private disputes between two or more parties and can provide for the recovery of one party's losses. These losses mainly flow from death or personal injury, interference with property, or frequently are simply financial losses.

Historically, the main areas of the civil law were contract and tort, but the law of property, trusts, judicial review, and employment, among others, all fall under the umbrella term of civil law. These areas of law essentially provide a system of rights and remedies. The most obvious perhaps is the law of contract. Treitel, in *The Law of Contract*, defines a contract as 'an agreement giving rise to obligations which are enforced or recognised by law'. Thus, obligations may be created by the parties' agreement and, should a party fail to perform their side of the agreement, the other will have a remedy for this failure, for example, there could be an express penalty or a further liability written into the contract. The law of tort, on the other hand, encompasses a number of situations where the law imposes a duty (in contract law the duties are usually imposed by the contractual terms or are implicit in the agreement) to act in accordance with a certain standard of care. This is a legal duty and the existence of that duty does not depend upon there being a contract. One of the main torts you will learn about, where such duties are imposed, is the tort of negligence, where the main remedy being sought is compensation by way of damages.

Taking the example above, the person who has been subjected to a battery may derive some comfort from the criminal law convicting and punishing the individual, However, what about the losses he has suffered in the form of pain, suffering, shock, possible medical or dental costs if the injuries require treatment, and/or time off work? It is the civil law, and in this case the tort of battery, that would provide a system for the compensation of such losses.

Table 2.3 summarises the differences between criminal and civil law and includes differences that are also discussed at 2.4. You will no doubt become more familiar with these differences when you begin your studies in both English Legal System and other areas such as criminal law and the law of tort.

Key point

The same set of facts may give rise to various legal consequences, sometimes both criminal and civil in nature.

2.2 **Common law and equity**

Another important classification of law that will be encountered in the early stages of a law course is that between common law and equity.

2.2.1 **Common law**

The term 'common law' often gives rise to difficulty as it can carry several meanings. The meaning of the term will depend upon the context in which the term is used.

- Common law may mean the law created by the common law courts in contrast to the law created by the Court of Chancery which first developed the law of equity.
- Common law may mean all the law created by the courts over time, including the law of equity, as opposed to the law created by Parliament—that is, legislation. In this sense, common law may be termed case law, i.e. 'judge-made' law.
- Similar to the interpretation above, common law may refer to a legal tradition which defines the English legal system in contrast to other legal systems that are followed in mainland Europe. Apart from England and Wales, other examples of

a system that follows a common law tradition include the United States (with the exception of Louisiana), Canada, and Australia. This common law tradition refers to judge-made law or case law and the system that is governed by the doctrine of judicial precedent. For instance, the English law of contract is not exclusively codified in a formal document (although there is often legislation, e.g. the Sale of Goods Act 1979) but is to be found mainly in the decisions of judges in cases, with some cases which were heard a hundred years ago still being authoritative. The common law tradition can also refer to the slightly different roles of judges and lawyers compared with other systems that have a civil law tradition. For instance, in civil law countries such as France, judges take a lead and pro-active role in criminal investigations and establishing the facts. They are therefore less reliant on the competing oral arguments that are advanced by the prosecution and defence.

First, it is worth briefly elaborating on the notion of the common law, as understood in its most frequently used, case law sense.

2.2.2 **Common law as case law**

See Chapter 5, 'The doctrine of judicial precedent'.

Most of English law comes from legislation and case law. The decisions of judges in cases brought before the courts are a major source of law. Such decisions are recorded in law reports and are used by lawyers to determine what the law is. In deciding cases, judges must look at relevant previous case law. In doing so, judges have to operate within the doctrine of binding precedent, which means that like cases must be decided alike. Courts are arranged hierarchically and a judge in a lower court must follow the law as laid down by the higher courts. There are two elements to the doctrine of precedent:

- the doctrine of *stare decisis* (stand by what is decided), indicating when one court is bound by a principle of law coming from another court; and
- a principle of law that crucially helped to decide a previous case which is binding and must be applied to a current case based on similar facts.

This system promotes certainty and makes the law more predictable. It allows lawyers to consult case law, secure in the knowledge that, for example, principles stated in the Supreme Court must be applied by the lower courts, such as the Court of Appeal or the High Court. Under this system, when a principle of law is established it operates prospectively, in the sense of applying to future cases. This newly established principle can equally have retrospective effect and may therefore be the basis for a new case or even a new appeal

Case law is different from the form of law made by Parliament. As Twining and Miers note in *How to Do Things with Rules*, statute law is in a fixed verbal form, whereas judge-made law is in a non-fixed verbal form. This means that the text in a statute is fixed unless amended by a subsequent Act of Parliament, whereas judge-made law has first to be ascertained from a case and may be clarified and developed in later cases. This leads to a difference in approach to the interpretation of the law. Lord Reid, commenting on the nature of case law in *Broome v Cassell & Co Ltd* [1972] AC 1027, said (at p.1085):

> [E]xperience has shown that those who have to apply the decision to other cases and still more those who wish to criticise it seem to find it difficult to avoid treating sentences and phrases in a single speech as if they were provisions in an Act of Parliament. They do not seem to realise that it is not the function of . . . judges to frame definitions or to lay down hard and fast rules. It is their function to enunciate principles and much that they say is intended to be illustrative or explanatory and not to be definitive.

See 5.2, 'Nature of judge-made law'.

Beyond legislation and case law, you may encounter some historical sources of law. These are custom, Roman law, and authoritative texts, such as *Blackstone's Commentaries* and *Coke's Institutes*. Custom as a source of law consists of rules that have their origin in the fact of their long usage. Indeed, the same may be said, although to a lesser extent, of Roman law (the system springing from Ancient Rome). The roots of jurisdictions in mainland Europe, and to a degree the law of Scotland (Scots Law) can be traced to Roman law. The courts have in certain instances drawn upon Roman law to deal with situations where there was a lack of decided case law. See, for example, in the law of contract *Taylor v Caldwell* (1863) 3 B & S 826, where Blackburn J referred to Roman law in creating a general excuse for obligations in a contract where a contract became impossible to fulfil, often due to an unforeseen event. Finally, authoritative texts—the legal writings of judges and academic lawyers—have played a small role in the development of the common law. Such writings may also be consulted by the courts when seeking to interpret a statute—see, for example, *R v JTB* [2009] UKHL 20. An example of the limits of these texts may be seen in *R v R* [1992] 1 AC 599.

Finally, the courts may take into account relevant academic literature, textbooks, and journal articles in deciding cases. This may form part of a majority or a minority dissenting decision. An academic article by Professor Glanville Williams was cited as persuasive in the case of *R v Shivpuri* [1986] 2 All ER 334, which criticised the state of the law on attempted crimes. Alternatively, and to illustrate with a topical example, in 2017 the UK Supreme Court decided that it would be unlawful for the government to notify the EU of its withdrawal by triggering Article 50 of the Treaty of the European Union, because it would change domestic law, specifically the European Communities Act 1972. The effect of the decision was that, in these circumstances, another Act of Parliament was required to authorise the notification. Lord Carnwarth disagreed. In his dissenting judgment, he relied not only on an academic article by Professor Gavin Phillipson in the *Modern Law Review* but also commentary by various academics in online blogs.

2.2.3 **Equity**

One interpretation of equity or equitable refers to everyone being treated fairly and impartially. However, the first legal point to note about equity is that it is in fact a body of law developed by the judges, subject to the doctrine of precedent. In this regard it is the same as other judge-made law. However, the origins, development, and substance of equity are very different from those of the common law. Equity developed because of the rigidity of the common law; the price of certainty is sometimes injustice, particularly when the common law tends to develop slowly. To remedy injustices, it was possible to petition the Chancellor as 'keeper of the King's conscience', acting on behalf of the King as the fountain of justice. At first, equity was merely the Chancellor acting according to conscience. There was no system and therefore no certainty with equity; it was said that equity depended upon the 'length of the Chancellor's foot', meaning the type of justice dispensed was determined by who the Chancellor was. Led by the Chancellor, the Court of Chancery became established and began to administer the law on equity.

The Chancellor was commonly an ecclesiastic and thus the law on equity was based upon moral and religious principles, particularly on what was thought to be conscionable. Over time, these principles eventually crystallised as a body of law governed by the doctrine of precedent. Today, the law on equity tends to encompass the law on trusts (e.g. when ownership of money or assets are contested, say, when they remain in the legal name of one person but are alleged to have been held for the benefit of others), or the law of breach of confidence (e.g. when someone abuses their duty of trust and confidence towards you by disclosing confidential information) or the law on estoppel (e.g. when a person is prevented from breaking a promise that you have relied on to your detriment).

Having these two jurisdictions, one common law and one equitable, operating in parallel and administered by separate courts inevitably led to conflict. To illustrate, it was possible for the common law and the law on equity to apply simultaneously to the same set of facts and yet reach directly opposing conclusions. Ultimately it was determined that where common law rules and equitable rules conflicted, the rules of equity were to prevail.

Example

In the law of property and the law of contract you will see the operation of common law rules and those of equity. At common law, merely part-paying a debt does not discharge a full debt, even if there is an accompanying promise by the creditor (someone who is owed a sum of money) that the part-payment does discharge the full debt. However, a principle of equity—that of estoppel—can be used to prevent a creditor going back on a promise to accept less, in circumstances where a debtor had relied upon the promise. You will learn much more about this when you begin your study of the law on contract. See *Hughes v Metropolitan Railways* (1877) 2 App Cas 439 and *Central London Property Trust v High Trees House Ltd* [1947] KB 130.

By the 1800s, equity was beset by major problems. For those of you that enjoy literature, Charles Dickens in his novel *Bleak House* gave a particularly damning verdict of the Court of Chancery, using the fictional case of Jarndyce v Jarndyce as a central feature in the book. Among these problems was an expensive, unduly complex, and extremely slow procedure, and where a party sought both common law and equitable remedies, it was necessary to commence proceedings in both the common law courts and the Court of Chancery. The Judicature Acts 1873–75 reformed this situation by fusing the administration of law and equity, so that both legal and equitable remedies could be awarded by the same court. The old common law courts and the Court of Chancery were replaced by the High Court (see later at 2.5).

2.3 **Parliamentary or legislative supremacy**

Before turning to Parliament it is worth clarifying that the *government* exercises executive power. The term executive can be used interchangeably to describe the government (and its powers)—because one thinks of the government, led by the prime minister and his Cabinet ministers, as the one ultimate authority—responsible for law enforcement and the execution of the law. The winning party in an election is the one that can form a government by (usually) commanding a majority in the House of Commons and is then able to propose and help pass new laws in Parliament. A Parliament where no one party gains a majority is said to be hung and may require a coalition to form a new government, as happened in 2010.

It is Parliament itself that is the supreme law-making body and may make laws on any subject it chooses. In the United Kingdom there is no higher law-making body than Parliament. This is often termed parliamentary supremacy (or 'sovereignty'). It is one of the cornerstones of the UK's constitution—the set of largely unwritten rules and principles that help to govern, organise, and structure how the state operates, including the extent of the government's powers and the rights that should be guaranteed to all people within the state. The commonly cited description of parliamentary supremacy is that attributed to Albert Venn Dicey who wrote in the *Law of the Constitution* (1885):

> The principle of Parliamentary sovereignty means neither more nor less than this, namely, that Parliament . . . has, under the English constitution, the right to make or unmake any law whatever; and, further, that no person or body is recognised by the law of England as having a right to override or set aside the legislation of Parliament.

Sir Ivor Jennings, in *The Law and the Constitution*, wrote that Parliament could even legislate to outlaw the smoking of cigarettes on the streets of Paris. Of course, the effect of parliamentary supremacy would mean that this was legally possible but from a political and practical point of view (e.g. there would be no way to enforce such a law), Parliament would scarcely contemplate doing so.

To be clear, when an Act of Parliament and a common law precedent, as expressed by a judge, conflict then it will be the Act of Parliament that will prevail. A judge-made

See Chapter 4, 'The interpretation of statutes' and Chapter 7, 'Human rights in the United Kingdom'.

law cannot repeal or override a declared rule in an Act of Parliament. By contrast, it is clear that an Act of Parliament may alter, in whole or in part, the direction that the common law has taken, and that is often the motive for legislative intervention if the common law is unclear, prone to unfairness, or simply in a state that requires legislative input.

To briefly digress, it is worth making a few observations about Treaties. A treaty is formally an agreement made by states. It is the UK government, acting in the name of the Crown (the Queen) that enters and agrees to a treaty. Examples of treaties entered into by the UK are the Treaty of Rome 1957, which established the European Economic Community (and which later became today's European Union—the EU), and the European Convention on Human Rights (ECHR) 1950.

However, while such treaties bind the UK in international law, they form no part of domestic law unless incorporated by Act of Parliament. Our system requires treaties to be incorporated into domestic law and thus our membership of the then European Economic Community was confirmed by the European Communities Act 1972. Although not strictly required for membership, the UK's Human Rights Act 1998 underlined the UK's membership of the ECHR by directly incorporating Convention rights (what we ordinarily label as human rights, such as the right to fair trial, or the right to freedom of expression) into UK law.

That is not to say that the international treaties that remain unincorporated into English law have no effect. There is a presumption of statutory interpretation that Parliament does not intend to legislate in contravention of an international treaty to which the UK is a signatory. Of course, this is only a presumption, and should Parliament by clear words indicate an intention not to comply with a treaty obligation, then the courts must give effect to this intention.

Under the vision of parliamentary supremacy as expressed by Dicey, Parliament is not bound by past parliaments and nor therefore may it bind future parliaments. This means that no Act of Parliament may be 'entrenched', that is, made impossible to repeal or overrule. To amend or repeal any Act of Parliament, no special procedure is required; the amending or repealing Act must pass through both the House of Commons and the House of Lords and then receive royal assent. Once an Act of Parliament has been made, its validity may not be questioned in the courts or by other bodies: see *British Railways Board v Pickin* [1974] AC 765.

Example

An example of an attempt to challenge the validity of an Act of Parliament was seen in *Jackson v Attorney General* [2006] 1 AC 262. The facts and legal issues were complex. You will certainly learn much more about this case when you study constitutional law. However, put simply, the case concerned the Hunting Act 2004, which made it an offence to hunt wild animals with dogs except in limited circumstances. In *Jackson v Attorney General*, a challenge to the validity of the Act was mounted. The argument in essence concerned the procedure for enacting (or passing) the Hunting Act 2004. The Parliament Acts 1911 and 1949 were used to pass the Hunting Act 2004. The combined effect of the Parliament Acts was to allow a bill (a draft Act) to become an Act of Parliament without the assent of the House of Lords, with the 1911 Act imposing at best a two-year delay and the 1949 Act shortening the delay period to one year. The 1949 Act itself was passed using the Parliament Act 1911 (i.e. without the assent of the House or Lords). It was argued that by passing the Parliament Act of 1949 using the 1911 Act, the Commons had sought to enlarge its powers. This was in contravention of the established principle that powers conferred on a body (the House of Commons) by an enabling Act (the Parliament Act 1911) may not be modified by that body unless there are express words in the Act authorising the modification. In other words, the argument was that the Parliament Act 1949 should have required the assent of the House of Lords; without such assent it was not valid and any legislation made under it—the Hunting Act 2004—was likewise invalid.

This was rejected by the House of Lords who took a matter of fact approach. The Lords declared that the Parliament Act 1911 was a law that created a parallel route to enacting a bill into an Act of Parliament. The scope of the 1911 Act permitted it to be validly amended, as it later was by the 1949 Act. The overall object of the 1911 Act was . . . to restrict . . . the power of the Lords to defeat measures supported by a majority of the Commons. The 1949 Act had been used subsequently to create other legislation before the Hunting Act 2004. Therefore any Act made using the Parliament Acts 1911-1949 was validly enacted and was a recognised Act of Parliament.

An Act of Parliament may create new law or may affect existing law. You may find references in the long title of an Act that indicate it is intended to amend or repeal existing legislation or common law rules, or to simply consolidate or codify rules that are now confusingly found across various Acts of Parliament. Table 2.1 explains and gives examples of the types of legislation.

The volume and complexity of legislation can give cause for concern and have done so for many years. In 2013, the Office of Parliamentary Counsel (made up of lawyers specialising in drafting government bills) published a report entitled *When Laws Become Too Complex—A Review into the Causes of Complex Legislation*. The report highlighted a number of issues: that the average length of bills introduced into Parliament has increased significantly; that multi-purpose bills (bills covering more than one legal area) are more common than they were; and, to illustrate the problem, between 1983 and 2009 Parliament passed into law 100 criminal justice bills creating over 4,000 new criminal offences. The causes of legislative complexity are considered in the report, which may be found at **www.gov.uk/government/publications/when-laws-become-too-complex**.

Table 2.1 Table of legislation—explanation and examples

Types of legislation or legislative provision	Explanation	Examples
Repealing	An Act of Parliament does not stop becoming law due to the passage of time or by falling into disuse. For a statute or a statutory provision to cease to be law it must be repealed by a further Act of Parliament. A schedule of repeals is a usual feature of an Act of Parliament. Additionally, the Law Commission (see 2.6.7) keeps statutes under review and will seek to repeal obsolete Acts of Parliament.	The Larceny Act 1916 was repealed by the Theft Act 1968. A provision of the Caravans Sites Act 1968 s.6, was repealed by the Criminal Justice and Public Order Act 1994. s. 1 of The European Union (Withdrawal) Act 2018 expressly states that the European Communities Act 1972 will be repealed on exit day.
Amending	An Act may seek to amend existing statutes or alter the common law.	The Law Reform (Frustrated Contracts) Act 1943 amended the existing common law on the frustration of contracts.
Consolidating	Consolidating legislation brings together in one Act of Parliament all the statutory provisions on a particular subject area. It is designed to make the law more coherent and easier to find, and therefore comply with.	The long title to the Employment Rights Act 1996 simply states that it is 'An Act to consolidate enactments relating to employment rights'. Although not expressly mentioned, it has been argued that the effect of the Equality Act 2010 was to consolidate protections in various pieces of equality legislation (e.g. Equal Pay Act 1970, Sex Discrimination Act 1975, and Race Relations Act 1976) into one source.
Codifying	Whereas consolidation concerns bringing together statutory provisions, codification is designed to bring all law, statutory and case law, together in a single statute. Such Acts again make the law easier to find.	The Sale of Goods Act 1893 was a codifying measure. Subsequently, the Act was amended and the Act and amendments were consolidated in the Sale of Goods Act 1979.

In relation to Acts of Parliament, the role of judges is to give effect to the intention of Parliament. This is done by interpreting the words in the statute. As Lord Diplock expressed in *Duport Steel v Sirs* [1980] 1 WLR 142, at p.157:

> Parliament makes the laws, the judiciary interpret them. When Parliament legislates to remedy what the majority of its members at the time perceive to be a defect or a lacuna in the existing law (whether it be the written law enacted by existing statutes or the unwritten common law as it has been expounded by the judges in decided cases), the role of the judiciary is confined to ascertaining from the words that Parliament has approved as expressing its intention what that intention was, and to giving effect to it. Where the meaning of the statutory words is plain and unambiguous it is not for the judges to invent fancied ambiguities as an excuse for failing to give effect to its plain meaning because they themselves consider that the consequences of doing so would be inexpedient, or even unjust or immoral.

Lord Diplock is emphasising the idea we mentioned earlier—the 'separation of powers'— between Parliament and the courts. The role of judges is to apply and interpret law made by Parliament. They must be careful not to encroach on Parliament's law-making function. However, the greatest challenge is often in the interpretation. The words as expressed in an Act of Parliament can have various interpretations, depending on how one approaches the task and to what degree the courts will look at the broad aim, context, and purpose of the Act. You will find more coverage and detail about this challenge in Chapter 4.

Parliament may empower other persons or bodies to make law on its behalf, such as government ministers, departments, and local authorities. This can be termed the power to make delegated legislation, i.e. the role and task of law-making are given to others. This is an important source of law as it fills in the gaps in an Act of Parliament. These gaps are where more practical and operational rules are required to ensure the Act is being observed. Those delegated are more likely to be in a position to assess those practical requirements accurately. It also allows parliamentary time to be saved in the process. The power to make delegated legislation is given in an Act of Parliament (which is referred to as the parent or enabling Act). Unlike primary legislation, the validity of delegated or secondary legislation may be challenged in the courts if the maker has acted *ultra vires*, which means beyond the powers permitted by the parent Act.

See 3.5, 'Secondary legislation'.

2.3.1 Relationship between the law of the UK and the law of the European Union (EU)

When the UK government signed the treaty confirming its membership of the then European Economic Community, the obligation under the treaty had no legal effect. Under the UK's constitution it was necessary for an Act of Parliament to be passed, incorporating such obligations into domestic law. By reason of enacting the European Communities Act 1972, the UK's legal system became bound up with the law-making institutions of the eventual European Union (EU). So, for instance, s.2(1) of this Act ensures that EU treaties and even EU Regulations are directly applicable in domestic law. In this respect it was confirmed in the European Court of Justice and later in the case of *R v Secretary of State for Transport, ex parte Factortame (No 2)* [1991] AC 603, that in cases of conflict between national law and the law of the European Union, the latter would prevail and be supreme. For extensive coverage of the detail on the relationship between the UK legal system, domestic law, and EU law, see Chapter 6.

See 3.5 for 'Secondary legislation' and 3.5.3 for 'Henry VIII clauses'.

The future political and economic relationship between the UK and the EU is rather uncertain. The UK formally left the EU on 31 January 2020 and is currently in a transition period until 31 December 2020. Leaving this uncertainty to one side, it is worth highlighting that the date of withdrawal signalled the detachment of the UK's legal system from direct EU and EU-derived legislation, such as EU regulations or directives. In that regard it will end supremacy of EU law (s.5 European Union (Withdrawal) Act 2018). However, there is a huge volume of domestic law created over the course of many decades of EU membership, that is influenced or shaped by, or simply implements EU law. In recognition of this, the government passed the EU (Withdrawal) Act 2018. This Act repeals the ECA 1972 on the day of exit and therefore ends the authority of the EU in the UK, but it also retains and preserves all existing EU law operating on the day before exit into domestic law. The Act is intended to promote short to medium-term certainty in the law for all individuals and businesses, until such time as those laws are subsequently amended or repealed by later Acts of Parliament. Diagram 2.1 shows the law-making bodies and the forms that law may take.

2.3.2 **Relationship between the law of the UK and the European Convention on Human Rights (ECHR)**

In 1949, the UK became an original founding member of the Council of Europe: an organisation that promotes democracy, human rights, and the rule of law in Europe. It currently has forty-seven member states. All members are signatories (technically labelled 'High Contracting Parties') to the European Convention on Human Rights. The European Court of Human Rights interprets this Convention and can hear applications from individuals or groups alleging that one of the member states has breached one or more human rights laid out in the Convention. Both the Council and the Court are based in Strasbourg, France. One of the most important points to note is that the Council of Europe is a wholly distinct body from the EU and any of its institutions such as the EU Parliament or Commission. The respective courts, the Court of Justice of the EU, based in Luxembourg, and the European Court of Human Rights in France have different roles, functions, and jurisdiction over the Member States. For instance, the Court of Justice of the EU can issue rulings to ensure that EU law is interpreted and applied in the same way, and it can also determine disputes between

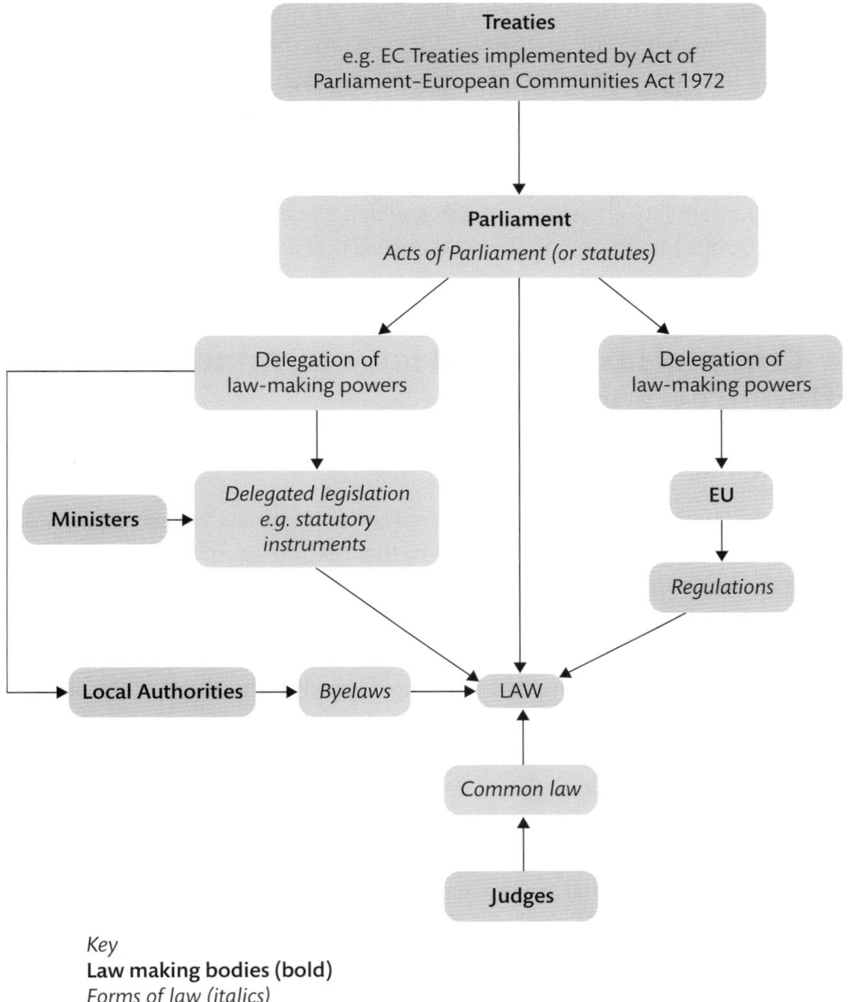

Diagram 2.1 Law-making bodies and forms of law

institutions of the EU and members. The ECtHR has no such role. There are currently 28 Member States of the EU (including, at least for now, the United Kingdom).

Despite popular media coverage often confusing the two Courts, and the Council of Europe with bodies of the EU, you should understand the clear differences between these two. Reading Chapters 6 and 7 will be of considerable assistance.

As mentioned earlier in this chapter, the Human Rights Act 1998 incorporated the rights outlined in the ECHR into domestic law. It is an Act of considerable constitutional significance. In accordance with s.2 of the 1998 Act, the English courts must take into account any judgment, decision, declaration, or advisory opinion of the European Court of Human Rights. The Act does not permit the courts to overrule or strike down legislation—that would be against the principle of parliamentary supremacy. Instead, s.3 of the Act requires the courts to seek to interpret and apply primary legislation and subordinate legislation, in a way, as far as is possible, that is compatible with Convention rights. If it is not possible to read the legislation so as to be compatible with Convention rights then the domestic court must make a declaration of incompatibility under s.4 of the Act, which places the onus upon the government to introduce legislation that would ensure that a compatible interpretation is possible.

2.4 **Criminal law and civil law—terminology, differences, and themes**

2.4.1 **Criminal**

We discussed the basic difference in criminal law and civil law earlier on pages 33–4. They serve different aims. Let's now turn to the differences in language and procedure. First, in criminal law, and in a criminal trial, the burden of proof is upon the prosecution to prove the defendant's guilt. This means that the onus falls on the prosecution to prove all the ingredients of the alleged crime with which a defendant is charged; a defendant is innocent until proven guilty. The standard of proof that the prosecution is required to meet is that the defendant's guilt is *beyond reasonable doubt*. Note that, in certain instances the burden of proof is placed upon a defendant, for example, if the defendant raises a defence of insanity or diminished responsibility. In these circumstances, the defendant has the burden but is required only to prove the defence to a civil standard of proof (see 2.4.2).

The criminal courts of trial are the magistrates' court and the Crown Court. In the former court, questions of fact (e.g. was the defendant at a particular location, was he carrying a weapon etc.) are determined by the magistrates or a district judge, whereas in the Crown Court, those findings of fact are made by a jury, consisting of twelve randomly selected people. A characteristic of the criminal process is that it is said to be adversarial, i.e. a battle between two sides, led by the prosecution and defence barristers, presenting their own version of the facts. The rules of criminal procedure and evidence govern this process and help to ensure that the trial is as fair as it possibly can be for both sides. The balance is between respecting the rights of the defendant and ensuring he or she receives a fair trial, with, on the other hand, respecting the state's interest in bringing the case on behalf of the complainant and society at large. Ultimately, this process is about fairly testing the strength of the case against the accused and, if proven, ensuring any due punishment is meted out to the defendant. It is worth highlighting that criminal trials are not necessarily about the pursuit of truth, although many observers hold that a particular verdict (guilty or not guilty) will vindicate their own story of what happened.

The criminal justice system has been the subject of major cost-saving changes in recent years. Like other public services, there has been a constant drive to make the process more efficient and less expensive. Many observers have criticised the effect this has had on the quality of justice the criminal justice system is able to provide to both defendants and complainants. The Further reading section at the end of this chapter has an example of one such observer–'The Secret Barrister' who has been particularly vocal about the impact of a range of political and policy changes on criminal justice in England and Wales.

Thinking point
What price for justice?

What are the benefits and risks in ensuring that the criminal justice system is ever more efficient and inexpensive? What are the particular benefits or risks for various groups in the criminal justice system, for example, the police, the Crown Prosecution Service, victims of crime, judges, lawyers, potential perpetrators of crimes, but also ordinary taxpayers and members of the public?

Finally, in criminal cases, a prosecution will be undertaken by the state in the name of the monarch or in the name of the Crown. The case will usually be reported as *R v Defendant's surname* (e.g. *R v Thornton or R v Smith*) followed by the citation of the law report. The R is for Regina (for a reigning Queen) or Rex (for a reigning King). Please note the best way to verbally express this case would be 'The Crown against Smith' or 'The Crown against Thornton'. Please try to avoid saying 'versus' as this is not conventionally used in England and Wales (but will no doubt have been said in many American legal dramas on TV!).

Note that in some older cases a prosecution before a magistrates' court would be made in the name of a police officer involved in the case. Often such cases were appealed to the Divisional Court of the Queen's Bench Division of the High Court and were then reported under the names of defendant and prosecutor, for example *Brutus v Cozens* [1972] 1 WLR 484. Sometimes a civil case will be also applicable in criminal law where a concept has been defined or developed. If a prosecution is successful, say, for offences of murder or manslaughter, a defendant is said to have been found *guilty*.

See further Chapter 13, 'The criminal process: pre-trial and trial'.

2.4.2 **Civil**

In civil trials the burden of proof is placed upon a party who is bringing the claim and making the allegation. Usually a claimant will bear the burden of proof and the standard of proof is that of the balance of probabilities, that is, the facts alleged must be more likely to be true than not. This is basically at least a 51 per cent likelihood, on balance between two competing options. However, the rules on both burden and standard of proof can change depending on the area of civil law you are studying. It is important in studying these substantive subjects, such as contract and tort, to note any special exceptions or rules relating to the burden of proof.

 Example

In the law of contract, note the following situation where the ordinary burden of proof is reversed: s.11(5) of the Unfair Contract Terms Act 1977 provides that where an exemption clause is subject to the test of reasonableness under the Act then it is for the person who relies on the clause to show that it is reasonable.

The adversarial model is also the basis for civil justice. However, the Civil Procedure Rules now permit a judge to take a much more active case management role to ensure that cases are dealt with justly and at proportionate cost to the amount of money involved, the complexity of the case, and its significance. This is often termed the 'overriding objective' of civil justice.

In terms of reporting civil cases, a person or organisation commencing proceedings is called the claimant, i.e. they are bringing the claim. In the older cases you will still encounter the term plaintiff in reference to the claimant. The person against whom the claim is brought, and who is therefore defending the claim, is termed a defendant. The names of these case are therefore *Claimant Surname v Defendant Surname* (e.g. Donoghue v Stevenson or Foakes v Beer) followed by the citation of the law report. If a claim is successful, then the defendant is said to have acted unlawfully and is found *liable*.

2.5 **Classification of the courts**

A court of first instance *A case will commence in a court of first instance (that is, a court of trial). This jurisdiction is also termed original jurisdiction. Decisions of courts may be challenged on appeal and erroneous decisions corrected. Courts hearing appeals are said to have appellate jurisdiction.*

The courts of England and Wales can generally be placed into two categories: superior and inferior. Put simply, superior courts are not limited or restricted in their jurisdiction, for example, in terms of money or geographical limits. They exercise supervisory jurisdiction over the inferior courts and are therefore able to hear appeals from decisions in those lower courts. In terms of legislation, the Judicature Acts 1873–1875, the Senior Courts Act 1981, and the Constitutional Reform Act of 2005 all variously and rather confusingly confirm the established hierarchy and the roles and powers of the various courts. Generally speaking, the superior courts in the UK are understood to be the Supreme Court (previously the Appellate Committee of the House of Lords), the Court of Appeal, High Court, Crown Court, Privy Council, and Employment Appeal Tribunal; the inferior courts include the magistrates' courts, the County Court and other ***first instance*** tribunals.

2.5.1 **Overview of the composition and jurisdiction of the courts**

This section now turns to briefly describe various courts in the hierarchy of England and Wales. As students of the law you will find a working grasp of the composition and jurisdiction of these courts useful. It will provide some useful background that will inform your understanding of the doctrine of judicial precedent—see Chapter 5—and also explain why decisions in particular courts carry more significance than others. Unfortunately, it is not possible to simply classify courts as criminal or civil courts, as some courts exercise both criminal and civil jurisdiction. However, the organisation of the courts allows for some courts to have particular specialisms.

See 8.1.15, 'Coroners'.

This present discussion focuses on the main courts where the overwhelming majority of cases and issues are determined. There are some more specialised courts, such as the ***coroner***'s court that are not detailed here, although you can find more information later in this book and more online such as at **https://www.gov.uk/government/publications/guide-to-coroner-services-and-coroner-investigations-a-short-guide**. Instead, the focus in this section will be on the two main courts of first instance, the magistrates' court and the County Court, and the appellate courts.

Coroner
A coroner is an independent judicial office holder, appointed by a local council and they investigate deaths that have been reported to them if it appears that the death was violent or unnatural, the cause of death is unknown, or the person died in prison, police custody, or another type of state detention. If necessary, a coroner can hold a special hearing to determine the cause of death that is termed an inquest.

2.5.2 **Magistrates' courts**

Magistrates' courts are presided over by Justices of the Peace (alternatively termed magistrates). They are sometime referred to as 'lay justices' as they are volunteers, will not be salaried, and may not be legally qualified so they may be advised in court by a legal adviser. Nonetheless, they will have undergone a training programme that includes court and prison visits as well as other appropriate preparation. Under s.121 of the Magistrates' Courts Act 1980, cases are normally heard before a bench of two or three Justices of the Peace. A single Justice of the Peace may try a summary offence, not punishable with imprisonment, on papers under s.16A Magistrates' Courts Act 1980, and these offences may include driving without insurance or non-payment of TV licences. The magistrates' courts have some limited civil jurisdiction (e.g. where it is given by statute, and tends to consist primarily of licensing laws, and the recovery of civil debts such as income tax or unpaid council tax). Otherwise, the magistrates predominantly exercise criminal jurisdiction.

See Chapter 8, 'The judiciary' and Chapters 12, 13, and 15 on criminal and civil procedure.

Criminal jurisdiction

All criminal cases commence in the magistrates' courts and more than 90 per cent of cases will be completed there. However, where a defendant is charged with a more serious offence a magistrates' court can send the defendant to the Crown Court for trial. To understand the circumstances in which the magistrates' court will do this, you need to first understand the classification of criminal offences. The classification is an essential element in the process of deciding where an offence is to be tried (see Table 2.2).

Table 2.2 Classification of criminal offences

Type of Offence	Explanation
Summary Only	These are less serious cases, such as motoring offences and minor assaults, where the defendant is not entitled to trial by jury. They are generally disposed of in magistrates' courts. Offences will carry no more than six months' imprisonment for a single offence.
Triable Either Way	These can be dealt with either by magistrates or before a judge and jury at the Crown Court. Such offences include theft and handling stolen goods. Magistrates can also decide that a case is so serious that it should be dealt with in the Crown Court. If the magistrates decide that they can try the case, a defendant can nonetheless insist on their right to trial in the Crown Court in front of a jury.
Triable Only on Indictment	Indictable only offences are the most serious criminal offences. These include, amongst others, murder, manslaughter, rape, and robbery. These must be heard at a Crown Court in front of a jury.

Table 2.3 Contrasting criminal and civil law

Criminal Law	Civil Law
Conduct which society and the state disapproves of and thus criminalises.	Involves the alleged unlawful conduct of someone in the course of an interaction or relationship between individuals/organisations.
Enforces particular forms of behaviour	Resolves the dispute between individuals
The case is brought in the name of the Crown and will begin (R v ***Defendant's Surname***).	The case is brought by the party alleging wrongdoing (the claimant) v defendant).
The burden of proof is on the prosecution and the standard of proof is beyond reasonable doubt.	The burden of proof is on the claimant and the standard of proof is on balance of probabilities (i.e. more likely than not).
Regulates society by the threat of punishment and sanction (with the police force used to enforce the law).	Regulates relationships by declaring rights, duties, principles, and other requirements that, if not observed, leave persons at risk of legal liability.
The court imposes a sentence that is required to reflect the seriousness of the crime and often imposes some form of punishment, e.g. with a community or custodial sentence.	The court makes an order for a remedy to the successful party, usually in the form of damages.

To summarise, if the offence is 'triable only on indictment', the magistrates' court must send the defendant to the Crown Court; if the offence is 'triable either way' then a magistrates' court must determine in which court the trial will be held, that is, whether a defendant is to be tried in the Crown Court or a magistrates' court. They will consider, amongst other things, the limits of their sentencing powers: a term of six months' imprisonment for a single offence or a maximum of twelve months if there is more than one offence charged. The defendant will retain a right to elect a trial at the Crown Court (in front of a jury) even where the magistrates decide that a trial in the magistrates' court would be appropriate. If the defendant is charged with a summary only offence the magistrates' court themselves may try the defendant. Statutory offences will usually indicate which classification an offence falls under by referencing the punishment and, in the case of an either way offence, express alternative punishments. For instance, consider the following examples from the Theft Act 1968.

Example

Section 8(2) of the Theft Act 1968 provides: 'A person guilty of robbery, or of an assault with intent to rob, shall on conviction on indictment be liable to imprisonment for life.'

Section 12(2) of the Theft Act provides the following penalty for taking a motor vehicle: the guilty person 'shall . . . be liable on summary conviction to a fine not exceeding level 5 on the standard scale, to imprisonment for a term not exceeding six months, or to both'.

2.5.3 **Crown Court**

The Crown Court is part of the Senior Courts and has jurisdiction throughout England and Wales. It is subject in certain instances to the supervisory jurisdiction of the High Court. The basic position in the Crown Court is that proceedings will be before a single judge. The main jurisdiction of the Crown Court is that of trial on indictment, before judge and jury: s.46 Senior Courts Act 1981. However, following the Criminal Justice Act 2003 it is possible for a judge to sit without a jury where there is a danger of jury tampering, such as threats made to the jury or offers of bribes etc. The Crown Court can also deal with cases that have been committed by the magistrates' court for sentencing, where, say, the magistrates' court is of the opinion that its sentencing powers are inadequate or when a co-accused is being tried in the Crown Court for a related offence. There are various rights of appeal to the Crown Court from the magistrates' courts, including against sentence or conviction where a defendant pleads not guilty or against sentence where a defendant pleads guilty.

Thinking point

The right to a jury trial

Trial in the Crown Court is more time-consuming and costly than trial in the magistrates' courts. However, a defendant is entitled to be tried by a jury at the Crown Court. To what extent do you think that offences should be more readily tried at the magistrates' court (or that more offences should be reclassified as summary only)? Would such an approach be defensible and to what extent would the interference with the defendant's right to be tried by a jury be justified?

2.5.4 **County Court**

The County Court is governed by the County Courts Act 1984 and deals exclusively with the entire range of cases in civil matters. These cases may include businesses trying to recover debts, personal injury claims, landlord and tenant disputes, and many others. The court's jurisdiction is conferred by statute and includes, for example, actions founded on contract, tort, recovery of land and money, as well as cases that proceed in equity (up to a limit of £350,000) By s.5 of the County Courts Act 1984, various judges may sit in the Country Court including a circuit judge, a district judge, and a deputy district judge. The judges usually sit alone and in most cases there will be no juries (cases in relation to libel are one of the main exceptions).

One of the most important roles of civil judges is to actively manage the proceedings in line with the overriding objective of the civil justice system (to deal with cases justly and at proportionate cost). This includes ensuring that the case is a last resort. Therefore, the judge will try to ensure that the parties cooperate with each other in the conduct of the case, help the parties to settle (to avoid spiralling legal bills and costs), encourage the parties to use alternative dispute procedures (e.g. negotiations or a mediation process), and will also issue directions to the parties to help control the progress of the case.

Commencing proceedings—the County Court or High Court?

The main courts of trial are the County Court and the High Court. At one time, whether an action proceeded in the County Court or the High Court was determined simply on the basis of the amount of the claim. However, this was not deemed to be the best use of resources, especially when the case was reasonably straightforward. One has to take into account the difficulty of the case in hand because cases with a relatively small monetary value may give rise to novel and complex points of law, which may have a significant impact on other cases. In light of this, the current rules on allocation of cases between the County Court and the High Court are as follows.

In most cases, such as those that involve contract or claims in tort, a claimant has a choice of where to commence proceedings, but the case may not commence in the High Court unless, in a claim for money, the value of the claim is more than £100,000 and, if applicable, it must not start in the High Court unless a personal injury claim is above £50,000. Using these ranges the claimant will be assisted in deciding where to commence the case and should generally do so in the High Court, taking into account (a) the financial value of the claim or the amount in dispute (influenced by the figures outlined above); (b) the complexity of the facts, legal issues, remedies, or procedures; and (c) the importance of the claim, for example, does it involve a point of law of general public interest? In any event, cases commenced in the County Court or the High Court may be transferred from one court to the other where appropriate under ss.40–42 of the County Courts Act 1984.

Small claims jurisdiction

Much of the County Court's work involves jurisdiction in cases that are allocated to a route that is known as 'small claims'. This jurisdiction, for example, covers breach of contract, personal injuries claims, and some landlord and tenant disputes. A claim may be allocated to the small claims track by a district judge, depending upon the amount of the claim and the complexity of the case. In general, where a claim is for £10,000 or less it will be allocated to the small claims track, subject to the following: if it is a personal injury claim or a claim against a landlord by a tenant it will be allocated to the small claims track if it is for £1,000 or less. The procedure involved allows litigants to appear without legal representation (these are known as litigants in person). The hearing is more informal and the court may adapt procedures in a way that it considers to be more accessible and fair to all parties; the strict rules of evidence do not apply. The perceived advantages are that the small claims process is quicker, less costly, and more flexible.

There is a limited appellate jurisdiction whereby circuit judges may hear appeals from the decisions of district judges.

Thinking point

Is 'speedy' justice, justice?

To what extent do you think increasing the small claims limit or insisting that parties avoid the courts at all costs, and/or simply ensuring that cases are dealt with at low cost and efficiently as possible, is desirable? What are the benefits and risks for speedy justice? Consider the ethical and financial implications for claimants, defendants, lawyers, and even ordinary taxpayers that help pay for the civil justice system?

2.5.5 **Family Court**

It is worth briefly acknowledging the specialist structure of Family Courts. The Crime and Courts Act 2013 helped to formally establish the current single Family Court system. Previously, the 'Family Court' under Matrimonial and Family Proceedings Act 1984 sat in the Family Division of the High Court, or relevant cases were heard by district judges in County Courts and in specialist magistrates' courts (with trained magistrates) that are then labelled as Family Proceedings Courts. However, since April 2014 the Family Court can now sit anywhere and can hear various types of case including adoption, divorce matters, local authority proceedings in relation to children in care, maintenance issues (payments) for children after a relationship breakdown, as well as access/custody matters in respect of children with parents who are now separated or divorced. There is now a broader range of judge who can sit on family law cases, and most hearings will take place in a designated family centre (although they still use the same buildings as county and magistrates' courts).

Thinking point

Will online courts be 'open' and transparent?

In the opening chapter, reference was made to proposals for an increasing role for information technology to be adopted in dispute resolution. One such proposal that has been recommended is the introduction of an Online Solutions Court. This court would comprise three stages: first, the pre-issue stage of litigation; second, online processes that actively manage cases and facilitate settlement by the promotion of alternative dispute resolution, such as mediation; and finally, online or video-link adjudication by a judge. It has been argued that such a proposal will increase access to justice, as it will be less daunting, cheaper, and more convenient to parties in dispute. The physical courts of the civil justice system will have a reduced caseload to process. However, one concern raised is that it would prevent the courts from being open to the public and prevent justice from being seen to be done. Would an Online Solutions Court damage this basic principle and if it does, would that outweigh the potential benefits?

For further reading see Sir Thomas Etherton MR, 'The Civil Court of the Future', **www.judiciary.gov.uk/wp-content/uploads/2017/06/slynn-lecture-mr-civil-court-of-the-future-20170615.pdf**.

2.5.6 **High Court**

The High Court is mainly a civil court (although there is limited criminal jurisdiction exercised by the Queen's Bench Division). The jurisdiction of the High Court is in part based upon statute—the Senior Courts Act 1981—and in part inherent, as a result of the development of the old common law courts. It is particularly important to appreciate that the High Court has both first instance (original) and appellate (hearing of appeal against previous decisions) jurisdiction. At first instance the High Court has unlimited civil jurisdiction of a general nature.

Unsurprisingly, High Court judges can sit in the High Court. Judges are referred to as Mr Justice or Mrs Justice [name]; Justice may be abbreviated to J as in, for example, Smith J or Foskett J. The maximum number of full-time equivalent judges that are permitted is 108 and at the time of writing in October 2019 the current number is ninety-six. The judges are attached to divisions of the High Court and there are thirteen attached to the Chancery Division, seventeen in the Family Division, and the remaining sixty-six in the Queen's Bench Division. At first instance one High Court judge sits to hear a case.

The three divisions based on the Senior Courts Act 1981 allow for the Court to be specialised. Within the Queen's Bench Division there are specialist courts: the Administrative Court, Admiralty Court, Commercial Court, Circuit Commercial Courts (formerly Mercantile Courts), and the Technology and Construction Court. There are specialist courts also attached to the Chancery Division, for example, the Patents Court. Table 2.4 gives an indication of the subject matter of the jurisdiction of each division.

Table 2.4 Jurisdiction of the High Court (see s.61 of and Sch.1 to the Senior Courts Act 1981)

Queen's Bench Division	Chancery Division	Family Division
Jurisdiction includes cases concerning contract and tort. Also, the following specialist courts fall within the Queen's Bench Division: *Administrative Court* Main jurisdiction is public and administrative law cases including, judicial review, statutory appeals, and habeas corpus; *Admiralty Court* Jurisdiction over cases concerning maritime issues, such as collision of ships; *Commercial Court* Jurisdiction includes complex cases concerning business such as: shipping, commodities, insurance, banking and financial services, and arbitration; *Technology and Construction Court* Jurisdiction over technically complex cases, such as building cases.	Jurisdiction includes cases concerning: property; the execution of trusts; the administration of estates; bankruptcy; partnerships; probate business, other than non-contentious business; companies. *Patents Court* Hears issues concerning patents; see Patents Act 1977 and Senior Courts Act 1981 s.6 There are other specialist courts in the Chancery Division.	Jurisdiction includes cases concerning: all matrimonial causes and matters; legitimacy; proceedings under the Children Act 1989; adoption; non-contentious probate business; all proceedings under the Child Support Act 1991; all proceedings under ss.6 and 8 of the Gender Recognition Act 2004; all civil partnership causes and matters. See 2.5.5 which deals with the creation of the Family Court.

Since October 2017, specialist civil courts known collectively as 'The Business and Property Courts of England and Wales' now operate across the country. This umbrella term encompasses several of the Chancery and Queen's Bench Division Courts described above including the Commercial Court, Admiralty Court, Technology and Construction Court, and Patents Court, among others. The rationale for the change was to offer this aspect of the High Court's work an intelligible name, to enable the flexible deployment of judges, and to allow for a greater connection between the courts sitting in the regions, with the Court's main centre in the Rolls Building, Fetter Lane, London. For further explanation of this development see **www.judiciary.gov.uk/wp-content/uploads/2017/03/bpc-explanatory-statement-final-20170518-v2.pdf**.

Appellate jurisdiction

The High Court also acts as *a* Court of Appeal in certain instances. For instance, the major appellate function is exercised by the *Divisional Court* of the Queen's Bench

Division. In criminal matters, appeals are heard following summary trial before a magistrates' court by way of case stated where it is alleged that the decision is wrong in law or was given in excess of jurisdiction. In addition, an appeal from a magistrates' court to the Crown Court following summary trial may be appealed again, by defence or prosecution, by way of case stated to the Divisional Court of the Queen's Bench Division: s.28 Senior Courts Act 1981. Again, the grounds for such an appeal are that the decision is wrong in law or is in excess of jurisdiction. In the case of civil appeals from the County Court, much depends on the judge who hears the case originally, although permission is required either by the original court or the appellate court, such as the High Court, that will hear the appeal. The test adopted is whether the court considers that the appeal would have a real prospect of success; or there is some other compelling reason why the appeal should be heard. An appeal will be allowed if the decision of the lower court was wrong, or unjust because of a serious procedural irregularity in the proceeding in the lower court. The appeal court can affirm, set aside, vary any order or judgment of the lower court, or refer any claim back to the lower court for a re-determination of an issue or point.

Divisional Courts *These consist of two or more judges: s.66(3) of the Senior Courts Act 1981.*

Supervisory jurisdiction

The Queen's Bench Division of the High Court exercises supervisory jurisdiction by means of judicial review. Essentially, this means that the High Court can exercise its jurisdiction over the proceedings and decisions of inferior courts, tribunals, and other (public) bodies or persons who carry out public or judicial functions. Put simply, judicial review is not an appeal and does not consider the merits of the case, rather, it concentrates on the process by which a decision is made. Amongst other things, a decision-making body must act within its powers, take into account relevant considerations, and act in accordance with the rules of natural justice, such as ensuring there was a fair and impartial hearing, that parties are properly consulted, and that everyone's views were adequately represented.

2.5.7 **Court of Appeal**

Since 1875, the Court of Appeal has been established as the penultimate appellate court in the UK's hierarchy of courts. It deals only with appeals from other courts or tribunals. It is divided into two divisions, criminal and civil. The Criminal Division can hear appeals from proceedings in the Crown Court, including those against convictions and sentences, as well as handling applications for permission to appeal. It can also hear other types of appeals, including referrals from the Attorney General where there is a concern that a sentence imposed by the Crown Court is too lenient. The Civil Division can hear appeals against most decisions by all three divisions of the High Court, the County Court, the Family Court, as well as a range of tribunals. Judges in the Court of Appeal are termed a Lord Justice of Appeal or Lady

Justice of Appeal (abbreviated to LJ). The maximum number of Lord or Lady Justices is thirty-nine in total. Usually three Lord or Lady Justices of Appeal will hear an appeal, although in a complex or very significant case a five-judge Court of Appeal may be convened. There are currently thirty-nine Lord and Lady Justices of Appeal in addition to the Lord Chief Justice, Master of the Rolls, and the respective heads of each division.

2.5.8 **Supreme Court**

Visit the online resources to watch a video on the Supreme Court.

On 1 October 2009 the Supreme Court of the UK replaced the Appellate Committee of the House of Lords as the highest court and final court of appeal in the UK. The then judges of the House of Lords—the Lords and Ladies of Appeal in Ordinary, were retitled as Justices of the Supreme Court. This change was brought about by the Constitutional Reform Act 2005.

There were many reasons for the Court's creation but the most significant was the following. The Appellate Committee of the House of Lords was located in the Palace of Westminster, within Parliament (the legislature). The judges sat inside the legislature too. Under the doctrine of the separation of powers the judicial and legislative functions should be physically and legally distinct to avoid any conflicts of interest or bias and to preserve the independence of each constitutional role. In other words, those charged with independently applying and interpreting the law should not also be capable of having a role in creating and making the law too. The existence of the Appellate Committee in the House of Lords offended that principle, because there was no strict separation. The integrity and independence of the individual judges was rarely questioned because of this arrangement but, nevertheless, the lack of separation gave the appearance of a lack of impartiality and independence. The creation of the Supreme Court of the UK addressed these concerns by (a) physically separating the Court from the legislative chamber: the Supreme Court is located in the former Middlesex Guildhall in Parliament Square, Westminster (a short walk away from Parliament but in a separate building); and (b) removing the right of the members of the Appellate Committee to take part in the legislative business and debates within the House of Lords.

Membership and jurisdiction

The first Justices of the Supreme Court were the 'Law Lords' or Lords of Appeal in Ordinary from the House of Lords. They still carry the title of Lord or Lady but are given the title out of ceremonial courtesy. The first new appointment to the Supreme Court of the UK was Sir John Dyson (now Lord Dyson), who had previously sat in the Court of Appeal.

By s.23 of the Constitutional Reform Act 2005, the Court consists of twelve justices. The justices usually sit in panels of five but may also sit in panels of seven or nine. The panels of seven or nine are constituted, for example, when a previous decision is asked to be, or may be, departed from; if the case raises an issue of constitutional significance; or if the issue raised is one of great public importance.

In rare circumstances, all twelve of the Justices may sit. These are usually cases of major constitutional significance and public interest. The most notable examples in recent years are the two 'Brexit' cases brought by Gina Miller. The first concerned whether the government alone had the right to trigger Article 50 of the Treaty of the European Union to commence the UK's process of withdrawing from membership of the EU. The second concerned whether the current prime minister's advice to the Queen that Parliament be prorogued (suspended) in September 2019 was lawful. The government lost both cases. The proceedings captured significant public attention and attracted, at times, hostile media coverage. Notoriously in November 2016, one newspaper, the *Daily Mail*, ran a front page headline—'Enemies of the People'—in reference to the three High Court judges that initially heard the first *Miller* case. The cases have led to ample debate about the role of the courts in a democracy within our current unwritten constitution. Both of the cases can be found on the UKSC website and are, respectively, *R (on the application of Miller and another) v Secretary of State for Exiting the European Union* [2017] UKSC 5 and *R (on the application of Miller) v The Prime Minister* [2019] UKSC 41. We strongly recommend reading them.

The jurisdiction of the Supreme Court is as the ultimate court of appeal in the UK. It can hear civil and criminal appeals from the Court of Appeal in England and Wales, and the Court of Appeal in Northern Ireland. It can also hear appeals from the Court of Session in Scotland on civil matters only. In some cases it can hear an appeal from the High Court in England and Wales in what are known as leapfrog appeals. You need permission (or leave) to appeal from the Court of Appeal (or in certain cases the High Court) to the UK Supreme Court. Permission will only be granted if either court certifies that the case raises an arguable point of law of general public importance which ought to be considered by the UK Supreme Court at that time. If the Court of Appeal does not grant permission, then permission can be requested directly from the UK Supreme Court.

Since October 2014 it has been possible to watch Supreme Court cases live through the Court's streaming service. You can also search the archive record which will store the recordings of the hearings for one year. We would wholeheartedly recommend taking time to watch these from time to time and especially cases of significance. You will learn a lot about advocacy and arguing a case at the highest level and the types of interventions one can expect from the panel of judges. Please visit the Court's excellent website where you will find the relevant details, facts, history, videos, and much more: **www.supremecourt.uk/**. For further information on the appeals procedures and how to bring a case to the UKSC see **https://www.supremecourt.uk/docs/a-guide-to-bringing-a-case-to-the-supreme-court.pdf**.

Example

How 'regular' is *regular*? This is a question that aptly sums up the case of *Isle of Wight Council v Platt* [2017] UKSC 28. It is a case that triggered public attention, particularly among parents with children at school. The case fundamentally concerned the freedom to take one's child on holiday outside of terms. Put more specifically, the question was whether a parent of a child of compulsory school age could take a child on holiday during term time without the leave of the school. Under the law, a parent is guilty of an offence if a child of compulsory school age 'fails to attend regularly'. The father in this case took his six-year-old daughter out of school during term time, after the headteacher expressly refused permission to do so. The father was prosecuted before a magistrates' court under s.444(1) Education Act 1996 which stipulated that *'if a child of compulsory school age who is a registered pupil at a school fails to attend regularly at the school, his parent is guilty of an offence'*.

He was prosecuted under the Act but pleaded not guilty on the basis of his daughter's excellent attendance record throughout the year. The magistrates' court took into account the child's overall attendance, rather than the attendance during the specified absence, and as it was still above 90 per cent, decided in favour of the father. They resolved that the requirement that his child had failed to attend regularly could not be satisfied on the facts.

The Council representing the school appealed by way of case stated to a Divisional Court of the Queen's Bench Division in the High Court and the Divisional Court also agreed with the magistrates' court. The Divisional Court then certified a point of law of general public importance for consideration by the Supreme Court, under s.1 Administration of Justice Act 1960. The Supreme Court distilled this point of law, with Lady Hale expressing simply: 'The essential question for this court is the meaning of "fails to attend regularly" in section 444(1) of the Education Act 1996.' Without giving anything away here, you will find out more about this case, the interpretations the UKSC considered, and their final conclusion in Chapter 4. Alternatively, you can read the case here **https://www.supremecourt.uk/cases/docs/uksc-2016-0155-judgment.pdf**.

Example

Popularly known as the 'gay cake' case, *Lee v Ashers Baking Company Ltd* [2018] UKSC 49 is another case demonstrating the UKSC's role in deciding cases of considerable public importance. The facts were that Mr and Mrs McArthur, owners of a bakery business (Ashers) were Christians who held the religious belief that the only form of marriage acceptable is that between a man and a woman. In May 2014, Mr Lee, a gay man, wished to take a cake to an event organised by campaigners for same-sex marriage in Northern Ireland. He wanted to utilise the Ashers' 'Build-a-cake' service by which customers could request images or inscriptions to be iced onto a cake. He placed an order with Ashers for a cake iced with a depiction of the cartoon characters 'Bert and Ernie' and the words 'Support Gay Marriage' (see Image 2.1). At first, Mrs McArthur took the order but later refused and informed Mr Lee that in conscience she could not supply such a cake and gave him a refund.

Image 2.1 The cake Ashers Bakery refused to supply

Source: Queer Space

Mr Lee brought a claim against both the McArthurs and the bakery for direct and indirect discrimination on the grounds of his sexual orientation under Equality Act legislation and other regulations guaranteeing fair treatment. His claim was successful in the first instance. The case, after unsuccessful appeals, reached the UKSC.

This time, the UKSC allowed the appeal and found in favour of the McArthurs. They found, amongst other reasons, that they had not broken the law. They had a lawful objection to supplying the cake not on the basis of Mr's Lee's personal sexual orientation but in supplying the particular cake with the particular message. Their right to freedom of thought and expression included a right not to be obliged to manifest a belief that they do not hold and/or profoundly disagree with. Their refusal to provide Mr Lee with a cake was not on the basis that *he* was gay, or that *he* supported gay marriage, but about supplying a cake that expressed a message that was not necessarily personal to him, i.e. the benefit of the message might equally appeal to the wider community beyond gay or bisexual people. There was no discrimination in this case.

What do you think of this case? Do you agree with the decision? Could it possibly lead to dangerous results? For further discussion of the human rights raised by such a case, see Chapter 7.

2.5.9 Judicial Committee of the Privy Council

The Judicial Committee of the Privy Council is not strictly speaking part of the UK's court hierarchy. It is in fact the highest court of appeal for many Commonwealth countries, as well as the United Kingdom's overseas territories, crown dependencies, and military sovereign base areas. It also hears very occasional appeals from a number of ancient and ecclesiastical courts. The membership of the Judicial Committee of the Privy Council is made up mainly of Justices of the Supreme Court and others who have held high judicial office, sometimes from Commonwealth countries. The governing statute is the Judicial Committee Act 1833. Decisions of the Judicial Committee of the Privy Council, while not binding on the English courts, are persuasive and can have an important impact upon the development of English law. This statement must now be read subject to the decision of the Supreme Court in *Willers v Joyce and another (No 2)* [2016] UKSC 44, which is discussed in Chapter 5. Again, further detail can be found at the Court's excellent website: **www.jcpc.uk**.

2.5.10 Court of Justice of the European Union (CJEU)

The UK remains, for now, a member of the European Union. Member States of the European Union accept the jurisdiction of the Court of Justice of the European Union (CJEU). The Court's role is to ensure that EU law is interpreted and applied consistently in every EU country, and thus seeks to ensure that countries and EU institutions abide by EU law by settling disputes between national governments and EU institutions. The Court gives rulings on cases before it, including making 'preliminary rulings' that assist national courts of EU Member States on questions of legal interpretation. In addition, it can make enforcement rulings that essentially declare a country to be at fault because they have infringed EU law, and it can also sanction EU institutions and offer damages to those persons or companies that have had their interests harmed.

The Court is technically divided into two courts, the Court of Justice which deals with preliminary rulings, and certain actions for annulment of EU actions or law, as well as appeals. There is also a General Court, which rules on actions for annulment brought by individuals, companies, and, in some cases, governments. In practice, it means that this Court deals mainly with competition law, the laws on whether governments can lawfully offer their own industries aid and financial assistance, as well as the laws on trade, agriculture, and trademarks.

There is no doubt that the UK's existing and future relationship with the EU will continue to be keenly debated and contested. Since the date of exit on 31 January 2020, the UK is in a transitional period (set to expire on 31 December 2020) in which the CJEU continues to have jurisdiction and the UK will continue to apply EU Law.

However, since the date of exit, section 6 of the EU Withdrawal Act 2018 confirms that UK courts will not be bound by principles laid down by the CJEU, and will not be able to refer any matter to the Court. It may nonetheless have regard to any subsequent CJEU decision insofar as it is relevant to an issue that the Court is considering. For more on the Court see **https://curia.europa.eu/jcms/jcms/j_6/en/**.

2.5.11 European Court of Human Rights (ECtHR)

The UK is a signatory to the European Convention for the Protection of Human Rights and Fundamental Freedoms. The European *Court* of Human Rights has jurisdiction over all cases involving the interpretation or application of the Convention. As mentioned earlier in this chapter, this is a court which is completely distinct from the CJEU, so do not fall into the trap of confusing the two courts. The Court has issued a series of judgments ruling on a range of Convention rights, from freedom of religion, freedom of expression, the prohibition of torture, the right to a fair trial, and the right to respect for private and family life. The Court has provoked controversial debate and one such case is *Hirst v United Kingdom (No 2)* (2005) ECHR 681, which ruled that the UK's blanket ban on British prisoners exercising the right to vote infringed the Convention because the nature of the ban was a disproportionate infringement of the UK's obligation to guarantee rights to all within the state's jurisdiction.

The composition of the Court is currently forty-seven judges with a judge from each state; judges are independent and are not appointed in a representative capacity. The Parliamentary Assembly of the Council of Europe elects judges from a list of three proposed by each state. Cases may be filtered out by a single judge in clearly inadmissible cases (i.e. those cases in which the Court has no jurisdiction or there is no case to address). Chambers of seven judges deal with the majority of cases, but a case may be referred to a Grand Chamber of seventeen judges where it raises 'a serious question affecting the interpretation or application of the Convention or the protocols thereto, or a serious issue of general importance'.

Attempts to address the problems faced by the European Court of Human Rights have been accommodated in two additional Protocols that are yet to enter into force. Protocol 15 reduces the time limit within which an application may be made to the Court after a final decision of domestic courts from six months to four months. The Protocol also seeks to enhance the principle of subsidiarity (a principle that means that member states have the primary responsibility to secure the rights defined in the Convention). Protocol 16 allows the 'highest courts and tribunals' of domestic jurisdictions to seek an opinion from the European Court of Human Rights on questions of principle regarding the interpretation and application of the Convention in cases before the domestic courts. By this latter protocol, it is hoped that, by creating a dialogue between the European Court and national courts, cases may be concluded domestically, rather than risk them ultimately going up to the European Court. For further information on the Court please see **www.echr.coe.int/**.

 Key point

It is important to know and understand the hierarchy and organisation of the courts as this is essential to the doctrine of binding precedent.

2.6 Legal personnel and bodies

In the final part of this chapter, we turn to consider various legal persons and bodies that you may come across in your studies. This section briefly summarises the roles, functions, and composition of various bodies. We would encourage you to hit the links and conduct any further research you may find useful.

2.6.1 The Ministry of Justice

Responsibility for aspects of the legal system has vested in various government departments in the recent past; in 2003 the Lord Chancellor's Department became the Department for Constitutional Affairs, which in 2007 assumed certain responsibilities from the Home Office. This is now known as the Ministry of Justice. The Ministry of Justice has responsibility for courts, tribunals, prisons, the probation service, and attendance centres. It is therefore responsible for developing policy in relation to all criminal and civil matters as well as the administration of the justice system at large. This includes its policy on everything from legal aid, the composition of the judiciary, to issuing guidance on ongoing updates and reform of legal bodies and services. Further detail on the work of the Ministry of Justice is available at **www.gov.uk/government/organisations/ministry-of-justice**.

2.6.2 Lord Chancellor

For centuries the Lord Chancellor has played a pivotal role in the English legal system. Traditionally, the role of the Lord Chancellor encompassed membership of the government as a Cabinet minister; a law-making role as the speaker of the second legislative chamber, the House of Lords; and also enjoyed the role of Head of the Judiciary, including the ability to sit as a judge in the Appellate Committee of the House of Lords. Additionally, the Lord Chancellor was able to appoint judges or recommend judges for appointment. In that regard, the role was vested with significant constitutional power.

However, the role in various ways offended the separation of powers as it enabled the individual occupying the position to exert power and influence in all arms of the state (executive, legislative, and judicial). It was criticised as being undemocratic and lacking impartiality because the individual could have several conflicts of interest and there was therefore a risk that power could be abused.

See further 8.1.1, 'The Lord Chancellor'.

The office of the Lord Chancellor was altered by the Constitutional Reform Act 2005. The creation of the Judicial Appointments Commission for England and Wales curtailed the Lord Chancellor's role in relation to the appointment of judges. The Lord Chancellor no longer acts as speaker for the House of Lords. The Lord Chief Justice is now the Head of the Judiciary and the Lord Chancellor can no longer sit as a judge.

The holder of the office of Lord Chancellor is also Secretary of State for Justice (and oversees the Ministry of Justice). One of their fundamental responsibilities is to defend and maintain the independence of the courts. There is no requirement that the Lord Chancellor be a lawyer and several previous office-holders such as Liz Truss MP and Michael Gove MP did not have a professional legal background.

2.6.3 **The Lord Chief Justice**

The Lord Chief Justice is the Head of the Judiciary of England and Wales and also (usually) serves as the President of the Court of Appeal (Criminal Division). He sits on the most important criminal, civil, and family cases. One such case was the first instance judgment in the case that determined the legality of the government proroguing (suspending) Parliament in September 2019. He is also the President of the Courts of England and Wales and may hear cases in any English court including magistrates' courts. Under the Constitutional Reform Act 2005 the Lord Chief Justice has approximately 400 statutory duties, and these include being responsible for representing the views of the judiciary to Parliament and the government, deploying judges, and allocating work to courts in England and Wales. He also has a lead responsibility in handling complaints against other judges as well as serving on the Sentencing Council, an organisation that promotes clarity and consistency in sentencing.

2.6.4 **The Attorney General**

The Attorney General is the chief legal adviser to the government. The Attorney General also oversees the Law Officers' departments which include the Crown Prosecution Service and the government Legal Department. The office-holder's role is varied and includes advising the government on questions of international law, bringing proceedings for contempt of court, and responding to questions of law that arise from government bills. In relation to criminal offences the Attorney General may prosecute, or take over the prosecution, in very important cases. In relation to certain offences where there are consequences for public policy, national security, or relationship with other states, the consent of the Attorney General is required to prosecute. Another of the Attorney General's roles is to review 'lenient' sentences handed down by the Crown Court. Should the Attorney General take the view that the sentence is too lenient, a case may be referred to the Court of Appeal. In September 2019 the current Attorney General, Geoffrey Cox, was heavily criticised after it emerged he had advised the government that its prorogation of Parliament was lawful and constitutional. The UK Supreme Court declared the prorogation to be unlawful and, despite political pressure to do so, his full advice to the government has not been published.

2.6.5 **The Director of Public Prosecutions (DPP) and the Crown Prosecution Service (CPS)**

The Director of Public Prosecutions (DPP) is the head of the Crown Prosecution Service—the CPS. The Director manages and oversees the operation of the CPS, an independent organisation that prosecutes criminal cases that have been investigated by the police and other investigative organisations in England and Wales. The CPS was created by the Prosecution of Offences Act 1985 and started operating in 1986, replacing the old inconsistent system of allowing regional police forces to both investigate and initiate prosecutions. The CPS decide which cases should be prosecuted according to a prosecution code, determine the appropriate charges to bring against individuals (especially in complex cases), prepare and present cases at court with the use of its own or independent barristers, and provide information and support to victims and prosecution witnesses. In recent years, the CPS has been criticised for errors in its disclosure of evidence that has risked injustice and unfair trials, as well as controversies about the drop in the rate of prosecutions (and convictions) for rape.

2.6.6 **Legal Aid Agency**

The Legal Aid Agency came into being on 1 April 2013 and is the agency that provides civil and criminal legal aid (funding) in England and Wales. Individuals, whether pursuing a civil claim, or when they are charged with a criminal offence, require access to legal advice and representation. The question of funding for such advice and representation is the question that naturally follows. To paraphrase a common expression that captures some of the criticism: the courts should be open to all—like the Ritz Hotel. In response to what the government argued was a spiralling legal aid budget, the Legal Aid, Sentencing and Punishment of Offenders Act 2012 was introduced and is the main piece of legislation that heavily curtailed civil legal aid. Criminal legal aid for defence barristers has also been cut, leading to many criminal barristers striking and refusing to take on new work in early 2018. The issues remain controversial and sensitive. Many have argued that there has been an inevitable impact on access to justice as well as a lack of representation for defendants due to a lack of criminal barristers that are now willing to take on work for such low rates of pay. This is an issue that occupies popular press coverage which continues to highlight the challenges facing both solicitors and barristers and is a topic worthy of your own independent research.

See Chapter 11, 'Access to justice'.

2.6.7 **The Law Commission**

The law is dynamic. Every week there are new cases clarifying or developing novel points of law. The ever-increasing growth of legislation reflects the fact that the law is very fast-moving. The English legal system therefore accommodates a statutory independent body called the Law Commission. The founding legislation is the Law Commissions Act 1965 and its aim is to ensure that the law is as fair, modern, simple, and cost-effective as possible; to make recommendations for consideration by Parliament; and to codify the law, eliminate anomalies, repeal obsolete and unnecessary enactments, and reduce the number of separate statutes.

The Law Commission is an independent body but it will regularly consult a wide range of persons, including the general public and government departments to determine which areas of law require a fresh examination. Otherwise, the Commission will identify those areas where it has expertise and where, for example, there have been miscarriages of justice, public pressure for changes in the law, technological developments that require a new legal framework, or when judges have identified a need for legislative intervention. Normally, after a thorough review of the law, a further consultation will be conducted, asking for input from lawyers, and other interested parties, bodies, or individuals including members of the public, before a final report is produced. Such reports will usually contain recommendations, and perhaps a draft bill, and will then be issued to the government. It is then up to the government to propose the reforms by first securing parliamentary time for the enactment of the proposal. This may depend on whether the government agree with the recommendation and the extent to which reforming the area of law is a priority. There remain many Law Commission reports that have not been implemented.

 **Example**

In recent years, the Law Commission has produced reports on *The Electronic Execution of Documents* (Law Com No. 386, 2019), *Anti Money Laundering* (Law Com No. 384, 2019), and *The Sentencing Code* (Law Com No. 382, 2018). Visit **www.lawcom.gov.uk/our-work/implementation/table/** and identify the status of these reports. Click on the relevant titles and consider what problem the Law Commission was seeking to tackle. Then read the recommendation and any proposals. To what extent do you think the Law Commission's suggestions remedy the problem it sought to address?

2.6.8 **Lawyers**

See Chapter 9, 'The legal profession'.

Lawyers are involved in the provision of legal services, such as dispensing advice; conducting routine legal work such as drafting a claim, a defence, or a witness statement; and of course the representation of clients before the courts. In England and Wales, lawyers are divided into two professions: solicitors and barristers. Traditionally it was left to barristers to conduct ***advocacy*** before the courts, and solicitors would prepare the case and have a closer relationship with the client. However, there has been an increasing overlap between the two branches of the profession, with many barristers undertaking direct access work that sees them prepare the case from the outset and from the first meeting with a client. Similarly, solicitors are now able to undertake a higher rights of audience course, and qualify as solicitor advocates. This will enable them to advocate in the senior civil and criminal courts in England and Wales. There are other important professionals in the provision of legal services such as paralegals, legal executives, and licensed conveyancers—specialists in property law.

Advocacy *is a specialist professional skill and in a legal context refers to the means by which a barrister puts his or her client's case to the court. It may be written or oral.*

Summary

- Defining law is problematic but it is important to recognise the various sources of law.
- The term 'common law' has various meanings which depend upon the context in which the term is used.
- The role of the judges is to interpret statutes and to develop the common law through the rules of judicial precedent.
- Law made by Parliament, on the one hand, and by judges, on the other, differs in a number of important respects.
- In the UK there is no higher law-making body than Parliament. Parliament is said to be supreme.
- The validity of an Act of Parliament may not be questioned in the courts or by other bodies.
- Criminal and civil proceedings have different terminology, different rules relating to burden and standard of proof, and different outcomes.
- For treaties, such as those relating to the EU and the ECHR, it is necessary for Parliament to pass legislation incorporating obligations within the respective treaties into domestic law.
- The courts are arranged hierarchically and act as courts of first instance (or trial) or courts of appeal. The courts are not arranged as civil or criminal courts but exercise jurisdiction in relation to civil proceedings or criminal proceedings or both.

Questions

1 What is the difference between a crime and a civil wrong?

2 What is the meaning of the term 'common law' and what are the characteristics of a 'common law' legal system?

3 Explain the concept of parliamentary supremacy.

4 What is the significance of the European Convention on Human Rights for English law?

5 What factors determine whether:

(a) a criminal case commences in a magistrates' court or the Crown Court;

(b) a civil case commences in the County Court or the High Court?

6 What are the main functions of:

(a) the Ministry of Justice;

(b) the CPS;

(c) the Law Commission?

Further reading

You should aim to read as widely as possible to support your understanding of the dynamic nature of law and the English legal system. Apart from books and articles, do get into the habit of reading the newspapers and listening to speech radio to keep up to date with current legal and political developments. There are also a number of useful websites you should access throughout your study of the English legal system. Your tutors will direct you to those. The selection below picks up on some of the themes raised in this chapter

- ***The Secret Barrister.*** *The Secret Barrister: Stories of the Law and How It's Broken,* Picador (2019)

  This is a very well written and eye-opening book from an anonymous practising criminal barrister. The book exposes a range of practical problems and failures in the criminal justice system, from the point of arrest to the final imposition of punishment. These problems all have a considerable impact on the provision of a fair trial and access to justice for those that have been wronged by a crime. It also incidentally serves as a very useful guide to understanding the system. This is a very thought-provoking read and will certainly stimulate opinion and reflection.

- ***Bingham, T.*** *The Rule of Law,* Penguin (2011)

  A short and very accessible book and an absolute *must-read* for law students. The author was a former Law Lord and someone whose judgments you will no doubt be reading. The book explores the notion of the 'rule of law', what it means, and why it is so fundamental in a fair and just society. It provides a clear and concise discussion of the challenges facing the rule of law as well as coverage of key principles such as parliamentary supremacy.

- ***(Lady) Hale, B.M.*** (Current President of the Supreme Court). *What is the United Kingdom Supreme Court for?* Macfadyen Lecture, Edinburgh, 28 March 2019

  This is a public lecture given by Lady Hale of Richmond, in which she defends the existence of the UK Supreme Court. She traces the historical origins of the Appellate Committee of the House of Lords before focusing on a constitutional defence of the Supreme Court and its advantages beyond that of other appellate courts. Her lecture can be found at **https://www.supremecourt.uk/docs/speech-190328.pdf**. We would also recommend a lecture by the Court's then Deputy President (and now President), Lord Reed, *The Supreme Court Ten Years On*, The Bentham Association Lecture 2019, University College London, 6 March 2019, in which he discusses a range of practical advantages and disadvantages of the Court's existence from the experience of its first decade since opening. See **https://www.supremecourt.uk/docs/speech-190306.pdf**.

- ***Sumption, J.*** *Trials of the State: Law and the Decline of Politics*, Profile Books (2019)

  Again another short read, this time by a former Justice of the Supreme Court. The book is based on BBC Radio 4's Reith Lectures 2019. This is a stimulating and at times challenging analysis of the relationship between the courts and Parliament. There are some excellent illustrations of the differences between our constitutional arrangements and those adopted in the USA. Jonathan Sumption asks several questions about the role of law in public life and where the limits should be drawn to enable politicians and those that we elect to decide matters that are highly contested, rather than it being determined in courtrooms. This is well worth a read, especially for those interested in a more advanced and critical understanding.

- ***Wacks. R.*** *Law: A Very Short Introduction*, Oxford University Press (2015)

  A short, pocket-sized, and very accessible read that will complement this textbook. The book provides a general account of various legal systems and considers modern challenges facing the law, including the threat from terrorism, cyber-crime, and the increasing role of digital technologies. It avoids jargon and offers matter-of-fact explanation of both civil and criminal justice. The book also addresses some philosophical themes such as the relationship between law and morality.

Online resources

You should now attempt the supporting self-test questions and end-of-chapter questions available at: **www.oup.com/he/wilson-rutherford4e**

Chapter 3

Legislation and the law-making process

Learning objectives

By the end of this chapter you should:

- be able to describe the composition of the various bodies which form the United Kingdom (UK) Parliament;
- be able to understand the procedure by which primary legislation is produced in the UK, including derogations from it, in particular the Parliament Acts procedure;
- be able to assess the effectiveness of the parliamentary stages of law-making in the UK;
- be able to compare and contrast government bills and private members' bills, and evaluate their relative success rates;
- be able to identify and explain the different forms of secondary legislation;
- be able to evaluate the need for secondary legislation and the effectiveness of Parliament's ability to prevent the abuse of delegated law-making powers.

Talking point

In the UK, all legislation is made either by, or using powers granted by, Parliament. It is therefore essential to understand what Parliament is. The UK Parliament comprises three bodies: the House of Commons, the House of Lords, and the monarch. The House of Commons (sometimes referred to as the lower house) is an elected body and its membership is fixed at 650. The House of Lords (sometimes referred to as the upper house), on the other hand, is a largely unelected body—most of its members are appointed—and its membership is not fixed. At the time of writing this book, there are around 800 members in the upper house. That makes it the second largest legislative body in the whole world—only China's People's Congress is bigger. As a general rule, the consent of all three bodies is required to produce an Act of Parliament.

The notion that the (largely unelected) upper house of the UK Parliament should have more members than the (elected) lower house is controversial. Indeed, the notion that the UK Parliament should comprise any unelected members, let alone more of them than there are elected members, is controversial. By way of contrast, the two bodies that comprise Congress in the USA are both elected, with fixed membership, and the upper house is much smaller than the lower house.

Consider any views you may already have on the following questions:

- What do you think about the current composition of the UK Parliament?
- Why do you think that we have two houses of Parliament?
- How do you think that members of the upper house should be chosen—by election, by appointment, or by a combination of the two?
- Do you think that there should be a fixed number of members in the upper house?
- What do you think should happen in the event that the two houses of Parliament disagree with each other?

In October 2017, a Report was published which suggested various reforms to the size of the upper house in the UK Parliament and the way in which its members are appointed. The proposals in this Report will be considered in detail later in this chapter (see 3.1.4). Compare the proposed reforms with your own responses to the questions above.

Introduction

This chapter examines 'legislation', which is a very broad term describing all the law made by, or under powers granted by, the UK Parliament. Legislation made by Parliament itself, in the form of 'Acts of Parliament', is described as 'primary' legislation because it is the highest form of UK law. Legislation made by other bodies under powers granted to them by Parliament is known as 'secondary' or 'delegated' legislation. You should not assume, however, that primary legislation is automatically or necessarily more important than secondary legislation. For example, take the broad subject of 'prohibition of discrimination in the workplace'. Until recently, there were numerous pieces of legislation that prohibited discrimination at work, but while some forms of discrimination were prohibited by primary legislation, others were prohibited by secondary legislation. For example:

 **Example**

Discrimination at work on grounds of sex, race, and disability was prohibited by primary legislation: the Sex Discrimination Act 1975, the Race Relations Act 1976, and the Disability Discrimination Act 1995, respectively. Discrimination at work on grounds of sexual orientation, religion or belief, and age were prohibited by secondary legislation, in the form of the Employment Equality (Sexual Orientation) Regulations 2003, the Employment Equality (Religion or Belief) Regulations 2003, and the Employment Equality (Age) Regulations 2006, respectively.

Is there any logical reason why this should have been? The answer appears to be 'no'. It makes perfect sense, therefore, that Parliament subsequently passed the Equality Act 2010, which consolidated all of the primary and secondary legislation above. Discrimination on grounds of age, disability, religion or belief, sex, and sexual orientation is now prohibited by **primary** legislation.

Moreover, very often the 'law' on a particular subject comprises a *combination* of primary and secondary legislation and it is necessary to be aware of both. Typically, where this does occur, primary legislation will lay down a framework of general principles and rules, with the secondary legislation providing more details.

The most significant difference between primary and secondary legislation is that while the latter can be subject to 'judicial review' in the courts, Acts of Parliament are immune from challenge in the courts. This general principle was accepted by the judiciary in *British Railways Board v Pickin* [1974] AC 765, although it is subject to one important exception. When the provisions of an Act conflict with a 'directly effective' provision of European Union (EU) law, the latter has to be enforced instead—a concept known as the 'supremacy' or 'primacy' of EU law. This exception was confirmed to exist by the Judicial Committee of the House of Lords in *R v Secretary of State for*

Transport, ex parte Factortame Ltd and Others [1991] 1 AC 603, a case involving a conflict between certain provisions of the Merchant Shipping Act 1988 and (what is now) Article 49 of the Treaty on the Functioning of the European Union. The House of Lords 'disapplied' the Act and applied Article 49 instead. (Note: when the UK leaves the EU (Brexit), which is scheduled for the end of January 2020, the supremacy of EU law over UK will come to an end. For further discussion of this and other provisions contained in the European Union (Withdrawal) Act 2018, see 6.8.)

3.1 **Parliament**

3.1.1 **The nature and functions of Parliament**

The UK Parliament has three main functions: first, to legislate—Parliament passes the laws by which the country operates; second, to deal with public finance—the government raises money by Acts of Parliament; third, to provide a forum in which the actions and policies of the government may be publicly scrutinised. This chapter will concentrate on the first of these functions, Parliament's legislative function.

The UK Parliament (as seen in Image 3.1) is actually composed of three bodies. These are the Queen in Parliament, the House of Lords, and the House of Commons.

Image 3.1 The Palace of Westminster, also known as the Houses of Parliament

Source: Claudio Divizia/Shutterstock

In theory, the most important of these bodies is the Queen; in practice, however, the real power lies with the House of Commons as the only directly elected body in Parliament. Most legislation originates from the Government and is introduced first into the House of Commons, where it is known as a bill. In certain circumstances, the Commons has the power to legislate without the consent of the House of Lords—but the converse situation does not apply. The House of Lords used to have the power to veto any bills sent to it by the House of Commons. This power is now limited to a temporary veto, following the enactment of the Parliament Acts (see 3.4). However, the Lords still plays an important role in the working of Parliament by suggesting amendments to bills introduced in the Commons and therefore providing an extra check on legislative proposals. In addition, bills can originate from the Lords. Such legislation tends to be of a non-contentious nature, and initiation in the Lords can save valuable parliamentary time. (See 3.3 for an explanation of how a bill becomes an Act of Parliament.)

You should note that, following devolution, there is now a Scottish Parliament (under the Scotland Act 1998) and National Assemblies for Wales (under the Government of Wales Act 1998) and Northern Ireland (under the Northern Ireland Act 1998), each of which has (limited) law-making power within those jurisdictions. However, there is no English Parliament; the UK Parliament fulfils this function. This post-devolution situation is uneven and arguably unfair. For example, Scottish MPs could (at least until very recently) vote in the UK Parliament on matters that only or primarily affect England, but there is no such right for English MPs to vote in debates before the Scottish Parliament. As a result, there have been calls for the creation of a separate English Parliament (see 3.3.4).

'Parliament' should not be confused with 'government'. The UK government is, generally speaking, formed by the political party which secured the most seats in the House of Commons at the last general election. Following the general election in December 2019, that party is the Conservative Party. Many other political parties are represented in Parliament, including the Labour Party (the official opposition), the Liberal Democrats, the Scottish National Party, Plaid Cymru, Sinn Fein, and so on. There are also a small number of independents. The prime minister and all government ministers (the Cabinet) have to be members of one or other house of Parliament; in practice, most are members of the House of Commons.

The UK Parliament is relatively unusual in that members of the government also sit in Parliament. This may be contrasted with other countries, such as the United States, where the government, represented by the President, are chosen in an entirely separate process from the country's parliament, Congress.

3.1.2 **The House of Commons**

The House of Commons dates from the fourteenth century. There are presently 650 seats in the House of Commons, each one representing a 'constituency';

the person elected to fill that seat is called a Member of Parliament (MP). The 650 constituencies cover the whole of the UK (England, Scotland, Wales, and Northern Ireland). All MPs are directly elected at a general election, through the system known as majoritarian vote (or more commonly first-past-the-post). The Parliamentary Voting System and Constituencies Act 2011 provided for the first-past-the-post system to be replaced with the 'alternative vote' system, although this was subject to ratification at a national referendum, which was held in May 2011. In the referendum (the first national referendum to be held in the UK since 1975), the result was a comprehensive rejection of the 'alternative vote' (68 per cent of voters said 'no'), meaning that the first-past-the-post system remains in place.

The Fixed-term Parliaments Act 2011 set the date of the next general election following its enactment as 7 May 2015, with subsequent elections to be held every five years, subject to a power vested in the prime minister to modify the date by up to two months. The next general election under the 2011 Act was set for 7 May 2020. However, in April 2017 the UK's then Prime Minister Theresa May called a 'snap' general election to be held in June. This is permitted under the 2011 Act but only in two situations: (a) where there is a vote of 'no confidence' in the government or (b) where two-thirds of MPs in the House of Commons (434 out of 650) vote in favour of an earlier election. The next day, 522 MPs voted in favour, which permitted the general election to go ahead in June 2017, nearly three years earlier than scheduled. This meant that the next general election should have been held in June 2022. Mrs May's successor as Prime Minister, Boris Johnson, made several attempts to call a general election in the autumn of 2019 under the same procedure as Mrs May but failed to secure the support of two-thirds of MPs. However, Mr Johnson succeeded in calling for the election in December 2019 by introducing the bill which became the Early Parliamentary General Election Act 2019. This bill was subject to the ordinary process for passing bills (see 3.3), which simply requires a majority (rather than two-thirds) of MPs to support it.

Disqualification from membership of the House of Commons

No formal qualifications (educational, professional, or otherwise) are required for MPs. However, a number of people are disqualified by law from being members of the House of Commons:

- persons under eighteen years of age;
- aliens (that is, not British, Irish, or Commonwealth nationals);
- members of the House of Lords (peers);
- undischarged bankrupts;
- those convicted of 'corrupt or illegal practices';

- people listed in s.1 of the House of Commons Disqualification Act 1975, such as judges, civil servants, members of the Armed Forces, and members of any police force;
- people currently serving a sentence of imprisonment of one year or more.

Clergy ordained in a number of churches (including the Church of England) used to be disqualified from membership. However, this was abolished by s.1 of the House of Commons (Removal of Clergy Disqualification) Act 2001. Until very recently, persons suffering from mental illness were disqualified from becoming MPs. The law was changed in this respect by s.1 of the Mental Health (Discrimination) Act 2013.

Thinking point

Who should be eligible to sit as an MP in the House of Commons, and how frequently should elections take place?

No formal qualifications (educational, professional, or otherwise) are required for MPs, yet they are responsible for producing legal rules to regulate a complex society with little outside help. Parliamentary time is constrained (in the Commons at least) by the need to balance other commitments, especially to constituencies. Short-term thinking is inevitable because of the recurring need for re-election. Party political debates (especially in the Commons) often distract from the need to get the wording of the legislation right.

In light of this:

1. Consider whether, and if so how, the composition of the House of Commons should be changed.
2. What advantages, if any, are there in the adoption of fixed-term parliaments under the Fixed-term Parliaments Act 2011?

Removal of MPs

The Recall of MPs Act 2015 sets out a process by which an MP will lose his or her seat in the House of Commons as a result of a successful 'recall petition', which will then trigger a by-election. There are three alternative conditions for such a petition:

1. where the MP is convicted of an offence in the UK and receives a custodial sentence;
2. where the House of Commons orders the suspension of the MP from the House for at least ten sitting days following a report from the Committee on Standards;
3. where the MP is convicted under s.10 of the Parliamentary Standards Act 2009 (offence of providing false or misleading information for allowances claims), regardless of the sentence imposed.

3.1.3 **The House of Lords**

The House of Lords dates from the early thirteenth century. It is composed of two main groups, the Lords Temporal and the Lords Spiritual. The Lords Temporal group consists of hereditary peers, life peers, and judicial peers.

Hereditary peers

Until November 1999, more than 750 hereditary peers were entitled to sit and vote in the House of Lords by virtue of birthright. There was much opposition to this hereditary principle, primarily on the basis that birthright alone should not justify a seat in Parliament. In 1999, therefore, the then Labour government introduced into Parliament a bill which duly became the House of Lords Act 1999. Section 1 of the 1999 Act removed the automatic right of all hereditary peers to seats in the House of Lords, although as a result of a compromise agreement during the progress of the bill, ninety-two hereditary peers were allowed to remain by virtue of s.2(2).

Life peers

Life peers are appointed under the Life Peerages Act 1958 by the Queen on the advice of the prime minister and, since 2000, with the approval of the House of Lords Appointments Commission (see later). The 1958 Act was intended to produce a more representative second chamber and to allow people who had achieved a position of national prominence in their field to be recognised with a seat in Parliament. It also allowed for people other than 'professional' politicians to participate in the law-making process. The life peers include among their number former members of the Commons, former senior police officers, and people prominent in the professions and arts. In November 2019, there were 675 life peers (excluding those on leave of absence, suspended, or disqualified—see later for further discussion of disqualification).

Judicial peers

The UK's highest court, the Supreme Court, was established on 1 October 2009 by s.23 of the Constitutional Reform Act 2005, replacing the Judicial Committee of the House of Lords. When a judge was appointed to the Judicial Committee (under the Appellate Jurisdiction Act 1876) and made a 'law lord' (or rather a 'Lord of Appeal in Ordinary', their official title), he was *also* made a judicial peer, a form of life peerage. This entitled the judge to sit in the House of Lords and participate in debates on proposed legislation and other matters. This presented a problem, as the law lords were simultaneously members of both the UK's legislature (Parliament) and its highest court (the Judicial Committee)—a clear breach of the doctrine of 'separation of powers', according to which no one should be simultaneously a member of more than one branch of government (legislature, executive, and judiciary).

This problem has now been resolved. When the Supreme Court was established and the Judicial Committee abolished in October 2009, the existing 'law lords' became the first judges of the Supreme Court. More significantly, however, all judges of the Supreme Court are disqualified from sitting in the House of Lords, which means that the 'separation of powers' is now respected. This disqualification does not apply to retired law lords. Furthermore, new judges appointed to the Supreme Court after 1 October 2009 are not given peerages. Thus, for example, when Lord Dyson was promoted from the Court of Appeal to take up a seat in the Supreme Court in April 2010, he was not given a peerage.

The Lords Spiritual

This is a group of twenty-six Bishops of the Church of England. Uniquely among the present members of the House of Lords, the spiritual peers must retire on reaching the age of seventy. The presence of the spiritual peers is controversial for several reasons. First, the very concept of 'spiritual peers' is debatable. The UK and Bhutan are the only countries in the world whose parliaments automatically give seats to spiritual leaders. It has been argued that these peers' continued presence is anachronistic, a throwback to the early years of the British Parliament when spiritual leadership was regarded as a far more important matter than it is today. Secondly, if the UK is to retain spiritual peers, why do they only represent one church (the Church of England)? In a multicultural, multi-faith nation, as the UK undoubtedly is today, why are no other churches officially represented?

Appointment of women bishops

Following the General Synod of the Church of England's November 2014 decision to allow women to become bishops, Parliament passed the Lords Spiritual (Women) Act 2015. Section 1 provides that, when a vacancy among the Lords Spiritual arises, that vacancy must be filled by the most senior *female* bishop (if there is one). The Act was passed after the Archbishop of Canterbury requested, on behalf of the Church of England, that the government make arrangements to enable the accelerated entry of female bishops to the House of Lords, and the government agreed. Before the Act, eligibility for the appointment of new spiritual peers (other than the five 'ex officio' spiritual peers) was based purely on seniority (in terms of length of tenure as a diocesan bishop). Had the new Act not been passed, then it would probably have taken many years before the most senior woman bishop became eligible for a seat in the House of Lords.

The Act does not apply to the five 'ex officio' spiritual peers: the Archbishops of Canterbury and York and the bishops of Durham, London, and Winchester. The holders of those positions are automatically given seats in the House of Lords regardless of their length of tenure. The Act is also limited in time: it runs for ten years, from

18 May 2015 (the date of the first sitting of Parliament after the 2015 general election). The Act will therefore expire on 18 May 2025, and the procedure for appointing new spiritual peers will once again be based purely on seniority regardless of gender.

The cross-benchers

The cross-benchers are those members of the Lords who are politically neutral. Their name derives from the fact that they literally sit in seats which 'cross' the Lords, rather than siding with the government benches or those of the opposition. Their number comprises some hereditary peers, some life peers, and all the retired law lords. They are quite significant in terms of numbers and provide an important contrast with the Commons, where virtually every MP represents a political party.

The House of Lords Appointments Commission

This body was established in 2000. Despite its name, the Commission has no power to appoint life peers. Instead, it has two functions: to encourage members of the public to nominate non-party political life peers as so-called 'People's Peers' and to 'vet' nominees put forward by the prime minister and the political parties. In April 2001, the first 'People's Peers' were nominated by the Commission and duly recommended to the Queen by the prime minister. The list attracted severe criticism: there were seven knights and one lady, and three professors—ironically, just the sort of people who would in any event have been nominated by the prime minister.

In March 2006, the Commission refused to approve four prime ministerial nominees owing to certain alleged financial irregularities, sparking the 'cash for honours' scandal. It transpired that three people nominated for life peerages by the then prime minister Tony Blair had had their nominations blocked by the Commission on the basis that the nominees had made undisclosed loans to the Labour Party. Although the police investigated the allegations (which, if true, would have amounted to a criminal offence), no charges were ever brought. However, the scandal raised awareness of the potential for 'cronyism' inherent in the present system whereby life peerages are conferred by the prime minister.

Disqualifications from membership of the House of Lords

These are as follows:

- aliens (not citizens of the UK, Ireland, or a Commonwealth country);
- judges;
- members of the House of Commons or members of the European Parliament;
- persons under the age of twenty-one;
- undischarged bankrupts;

- persons convicted of serious crimes;
- members who have been expelled by the House.

As of November 2019, four peers are disqualified on the ground that they are judges (Baroness Hale and Lord Kerr are judges in the UK Supreme Court; Lord Burnett is the Lord Chief Justice of England and Wales; Lord Boyd is a judge in the Court of Session in Scotland). One peer (Baroness Mobarik) is disqualified as she is an MEP.

Retirement or resignation of members of the House of Lords

Section 1 of the House of Lords Reform Act 2014 (HLRA) provides that a member of the House of Lords may retire or otherwise resign as a member of the House of Lords by giving notice. This formalised a voluntary retirement policy introduced in June 2011. To date, more than 100 peers have retired since 2011.

Removal of members of the House of Lords on grounds of non-attendance

Section 2 of the HLRA provides—for the first time—that a member of the House of Lords who does not attend the House during a parliamentary session will cease to be a member of the House at the beginning of the following session. There are a number of exceptions:

- where the member had a leave of absence;
- where the member was disqualified or suspended from sitting during the whole session;
- where the House resolves that by 'reason of special circumstances' the member should not be suspended;
- where the session is shorter than six months.

To date, six peers have ceased to be members of the House of Lords as a result of non-attendance.

Removal of members of the House of Lords following conviction of a serious offence

Section 3 of the HLRA provides—again for the first time—that a member of the House of Lords who has been convicted of a 'serious offence' will cease to be a member of the House of Lords. This will apply if the Lord Speaker of the House certifies that the member has been (a) convicted of a criminal offence, and (b) sentenced to be imprisoned for more than one year. It is irrelevant whether the person was a member of the House of Lords at a time when the offence was committed (provided that they were a member *when convicted*). It is also irrelevant whether the offence, conviction, sentence, or imprisonment occurred in the UK or anywhere else. However, the Act only applies to offences committed 'on or after the day on which this section comes into force'.

Expulsion or suspension of members of the House of Lords

The House of Lords (Expulsion and Suspension) Act 2015 allows for members of the House to be expelled or suspended. Prior to this Act, the House of Lords had no power to expel a member. The House did hold the power to suspend a member, but this power was limited in time. Under the Act, a suspension could be indefinite.

3.1.4 **Reform of the House of Lords**

The House of Lords has been the subject of a great deal of criticism in recent years. Some of the major criticisms are as follows:

- the composition of the Lords is too restricted. The typical peer is male, middle-aged or older, based in the south of England, and comes from a middle-class or higher socio-economic background and is therefore unrepresentative of the general population;
- the Lords is an unelected body. This is obviously undemocratic, in the sense that the electorate have virtually no say in the composition of one of their parliamentary bodies;
- the Lords is too large. As of November 2019 there are around 800 peers (excluding those on leave of absence or temporarily disqualified);
- the presence of the spiritual peers is controversial.

Visit the online resources to watch a video on the House of Lords Reform Bill.

Reform proposals to date

The removal of more than 600 hereditary peers by the House of Lords Act 1999 (discussed previously) was intended to address the first criticism. However, the 1999 Act did not address the other criticisms and so debate continues as to the possibility of further reform. Since 2000, a number of reform proposals have come and gone, including no fewer than four government White Papers (see 3.3.1 for an explanation of White Papers). However, one option which has attracted support is a 'hybrid' of elected members (to ensure some democratic input and, with it, legitimacy) and appointed members (allowing for the retention of independent, non-political members and experts). However, there is disagreement over the exact proportion of the two groups. There is also disagreement over various other details, such as what form of electoral system should be used, how long the terms of office should be, whether the elected and/or appointed members should be entitled to stand for re-election or re-appointment, and whether or not the spiritual peers should be retained.

Following the general election in May 2010 and the formation of the Liberal Democrat/Conservative coalition government, it was announced that the new government had reached an agreement that the House of Lords should be replaced by either a wholly or mostly elected body, with a system of proportional representation (PR) to be used in the election. In June 2012, the House of Lords Reform Bill was introduced into the House of Commons to put this agreement into effect. Specifically, the bill provided for a reformed House of Lords consisting of 360 elected members, ninety appointed members, twelve Lords Spiritual, and an unspecified number of 'ministerial members'. However, at the second reading stage in July, a significant number of Conservative MPs opposed the bill, forcing the government to abandon it.

The notion of replacing the House of Lords with an *entirely* elected upper chamber is particularly controversial. Although such a body exists in many other countries, such as Australia and the United States, it risks duplication of the House of Commons, and hence would put the two Houses on a possible collision course, with both claiming equal democratic legitimacy. There is also the potential for deadlock during the legislative process if each House is dominated by a different political party, or alternatively 'rubber-stamping' of bills if both Houses are dominated by the same party.

In October 2017, a Report into the composition of, and appointment methods used for, the House of Lords was published. The Report did not go so far as to suggest replacing the upper house with an elected body. Instead, its proposals focused on the size of the House of Lords and the process by which peers are appointed. The Report was produced by a committee chaired by Lord Burns, a cross-bencher in the present House of Lords. On publication of the Report, he said:

> With over 800 members—about 150 more than the Commons—we are too large. The time has now come to take action to correct this and put a cap on numbers for the future . . . A smaller, more effective house will be able to build public confidence and support for its crucial constitutional role in checking bills before they become law . . . While no set of proposals will ever be perfect, we believe that ours would provide a fair solution, which could prove sustainable for as long as this remains an appointed chamber.

The key proposals are as follows:

- The number of peers to be capped at 600—but not until 2027. Numbers will be gradually reduced over ten years using a policy of 'two out, one in' (that is, two existing members would have to leave before a new member could be appointed).
- Newly appointed members to serve for a maximum of fifteen years before retiring.
- Appointment of new peers to be managed to ensure no one political party enjoyed a majority. Appointments to be shared between the parties, based on an average of the vote share at the most recent general election and the total number of each party's MPs in the House of Commons. This is designed to ensure that the composition of the Lords 'reflect[s] the political views of the country over the medium term'.

- At least 20 per cent of peers to be independent cross-benchers, appointed by the House of Lords Appointment Commission.
- The spiritual peers are unaffected.

The Burns Report is available at **www.parliament.uk/documents/lords-committees/size-of-house/size-of-house-report.pdf**.

Critical debate

In February 2007, an editorial in *The Times* newspaper commented that '[t]he quest for Lords reform is akin to looking for the Goldilocks option. The Upper House has to have enough (electoral) legitimacy to be able to challenge a government but not so much that it leads regularly to gridlock.'

This comment reflects the twin imperatives for Lords reform of (a) legitimacy and (b) difference. The 'legitimacy' imperative is the need for the House of Lords to be taken seriously, not just by the government but by the general public. Replacing the presently unelected, primarily appointed House with a democratically elected body would go a long way to satisfying this. The 'difference' imperative is the need for the House of Lords to not simply replicate the House of Commons. The current House achieves this, but a democratically elected body may not do so. As the *Times* editorial points out, replacing the House of Lords with an elected body may lead to 'gridlock' involving the two Houses of Parliament, a situation which is particularly likely to happen if each House is controlled by a different political party. (This problem often afflicts the US Congress, with the House of Representatives often controlled by one party while the Senate is controlled by the other. As both House and Senate are directly elected, each can claim equal legitimacy, and hence 'gridlock' often ensues.)

In light of this, consider whether the present House of Lords should be replaced by a directly elected body. If you accept the arguments that (a) democratic legitimacy is essential, but (b) simply replacing the House with a directly elected body creates too great a risk of 'gridlock', how might the composition of a reformed Lords be modified to avoid that risk?

3.2 **Primary legislation**

Primary legislation, in the form of Acts of Parliament—otherwise known as statutes—typically contains the fundamental principles of English law (other than those still regulated by the courts, known as the common law). As noted at the beginning of this chapter, there is also secondary legislation, which typically contains more detailed provisions. Secondary legislation will be dealt with in 3.5. The remainder of this section will concentrate on primary legislation.

There are literally thousands of Acts of Parliament in existence at any given time, covering just about any subject you care to name. There is no such thing as a 'typical' statute, although they do have various features in common. Statutes can range in size from a few lines to hundreds of pages. For example, at one extreme there is the Public Order (Amendment) Act 1996, which comprises a mere two sections. At the other there is the Income Tax Act 2007, with 1,035 sections, while the Companies Act 2006 is so big that it is subdivided into forty-seven separate parts and contains a grand total of 1,300 sections.

3.2.1 **Public, private, and hybrid legislation**

Primary legislation may be either 'public', 'private', or 'hybrid'.

Public legislation

Public legislation affects the general law of the land, while private legislation is of a local or personal nature. The Human Rights Act 1998, the House of Lords Act 1999, and the Constitutional Reform Act 2005 are all examples of public Acts of Parliament.

Private (or local) legislation

Private (or local) legislation is designed to confer particular powers or benefits on any person(s) in excess of, or in conflict with, the general law. The promoters of such legislation are often local authorities, but private companies and occasionally individuals can also put forward proposals for such legislation, seeking special powers not available in the general law. Examples of private (or local) legislation from recent years include the Allhallows Staining Church Act 2010, the Humber Bridge Act 2013, the Leeds City Council Act 2013, and the Faversham Oyster Fishery Company Act 2017.

Hybrid legislation

Hybrid legislation refers to public legislation which affects a private person or interest in a particular way. The Channel Tunnel Act 1987 is a good example. It is public legislation in that, by allowing for the construction of a rail tunnel between the UK and France, it potentially affects everyone in the UK. However, it is also private, as certain parts of the Act have very specific application. For example, Part IV of the Act is headed 'Construction and Improvement of Roads near Folkestone'. The most recent piece of hybrid legislation to be passed is the High Speed Rail (London–West Midlands) Act 2017, an Act 'to make provision for a railway between Euston in London and a junction with the West Coast Main Line at Handsacre in Staffordshire, with a spur from Water Orton in Warwickshire to Curzon Street in Birmingham; and for connected purposes'.

3.2.2 **'Constitutional' and 'ordinary' legislation?**

There is a long-standing principle in English law that Parliament cannot bind itself. In other words, Parliament is free at any time to legislate on a subject and, to the extent that there is pre-existing, inconsistent legislation on the same subject, that earlier legislation is, either expressly or impliedly, repealed. This point was confirmed by the Divisional Court in *Thoburn v Sunderland City Council* [2002] EWHC 195 (Admin), [2003] QB 151. However, in the same case, the Divisional Court declared that there was an exception to the principle, which is when the pre-existing legislation is 'constitutional' in nature. Such legislation is, according to the Court, immune from implied repeal, albeit not express repeal. Laws LJ stated:

> We should recognise a hierarchy of Acts of Parliament: as it were 'ordinary' statutes and 'constitutional' statutes. The two categories must be distinguished on a principled basis. In my opinion a constitutional statute is one which (a) conditions the legal relationship between citizen and state in some general, overarching manner, or (b) enlarges or diminishes the scope of what we would now regard as fundamental constitutional rights.

Laws LJ listed several examples of 'constitutional' statutes: Magna Carta 1297; the Bill of Rights 1689; the Union with Scotland Act 1706; the Representation of the People Acts 1832, 1867, and 1884; the European Communities Act 1972; the Human Rights Act 1998; the Scotland Act 1998; and the Government of Wales Act 1998. In the UK Supreme Court case of *Buckinghamshire County Council and Others v Secretary of State for Transport* [2014] UKSC, [2014] 1 WLR 324, Lord Neuberger and Lord Mance (with whom Baroness Hale, Lord Kerr, Lord Sumption, Lord Reed, and Lord Carnwath agreed) lent support to Laws LJ's proposition about 'constitutional statues' when they said:

> We have a number of constitutional instruments. They include Magna Carta, the Petition of Right 1628, the Bill of Rights and (in Scotland) the Claim of Rights Act 1689, the Act of Settlement 1701 and the Act of Union 1707. The European Communities Act 1972, the Human Rights Act 1998 and the Constitutional Reform Act 2005 may now be added to this list.

More recently, in *Miller v Secretary of State for Exiting the European Union* [2016] EWHC 2768 (Admin), [2017] 1 CMLR 34, Lord Thomas CJ, Sir Terence Etherton MR, and Sales LJ said that 'the status of the European Communities Act 1972 as a constitutional statute is such that Parliament is taken to have made it exempt from the operation of the usual doctrine of implied repeal by enactment of later inconsistent legislation'.

3.2.3 **The origins of legislation**

Government legislation

At the beginning of each parliamentary session, the monarch opens Parliament with a speech (the Queen's Speech) from the throne which outlines the government's main proposals for the session. Legislation is passed for various reasons:

- Most primary legislation is designed to implement government policy. For example, the Human Rights Act 1998 was a long-term objective of the Labour Party even when in opposition, as was the House of Lords Act 1999. More recent examples of policy legislation include the Deregulation Act 2015, the Investigatory Powers Act 2016, and the National Citizen Service Act 2017.

- There are annual measures, such as the Finance Act (which implements the government's Budget) and the Supply and Appropriation Act (which authorises public expenditure).
- Ad hoc measures arise in the course of every parliamentary session. Recent examples are:
  - the Anti-terrorism, Crime and Security Act 2001, passed in the wake of the terrorist atrocities of 11 September 2001;
  - the London Olympic Games and Paralympic Games Act 2006 (passed in response to the decision of the International Olympic Committee to award the 2012 Olympic Games to London—had the Games gone to Paris instead, there would have been no need for this statute);
  - the Banking (Special Provisions) Act 2008, passed in order to allow the government to nationalise stricken banks (the first candidate being Northern Rock, which was in danger of collapse at the time).
- Some legislation is a response to decisions of the courts. For example:
  - the Contempt of Court Act 1981—in part a response to the decision of the European Court of Human Rights in *Attorney General v Times Newspapers Ltd* [1979] 2 EHRR 245 that the law of contempt of court as stated by the House of Lords in the case contravened the right to freedom of expression;
  - the Theft (Amendment) Act 1996—a response to the House of Lords decision in *R v Preddy* [1996] AC 815;
  - the Sexual Offences (Amendment) Act 2000—a response to the decision of the European Court of Human Rights in *Sutherland v United Kingdom* (1997) 24 EHRR CD 22;
  - the Criminal Evidence (Witness Anonymity) Act 2008—passed in response to the House of Lords' decision in *R v Davis* [2008] UKHL 36.
- Some legislation is required to give effect to the UK's international obligations, primarily under the various treaties that relate to membership of the EU. Thus, when the British government agreed to join what was then called the European Economic Community (EEC) by signing the European Community Treaty, legislation was needed to give effect to this, and Parliament duly passed the European Communities Act 1972. Since then, the government has agreed to sign a number of other EU Treaties, and each time a new Act of Parliament has been passed in order to confirm this.
- Some legislation is required to implement EU directives (see later for more detail).
- Consolidation Acts are also passed from time to time. These bring various statutes which have been passed over the years on the same subject into one place,

primarily for convenience. A good example is the Equality Act 2010, mentioned at the beginning of this chapter, which consolidates several earlier statutes.

- Codification Acts are similar to consolidation statutes, but with a broader scope. Codification statutes will bring together not just pre-existing statutes on one subject but also the case law that has built up on the subject. Good examples of such statutes are the Theft Act 1968 and the Police and Criminal Evidence Act 1984 (PACE).
- Once legislation has been passed by Parliament, it can only be repealed by Parliament itself. As a result, legislation is sometimes passed simply in order to repeal old statutes which would otherwise remain in force indefinitely, far beyond their useful life. The most recent example is the Statute Law (Repeals) Act 2013, which repeals dozens of old Acts of Parliament such as the Female Orphan Asylum Act 1800 and the Hospital for Poor French Protestants Act 1808.

Implementation of EU directives

A significant amount of UK legislation is passed in order to bring the UK into line with legislation produced by the EU's law-making bodies. There are various forms of EU legislation—discussed in detail in Chapter 6—one of which is called a directive.

Directives are binding on the governments of the EU's Member States, including the UK (at least, until the UK leaves the EU at the end of January 2020), but only as to 'the result to be achieved', while leaving to the Member States the choice of 'form and methods' (according to Article 288 of the Treaty on the Functioning of the European Union). This means that a directive, on its own, has no legal force. The Member States must pass their *own* legislation, to achieve whatever '*result*' the directive requires.

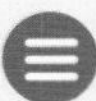 Example

Implementation of Directive 92/85 into UK law

Part VIII of the Employment Rights Act 1996 was passed in order to give effect to Directive 92/85 on the rights of pregnant workers. Article 8 of the directive states that 'Member States shall take the necessary measures to ensure that workers . . . are entitled to a continuous period of maternity leave of at least 14 weeks'. Section 73(1) of the 1996 Act (when first enacted) stated that 'an employee's maternity leave period continues for the period of 14 weeks from its commencement or until the birth of the child, if later'. Thus, the UK government had to achieve the 'result' stipulated in the directive of guaranteeing pregnant workers at least fourteen weeks' maternity leave. The 1996 Act clearly achieved this result. (As it happens, s.73 was amended in 1999 in order to increase the minimum maternity leave period to eighteen weeks, and again in 2006 to increase it to twenty-six weeks—an option provided for by the directive, which refers to a 'period of maternity leave of *at least* 14 weeks'.)

In practice, the majority of directives are given effect in the UK via secondary legislation, which will be discussed in detail later. See also 6.8 for discussion of what will happen to this UK legislation after the UK leaves the EU at the end of January 2020.

Private members' bills

During the course of the parliamentary session, there are limited opportunities for backbench MPs (in the Commons) and for members of the House of Lords to introduce proposals for legislation. These are called private members' bills. Often, the bill put forward has little chance of becoming law but is designed to draw attention to a particular issue and/or try to embarrass the government into introducing a government bill. For example, between 1988 and 2002, no less than eight private members' bills were put forward relating to the control of high residential hedgerows. None of them became Acts; however, the then Labour government eventually responded and now ss.65–67 of the Anti-social Behaviour Act 2003 (which was a piece of government legislation) deals with the problems created by high hedges. Most often, private members' bills are either discontinued by the MP or peer who introduced them, or simply fail through lack of time.

However, that is not to suggest that backbench MPs have no chance of introducing important, and sometimes controversial, legislation. In fact, the government of the day may quietly provide assistance behind the scenes for such bills, although politically it may not wish to be too closely associated with them.

Key point

The distinction between government bills and private members' bills is simply that the former are endorsed by the government whereas the latter are introduced into Parliament by individual MPs or peers. However, if/when a government or private members' bill becomes an Act of Parliament, the final legislation has exactly the same legal status.

Examples of private members' bills becoming important Acts of Parliament include the following:

- Abortion Act 1967 (which legalised abortions);
- Sexual Offences Act 1967 (which decriminalised homosexual acts between consenting male adults);
- Criminal Procedure (Insanity and Unfitness to Plead) Act 1991 (this Act abolished mandatory indefinite detention in a secure mental hospital following a verdict of insanity in a criminal trial, except in murder cases);
- Law Reform (Year and a Day Rule) Act 1996 (by this Act the ancient 'year and a day' rule in murder was abolished);

- Gangmasters (Licensing) Act 2004 (which created a Gangmasters Licensing Authority to regulate vulnerable workers in the agriculture and shellfish-gathering sectors);
- Presumption of Death Act 2013 (which provides that a person missing for seven years is presumed to have died);
- House of Lords Reform Act 2014 (discussed earlier);
- Citizenship (Armed Forces) Act 2014 (which allows for foreign nationals who were members or former members of the British armed forces to become UK citizens);
- Organ Donation (Deemed Consent) Act 2019 (which changed the system of organ donation in England and Wales from opt-*in* to opt-*out*).

Private members' bills take four forms:

1. **The ballot.** At the beginning of each parliamentary session, those MPs who wish to do so enter a ballot. Twenty names are drawn out and those members, in order, have the opportunity to present their chosen bills to Parliament. The successful members are invariably lobbied from various sources to adopt their ideas for legislation, although typically fewer than half the bills introduced will become Acts of Parliament. Some recent Acts produced via this route are the Riot Compensation Act 2016, the Homelessness Reduction Act 2017, the Assaults on Emergency Workers (Offences) Act 2018, and the Stalking Protection Act 2019.
2. **The 'ten minute rule' procedure.** This is given its name because members are not permitted to make a full speech, but are allowed a 'brief explanatory statement' (of about ten minutes) regarding the desirability of the bill. In reality, this procedure is used to gain publicity for a measure, as there is rarely enough support, or time, to take the bill further. The most recent example of a ten minute rule bill becoming law is the Holocaust (Return of Cultural Objects) (Amendment) Act 2019.
3. **Standing order 57 (presentation bills).** Under this procedure a member may present a bill when a gap in the Commons timetable occurs. As with ten minute rule bills, it is primarily a publicity opportunity rather than a serious attempt at introducing legislation. The most recent statutes produced via this procedure are the Health & Social Care (National Data Guardian) Act 2018 and the Animal Welfare (Service Animals) Act 2019.
4. **Peers' bills.** This refers to bills introduced by peers in the Lords, some of which are subsequently adopted by a backbench MP and guided through the Commons. The most recent statute produced via this route is the Children Act 1989 (Amendment) (Female Genital Mutilation) Act 2019.

3.3 The passage of legislation through Parliament

In order to become an 'Act of Parliament', a legislative proposal—known as a 'bill'—must normally be passed by the House of Commons and the House of Lords and given royal assent before it becomes law. As already indicated, most bills—whether government or private members'—originate in the House of Commons (and are known as 'Commons Bills'), although some bills may be introduced in the House of Lords (and are referred to as 'Lords Bills'). Generally speaking, bills relating to public finance, such as the annual Supply and Appropriation Bills and Finance Bills, start in the Commons, while more technical bills typically start in the Lords.

3.3.1 Procedure for the passage of a public bill

All bills must pass through five stages in each House of Parliament before being sent for royal assent. However, there are certain steps that most bills go through before reaching that point.

Pre-legislative steps

Government bills are drafted by specialist lawyers in the Parliamentary Counsel Office (PCO), as instructed by the minister concerned. Even before that point, there may have been either a 'Green Paper' or 'White Paper', or both, prior to a government bill coming into existence. Green Papers are purely consultation papers on a particular subject, whereas White Papers set out the government's policy in more detail. Over the past ten years or so it has become increasingly common for the government to publish draft bills and invite further comment and feedback. Sometimes, these draft bills are subjected to parliamentary scrutiny by Pre-legislation Committees.

Many government bills (and hence Acts) owe their existence to the work of the Law Commission. This body was established by Parliament in 1965 to review the law in England and Wales and to recommend proposals for law reform. Such reforms may be necessary for a variety of reasons: to modernise outdated law, to simplify overly complicated law, to make the law on a particular subject more accessible, and so on. The Law Commission works on a number of different proposals simultaneously. When it is ready to do so, it issues a Consultation Paper on an area of law, typically setting out the problems which it has identified with that area and proposing a range of options for reform. The paper will invite feedback on its proposals. This will typically be followed by a report summarising the responses to the Consultation Paper and setting out the Law Commission's preferred option for reform. It is then up to the government to decide whether to translate the Law Commission's proposal into a government bill, although the government may well issue a Green and/or White Paper of its own first—especially if the government agrees with the Law Commission about the need for reform, but not necessarily with the Law Commission's preferred option for reform.

For example, the law of voluntary manslaughter (the area of criminal law where the accused is charged with murder but invokes a special defence, reducing his or her liability to manslaughter) was completely overhauled by Parliament in the Coroners and Justice Act 2009. Briefly, this Act reformulated the defence of diminished responsibility, abolished the ancient common law defence of provocation, and introduced a new statutory defence of 'loss of control'. But how and why did this Act come into existence? The following chronology summarises the key steps:

- October 2003—having taken the view that the law of voluntary manslaughter was out of date and overly complicated, the Law Commission published a Consultation Paper entitled 'Partial Defences to Murder' inviting responses to its proposals to reform the area.
- August 2004—following consultation, the Law Commission published a Report, also entitled *Partial Defences to Murder*, recommending how the law of voluntary manslaughter should be reformed.
- December 2005—the Law Commission published a second Consultation Paper, entitled 'A New Homicide Act for England and Wales?' This was more ambitious and wide-ranging than the 2003 Consultation Paper and 2004 Report, covering the whole range of homicide offences.
- November 2006—following consultation, the Law Commission published another Report, also entitled *A New Homicide Act for England and Wales?*, recommending how the law of murder (including all forms of manslaughter) should be reformed.
- July 2008—the Labour government published its own Consultation Paper, entitled 'Murder, Manslaughter and Infanticide: Proposals for Reform of the Law'. This adopted some, but by no means all, of the Law Commission's recommendations; it also amended some of the Law Commission's proposals for reform of the law of homicide. It included a draft bill.
- January 2009—following consultation, the Coroners and Justice Bill was introduced into Parliament. It closely resembled the government's draft bill, although there were some changes.
- November 2009—the bill received royal assent and became the Coroners and Justice Act 2009.

The first reading

This is a purely formal stage. The title of the bill is read out, an order made for the bill to be published, and a date fixed for the second reading. Before a government bill can progress to the next stage, s.19 of the Human Rights Act 1998 requires the relevant minister to issue a statement, which must be to the effect that:

- in his view, the provisions of the bill are compatible with the Convention rights ('a statement of compatibility'); or
- although he is unable to make a 'statement of compatibility', the government nevertheless wishes the House to proceed with the bill.

The reference to 'minister' and 'the government' in s.19 would seem to exclude both private and private members' bills from this requirement.

The second reading

At this stage, the House considers the principles and purposes of the bill. The minister or member will outline the bill's provisions and justifications. The opposition gives its views. This will not automatically or necessarily be negative, even for government bills. If the proposed legislation is uncontroversial or welcomed by all concerned, then it should attract 'cross-party' support. Backbenchers may draw attention to any weaknesses, particularly in regard to those they represent. For example, during the passage of the National Lotteries Bill in 1992/93, many backbench MPs from constituencies in which football pools companies' headquarters were based drew attention to the impact that the lottery would (and in fact did) have on employment.

The bill is then voted on. If the bill is 'read' a second time, the House is deemed to have approved the bill in principle. If the second reading is defeated then that is the end of the bill. It is *extremely* unlikely that a government bill will fail a second reading. It may do so if the government has no overall majority and its opponents combine against it. This happened twice in the twentieth century—with the Rent Restrictions Bill in 1923/24 and the Reduction of Redundancy Rebates Bill in 1976/77. In 1985/86, the Conservative government's Shops Bill was so unpopular that seventy-two of its own backbenchers voted against it at second reading and the bill was lost. So far this century, one government bill has already been lost—the House of Lords Reform Bill 2012 (discussed at 3.1.4).

Committee stage

In the Commons, the bill is typically next sent to a Public Bill Committee (formerly known as a Standing Committee) of between sixteen and fifty MPs (usually about eighteen). The composition of the Committee will reflect the political composition of the whole House. A new committee will be set up for each bill, and will be named after the bill—thus, for example, the committee dealing with the Welfare Reform Bill in 2010/12 was called the Welfare Reform Bill Committee. Each committee must consider the details of its bill (in theory, line by line). Amendments will usually be proposed and considered. Public Bill Committees have the power to take written and oral evidence from people and organisations outside of Parliament regarding the contents of their bill, the idea being that this will improve the scrutiny process.

The advantage of the committee stage is that it allows for several bills to progress through the House of Commons simultaneously, and it is also easier for detailed discussion to take place in a small committee room than on the floor of the House of Commons itself. However, some bills do have their 'committee stage' on the floor of the House of Commons, thus enabling all MPs to participate in the detailed debate if they wish to do so. This is known as a 'Committee of the Whole House'. This procedure may be used for the following:

- bills of constitutional importance (such as the bills which became the Human Rights Act 1998 and the European Union (Withdrawal) Act 2018) and bills which are required to endorse the government's signing of international treaties, such as the bill which became the European Union (Amendment) Act 2008;

- bills which need to be passed quickly (such as the bill which became the Anti-terrorism, Crime and Security Act 2001, the bill which became the Banking (Special Provisions) Act 2008, and the bill which became the Criminal Evidence (Witness Anonymity) Act 2008);
- the major clauses of each year's Finance Bill(s);
- non-controversial bills which go through 'on the nod'.

In the Lords, meanwhile, the committee stage will normally be taken on the floor of the House (potentially allowing all peers to participate).

Report stage

After detailed scrutiny by the Public Bill Committee, the bill is reported back to the House, allowing those MPs who were not on the Committee to participate in further scrutiny. Amendments made by the Committee will either be endorsed or reversed by the House. Occasionally, further amendments, usually government-sponsored, may be made at this stage and new clauses added. Where a bill was considered by a committee of the Whole House and not amended, then the bill progresses immediately to the third reading stage without a report stage.

Third reading

Once again, the whole House considers the proposals behind the legislation. In the Commons, there are strict limits on further amendments. Except in the case of major bills, this stage is usually short.

The other House

These stages are then repeated in the other House. Each House has discretion to amend bills passed originally in the other House. Where this happens, the amended bill must return to its original House for consideration of the amendments. Thus, if a Commons bill is amended in the Lords, the amended bill must be returned to the Commons. If the Commons votes to agree to the amendments, then the bill can be presented for royal assent (see later). If, however, the Commons rejects one or more of the Lords' amendments (or amends them) then the bill must go back to the Lords for them to decide whether to persist with their amendments.

If the Lords drop their amendments, then the bill can be presented for royal assent; however, if not, the bill must return to the Commons. This process can go on several times and is referred to as 'ping-pong', with a bill potentially shuttling back and forth between the two Houses several times. The process cannot go on indefinitely, however, because ultimately, if no agreement is reached before the end of the parliamentary session (when Parliament is 'prorogued'), then all outstanding bills are lost unless either agreement had been made to carry the bill over to the next session (about which see later at 3.3.2) or the provisions of the Parliament Act apply.

An example of the latter situation is the bill which became the Hunting Act 2004, which shuttled between the two Houses in November 2004. The bill passed by the Commons banned fox-hunting, but the Lords amended it to allow some form of licensed fox-hunting to continue. The Commons refused to accept these amendments and the Lords refused to withdraw them, and eventually the 2003/04 session ended with no agreement. However, the bill was passed under the Parliament Act provisions.

Visit the online resources to watch a video on how the Lords works with the Commons to make a bill law.

Royal assent

Once the bill has been passed by both Houses of Parliament it receives royal assent. This is now a purely formal stage, although governed by the Royal Assent Act 1867. The last monarch to refuse to grant royal assent was Queen Anne in the 1706/07 session.

Commencement

On the date of royal assent, a bill becomes an Act of Parliament. That does not necessarily mean that it has force of law, however. Unless otherwise provided in the Act of Parliament, the Act will come into force immediately but, very often, it is deemed desirable for commencement to be delayed, either for the whole Act or parts of it. The delay may be until a specified date or until such day as the relevant government minister 'may' prescribe. It follows that, sometimes, an Act—or at least part of it—never comes into force at all. An example is the Easter Act 1928, which aimed to set a fixed date for Easter, but is still not in force over ninety years later.

A good example of an Act coming into force long after royal assent is the Human Rights Act 1998. This received royal assent in November 1998, but did not come into force in England and Wales until 2 October 2000. The delay was quite deliberate—to give those persons and bodies affected by the Act (including judges and magistrates) time to adjust to it. The date of the Act coming into force was determined by the then Home Secretary Jack Straw in the Human Rights Act 1998 (Commencement No.2) Order 2000 (SI 2000/1851) (a form of secondary legislation called a 'commencement order'—see 3.5.1).

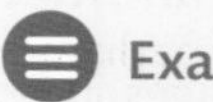

Example

The following is an example of a bill becoming an Act: the Racial and Religious Hatred Act 2006.

The Racial and Religious Hatred Bill, a government bill, was designed to extend the racial hatred offences in the Public Order Act 1986 to cover stirring up hatred against persons on religious grounds. There was a variety of offences under the 1986 Act, each offence requiring that words, behaviour, written material, recordings, or programmes must be threatening, abusive, or insulting and intended or likely to stir up *racial hatred*. Under the new bill, these offences would be amended so that each would apply to the stirring up of either racial *or religious* hatred, 'religious hatred' being defined as hatred against a group of persons defined by reference to religious belief or lack of religious belief.

Opponents of the bill argued strongly that it would, if enacted in its original form, inhibit freedom of speech. The Reverend James Jones, the Bishop of Liverpool, wrote in *The Telegraph* (24 October 2005) that:

> the probable consequences of this Bill will be not only unintended but also unacceptable . . . bringing a person before the courts for their beliefs, however odious or innocuous, introduces to our society an element hitherto foreign and starts to shape our culture differently. It makes people hesitant to express convictions which explicitly or implicitly criticise another faith. It begins to stifle and silence serious and robust debate about religion in a modern, pluralist and democratic culture . . . Sometimes religion needs to be criticised.

The Racial and Religious Hatred Bill was introduced into the Commons on 19 June 2005 and received its first reading that day. It received its second reading on 21 June and was then referred to Standing Committee A. It cleared that stage on 30 June 2005 and the report and third reading were taken together on 11 July, when it was ready to go on to the Lords.

There it had its first reading on 12 July and a second reading on 11 October. However, after that it suffered a torrid time, especially at the Committee stage on 25 October, where it was significantly amended. In particular, the Lords deleted references to words that could be regarded as 'abusive or insulting', limiting the new offence to 'threatening' words. A second amendment deleted the word 'recklessness' from the new offence of inciting religious hatred, meaning that it could only be committed intentionally. The bill was reported on 8 November 2005 and the amended bill duly received its third reading on 24 January 2006 and thus cleared the Lords. The bill was returned to the Commons for consideration of the Lords' amendments on 31 January.

There, in a shock development, a Labour backbench rebellion led to the Lords' amendments being approved by the Commons, despite government opposition. With Prime Minister Tony Blair absent from the Commons, apparently satisfied that Labour's sixty-five-seat Commons majority was big enough to overturn the Lords' amendments, the Commons instead approved the Lords' amendments on deleting the word 'recklessness' by 288 votes to 278 and on the deletion of the words 'abusive or insulting' by 283 votes to 282—a difference of just one vote. These defeats constituted only the second and third times that Labour had lost votes in the Commons since being elected in June 1997.

The bill—having had a version agreed by both Houses of Parliament—received royal assent on 16 February 2006 and became the Racial and Religious Hatred Act 2006.

3.3.2 **Carrying over bills from one parliamentary session to another**

The long-standing rule that all public bills must complete all their stages in both Houses and receive royal assent within the same session of Parliament no longer applies. Instead, there is now an option to allow bills to carry over from one session to another. It was used for the first time when the bill which became the Financial Services and Markets Act 2000 was carried over from the 1998/99 session to the 1999/2000 session. Several more Acts have now been passed having been carried over, including the Constitutional Reform Act 2005 and the Corporate Manslaughter and Corporate Homicide Act 2007.

This brings the procedure for public bills into line with the procedure for passing private and hybrid bills, where carry-over has been accepted for some time. The Crossrail Act 2008, for example, was originally introduced as a hybrid bill in the 2004/05 session and was carried over three times before eventually becoming an Act of Parliament in the 2007/08 session. The High Speed Rail (London–West Midlands) Act 2017 (also originally introduced as a hybrid bill) was introduced in 2013/14 and was also carried over three times before eventually becoming an Act of Parliament in the 2016/17 session.

The advantage of carry-over is that it avoids the hectic 'ping-pong' sessions which often occur at the end of every parliamentary session as the government desperately tries to get all of its bills through before Parliament is prorogued and all outstanding bills are lost. The danger of 'ping-pong' was that modifications and alterations to bills would be made in haste, and compromises made, without full consideration of their implications. However, there is a possible disadvantage of the new 'carry-over' facility: bills that are carried over may cause congestion in future parliamentary sessions, with time having to be found for debate on them.

3.3.3 **The effectiveness of parliamentary scrutiny of legislation**

The effectiveness of Parliament in scrutinising legislation is limited by various factors.

The government's majority

The government can control its own supporters most of the time by relying on party loyalty and the whip system. Government bills are rarely lost in their entirety (but see the passage of the Racial and Religious Hatred Act 2006, described earlier, for a situation where the government failed to prevent one of its bills being amended).

The government's control of the timetable

The government has control of the parliamentary timetable and can normally ensure that there is time for its measures to be considered. It can use various procedural devices such as the 'closure' motion and the 'guillotine' to ensure that measures are voted on and not talked out. The 'guillotine'—officially known as an Allocation of Time Motion—is a procedure available in the House of Commons which sets a limit on the amount of time that may be spent on a particular stage(s) of a bill. It was first used in response to the delaying tactics, known as 'filibustering', of certain MPs who were wasting huge amounts of time delaying the Criminal Law (Amendment) Bill in 1886/87. Some bills may be guillotined more than once. For example:

- Dangerous Dogs Bill 1990/91—every stage, including consideration of Lords' amendments, was guillotined;
- Prevention of Terrorism (Additional Powers) Bill 1995/96—second reading (three hours), Committee (two hours), report and third reading (one hour);
- Human Reproductive Cloning Bill 2001—every stage guillotined.

In recent years, however, guillotines have been deployed sparingly. In the whole of the 2006/07 session, for example, guillotine motions were used only twice, on the second reading of the bills which became the Investment Exchanges and Clearing Houses Act 2006 and the Northern Ireland (St Andrews Agreement) Act 2006.

Programme motions

In 1997/98, a trial was introduced to programme certain bills. The first programme was set down in January 1998 on the bill which became the Scotland Act 1998. Programme motions require a debate, which usually takes place immediately after the second reading. A programme motion (which is amendable) should state, among other things, the date by which the bill should be reported from Committee, the amount of time proposed for report and third reading, and provisions for carrying over to a subsequent session (if any). It is evident that there has been a dramatic increase in the number of programme motions since their introduction in 1998. Over the same period, there has been a significant reduction in the use of guillotine motions, which suggests that programme motions have *effectively* replaced the guillotine as a means of controlling debate in the Commons.

Limited power of MPs

MPs have limited ability to scrutinise the activities of government effectively. This is caused by the following factors:

- lack of time: the amount of legislation being dealt with is extensive;
- lack of expertise: the complexity and technical nature of much legislation makes it difficult for the average MP to comment;
- lack of independent information: most information comes via the Whips.

The role of the opposition parties

There is a basic conflict between the need for technical scrutiny of legislation and the need for the opposition parties to be seen opposing government measures. It has been said that 'the purpose of many Opposition amendments is not to make the bill more generally acceptable but to make the government less generally acceptable'.

The role of the House of Lords

The power of the House of Lords to amend legislation has been limited by the Parliament Act procedure (described later) and by self-imposed limitations arising from its own concern about its lack of credibility. However, there are indications that after the passage of the House of Lords Act 1999, the House regards itself as more 'legitimate' and more willing to exercise its powers to amend and even reject government legislation.

3.3.4 **English Votes for English Laws (EVEL)**

Following the Scottish independence referendum in September 2014, the government promised to devolve more powers to the Scottish Parliament (and in due course the Scotland Act 2016 was passed to effect this). The government also proposed to amend the procedure by which some primary legislation is passed through the UK Parliament by giving England's MPs a veto over government bills that only affect England. (A similar procedure will be used for government bills covering only England and Wales but not the rest of the UK, with both English and Welsh MPs involved.) Whether a bill affects only England (or England and Wales) will be a decision for the Speaker of the House of Commons. In October 2015 the House of Commons voted to approve the new procedures, although the vote was quite close: 312 in favour and 270 against. The new procedure is known as 'English Votes for English Laws', or EVEL.

Under the new procedure, any government bills that, in the opinion of the Speaker, concern only England (or England and Wales) will be debated by the House of Commons in the usual way up to and including the second reading but, after that, only English (or English and Welsh) MPs will participate (and vote) in the Committee stage. If they vote in favour, the bill will pass to the report stage as usual, but a 'no' vote will result in the bill being dropped. The procedure in the House of Lords is unaffected, although any amendments made by the House of Lords will be subject to 'double majority' approval by all MPs and by all English (or English and Welsh) MPs in the House of Commons.

Similarly, if most of a government bill applies to the whole of the UK but, in the opinion of the Speaker, it contains some clauses that only concern England (or England and Wales), the bill will be debated by the House of Commons in the usual way up to and including the report stage. However, instead of proceeding to the third reading, there will be a new 'Legislative Grand Committee' stage, at which only the English (or English and Welsh) MPs will be able to debate (and vote on) those clauses. If they vote in favour, the bill will pass to its third reading as usual, but a 'no' vote would result in the bill being dropped. Again, the procedure in the House of Lords is unaffected.

The new EVEL procedures are designed to address the 'West Lothian Question', the paradoxical situation under which Scottish MPs can vote on issues such as health and education affecting only England (or England and Wales) but the English and Welsh MPs in the House of Commons have no say on similar matters relating to Scotland, because they have been devolved to the Scottish Parliament in Edinburgh. The government issued an 'Explanatory Guide' in July 2015 in which it set out the case for the new procedures:

> As devolution to Scotland, Wales and Northern Ireland is strengthened, the question of fairness for England becomes more acute. These proposals change the process by which legislation is considered by the House of Commons so that MPs with constituencies in England (and where relevant England and Wales) are asked to give their consent to legislation that only affects England (or England and Wales), and is on matters that are devolved elsewhere in the UK. Those MPs will therefore have the opportunity to veto such legislation. The change will strengthen England's voice, just as devolution has strengthened the voices of Scotland, Wales and Northern Ireland within the Union, so that the legislative process is fair for everyone. All MPs will continue to be able to amend and vote on all legislation, as they can now.

However, other political parties were less enthusiastic. The Scottish National Party (SNP) in particular was critical of the new procedures, on the basis that they complicate the legislative procedure and reduce the influence that MPs representing Scottish constituencies have in the UK Parliament. Pete Wishart, the SNP's shadow leader of the Commons, told BBC Radio 4's Today programme at the time: 'They will make Scottish MPs second class in the unitary UK parliament, they will politicise the office of Speaker in forcing him to take the decision to exclude Scottish MPs from bills and they create an unnecessary new level of parliamentary procedure in a very tight parliamentary timetable.'

In November 2015, the then Speaker of the House of Commons, John Bercow, certified that the government's Housing and Planning Bill 2015/2016 exclusively concerned England and/or Wales (but not the rest of the UK) and it therefore became the first bill to be dealt with under the EVEL procedure.

Thinking point

Is it time for an English Parliament?

The controversy and debate around the new EVEL procedure has reignited another debate: should there be a separate English Parliament? (Bear in mind that England had a separate Parliament from 1215 to 1707, until the Union with England Act 1707 merged the English Parliament with that in Scotland.) Given that Scotland, Wales, and Northern Ireland now have their own legislative bodies, consider the case for and against doing the same for England. (Note: such a body would not replace the UK Parliament but would comprise only English MPs and would carry out the same functions for England as the devolved legislatures already do for the other parts of the UK.)

3.4 **Resolving inter-House conflicts using the Parliament Act procedure**

Prior to 1911, both Houses of Parliament had equal powers over legislation—in effect, both Houses enjoyed an absolute veto over bills and the agreement of both Houses was needed before a new Act of Parliament could be created. However, this was changed after the House of Lords refused to pass the Finance Bill in 1909, despite the fact that the bill had already cleared the Commons. The Liberal government of the time responded by introducing the Parliament Bill, which was duly passed by both Houses and became the Parliament Act 1911. Under the 1911 Act, the House of Commons is permitted to override the House of Lords' refusal to allow a bill to pass, provided that certain conditions are met (see 3.4.2). Now, the House of Lords has merely a temporary veto over legislative measures. A 'money' bill must pass almost immediately, but other public bills may be delayed by a year.

You may be wondering why the House of Lords passed the Parliament Bill, given that, at the time, it still had its absolute veto over all bills. The reason is that the Lords was threatened with something far worse if it did not do so. Bear in mind that, at this time, the great majority of the Lords' membership comprised hereditary peers, most of whom supported the Conservative Party. The Liberal government therefore made it known that King George V would be prepared, if necessary, to flood the Lords with hundreds of new Liberal-supporting hereditary peers. To the Conservative-supporting hereditary peers in the Lords, that was a much less attractive prospect than the loss of their veto, hence their support for the Parliament Act.

3.4.1 **Money bills**

A money bill is one which, in the opinion of the Speaker of the House of Commons, relates exclusively to central government expenditure, taxation, or loans. For money bills, s.1(1) of the Parliament Act 1911 (as amended) applies. The effect of this provision is that the bill may be presented for royal assent and become an Act of Parliament—with or without the consent of the House of Lords—after one month. The bill must be sent to the Lords at least one month before the end of the session.

3.4.2 **Other bills**

For any other public bill (except a bill containing a provision to extend the maximum duration of Parliament beyond five years), s.2(1) of the Parliament Act 1911 (as amended) applies. When originally passed, s.2(1) of the 1911 Act required a bill to have been presented to the Lords in three successive parliamentary sessions. Only after three successive Lords rejections would the Commons then have the authority to send the bill to the monarch for royal assent. This effectively allowed the Lords to delay by two years any bill of which it did not approve.

However, the 1911 Act was to be amended when the Parliament Act 1949 was passed. Controversially, the 1949 Act was itself passed under the 1911 Act provisions, after the Lords rejected the bill three times. Section 2(1) of the 1911 Act (as amended) now provides that the Commons may submit a bill for royal assent after just two Lords rejections. This effectively reduces the Lords' ability to delay any bill to one year.

The amended section provides, in full, as follows:

> Parliament Act 1911 (as amended—1949 amendments in CAPITALS) 2(1) If any Public Bill is passed by the Commons in TWO SUCCESSIVE SESSIONS and having been sent to the Lords at least one month before the end of the session, is rejected by the Lords in each of these sessions, that Bill shall on the SECOND rejection by the Lords, unless the Commons directs to the contrary, be presented to the Sovereign for the royal assent and thereupon become an Act of Parliament without the Lords' consent. But the foregoing provision is not to take effect unless ONE year has elapsed between the date of the second reading in the first of the sessions in the Commons and the date of its passing the Commons in the second session.

Since 1911, the Parliament Act procedure has only been used seven times, as follows:

- Government of Ireland Act 1914;
- Welsh Church Act 1914;
- Parliament Act 1949;
- War Crimes Act 1991—which allowed for the prosecution in the UK of suspected Nazi war criminals;
- European Parliamentary Elections Act 1999—which introduced proportional representation for the 1999 UK elections to the European Parliament;
- Sexual Offences (Amendment) Act 2000—which lowered the age of consent for homosexual sexual intercourse from eighteen to sixteen;
- Hunting Act 2004—which prohibits the hunting of wild mammals (particularly foxes) with dogs in England and Wales.

The *Jackson* case: *R (on the application of Jackson and Others) v Her Majesty's Attorney General* [2005] UKHL 56, [2006] 1 AC 262

After the Hunting Act 2004 was passed, various members of the Countryside Alliance brought a court case which involved not only a direct challenge to the Hunting Act 2004 but also an indirect challenge to the Parliament Act 1949. The Alliance alleged that while the Parliament Act 1911 was valid, being an Act passed by both the Commons and the Lords, the amendments made to it in the Parliament Act 1949 were invalid. That was because the 1949 Act was itself made under the 1911 Act powers—that is, it was passed by the Commons only. The Alliance argued that Parliament in 1911 never intended that the Parliament Act itself could be amended without the express agreement of the Lords. The Alliance further argued that all legislation passed under the amended Parliament Act procedures was invalid too. Alternatively, it was suggested that the Hunting Act was a form of 'delegated' legislation, and therefore (unlike primary legislation) capable of being challenged judicially.

In February 2005, the Court of Appeal rejected these arguments. Lord Woolf CJ accepted that the Commons did have the power to amend the Parliament Act 1911, using the Parliament Act procedure itself. He said that once the 1911 Act had made the 'fundamental change' of allowing the House of Lords' consent to bills to be dispensed with, the reduction of the two-year period in the original s.2(1) to the one-year period in the amended Act was a 'relatively modest and straightforward amendment'. A subsequent appeal to the Judicial Committee of the House of Lords was dismissed in October 2005, although the law lords rejected the suggestion that the 1911 Act permitted only 'relatively modest and straightforward' amendments. Lord Bingham (the senior law lord) stated:

> I agree with the appellants that the change made by the 1949 Act was not, as the Court of Appeal described it, 'relatively modest', but was substantial and significant. But I also agree with them and also the Attorney General that the breadth of the power to amend the 1911 Act in reliance on s.2(1) cannot depend on whether the amendment in question is or is not relatively modest . . . The 1949 Act and the 2004 Act are Acts of Parliament of full legal effect.

Lord Hope observed that 'each of the two main parties' had made use of the amended Parliament Act procedure (the War Crimes Act 1991 had been passed by a House of Commons under a Conservative government). He added that 'the political reality is that of a general acceptance by all the main parties and by both Houses of the amended timetable which the 1949 Act introduced. I do not think that it is open to a court of law to ignore that reality.' Lord Carswell hinted that there may be some limits to the uses that could be made of the 1911 Act's procedures, 'though the boundaries appear extremely difficult to define'. He noted that 'no government in the real political world' would attempt to use those powers for the purpose of 'fundamental constitutional change'.

Similarly, Baroness Hale pointed out that Parliament, in passing the Parliament Act 1911, had specifically excepted bills that would prolong the maximum life of Parliament beyond five years. She concluded that this meant that bills could be passed under the 1911 Act procedure even where they amended the 1911 Act itself, except one to remove that exception. Baroness Hale said that Parliament had effectively 'disabled' itself from using the 1911 procedure to 'remove the exception'. This must be correct; otherwise a powerful government could effectively use the Commons to pass legislation extending the lifespan of Parliament indefinitely, removing the need for future elections and converting the UK into an elected dictatorship.

Lord Nicholls concentrated on the appellants' argument that the 1911 Act created a new delegated law-making body (comprising the Commons and the monarch) and that this body could not use its delegated powers to enlarge those powers. He stated:

> It would be inappropriate to liken the House of Commons to a 'delegate' or 'agent' when applying the 1911 Act procedure. The appropriate approach, rather, is to

recognise that when it enacted s.2 the intention of Parliament was to create a second, parallel route by which . . . any public bill introduced in the Commons could become law as an Act of Parliament. It would be inconsistent with this intention to interpret s.2 as subject to an inherent, over-arching limitation comparable to that applicable in delegated legislation . . . The Bill to the Parliament Act 1949 was within the scope of s.2 of the 1911 Act. From this it follows that the legal challenge to the enactment of the Hunting Act 2004 also fails.

 **Key point**

The Parliament Act procedure allows for a bill to be passed by the House of Commons and the monarch without the consent of the House of Lords. There is no equivalent procedure allowing for a bill to be passed by the House of Lords and the monarch without the consent of the House of Commons.

3.5 Secondary legislation

Not all legislation is made directly by Parliament. The sheer complexity of modern society means that Parliament has neither the time nor the detailed knowledge to enact all the various provisions that are required. Accordingly, power may be delegated by Act of Parliament (often called the 'parent' or 'enabling' Act) to the Privy Council, government ministers, local authorities, or other regulatory agencies to enable them to make 'secondary' or 'delegated' legislation.

 **Key point**

Legislation can only be made by Parliament (primary legislation) or by other bodies on whom law-making power has been conferred by Parliament (secondary legislation). Other than Parliament itself, no body in the English legal system has independent law-making powers.

3.5.1 Forms of delegated legislation

Delegated legislation can be made in a variety of forms.

Statutory instruments

The most significant form of delegated legislation, numerically speaking, are those made by government ministers (and occasionally by other bodies) and called 'statutory instruments' (SIs). Typically, 3–4,000 SIs are produced every year. All statutory instruments are regulated by the Statutory Instruments Act 1946, which lays down certain procedural requirements for their making (see 3.5.4). Statutory instruments are given titles as well as reference numbers, known as the SI number. An SI number might appear as 2008/123, meaning that it is the 123rd statutory instrument produced in the year 2008. Here are some examples (note the variety of names):

- the Building (Electronic Communications) *Order* 2008 (SI 2008/2334);
- the Trade Marks (Amendment) *Rules* 2008 (SI 2008/2300);
- the Veterinary Medicines *Regulations* 2008 (SI 2008/2297);
- the Workmen's Compensation (Supplementation) (Amendment) *Scheme* 2008 (SI 2008/721).

Specific types of statutory instrument

Commencement orders

A number of statutory instruments are used to bring parts of pre-existing Acts of Parliament into effect. These are called 'commencement orders'. There may be more than one such order per Act, especially if the statute is large. A good example of a commencement order was given earlier in this chapter: the Human Rights Act 1998 (Commencement No. 2) Order 2000 (SI 2000/1851), which brought the 1998 Act into effect on 2 October 2000.

Remedial orders

These are special statutory instruments made under s.10(2) of the Human Rights Act 1998, which applies 'if a provision of legislation has been declared under s.4 to be incompatible with a Convention right'. Although subject to certain preconditions, s.10(2) states that '[i]f a Minister of the Crown considers that there are compelling reasons for proceeding under this section, he may by order make such amendments to the legislation as he considers necessary to remove the incompatibility'. A case illustrating this procedure is *R (on the application of H) v Mental Health Review Tribunal for North & East London Region* [2001] EWCA Civ 415, [2002] QB 1. Here, the Court of Appeal declared an incompatibility between ss.72 and 73 of the Mental Health Act 1983 and Articles 5(1) and 5(4) of the European Convention (the right to liberty). Subsequently, the Health Secretary made a remedial order under s.10(2) of the 1998 Act—the Mental Health Act 1983 (Remedial) Order 2001 (SI 2001/3712)—which amended the 1983 Act.

Regulatory reform orders

The Legislative and Regulatory Reform Act 2006 had a controversial passage through Parliament before being enacted. This is not surprising, as s.1(1) of the Act states that a minister 'may by order under this section make any provision which he considers would serve the purpose in subsection (2)', while s.1(2) states that '[t]hat purpose is removing or reducing any burden, or the overall burdens, resulting directly or indirectly for any person from any legislation'. Notice the reference to 'any provision' and 'any legislation'. The Labour government which promoted the bill was unapologetic: the Explanatory Notes to the Act published on the UK legislation (**www.legislation.gov.uk**) website state that '[t]he power is a broad one, and it is intended to be so'. However, so sweeping are these powers that a number of special controls are placed on ministers seeking to exercise them. Section 3(2) lists a total of six conditions that must be met before a reform order can be made.

Orders in council

The highest form of delegated legislation is called an 'order in council'. Theoretically, these are made by the Privy Council, but in practice they are made by a government minister. Orders in council may (if made under statutory authority) be published as statutory instruments and subject to the provisions of the Statutory Instruments Act 1946. An example is provided by s.30(1) of the Civil Aviation Act 1980, which states: 'Her Majesty may by order in council direct that any of the provisions of this Act shall extend with such modifications (if any) as may be specified in the order to any relevant overseas territory.'

Byelaws

Local Authorities have power under a number of statutes to make 'byelaws' for the regulation, administration, and management of their affairs. Section 235(1) of the Local Government Act 1972, for example, allows a district council to make byelaws for the 'good rule and government of the whole or any part of the district and for the prevention and suppression and nuisance therein'. Other bodies have power under other statutes to make byelaws. The Strategic Rail Authority was, prior to its abolition, given power to create byelaws regulating rail transport under s.219 of the Transport Act 2000.

3.5.2 **Why is delegated legislation necessary?**

Time constraints

If all legislation took the form of primary legislation, Parliament would struggle to cope with the mass of detail required. Instead, an enabling (or 'parent') Act lays down broad principles, leaving the details to be filled in by delegated legislation. For example, the primary legislation that deals with loans for students in higher education—originally the Education (Student Loans) Act 1990, subsequently repealed and replaced by Part II of the Teaching and Higher Education Act 1998—confines itself to dealing with the question of students' eligibility to apply for a loan. Other matters, most importantly the maximum amount that can be borrowed per year, are dealt with by regulations, produced annually by the government. If Parliament had to deal with this amount of detail the parliamentary timetable would soon be full, as a new Act would be required every year.

Complexity

The subject matter of much legislation is technical and highly complex. It would be inappropriate to include this in an Act of Parliament. Not only would consideration of detailed, technical legislation be ineffective in the contentious atmosphere of Parliament, but the principles of the resultant legislation would be difficult to comprehend. The procedure for making delegated legislation also makes it easier to consult experts during its formulation than is the case with primary legislation. Notable areas in which this approach is adopted include health and safety regulations made under the Health and Safety at Work, etc. Act 1974 and the Food Safety Act 1990. Recent examples of complex, technical delegated legislation are the Waste Electrical and Electronic Equipment Regulations 2006 (SI 2006/3289) and the Horses (Zootechnical Standards) (England) Regulations 2006 (SI 2006/1757).

Flexibility

The use of delegated legislation can, for example, allow account to be taken of local conditions. For example, s.18(1) of the Clean Air Act 1993 provides that a local authority may, by order, declare the whole or any part of the district of the authority to be a smoke control area; any order made under this section is referred to in this Act as a 'smoke control order'. This empowers local authorities to make smoke control orders in those areas where it is considered appropriate. An example of extremely specific delegated legislation is the A282 Trunk Road (Dartford–Thurrock Crossing Charging Scheme) Order 2008 (SI 2008/1951).

Emergencies

Use of regulations means emergency powers can be brought into effect very quickly to deal with outbreaks of disease, typically involving agricultural products. Examples of such 'emergency' legislation include the Food Protection (Emergency Prohibitions) (Radioactivity in Sheep) Order 1991 (SI 1991/20) and the Food (Peanuts from China) (Emergency Control) (England) Regulations 2002 (SI 2002/774).

Incorporation of EU directives

As already indicated, most EU directives are implemented in the UK using delegated legislation. In this situation the 'parent' Act is usually the European Communities Act 1972, which lays down very broad law-making powers on government ministers to introduce delegated legislation as required to ensure that the UK complies with its obligations as a Member State of (what is now) the EU by implementing directives.

Although primary legislation is occasionally used to implement directives, if a separate Act of Parliament was required for every directive, Parliament would be so busy enacting those statutes that it would have little time to do anything else. Important examples include:

- the Health and Safety (Display Screen Equipment) Regulations 1992 (SI 1992/2792), which implement Directive 90/270;
- the Working Time Regulations 1998 (SI 1998/1833), which implement Directive 93/104;
- the Consumer Protection (Distance Selling) Regulations 2000 (SI 2000/2334), which implement Directive 97/7.

The European Union (Withdrawal) Act 2018 will repeal the European Communities Act 1972 on the day that the UK leaves the EU (currently scheduled for the end of January 2020). The repeal of the 1972 Act (without remedial provisions) would mean that all of the delegated legislation passed under the Act since January 1973—estimated to be some 7,900 statutory instruments—would cease to exist. Hence, the Withdrawal Act provides that this delegated legislation will be 'saved' despite the repeal of the 1972 Act. See further 6.8.

3.5.3 **Possible dangers inherent in secondary legislation**

Lack of accountability

Delegated legislation is not used simply to fill in details but also to establish matters of principle. In some instances, Parliament passes framework legislation which means little without the many regulations made under it. Ministers may be given sweeping powers to amend primary legislation (known as 'Henry VIII' clauses, on which see later). Yet, delegated legislation is rarely subject to the same level of scrutiny as primary legislation. The normal methods of scrutiny are avoided and, as is demonstrated later, the particular methods of scrutinising delegated legislation are patchy.

Potential for abuse

In many instances, the 'parent' Act will give the minister wide discretionary powers. A common formulation is to give the minister the power to 'make such regulations as he considers appropriate'. Where such wide discretion is given it can be extremely difficult to control the exercise of the power through the traditional operation of the *ultra vires* rule. (The *ultra vires* rule allows the courts to intervene if the minister making the regulations has gone beyond the limits of the powers granted to him by the enabling Act.)

There is also the risk that a minister might commit a constitutional impropriety, for example by creating regulations which operate retrospectively or attempt to impose a tax without having express authority to do this under the parent Act.

'Henry VIII clauses'

There is a particular danger where a minister is given the power to amend primary legislation by delegated legislation. Any section in an Act by which this power is given will often be referred to as a 'Henry VIII' clause. A good example is s.207 of the Equality Act 2010, which allows a minister to amend 'an enactment', including some provisions of the 2010 Act itself.

The European Union (Withdrawal) Act 2018 has attracted controversy and criticism for containing some extremely wide 'Henry VIII' clauses. The Withdrawal Act, which will maintain or convert existing EU law into UK law (referred to as 'retained EU law') once the UK leaves the European Union (scheduled for the end of January 2020), provides that government ministers will then be able to amend or repeal that legislation using statutory instruments. Section 8 of the Withdrawal Act 2018 provides that, after leaving the EU, a government minister may 'make such provision as the Minister considers appropriate to prevent, remedy or mitigate (a) any failure of retained EU law to operate effectively, or (b) any other deficiency in retained EU law, arising from the withdrawal of the UK from the EU'. Critics such as Keir Starmer QC, the former DPP and Shadow Secretary of State for Exiting the EU at the time of the bill's passage through Parliament, argued that government ministers should not be given such sweeping powers and that Parliament should have greater control over this legislation. The European Union (Withdrawal) Act 2018 is examined in detail in Chapter 6 (see 6.8).

3.5.4 **Control over delegated legislation**

Widespread use of delegated legislation clearly has its dangers, particularly when it is used not simply for matters of a detailed or technical nature but to effect changes of substance in the law. Then it could be argued that too much power is concentrated in the hands of the executive, creating the opportunity for abuse. It is, therefore, considered important that the use of delegated powers is properly controlled. This control can be exercised in a number of ways.

The enabling Act

It is up to Parliament, when passing the enabling Act, to give the minister, or other subsidiary body, powers—which may be as wide or narrow as it chooses. If the resultant subordinate legislation goes beyond the limits of the parent Act, then it will be possible to challenge it in court as being *ultra vires*. The grant of wide discretionary power makes it much more difficult to control the exercise of power as the limits of the authority are not clearly stated. In the House of Lords, the Delegated Powers and Regulatory Reform Committee examines bills in the Lords and reports on any clauses that will give ministers powers to enact secondary legislation.

Laying before Parliament

Parliament can ensure greater control of delegated legislation by requiring that it should be laid before Parliament. It should be noted that:

- Not all delegated legislation is required to be laid before Parliament (in particular, commencement orders—which simply bring parts of pre-existing primary legislation into force—do not have to be laid).
- There are a number of different laying procedures. The enabling Act will specify which procedure applies. These range from a requirement to lay the delegated legislation before Parliament for information only, via a requirement that legislation be laid for a forty-day period during which it is subject to possible annulment (the negative procedure), to a requirement that the legislation will only come into effect after it has been approved by both Houses of Parliament (the affirmative procedure).

The negative procedure

The most common procedure is where delegated legislation is required to be laid before Parliament, usually for forty days, subject to a negative resolution. Here, the onus is on Parliament to pass a motion (called a 'prayer') to annul the legislation. An example is s.48(3) of the Food Safety Act 1990, which states: 'Any statutory instrument [made] under this Act . . . shall be subject to annulment in pursuance of a resolution of either House of Parliament.'

To bring a successful prayer to annul is difficult to achieve, certainly in the Commons, usually because the government can use its majority to defeat such a motion. The Commons last annulled a statutory instrument in October 1979, and the House of Lords last did so in February 2000, when a successful prayer was passed to annul the Greater London Authority Elections Rules 2000 (SI 2000/208).

The affirmative procedure

The most demanding form of laying procedure, at least in theory, is the affirmative procedure. This is where a piece of delegated legislation is laid, in draft, and has to be approved by *both* Houses of Parliament before it comes into effect. The government must therefore arrange for an appropriate motion of approval to be passed. However, this rarely poses problems for the government; indeed, the last occasion on which a draft statutory instrument failed to secure approval was in November 1969. In practice, the whole House of Commons never votes to approve a statutory instrument. Rather, they are referred to a Delegated Legislation Committee comprising around seventeen MPs. There are often debates about the SI leading up to the vote, but there is no power to amend the proposed legislation. The affirmative procedure is reserved only for the most important (about 10 per cent of all statutory instruments).

A good example of a delegated law-making power subject to the affirmative procedure is s.1(6) of the Education (Student Loans) Act 1990, which (prior to its repeal) stated that 'the power to make orders under [this section] shall be exercisable by statutory instrument and no such order shall be made unless a draft of it has been laid before and approved by a resolution of each House of Parliament'.

Thinking point

What is the best way of allowing Parliament to exercise control over secondary legislation?

Which laying procedure would you prescribe to achieve the most effective parliamentary control over delegated legislation?

Failure to comply with laying arrangements

Failure to comply with any laying requirement will be a procedural irregularity, leaving the statutory instrument potentially open to challenge in the courts. However, the courts have never been entirely clear as to the effect of failure to comply with laying requirements. Would this invalidate the statutory instrument?

In the leading case on the subject, *R v Sheer Metalcraft Ltd* [1954] 1 QB 586, Streatfeild J said:

> I do not think that it can be said that to make a valid statutory instrument it is required that all these stages should be gone through, namely the making, the laying before Parliament, the printing and the certification of that part of it which it might be unnecessary to have printed. In my judgment the making of an instrument is complete when it is first of all made by the Minister concerned and after it has been laid before Parliament. When that has been done it then becomes a valid statutory instrument, totally made under the provisions of the Act.

This seems to suggest that a failure to comply would not invalidate a statutory instrument.

Scrutiny by parliamentary committee

There are two such committees, both of which check to see whether the attention of the Houses should be drawn to particular secondary legislation. The Parliamentary Joint Committee on Statutory Instruments (which consists of members from each House of Parliament), known as the Scrutiny Committee, considers whether the legal technicalities have been complied with. The Committee looks to see whether the legislation has been unduly delayed, purports to have retrospective effect, makes some 'unusual or unexpected' use of the powers conferred by the enabling Act, and so on. The Lords Secondary Legislation Scrutiny Committee, which was established in 2012, 'examines the policy merits of any statutory instruments or regulations laid before the House of Lords'.

Summary

- The UK Parliament is the body responsible for making all UK legislation. It comprises three constituent parts: the House of Commons, the House of Lords, and the monarch.
- The present House of Lords (non-elected) is complementary to the House of Commons (elected). The Commons has democratic legitimacy but is highly political and adversarial; MPs do not have the wealth of specialist knowledge and experience to be found in the Lords.
- Since the House of Lords Act 1999, there have been several reform proposals relating to the House of Lords. Most of these have recommended a 'hybrid' body comprising a combination of elected and appointed members.
- The legislative process in the UK Parliament (standard procedure) consists of a bill receiving, in each House: a first reading, second reading, committee stage, report stage, and third reading. If agreement is reached the bill receives royal assent, at which point the bill becomes an Act. If not, the bill fails, subject to the Parliament Act procedures.
- In 2015, a new procedure was introduced: English Votes for English Laws (EVEL). Under the new procedure, government bills which only affect, in whole or in part, England (or England and Wales) will still be debated and voted on by the House of Commons at the second reading, report, and third reading stages, but will have a special Committee stage in which only English (or English and Welsh) MPs will participate.
- There are government bills and private members' bills. The latter take various forms—ballot, ten minute, presentation, and peers' bills. The success rate of private members' bills is low. Most private members' bills are really just designed to raise awareness.
- The Parliament Act 1911 procedure (as amended) is used to resolve inter-House conflicts. It allows the Commons and the monarch to pass bills without the consent of the Lords, provided certain conditions are satisfied.
- Secondary legislation is usually produced by government ministers in the form of statutory instruments. There are also byelaws, typically produced by local authorities. Statutory instruments may be subject either to a negative laying procedure or an affirmative laying procedure.
- Potential dangers of secondary legislation include the lack of parliamentary scrutiny and Henry VIII clauses (provisions within primary legislation conferring power on a government minister to amend that legislation by statutory instrument) which may be abused.

Questions

1 Explain public legislation, private legislation, and hybrid legislation.
2 Explain the differences between government bills and private members' bills.
3 What are the conditions that must be satisfied before a public bill (other than a money bill) can be passed under the terms of the Parliament Act procedure?
4 Explain the differences between the affirmative laying procedure and the negative laying procedure for statutory instruments.
5 Give three justifications for the existence of secondary legislation.
6 Give three possible dangers posed by the existence of secondary legislation.

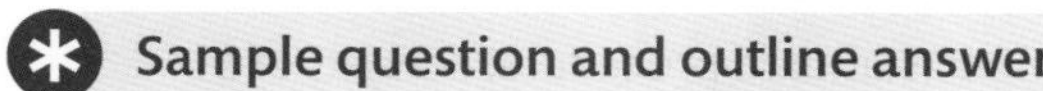

Sample question and outline answer

Question

The changes to the composition of the House of Lords that have taken place over the past sixty years mean that the procedure for passing legislation under the Parliament Act 1911 (as amended) is no longer justified. Explain the legislative procedure under the Parliament Act 1911 (as amended) and consider whether it is still justified in the twenty-first century.

Outline answer

Answers should explain the (amended) Parliament Act procedure, which allows for bills to become Acts of Parliament without the consent of the House of Lords provided certain criteria are satisfied (that is, it must be a Commons bill; the bill must have been rejected twice in successive sessions; it must be substantially the same bill in each session, and so on). Give some examples of bills that have become Acts under the procedure, such as the War Crimes Act 1991 and the Hunting Act 2004.

Answers should explain the changes to the composition of the House of Lords 'over the past sixty years', that is, since the late 1950s. This includes the creation of the first life peers under the Life Peerages Act 1958, the removal of most hereditary peers under the House of Lords Act 1999, the establishment of House of Lords Appointments Commission in 2000, the ability of peers to retire from the Lords, and the removal of peers for non-attendance or following conviction of a serious offence under the House of Lords Reform Act 2014.

Answers should assess (a) whether the Parliament Act was justified in 1911, when it was originally enacted; and (b) whether it is justified in the twenty-first century.

When the 1911 Act was passed the House of Lords was composed primarily of hereditary peers, whereas the House of Commons was directly elected; the Commons could therefore make a strong claim to have significantly more democratic legitimacy than the Lords. It logically follows that an unelected body should not be able to thwart the wishes of an elected body and, therefore, the democratically elected Commons should get its way eventually. This fundamental position has not changed since 1911, despite the various reforms since 1958; the Lords is still unelected and hence should not be able to stop legislation which has been approved by the Commons.

This is especially true if the bill in question was designed to enact a proposal contained in the government's election manifesto, and which can therefore be taken to have attracted public support. These arguments can be countered by the fact that voter apathy means turnout at elections is often low, which undermines to some extent the Commons' claim to be more democratic. On the manifesto point, it is fanciful to suggest that all voters who voted for the eventual government supported (or were even aware of) every proposal in the party's manifesto. Moreover, the first-past-the-post electoral system used in the UK also means that governments can be voted into office on less than 50 per cent of the turnout, which indicates that government proposals are not necessarily backed by a majority of the public after all.

Answers should discuss the fact that the legitimacy of the Hunting Act 2004 and Parliament Act 1949 was challenged in the courts in *Jackson and Others v Attorney-General* (2005), culminating in a hearing before nine law lords in the Judicial Committee of the House of Lords (now the Supreme Court). The law lords unanimously upheld the legitimacy of both Acts (Lord Hope describing the procedure as a 'political reality' which had achieved 'general acceptance' by all of the main political parties), although some of their Lordships discussed the possibility that there might be some limits on its use (Lord Steyn gave an example of a bill to abolish judicial review).

Students could therefore conclude that the Parliament Act procedure remains justified. Nevertheless, it would be legitimate to take the position that the House of Lords in 1911 and that in the twenty-first century are sufficiently different (in terms of their composition and therefore democratic legitimacy) such that the Parliament Act procedure was no longer justified (in light of the reforms that have taken place). If so, it would be appropriate to consider that another means of resolving inter-House conflicts would be desirable to avoid deadlock. Possibilities include conciliation committees, where selected members of both houses meet to try to work out a compromise solution (found in the US Congress), or even dissolution of Parliament, which then gives the electorate the power to cast the deciding vote (an option of last resort available in Australia).

Further reading

- ***Brazier, R.*** *'Royal Assent to Legislation'* (2013) 129 LQR 184

  Provides 'a comprehensive analysis of the mechanics of royal assent to legislation in the United Kingdom'.

- ***Lord Burns***, *'Report of the Lord Speaker's Committee on the Size of the House'* **www.parliament.uk/documents/lords-committees/size-of-house/size-of-house-report.pdf**

- ***Gover, D.*** and ***Kenny, M.*** *'Finding the Good in EVEL: An Evaluation of "English Votes for English Laws" in the House of Commons'* **www.ucl.ac.uk/constitution-unit/news/EVEL_Report_A4_FINAL.pdf**

- ***Harlow, A.***, ***Cranmer, F.***, and ***Doe, N.*** *'Bishops in the House of Lords: A Critical Analysis'* [2008] PL 490

- ***Muylle, K.*** *'Improving the Effectiveness of Parliamentary Legislative Procedures'* (2003) 24 Stat LR 169

  Identifies problems with the legislative process and discusses various options for reform.

- ***Phillipson, G.*** *'The Greatest Quango of them all, a Rival Chamber or a Hybrid Nonsense? Solving the Second Chamber Paradox'* [2004] PL 352

  Discusses the various options for reforming the House of Lords.

- ***Weill, R.*** *'Centennial to the Parliament Act 1911: The Manner and Form Fallacy'* [2012] PL 105

  Examines the passage of the Parliament Acts of 1911 and 1949 and the House of Lords' ruling in *Jackson and Others* (2005).

Online resources

You should now attempt the supporting self-test questions and end-of-chapter questions available at: **www.oup.com/he/wilson-rutherford4e**

Chapter 4

The interpretation of statutes

Learning objectives

By the end of this chapter you should:

- understand how problems of statutory interpretation may arise;
- know and understand the constitutional role of the courts in relation to statutory interpretation;
- be able to explain the nature and content of the 'rules' of statutory interpretation;
- appreciate the various approaches to the discovery of the intention of Parliament as expressed in the words of an Act of Parliament and the courts' use of a contextual and purposive approach to interpretation;
- be aware of the role of internal and external aids to interpretation of an Act of Parliament;
- be able to analyse the reasons for the rules and aids and their effectiveness in determining legislative intent;
- be capable of evaluating the impact of the United Kingdom's (UK) membership of the European Union (EU) and the enactment of the Human Rights Act 1998 upon the process of statutory interpretation.

Talking point

An issue often reported in the newspapers is that of parents taking their children out of school during term-time to go on holiday. In *Isle of Wight Council v Platt* [2017] UKSC 28, Mr Platt had sought permission from the head-teacher to take his daughter out of school during term time. His request was refused. Despite the refusal, Mr Platt took his daughter out of school and went on holiday, with the result that his daughter missed seven school days. In consequence, the local authority issued a fixed penalty notice under the Education Act 1996 requiring Mr Platt to pay £60. As this sum was not paid within twenty-one days, the penalty increased to £120. The increased sum was not paid, so the local authority sought to prosecute Mr Platt before the Isle of Wight magistrates' court under s.444(1) Education Act 1996. By this subsection, a parent is guilty of an offence 'if a child of compulsory school age who is a registered pupil at a school fails to attend regularly at the school'. The issue before the court was a simple question: had the child failed to attend 'regularly' at school? The court thus had to determine the meaning of 'regularly'. There are three broad meanings which may be given to the word 'regularly':

1. Evenly spaced, as in 'I attend school every Monday';
2. Sufficiently, as in 'I have attended 95 per cent of classes';
3. In accordance with rules, as in 'I have to attend every day as required, unless excused'.

In this case, the magistrates' court found in favour of Mr Platt, basing its decision on the child's percentage attendance outside the dates of the absence, which amounted to 90.3 per cent. The court adopted the second interpretation of 'regularly', i.e. to mean sufficiently. An appeal by way of case stated was made to the Divisional Court of the Queen's Bench Division, which agreed with the decision of the magistrates' court. The Divisional Court certified a point of law of general public importance to be heard on appeal in the Supreme Court. The Supreme Court had to decide what was meant by 'fails to attend regularly' in s.444(1) Education Act 1996.

This case presents an excellent example of a problem that requires the process of statutory interpretation. Lawyers and judges have to be able to identify the meaning of the words in an Act of Parliament. This process raises several questions. When words have contested meanings, how is the final and decisive meaning to be identified? Should one look at the meaning of the words as written down, or should one also consider the intention of those persons that essentially drafted those words into the Act? If the latter, what do you think the court is permitted to consider in the search for the 'intention' of Parliament? In this chapter, you will learn much more about how courts decide the meaning of words in legislation. You will also discover what the UKSC decided in the case of *Platt* later on in the chapter. However, in the meantime, consider the following questions:

- Consider the word 'regularly'? What would your definition of the word be, and to what degree do you think it depends on the context in which you are saying it?
- Imagine you are one of the UK Supreme Court judges hearing this case. What arguments do you think the local authority are likely advance? You may want to think about the consequences of a policy that would permit holidays during term time.
- Do you agree with the magistrates' court in finding for Mr Platt? Or are you persuaded by any alternative arguments that might help you find in favour of the local authority.

Introduction

At its most basic level, the interpretation of statutes is about the problem of communication. It is about the limits of the language we use and the words that we use to convey what we mean. There are several perspectives that need to be considered in the process of interpretation. The words used in a statute are drafted to convey a particular meaning, that is, the intention behind the words used. Who are the words aimed at and what does the person reading the words take them to mean? What do the words actually used say and are those words capable of bearing only one meaning? Ideally, the words used will clearly express the intention of the maker of the legislation, and that intention will be clearly communicated to the person reading the words of the statute. However, that is not always the case and problems of interpretation arise when words do not convey the intention clearly. The chapter begins by considering two frequent problems with interpreting language in statutes.

4.1 **Problems of language**

There are two problems that frequently arise in the process of statutory interpretation. First, that the language used in a statute is vague or ambiguous; secondly, that new situations may arise that were unforeseen at the time the legislation was drafted and passed.

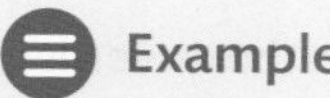

Vague or ambiguous language

Words may be vague, particularly when describing an abstract concept rather than a physical entity. For instance, the word 'obscenity' is difficult to precisely describe, as is an inherently vague word such as 'reasonable'. In other cases, physical words that describe objects or structures can also be vague. For example, what is the definition of a 'building'? Is there a finite list of attributes that a building must have? Alternatively, what attributes must or ought a building to have? Would a static caravan on a brick foundation constitute a 'building'?

Ambiguity arises when words have more than one possible meaning. A word may be used in its ordinary sense or in a technical sense. For example, in *Fisher v Bell* [1961] 1 QB 394, it had to be decided whether a display of goods, in this case a flick knife, in a shop window was an 'offer'. This was because an Act expressly prohibited someone to '*offer* for sale or hire' certain offensive weapons. The ordinary dictionary definition would probably encompass someone making something available for sale, as in placing goods in a shop display for purchase. However, the technical legal meaning of offer from the law of contract is as follows: a party makes a proposal, containing terms which are certain, together with an intention to be bound by the terms, which will become binding should the party to whom the proposal is addressed accept the proposal. In other words, technically an offer is an attempt at making a binding contract and, in this case, placing an item in a shop window is not to make an offer, but to an invite a potential purchaser to make an offer. On this occasion, the Court in *Fisher v Bell* decided that Parliament had used the word in its technical legal sense so that a shopkeeper had not made an offer in displaying the flick knife in a shop window (see 4.3.1).

Unforeseen developments

In *Royal College of Nursing of the United Kingdom v Department of Health and Social Security* [1981] AC 800, the Court had to consider the meaning of s.1(1) of the Abortion Act 1967. This section provides that 'a person shall not be guilty of an offence under the law relating to abortion (ss.58 and 59 Offences Against the Person Act 1861) when a pregnancy is terminated by a registered medical practitioner'. At the time that the Act was passed, the main method of abortion was surgical and thus required a doctor; by 1980, the most common method was medical induction (injecting a chemical fluid into the womb to trigger premature birth of the foetus) which could be carried out by a nurse. In the light of this latter procedure, the House of Lords was asked to consider whether s.1(1) of the Abortion Act 1967 protected a non-registered medical practitioner—a nurse who, under the instructions of a registered medical practitioner—a doctor—effectively caused the abortion by introducing into a mother's womb an abortifacient fluid. Put another way, the question was whether Parliament in s.1(1) intended to prohibit nurses from conducting this new method of abortion.

By a 3:2 majority, the Court decided no. The majority decided that the creation of the Act was motivated by legalising and preventing back-street and unsafe abortions. In light of this aim—described in the Act as to amend and clarify the law relating to 'termination of pregnancy', the intention was to ensure that abortions were carried out in safe and hygienic conditions. Doctors and nurses were part of a treatment team and thus the latter were permitted to conduct the procedure. It is, however, worth noting some of the risks of taking such an approach to interpretation. Lord Wilberforce, in a dissenting opinion, said (at p.822):

> When a new state of affairs, or a fresh set of facts bearing on policy, comes into existence, the courts have to consider whether they fall within the parliamentary intention. They may be held to do so, if they fall within the same genus of facts as those to which the expressed policy has been formulated. They may also be held to do so if there can be detected a clear purpose in the legislation which can only be fulfilled if the extension is made. How liberally these principles may be applied must depend upon the nature of the enactment, and the strictness or otherwise of the words in which it has been expressed. The courts should be less willing to extend expressed meanings if it is clear that the Act in question was designed to be restrictive or circumscribed in its operation rather than liberal or permissive. They will be much less willing to do so where the subject matter is different in kind or dimension from that for which the legislation was passed. In any event there is one course which the courts cannot take, under the law of this country; they cannot fill gaps; they cannot by asking the question 'What would Parliament have done in this current case—not being one in contemplation—if the facts had been before it?' attempt themselves to supply the answer, if the answer is not to be found in the terms of the Act itself.

How a court interprets a statute when faced with a situation that was unforeseen by Parliament at the time of the passage of an Act, ultimately, depends upon the nature of the legislation. For instance, it can depend on whether the Act is designed to be highly certain and restrictive in that area, or it is designed to be more flexible and liberal. Note that Lord Wilberforce's statement as to how to approach this problem of the unforeseen development was approved by the House of Lords in *Fitzpatrick v Sterling Housing Association Ltd* [2001] 1 AC 27.

A similar problem was also seen in *R (Quintavalle) v Secretary of State for Health* [2003] 2 AC 687 (see later at 4.3.5).

4.2 **Preliminary issues**

To begin, a number of preliminary questions need to be addressed in order to understand the process of statutory interpretation. These questions also highlight some of the complexity and uncertainty of the process. This section address three significant preliminary questions.

First, in interpreting a statute, consider what are the courts precisely being asked to do? The primary task of the courts is to search for and give effect to the intention of Parliament (or the legislature) as found in the words of the statute. Lord Watson, in *Salomon v Salomon* [1897] AC 22, said (at p.38):

> 'Intention of the Legislature' is a common but very slippery phrase, which, popularly understood, may signify anything from intention embodied in positive enactment to speculative opinion as to what the Legislature probably would have meant, although

> there has been an omission to enact it. In a Court of Law or Equity, what the Legislature intended to be done or not to be done can only be legitimately ascertained from that which it has chosen to enact, either in express words or by reasonable and necessary implication.

This quotation emphasises the relationship between parliamentary intention and the words used in the statute; whatever Parliament's intention might or might not have been, the exact words used in the statute must be capable of bearing such a meaning.

The task for a court is to search for the true meaning of what Parliament has said. However, there are limits on how a court may interpret a statute. In *Jones v DPP* [1962] AC 635, Lord Reid said the words of a statutory provision were only to be given a meaning that they could reasonably bear; in the event of a word being ambiguous, a court could choose between the meanings. In general terms this principle continues to apply but it would now need to be read subject to s.3 of the Human Rights Act 1998 (see 7.2).

Secondly, is there a clear method for ascertaining the purpose of Parliament? You will find that there is no certain way of ascertaining the purpose of Parliament and in searching for such purpose the courts are asked to make choices between rival interpretations. The argument as to what is the 'correct interpretation' of a statutory provision is aided by use of the so-called 'rules' of statutory interpretation. As Lord Reid explained in *Maunsell v Olins* [1975] AC 373, 382, 'they are not rules in the ordinary sense of having binding force. They are our servants not our masters.' The rules of statutory interpretation are used as aids to construction but may operate inconsistently, as different rules may point to different answers (for an example, see the case study on *Coltman v Bibby* [1988] 2 AC 276 at 4.3.6).

It is thus clear that the rules of statutory interpretation are not to be followed slavishly; they are helpful tools in the search for the intention of Parliament, but their use is not certain to provide a 'right answer'. The rules may be used to support arguments as to the meaning of a statute, but as the courts are not bound by the rules, which rule or rules are to apply is ultimately a choice for the court's judgment. It is worth pointing out that the rules of statutory interpretation also may be employed in the interpretation of contracts, wills, and other legal documents, so do not compartmentalise this topic as solely a part of your studies on English Legal System module. These rules can have a broader application in the law. One last observation: the statements made by the courts concerning how to interpret statutes are not strictly binding in term of the doctrine of precedent sense, but they are *obiter dicta* (see 5.4).

Thirdly, if it is discovered that the words of a statute do not clearly communicate the intention or purpose of Parliament, from where is such intention to be considered and identified? This raises the issue of what a court can consult beyond the four corners of the precise statute. Rules have been developed as to what may and may not be considered in seeking the intention and purpose of Parliament.

Key point

The rules of statutory interpretation are techniques for finding the true meaning of a statute, but do not comprise a system, application of which will ultimately produce the 'right' answer.

4.3 The approach to statutory interpretation

Traditionally, students begin their learning of statutory interpretation by understanding three essential rules: the literal rule, the golden rule, and the mischief rule.

4.3.1 The literal rule

The literal rule concentrates upon the words of the statute. Meaning is to be ascertained by application of the rules of grammar and the finding of dictionary definitions. It is the usual starting point in the process of interpretation. As Lord Diplock said in *Duport Steels Ltd v Sirs* [1980] 1 WLR 142, 157, 'the role of the judiciary is confined to ascertaining from the words that Parliament has approved as expressing its intention what that intention was and to give effect to it.' At its most extreme, an application of the literal rule only considers the words of the statute in the search for the intention of Parliament.

Thinking point

Is the literal rule still useful, literally?

The literal rule operates on the assumption that the meanings of words and sentences are clear, which, of course, is quite often not the case. It is also apparent that sometimes the words of a statute and the perceived purpose of a statute may be at odds. The literal rule is now deemed to be out-dated and has largely been succeeded by the more contextual approach to interpretation (see later at 4.3.5). However, consider whether the literal approach has any role to play in the interpretation of statutes? Do you think it is a useful starting point for a judge?

A classic example of the literal rule is the case of *Fisher v Bell* [1961] 1 QB 394. As outlined earlier, this case concerned a shopkeeper who displayed in his shop window a flick knife with a ticket stating: 'Ejector knife—4s'. The Restriction of Offensive Weapons Act 1959 s.1, provided that '[a]ny person who manufactures, sells or hires or offers for sale or hire' a flick knife shall be guilty of an offence. The prosecution argued that the knife was offered for sale in contravention of the Restriction of Offensive Weapons Act 1959. The defendant said that no such offer had been or was being made.

It was held by the Divisional Court of the Queen's Bench Division that an offer had not been made. The Court gave the word 'offer' a technical legal meaning by reading the statute against its meaning in the general law of contract. The Act was therefore not contravened and no offence was committed. Lord Parker CJ said that under the ordinary law of contract the display of an article with a price on it in a shop window is merely an 'invitation to treat' and not a legal offer for sale, the acceptance of which would constitute a binding contract. In addition, there was no indication in the statute that Parliament had intended that the word 'offer' in the 1959 Act should have a meaning other than the one supplied by the general law of contract. In consequence, the defendant was not guilty of the offence charged.

See 4.6.2, 'Presumptions of legislative intent in cases of doubt or ambiguity'.

The case may be viewed as an example of the literal rule. Alternatively, it may be seen, as Cross argues in *Statutory Interpretation* (p.73), 'as an example of the presumption that penal statutes should be strictly construed in favour of the accused'. In other words, in cases where there is doubt about the law and its criminalisation of conduct, the starting point should be that the person accused is given the benefit of any doubt.

Of course, one might criticise the approach taken because it might be said to go against the purpose and thrust of the Act—to restrict the sale and supply of offensive weapons. It is interesting to note that the 1959 Act was later amended by the Restriction of Offensive Weapons Act 1961, the offence in s.1 being expanded to include where a person 'exposes . . . for the purpose of sale' a flick knife.

4.3.2 **The golden rule**

The classic statement of this rule is to be found in the words of Lord Wensleydale in the case of *Grey v Pearson* (1857) 6 HL Cas 61, 106 (note that this case concerned the interpretation of a will, but the rule also applies to statutes). The golden rule may be used where a literal interpretation of the words of a statute leads to an absurdity or to an inconsistency or repugnance with the rest of the statute. The inference drawn is that the meaning discovered by an application of the literal rule cannot, in reality, have been intended by Parliament. When applicable, Lord Wensleydale said, the grammatical and ordinary sense of the words of a statute may be modified to avoid absurdity, inconsistency, or repugnance. In deciding how to avoid the absurdity or inconsistency the court will look at Parliament's purpose in passing the legislation.

Adler v George [1964] 2 QB 7 illustrates how the golden rule may be used. By s.3 of the Official Secrets Act 1920 it is an offence for a person 'in the vicinity of any prohibited place' to obstruct any member of Her Majesty's forces. The defendant, Adler, had entered a Royal Air Force station, a prohibited place, and obstructed a member of Her Majesty's forces, and was convicted by magistrates. On appeal, the defendant contended that no offence could be committed as the defendant was *in* the prohibited place and not, as s.3 provides, 'in the *vicinity* of any prohibited place'. It was argued that literally, 'in the vicinity of' meant 'near' or 'close to', but did not mean 'in' or 'on'. Lord Parker CJ rejected this interpretation and said that s.3 was designed to prevent interference with Her Majesty's forces when performing duties relating to security of prohibited places. Viewed against this purpose it would be absurd that an offence was created by obstructing near a prohibited place and not within the place itself. His Lordship said that the words 'in or' may be inserted before 'in the vicinity of any prohibited place'. Clearly, it was strange that the more serious offence, obstructing in the prohibited place, was omitted while an offence of obstruction near the prohibited place was created. No doubt this anomaly convinced the Court that the intention of Parliament must have been to cover both situations.

It can be seen that Lord Parker CJ refers to absurdity to indicate that the words of the statute cannot wholly reflect the intention of Parliament and so words may be necessarily 'read into' the statute. This is particularly so having regard to the context of the Act, which is designed to prevent interference with members of Her Majesty's forces in respect of a prohibited place. His Lordship, in this sense, is having regard to the purpose of s.3 of the Act.

Thinking point

Was *Grey v Pearson* a step too far?

Perhaps ironically, Lord Wensleydale in *Grey v Pearson* does not indicate what is precisely meant by 'absurdity' or 'inconsistency'. Is there a particular threshold when something definitively becomes absurd or inconsistent? Similarly, he gives no clear indication as to the method to be followed when one encounters an absurd or inconsistent outcome. His Lordship was also somewhat cryptic when he said: 'the grammatical and ordinary sense of the words may be modified.' Does this mean that the words of the statute must be capable of bearing an alternative meaning, and the golden rule simply indicates that the meaning that does not lead to absurdity or inconsistency is to be favoured? Or, more radically, does the rule allow for the reading in or ignoring of words expressly written into the words of the Act? *Adler v George* offers an illustration of judges reading words in to the statute. Consider the constitutional implications of this. Remember, under the theory of the separation of powers, Parliament makes the law and a judge must not legislate but only interpret and apply those statutes. Do you think Lord Parker and his application of the golden rule crosses this constitutional boundary?

4.3.3 **The mischief rule**

The mischief rule is one of some antiquity. A classic formulation of the rule is to be found in *Heydon*'s case (1584) 3 Co Rep 7a, 7b, where it was said:

> And it was resolved by them that for the sure and true interpretation of all statutes in general (be they penal or beneficial, restrictive or enlarging of the common law), four things are to be discerned and considered:
>
> 1. What was the common law before the making of the Act,
> 2. What was the mischief and defect for which the common law did not provide,

> 3. What remedy the Parliament hath resolved and appointed to cure the disease of the Commonwealth, and
> 4. The true reason of the remedy;
>
> and then the office of all the judges is always to make such construction as shall suppress the mischief and advance the remedy.

As seen from the above, the courts were to interpret an Act so as to suppress the mischief and give effect to the remedy. However, the problem with this approach relates to the words of an Act and the extent to which it was permissible for a court to give a meaning to the words used that they were not capable of bearing. Additionally, the rule assumes that legislation is 'only designed to deal with evil and not to further a positive social purpose' (*The Interpretation of Statutes*, Law Commission (Report No. 21) 1969). While it is evident that the courts have embraced the notion of a purposive approach to interpretation (see page 125), nonetheless references to 'mischief' are still to be found in the judgments of the courts. For an example of the use of the mischief rule see *Royal College of Nursing of the United Kingdom v Department of Health and Social Security* [1981] AC 800, a case considered at the beginning of this chapter.

The mischief rule is also illustrated by the following case. In *Smith v Hughes*, prostitutes in a house sought to attract the attention of men passing in the street by beckoning from balconies or tapping on windows. Under s.1(1) of the Street Offences Act 1959 it was 'an offence for a common prostitute to loiter or solicit in a street or public place for the purpose of prostitution'. It was argued on behalf of the defendant prostitutes that a balcony was not 'in a street' or 'public place', nor was tapping on a glass window from within a house. The defendants were convicted by magistrates and appealed to the Divisional Court of the Queen's Bench Division.

The problem was that the Act did not make clear where the prostitute had to be when the solicitation took place. Lord Parker referred to the mischief of the 1959 Act, which was well known, as a measure 'intended to clean up the streets' and to enable people to walk without being solicited by prostitutes. Against this background it mattered not that the prostitutes were indoors or on balconies; the solicitation was projected into the street and was aimed at a person walking in the street, and fell within s.1(1) of the Street Offences Act 1959. The defendants' conviction was upheld.

Thinking point

'Up to Mischief': Who and how to decide?

Who decides upon the formulation of the 'mischief'? Which materials may a judge rely upon in determining the 'mischief' of a statute? You may find this useful to contemplate when you consider the later discussion on aids to interpretation, either inside the Act of Parliament or outside the Act of Parliament. Identifying a mischief may also require its own exercise in interpretation too because, for instance, the mischief might not be clear, may not attract firm agreement and there may well be more than one mischief.

Purposive approach—*Heydon's* case and the purposive approach contrasted

Strictly speaking, it is possible to differentiate between the rule in *Heydon's* case and what is known as a purposive approach, i.e. a rule that looks more squarely at the aim and purpose underlying the statute and that permits looking inside and outside the Act to discover that purpose (although there are limits in how far one can go beyond the words of a statute and in terms of the external aids that can be relied on; these will be considered later). The rule in *Heydon's* case was stated at a time when the role of Parliament was different—Parliament met infrequently and its supremacy had not been established, so the courts were more willing to go beyond the words of the statute to 'suppress the mischief and advance the remedy'. In ascertaining the mischief, the courts tended to look only within the four corners of the statute itself and not to external sources. Otherwise, it is fair to say that whether one calls it the mischief rule or the purposive rule/approach, the difference in method and outcome is not likely to be substantial. One way of thinking about it is that the purposive approach necessarily encompasses the mischief rule—it is a slightly expanded form of the rule.

4.3.4 **Application of the literal, golden, and mischief rules**

The problem encountered with application of these three rules, that is, the literal, golden, and mischief rules, was the question of which rule was to be applied in any given situation. Professor John Willis, in 'Statute Interpretation in a Nutshell' (1938) 16 Can Bar Rev 1, said: 'a court invokes whichever of the rules produces a result that satisfies its sense of justice in the case before it.' The literal rule was the one most frequently referred to by the courts expressly, but all three rules were valid and reference could be made to them as the situation demanded; however, no justification was given by the courts for their use, or indeed any indication given of the circumstances of when each rule was to be employed. See Diagram 4.1 giving an overview of the approaches to statutory interpretation.

The obvious shortcomings of this situation—excessive literalism and the lack of a systematic approach—led to calls for legislative reform in this area. In 1969 the Law Commissions produced a report, *The Interpretation of Statutes*, which proposed that 'a limited degree of statutory intervention is required in this field . . . to clarify, and in some respects to relax the strictness of, the rules which . . . exclude altogether or exclude when the meaning is unambiguous, certain material from consideration'. No legislation was ever passed in response to this report but since then, academic writers have sought to make sense of the mass of conflicting *obiter dicta* comments by judges. Foremost in seeking to systematise have been Sir Rupert Cross and Francis Bennion, in separate books both entitled *Statutory Interpretation*. Their success may be measured by the frequent references made to their work by the courts. An approach identified by Cross is considered next.

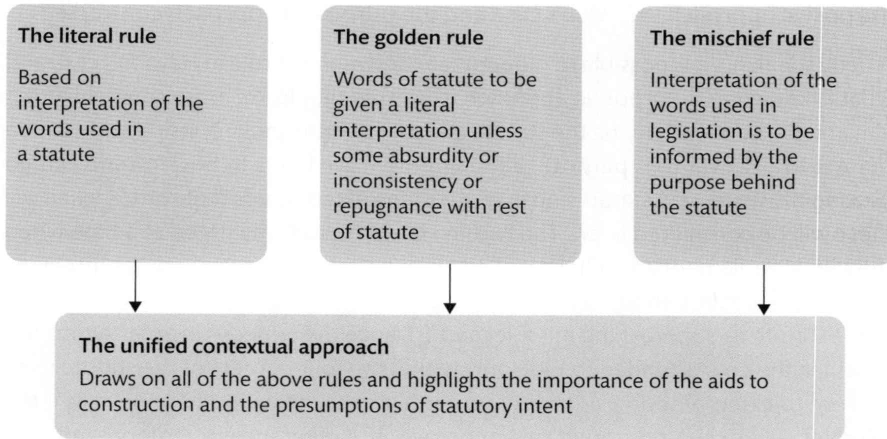

Diagram 4.1 Approaches to statutory interpretation

4.3.5 The unified contextual approach

Sir Rupert Cross felt that judges in practice used a combination of these rules in interpreting any one statutory provision. He called this a unified contextual approach and it broadly reflects a purposive approach to interpretation. He described it as follows (at p.49):

1. The judge must give effect to the [grammatical and] ordinary, or, where appropriate, the technical meaning of words in the general context of the statute; he must also determine the extent of general words with reference to that context.
2. If the judge considers that the application of the words in their grammatical and ordinary sense would produce a result which is contrary to the purpose of that statute, he may apply them in any secondary meaning that they are capable of bearing.
3. The judge may read in words which he considers to be necessarily implied by words which are already in the statute and he has a limited power to add to, alter or ignore statutory words in order to prevent a provision from being unintelligible or absurd or totally unreasonable, unworkable, or totally irreconcilable with the rest of the statute.
4. In applying the above rules the judge may resort to certain aids to construction and presumptions . . .
5. The judge must interpret a statute so as to give effect to directly applicable European Community law, and, in so far as this is not possible, must refrain from applying the statutory provisions which conflict with that law.

See further 4.8 'Interpretation of legislation and the Human Rights Act 1998'.

To these points there must now be added a sixth, arising out of s.3 of the Human Rights Act 1998. In the 1998 Act, it is provided that a judge must interpret and give effect to primary legislation and subordinate legislation, in so far as it is possible to do so, in a way which is compatible with the Convention rights.

In considering the words of a statute, the courts must consider the context in which they are being used. Lord Simon, in *Maunsell v Olins* [1975] AC 373, at p.391, explained:

> Statutory language, like all language, is capable of an almost infinite gradation of 'register'—i.e., it will be used at the semantic level appropriate to the subject matter and to the audience addressed (the man in the street, lawyers, merchants, etc.). It is the duty of a court of construction to tune in to such register and so to interpret the statutory language as to give to it the primary meaning which is appropriate in that register (unless it is clear that some other meaning must be given in order to carry out the statutory purpose or to avoid injustice, anomaly, absurdity or contradiction). In other words, statutory language must always be given presumptively the most natural and ordinary meaning which is appropriate in the circumstances.

This makes the point that the intended meaning of words depends upon the circumstances in which they are used. Words may have an ordinary meaning or a technical meaning. See, for example, *Fisher v Bell* [1961] 1 QB 394. The aids to construction both internal and external to an Act, which are explained later in the chapter, help to establish the context of an Act. Lord Simon also explains that if the primary meaning to be given to the words do not fulfil the statutory purpose or would otherwise lead to injustice, anomaly, absurdity, or contradiction then a secondary meaning may be given if the words are capable of bearing such meaning.

In a contextual approach to interpretation, the appreciation of the purpose of the Act is essential. Again, the internal and external aids to interpretation may be consulted to establish such purpose. In *R v Montila* [2004] 1 WLR 3141, the House of Lords, in a single opinion delivered by Lord Hope, said (at p.3151): 'it has become common practice for their Lordships to ask to be shown the Explanatory Notes when issues are raised about the meaning of words used in an enactment.'

See 'Explanatory Notes' in 4.4.2.

Statements by the House of Lords suggest that a contextual and purposive approach to the interpretation of statutes is to be adopted. Lady Hale in *R (on the application of Black) v Secretary of State for Justice* [2017] UKSC 81, stated: 'The goal of all statutory interpretation is to discover the intention of legislation . . . in light of their context and their purpose.' Earlier still, Lord Steyn, in *R (Quintavalle) v Secretary of State for Health* [2003] 2 AC 687, more cautiously said (at p.700): 'nowadays the shift towards purposive interpretation is not in doubt. The qualification is that the degree of liberality permitted is influenced by the context, e.g. social welfare legislation and tax statutes may have to be approached somewhat differently.' In this respect, Lord Steyn is advocating that a more cautious approach may be required in certain areas of social or economic policy because a broad interpretation may lead to unintended economic and social consequences. See Bell, J. and Engle, G. *Cross Statutory Interpretation*, pp.180–3.

The following cases give examples of the application of the contextual and purposive approach.

In *R v Z (Attorney General for Northern Ireland's Reference)* [2005] UKHL 35, [2005] 2 AC 645, Z and others were charged under s.11(1) of the Terrorism Act 2000 with belonging to a proscribed organisation, the Real Irish Republican Army (the 'Real IRA'). By s.3(1) of the Act, 'an organisation is proscribed if (a) it is listed in Sch.2, or (b) it operates under the same name as an organisation listed in that schedule'. Schedule 2 included the Irish Republican Army (the IRA), but did not include the 'Real IRA'. The question for the House of Lords was simply whether the 'Real IRA' was a proscribed organisation.

It was argued on behalf of Z that the words used by Parliament had not made clear an intention to proscribe the 'Real IRA'; the organisation was not included in Sch.2, nor did the 'Real IRA' fall within s.3(1)(b) as it had a different name, separate membership, and different aims from the IRA. Reliance was also placed on the principle of legal policy that any doubt in a penal statute should be resolved in favour of a defendant, as seen in *Tuck & Sons v Priester* (1887) 19 QBD 629. It can be seen that Z's argument was based upon a literal interpretation of the Terrorism Act 2000, supported by a presumption of legislative intent.

However, Lord Bingham said (at p.655):

> [T]he interpretation of a statute is a far from academic exercise. It is directed to a particular statute, enacted at a particular time, to address (almost invariably) a particular problem or mischief. As was said in *R (Quintavalle) v Secretary of State for Health* [2003] 2 AC 687, 695 para 8: 'The court's task, within the permissible bounds of interpretation, is to give effect to Parliament's purpose. So the controversial provisions should be read in the context of the statute as a whole, and the statute as a whole should be read in the historical context of the situation which led to its enactment.'

His Lordship concluded that in approaching the issue in the present case, the historical context was of fundamental importance. Looking at the legislation passed prior to and including the Terrorism Act 2000, the common object, with a limited exception, was the suppression of Irish terrorism. Parliament had previously enacted statutes mindful of the IRA having split into two groups—the Official IRA and the Provisional IRA—and used the general label 'the Irish Republican Army' for the purposes of proscription. This approach employed a blanket term 'to embrace all emanations, manifestations and representations of the IRA, whatever their relationship to each other'. The Terrorism Act 2000 was enacted against this background, of which Parliament must have been aware.

Lord Woolf agreed with Lord Bingham, and, applying the approach of reading s.3 not only in the context of the Act as a whole but also in the light of the situation which led to its enactment, said (at p.660): 'there can be no doubt and any other view would be absurd, that the words of s.3 and Sch.2 were intended to include the Real IRA which was the most active of the different organisations at the time of enactment.' All of their Lordships agreed that the 'Real IRA' fell within the term 'the IRA', although they differed in their reasoning.

The case illustrates the purposive approach to interpretation with express reference made to the object of the Terrorism Act 2000. The process of identifying Parliament's intention was reinforced by considering the absurdity that would result if the 'Real IRA', an active terrorist organisation at the time of enactment, were not included within the scope of that intention.

Another example of the purposive approach to interpretation is seen in *R (Quintavalle) v Secretary of State for Health* [2003] 2 AC 687. This case raised the issue of an unforeseen development. As previously outlined, the question that often arises is: could legislation be applied to a development that was unknown at the time of the passage of an Act? The Human Fertilisation and Embryology Act 1990 was passed against a background of fast-moving scientific developments. Under the Act a statutory licensing authority was established to regulate the creation of human embryos outside the human body. Importantly, at the time of enactment it was thought that a human embryo could only be created by a process of fertilisation.

Later scientific developments allowed the creation of a human embryo by cell nuclear replacement (CNR), a process not involving fertilisation. By s.1(1), '(a) embryo means a live human embryo where fertilisation is complete, and (b) references to an embryo include an egg in the process of fertilisation, and, for this purpose, fertilisation is not complete until the appearance of a two cell zygote', and by s.1(2) it was stated that the Act applies only to the 'bringing about the creation of an embryo outside the human body'. The House of Lords was asked whether an embryo created by CNR fell within the regulatory scheme established by the 1990 Act. It was argued that by defining 'embryo' by reference to fertilisation, Parliament excluded embryos created by CNR. However, Lord Bingham, having considered the background to the 1990 Act, said that embryos created by CNR were subject to regulation.

His Lordship reasoned that the Act was directed to the creation of human embryos outside the human body and Parliament clearly could not have intended to distinguish between embryos on the basis of method of creation given the state of scientific knowledge in 1990. Lord Millett, relying in part upon the long title to the Act, 'an Act to make provision in connection with human embryos and any subsequent development of such embryos', said (at p.708):

> Parliament intended to make comprehensive provision for the protection of human embryos however created, and that the failure of particular provisions to capture embryos produced by a process not involving fertilisation is not because Parliament intended to leave them unregulated but because Parliament did not foresee the need to deal with them.

In the light of the purpose behind the Act, s.1(1)(a) had to be read as directed to live human embryos created outside the body, irrespective of their manner of creation. Consequently, the words 'where fertilisation is complete' in s.1(1)(a) were interpreted as not being an essential part of the definition of an embryo, but referring to the time at which an embryo became such. Was this interpretation consistent with the guidance of Lord Wilberforce (see 4.1)?

Lord Bingham posed and answered the following questions:

- Did live human embryos created by CNR fall within the same genus of facts as those to which the expressed policy of Parliament had been formulated? His Lordship answered yes, as the embryos were similar and both forms were in need of regulation given the purpose of the Act.
- Was the operation of the 1990 Act to be regarded as liberal and permissive in its operation or restrictive and circumscribed? While considering this to be 'not an entirely simple question', his Lordship considered that the purpose of the Act required the regulation of 'activities not distinguishable in any significant respect from those regulated by the Act'.
- Was the embryo created by CNR different in kind or dimension from that for which the Act was passed? In his Lordship's view, given the reasons for the legislation, that is, to address difficult moral, religious, and scientific issues relating to human embryos, the answer was no.

Lord Steyn said (at p.703): 'in order to give effect to a plain parliamentary purpose a statute may sometimes be held to cover a scientific development not known when the statute was passed. Given that Parliament legislates on the assumption that statutes may be in place for many years, and that Parliament wishes to pass effective legislation, this is a benign principle designed to achieve the wishes of Parliament.'

Thinking point

Do judges interpret or do they legislate?

Can this statement of Lord Steyn be reconciled with the comments made by Lord Wilberforce (see 4.1) in *Royal College of Nursing of the United Kingdom v Department of Health and Social Security* [1981] AC 800? Why did the majority of the House of Lords in the *Royal College of Nursing* case disagree with the decision reached by Lord Wilberforce?

Let us return to another case that we mentioned in this chapter's Talking Point on p.116. The Supreme Court, in *Isle of Wight Council v Platt* [2017] UKSC 28, had to decide what was meant in s.444(1) Education Act 1996 by the words 'fails to attend regularly'. In the end, the UKSC found for the school and the local authority.

Visit the online resources to watch the Supreme Court judgment.

Lady Hale, having reviewed the section in its historical context, rejected two possible interpretations of 'regularly': 'at regular intervals', and 'sufficiently frequently'. She preferred an interpretation of regularly as 'in accordance with the rules prescribed by the school'. 'Sufficiently frequently' was rejected as it ran counter to the purpose of the Education Act 1944, which was to 'increase the scope and character of compulsory state education'. Other features of the Act pointed to an intention to restrict the excuses for non-attendance. Furthermore, an interpretation of 'regularly' as 'sufficiently frequently' was too uncertain to found a criminal offence. Finally, there were, in Lady Hale's opinion, good policy reasons against the desirability of such an interpretation, for example the disruptive effect on the pupil's education, the potential disruption to other pupils' education, and the impact upon the effective management of a school. In conclusion, Lady Hale said the above reasons also pointed towards the correct interpretation being 'in accordance with the rules prescribed by the school'. She said that any argument that a single absence without leave or acceptable excuse would lead to criminal liability, could be managed by a sensible prosecution policy.

You may also want to reflect on the following fundamental question. To what extent does a purposive approach allow the courts to depart from the words of a statute? If the courts do so, is that justifiable? The cases generally disclose that the courts, within very narrow limits, are willing to read words in and out as stated in Cross's third point. We discussed this a little earlier and we can briefly reflect on this next.

Reading words in and Reading words out

Cross, in point three, said that judges may read words into a statute when the words are necessarily implied, in light of words already present in the statute. This was seen in *Adler v George* [1964] 2 QB 7, discussed earlier.

Cross said that a judge, using the yardstick of a statutory provision being absurd or unintelligible or totally irreconcilable with the rest of the statute, has a limited power to add to, alter, or ignore statutory words. In *McMonagle v Westminster City Council* [1990] 2 WLR 823, the House of Lords ignored words contained in the Local Government (Miscellaneous Provisions) Act 1982 as amended by the Greater London Council (General Powers) Act 1986. The appellant had been convicted of knowingly using premises as a 'sex encounter establishment' without a licence. 'Sex encounter establishment' was defined, inter alia, as '(c) premises at which entertainments *which are not unlawful* are provided' (emphasis added). It was argued on behalf of the appellant that the prosecution had to prove the activities at the appellant's premises were not unlawful; that is, that the activities were not so indecent in character as to amount to a common law offence.

Lord Bridge said that the purpose of the 1982 Act was to control sex establishments and that a literal interpretation of the words would have the effect of frustrating this purpose. To avoid this construction, his Lordship treated the words 'which are not unlawful' as the product of poor draftsmanship, and unnecessary. Usually effect must be given to every word of a statute, but if no sensible meaning can be given to a word or phrase and it frustrates the object of the legislation then such may be disregarded.

It is important to consider how far courts may depart from the wording of an Act of Parliament in the process of interpretation and whether the courts are consistent in this practice. Remember, of course, that when legislation's compatibility with the European Convention on Human Rights (ECHR) is in question, the courts, by s.3 of the Human Rights Act 1998, are under a duty to interpret and give effect to legislation to ensure such compatibility, in so far as it is possible to do so. This raises the same question about how far the courts are able to depart from the strict wording of the Act. This will be discussed later but for now, you can appreciate how statutory interpretation operates in practice by looking at a case in much closer detail.

4.3.6 The rules of statutory interpretation in action

The case of *Coltman v Bibby* [1988] 2 AC 276 illustrates how the rules of statutory interpretation may be employed to determine the intention of Parliament.

The facts of the case were that Leo Coltman died when a ship of some 90,000 tons in which he worked, called the *Derbyshire*, sank. Damages were sought by the claimants, who were administering the estate of Coltman, from the defendant employers, Bibby Tankers Ltd. Under s.1(1) of the Employer's Liability (Defective Equipment) Act 1969, should an employee suffer personal injury in the course of his employment because of a defect in equipment provided by an employer, for the purposes of the employer's business, and the defect is due to the fault of a third party (for example, a manufacturer that supplied the equipment), then the injury is attributable to the negligence of an employer. The employer would be vicariously liable to the employee even if the fault was of the third party, and the employer would have a right to proceed against the third party to recover damages.

The case illustrates the difficulties that arise over the use of definitions in statutes: the House of Lords had to decide whether a ship was 'equipment' for the purposes of the Employer's Liability (Defective Equipment) Act 1969. If it was, the defendants would be liable to pay damages to the estate of Leo Coltman.

A starting point when considering the meaning of words in a statute is to see if Parliament has provided definitions of the terms used. These may sometimes be found in the section where the term is used or in the Interpretation section which is located at the end of a Part of an Act or at the end of an Act. The Employer's Liability (Defective Equipment) Act 1969 provided in s.1(3) that 'in the section "equipment" includes any plant and machinery, vehicle, aircraft and clothing . . . "personal injury" includes loss of life'.

The High Court held that the ship was 'equipment', whereas the Court of Appeal, by a majority, decided that it was not. The case was appealed to the House of Lords.

It is helpful to consider the arguments put forward by both sets of counsel before the House of Lords.

Arguments for the claimants

- There is no exhaustive definition of 'equipment' in the Act; note that s.1(3) uses the word 'includes', not 'means'. Parliament has used wide words and a ship therefore falls within the meaning of 'equipment' or 'plant' or 'vehicle'.
- Equipment' is provided 'for the purposes of the employer's business', which is wider than providing equipment to a particular employee for use in the course of his work.
- The purpose of the Act is to protect employees who are injured due to defective equipment when that fault is attributable to the fault of a third party and not an employer.
- The 1969 Act applies to hovercrafts, and for the purposes of taxation legislation a ship is treated as 'plant'.
- Given that Parliament has used wide words and has not expressly excluded ships from the definition of 'equipment', ships ought to be included; to arrive at any other interpretation would create absurd anomalies—for example, a cross-Channel hovercraft is covered by the 1969 Act, but a cross-Channel ferry would not be so covered.

Arguments for the defendants

- The ordinary use of the word 'equipment' is something with which a person or thing is 'fitted out'. Support for this meaning is to be found in the *Oxford English Dictionary*.
- The claimants conceded that a factory or a hotel could not be 'equipment'. A large ship is like a factory, a place where an employee works. Liability attaches to 'equipment' within a factory or ship but not to the structure of the factory or ship.
- For the purposes of the Occupiers Liability Act 1957 and the Factories Act 1961, a ship is within the definition of 'premises'.
- 'Equipment' must be read in its context, particularly in the light of the word 'provided' which means 'supplied or furnished for use'. An interpretation which suggests that a ship is provided to the crew surely cannot be correct.
- Section 1(3) extends the ordinary meaning of 'equipment' to cover, for example, 'aircraft' and 'plant' that would not normally be covered. The meaning of 'plant', defined by the *Oxford English Dictionary* as '[t]he fixtures, implements, machinery, and apparatus used in carrying out an industrial process', is not apt to include a ship. The same is true of 'vehicle', as a means of conveyance on land. If the word 'vehicle' was given a wider meaning, as encompassing any form of conveyance, so as to include a ship, then it would also cover an aircraft; however, Parliament has included an aircraft expressly, but made no mention of a ship. 'The Act is drafted in terms of inclusion, and anything not within the words of inclusion are excluded *sub silentio*—excluded by silence.'

The reasoning in the House of Lords

Lord Oliver delivered the leading opinion, with which the other Lords agreed, finding that the ship was indeed 'equipment'.

His Lordship first pointed to the mischief behind the 1969 Act that employees in the course of their employment may be injured by defective equipment provided by an employer. While the employer at common law might not have been negligent in supplying the defective equipment, an employee might not be able to claim against the third person supplying the employer with such, as the third person may no longer be traceable, or be insolvent (have no money), or have ceased to trade. Parliament in consequence imposed a vicarious responsibility on an employer for defective equipment, making the employer liable to an employee, with the employer then having a right of action against the third party. The purpose of the Act, said Lord Oliver, was to be found in the long title to the Act: 'to make further provision with respect to the liability of an employer for injury to his employee which is attributable to any defect in equipment provided by the employer for the purposes of the employer's business; and for purposes connected with the matter aforesaid.'

The word 'equipment' had to be read in its context of 'equipment provided by his employer for the purposes of the employer's business'. To carry on business, a ship owner clearly needs ships; it is no misuse of language to say that these are the equipment of the business.

The analogy with a factory was rejected as a small boat would be 'equipment'—for example, a powerboat used for water-skiing training—so the size of the vessel and the fact that it also accommodates crew is not a justification to exclude it from falling within the definition of 'equipment'.

A major argument that stood in the way of a ship being 'equipment', in his Lordship's view, was the need to read s.1(1) subject to s.1(3). 'Equipment' in s.1(1) may be given a wide meaning, but s.1(3) indicated how far the definition may extend, that is, 'equipment' includes 'any plant and machinery, vehicle, aircraft and clothing'; the extended meaning does not include vessels and this must be deliberate, given the enumeration of what 'equipment' includes. Lord Oliver rejected this argument, saying that s.1(3) was not restrictive as it used the word 'includes' and the items in the list are for the purpose of clarification. The use of the word 'any' in s.1(3) indicated, in the light of the purpose of the Act, that 'it should be widely construed so as to embrace every article of whatever kind furnished by the employer for the purposes of his business'.

Lord Oliver concluded (at p.300):

> The omission is certainly curious but I find myself entirely unpersuaded that there can be deduced from it an intention to cut down the very wide meaning of 'equipment' in subsection (1) which is indicated both by the legislative purpose of the statute and by the width of the clarifying definition.

As the expression 'plant and machinery' includes machinery installed or affixed to a ship, it would be absurd if an employer were liable for injury caused by defects in such machinery, but not for injury caused by defects in the structure of the ship itself. If this approach were to be adopted, problems of demarcation would arise. Equally, to exclude all vessels of whatever size would seem to run counter to the purpose of the Act. Undoubtedly, some vessels must be 'equipment' of a business; for example, a dredger. If some vessels are 'equipment', then there is no justification for seeking to distinguish between vessels of different sizes.

As can be noted, his Lordship used various techniques to justify his decision that a ship was 'equipment' for the purposes of the Employer's Liability (Defective Equipment) Act 1969. An application of the literal rule was not possible as there was clearly an uncertainty caused by ss.1(1) and 1(3). Reference was made to the mischief and purpose of the Act and the various absurdities that would arise if vessels were not included in 'equipment'. The nature of definitions was considered and the use of the word 'includes' in s.1(3) meant that there was only a partial definition of 'equipment', which did not cut back the meaning of this word as used in s.1(1).

Critical debate

We encountered the case of *Royal College of Nursing of the United Kingdom v Department of Health and Social Security* [1981] AC 800 earlier. To briefly refresh the facts, this case concerned the Abortion Act 1967. When the Act was passed, the method of abortion was surgical and carried out by doctors, but by the early 1970s another method of abortion, medical induction, had replaced the need for surgery and was now commonly carried out by nurses. With this advance in abortion techniques, actions by a nurse became the effective cause of an abortion. Under the wording of the Act under s.1(1)—that referred to it not being an offence when a 'termination of pregnancy [is] carried out by a registered medical practitioner', the question was whether it was lawful for nurses to be inducing an abortion. The majority of the House of Lords arrived at a decision in favour of the interpretation placed on the 1967 Act by the DHSS and that it was lawful for nurses to conduct the procedure. In doing so the House of Lords employed the mischief rule to identify the intention of Parliament.

Read the case. In light of what you know now, including the details of the relevant rules, did the majority of the House of Lords go beyond the expressed intention of Parliament? Should the issue have been left to Parliament to resolve? What would have been the consequences had the House of Lords declared that it was not lawful for nurses to be involved in the termination of pregnancies by this procedure?

4.4 **Aids to construction**

In construing the words of a section of an Act the court may encounter ambiguity or uncertainty, or the provision may appear pointless. In such a situation a court may consult other parts of an Act as guides to the intention of Parliament or, within limits, go outside the Act in search of such intention. Table 4.1 identifies the aids to construction.

Table 4.1 Aids to construction of statutes

Internal aids to construction—found within an Act of Parliament	External aids to construction—found within an Act of Parliament
Long title	Explanatory Notes
Preamble	Interpretation Act 1978
Short title	Pre-parliamentary materials
Cross-headings	Parliamentary materials—Hansard
Side or marginal notes	Statutes *in pari materia*
Punctuation	Dictionaries

4.4.1 Aids to construction found within an Act of Parliament

The features of an Act that may be used as aids to construction are: the long title, the preamble (if an Act has one), the short title, cross-headings, side or marginal notes, and punctuation. Lord Reid, in *DPP v Schildkamp* [1971] AC 1, said that although punctuation, side or marginal notes, and cross-headings are not the product of anything done in Parliament (they are not capable of being amended by Parliament and are put in a statute by Parliamentary Counsel) (at p.10), 'it may be more realistic to accept the Act as printed as being the product of the whole legislative process, and to give due weight to everything found in the printed Act.'

Thinking point

Internal aids—part of the Act or not?

It is necessary to understand how legislation is made in order to follow the courts' approach to the internal aids to construction. The long title, preamble, and short title all may be amended by Parliament during the passage of a bill, but they do not create rules of law.

The marginal or side notes are part of a bill not for the purposes of debate, but for ease of reference. They are included by Parliamentary Counsel, who is responsible for the drafting of a bill. While they cannot be amended by Parliament, they are a feature of a bill and ultimately part of the resulting Act of Parliament.

What is important is that all the internal aids are part of the context of the Act and may be used to inform the reader of the purpose of an Act, but they are not the enacting words of the statute, that is, the words of the sections, and therefore must carry less weight. What do you think are the appropriate limits for the use of internal aids?

It is important to appreciate the limits within which these aids operate. In Figure 4.1 you will find an annotated statute which indicates the various features of an Act of Parliament.

Changes to legislation: There are currently no known outstanding effects for the Tenant Fees Act 2019. (See end of Document for details)

Tenant Fees Act 2019

Short Title indicating the basic subject matter of the Act.

2019 CHAPTER 4

An Act to make provision prohibiting landlords and letting agents from requiring certain payments to be made or certain other steps to be taken; to make provision about the payment of holding deposits; to make provision about enforcement and about the lead enforcement authority; to amend the provisions of the Consumer Rights Act 2015 about information to be provided by letting agents; to make provision about client money protection schemes; and for connected purposes. [12th February 2019]

The Long Title indicates the mischief the Act is directed towards and/or the Act's Contents and Purpose. This Act's key purpose was to restrict and control payments to a landlord or letting agent in connection with a tenancy of housing in England. This includes tenancies of student accommodation.

The Date of Royal Assent.

BE IT ENACTED by the Queen's most Excellent Majesty, by and with the advice and consent of the Lords Spiritual and Temporal, and Commons, in this present Parliament assembled, and by the authority of the same, as follows:—

Prohibitions etc applying to landlords and letting agents

This is a cross-heading and can be useful for a reader to find their way around the act. The heading signals what the subsequent sections will cover.

1 Prohibitions applying to landlords

(1) A landlord must not require a relevant person to make a prohibited payment to the landlord in connection with a tenancy of housing in England.

(2) A landlord must not require a relevant person to make a prohibited payment to a third party in connection with a tenancy of housing in England.

(3) A landlord must not require a relevant person to enter into a contract with a third party in connection with a tenancy of housing in England if that contract is—

(a) a contract for the provision of a service, or

(b) a contract of insurance.

(4) Subsection (3) does not apply if the contract is for—

(a) the provision of a utility to the tenant, or

(b) the provision of a communication service to the tenant.

(5) A landlord must not require a relevant person to make a loan to any person in connection with a tenancy of housing in England.

Figure 4.1 The Tenant Fees Act 2019, annotated.

Source: UK Parliament, Crown copyright

(Continued)

Tenant Fees Act 2019 (c. 4) 3
Document Generated: 2019-08-19

***Changes to legislation:** There are currently no known outstanding effects for the Tenant Fees Act 2019. (See end of Document for details)*

This box is repeated after sections in the Act and clarifies the date of commencement of the provision: here the 1st of June 2019. s34 of the Act clarifies that the date the Act comes into force is delegated to a Minister to declare in regulations.

Commencement Information

I1 S. 1 in force at 1.6.2019 by S.I. 2019/857, **reg. 3(a)**

2 Prohibitions applying to letting agents

(1) A letting agent must not require a relevant person to make a prohibited payment to the letting agent in connection with a tenancy of housing in England.

(2) A letting agent must not require a relevant person to make a prohibited payment to a third party in connection with a tenancy of housing in England.

(3) A letting agent must not require a relevant person to enter into a contract with the agent or a third party in connection with a tenancy of housing in England if the contract is—

(a) a contract for the provision of a service, or

(b) a contract of insurance.

(4) A letting agent must not require a relevant person to make a loan to any person in connection with a tenancy of housing in England.

(5) For the purposes of this section, a letting agent requires a relevant person to make a payment, enter into a contract or make a loan in connection with a tenancy of housing in England if and only if the letting agent—

(a) requires the person to do any of those things in consideration of arranging the grant, renewal, continuance, variation, assignment, novation or termination of such a tenancy,

(b) requires the person to do any of those things pursuant to a provision of an agreement with the person relating to such a tenancy which requires or purports to require the person to do any of those things in the event of an act or default of a relevant person,

(c) requires the person to do any of those things pursuant to a provision of an agreement with the person relating to such a tenancy which requires or purports to require the person to do any of those things if the tenancy is varied, assigned, novated or terminated,

(d) requires the person to do any of those things—

(i) as a result of an act or default of a relevant person relating to such a tenancy or housing let under it, and

(ii) otherwise than pursuant to, or for the breach of, an agreement entered into before the act or default, or

(e) requires the person to do any of those things in consideration of providing a reference in relation to that person in connection with the person's occupation of housing in England.

(6) For the purposes of this section, a letting agent does not require a relevant person to make a payment, enter into a contract or make a loan if the letting agent gives the person the option of doing any of those things as an alternative to complying with another requirement imposed by the letting agent or the landlord.

(7) Subsection (6) does not apply if—

(a) the other requirement is prohibited by this section or section 1 (ignoring subsection (6) or section 1(7)), or

Figure 4.1 *(Continued)*

(10) In paragraph 10 of Schedule 5 to the Consumer Rights Act 2015 (duties and powers to which Schedule 5 applies), at the appropriate place insert " section 26 of the Tenant Fees Act 2019 ".

Commencement Information

I28 S. 26 in force at 15.4.2019 for specified purposes by S.I. 2019/857, **reg. 2(c)**

I29 S. 26 in force at 1.6.2019 in so far as not already in force by S.I. 2019/857, **reg. 3(u)**

General interpretation

This series of sections offers guidance on defining and interpreting key terms found in the Act.

27 Meaning of "letting agent" and related expressions

(1) In this Act "letting agent" means a person who engages in letting agency work (whether or not that person engages in other work).

(2) In this Act "letting agency work" means things done by a person in the course of a business in response to instructions received from—

- (a) a landlord who is seeking to find another person to whom to let housing, or
- (b) a tenant who is seeking to find housing to rent.

(3) A person is not a letting agent for the purposes of this Act if the person engages in letting agency work in the course of that person's employment under a contract of employment.

(4) A person who is an authorised person in relation to a reserved legal activity is not a letting agent when carrying on legal activity in response to instructions from a landlord or tenant who does not instruct that person to do other things within subsection (2).

(5) In subsection (4)—

- (a) "legal activity" and "reserved legal activity" have the meanings given by section 12 of the Legal Services Act 2007;
- (b) "authorised person" has the meaning given by section 18 of that Act.

Commencement Information

I30 S. 27 in force at 1.6.2019 by S.I. 2019/857, **reg. 3(v)**

28 Interpretation

(1) In this Act—

"assured shorthold tenancy" has the same meaning as in Part 1 of the Housing Act 1988;

"communication service" has the meaning given by paragraph 11(3) of Schedule 1;

"enforcement authority" has the meaning given by section 7(5);

"excluded licence" means a licence which is granted to a licensee by a licensor who resides in the housing where—

(Continued)

***Changes to legislation:** There are currently no known outstanding effects for the Tenant Fees Act 2019. (See end of Document for details)*

Schedules are part of an Act that collects practical and technical details about how the Act works in one place. This keeps the sections that outline key principles concise and clear.

SCHEDULES

SCHEDULE 1

Section 3

PERMITTED PAYMENTS

Rent

1 (1) A payment of rent under a tenancy is a permitted payment.

(2) But, subject as follows, if the amount of rent payable in respect of any relevant period ("P1") is more than the amount of rent payable in respect of any later relevant period ("P2"), the additional amount payable in respect of P1 is a prohibited payment.

(3) Where there is more than one later relevant period in respect of which the amount of rent payable is lower than the amount of rent payable in respect of P1—

(a) if different amounts of rent are payable for different later relevant periods, P2 is the relevant period for which the lowest amount of rent is payable;

(b) if the same amount of rent is payable for more than one later relevant periods, P2 is the first of those periods.

(4) The following provisions apply for the purposes of determining—

(a) whether the amount of rent payable in respect of a relevant period is more than the amount of rent payable in respect of a later relevant period, and

(b) the difference between the amount of rent payable in respect of the earlier relevant period and that payable in respect of the later relevant period.

(5) Where the later relevant period is a different length of time to the earlier relevant period, the amount of rent payable in respect of the later period is to be treated as the proportionate amount of rent that would be payable in respect of that period if it were the same length of time as the earlier period.

(6) There is to be left out of account any difference between the rent payable in respect of the earlier relevant period and the rent payable in respect of the later relevant period as a result of a variation of the rent payable in respect of the later period—

(a) pursuant to a term in the tenancy agreement which enables the rent under the tenancy to be increased or reduced, according to the circumstances, or

(b) by agreement between the landlord and the tenant after the tenancy agreement has been entered into.

(7) In this paragraph "relevant period", in relation to a tenancy, means any period of time in respect of which rent is payable under the tenancy.

(8) But "relevant period" does not include a period of time which begins after the end of one year beginning with the first day of the tenancy.

Figure 4.1 *(Continued)*

The long title

This gives an indication of the purpose of an Act. In *R v Bates* [1952] 2 All ER 842, Donovan J said that upon reading the words of a section, should doubt or ambiguity arise, then the long title may be consulted as an aid to resolving the doubt or ambiguity. However, if the words of the section make a meaning clear, the long title cannot be used to restrict such meaning.

The preamble

Preambles are rarely seen in modern statutes but were more common in older statutes. Where a preamble exists it may set out the reasons for the passing of the statute. It may be consulted as part of reading the statute as a whole. Viscount Simonds said in *AG v Prince Ernest Augustus of Hanover* [1957] AC 436 (at p.461):

> So it is that I conceive it to be my right and duty to examine every word of a statute in its context, and I use 'context' in its widest sense, which I have already indicated as including not only other enacting provisions of the same statute, but its preamble, the existing state of the law, other statutes *in pari materia*, [see later at 4.4.2] and the mischief which I can, by those and other legitimate means, discern the statute was intended to remedy.

Once again the indication is that the courts are able to read beyond the words of a statute to establish the circumstances surrounding the making of the legislation. So a preamble may inform a court's reading of the words of an Act, but it cannot be used to cut down the plain meaning of the words.

The short title

The short title, while being part of an Act, is of limited interpretative value as it is merely a brief way of referring to an Act. Indeed, the short title may be positively misleading. For example, the Unfair Contract Terms Act 1977 does not cover all potentially unfair terms of a contract and its scope extends beyond contract terms to non-contractual notices also.

Cross-headings

These are to be found above a section or group of sections; they are there to help the reader find their way around an Act. A cross-heading may be consulted when the words of a section are ambiguous or unclear. However, in the light of a more contextual approach to the construction of statutes, it would appear (by analogy with Explanatory Notes and marginal and side notes) that ambiguity is not necessary to permit the use of cross-headings; see later *R (Westminster City Council) v National Asylum Support Service* [2002] 1 WLR 2956 and *R v Montila* [2004] 1 WLR 3141.

Side or marginal notes

So called because they originally appeared in the margin to an Act, side or marginal notes signpost the content of a specific section. Since 2001, the note is placed in bold above the section to which it relates. As an aid to construction, a side note may be used in considering what the purpose of the section is and the mischief it sought to address, but it cannot be used to restrict the clear meaning of a section ascertainable from its words. In *R v Montila* [2004] 1 WLR 3141, the House of Lords said that as side notes are included for ease of reference and not for debate before Parliament, they are to be accorded less weight; nonetheless, they provide a context for the examination of an Act.

An example of the use of side or marginal notes is seen in *Tudor Grange Holdings Ltd v Citibank NA* [1991] 3 WLR 750. In this case the claimants under a contract with the defendant bank alleged a breach of contract. This claim was contractually settled. The claimants later alleged that the settlement of the claim was subject to a test of reasonableness by reason of s.10 of the Unfair Contract Terms Act 1977.

Section 10 provides:

> A person is not bound by any contract term prejudicing or taking away rights of his which arise under, or in connection with the performance of, another contract, so far as those rights extend to the enforcement of another's liability which this Part of this Act prevents that other from excluding or restricting.

It was argued by the claimants that the terms of the contractual settlement by its terms took away certain rights under the first contract with the defendant bank.

The High Court decided that Parliament never intended s.10 to apply to settlements of claims. In arriving at this conclusion, Browne-Wilkinson VC looked for the mischief behind the section and relied, in part, upon the marginal note which said: 'Evasion by means of secondary contract'. This indicated that s.10 was aimed at the use of exemption clauses in secondary contracts to evade the control of Part 1 of the 1977 Act, which read:

> [A] contract to settle disputes which have arisen concerning the performance of an earlier contract cannot be described as an evasion of the provisions in the Act regulating exemption clauses in the earlier contract. Nor is the compromise contract 'secondary' to the earlier contract.

This case is considered later in the chapter when considering Law Commission reports as an example of an external aid to construction.

Punctuation

As has been seen in the words of Lord Reid in *DPP v Schildkamp*, punctuation may be considered as part of a statute and may be used as an aid to interpretation in the event of ambiguity.

4.4.2 **Aids to construction found outside an Act of Parliament**

Explanatory Notes

Since 1999, Explanatory Notes accompany a bill introduced by a government minister during its parliamentary passage. The Explanatory Notes are updated during this time and are published along with the new Act. They seek to explain the impact of the legislation in layman's terms and may be used as an aid to construction of the statute. In *R (on the application of S) v Chief Constable of South Yorkshire* [2004] 1 WLR 2196, Lord Steyn said that, although Explanatory Notes are not approved by Parliament, they may cast light on the context of the statute and the mischief at which it is aimed.

The Explanatory Notes thus give the context of an Act and an indication of what the Act is intended to achieve and may be consulted. They may be used even in the absence of an ambiguity, as it is permissible to read an Act of Parliament in its context. See the opinion of Lord Steyn in *R (Westminster City Council) v National Asylum Support Service* [2002] 1 WLR 2956 (at p.2959): '[i]n so far as the Explanatory Notes cast light on the objective setting or contextual scene of the statute, and the mischief at which it is aimed, such materials are therefore *always* admissible aids to construction' (emphasis added). Lord Steyn also indicated that Explanatory Notes may be accorded greater weight than Law Commission reports or government Green or White Papers, as there is a closer connection between the Explanatory Notes and the proposed legislation than with pre-parliamentary materials.

Interpretation Act 1978

This Act is important, but its title promises more than it actually delivers. It deals with details. Some examples serve to illustrate what it does.

1. Section 4 indicates that an Act comes into force either: (a) when provision is made for it to come into force on a particular day; or (b) if there is no such provision then on the day the Act receives royal assent. In each case, the Act is in force from the beginning of the day on which it comes into force.
2. Section 6 provides that unless a contrary intention appears in an Act:
    - where words used in an Act refer to the masculine gender they also include the feminine gender and vice versa;
    - words appearing in the singular include the plural and words in the plural include the singular.

Pre-parliamentary materials

Before a bill is presented to Parliament and it then passes into law it may have been preceded by a royal commission, Law Commission, or other official committee report. Such reports may have explored problems in existing law or considered remedying perceived injustice. To what extent may such pre-parliamentary materials be used in the process of construction? It was said by the majority of the House of Lords in the *Black Clawson* case [1975] AC 591, that pre-parliamentary materials could be consulted to ascertain the state of the law before the Act and the mischief at which the Act was directed. However, the recommendations contained in a report, the draft bill, and any comments thereon cannot be used in ascertaining the meaning of the words used in an Act.

Thinking point

The value of pre-parliamentary materials

Lord Reid said that as the courts (at that time) did not consult Hansard in ascertaining the intention of Parliament then, with stronger reason, the courts should 'disregard expressions of intention by committees or royal commissions which reported before the Bill was introduced'. Now it is permissible for the courts to use Hansard (see the next section), should the courts be able to consult the recommendations in a report as an indication of the intention of Parliament? See Lord Simon's opinion in the *Black Clawson* case that a draft bill and commentary annexed to a draft bill could be used to establish parliamentary intent. His Lordship said (at p.651):

> To refuse to consider such a commentary, when Parliament has legislated on the basis and faith of it, is for the interpreter to fail to put himself in the real position of the promulgator of the instrument before essaying its interpretation. It is refusing to follow what is perhaps the most important clue to meaning. It is perversely neglecting the reality, while chasing shadows. As Aneurin Bevan said: 'Why read the crystal when you can read the book?' Here the book is already open: it is merely a matter of reading on. Certainly, a court of construction cannot be precluded from saying that what the committee thought as to the meaning of its draft was incorrect. But that is one thing: to dismiss, out of hand and for all purposes, an authoritative opinion in the light of which Parliament has legislated is quite another.

Obviously this must be read subject to the warning that Parliament might not have followed the recommendations of the committee in which case they will be of little or, more likely, no interpretative value.

An illustration of the use of pre-parliamentary materials is seen in *Tudor Grange Holdings Ltd v Citibank NA* [1992] Ch 53. Browne-Wilkinson VC, in seeking the mischief of the Unfair Contract Terms Act 1977, consulted the second report on exemption clauses of the Law Commission on Exemption Clauses (1975) (Law Com No. 69). He commented (at p.66):

> This report was the genesis of the Act of 1977. The report is wholly concerned with remedying injustices which are caused by exemption clauses in the strict sense. So far as I can see, the report makes no reference of any kind to any mischief relating to agreements to settle disputes.

This allowed him to conclude that the Act was not seeking to control contractual settlements of disputes, and as outlined earlier, strengthening his interpretation of s.10.

Parliamentary materials—Hansard

For many years the courts refused to allow the use of Hansard—the official record of parliamentary debates—as an aid to construction of an Act of Parliament. This practice was confirmed by the House of Lords in *Davis v Johnson* [1979] AC 264. However, the refusal to do so was heavily criticised on the basis that an obvious source of elucidating Parliament's intention was being unnecessarily ignored.

In the case of *Pepper v Hart* [1993] AC 593, the House of Lords, consisting of seven law lords, decided by a majority of 6 to 1 that Hansard could be used as an aid to interpretation. However, the Lords in the majority recognised the limits to the use of such materials. Hansard is only to be used within the following limits:

> [F]irst, the legislation must be ambiguous or obscure or a literal interpretation would lead to an absurdity; second, the statement or statements relied on were made by the minister or other promoter of a Bill, together if necessary with such other Parliamentary material as is necessary to understand such statements; and third, the statements relied upon are clear.

A literal interpretation of legislation is not possible where the words used are ambiguous or uncertain, so another meaning may be sought by reference to clear statements made in Parliament by the promoter of the legislation. Reference may be made to Hansard where the material identifies the mischief behind the Act or the legislative intention behind the unclear language used. The House of Lords further seemed to indicate that reference to Hansard would only be permitted where Parliament addressed the very issue that a court was being asked to decide. In this regard, the use of Hansard should have its limits.

The leading opinion of Lord Browne-Wilkinson and the dissenting opinion of Lord Mackay illuminate the reasons for and against the use of Hansard in the interpretation of a statute. In essence the argument is, on one side, a matter of principle, that is, that access to parliamentary words may throw light on the mischief behind a statute or the legislative intent; this is as opposed to, on the other side, considerations of cost, uncertainty in the parliamentary words themselves, and even problems of access to Hansard.

Thinking point

Hands on Hansard: Is its use desirable?

Hansard is a controversial external aid to interpretation. Be prepared to evaluate the reasons for and against the use of Hansard. In this respect, you will want to consider the cases subsequent to *Pepper v Hart*. How useful has Hansard been in those cases? Note that Lord Mackay's comments were delivered before the power of the internet was apparent. Nonetheless, consider whether having lawyers poring over Hansard will lead to increased costs and whether it is definitively more likely to help find the 'correct' answer. Are there other risks associated with consulting Hansard that might lead to constitutionally dubious results (think of who sits in Parliament and whose statements will be more likely to be relied on).

The debate over the legacy of *Pepper v Hart* has continued. Lord Steyn, writing extra-judicially ('*Pepper v Hart*: A Re-examination' (2001) 21 OJLS 59), has said that in his view, *Pepper v Hart* has substantially increased the costs of litigation to 'very little avail'. His Lordship also argued that the decision may have led to a change in the behaviour of the executive, encouraging the making of statements in Parliament as to the *government's* intention behind the introduction of legislation. The courts are aware of the constitutional risk of relying on and then interpreting the government's intention when, in fact, they should be interpreting that of Parliament's. In *Evans v Amicus Healthcare* [2004] 3 WLR 681, Thorpe and Sedley LJJ said (at p.685):

> In the absence of any intractable ambiguity of the sort contemplated in *Pepper v Hart*, it seemed at first sight an endeavour by the department of state responsible for drafting the legislation to introduce its own intentions as an aid to construction, something which is no more permissible in the construction of legislation than it is in the construction of contracts.

It is important to evaluate how the rule that permits Hansard to be consulted has worked in practice, as seen in the subsequent case law.

The case of *Pepper v Hart* raised a problem that had been considered during parliamentary debates leading to the passing of the Finance Act 1976, and the minister had given a clear answer to the issue that had come before the courts. So the uncertainty in the meaning of the Finance Act 1976 was resolved by looking at the legislative history of the Act. It was fortunate that Hansard provided a clear answer. Another example of Hansard being used to successfully support a particular interpretation of a legislative phrase was seen in *Stevenson v Rogers* [1999] QB 1028. In *R v JTB* [2009] UKHL 20, Hansard was used when the House of Lords decided that the defence of *doli incapax* for children between the ages of ten and fourteen had been abolished by s.34 of the Crime and Disorder Act 1998. Lord Philips accepted that that conclusion could not be reached from the words of s.34 but once extrinsic aids were considered (e.g. the pre-legislative materials such as the consultation and White Papers, and the statements made in Parliament), the intention of Parliament became much clearer. However, the rule in *Pepper v Hart* specifies that Hansard may only be used where the legislation is ambiguous or obscure, the statements to be relied upon are those of ministers or other promoters of a bill, and the statements are clear. It may be observed that in *R v JTB*, first, the legislation was not ambiguous and secondly, the statements made in Parliament during the passage of the Crime and Disorder Act 1998 were not clear. See further Francis Bennion, 'Mens Rea and Defendants Below the Age of Discretion' [2009] Crim LR 757, where the use of Hansard is criticised. In *R (on the application of Jamar Brown (Jamaica)) v Secretary of State for the Home Department* [2015] UKSC 8, the Supreme Court reiterated the need for clear ministerial answers to questions in Parliament before the courts should admit statements under *Pepper v Hart*.

The opinions of the judiciary, particularly in the House of Lords, are divided on how Hansard is to be used. In *Jackson v Attorney General* [2006] 1 AC 262, the difference was apparent in the opposing views of Lords Nicholls and Steyn. Lord Nicholls, restating an opinion given in *R v Secretary of State for the Environment, Transport and the Regions, ex parte Spath Holme* [2001] 2 AC 349, said that it was permissible to consult clear ministerial statements in Hansard to discover the *purpose* that the words in a statute are seeking to achieve. In contrast, Lord Steyn sought to limit the operation of *Pepper v Hart* when he said (at p.301):

> [It] should be confined to the situation which was before the House in *Pepper v Hart*. That would leave unaffected the use of Hansard material to identify the mischief at which legislation was directed and its objective setting. But trying to discover the intentions of the Government from ministerial statements in Parliament is constitutionally unacceptable.

Reliance was placed upon the opinion of Lord Hope in *Spath Holme*, where he said (at p.408):

> [T]he decision in *Pepper v Hart* should be confined to cases where the court is concerned with the meaning that is to be given to the words used in legislation by Parliament. It would be contrary to fundamental considerations of constitutional principle to allow it to be used to enable reliance to be placed on statements made in debate by ministers about matters of policy which have not been reproduced in the enactment. It is the words used by Parliament, not words used by ministers, that define the scope within which the powers conferred by the legislature may be exercised.

Thinking point

Mistaken identity: How can one identify Parliament's intention?

The use of Hansard may be contrasted with another method of discovering parliamentary intention, that of the golden rule. According to the golden rule, it may be argued that Parliament cannot have intended a meaning where it leads to absurdity. Such an approach is inferential, not direct, whereas Hansard, in *Pepper v Hart*, provided direct evidence of what was meant by s.63(2) of the Finance Act 1976. Consider other ways in which the intention of Parliament may be identified.

The case law seems to suggest that it is rare that Hansard will be determinative of a question of interpretation. In *R (Quintavalle) v Secretary of State for Health* [2003] 2 AC 687, Lord Hoffmann said: 'As it is almost invariably the case when such statements are tendered under the rule in *Pepper v Hart*, I found neither of assistance.' Again, in *R v Clinton* [2012] EWCA Crim 2, Lord Judge CJ said: '[e]ven on the most generous interpretation of *Pepper (Inspector of Taxes) v Hart* . . . the debates did not reveal anything which assisted in the process of legislative construction.' However, his Lordship explained that the construction reached by the court was consistent with the views expressed in Parliament during the passage of the legislation.

Where a criminal statute is ambiguous then Hansard will not be used to extend the scope of criminal liability created by the statute; a defendant is to receive the benefit of the ambiguity: see *Massey and Another v Boulden and Another* [2003] 1 WLR 1792. This principle is supported by the comments of Lord Phillips LCJ in *Thet v DPP* [2006] EWHC 2701, who said: '[i]f a criminal statute is ambiguous, I would question whether it is appropriate by the use of *Pepper v Hart* to extend the ambit of the statute so as to impose criminal liability upon a defendant where, in the absence of the parliamentary material, the court would not do so. It seems to me at least arguable that if a criminal statute is ambiguous, the defendant should have the benefit of the ambiguity.' It may be further noted that Hansard was of no value in *Thet v DPP* as the statement by the minister indicated that the meaning of 'reasonable excuse' in the Asylum and Immigration (Treatment of Claimants) Act 2004 was best 'left to the circumstances of each individual case' and that ultimately it was for the courts to decide!

Statutes *in pari materia*

Sometimes there will be a number of statutes on the same subject area. These are known as statutes *in pari materia*. Hence, should the words of a statute be uncertain or ambiguous, a court may consider as an aid to construction other statutes which are *in pari materia*. Unfortunately, it is not clear when statutes are, in fact, *in pari materia*. As a starting point, judges will first look to Acts that are on the same subject before considering the validity of another Act of Parliament in helping to interpret the particular provision.

In *R v Wheatley* [1979] 1 WLR 144, the Court of Appeal was asked to decide whether the definition of 'explosive substance' in the Explosive Substances Act 1883 should be construed with the assistance of the Explosives Act 1875. The Court looked to the long titles to the Acts and noted that the 1875 Act dealt with 'explosive substances' and the 1883 Act was 'to amend the law relating to explosive substances'. The 1883 Act was evidently intended to amend the 1875 Act. Section 9(1) of the 1883 Act provides that 'explosive substance shall be deemed to include . . .' but the list in the section did not provide a complete definition and it was taken to be simply expanding the existing meaning of 'explosive substance'. Section 3 of the 1875 Act, however, gave a definition of 'explosive' (referring to gunpowder, nitro-glycerine, and dynamite amongst others). In the light of this, the Court was convinced that both Acts were *in pari materia* and therefore when construing the 1883 Act it was permissible to use the definition in the 1875 Act.

An illustration of where statutes were considered not to be *in pari materia* was seen in *Stevenson v Rogers* [1999] QB 1028, where the phrase 'in the course of a business' in the Unfair Contract Terms Act 1977 and in the Sale of Goods Act 1979 was given different meanings.

Dictionaries

It is permissible to consult a dictionary if the meaning of a word used in a statute is unclear. Obviously, if a statute defines a word then that is the definition to be used. However, dictionaries are to be treated with caution. In *Customs and Excise Comrs v Top Ten Promotions Ltd* [1969] 1 WLR 1163, Lord Upjohn said (at p.1171):

> It is highly dangerous, if not impossible, to attempt to place an accurate definition on a word in common use; you can look up examples of its many uses if you want to in the Oxford Dictionary but that does not help on definition; in fact it probably only shows that the word normally defies definition. The task of the court in construing statutory language such as that which is before your Lordships is to look at the mischief at which the Act is directed and then, in that light, to consider whether as a matter of common sense and everyday usage the known, proved or admitted or properly inferred facts of the particular case bring the case within the ordinary meaning of the words used by Parliament.

4.5 Rules of language

These rules give an indication of the intention behind the use of words. They are really rules relating to grammar. It is important to note the limits to their operation. You will find the rules of language illustrated in the following sections.

4.5.1 *Expressio unius est exclusio alterius* rule

Under this rule the mention of one or more things of a particular class excludes silently all other members of the class. A classic example of the use of the rule is seen in the interpretation of the following phrase: 'land, houses and coalmines'. The word 'land' potentially includes mines. However, the express inclusion of the word 'coalmines' in the phrase must be taken to mean that no (other) mines are intended to be included.

The limits of the rule were explained in *Galinski v McHugh* (1989) P & CR 359. In this case, the claimant landlord wished to serve a notice under s.4 of the Landlord and Tenant Act 1954 on the defendant tenant. This was done by serving the notice on solicitors who were representing the defendant. The defendant claimed that this service was invalid and relied on s.4(1) of the 1954 Act which requires notice 'to be given to the tenant.' The landlord relied on s.66(4) of the Act, which deals with service of notices and incorporates s.23 of the Landlord and Tenant Act 1927, which provides, inter alia, 'in the case of a notice to a landlord, the person on whom it is to be served shall include any agent of the landlord duly authorised in that behalf'. Put another way, this meant that service could include the landlord authorising an agent to serve it on the tenant, and that by analogy, the landlord serving the notice on the defendant's solicitor was sufficient. However, it was argued by the defendant, using the *expressio unius est exclusio alterius* rule, that as s.66(4) indicated expressly that a notice to a landlord could be served on any agent *of the landlord*, but did not explicitly mention service on an agent of a tenant (in this case the defendant's solicitor), such latter service was excluded.

The Court of Appeal held that the *expressio unius* rule was no more than an aid to construction, and it may not operate where it is possible to explain an express inclusion on grounds other than an intention to exclude other categories. Parliament may have made an express reference to service on a landlord's agent as landlords are more likely to have agents than tenants are, and furthermore tenants may be accustomed to dealing with the agents of landlords. In light of this, an express reference to agents of tenants was unnecessary, and s.66(4) did not expressly prohibit other modes of service. In summary, Parliament did not intend for notices to tenants to exclusively be served upon them personally.

4.5.2 ***Ejusdem generis* rule**

Where general words follow specific words which form a class (or a genus) then the general words are to be read in light of the specific words. The rule only applies where the specific words form a class. For example, Lord Simon, in a debate in the chamber of the House of Lords, said if an animal transportation measure applied to 'calves, lambs and other animals', the general words 'other animals' taken out of context could cover the whole of the animal kingdom. But this is not the intention of Parliament, as the specific words refer to the young of farm animals and are meant to cover, say, kids and foals. The rule was applied in *Powell v Kempton Park Racecourse* [1897] 2 QB 242, in which the House of Lords were asked to consider whether an outdoor betting stall was illegal. In reference to the relevant Act, the Betting Act 1853, the relevant prohibited places were 'house, office, room or other place for betting'. The Court decided that the provision did not include open-air spaces, as the class—the specific list of places—were all indoors.

In *Massey and Another v Boulden and Another* [2003] 1 WLR 1792, the Court of Appeal had to decide whether a village green fell within s.34(1)(a) of the Road Traffic Act 1988, which prohibited the driving of a motor vehicle, without lawful authority, on 'any common land, moorland or land of any other description, not forming part of a road'. It was decided that the specific words 'common land' and 'moorland' did not create a class, and therefore 'land of any other description' was sufficiently wide to encompass a village green. In this case, one might also argue that the general words ('or land of any other description') are so general that it need not be read in the light of the specific words, but can simply be given its natural meaning.

4.5.3 ***Noscitur a sociis* rule**

Simply put, words derive their meaning from, and so must be read subject to, the context in which they appear. As Viscount Simonds said in *AG v Prince Ernest Augustus of Hanover* [1957] AC 436, 'words, and particularly general words, cannot be read in isolation: their colour and content are derived from their context.' An example of the rule is seen in *Pengelley v Bell Punch Co. Ltd* [1964] 1 WLR 1055, where the Court of Appeal had to determine the meaning of s.28(1) of the Factories Act 1961. Section 28(1) provided:

> All floors, steps, stairs, passages and gangways shall be of sound construction and properly maintained and shall, so far as is reasonably practicable, be kept free from any obstruction and from any substance likely to cause persons to slip.

The Court was asked if it was permissible to store boxes on a factory floor. The word 'floors' had to be read in context of the other words 'steps, stairs, passages and gangways', which indicated places used for the purposes of passage. However, in light of the word 'obstruction', which means to block or make impassable, s.28(1) was referring to floors used for the purposes of movement and did not generally apply to all 'floors'. So factory floors could be used to store materials.

4.6 Presumptions of statutory intent

Cross identifies two types of presumption, although there is a tendency for these to merge into each other. First, there are presumptions of general application, such as when Parliament legislates against the background of constitutional and administrative principles; secondly, there are presumptions of legislative intent in cases of doubt or ambiguity as to the words in an Act.

4.6.1 Presumptions of general application

These presumptions apply even if there is no ambiguity in the text of the legislation. They assume that a statute is drafted against the background of legal principles and thus allow for brevity on the part of the draftsman. Cross comments (at p.166) that the 'presumptions of general application not only supplement the text, they also operate at a higher level as expressions of fundamental principles governing both civil liberties and the relations between Parliament, the executive and the courts'. The presumptions have also been explained in terms of a principle of legality; this principle protects both procedural safeguards and substantive basic or fundamental rights. See *R v Secretary of State for the Home Department, ex parte Simms* [2000] 2 AC 115. However, the principle only has prima facie force and can be displaced by clear unambiguous words of a statute. See *R v Secretary of State for the Home Department, ex parte Pierson* [1998] AC 539 at pp.587–90, for Lord Steyn's explanation of the basis of presumptions of general application and a number of examples. These examples include (i) that decision makers acting under statutory powers should exercise their discretion reasonably and that bodies and tribunals should act in accordance with natural justice (i.e. honour the principles of a fair and impartial hearing), and

(ii) the presumption that a criminal offence-creating statute ought to be construed as requiring the element of *mens rea* (see *Sweet v Parsley* [1970] AC 132 and *R v Sally Lane and John Letts* [2018] UKSC 36) and this would apply when the statute was silent and/or ambiguous.

4.6.2 **Presumptions of legislative intent in cases of doubt or ambiguity**

Presumption of intent may also be employed when a statute is unclear or so ambiguous that the intention of Parliament cannot be established. The following are examples of such presumptions.

Presumption in relation to penal statutes

If a penal statute is ambiguous, then the presumption of intent is that the statute should be strictly construed so as to avoid criminal liability. Lord Esher MR, in *Tuck & Sons v Priester* (1887) 19 QBD 629, 638, stated:

> If there is a reasonable interpretation which will avoid the penalty in any particular case we must adopt that construction. If there are two reasonable constructions we must give the more lenient one. That is the settled rule for the construction of penal sections.

A good illustration of how this presumption operates was seen in *Hobson v Gledhill* [1978] 1 WLR 215. Section 1(1) of the Guard Dogs Act 1975 provides that:

> A person shall not use or permit the use of a guard dog at any premises unless a person ('the handler') who is capable of controlling the dog is present on the premises and the dog is under the control of the handler at all times while it is being so used *except* while it is secured so that it is not at liberty to go freely about the premises. (emphasis added)

The section contains an ambiguity which relates to when the exception applies. Two possible meanings are apparent:

(a) there is no offence if there is always a handler, capable of controlling the dog, on the premises where a dog is being used *and* the dog is under the control of the handler unless the dog is secured; or

(b) there is no offence if there is a handler capable of controlling the dog where a dog is being used and the dog is under the control of the handler *or* when there is no handler on the premises but the dog is nevertheless secured.

In relation to meaning (a), the exception applies only to the words 'and the dog is under the control of the handler at all times while it is being so used', whereas for meaning (b), the exception applies to all of the preceding words of the paragraph.

Having understood the ambiguity, the question for a court is how to resolve the problem. Lord Widgery CJ, in the Divisional Court of the Queen's Bench Division, said (at p.219) that he was unable to say 'which of the solutions canvassed was the intention of Parliament, and the right course in those circumstances is to favour the citizen'. Peter Pain J said (at p.218), in favouring meaning (b), that 'one comes to the rule that a penal statute, where there is an ambiguity, should always be construed in favour of the citizen who may find himself the subject of the penalty'. This restricted duty placed on the citizen was consistent with the mischief which Parliament was seeking to address, that is, dogs should be secured so that persons entering premises, whether lawfully or not, would be able to remove themselves from the area of attack by a dog.

Presumption against the retrospective operation of a statute

It is a fundamental principle of any legal system that a citizen should be able to discover the law and be able therefore to avoid the consequences of breaking the law. If an Act of Parliament is retrospective this may mean that a citizen has broken laws at a time when the law did not exist. While Parliament is able to pass legislation that does have retrospective operation, in order to do so clear words must be used. Should Parliament not make this intention clear, the presumption is that no retrospective effect was intended.

Presumption against ousting the jurisdiction of the courts

Should a statute seek to exclude the jurisdiction of the courts then the words used must be clear; such provisions will be construed strictly so as to preserve the jurisdiction of the courts. In *Anisminic Ltd v Foreign Compensation Commission*, s.4(4) of the Foreign Compensation Act 1950 provided that the 'determination by the commission of any application made . . . shall not be called in question in any court of law'. The House of Lords, by a majority, said that while a valid determination of the commission could not be questioned, s.4(4) did not prevent the courts from inquiring whether an order of the commission was made on the basis of a misconstruction of their jurisdiction. The judgment would not be a 'determination' within s.4(4) and therefore the courts could declare it a nullity.

This case was analysed in considerable detail in *R (Privacy International) v Investigatory Powers Tribunal* [2019] UKSC 22. In this case the majority upheld a common law presumption against ousting the jurisdiction of the High Court. The presumption applied to quash a legally erroneous decision of the Investigatory Powers Tribunal (a tribunal that can examine the conduct of the Security and Intelligence Services). The drafting of s.67(8) of the Regulation of Investigatory Powers Act 2000 did not prevent a determination that was legally invalid, whether by jurisdiction or another error of law, from being judicially reviewed by the High Court. Lord Carnwarth added that only the most clear and explicit terms in the statute could have excluded such jurisdiction.

Presumption against Parliament being in breach of international law

The UK may enter into treaties with other sovereign states which have effect in international law, but do not become part of UK domestic law (remember that, to incorporate treaty obligations into domestic law, Parliament would have to pass an Act to that effect). Should an Act of Parliament be ambiguous it is presumed that Parliament does not intend to be in breach of its international obligations.

4.7 **Interpretation of legislation and the EU**

First, this topic is considered in further detail in Chapter 6. However, to offer a brief summary, by enacting the European Communities Act 1972, the judiciary's flexibility in interpretation was significantly reshaped. By s.2(4) of the Act, 'any such provision as might be made by Act of Parliament . . .' shall be construed as to comply with binding EU law. The most famous discussion of this provision was by Lord Bridge in the case of *R (Factortame Ltd) v Secretary of State for Transport* [1990] UKHL 7, where a domestic Act of Parliament—the Merchant Shipping Act 1988—had to be effectively disapplied.

The UK is therefore bound to implement European Union law (at least while the UK remains a member of the EU). This means that domestic legislation (whether primary or secondary) must be passed in order to implement, say, EU directives. The courts must then adopt a purposive approach when interpreting this legislation, using the directive as an aid to interpretation. In *Litster and Others v Forth Dry Dock Co Ltd and Another* [1990] 1 AC 546, 559, Lord Oliver, when considering domestic regulations made to implement a directive, said:

> [I]f the legislation can reasonably be construed so as to conform with those obligations, obligations which are to be ascertained not only from the wording of the relevant directive but from the interpretation placed on it by the Court of Justice of the European Communities, such a purposive construction will be applied even though, perhaps, it may involve some departure from the strict and literal application of the words which the legislature has elected to use.

As can be seen, the courts may only give effect to the purpose of a directive where domestic legislation is reasonably capable of bearing the meaning to be given to it.

The case of *Robertson v Swift* [2014] UKSC 50 illustrates a purposive interpretation of domestic legislation in the light of a European Council directive. Briefly, the facts concerned a contract which was made following an inquiry for removal services by a consumer, Robertson, to Swift, who ran a removals business. Subsequently, Swift called at Robertson's house and a written contract for removal services was concluded there.

Later Robertson, having paid a deposit, sought to cancel the contract orally and then posted a letter of cancellation to Swift before the removal date. Swift responded by seeking to claim cancellation charges under the cancellation provisions in the written contract, and refused to return the deposit.

The case fell to be decided under the Cancellation of Contracts made in a Consumer's Home, or Place of Work etc. Regulations 2008 (now since replaced by the Consumer Contracts (Information, Cancellation and Additional Charges) Regulations 2013). Under the 2008 Regulations, reg. 7(1) gave a consumer the right to cancel a contract within a cancellation period (seven days) and reg. 7(2) 'required a trader to give a consumer written notice of his right to cancel the contract. By reg. 7(6): 'A contract to which these Regulations apply shall not be enforceable against the consumer unless the trader has given the consumer a notice of the right to cancel and the information is in accordance with this regulation.' Regulation 8(1) provided that if a consumer serves a cancellation notice within the cancellation period the contract is cancelled, and by reg. 10(1), on cancellation, any sum paid by a consumer is recoverable.

The Court of Appeal decided that the 2008 Regulations did apply. However, although the contract was not enforceable against Robertson (by virtue of reg. 7(6)), as no written notice of the consumer's right to cancel had been given by Swift, Robertson (under reg. 7(2)) was not entitled to cancel the contract, so the contract remained in being and the deposit could not be recovered. This decision was appealed to the Supreme Court.

The Supreme Court stated that the correct approach to the interpretation of the Regulations was that a national court was to interpret domestic legislation, 'so far as was possible, in the light of the wording and the purpose of directive in order to achieve an outcome consistent with the objective pursued by the directive' (*Schulte v Deutsche Bausparkasse Badenia AG* (Case C-350/03) [2006] 1 CMLR 11 [71], CJEU). The purpose of the Directive (Council Directive (85/577/EEC)) was the enhancement of consumer protection. Lord Kerr, relying on *Martín Martín v EDP Editores SL* (Case C-227/08) [2010] 2 CMLR 27 CJEU, said (at [25]):

> To hold that the consumer did not have the right to cancel because the trader had not served written notice of the right to cancel would run directly counter to the overall purpose of the Directive in ensuring that a consumer has the opportunity to withdraw from a contract without suffering significant adverse consequences . . . But if the right to cancel could be effectively nullified by a failure (or refusal) of a trader to give written notice of the right to the consumer, this would create a considerable gap in the level of protection that the Directive sought to provide.

Lord Kerr said that the question of entitlement to cancel, in the absence of a written notice from a trader, informing of a right to cancel, had been decided by the Court of Justice of the EU in *Heininger* (Case-481/99) [2003] 2 CMLR 42 [45] and *E Friz GmbH v Carsten von der Heyden* (Case C-215/08) [2010] 3 CMLR 23 [37]–[39]; a consumer can exercise a right of cancellation at any time in the absence of a notification of such a right by a trader.

Could this result be achieved under the 2008 Regulations? Lord Kerr said that the 2008 Regulations should be given a purposive interpretation both under EU and domestic law. It was accepted by the Supreme Court that the word 'within' in regs 7(1) and 8(1) could be read as meaning 'at any time prior to the expiration of' the cancellation period. So the cancellation period would either expire seven days after the consumer received notice of the right to cancel from the trader or, should no such notice be served, as in the present case, there would be no expiration and the consumer would remain free to cancel.

In consequence, the failure by Swift to give notice to Robertson of the right to cancel did not prevent Robertson from cancelling, as he had done. The Court confirmed that, 'a failure by a trader to give written notice of the right to cancel does not deprive a consumer of the statutory right to cancel under regulation 7(1) of the 2008 Regulations. Dr Robertson was therefore entitled to cancel the contract as he did by his letter . . . He is therefore entitled to recover his deposit of £1000.'

The issue in the *Robertson* case arose out of a gap in the wording of the 2008 Regulations. Lord Kerr confirmed (at [30]) that 'a purposive construction is one which eschews a narrow literal interpretation in favour of one which is consonant with the purpose of the relevant legislation, in this case, the comprehensive protection of the consumer in the event of the cancellation of the contract'. Here, by using the Directive and the supporting case law of the Court of Justice of the EU, the Supreme Court was able to interpret the 2008 Regulations to ensure the purpose was achieved.

Key point

The approach to the interpretation of EU law is similar to the approach under s.3 of the Human Rights Act 1998 in relation to the ECHR. See *Vodafone 2 v Commissioners for Her Majesty's Revenue and Customs* [2010] Ch 77; *Robertson v Swift* [2014] UKSC 50, [2014] 1 WLR 3438; and *Lock v British Gas Trading Ltd* [2016] EWCA Civ 983.

What happens, however, if the UK fails to implement the directive (in other words, there is no domestic implementing legislation)? The answer is that the UK courts are nevertheless still obliged to adopt a purposive approach to any pre-existing domestic legislation that may exist in the same subject area, again using the directive as an aid to interpretation.

Such a situation occurred in *Webb v EMO Air Cargo (UK) Ltd* [1993] 1 WLR 49. The claimant was employed initially to replace a pregnant employee during her taking a period of maternity leave, but was to continue to be employed after the return of that employee. Shortly after commencing her employment the claimant found that she too was pregnant and her employer dismissed her. Her claim under s.1 of the Sex Discrimination Act 1975 was rejected by an industrial tribunal, the Employment Appeal Tribunal, and the Court of Appeal. On appeal to the House of Lords, the claimant argued that the 1975 Act should be interpreted purposively using the Equal Treatment Directive (Directive 76/207). The dilemma for the claimant was that this directive was adopted in 1976 subsequent to the enactment of the Sex Discrimination Act 1975.

Lord Keith stated that a UK court would have to interpret domestic legislation in any area subject to a directive in a way which accords with the purpose of the directive 'if that can be done without distorting the meaning of the domestic legislation'. His Lordship added, relying on *Marleasing SA v La Comercial Internacional de Alimentacion SA* (Case 106/89) [1990] ECR I-4135, that this approach applied whether the domestic legislation was passed *before or after* the relevant directive. The important point is that domestic law must be capable of bearing the meaning which accords with the purpose of a directive; if not, then it is for Parliament to legislate, not for the courts to arrive at a construction which the words will not bear. Before determining the claimant's appeal, a ruling concerning the Equal Treatment Directive was sought from the European Court of Justice. The Court of Justice ruled that the Directive precluded a dismissal in the claimant's circumstances on the grounds of pregnancy. In *Webb v EMO Air Cargo (UK) Ltd (No. 2)* [1995] 1 WLR 1454, the House of Lords decided that ss.1(1)(a) and 5(3) could be interpreted in a way which was consistent with the Directive.

 **Example**

The Consumer Rights Act 2015 makes reference to 'good faith' in s.62(4), but does not indicate what the term means. (Note that this provision had previously been part of a statutory instrument, the Unfair Terms in Consumer Contracts Regulations 1994, that did expressly indicate the factors that were to be considered in assessing good faith.) It is permissible to consult the recitals to Directive 93/13 on Unfair Terms in Consumer Contracts [1993] OJ L95/29 in order to gain guidance on this term. The recitals provide:

> [I]n making an assessment of good faith, particular regard shall be had to the strength of bargaining positions of the parties, whether the consumer had an inducement to agree to the term and whether the goods or services were sold or supplied to the special order of the consumer; whereas the requirement of good faith may be satisfied by the seller or supplier where he deals fairly and equitably with the other party whose legitimate interests he has to take into account.

See *Director General of Fair Trading v First National Bank plc* [2002] 1 AC 481.

4.8 **Interpretation of legislation and the Human Rights Act 1998**

The Human Rights Act 1998 places a duty upon the courts to interpret legislation to ensure compatibility with the ECHR. Section 3(1) of the Act provides:

> So far as it is possible to do so, primary legislation and subordinate legislation must be read and given effect to in a way which is compatible with the Convention rights.

The subsection applies to all legislation, existing and future. The use of the word 'possible' gives rise to some uncertainty: how far may the courts depart from the wording of legislation in seeking to achieve compatibility? Parliament envisages that some legislation may not be compliant and by s.4 a court may make a declaration of incompatibility, so there is a limit to the judicial task under s.3(1).

Where a legislative provision is ambiguous then the court must choose the meaning which is compatible with Convention rights. However, it is not necessary for there to be ambiguity for s.3 to apply, as was seen in *R v A* [2002] 1 AC 45, where words were read into s.41 of the Youth Justice and Criminal Evidence Act 1999 to ensure compliance with a defendant's right to a fair trial under Article 6 of the ECHR. This is a departure from the traditional approach to statutory interpretation where the task is to discover the meaning of legislation from the words used by Parliament.

The main question to be answered is: to what extent are the courts constrained in their task under s.3 by the words used in legislation? This question was considered in *Ghaidan v Godin-Mendoza* [2004] UKHL 30 and is discussed in further detail at 7.2.

Visit the online resources to watch a video on reading and interpreting statutes.

Summary

- The role of a judge in interpreting a statute is to discover and give effect to the intention of Parliament. However, the concept of intention of Parliament is difficult to determine.
- The principles of statutory interpretation are not binding rules but simply tools that the courts may use to identify and locate the intention of Parliament.
- The traditional approach to interpretation consists of three distinct 'rules' of statutory interpretation: the literal rule, the golden rule, and the mischief rule.
- Arguably, the traditional rules are of limited value and have generally given way to a contextual and purposive approach.
- A court may read the whole of an Act of Parliament, but not every part of an Act carries equal weight and value in interpreting particular provisions.
- The sections of an Act express the intention of Parliament and are paramount; the aids to construction cannot be used to give the words of a section a meaning they cannot bear, except in limited circumstances (subject to the operation of s.3 of the Human Rights Act 1998).

- Internal aids—the long title, preamble, cross-heading, marginal or side notes, punctuation—may be used to establish the context and purpose of an Act but they cannot be used to restrict the clear meaning of the words of a section.
- External aids may be consulted subject to the limits to their use. These aids are outside of an Act and include: Explanatory Notes; the Interpretation Act 1978; pre-parliamentary materials; parliamentary materials—Hansard; statutes on the same subject area; statutes *in pari materia*; and dictionaries.
- One of the external aids—the use of Hansard—is complex and controversial. Hansard ought only to be used within the following limits:

  (a) The legislation must be ambiguous or obscure or a literal interpretation would lead to an absurdity;

  (b) The statement or statements relied on were made by the minister or other promoter of a bill;

  (c) The statements relied upon are clear.
- Presumptions are used as a last resort should an Act prove to be wholly unclear or ambiguous. These are presumptions of legislative intent and can either be of general application or may apply when statutory provisions are ambiguous or unclear.
- The courts of the UK are to construe domestic legislation in any area subject to an EU directive in a way which accords with the purpose of the directive if that can be done without distorting the meaning of the domestic legislation.
- The Human Rights Act 1998 has changed the role of the courts in interpreting legislation when issues of Convention rights are raised. Under s.3, the courts may go beyond the words of the legislation in seeking to ensure the Act is complaint with Convention rights.

? Questions

1 Why is it misleading to refer to the 'rules' of statutory interpretation?

2 Using authority, define and explain the literal rule, golden rule, and mischief rule.

3 What is meant by the purposive approach to statutory interpretation and explain a case where it was applied?

4 Using examples, contrast and analyse the value of internal and external aids to interpretation.

5 Critically evaluate the permission, as established in *Pepper v Hart*, to use Hansard as an external aid to construction?

6 What is the impact on statutory interpretation of: (a) the UK's membership of the EU; (b) the Human Rights Act 1998?

Sample question and outline answer

Question

The use of Hansard as an aid to statutory interpretation is fraught with difficulty. The courts have not found it a useful guide to the interpretation of statutes. Discuss.

Outline answer

This question raises three main issues: first, when Hansard can be used as an aid to statutory interpretation; secondly, whether using Hansard is fraught with difficulties (this requires an evaluation of the basis for its use); thirdly, the experience of the courts in cases subsequent to *Pepper v Hart*.

In *Pepper v Hart* it was stated by Lord Browne-Wilkinson that the rule against the use of Hansard should be relaxed so as to permit reference to parliamentary materials in the following circumstances: first, the legislation must be ambiguous or obscure or a literal interpretation would lead to an absurdity; secondly, the statement or statements relied on were made by the minister or other promoter of a bill, together with such other parliamentary material as is necessary to understand such statements; thirdly, the statements relied upon are clear.

The House of Lords was setting out a limited relaxation of the rule against the use of Hansard in the interpretation of statutes. Indeed, Lord Bridge suggested that Hansard should only be used where Parliament has considered the very issue of interpretation which the court faces and the minister has provided a clear answer to that issue. That was the very situation in *Pepper v Hart*. The reason for the limited approach was to ensure legal certainty.

An argument against the relaxation of the rule excluding the use of Hansard was that the costs of litigation would increase with the increased workload of consulting Hansard. One of the main difficulties is convincing a court that the conditions laid down in *Pepper v Hart* have been satisfied. It should be noted that even the judges are not in agreement as to how *Pepper v Hart* is to be interpreted: see, for example, *Jackson v Attorney General* and the criticisms made by Bennion on the reasoning in *R v JTB*.

The case law subsequent to *Pepper v Hart* does not present a clear picture as to the value of Hansard as an aid to interpretation. Some cases demonstrate the use of Hansard, for example, *Warwickshire County Council v Johnson* [1993] AC 583. In this case the House of Lords used Hansard to interpret s.20(1) of the Consumer Protection Act 1987. Under s.20(1) it was an offence to give a misleading price indication 'in the course of any business of his'. Here an employee of an electrical retailer was found by the Divisional Court to have given a misleading statement 'in the course of [a] business of his'. It was argued on the employee's behalf that s.20(1) was ambiguous. The House of Lords agreed and resolved this issue by looking at the clear words of the minister in Parliament, which indicated that the intention of the statute was not to cover individual employees but to cover the 'business' of an employer. Equally, in *Stevenson v Rogers* Hansard was employed successfully.

However, there is a considerable case law which shows circumstances where Hansard has been of no assistance. In *R v Secretary of State for the Environment, Transport and the Regions, ex parte Spath Holme* the House of Lords refused to permit the use of Hansard, as the statute, the Landlord and Tenant Act 1985, was not ambiguous, obscure, or giving rise to absurdity, nor were the statements made by ministers in Parliament clear. Indeed, certain judicial comments suggest that Hansard is rarely of use: see Lord Hoffman's remarks in *R (Quintavalle) v Secretary of State for Health*. Usually Hansard may not be used, where a criminal statute is ambiguous, to extend the scope of criminal liability created by the statute: see *Massey and Another v Boulden and Another* and Lord Phillips in *Thet v DPP*. There is also some caution adopted when relying on Hansard because of the risk that it may obscure the intention of Parliament with the intention of the government.

While the use of Hansard does give rise to difficulties, including what the precise limits of its operation are, it has been used by the courts as an aid to the interpretation of statutes in some cases. The problems encountered by the courts revolve around whether the conditions for Hansard's use have been met. It would seem that in the case law subsequent to *Pepper v Hart* the courts have sought to limit the use of Hansard.

Further reading

If you want to fully appreciate how the rules of statutory interpretation apply in practice then read the leading cases. Nothing will replace the value of doing so. In particular, we would recommend you pay attention to the arguments raised by counsel in advancing the competing arguments about interpretation.

- ***Bell, J.*** and ***Engle, G.*** *Cross Statutory Interpretation*, 3rd edn, Oxford University Press (1995)

  This book, albeit dated and prior to recent cases, is still one of the classics of statutory interpretation. It is described as a 'short, systematic introduction to the general principles of statutory interpretation' and includes coverage of the history, traditional rules, the aids and the presumptions.

- ***Bennion, F.*** *Statutory Interpretation*, 7th edn, LexisNexis (2019)

  This is an advanced and exhaustive reference text and is the leading work on interpretation. Primarily for practitioners, it explains the detailed range of factors that the courts would consider in deciding the meaning and effect of all types of legislation. We would recommend referring to this cautiously and only to the extent that you are pursuing an advanced understanding of the law.

- ***Katzmann. R. A.*** *'Judging Statutes'* Oxford University Press (2016)

  This is a very concise book by an American Judge of the US Court of Appeals for the Second Circuit. In it he deftly summarises a range of challenges faced by the American judiciary in interpreting Acts of Congress, including the approach taken to legislative history. There is an excellent discussion of the broad purposive approach as adopted across the Atlantic alongside the more restrictive 'textualist' approaches to interpretation favoured by some judges. This is a good read if you want a comparative and more global understanding of the process of statutory interpretation.

- ***Kavanagh, A.*** *'Pepper v Hart and Matters of Constitutional Principle'* (2005) 121 LQR 98

  This article examines the constitutional reasons against the use of Hansard in the process of interpretation and argues in favour of the courts giving greater effect to the intention as precisely enacted in the words of a statute.

- ***Millett, Lord.*** *'Construing Statutes'* (1999) 20 Stat LR 107

  In this short article Lord Millett concisely considers the problems surrounding the discovery of the meaning of legislation as well as the arguments against the ruling in *Pepper v Hart*.

- ***Sales, Lord Justice.*** *'Modern Statutory Interpretation'* (2017) 38 Stat LR 125

  Now a Justice of the Supreme Court, Lord Sales analyses the relationship between Parliament and the courts' function in interpreting Acts of Parliament. It offers an excellent chronological background to the interpretation of statutes over time and contains an excellent discussion of the constitutional themes at play when the courts undertake statutory interpretation.

- ***Steyn, Lord.*** *'Pepper v Hart: A Re-examination'* (2001) 21 OJLS 59

  This is a must read for those of you who want to develop a more detailed analysis of the arguments surrounding the use of Hansard. Lord Steyn also highlights a range of legal and practical consequences of the decision in *Pepper v Hart* before providing his own constitutional analysis and solution to the problem.

- ***Twining, W.*** and ***Miers, D.*** *How to Do Things with Rules*, 5th edn, Cambridge (2010)

  Although a little dated, this is still an excellent and insightful textbook that critically explores the context, method, and system of statutory interpretation. It includes coverage on both the impact of EU membership and the effect of the HRA 1998 on issues of interpretation.

- ***Vogenauer. S.*** *A Retreat from Pepper v Hart? A Reply to Lord Steyn* (2005) 25(4) OJLS 629

  This article is an incredibly detailed reply to Lord Steyn's article (included above). It seeks to show how the House of Lords embarked on a retreat from its landmark decision in *Pepper v Hart* and attempts to refute the reasons advanced in support of the retreat. In addition, it argues that the alternative solution proposed by Lord Steyn creates both conceptual and practical difficulties.

Online resources

You should now attempt the supporting self-test questions and end-of-chapter questions available at: **www.oup.com/he/wilson-rutherford4e**

Chapter 5

The doctrine of judicial precedent

Learning objectives

By the end of this chapter you should:

- understand the principles of the doctrine of judicial precedent;
- be able to recognise the characteristics of *ratio decidendi* and *obiter dicta*;
- appreciate the factors involved in identifying both *ratio decidendi* and *obiter dicta*;
- know the hierarchy of the courts;
- be able to explain the rules of binding precedent in relation to the courts in the hierarchy.

Talking point

In *ParkingEye Ltd v Beavis* [2015] EWCA Civ 402, Mr Beavis parked his car next to a retail park. Signs warned that failure to comply with the parking terms displayed would result in a charge of £85. Mr Beavis overstayed the period of permitted free parking and was sent a notice requiring the payment of £85 or a reduced sum if paid within fourteen days. Mr Beavis challenged the notice and argued it was a penalty that was unenforceable at common law. The law on penalties was to be found in a House of Lords case, *Dunlop Pneumatic Tyre Co Ltd v New Garage and Motor Co Ltd* [1915] AC 79. There had been numerous cases since this case was decided and the principles underlying the case, it may be argued, had become uncertain. *ParkingEye Ltd v Beavis* was first heard in the County Court, where the payment of the sum was held to be enforceable. An appeal went to the Court of Appeal (Civil Division) where the court affirmed the decision of the County Court, holding that the sum charged was neither extravagant nor unconscionable and was therefore enforceable. A further appeal was made to the Supreme Court in the conjoined appeals of *Cavendish Square Holding BV v El Makdessi* and *ParkingEye Ltd v Beavis* [2015] UKSC 67. The Supreme Court reviewed the common law relating to penalty clauses and considered whether the common law rule relating to penalties should be abolished. The UKSC dismissed the appeal. Mr Beavis lost.

The legal journey of the case from the County Court up to—finally—the UK Supreme Court requires an understanding of the doctrine of precedent. Ask yourself the following questions:

- What do you understand the word 'precedent' to mean in its everyday use? In what context does it arise and what is the significance when someone is said to have 'established or set a precedent'?
- Why do you think having a hierarchy of courts is significant for parties or persons in a dispute?
- Once a decision is made by the most senior court—the UK Supreme Court—how do you think this decision will affect similar cases that are heard in the same or other courts in the future?

Introduction

This chapter takes you through the key features of the doctrine of judicial precedent. The doctrine of judicial precedent is one of the most fundamental topics of the English legal system. It is the one that most lawyers are required to grasp and work within during the everyday course of their professional lives. This chapter contains a considerable amount of new terminology; however, once you fully absorb the doctrine, the terms will become very familiar. Similarly, there are a lot of cases covered in this chapter and unfortunately, there won't always be opportunities to discuss the facts in detail or in depth. They are included to demonstrate the rules of precedent in action, rather than discuss the facts or decisions in those cases. Do feel free to follow up those cases should you find yourself curious about a particular case. Finally, it is worth bearing in mind the ordinary definition of precedent—an early action or decision that is used as an example or guide to be followed should the situation require. In many respects, this is at the centre of the ideas and principles of judicial precedent.

Let's start at the beginning. When a dispute arises a lawyer is usually consulted. Having identified the issue raised by the facts, the lawyer will discover the law that is applicable to the problem. If the problem is largely governed by case law, such as contract and tort, then the lawyers will consider the state of the common law, that is, identify relevant decisions of judges that can be found in law reports. The lawyer will need to extract from relevant cases the principles or rules which will assist in resolving the problem. What a lawyer is seeking is a principle or rule upon which a ***decision*** in a case is based; this is called the *ratio decidendi* of the case. Within a system of ***binding*** precedent, the ratio is the binding part of a case.

Bound by a case or decision
Lawyers may refer to being bound by a case or a decision. The context should make clear [however] that the words are being used as synonyms for the binding part of the case, the ratio decidendi. *As will later become clear, the reasons for the ratio, the decision, or the case in its entirety are not binding in terms of the doctrine of precedent.*

The basis of the doctrine of judicial precedent is that like cases should be decided alike. So if the facts of a case are materially the same as the facts of a previous case, then the principle or rule (the *ratio decidendi*) used to decide the previous case should be used to decide the instant case and in this way certainty in the legal system is promoted. This also enables lawyers to give legal advice with a degree of predictability about the strength of a client's case.

In English law, and albeit within limits, the lower courts must apply the relevant *ratio decidendi* of a higher court in the hierarchy. Cross and Harris, in *Precedent in English Law*, pithily sum up the operation of the doctrine of binding precedent in the following words:

> Every court is bound to follow any case decided by a court above it in the hierarchy, and appellate courts (other than the House of Lords) [now the Supreme Court] are bound by their previous decisions.

The doctrine therefore ensures that the courts decide cases in an orderly way, that the authority of senior courts is respected, and that, ultimately, change occurs incrementally.

 **Key point**

The operation of a system of binding precedent depends upon three things: the availability of reliable records of decisions; the identification of rules of law from the decisions in cases; and, where there are several courts in a legal system, a settled hierarchy of courts.

5.1 Judicial precedent and law reporting

The prerequisite for the operation of a doctrine of judicial precedent is an effective system of law reporting. When judges make decisions, there must be a mechanism to discover the rules that emerge from the cases. Accuracy is at a premium. In the English legal system, law reporting falls into two distinct phases: before 1865 and after 1865.

Focusing on recent history, in 1865, the Incorporated Council of Law Reporting commenced publishing the most authoritative set of reports, the *Law Reports*. While not published by the state, they are the nearest that English law has to an official set of reports. They are systematic and accurate. The system follows the organisation of the courts: Appeal Cases (AC) comprise decisions of the Supreme Court/House of Lords and the Privy Council; and Chancery Division (Ch), Queen's Bench Division (QB), and Family Division (Fam) comprise both cases decided at first instance and appeals to the Court of Appeal. The organisation of the series of *Law Reports* has varied from time to time, mirroring the organisation and changes in the organisation of the courts. The criteria for inclusion in the *Law Reports* are that: a case introduces a new principle or rule, an existing principle or rule is materially modified, a doubt in the law is settled, or a case is peculiarly instructive.

The accuracy of the *Law Reports* is ensured by the editorial process, which includes reporting by a barrister and checking by the judge(s) involved in the decision.

The Incorporated Council of Law Reporting also publishes the *Weekly Law Reports*, which provide, as the name suggests, a regular source of recently decided cases. Many of the cases reported in the *Weekly Law Reports* will ultimately be included in the *Law Reports*. While the *Law Reports* may be considered the most authoritative set of reports, other series of reports are published. Foremost among these are the *All England Law Reports* published by LexisNexis in a weekly series. The *Weekly Law Reports* and the *All England Law Reports* are general in scope and include coverage of cases on many areas of English law. Additionally, there are many specialist sets of reports dealing with cases on particular areas of law. Examples of these include the *Building Law Reports*, *Industrial Relations Law Reports*, and *Housing Law Reports*.

Of course, law reports are now increasingly and in some cases exclusively available electronically. You are more likely to access them online than in hard copy in the library. LexisLibrary and Westlaw each provide a very detailed searchable database of case law. There are other databases where you can find more recent cases such as Lawtel. The UK Supreme Court website and that of the Court of Appeal and High Court also have search functions on their own respective sites. Finally, the British and Irish Legal Information Institute's website—**www.bailii.org**—is another popular free website that contains case reports, amongst other legal materials.

5.2 Nature of judge-made law

Judges are responsible for the development of case law. In this way, it is the judges themselves that develop or make law. Before discussing the doctrine of precedent it is important to understand some basic points about the nature of judicial law-making. The first point is that judges only have the opportunity to make pronouncements on an area of law should a relevant case be brought before them. It is not uncommon for a problem in the law to lie unresolved for many years due to no case being brought that would enable the courts to address it. Secondly, the courts are constrained by precedents created by previous cases; they must work within the existing rules of the doctrine of judicial precedent. Thirdly, the courts are always wary of the retrospective effect of case law because of its implication for the rule of law and how it can unfairly affect individuals who at the relevant time thought they were acting lawfully. Fourthly, the courts are constitutionally required to respect parliamentary supremacy and in some areas the judges consider that the development of the law should be left to those democratically elected in Parliament.

To provide some background, there was once a time when judges adhered to the 'declaratory theory' of the common law. This theory stated that when the judges made decisions, they were merely declaring what the law was and had always been, as if the law mysteriously existed in the ether. This concealed two important points. First, judge-made law is retrospective; a statement of law in a later case applies to situations that may have already occurred. So, for example, if at the time an act takes place there is no clear law governing it but a later case then makes clear that the law does in fact apply to such an act, then the law as clarified will retrospectively apply. As mentioned, this is generally objectionable as citizens have no way of knowing what the law is at the time of the act. The declaratory theory, rather artificially, held that the law had always been in existence and that the later judge merely declared what it was. Secondly, it was also argued that unelected judges should not be making laws in a democratic society. For obvious reasons, the declaratory theory simply sought to mask and rebuff this criticism.

The declaratory theory is now seen for what it is: a fiction, and this has been recognised by the courts. Lord Lloyd in *Kleinwort Benson Ltd v Lincoln City Council* [1999] 2 AC 349 said (at p.393):

> Nobody now suggests that the common law is static. It is capable of adapting itself to new circumstances. Is it then capable of being changed? Or is it only capable of being developed? The common-sense answer is that the common law is capable of being changed, not only by legislation, but also by judicial decision. This is nowhere clearer than when a long-standing decision of the Court of Appeal is overruled. Indeed in a system such as ours, where the Court of Appeal is bound by its own previous decisions, the main justification for the existence of a second tier appeal is that it enables the House to redirect the law when it has taken a wrong turning.

While judges do make law, they do so within limits. C. K. Allen, in *Law in the Making*, explains that: 'the creative power of the courts is limited by the existing legal material at their command. They find the material and shape it. The legislature may manufacture entirely new material.' One writer likened judge-made law to a tapestry: all that the judges may do is insert stitches here and there but only when a dispute raising the same area of law is brought before the courts. The insertions are limited by the surrounding fabric and judges must ensure that they are consistent with the existing body of law. In this sense judges make partial and piecemeal changes to the law; this is not to say that judges do not make significant changes to the law. They do. However, on the other hand, Parliament can remove and replace sections of the tapestry or undertake sweeping reforms of the law by wholly replacing the fabric.

Under the UK's unwritten constitution, the role of judges is to interpret and help to enforce the law. Parliament is to make laws. This generalisation, of course, needs to be qualified because of the judges' role in relation to the common law—at the centre of the doctrine of precedent. Traditionally, judges, in developing the common law, have adopted a low-key role in relation to law-making, avoiding as far as possible controversial issues of policy so as to avoid accusations of undemocratic activity. The development of the law of contract, tort, and to a lesser extent property does not generate great public interest. In other areas such as administrative law (judicial review) when individuals are claiming against public bodies and often government and ministerial departments, the development of the law does trigger considerable interest. The Brexit-related cases brought by Gina Miller in first, successfully challenging the government in its intention to trigger Article 50 of the Treaty of the European Union to commence the process of withdrawal with parliamentary authority, and, secondly, in successfully demonstrating that the Prime Minister's advice to Her Majesty to prorogue Parliament in September 2019 was unlawful, attracted considerable public and media attention. It led to ample debate about the 'correct' limits of judicial power in a parliamentary democracy. In a similar vein, the role of judges in the process of interpretation of statutes, especially under the Human Rights Act 1998, often triggers considerable public attention.

The judicial role in relation to law-making was explained in *Knuller v DPP* [1973] AC 435 by Lord Simon when he said (at p.490):

> [I]t has been suggested that the speeches in *Shaw v. Director of Public Prosecutions* indicated that the courts retain a residual power to create new offences. I do not think they did so. Certainly, it is my view that the courts have no more power to create new offences than they have to abolish those already established in the law; both tasks are for Parliament. What the courts can and should do (as was truly laid down in *Shaw v. Director of Public Prosecutions*) is to recognise the applicability of established offences to new circumstances to which they are relevant.

Lord Lowry, in *C (A Minor) v DPP* [1996] AC 1, set out some general guidance in relation to judicial law-making when he said (at p.28):

> [I]t is hard, when discussing the propriety of judicial law-making, to reason conclusively from one situation to another . . . I believe, however, that one can find in the authorities some aids to navigation across an uncertainly charted sea. (1) If the solution is doubtful, the judges should beware of imposing their own remedy. (2) Caution should prevail if Parliament has rejected opportunities of clearing up a known difficulty or has legislated, while leaving the difficulty untouched. (3) Disputed matters of social policy are less suitable areas for judicial intervention than purely legal problems. (4) Fundamental legal doctrines should not be lightly set aside. (5) Judges should not make a change unless they can achieve finality and certainty.

In relation to judicial law-making consider *R v R (Rape: Marital Exemption)* [1992] 1 AC 599. The House of Lords overruled what was believed to be the law that a wife had given irrevocable consent to sexual intercourse with her husband, and therefore a husband could not be convicted of raping his wife. Do you think the House of Lords was making law? If so, is this objectionable? For further discussion of this case see Giles, M. 'Judicial Law-Making in the Criminal Courts: The Case of Marital Rape' [1992] Crim LR 407.

Thinking point

Parliament v. Courts?

It is clear that the judges do make law. The questions to be addressed are: first, in what circumstances does such law-making occur; secondly, to what extent *should* the judges be making law? Is there a distinction to be drawn between the types of issues suitable for law-making by judges or by the parliamentary process that may (or may not) lead to legislation? On what basis or information should judges base these decisions? Consider and contrast the processes that may be employed in preparing and passing legislation through Parliament.

It should be noted that sometimes judges will indicate that the law has been developed by the courts as far as it can be, and it is now for Parliament to further develop or amend it.

Critical debate

The debate about a so-called 'right to die' was highlighted in the case of *R (on the application of Nicklinson) v Ministry of Justice* [2014] UKSC 38. The case brought into focus the interplay of law and morality, the limits of judge-made law, and the relationship between the courts and Parliament. Mr Nicklinson, who had suffered a severe stroke and was paralysed from the neck down, lost his case. The judges refused to develop the common law and deferred to Parliament to assess the question of whether the current law on assisted suicide infringed an individual's right to a private life. Why do you think the courts left the responsibility to develop the law to Parliament? Do you agree with the judges in doing so, or was this a missed opportunity?

5.3 *Ratio decidendi*

Cross and Harris, in *Precedent in English Law* (p.72), describe *ratio decidendi* in the following terms:

> any rule of law expressly or impliedly treated by the judge as a necessary step in reaching his conclusion, having regard to the line of reasoning adopted by him, or a necessary part of his direction to the jury.

In terms of the doctrine of precedent, a previous court decision will only be binding if the facts of the instant case are sufficiently similar so that the *ratio decidendi* or rule of law from the previous case should be applied. Note that it is not the actual decision that is binding; under the doctrine of judicial precedent, the binding part of the case is the *ratio decidendi*. The *ratio* must be the basis or a basis for the determination of the decision, as decided by the majority of judges. To complicate matters, the nature of case law is such that usually a judge or judges will not explicitly state the *ratio decidendi*. In addition, a judge may also state other principles of law which do not relate directly to the basis for the decision in the case. These statements are termed *obiter dicta* (other things said). So, lawyers therefore must identify and then 'construct' the *ratio decidendi* from the judgment or judgments of the court. This should be an essential skill that you will learn and develop throughout your studies.

Key point

The *ratio decidendi* of a case is not the decision reached in a case but the rule of law upon which the decision is based.

Ratio decidendi also has to be distinguished from the term *res judicata*. The decision in a case is binding on the parties to that case and is said to be *res judicata*; subject to any appeal, the same parties cannot re-litigate the same points already judicially determined. The *ratio decidendi* of a case, in accordance with the rules of binding precedent, is binding on other courts.

5.3.1 Identification of the *ratio decidendi* of a case

Twining and Miers, in *How to Do Things with Rules*, helpfully explain that the search for the *ratio* of a case is not like a hunt for buried treasure, meaning that if you continue to dig, the *ratio decidendi* will ultimately be found. A characteristic of the *ratio decidendi* of a case is that it is not in a 'fixed verbal form'; the words of a *ratio* must be chosen and the rule 'constructed'. Also, our appreciation of the *ratio decidendi* may be changed by subsequent case law. Crucial in this search is the identification of the legal issues raised before the court; in other words, what has the court been asked to decide?

Example

Invitations to tender are requests for individuals or companies to make bids in relation to the completion of work and/or the supply of goods. The person inviting the tenders gives details of the work or goods required and interested parties submit 'tenders' that will include an indication of the price charged. When you study the Law of Contract module, it is likely you will be asked: does an invitation to tender amount to a promise to be bound by the lowest or highest bid submitted (i.e. an offer), or does it merely constitute an invitation to treat, inviting the bidders themselves to make an offer? The formal basis of a contract only begins when an actual offer is made.

In *Spencer v Harding* (1870) LR 5 CP 561, the defendants issued a circular which identified goods which they were 'instructed to offer to the wholesale trade for sale by tender'. The claimants submitted the highest tender, but the defendants refused to sell to them. The Court was asked to decide if the circular amounted to an offer or whether it was merely an invitation to treat. If the circular was an offer then the claimants had accepted and a contract was formed; if the circular was an invitation to treat then the claimants, by submitting a tender, had made an offer which the defendants had not accepted and hence there was no contract.

It was decided that the circular was an invitation to treat and judgment was given for the defendants. This statement does not indicate the rule underpinning the decision. The *ratio decidendi* of the case was:

> [I]n the absence of words expressing a promise to sell to the highest bidder, the circular was merely an invitation to treat. No intention to be bound was expressed in the circular.

Hence, this rule was a necessary part (or justification) of the decision, or required to answer the question.

The most useful analysis of how to find the *ratio decidendi* of a case was undertaken by Dr A. Goodhart in 1931 in his *Essays in Jurisprudence and the Common Law*. In his view, the *ratio decidendi* is to be found in the facts treated by the judge as material and the decision based upon such facts. This is considered to be a test for finding the *ratio* of a case. While Goodhart's test is undoubtedly useful, it is somewhat flawed. Cross and Harris identify a number of criticisms that may be made of Goodhart's approach. One major problem is highlighted by Professor J. Stone, who said that the search for material facts often involves an element of choice. Facts that are considered to be material may be defined at various 'levels of abstraction'.

For example, in *Pharmaceutical Society of Great Britain v Boots Cash Chemists* [1953] 1 All ER 482, it was asked whether a display of drugs and poisons, specified in the Pharmacy and Poisons Act 1933, in a self-service store amounted to an offer. It was decided that such a display was merely an invitation to treat and not an offer. It could be argued that the *ratio* of the case was that a display of drugs and poisons in a self-service store is an invitation to treat. The *ratio decidendi* of the case would therefore only apply when dealing with a display of drugs and poisons. However, is there any good reason to so restrict the *ratio*? Drugs and medicines fell within a wider class, that of 'goods', and therefore should the *ratio* of the case not govern displays of goods? The language of the judges in the *Pharmaceutical Society* case clearly indicated that the *ratio decidendi* concerned the display of *goods*. Thus, a working rule is often, the more general the term, (in this case 'goods') the wider the *ratio*. Conversely, the more restricted the term, (in this case 'drugs') the narrower the rule will be. For a further illustration of these points, see the case study on *Blackpool & Fylde Aero Club Ltd v Blackpool Borough Council* [1990] 1 WLR 1195 later in this chapter.

5.3.2 **Cases on the interpretation of statutes**

The rules of precedent apply to judge-made law, but also to cases interpreting statutes. When the courts interpret a statute in a particular manner, then that determination (e.g. the approach, or definition that is developed) becomes a precedent as to the meaning of the words or phrases used in the statute.

 **Example**

In criminal law, theft is defined by s.1 of the Theft Act 1968 as the dishonest appropriation of property belonging to another with the intention of permanently depriving the other of it. A question that caused the courts some difficulty was the role of consent in relation to appropriation, namely, could property be appropriated in circumstances where the property owner consents? In *Lawrence v Metropolitan Police Commissioner* [1972] AC 626, a non-English-speaking Italian, Mr Occhi, arriving in England for the first time, got into a taxi and showed to the defendant driver a piece of paper identifying an address to which he wished to be taken. The defendant said that the journey was long and would be expensive. Mr Occhi gave the defendant £1, but from his open wallet the defendant removed a further £6. In fact, the journey was much shorter and the correct fare was approximately 10s 6d (53p). The defendant was convicted of theft, but appealed on the main ground that Mr Occhi had consented to the taking of £6 and, in consequence, there was no appropriation. The House of Lords held that the consent of an owner to a defendant taking property is irrelevant in establishing appropriation.

In a later case, *R v Morris* [1984] AC 320, the House of Lords once again considered this issue of consent and appropriation. The appeal involved two related cases concerning the switching of price labels on goods in supermarkets; removing a price label from goods and replacing it with a label with a lower price. In both cases the defendant was convicted and their subsequent appeal dismissed. In the House of Lords, there was apparent approval of *Lawrence*. However, Lord Roskill said, in the context of the meaning to be given to appropriation in s.1(1) of the Theft Act 1968, appropriation involves 'not an act expressly or impliedly authorised by the owner but an act by way of adverse interference with or usurpation of those rights'. His remarks indicated, in making a finding of an appropriation, that the absence of consent was crucial.

In *DPP v Gomez* [1993] AC 442, the defendant—an assistant store manager—was asked by an accomplice to supply goods from the shop in return for two stolen building society cheques. The defendant agreed and convinced the store manager (his boss) to authorise the supply of the goods in return for one cheque, telling him that the cheque was 'as good as cash'. He agreed. Further goods were supplied in return for the second cheque. The defendant was convicted of theft. The House of Lords was asked to decide as a point of law of general public importance:

> When theft is alleged and that which is alleged to be stolen passes to the defendant with the consent of the owner, but that has been obtained by a false representation, has (a) an appropriation within the meaning of s.1(1) of the Theft Act 1968 taken place . . . ?

Lord Keith said:

> The actual decision in Morris was correct, but it was erroneous, in addition to being unnecessary for the decision, to indicate that an act expressly or impliedly authorised by the owner could never amount to an appropriation . . . Lawrence makes it clear that consent to or authorisation by the owner of the taking by the rogue is irrelevant. The taking amounted to an appropriation within the meaning of s.1(1) of the Act of 1968.

Thus, in *Gomez*, it was confirmed that Lord Roskill's comments in *Morris*, stated earlier, were an *obiter dictum*. Lord Keith clearly addressed the point and said Lord Roskill's opinion was 'unnecessary for the decision'. Additionally, Lord Roskill was wrong: the case of *Lawrence* authoritatively and clearly established that consent was irrelevant and a lack of consent was not a prerequisite for an appropriation.

In relation to the interpretation of statutes some caution must be exercised by the courts, as the same words or phrases may be used in a different context within the statute or across different statutes. In these circumstances, a later court may not be strictly bound by a previous court's interpretation of a statute if, on a true construction of the precise statutory provision, Parliament intended the words to carry a different meaning. This is simply a determination that the previous ratio was not binding because the material facts of the present case were different. In *Stevenson v Rogers* [1999] QB 1028, the meaning of 'in the course of a business' in s.14(2) of the Sale of Goods Act 1979 fell to be decided by the Court of Appeal. In an earlier decision of the Court of Appeal, *R & B Customs Brokers v UDT* [1988] 1 WLR 321, the meaning of this same phrase, but in s.12 of the Unfair Contract Terms Act 1977, had been decided. In *Stevenson*, the Court of Appeal gave a different interpretation to 'in the course of a business' and determined that the meaning adopted in *R & B Customs Brokers* was confined to the Unfair Contract Terms Act 1977. See 'Statutes *in pari materia*' in 4.4.2.

Nonetheless, the degree of caution depends on the particular case, and the particular judge in the interpretation they wish to reach. In *Partridge v Crittenden* [1968] 1 WLR 1204, the Court had to consider the meaning of the words 'offer for sale' in the Protection of Birds Act 1954. In considering the meaning, the Court referred to *Fisher v Bell* (see 4.3.1) and the interpretation question in that case, that of 'offer for sale' within the Restriction of Offensive Weapons Act 1959. Although a different statute, the approach in *Fisher v Bell* was useful in the case of *Partridge v Crittenden* because of the presumption that such provisions were to be read in light of the general law of contract.

5.3.3 **Looking to later cases in determining the *ratio decidendi* of a case**

A later case may indicate what is perceived to be the *ratio decidendi* of an earlier case. Additionally, a later case may clarify the *ratio decidendi* of an earlier case by, for example, reclassifying what are or are not the *material* facts.

 **Example**

The formation of contract depends upon the existence of an offer and a subsequent acceptance of the offer. The general rule is that there must be actual communication of the acceptance of the offer to the person making the offer. There is a well-known exception to this rule: when the parties contemplate that post will be used as the means of sending an acceptance, then acceptance is complete as soon as the letter of acceptance is posted. As new methods of communication were developed the courts were asked to decide, in a series of cases, when the postal rule applied.

In *Entores Ltd v Miles Far East Corporation* [1955] 2 QB 327, the Court of Appeal decided that when an acceptance to an offer is sent by telex, an instantaneous means of communication, the general rule of actual communication applies, not the postal rule.

However, the issue of which rule applies to an acceptance by telex was raised again before the House of Lords in the *Brinkibon* case [1983] 2 AC 34. The House of Lords agreed with the Court of Appeal that the rule of actual communication applied. However, the House of Lords sought to qualify the rule. Lord Wilberforce said (at p.42):

> Since 1955 the use of telex communication has been greatly expanded, and there are many variants on it. The senders and recipients may not be the principals to the contemplated contract. They may be servants or agents with limited authority. The message may not reach, or be intended to reach, the designated recipient immediately: messages may be sent out of office hours, or at night, with the intention, or upon the assumption, that they will be read at a later time. There may be some error or default at the recipient's end which prevents receipt at the time contemplated and believed in by the sender. The message may have been sent and/or received through machines operated by third persons. And many other variations may occur. No universal rule can cover all such cases: they must be resolved by reference to the intentions of the parties, by sound business practice and in some cases by a judgment where the risks should lie.

This statement indicates that the general rule as to communication of acceptance would only apply where telexes are sent and received by principals during office hours (those were the facts in both *Entores* and *Brinkibon*). Lord Wilberforce said that the rule was not 'universal' and another approach may have to be adopted where the facts are different. *Brinkibon* thus confirmed the *ratio* of *Entores*, approved it, but sought to clarify and explain its limitations. In doing so, it made the rule more nuanced.

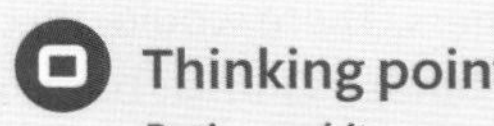

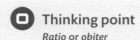

Thinking point

Ratio or obiter

Sometimes it can be difficult to determine the status of judicial comments—*ratio* or *obiter*? Consider whether Lord Wilberforce's statement forms part of the *ratio decidendi* of *Brinkibon*. Remember that the *ratio decidendi* must be necessary for the decision in the case; if the principle of law does not affect the outcome of the case it will not be the *ratio*. See the discussion of *obiter dicta* later in the chapter.

5.3.4 **Finding the *ratio decidendi*—an illustration**

In *Blackpool & Fylde Aero Club Ltd v Blackpool Borough Council* [1990] 1 WLR 1195, Blackpool Borough Council, the defendants, owned Blackpool Airport and operated pleasure flights. In 1983, Blackpool & Fylde Aero Club Ltd, the claimants, were invited along with six other parties, to tender for the operation of the flights. In the defendant's invitation to tender, it was provided: 'The Council do not bind themselves to accept all or any part of any tender. No tender which is received after the last date and time specified shall be admitted for consideration.' The claimants submitted their tender in the correct form and before the deadline. However, a failure by town hall staff to empty the postbox meant that the claimants' tender was not considered to have been received in time and, in consequence, was disregarded. The claimants sued the defendants.

Focusing on the issue in contract law, at first instance, the High Court judge found in favour of the claimants and held that there was a breach of contract. The defendants appealed to the Court of Appeal.

The issues and the material facts

The first part of an analysis of a case is a careful identification of the issues raised by the parties. What is the court being asked to decide upon? In this case, the claimants, in contract law, sought damages for breach of contract. Put simply, the legal issue relates to whether a contract has been formed and, specifically, whether there has been a valid offer and acceptance. In order to identify the material facts it is necessary to understand the law surrounding the legal issues that have been raised. Here, the question was whether an invitation to tender was an invitation to treat or an offer. The claimants alleged that it was an offer, and relied upon the council's promise 'that if a tender was returned to the town hall, Blackpool before noon on Thursday 17 March 1983 the same would be considered along with other tenders duly returned when the decision to grant the concession was made'.

The arguments

It was argued on behalf of the defendants that the invitation to tender was in fact an invitation to treat, that is, an invitation to simply receive offers. There would, therefore, be no obligation upon the defendants to accept any tender. On that basis, no contract could be formed unless and until the defendants accepted the claimant's offer. The defendants relied on *Spencer v Harding* (1870) LR 5 CP 561 and *Harris v Nickerson* (1873) LR 8 QB 286.

Counsel for the claimants accepted that normally an invitation to tender was merely an invitation to treat. However, they sought to argue that in certain situations contractual obligations could arise either from the express words of the invitation to tender or from the circumstances surrounding it. Counsel suggested that the relevant question should be 'How would an ordinary person reading the tender document construe it?' The claimants submitted that a timely and conforming tender would be considered along with all other submitted tenders.

The decision

The Court of Appeal decided that the judge at first instance was correct and that the invitation to tender was indeed an offer (but in the limited sense that the defendants would consider a timely and conforming tender). This had been accepted by the claimants submitting a compliant tender.

The *ratio decidendi*

The decision reached does not explain the basis upon which the case was decided. The basis for the decision, the *ratio decidendi*, may be stated as follows:

> [W]here a local authority invites a selected number of parties to submit tenders and where the invitation prescribes a clear, orderly and familiar tendering procedure, including draft contract conditions available for inspection and plainly not open to negotiation, a prescribed common form of tender, the supply of envelopes designed to preserve the absolute anonymity of tenderers and clearly to identify the tender in question, and an absolute deadline, that evinces an implied intention of the parties that *a conforming tender will be considered and to that extent an invitation to tender is an offer capable of being accepted.* (my emphasis)

Note that this formulation of the *ratio* raises a number of questions: does the *ratio* only apply to local authorities; is it necessary that the tenderers be selected; and what form of procedure must be involved? Until later cases consider and decide these points, uncertainty would still be attached to the application of the rule.

What, then, has happened to the precedent in *Blackpool & Fylde Aero Club Ltd v Blackpool Borough Council* in later cases?

In *Harmon CFEM Facades (UK) Ltd v The Corporate Officer of the House of Commons* (1999) 67 Con LR 1, the rule in the *Blackpool* case was considered to apply to tendering processes initiated by public sector bodies, thus implying that the rule in the *Blackpool* case would not apply to invitations to tender initiated by private sector bodies. It was later held in *Natural World Products Ltd v ARC 21* [2007] NIQB 19 that the impact of the *Blackpool* case was to create a rule 'in English law that in the public sector where competitive tenderers are sought and responded to, the contract comes into existence whereby the prospective employer impliedly agrees to consider all tenderers fairly', per Deeny J at [5].

Key point

Later cases may clarify and specify the *ratio decidendi* of a previous case. For instance, as a *ratio decidendi* is not in a fixed verbal form, a *ratio* may change due to a later court deciding that a fact is not material or reformulating how facts are classified.

5.3.5 **More than one *ratio***

It is possible that a case may have more than one *ratio decidendi*. This may occur where a court is asked to decide several issues, and thus different *rationes decidendi* are required. If there is more than one *ratio* then each of them can have their own binding effect when the material facts are relevant.

5.3.6 The *ratio decidendi* of appellate courts

In ascertaining the *ratio decidendi* of appellate courts, one might need to consider multiple judgments. There may be three in the Court of Appeal and five in the Supreme Court/House of Lords—and there is not always agreement among the judges. Nowadays, single majority judgments are common but sometimes a judge can agree to the outcome but disagree on the basis for doing so, that is, how a decision to, say, allow an appeal is reached. This will then require a separate judgment. Inevitably, this will impact on the *ratio decidendi* of the case. Hence, it is necessary to determine the basis for each judge's decision and then determine if the majority is in favour of a particular ground for the decision. If a majority can be identified then this will form the more authoritative *ratio* of the case, while a minority view may only be considered to be persuasive.

If a judge dissents as to the decision to be reached in a case then the judgment is not binding as far as the doctrine of precedent is concerned; the dissenting judgment will not be part of the *ratio decidendi* of the case. However, such dissent may point to an alternative view of the law which may be accepted by a later but higher court. In this regard a dissenting judgment can often be persuasive when the courts are asked to devise a new ratio or revise an existing binding one. For example, see the dissenting judgment of Denning LJ in *Candler v Crane Christmas & Co* [1951] 2 KB 164 which was approved in *Hedley Byrne & Co Ltd v Heller & Partners Ltd* [1964] AC 465.

5.4 *Obiter dicta*

In a case, other statements as to the law under consideration may be made by judges which do not affect the outcome of a case. Such statements are referred to as *obiter dicta* (note that a single pronouncement by a judge is termed an *obiter dictum*). *Obiter dicta* are not binding on later courts, they are merely persuasive. The reason why *obiter dicta* do not carry the same weight as the *ratio decidendi* of a case is that the statements are not the basis for the decision in the case. Hence, those comments may not have been the subject of full argument or judicial consideration.

As with the *ratio decidendi* of a case, the identification of *obiter dicta* is not without difficulty. If the statement of law is not the basis for the court's decision as such, then it will, by virtue of this, be an *obiter dictum*. A case from the law of contract, *Partridge v Crittenden* [1968] 1 WLR 1204, provides an illustration of this point. In that case the appellant was convicted of an offence, under s.6 of the Protection of Wild Birds Act 1954, of offering for sale a live wild bird, 'other than a close-ringed specimen bred in captivity'. The appeal raised two questions. First, were magistrates right to decide that an advert indicating the birds were for sale was an 'offer for sale'? Secondly, were they right to hold that a bird was not a close-ringed specimen bred in captivity if the ring was removable from the bird's leg? The High Court held that no offence was committed as the advert did not constitute an offer. The rule relating to this issue was the basis for the decision and would clearly form the *ratio decidendi* of the case. However, the Court considered in some detail what was meant by 'a close-ringed specimen bred in captivity' and concluded that the magistrates were correct in their decision, that is, that as the ring could be removed it was not a close-ringed specimen. This statement was not the basis of the decision, it supported a conviction rather than an acquittal, and therefore it is to be classified as an *obiter dictum*. Note that the *obiter dicta* of the Supreme Court/House of Lords, while still persuasive, carry more weight than *dicta* of the lower courts.

 **Example**

Many instances of *obiter dicta* occur when judges speculate as to what the outcome would have been had the facts of the case been different. For example, in *Spencer v Harding*, discussed previously, Willes J said: '*If the circular had gone on, "and we undertake to sell to the highest bidder"*, the reward cases would have applied, and there would have been a good contract in respect of the persons' (emphasis added), meaning that the circular would have been an offer which would have been accepted by the highest bid of the claimants. This is clearly not the *ratio decidendi* as it does not support the decision that the circular was an invitation to treat.

Hedley Byrne v Heller [1964] AC 465 provides evidence of *obiter dicta*, where the House of Lords said that a duty in the tort of negligence could be owed for statements that caused pure economic loss. However, this was not part of the *ratio* of the case because, on the facts, no such duty was owed as the bank making the negligent statements had expressly disclaimed responsibility for the statements. Although not binding, the *dicta* that such a duty could be owed formed the basis for later cases to develop the tort of negligent misstatement.

5.5 Nature of *stare decisis*

The doctrine of precedent rests on the principle of *stare decisis*—to stand by what is decided. This principle reflects a desire to promote certainty and to allow the law to develop in an orderly way. To this end, there is a hierarchical court system, indicated in Diagram 5.1. The hierarchy starts with the highest appellate courts and descends to the lowest courts of first instance.

5.5.1 The Court of Justice of the European Union (EU)

The European Communities Act 1972, and specifically, s.3(1)–(2), effectively binds UK courts to consider and take notice of the decisions of the Court of Justice of the EU (CJEU) in relation to matters of EU law. In addition, UK courts can refer matters that require a decision from the CJEU, such as on a particular point of interpretation of the Treaties.

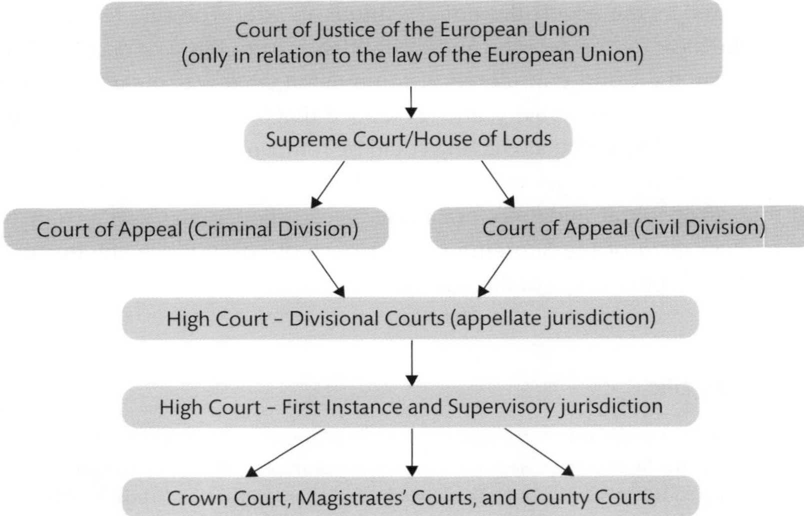

Diagram 5.1 Hierarchy of the courts

One of the consequences of the UK leaving the European Union is that the UK Parliament will have to clearly establish the continuing relationship between the UK courts and the CJEU. This is particularly the case in respect of rulings on retained EU law, that is, existing EU-derived domestic legislation that, say, implements an EU directive or other directly applicable EU Law. This issue is now dealt with by the EU (Withdrawal) Act 2018 which repealed the European Communities Act 1972 on 31 January 2020. The Act will simply convert the status of EU retained law into the domestic legal system. Section 6(1) of the EU (Withdrawal) Act 2018 states that a court or tribunal will not be bound by any principles or decisions of the European Court and cannot not refer any matter to the CJEU on or after the day of exit. Put simply, after the UK exits the EU, case law of the CJEU will not be binding but it may be persuasive, as s.6(2) confirms that a UK court or tribunal *may have regard* to a decision of the European Court, another EU entity, or the EU so far as it is relevant to any matter before the court or tribunal. Otherwise, the UK courts will have regard to retained case law or general principles of EU law until such time as, say, an appellate court, like the UK Supreme Court, departs from or overrules such precedents.

Please note that this Act will only come into force on 'exit day', that is, when a withdrawal agreement has been ratified by an Act of Parliament. Leaving with a 'deal' that is likely to be accepted by Parliament has been a complex and ongoing political process. As a result, the date of exit has been variously extended from the original date of 29 March 2019, to 31 October 2019 and to the current exit date (at the time of writing) of 31 January 2020.

5.5.2 **The Supreme Court (formerly the House of Lords)**

The Supreme Court is the highest court in the United Kingdom's hierarchy. Decisions of the Supreme Court (including its former existence as the House of Lords) bind all the courts beneath it in the hierarchy. References will, obviously, be made to the House of Lords in cases prior to 1 October 2009, and will be retained for the purposes of accuracy.

Until 1966, the House of Lords was bound by *its own* previous decisions, as established in *London Tramways Co. Ltd v London County Council* [1898] AC 375. In consequence, the development of areas of law was stifled, unless Parliament amended or reformed the law by passing legislation. This practice was altered by the Practice Statement (Judicial Precedent) [1966] 1 WLR 1234. It is worth noting that this Practice Statement is now of equal application in the Supreme Court, as confirmed in *Austin v Southwark London Borough Council* [2010] UKSC 28. This Practice Statement stipulates that:

> . . . the use of precedent [is] an indispensable foundation upon which to decide what is the law and its application to individual cases. It provides at least some degree of certainty upon which individuals can rely in the conduct of their affairs, as well as a basis for orderly development of legal rules. Their Lordships nevertheless recognise that too rigid adherence to precedent may lead to injustice in a particular case and also unduly restrict the proper development of the law. They propose, therefore, to modify their present practice and, while treating former decisions of this House as normally binding, to depart from a previous decision when it appears right to do so.
>
> In this connection they will bear in mind the danger of disturbing retrospectively the basis on which contracts, settlements of property and fiscal arrangements have been entered into and also the especial need for certainty as to the criminal law.
>
> This announcement is not intended to affect the use of precedent elsewhere than in this House.

This statement is limited in effect as it was only intended to affect the practice of precedent in the House of Lords, not in other courts. The Lords restated that the role of precedent was essential to provide some degree of certainty in judge-made law and, in consequence, previous decisions of the House of Lords will normally be binding. However, the Practice Statement indicates that the House could depart from a previous decision 'when it appears right to do so'.

See further on the retrospective nature of case law at 5.6.1.

The power to depart from its previous decisions was thus established. The question arises: when is it *right* to depart from a previous decision? The Practice Statement gives some guidance as to this. It may be right to depart from a previous decision, first, where there is a need to avoid injustice in individual cases, and secondly, if the development of the common law is being unduly restricted. This is clearly guidance of a very general and rather vague kind and thus it is difficult to predict when the power in the Practice Statement will be exercised. More specifically, the House of Lords said that caution needed to be exercised in departing from cases concerning

- contracts;
- settlement of property;
- taxation.

 **Example**

Consider why certainty and adhering to precedent might be more important in commercial dealings/interactions such as commercial contracts, property transactions, or tax liabilities. Let's say a solicitor advises a client on the creation of a contract relying on a precedent established by the Supreme Court/House of Lords. What would the implications be if in a subsequent decision of the Supreme Court the previous precedent was overruled? The consequence is likely to be that the solicitor's advice, although accurate when given, would need to be redrawn. The commercial and legal positions of the parties to that contract would be changed and that might have compromised the original negotiation of entering into that contract. Think of the other financial or administrative consequences that might follow the House of Lords overruling precedents in commercial, property, or tax matters.

There is also said to be an especial need to ensure certainty in the criminal law. If a Supreme Court *ratio decidendi* is overruled by a subsequent Supreme Court judgment because, say, the earlier Supreme Court decision was based on a *ratio* that is deemed to be legally erroneous, then there is a risk of injustice. This is because the later judgment would apply retrospectively and that actions or behaviour that were previously thought to be lawful would now not be (or actions that were unlawful, would now be lawful). This has consequences for individuals and the extent to which they know and can adhere to the law. It may even lead to a series of cases being reviewed and or appeals, say, in terms of whether earlier convictions were now safe.

Since 1966, the House of Lords has rarely exercised its power to overrule one of its previous decisions. Examples of such exercise of the Practice Statement power are seen in *R v Secretary of State for the Home Department, ex parte Khawaja* [1984] AC 74; *R v Shivpuri* [1987] AC 1; *Murphy v Brentwood District Council* [1991] 1 AC 398; and *R v G and Another* [2004] 1 AC 1034. You may want to use a legal database and research these cases and consider (a) the principle that was overruled, and (b) the reasons put forward by the House of Lords for doing so.

In *Jones v Secretary of State for Social Services* [1972] AC 944, Lord Reid said that certainty in the law required that the Practice Statement power should be 'used sparingly'. He drew a distinction between cases where an old decision of the House of Lords created a broad principle which might be ready for reconsideration and those cases that concern contractual and/or statutory interpretation. In relation to the latter, Lord Reid said that reconsideration should be rare, as answers to questions of interpretation and construction are difficult to evaluate precisely, and it is often a question of judgment as to the particular approach to be adopted, for example, a narrow literal approach or a mischief/purposive approach. In consequence, in *Re Dowling* [1967] 1 AC 725, the House of Lords declined to rely on the Practice Statement to depart from a previous House of Lords decision because it primarily concerned the construction of a statute and did not involve a 'broad issue of justice or public policy . . . nor . . . any question of legal principle'.

Otherwise, it is generally accepted that finality and certainty in the law are desirable. The Supreme Court/House of Lords is reluctant to overrule its earlier decisions merely on the basis that a previous decision is considered to be wrong. If the approach were otherwise, future litigants might argue that a decision is wrong in the hope that a differently constituted Supreme Court/House of Lords might agree. In *Doherty v Birmingham City Council* [2009] AC 367, the House of Lords was invited to overrule its recent reasoning in *Kay and Others v Lambeth London Borough Council* [2006] 2 AC 465. The facts are not especially relevant for present purposes but the case involved the right of a local authority to obtain an order for possession of a site that had been used for many years as a gypsy and travellers caravan site. The current occupier no longer had a right to remain on the site but was arguing his removal would be a breach of the right to respect for his private and family life, and his home under the European Convention on Human Rights. The House of Lords refused to expressly overrule the decision in *Kay*. Lord Hope said that the power to overrule a recent decision should not be exercised unless there was a good reason for doing so.

Again, in conjoined appeals of *Cavendish Square Holding BV v El Makdessi* and *ParkingEye Ltd v Beavis* [2015] UKSC 67, the Supreme Court was asked to abrogate, or restrict, the penalty rule in the law of contract (note that we considered the case of *Beavis* at the outset of this chapter). This would have required a departure from the decision of the House of Lords in *Dunlop Pneumatic Tyre Co Ltd v New Garage and Motor Co* [1915] AC 79. The Supreme Court refused to effectively repeal or nullify the rule; instead they sought to clarify and then restate it.

The following cases further illustrate the factors that the Supreme Court/House of Lords may take into account in determining whether or not to depart from a previous decision. In *Horton v Sadler* [2007] 1 AC 307, the House of Lords departed from its previous decision in *Walkley v Precision Forgings Ltd* [1979] 1 WLR 606. The latter case had constrained the exercise of a discretion under s.33 of the Limitation Act 1980 to extend the time limit an individual has to bring a personal injury claim beyond the usual three years. The House of Lords departed from the reasoning in *Walkley*. In doing so it considered that its decision would not impact upon contracts, settlements of property, or fiscal arrangements as it was not a rule which had been relied upon in entering upon such dealings. Similarly, the criminal law would be unaffected and there would be no detriment to public administration. Lord Bingham then gave three specific reasons for departing from *Walkley*: that it unfairly deprived claimants of a right to bring a claim that Parliament intended them to have; that it had driven the Court of Appeal to draw distinctions which, while correct, were so fine and granular that it demonstrated the lack of credibility in the law; and that it subverted the clear intention of Parliament. The decision was one that was plainly wrong and, in the circumstances, justice and certainty would be promoted by departing from it.

R v Shivpuri [1987] AC 1 was another House of Lords case that concerned the construction of a statute. The appellant had carried a package from India which he believed to contain heroin or cannabis, but which actually contained harmless vegetable matter. He was convicted of attempting to be knowingly concerned in dealing with and harbouring a controlled drug, namely heroin, the importation of which was prohibited, contrary to s.1(1) of the Criminal Attempts Act 1981 and s.170(1)(b) of the Customs and Excise Management Act 1979. The House of Lords was asked:

> [D]oes a person commit an offence under s.1 of the Criminal Attempts Act 1981 where, if the facts were as that person believed them to be, the full offence would have been committed by him, but where on the true facts the offence which that person set out to commit was in law impossible?

On the facts, the appellant had a guilty mind but was actually performing a lawful act; nonetheless, their Lordships thought the answer to the question posed was 'yes' and that an offence had been committed. However, this answer was inconsistent with that given in *Anderton v Ryan* [1985] AC 560, which had been decided by the House of Lords only the previous year.

The House of Lords departed from its decision in *Anderton v Ryan* on the basis that the decision was wrong. Lord Bridge, although recognising the need for certainty in criminal law, felt that it was permissible to depart from the decision having regard to the following considerations:

- Despite *Anderton v Ryan* being a recent decision it was better to correct an error sooner rather than later.
- In the present case, it was unlikely that the individual was acting on the belief that his actions were lawful as under *Anderton v Ryan*, thereby justifying the change to ensure his behaviour was criminalised.
- Finally, a failure to use the Practice Statement and depart from *Anderton v Ryan* would have the effect of nullifying the Criminal Attempts Act 1981, because it would uphold an earlier decision in *R v Smith (Roger)* [1975] AC 476 and leave the law unchanged.

The case of *Austin v Southwark London Borough Council* [2010] UKSC 28 concerned the interpretation of s.82(2) of the Housing Act 1985. The House of Lords considered the interpretation in *Knowsley Housing Trust v White (Secretary of State for Communities and Local Government intervening)* [2009] AC 636 and were invited to overrule a much earlier Court of Appeal decision that stated the meaning of the section: *Thompson v Elmbridge Borough Council* [1987] 1 WLR 1425. The court in *Knowsley* refused to do so. In *Austin* it was argued that *Knowsley* (and therefore overruling *Thompson*) should be departed from as the interpretation of s.82 (2) was incorrect. The court in

Austin similarly refused to do so. Although the Court noted that the interpretation of the section was possibly wrong, it cited, amongst other reasons, the fact that the *Thompson* definition had been relied upon in tens of thousands of cases, and the retrospective effect of overruling it would lead to incalculable uncertainty. In addition, Parliament had passed the Housing and Regeneration Act 2008. Therefore, stating that *Thompson* was no longer good law would have the effect of undermining the legislation and run counter to the intention of Parliament as it was introduced on the basis that the definition of *Thompson* was valid and upheld.

In *Knauer v Ministry of Justice* [2016] AC 908, a case concerning damages for death under the Fatal Accidents Act 1976, the Supreme Court was willing to depart from two House of Lords cases, *Cookson v Knowles* [1979] AC 556 and *Graham v Dodds* [1983] 1 WLR 808. The reason for doing so was that there had been 'a material change in the relevant legal landscape since the earlier decisions, namely the decision in *Wells v Wells* [1999] 1 AC 345 and the adoption of the Ogden tables' (a means of calculating damages for future losses in cases involving personal injury and/or death). This change, taken together with the unfair outcomes caused by the application of the two House of Lords decisions, required the law to be changed. The argument that such a change should be left to Parliament was rejected because the law that was under consideration had been made by judges. It should therefore be remedied by judges. In any event, the change would not have wider implications and it had been recognised by the Law Commission in a report that legislation was unnecessary.

In *R v Jogee* [2016] UKSC 8, the Supreme Court was asked to reconsider the criminal law relating to 'parasitic accessory liability'. Although, technically incorrect, it is often characterised as the law on 'joint enterprise'. The relevant background concerned secondary parties (D2) who have been engaged with one or more others in a criminal venture to commit crime A, but in doing so the principal (D1) commits a second crime, crime B. In many of the reported cases, crime B is murder committed in the course of some other criminal venture (e.g. group retaliatory violence) but it has been difficult to demonstrate who struck the fatal blow, despite everyone encouraging it. The precise question the UKSC were considering was: What is the mental element which the law requires of the secondary party (to hold him liable for crime B)?

The common law position was stated by the Privy Council in *Chan Wing-Siu* [1985] AC 168 and developed by the House of Lords in *R v Powell* and *R v English* [1999] 1 AC 1. Their approach to the kind of situation described above was that the mental element required of D2 was simply that he foresaw the possibility that D1 might commit crime B. If D2 did foresee this, his continued participation in crime A was not simply evidence that he intended to assist crime B, but an automatic authorisation of it. So D2 was guilty under this rule, even if he did not intend to assist in crime B at all. This set a lower test for D2 than for D1, who would only be guilty of crime B if he had the necessary mental element for that crime, usually intent. The approach also stood in contrast to the usual rule that secondary parties charged with assisting or encouraging the principal to commit crime B needed to demonstrate an intent on the part of the principal to do so. The net effect of this approach was that secondary party liability for murder involved a lesser degree of mental culpability than the crime of murder itself.

The Supreme Court decided that the Privy Council (subsequently developed by the House of Lords) had fallen into error and the legal approach should be effectively overruled. The UKSC argued it was right to do so for a number of reasons (see [79]–[87]). To cite only a few, the fundamental argument was about re-establishing the coherence of liability between the principal and secondary party so that the latter should be only liable when he has the intention to assist or encourage the principal to commit crime B. Secondly, in the Privy Council and the House of Lords not all relevant authorities were considered and those that were, were considered erroneously, often distorted by general policy arguments. The current state of the law had also led to significant practical issues including a large number of appeals.

It is worth highlighting that the Supreme Court rejected the argument that change should be left to Parliament, on the basis that the doctrine of secondary liability is a common law doctrine and should be corrected by the courts. In addition, such a correction would bring the common law into line with legislation made by Parliament in relation to inchoate criminal liability: see s.44 of the Serious Crime Act 2007. In consequence, the Supreme Court took the opportunity to restate the law to promote certainty, but was mindful of the likely new appeals that such a change would bring. We would certainly recommend reading the case.

Visit the online resources to watch the Supreme Court judgment on R v Jogee.

Finally, in *Murphy v Brentwood District Council* [1991] 1 AC 398, the House of Lords had to consider the development of negligence in the law of tort. The previous decision in *Anns v Merton London Borough Council* [1978] AC 728 was considered not to have proceeded on any basis of principle at all and, in the words of Lord Keith, 'constituted a remarkable example of judicial legislation'. The effect of the decision in *Anns* was to cause uncertainty in the law of negligence and it was not one that citizens or local authorities would rely upon to a significant extent in conducting their affairs. Lord Keith in *Murphy* continued that the decision in *Anns* was not supported by 'any coherent and logically based doctrine behind it' and its effect was to put the law of negligence into a state of confusion. In consequence, the decision in *Anns* was considered to be wrong and was departed from.

The evidence suggests that it can be difficult to identify the circumstances or conditions in which the Supreme Court/House of Lords may or may not be willing to depart from one of its previous decisions. Cross and Harris, in *Precedent in English Law*, argue that there are several factors that the House of Lords will consider in deciding whether to exercise its power.

First, the Lords must be persuaded that the change will improve the law. In *Miliangos v George Frank (Textiles) Ltd* [1976] AC 443, the Practice Statement was used to overrule an earlier precedent of *Re United Railways* [1961] AC 1007 and established that in an English civil case, the court may award judgment by way of damages in foreign currency (rather than in British Sterling). Secondly, something of significance must have been overlooked in arriving at the earlier decision or there has been a 'material change in circumstances': see *R v Shivpuri*, discussed earlier. Thirdly, given the retrospective nature of overruling, consideration will be given to any reliance placed upon the House of Lords precedent. Fourthly, if Parliament has passed legislation which assumes the existence of a decision of the House of Lords, it is unlikely that such a decision will be overruled: see *British Railways Board v Herrington* [1972] AC 877, in which the House of Lords held that a duty of care could be owed to trespassers and which overruled an earlier House of Lords precedent, *Addie v Dumbreck* [1929] AC 358. This particular line of case law was essentially superseded by the introduction of the Occupiers Liability Act 1984. Fifthly, and finally (at p.142),

> [T]here is some support for the view that the House should not overrule an earlier decision, even if thought to be mistaken, where the issue is moot—that is where, on the facts of the instant case, it would make no difference to the outcome whether the impugned ruling were part of the law or not.

If a Supreme Court/House of Lords decision is inconsistent with a later decision of the European Court of Human Rights, should a lower court follow the decision of the Supreme Court/House of Lords or that of the European Court of Human Rights? See the House of Lords decision in *Kay and Others v Lambeth London Borough Council* [2006] 2 AC 465, discussed later.

5.5.3 **Court of Appeal**

The Court of Appeal is split into two divisions: the Court of Appeal (Civil Division) and the Court of Appeal (Criminal Division). The rules of precedent that operate in each division, while largely the same, differ in some important respects. This section turns to identifying those differences.

Court of Appeal (Civil Division)

The Court of Appeal (Civil Division) is bound by the decisions of the Court of Justice of the EU and the Supreme Court/House of Lords. However, the Court binds all the courts beneath it in the hierarchy of courts. Is the Court of Appeal (Civil Division) bound by its previous decisions? The answer is normally 'yes', but subject to some limited exceptions.

The precedent practice operating in the Court of Appeal (Civil Division) was established in *Young v Bristol Aeroplane Co Ltd* [1944] KB 718. Lord Greene MR said that the Court of Appeal was bound by its own previous decisions and by decisions of courts of equal jurisdiction subject to the following exceptions:

(a) where the Court of Appeal is faced by two conflicting decisions of its own, the present court must choose which decision to follow (obviously leaving one that cannot be followed);

(b) the Court of Appeal must refuse to follow a decision of its own which conflicts with a Supreme Court/House of Lords decision, even though the decision of the Court of Appeal has not been expressly overruled (this is self-evident because the Supreme Court is higher in the court hierarchy);

(c) if a previous decision of the Court of Appeal is considered to have been given *per incuriam* then the present Court of Appeal is not bound to follow it.

Young v Bristol Aeroplane Co Ltd also confirmed that a full court, consisting of six or nine judges, has no greater power than a usual court consisting of three judges. Also, when the Court of Appeal sits with two judges, the decision has the same authority as a three-judge court: see *Langley v North West Water* and T. Prime and G. Scanlan, 'Stare Decisis and the Court of Appeal: Judicial Confusion and Judicial Reform?' (2004) 23 CJQ 212.

Returning to the *Young* exceptions mentioned above, this section proceeds to consider each of them in more detail.

(a) Conflicting decisions of the Court of Appeal

Normally, a later Court of Appeal is bound to follow previous binding decisions of the Court. But, infrequently, an inconsistency or conflict in the case law might arise that is only apparent to the latest court that is required to decide a particular matter.

This became evident in *Farley v Skinner* [2000] PNLR 441, which concerned a claim for damages for disappointment arising from a breach of contract. The rule which emerged from *Watts v Morrow* [1991] 1 WLR 1421 was that damages were payable for disappointment if the object of the *entire* contract was to give pleasure, relaxation, or peace of mind and this had not been achieved. *Watts v Morrow* was followed in *Knott v Bolton* (1995) 11 Const LJ 375. However, two Court of Appeal decisions, *Jackson v Chrysler Acceptances Ltd* [1978] RTR 474 and *Branchett v Beaney* [1992] 3 All ER 910, suggested that disappointment damages were recoverable where *one* of the objects of a contract (as opposed to being the object of the entire contract) was to provide enjoyment or peace of mind. Neither of these cases was cited in *Knott v Bolton*. In consequence, the Court of Appeal (Civil Division) in *Farley v Skinner* was faced with inconsistent authority. The Court, by a majority of 2 to 1, nonetheless decided the case by following *Watts v Morrow*. The decision of the Court of Appeal in *Farley v Skinner* was reversed by the House of Lords. See 5.6.2.

The general approach taken by the Court of Appeal was expressed in *Patel v Secretary of State for the Home Department* [2012] EWCA Civ 741, which stated that where the Court of Appeal must choose between conflicting authorities, the general rule is that the later decision is to be preferred *if* the latter case fully considered the earlier decision (Lord Neuberger MR at [59]).

In *Globe Motors Inc. v TRW Lucas Varity Electric Steering Ltd* [2016] EWCA Civ 396, a conflict between two previous Court of Appeal decisions had to be resolved. The Court considered, among other issues, the effect of a written clause that expressly prevented the terms being altered by an oral agreement (although the case was decided on other grounds). In *United Bank Ltd v Asif* (11 February 2000, unreported), it was held that such a clause prevented a later oral variation of the written contract. However, in *World Online Telecom v I-Way Ltd* [2002] EWCA Civ 413, the Court of Appeal left open the door after a more detailed consideration. This latter decision was given in ignorance of the decision in *United Bank Ltd v Asif*. Thus, in the *Globe Motors* case, the Court was faced with the prospect of determining which case to follow. Beatson LJ said that these previous decisions of the Court of Appeal were inconsistent and therefore not binding. The Court of Appeal preferred the approach in *World Online* which was based on freedom of contract, and that did leave an opportunity to permit a contract to be varied orally despite the existence of a clause that sought to limit this route of variation.

(b) A Court of Appeal decision, though not expressly overruled, cannot stand with a decision of the Supreme Court/House of Lords

Under the normal rules of judicial precedent, a Court of Appeal decision should not conflict with a decision of the Supreme Court/House of Lords. The exception is straightforward. In *Iqbal v Whipps Cross University NHS Trust* [2007] EWCA Civ 1190, this exception was clarified when the Court faced a slightly different problem. On this occasion, the Court of Appeal was faced with the problem of one of its own previous decisions being inconsistent with an *earlier* decision of the House of Lords. It was held that the exception does not apply where the inconsistency of a decision of the Court of Appeal is with a *previous* House of Lords decision, unless the Court of Appeal decision is given *per incuriam*. If an earlier Court of Appeal wrongly distinguishes or misinterprets an existing Supreme Court/House of Lords decision, a later Court of Appeal is still bound by the decision of the previous Court of Appeal. Simply expressing disagreement with the reasoning of the earlier court is an insufficient ground for not following the precedent. The correct approach is for the 'error' to be considered by the Supreme Court/House of Lords.

The more difficult question is where a previous Court of Appeal decision appears to be inconsistent with a *subsequent* decision of the Supreme Court/House of Lords. (See Cross and Harris, p.147.) In *R v Wood* [2008] EWCA Crim 1305, the Court of Appeal effectively overruled the earlier Court of Appeal judgment in *R v Tandy* [1989] 1 WLR 350. The issue concerned whether alcoholism amounted to an 'abnormality of mind' for the purposes of the diminished responsibility defence. The precise focus was whether the drinking was truly involuntary rather than simply failing to resist a craving for drink. The Court in *Wood* stated that the House of Lords decision in *R v Dietschmann* [2003] UKHL 10 required a re-assessment of the way in which *Tandy* is applied.

(c) Per incuriam

In *Morelle v Wakeling* [1955] 2 QB 379, Sir Raymond Evershed MR explained *per incuriam* in the following terms:

> As a general rule the only cases in which decisions should be held to have been given *per incuriam* are those of decisions given in ignorance or forgetfulness of some inconsistent statutory provision or of some authority binding on the court concerned: so that in such cases some part of the decision or some step in the reasoning on which it is based is found, on that account, to be demonstrably wrong. This definition is not necessarily exhaustive, but cases not strictly within it which can properly be held to have been decided *per incuriam* must, in our judgment, consistently with the stare decisis rule which is an essential feature of our law, be, in the language of Lord Greene MR, of the rarest occurrence.

In cases involving statutory childcare, in *R (on the application of W) v Lambeth LBC* [2002] 2 ALL ER 901, the Court of Appeal (Civil Division) held that its previous decision in *R (on the application of A) v Lambeth LBC* [2001] EWCA Civ 1624 had been given *per incuriam.* Brooke LJ said that, had the Court of Appeal in *A* been directed to s.122 of the Immigration and Asylum Act 1999 and s.17A of the Children Act 1989, alongside the housing allocation arrangements at the time, it must or would have decided *R (on the application of A) v Lambeth LBC* differently. In *Walsall MBC v Secretary of State for Communities and Local Government* [2015] JPL 1183, the Court of Appeal considered whether a previous decision, *Wendy Fair Markets Ltd v Secretary of State for the Environment* [1996] JPL 649, had been given *per incuriam* but concluded that the case was binding on the court.

In *CPS v Gohil* [2012] EWCA Civ 1550, the Court of Appeal thought the decision in *BOC Ltd v Instrument Technology Ltd* [2002] QB 537 was *per incuriam* as the previous court had failed to consider the presumption that Parliament legislates in conformity with the UK's international obligations.

In *Williams v Fawcett* [1986] QB 604—a case involving the notice requirements before committing someone to prison for contempt—Sir John Donaldson MR emphasised that the concept of *per incuriam* did not merely apply in instances of ignorance or forgetfulness of an inconsistent statutory provision or binding precedent, but also encompassed a 'manifest slip or error'. However, as already seen, such instances must be 'of the rarest occurrence'. Sir John Donaldson MR, in deciding that previous decisions of the Court of Appeal had been given *per incuriam*, said that the situation before him was 'exceptional'. The reasons for so deciding were: the growth of the error in the law could be clearly detected; the cases all concerned the liberty of the subject; and an appeal to the House of Lords, where the error could be corrected, was unlikely.

Further guidance as to what might be considered 'exceptional' was given by Lord Donaldson in *Rickards v Rickards* [1990] Fam 194. His Lordship said that a previous decision of the Court of Appeal could be treated as *per incuriam* where it concerned procedural rules (rather than substantive rules), where in error it had been denied that the court had jurisdiction, and where an appeal to the House of Lords to correct the error was unlikely.

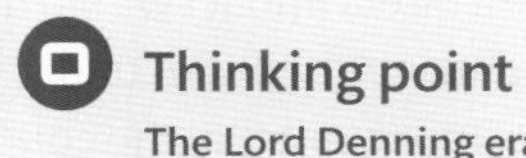

The Lord Denning era

During the 1970s, the ever-so-slightly controversial Lord Denning waged a campaign to free the Court of Appeal (Civil Division) from the bonds of precedent. He was ultimately unsuccessful. To illustrate this point please read *Davis v Johnson* [1979] AC 264 and compare Lord Denning's judgment in the Court of Appeal with the opinions of Lords Diplock and Salmon in the House of Lords.

The Court of Appeal is generally an intermediate court of appeal, not a final court of appeal, unlike the Supreme Court. Lord Diplock, in *Davis v Johnson*, said (at p.326): 'In an appellate court of last resort a balance must be struck between the need on the one side for the legal certainty resulting from the binding effect of previous decisions, and, on the other side the avoidance of undue restriction on the proper development of the law.' The 'proper development of the law' may safely be left to the 'court of last resort', in other words, an appeal to the Supreme Court; the need for legal certainty would be undermined if the Court of Appeal was not bound by its previous decisions. Do you agree? Do you think it is justified that the Court of Appeal is more strictly bound by its previous decisions, compared with what is now UK Supreme Court and their reliance on the Practice Statement?

Finally, another exception to the operation of precedent in the Court of Appeal was considered by the House of Lords in *R (on the application of RJM) v Secretary of State for Work and Pensions* [2009] AC 311. The question was whether a previous decision of the Court of Appeal that was inconsistent with a subsequent decision of the European Court of Human Rights, was binding on the current Court of Appeal. Lord Neuberger reaffirmed that the Court of Appeal should follow a decision of the House of Lords even if the decision of the House of Lords may be, or is, inconsistent with a subsequent decision of the European Court of Human Rights (save for wholly exceptional circumstances: see *Kay and others v Lambeth London Borough Council* [2006] 2 AC 465, [45]). However, his Lordship said that the situation is different when the Court of Appeal is considering the binding nature of its own previous decisions. While normally binding, Court of Appeal decisions may be departed from in certain situations, as stated in *Young v Bristol Aeroplane Co Ltd* [1944] KB 718, 729–30, but in the light of the Human Rights Act 1998 and in particular s.2(1)(a), the exceptions in *Young* may be developed. Lord Neuberger (at [66]) concluded that:

> the law in areas such as that of precedent should be free to develop, albeit in a principled and cautious fashion, to take into account . . . changes. Accordingly, I would hold that, where it concludes that one of its previous decisions is inconsistent with a subsequent decision of the ECtHR, the Court of Appeal should be free (but not obliged) to depart from that decision.

There are two points to note in this quotation. First, the 'changes' mentioned refer to the fact that when *Young* was decided, the decisions of international courts, in this instance the European Court of Human Rights, did not have a direct impact within the English legal system, until the enactment of the Human Rights Act 1998. Secondly, in order for the common law to develop in an orderly way it is important that the courts do not depart too freely from precedents. Lord Neuberger emphasised the need for caution when departing from otherwise binding precedent. It is undecided whether this practice outlined by Lord Neuberger will also apply to Divisional Courts in the High Court, as those courts are generally bound by their own previous decisions subject to the exceptions outlined in *Young*.

Court of Appeal (Criminal Division)

The Court of Appeal (Criminal Division) is bound by the decisions of the Supreme Court/House of Lords and binds all the courts beneath it. The rule in *Young v Bristol Aeroplane Co Ltd* also applies to the Criminal Division. A further exception was established by the Court of Criminal Appeal in *R v Taylor* [1950] 2 KB 368. In this case, Lord Goddard CJ said:

> The Court of Appeal in civil matters usually considers itself bound by its own decisions or by decisions of a court of co-ordinate jurisdiction. For instance, it considers itself bound by its own decisions and by those of the Exchequer Chamber . . . In civil matters this is essential in order to preserve the rule of stare decisis. This court, however, has to deal with questions involving the liberty of the subject, and if it finds, on reconsideration, that, in the opinion of a full court assembled for that purpose, the law has been either misapplied or misunderstood in a decision which it has previously given, and that, on the strength of that decision, an accused person has been sentenced and imprisoned it is the bounden duty of the court to reconsider the earlier decision with a view to seeing whether that person had been properly convicted.

The reference to the liberty of the subject justifies a different approach to *stare decisis* in the Court of Appeal (Criminal Division). It is argued that, in criminal cases, justice is more important than certainty.

An example of an application of this exception is to be found in *R v Simpson* [2004] QB 118, where the Court of Appeal (Criminal Division), sitting with five judges, concluded that the decision in *R v Palmer* [2002] EWCA Crim 2202 was wrong as the law had been misunderstood and misapplied. The Court said that, in exercising the discretion to decide that a previous case had been wrongly decided, the constitution of the court (i.e. number and/or seniority of the presiding judges) would be of relevance.

This exception to *stare decisis* and the *per incuriam* doctrine was considered in *R v Rowe* [2007] QB 975. In this case, the Court of Appeal (Criminal Division), consisting of five judges, considered *Simpson* and concluded that *R v M* [2007] EWCA Crim 298, a previous Court of Appeal (Criminal Division) decision, was wrongly decided as it was based upon 'wrong assumptions and false analysis'. However, the reason why the Court of Appeal (Criminal Division) refused to follow the decision in *R v M* was that it had been given, said Lord Phillips, 'in circumstances that were truly "*per incuriam*"'. Hence, *R v M* was not followed because:

- the reasoning of the previous court had not had regard to relevant authority and as a result arrived at false assumptions;
- the reasoning of the previous court had not followed the written submissions of the appellant, with the consequence that the respondent's written submissions had not dealt with the points upon which the Court based its reasoning;
- the judgment was effectively extempore, that is, at the time without time for research or reflection.

By contrast, in *R v Varma (Aloke) and Others* [2011] QB 398, the Court of Appeal (Criminal Division) refused to overrule its previous decision in *R v Clarke* [2010] 1 WLR 223, after it had been argued by the Crown that the decision in *R v Clarke* was given *per incuriam*. While noting that *R v Simpson* allowed the court discretion to escape a binding decision when it is legally wrong, the permissible discretion is limited. Lord Judge CJ said (at p.411):

> [W]hat Simpson does not establish, however, is that a five-judge constitution is entitled to disregard or deprive the only previous decision of the three-judge constitution of the court of its authority on a distinct and clearly identified point of law, reached after full argument and close analysis of the relevant legislative provisions. This principle applies with particular emphasis when the consequences of doing so would be to the disadvantage of the defendant.

The Court of Appeal held that the decision in *Clarke* was based on the full relevant information available at the time; there was no possibility of conflict among relevant authorities; earlier decisions had not been misunderstood; the Court had given a reserved judgment considered in meticulous detail; and, in consequence, it was not open to even a five-judge court to hold that *Clarke* was wrongly decided. (Note that *R v Varma (Aloke)* was appealed to the Supreme Court [2012] UKSC 42 where *R v Clarke* was overruled.)

Should a Court of Appeal be faced with conflicting Supreme Court/House of Lords and Privy Council (see at 5.5.8) decisions, the rules of precedent would seem to dictate that the Supreme Court/House of Lords decision, rather than that of the Privy Council, must be followed. However, there is at least one unique exception.

In *Smith (Morgan)* [2001] 1 AC 146, the House of Lords considered a partial defence to murder, and more precisely, the test for provocation (now termed loss of control). Put simply, this is a defence when a particular event or action, often by the victim, has led the defendant to lose control of their ordinary powers of restraint. The House were considering the legal test and determined that in judging whether a reasonable person in the defendant's position would have lost their self-control, all the personal characteristics (e.g. mental vulnerabilities or frailties) of the defendant could be considered. A few years later, in *Attorney General for Jersey v Holley* [2005] 2 AC 580, the Privy Council (consisting of nine Lords of Appeal in Ordinary, 75 per cent of the judges in the House of Lords) held by a majority of 6 to 3 that the test of provocation required judging whether a reasonable person in the defendant's position would have lost their self-control, but only by reference to a reasonable person exercising ordinary powers of self-control (i.e. irrespective of the defendant's personal characteristics). Lord Nicholls, delivering the judgment on behalf of the majority, said: 'This appeal, being heard by an enlarged board of nine members, is concerned to resolve this conflict and clarify definitively the present state of English law, and hence Jersey law, on this important subject.'

In *R v James (Leslie)* [2006] QB 588, the Court of Appeal (Criminal Division), sitting as a court of five judges, noted that the majority of the Privy Council had expressly stated that *Holley* was to 'clarify definitively' English law in relation to the defence of provocation, and that the deciding law lords in *Holley* largely still sat in the House of Lords, and in consequence, the Court of Appeal should follow *Holley* and not *Smith (Morgan)*. Strictly speaking, *Smith (Morgan)* was not overruled. It should be noted that the defendant in *James* sought leave to appeal to the House of Lords but this was refused by the Appeal Committee of the House of Lords.

Again, on the other hand, in *Sinclair Investments (UK) Ltd v Versailles Trade Finance Ltd (in administrative receivership) and Others* [2011] 3 WLR 1153, the Court of Appeal had to consider whether to follow a Privy Council decision, *Attorney General of Hong Kong* [1994] 1 AC 324, in preference to previous decisions of its own, *Metropolitan Bank v Heiron* (1880) 5 Ex D 319 and *Lister & Co v Stubbs* 45 Ch D 1. The Court of Appeal decided that it should follow its own previous decisions unless, in the words of Lord Neuberger, 'there are domestic authorities which show that the decisions of this court were per incuriam or at least of doubtful reliability'. The general position is that the Court of Appeal, where faced by a conflicting Privy Council decision, should follow its own precedents and leave it to the Supreme Court to overrule the precedent if appropriate. The approach of the Court of Appeal must now be viewed in the light of the judgment of the Supreme Court in *Willers v Joyce (No 2)* [2016] UKSC 44: see 5.5.8.

5.5.4 **High Court—Divisional Courts and at first instance**

It is important to identify the jurisdiction being exercised by the Divisional Courts of the High Court. Divisional Courts may exercise appellate jurisdiction and supervisory jurisdiction.

Appellate jurisdiction

A Divisional Court in civil cases is bound by the Supreme Court/House of Lords and the Court of Appeal. It is bound by its previous decisions, subject to the exceptions in *Young v Bristol Aeroplane Co Ltd*. This was established in *Huddersfield Police Authority v Watson* [1947] KB 842.

A Divisional Court in criminal cases is bound by the Supreme Court/House of Lords and the Court of Appeal. It is bound by its previous decisions, subject to the exceptions in *Young v Bristol Aeroplane Co Ltd*. A further exception was established in *R v Manchester Coroner, ex parte Tal* [1985] QB 67. In the latter case, Robert Goff LJ said that in criminal cases there was no material distinction between the exercise of appellate jurisdiction by a Divisional Court from decisions of magistrates by way of case stated and the exercise of appellate jurisdiction by the Court of Appeal (Criminal Division), with further appeals from each court lying to the House of Lords. In consequence (at p.79), '[i]t is difficult to imagine that nowadays, in such cases, a Divisional Court would adopt a different attitude from the Court of Appeal (Criminal Division) in *Reg v Gould* [1968] 2 QB 65'. So it appears that the precedent practice in the Court of Appeal (Criminal Division) also operates when a Divisional Court is exercising criminal jurisdiction.

In *Younghusband v Luftig* [1949] 2 KB 354, Lord Goddard CJ said that a Divisional Court of five judges had no more power than a court of three or two judges; a Divisional Court is bound by its own decisions, whatever the number of judges constituting it.

Supervisory jurisdiction

In *R v Manchester Coroner, ex parte Tal* [1985] QB 67, it was further decided that when a Divisional Court is exercising supervisory jurisdiction over inferior courts and tribunals by way of judicial review it is not bound by previous decisions of another Divisional Court. It was expected that the power to depart from previous decisions would be exercised rarely.

High Court at first instance

A judge sitting in the High Court at first instance is bound by the Supreme Court/House of Lords, the Court of Appeal, and Divisional Courts. Decisions of the High Court are binding on the County Court and magistrates' courts. At first instance, a judge will follow a decision of another judge of first instance, unless persuaded that that judgment is wrong; courts of equal jurisdiction do not bind each other (see *Huddersfield Police Authority v Watson* [1947] KB 842; for a recent example, see *R (on the application of Jollah) v Secretary of State for the Home Department* [2017] EWHC 330 (Admin)). A single judge exercising supervisory jurisdiction is not strictly bound, but the Court in *ex parte Tal* said that it was difficult to imagine a single judge departing from a decision of a Divisional Court.

While judges at first instance are not strictly bound by previous decisions of judges in the High Court, later judges will not depart from such a decision too readily. Judicial comity and a degree of respect among the judges means that previous decisions are likely to be followed. If a judge departs from an earlier decision, this then leaves a problem in the law for a later judge who will inevitably be facing two opposing High

Court decisions. The approach to adopt was outlined in *Colchester Estates (Cardiff) v Carlton Industries* [1986] Ch 80. Nourse J, relying upon statements made by Denning J in *Minister of Pensions v Higham* [1948] 2 KB 153, said that where there are conflicting decisions of the High Court at first instance, the later decision is to be preferred if it was arrived at after a full consideration of the earlier case.

Thinking point

How certain can one be?

The reasons behind the approach of Nourse J are, once again, certainty and finality. There has to be an end to argument on a point of law for the sake of certainty. Given the non-binding nature of a High Court decision on later sittings of the High Court, the point could be argued again and again. Obviously Nourse J's approach promotes certainty and invites a definitive ruling to be sought by way of an appeal to the Court of Appeal.

In the first instance case of *Miliangos v George Frank*, Bristow J faced what he thought were conflicting authorities from the appellate courts: *Re United Railways of Havana and Regla Warehouses Ltd* [1961] AC 1007 from the House of Lords, and *Schorsch Meier v Hennin* [1975] QB 416 from the Court of Appeal. Bristow J chose to follow the earlier decisions of the House of Lords, deciding that the Court of Appeal's later decision in *Schorsch Meier v Hennin* was given *per incuriam*. When the *Miliangos* case reached the House of Lords, Lord Simon declared that the Court of Appeal in *Schorsch* had considered *Re United Railways of Havana and Regla Warehouses Ltd* in reaching its decision and that it was not made *per incuriam*. In any event, his Lordship continued that in such instances of conflict, the decision of the immediately superior court ought to be followed. It was not for an inferior court to rule that a superior court's decision was *per incuriam*. Reliance was placed upon the words of Lord Diplock in *Baker v The Queen* [1975] AC 774, 788:

> [T]he *per incuriam* rule . . . does not apply to decisions of courts of appellate jurisdiction superior to that of the court in which the rule is sought to be invoked: *Broome v. Cassell & Co. Ltd.* [1972] A.C. 1027. To permit this use of the *per incuriam* rule would open the door to disregard of precedent by the court of inferior jurisdiction by the simple device of holding that decisions of superior courts with which it disagreed must have been given *per incuriam*.

Thinking point

Certainty at the expense of chaos

Lord Simon arrived at this conclusion on the basis that a failure to follow an immediately superior court invited chaos in the law. Should the Court of Appeal have erred in its decision, the correct way forward would be by way of appeal to the House of Lords (now the

Supreme Court), which could be achieved from the High Court by the 'leapfrog' procedure under the Administration of Justice Act 1969. By s.12 of that Act, an appeal may go directly from the High Court to the Supreme Court if a point of law of general public importance is involved and it is one 'in respect of which the judge is bound by a decision of the Court of Appeal or of the Supreme Court in previous proceedings, and was fully considered in the judgments given by the Court of Appeal or Supreme Court (as the case may be) in those previous proceedings'. In this way the costs of a needless appeal to the Court of Appeal could be avoided.

5.5.5 **The Crown Court**

The Crown Court is bound by all the courts above it in the hierarchy, including the Divisional Court of the Queen's Bench Division. Cross and Harris assert:

> It has been convincingly argued the precedential effect of Crown Court decisions does not vary with the status of the presiding judge and that, in view of the absence of any systematic reporting of such decisions, a Crown Court ruling does not bind another Crown Court or a magistrates' court.

Nevertheless, the decisions are persuasive.

5.5.6 **The County Court and magistrates' courts**

These courts are bound by all the courts above them in the hierarchy, but do not bind themselves or other courts.

5.5.7 **Family Court**

As was seen in Chapter 2, the jurisdiction of the courts in relation to family law is exercised by the Family Court in place of the High Court (in part), the County Court, and magistrates' courts. The jurisdiction of the court is exercised by judiciary of all levels, for example High Court judges (puisne judges), Circuit judges, district judges, District Judges (Magistrates' Court), and justices of the peace not being District Judges (Magistrates' Court). As the Family Court comprises various levels of the judiciary, an issue of judicial precedent arises, that is, are the decisions within the Family Court of equal status? Section 31C(2) of the Matrimonial and Family Proceedings Act 1984 (as amended by Sch.10 to the Crime and Courts Act 2013) deals with the issue of precedent by indicating which decisions of judges in the Family Court are to be followed by which other members of the judiciary sitting in the Family Court. For example, a decision of a High Court judge is to be followed by circuit judges, district judges, District Judges (Magistrates' Court), and justices of the peace.

5.5.8 **Judicial Committee of the Privy Council**

The Judicial Committee of the Privy Council hears appeals from many Commonwealth countries (e.g. Jamaica), as well as the United Kingdom's overseas territories (e.g. Gibraltar or the Falkland Islands) and Crown dependencies (e.g. the Isle of Man). Although likely to have similar common law origins, the law in these countries may differ from that of England and Wales. Uniquely, the judges sitting in the Judicial Committee of the Privy Council will predominantly be Justices of the Supreme Court. Nonetheless, decisions of this court are not officially binding on English courts but will be persuasive. Indeed, in some limited instances, they can be so persuasive as to be judged to be effectively binding in all but name.

First, the Judicial Committee of the Privy Council does not strictly bind itself, but a decision may be departed from only with the greatest hesitation: *Gideon Nkambule v R* [1950] AC 379. In terms of other appellate courts, in *Worcester Works v Cooden* [1972] 1 QB 210, Lord Denning confirmed that the Court of Appeal (Civil Division) was not bound by decisions of the Privy Council; he also said that where the Privy Council disapproved of a previous decision of the Court of Appeal, or cast doubt on it, then the present Court of Appeal was at liberty to depart from its own previous decision.

The latest statement of operation of the doctrine of judicial precedent in relation to the Judicial Committee of the Privy Council (JCPC) was in *Willers v Joyce (No 2)* [2016] UKSC 44. This was in fact a UK Supreme Court judgment composed of nine Justices on the bench. Having considered the hierarchical nature of precedent and the need for certainty, Lord Neuberger explained the position of the JCPC. The JCPC is not a court of any part of the United Kingdom, but it almost always applies the common law and the judges will almost always be Justices of the Supreme Court. Three consequences flow from these observations:

1. The starting point is that decisions of the JCPC cannot bind the courts of England and Wales and cannot override any decision of a court of England and Wales.
2. Nonetheless, given that the judges in the JCPC are also Justices of the Supreme Court and will be applying the common law, decisions are to be treated by all courts of England and Wales as of great weight and persuasive value.
3. The JCPC should regard itself as bound by decisions of the House of Lords or the Supreme Court, particularly if applying the law of England and Wales.

The doctrine of judicial precedent requires the courts of England and Wales to follow decisions of the courts above them in the hierarchy even if there is an inconsistent decision of the JCPC. The Supreme Court considered whether this was an absolute rule or subject to the qualification that the rule does not apply where a judge at first instance or the Court of Appeal takes the view that 'it is a foregone conclusion' that a decision already taken by the JCPC will be accepted by the Supreme Court. Lord Neuberger concluded that, subject to one qualification, the rule should be absolute; a binding precedent is to be followed, irrespective of an inconsistent decision of the

JCPC. The qualification is that if a party in the JCPC challenges a previous decision of the House of Lords, Supreme Court, or Court of Appeal involving an issue of English law, the members of the JCPC can, if they think it appropriate, decide that the previous decision is incorrect. They can then expressly direct that the courts of England and Wales should treat the decision of the JCPC as representing the law of England and Wales and thus it will become binding upon those courts. This approach is plainly a practical solution recognising the authority and composition of the judges of the Privy Council. Reading the judgment in this case is *highly recommended*. It is nine pages long and Lord Neuberger concisely discusses the nature of judicial precedent, the court hierarchy, and the role of the JCPC in this hierarchy. It can be found here: **https://www.supremecourt.uk/cases/docs/uksc-2015-0154a-judgment.pdf**.

5.5.9 Judicial precedent, the Human Rights Act 1998, and the European Court of Human Rights

See 7.6, 'The UK courts and the European Court of Human Rights'.

The Human Rights Act 1998 incorporates the European Convention on Human Rights into domestic law. By s.2(1) of the Human Rights Act 1998:

> A court or tribunal determining a question which has arisen in connection with a Convention right must take into account any
>
> (a) judgment, decision, declaration or advisory opinion of the European Court of Human Rights . . .
>
> whenever made or given, so far as, in the opinion of the court or tribunal, it is relevant to the proceedings in which that question has arisen.

Therefore, the English courts and tribunals are not strictly bound by the decisions of the European Court of Human Rights, they are under a duty to 'take into account' any relevant case law. This must be read alongside s.3 of the Human Rights Act 1998, which provides that the courts, so far as it is possible to do so, must read and give effect to primary legislation and subordinate legislation in a way which is compatible with the Convention rights. Finally, by s.6(1) it is unlawful for a public authority, which includes a court or tribunal, to act in a way which is incompatible with a Convention right.

Overall, the effect of these provisions might be to suggest that a court may depart from a previous binding decision in order for the law to be compliant with rights under the Convention. However, the House of Lords in *Kay and Others v Lambeth London Borough Council* [2006] 2 AC 465 reasserted the authority of judicial precedent. Lord Bingham declared;

> The Strasbourg court authoritatively expounds the interpretation of the rights embodied in the Convention and its protocols, as it must if the Convention is to be uniformly understood by all member states. But in its decisions on particular cases the Strasbourg court accords a margin of appreciation, often generous, to the decisions of national authorities and attaches much importance to the peculiar facts of the case. Thus it

> is for national authorities, including national courts particularly, to decide in the first instance how the principles expounded in Strasbourg should be applied in the special context of national legislation, law, practice and social and other conditions. It is by the decisions of national courts that the domestic standard must be initially set, and to those decisions the ordinary rules of precedent should apply.

Lord Bingham emphasised the need for certainty and for lower courts to respect the traditional rules of judicial precedent. The general approach is that should a lower court consider a binding precedent to be inconsistent with a later decision of the European Court of Human Rights, it may say so and give leave to appeal. Please note that the case of *Kay* and a further case, *Manchester City Council v Pinnock* [2010] UKSC 45, are discussed in further detail in Chapter 7.

The final question to consider is whether the European Court of Human Rights is bound by its own previous decisions. The answer is that it is not strictly bound; however, the underlying reasons for the system of precedent still apply in the operation of the Court. In *Coster v United Kingdom* (2001) 33 EHRR 20, the Court declared:

> While it is not formally bound to follow any of its previous judgments, it is in the interests of legal certainty, foreseeability and equality before the law that the European Court of Human Rights should not depart, without good reason, from precedents laid down in previous cases. Since the Convention is first and foremost a system for the protection of human rights, the court is to have regard to the changing conditions in contracting states and respond, for example, to any emerging consensus as to the standards to be achieved.

5.6 **Methods of avoiding precedents**

This final section now turns to consider when the court can avoid following a precedent (binding or otherwise). In other words, the situations when a court can determine that it is not bound by an earlier precedent by a court in the hierarchy. There are three situations that you need to be most familiar with.

5.6.1 **Overruling**

Overruling occurs when a later court decides that the law as stated in an earlier and different case is wrong and no longer represents the law. Clearly, overruling can only be done within the bounds of the doctrine of *stare decisis*. For example, the Supreme Court can overrule its previous decisions (using the Practice Statement) and those of lower courts, such as the Court of Appeal. However, self-evidently, the Court of Appeal cannot overrule a precedent of the Supreme Court/House of Lords. When a court overrules a previous case the effect is both prospective (i.e. established for the future) and retrospective (i.e. also applied to the past) and the new legal principle is now treated as if it had been the law all along. You will come across several examples of overruling, including those we have discussed in this chapter; see, for instance, the case of *R v Jogee* [2016] UKSC 8 mentioned earlier.

The courts are mindful of the legal uncertainty that overruling may create. This is because a principle of law in a case operates retrospectively, and this may operate unfairly should people have conducted their affairs in accordance with a law that has now been overruled. In some jurisdictions, such as the United States, there is a practice of prospective overruling; the newly established legal principle will only apply to the future; the overruled and older principle of law can remain in place for events and transactions occurring before the latest decision and, depending upon the type of prospective overruling, it may only be confined to the precise facts of the instant case.

The House of Lords considered the temporal operation of judicial decisions in *Re Spectrum Plus Ltd (in liquidation)* [2005] 2 AC 680. It was acknowledged that prospective overruling was not a practice adopted in the English legal system. This, it was argued, was consistent with the judicial role of deciding what the law is and applying it to a set of facts, as opposed to Parliament's role of making law. However, Lord Nicholls said that exceptionally the House of Lords could alter judicial practice and restrict their overruling to prospective matters only. Lord Nicholls (at p.699) said such overruling may be necessary

> to serve the underlying objective of the courts of this country: to administer justice fairly and in accordance with the law. There could be cases where a decision on an issue of law, whether common law or statute law, was unavoidable but the decision would have such gravely unfair and disruptive consequences for past transactions or happenings that this House would be compelled to depart from the normal principles relating to the retrospective and prospective effect of court decisions.

It is to be noted that Lord Nicholls suggested that this exceptional practice could potentially apply both to judge-made law and to the interpretation of statutes; however, in respect of the latter category, Lords Steyn and Scott ***dissented***. See also *Awoyami v Radford and Another* [2007] All ER (D) 183; Lord Rodger, 'A Time for Everything under the Law: Some Reflections on Retrospectivity' (2005) 121 LQR 57.

Dissent
When a judge disagrees with a decision reached by the other judges in a case, the judge is said to dissent.

5.6.2 **Reversing**

Technically speaking, this is not a way of avoiding precedent but simply confirms the powers of a court (that is higher in the hierarchy) in relation to a decision made by a lower court in the same case. By reversing a decision, a higher court is saying that the lower court's decision is wrong (and an appeal is said to be allowed). When a higher court states that a decision of a lower court is correct it is said to be affirmed (and an appeal against the lower court decision is said to be dismissed).

There are too many cases to mention that demonstrate the process of reversing. It essentially occurs when a party's appeal is allowed. However, you may want to consider the following examples (though feel free to find many more).

 Example

Let's return to the case of *Lee v Ashers Baking Company Ltd* [2018] UKSC 49 (the 'gay cake' case). We considered this case in Chapter 2. Read Lady Hale's judgment and consider the precise principles that influenced her to ultimately reverse the finding of discrimination by the Northern Ireland Court of Appeal.

Alternatively, you may want to consider some recent and important cases in the law of tort. Of particular significance is *Robinson v Chief Constable of West Yorkshire Police* [2018] UKSC 4. This case involved determining the circumstances in which the police would be under a duty of care to protect the public from personal injury. Have a look at Lord Reed's judgment that represented the majority, and try to determine the principles which led him to reverse the decision taken by the Court of Appeal.

Or to offer another recent case in the law of tort, read *Darnley v Croydon Health Services NHS Trust* [2018] UKSC 50. This case involved an individual who had suffered a head injury. Seeking treatment, he attended his local A&E department at a hospital in Croydon, London. An A&E receptionist then gave him misleading information about the waiting time before he would be seen, indicating that it would take 4–5 hours (rather than informing him he would be seen within 30 minutes by a triage nurse). Feeling too unwell to wait for hours, the individual left and returned home. He later collapsed, and despite undergoing an emergency operation, he was left with permanent brain damage and paralysis on one side of his body. The evidence suggested that had he been seen in the normal routine way by a triage nurse, he would been admitted for surgery earlier and would have gone on to make a complete recovery. He brought proceedings against the NHS trust in respect of the negligent information about waiting times provided by the receptionist.

The case can be found here: **https://www.supremecourt.uk/cases/docs/uksc-2017-0070-judgment.pdf**. The judgment by Lord Lloyd-Jones in this case is very clear and readable. Identify the final decision in this case and the particular *ratio decidendi* (note there is more than one!). Consider the law and principles that led the UKSC to allow the appeal (and therefore reverse the findings made by the Court of Appeal).

5.6.3 **Distinguishing**

This is arguably one of the most important and widespread methods of avoiding precedent. It is one that lawyers and judges will regularly adopt to escape following an otherwise binding precedent. It is one that you will no doubt analyse in considerable detail (and practise should you decide to engage in mooting) in lectures and seminars throughout your studies. The technique or process of distinguishing is to point to material differences in the facts of the case constituting the earlier precedent compared with the instant case. In this way, it is argued that the *ratio decidendi* in the previous case simply does not apply to the present case because of the material factual differences between the cases.

To offer an example, consider the case of *Holwell Securities v Hughes* [1974] 1 WLR 155. In this case, which concerned the law of contract, the Court of Appeal (Civil Division) had to decide whether a letter sent by post that accepted a contract but was never received would be a valid form of acceptance, leading to the formation of a contract. It was argued that it was valid because of the 'postal rule' as established in in *Henthorn v Fraser* [1892] 2 Ch 27. In that case it was clearly in the contemplation of the parties that post was to be used to communicate acceptance and there was nothing in the contract to specify the manner or method of how the acceptance was to be communicated. In *Holwell*, however, the offer provided that its acceptance was to be 'exercisable by notice in writing'. These words, said the Court, indicated that the letter of acceptance had to in fact be received. Thus *Henthorn* was distinguished.

Conduct some research and consider the following pair of cases: *Balfour v Balfour* [1919] 2 KB 571 and *Merritt v Merritt* [1970] 2 All ER 760. On what basis was *Merritt* distinguished from the precedent established in *Balfour*?

5.7 **Nature of the rules of judicial precedent**

Note that the rules of precedent are not themselves binding as they do not relate to a dispute before the court. The rules therefore cannot be part of a *ratio decidendi*. Nonetheless, the House of Lords, by the Practice Statement of 1966, changed the practice of precedent. The precise status of the Practice Statement has been the subject of academic commentary as to the authority for instituting such a change, but the de facto situation is that the Practice Statement has been followed. No successful challenge has been mounted in the courts or Parliament.

5.8 **Case analysis**

As a law student, it is important to develop good habits at the earliest opportunity. Regularly reading cases is one such habit but it is a skill that can be developed and nurtured. As a starting point, you may find following the template useful to help you in analysing a case:

- **Legal issues:** the first task in reading a case is to identify the questions or issues the court is being asked to decide. There may be more than one issue before a court and how the case is argued will indicate the question or questions asked of the court.
- **Material facts:** what are the *material* (i.e. key and most relevant) facts of the case that ultimately support the decision?
- **The decision in the case:** it is useful to appreciate the outcome which will be important to the parties involved, but for lawyers the decision is very much secondary to the *ratio decidendi* of the case.
- **Reasons for the *ratio decidendi*:** it is important to separate the reasons for the *ratio decidendi* from the *ratio decidendi* itself. Judges will seek to justify why a case is decided in a particular way; in other words, a justification will be given for the *ratio decidendi* of the case.

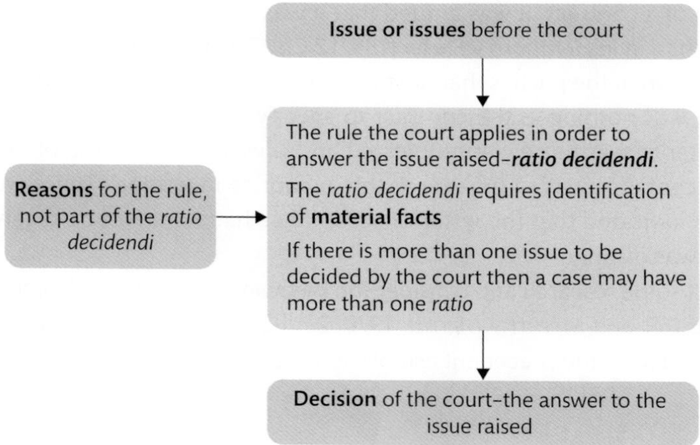

Diagram 5.2 Case analysis—finding the *ratio* of a case

- **The *ratio decidendi*:** in relation to new cases, lawyers will have to attempt to formulate the rule of law upon which the decision in the case is based. As we have seen, this is a difficult process, as judges will not usually neatly package a rule for the reader; instead the reader may need to 'construct' the *ratio*, looking for clues in the language used by the judge (or judges). If a case has been considered in later cases, then the later court may help you identify the *ratio decidendi* of the earlier case. See Diagram 5.2, which illustrates the relationship between the issue, the material facts, and the *ratio decidendi*.
- **Other statements of law—*obiter dicta*:** statements of law which do not affect the outcome of a case are classified as *obiter dicta* and are not binding on later courts. *Obiter dicta* are, however, persuasive.
- **The deciding court:** once the *ratio* of a case has been determined, the status of the deciding court must be noted so that one can consider the extent to which the *ratio* is binding. Such information will influence how the case may be used.
- **Later cases:** consider what has happened to a decision in later cases. Has it been affirmed, reversed, followed, distinguished, or overruled?

Summary

- Judicial precedent promotes certainty by ensuring that like cases are decided alike. Decision-making by the courts is governed by the doctrine of judicial precedent, which allows for the law to develop in an orderly way. However, this aim is sometimes achieved at the expense of justice.

- Law is made by judges, but the law-making power is a limited one. The courts ought not to usurp the role of Parliament as the main law-maker. For example, the courts should not effect a major change to the common law if there are conflicting views, especially in relation to social policy or if Parliament has refused to introduce such changes.
- The *ratio decidendi* of a case is the basis upon which a case is decided. A case may have more than one *ratio* depending on the ground of the decision.
- A distinction must be drawn between the *ratio decidendi* of a case, which may bind later courts, and *res judicata*, which indicates that the parties to a case, subject to any appeal, are bound by the decision in the case.
- When determining the *ratio decidendi* of a case, later cases are important for two reasons. First, a judge in a later case may state what the *ratio decidendi* of a previous case is; secondly, a judge or judges in a later case may clarify the *ratio* of a previous case by restating what the material facts are, thus narrowing or widening a *ratio*.
- Unlike the *ratio decidendi*, *obiter dicta* do not affect the decision in a case and are merely persuasive on other courts.
- In looking at the hierarchy of the courts, it is important to consider (a) which courts bind the particular court you are considering, and (b) whether the court binds itself.
- The Supreme Court will normally follow its previous decisions but may depart from such decisions when it 'appears right to do so'. This discretion is to be exercised sparingly.
- The Court of Appeal is bound by the *rationes* of the courts above it and by its previous decisions, subject to exceptions as outlined in *Young v Bristol Aeroplane Co Ltd* [1944] KB 718 (CA).
- The High Court is bound by the courts above it in the hierarchy. Whether it is bound by its previous decisions depends upon the jurisdiction that the court is exercising, that is, appellate, supervisory, or first instance. A Divisional Court exercising appellate jurisdiction is bound by its previous decisions, subject to the rule in *Young v Bristol Aeroplane Co Ltd*. At first instance the High Court is not bound by previous first instance decisions, but it will not lightly depart from such decisions.
- The Crown Court, magistrates' courts, and the County Court are bound by all the courts above in the hierarchy and do not bind themselves.
- There are three main ways of avoiding precedent: overruling, reversing, and distinguishing.

Questions

1 What is the doctrine of (binding) judicial precedent?
2 Under the doctrine of precedent, what is the binding part of a case?
3 Explain the characteristics of *obiter dicta.*
4 What factors does the Supreme Court/House of Lords take into account in exercising their power under the 1966 Practice Statement to depart from their previous decisions? Give examples of when the Practice Statement has been used
5 In what circumstances may the Court of Appeal (Civil Division) and (Criminal Division) refuse to follow its own previous decisions? Give examples of when those exceptions have been relied upon.
6 How does the precedent practice in the High Court differ according to whether the court exercises appellate or first instance jurisdiction?
7 In relation to the provision in the Human Rights Act 1998, to what degree do the traditional rules of precedent still apply?
8 Explain, with examples, the three main methods by which a court can avoid a precedent?

Sample question and outline answer

Question

The Practice Statement of 1966 indicated that the House of Lords (now the Supreme Court) would be more willing to depart from its own previous precedents. Discuss the reasons and circumstances for the House of Lords/Supreme Court departing from its own precedents in decided cases.

Outline answer

First, you may wish to begin with the principle of *stare decisis* and explain the principles behind judicial precedent, in particular that of certainty and stability in the legal system.

Secondly, you can turn to focus on the House of Lords/UK Supreme Court. Begin by establishing its overall significance in the hierarchy and then explore the Practice Statement, concentrating on the precise terminology and scope of the powers. You may note the vague 'appears right to do so' terminology.

One of the main issues arising out of the Practice Statement concerns the retrospective effect of precedents; they apply to the past as well as the future. The problems that this can cause need to be explored, especially the issue of reliance on a precedent by lawyers and citizens in ordering their affairs or as a guide to future action. The specific reference to contracts, settlements of property, and fiscal arrangements reflects the desire not to retrospectively disturb transactions or actions where reliance has been placed on existing precedent. It has been made clear in the case law that the Practice Statement power is to be used sparingly: *Jones v Secretary of State for Social Services* (1972).

Then you can turn to consider the main issue: in what circumstances will the House of Lords/Supreme Court consider it 'right' to depart from a previous decision? Here you need to explain and refer to a selection of decided cases to highlight the basis for the House of Lords/Supreme Court departing from its own previous precedents. The case law needs to be explained and analysed. There are several cases discussed in this chapter. You should take a sample of those in turn and explore the circumstances in which it has had to be used. You may want to consider whether the Supreme Court/House of Lords have been consistent in using the Practice Statement or whether it is very much on a discretionary case-by-case basis.

Clearly, the tension is between promoting certainty in the law while at the same time seeking to ensure that justice is done. This may be a theme of your discussion. Perhaps unfairly, the fact that a previous decision is perceived to be wrong will not, of itself, necessarily be a reason to depart from it; the need for certainty may outweigh this consideration. You may wish to consider whether that is fair. An explanation of the House of Lords' approach to the interpretation of statutes in previous precedents can also be given—see, for example, *Jones v Secretary of State for Social Services* (1972) and the refusal to depart from *Re Dowling* (1967). A comparison may be drawn with a discussion of *R v Shivpuri* (1987).

If an old case of the House of Lords raises a broad issue of justice, public policy, or legal principle, then reconsideration of it may be appropriate. For instance, in *British Railways Board v Herrington* (1972), the previous House of Lords case of *Addie & Sons v Dumbreck* (1929) was reconsidered. Lord Pearson said that 'the rule in Addie's case has been rendered obsolete by changes in physical and social conditions and has become an encumbrance to the proper development of the common law in this field'. It would seem that if Parliament does not seek to legislate on a defect in the common law then the Supreme Court may decide to depart from its own previous decisions, as exemplified by *R v Jogee* (2016).

In conclusion, you should answer the question directly. It is entirely up to you how you form your view. You may consider that the power to depart from previous precedents has been used sparingly by the Supreme Court/House of Lords and this is problematic. It may be due to concerns over the retrospective nature of precedent, but to what extent is that a good reason? There is evidence that the Court can and will use the Practice Statement in certain circumstances to develop the law and/or to do justice. Is that enough?

Further reading

At first-year level your reading should be directed to two essential goals: a knowledge and understanding of the rules of judicial precedent, and an appreciation of what underpins the rules. Reading what the judges have had to say in the case law is essential. Further case commentary may be available in journal articles.

- **Cross, R.** and **Harris, J.** *Precedent in English Law*, 4th edn, Oxford University Press (1991)

  This is the leading and authoritative text on the doctrine of judicial precedent but note its publication date. The coverage may be a little dated but the discussion of core principles such as *ratio decidendi* remains excellent.

- **Giles, M.** *'Judicial Law-Making in the Criminal Courts: The Case of Marital Rape'* [1992] Crim LR 407

  This is an older article but provides an apt illustration of how the common law may evolve to reflect developments in modern society.

- **Gillespie, A.** *'Precedent and the Limits of Simpson'* (2010) 74 J Crim L 492

  This article explores the precedent issue raised before the Court of Appeal (Criminal Division) in *R v Varma* (2010).

- **Mirfield, P.** *'A Novel Theory of Privy Council Precedent'* (2017) 133 LQR 1

  This article comes recommended. It provides a critical analysis of *Willers v Joyce* [2016] UKSC 44 and the Supreme Court's approach to the status of Privy Council decisions.

- **Prime, T.** and **Scanlan, G.** *'Stare Decisis and the Court of Appeal: Judicial Confusion and Judicial Reform?'* (2004) 23 CJQ 212

  This article concentrates on the principles of precedent at the Court of Appeal. It offers a review of the case law, from *Young v Bristol Aeroplane* onwards, that has informed the Court's practice towards its own precedents.

Online resources

You should now attempt the supporting self-test questions and end-of-chapter questions available at: **www.oup.com/he/wilson-rutherford4e**

Chapter 6

The law and institutions of the European Union (EU)

Learning objectives

By the end of this chapter you should:

- know what the main institutions of the EU are and how they are comprised;
- understand the respective functions of the institutions;
- know the various sources of EU law;
- be able to distinguish between the various legislative acts adopted by the Union;
- understand the purpose and mechanics of the preliminary rulings procedure;
- explain why reform of the preliminary rulings procedure is regarded as important, and critically analyse the various reform proposals that have been made;
- understand the doctrine of supremacy;
- understand the principles of direct effect and indirect effect;
- understand the justification for the development of the principle of state liability.

Talking point

The United Kingdom (UK) has been a Member State of the EU since January 1973, when a Conservative government took the UK into what was then the European Economic Community (EEC). The Labour government that followed held a national referendum in June 1975 on whether the UK should retain its membership of the EEC, which resulted in more than 67 per cent of the electorate voting 'yes'.

For more than forty years, that situation remained unchallenged (although the EEC gradually evolved into the present-day EU). However, in June 2016 a second referendum on EU membership was held, and this time 52 per cent voted in favour of the UK leaving the EU. Within days Prime Minister David Cameron had resigned; he was replaced with Theresa May, who famously declared that 'Brexit means Brexit'. The next step was to formally invoke the leaving process. This process (never before used) is set out in Article 50 of the Treaty on European Union. The new prime minister invoked this procedure at the end of March 2017, starting a two-year countdown towards the UK's exit from the EU. That process has been delayed several times, with the current departure date scheduled for the end of January 2020.

The question of whether or not the UK electorate made the right decision when it chose to leave the EU is a very complex and controversial one, involving issues of national identity, economics, politics, and law which are outside the scope of this book. Instead, this chapter will seek to explain the history and core legal principles of the EU, and the impact on the English legal system of the UK's membership of the EU. This will entail looking at key legal principles such as the 'supremacy' of EU law over conflicting national law, the 'direct effect' of EU law (which allows EU legislation to be enforced in UK courts and tribunals), the 'indirect effect' of EU law (which requires judges in UK courts and tribunals to interpret UK legislation to bring it into line with EU legislation), and the 'preliminary rulings' procedure (which enables judges in UK courts and tribunals to seek advice from the Court of Justice in Luxembourg on the true meaning of EU law).

All of this is due to end at the end of January 2020, but what exactly will happen then? Will EU law continue to enjoy 'supremacy' over UK law? Will it still be possible to enforce EU law in UK courts and tribunals? What will happen to the UK courts' ability to access the preliminary rulings procedure? At the time of writing, no one knows for sure. However, this chapter will also set out the key provisions in the European Union (Withdrawal) Act 2018, which goes a long way to answering those questions.

Introduction

The UK joined what was then called the European Economic Community (EEC) in January 1973. However, at that date the EEC had already been in existence for fifteen years, formed when the Treaty of Rome came into effect in January 1958. The idea behind the EEC was to promote economic cooperation between different Member States for their mutual benefit. Over the years, the EEC expanded both geographically (as more countries joined) and legally, particularly when the decision was made to create the EU in November 1993. No longer restricted to 'economic' matters, the EU is now a 'union' of twenty-eight Member States (with the UK scheduled to leave, but more countries waiting to join). It has its own institutions, including a parliament and courts, which ensure its (reasonably) smooth functioning. It has its own law-making powers, but the most important aspects of the 'law' of the EU are found in two international agreements: the Treaty on European Union of 1992 and the Treaty on the Functioning of the European Union of 2007. In addition, the Court of Justice of the EU has established a number of key principles of EU law, including the doctrines of 'supremacy' (the principle that EU law overrides any conflicting provisions of national law), 'direct effect' (the principle that certain provisions of EU law are enforceable in the national courts), and 'state liability' (the principle that Member States are obliged to compensate individuals for any losses caused to them by a breach of their EU legal obligations).

6.1 **The history of the EU**

6.1.1 **The European Coal and Steel Community (ECSC)**

The historical development of the EU dates back to the post-Second World War era. In 1951 the Treaty of Paris was signed by the governments of Belgium, the Netherlands, Luxembourg, France, West Germany, and Italy, establishing the European Coal and Steel Community (ECSC) and creating a 'common market' in coal and steel. It was seen as a way of promoting cooperation between countries which had been at war with each other less than a decade previously. It was also seen as a means of accelerating post-war recovery and, by removing the raw materials for war from the control of the Member States, making another war less likely.

For more detailed discussion of the institutions responsible for running the EU, see 6.2.

The ECSC was (for the time) an unusual organisation. There was a Council of Ministers, consisting of representatives of the Member States, with responsibility for the overall development and policies of the ECSC, and with supranational power (that is, the power to make legally binding decisions without the intervention of national parliaments or governments). There was a permanent executive called the High Authority (subsequently renamed the European Commission), responsible for the day-to-day running of the ECSC, to which power could be delegated by the Council. The Treaty of Paris also established a Court of Justice, which was to resolve any disputes that arose between the Member States and to enforce the law in accordance with the Treaty.

6.1.2 **The EEC**

The Treaty of Rome was signed in 1957, establishing the EEC in January 1958. Its purpose was to promote the general economic integration of the six Member States who had formed the ECSC six years earlier. The EEC had a much wider remit than the ECSC and was designed to promote cooperation in a variety of 'economic' fields, such as agriculture, employment, fishing, trade, and transport. It is very important to note that these fields of operation are finite: the EEC only had power to act in those areas identified in the Treaty itself. In other areas, for example direct taxation, the individual Member States retained full control. The Treaty of Rome also created the 'Common Market', an area comprising all of the Member States in which goods, people, services, and capital would be free to move.

A second Treaty of Rome was also signed in 1957, establishing the European Atomic Energy Community (EURATOM), which was intended to promote cooperation in the generation and distribution of nuclear energy. Thus, from January 1958, there were three distinct European Communities: the ECSC, the EEC, and EURATOM. However, from 1969 they were run by a single set of institutions.

6.1.3 **Geographical enlargement and legal expansion**

Since 1958, the EEC/EU has grown from an initial membership of six to twenty-eight, following the accession of the UK, Denmark, and Ireland in 1973; Greece in 1981; Spain and Portugal in 1986; Austria, Finland, and Sweden in 1995; Cyprus, the Czech Republic, Estonia, Hungary, Latvia, Lithuania, Malta, Poland, Slovakia, and Slovenia in 2004; Bulgaria and Romania in 2007; and Croatia in 2013. Following the collapse of the Berlin Wall in 1989, Germany was reunited and the former East Germany was absorbed into the EU. At present, five other states are involved in formal negotiations to join: Albania, Montenegro, North Macedonia, Serbia, and Turkey. Iceland applied for EU membership in 2009, but subsequently withdrew its application.

Meanwhile, in 1986, the governments of the Member States signed the Single European Act (SEA), which came into effect in 1987. The SEA made a number of modifications to the (first) Treaty of Rome, the most important being:

- The list of fields in which the EEC was competent to act was expanded. For example, environmental protection was added.
- The Court of First Instance was created, to relieve some of the workload from the European Court of Justice.
- The 'Common Market' was renamed the 'Internal Market' or 'Single Market'.

6.1.4 **The EU and other developments**

The legal expansion of the EEC, which began in 1986, continued when the Treaty on European Union (TEU) was signed in 1992 and came into effect in November 1993. Among other things, the TEU:

- established the EU;
- renamed the EEC as simply the EC;
- made various amendments to the (first) Treaty of Rome;
- renamed the Council of Ministers as the Council of the European Union;
- recognised the European Council as an institution of the EU;
- established the concept of 'citizenship' of the Union;
- paved the way for the adoption of the single European currency, the euro, in 2002.

Two further treaties were signed: the Treaty of Amsterdam in 1997 and the Treaty of Nice in 2001. These made further amendments to both the (first) Treaty of Rome and the TEU but did not make any fundamental changes to the way in which either the EC or EU operated. In December 2000, the Charter of Fundamental Rights (the Charter) was approved by the governments of the EU's Member States. The Charter did not, initially, have binding legal force, but that changed in December 2009 (see later at 6.3.1).

The Treaty of Paris, signed in 1951, was only ever intended to last for fifty years and it duly lapsed in 2002. As a result, the ECSC ceased to exist. The provisions of the Treaty of Rome were applied to the coal and steel industries instead. The same year saw the introduction of the single European currency, the euro, in twelve Member States: Austria, Belgium, Finland, France, Germany, Greece, Ireland, Italy, Luxembourg, the Netherlands, Portugal, and Spain. Slovenia adopted the euro in 2007, followed by Cyprus and Malta in 2008, Slovakia in 2009, Estonia in 2011, Latvia in 2014, and Lithuania in 2015. There are now nineteen Member States in the 'eurozone', overseen by the European Central Bank (ECB), which is based in Frankfurt in Germany.

6.1.5 **The state of the Union**

The latest EU Treaty is the Lisbon Treaty, signed in 2007, which came into effect in December 2009. The main features are:

See 6.3 for discussion of the TEU, TFEU, and Charter.

- the EC was abolished;
- the (first) Treaty of Rome was amended and renamed the Treaty on the Functioning of the European Union (TFEU);
- the TEU was amended;
- the Charter of Fundamental Rights was given legal force;
- the EU committed to becoming a signatory to the European Convention on Human Rights (ECHR);

- a president and foreign minister of the EU were established;
- combating climate change and global warming become official policies of the EU;
- the Court of First Instance (CFI) was renamed as the General Court.

6.1.6 What next for the UK?

At the time of writing it is inherently speculative what will happen after the UK's exit from the EU (so-called Brexit), which is scheduled for the end of January 2020. Shortly after becoming prime minister in July 2016, Theresa May declared that 'Brexit means Brexit'. In September 2017, she confirmed that the UK government intended to leave the EU entirely, including both the single market (the free movement of goods, people, services, and capital) and the customs union (which precludes the imposition of import or export tariffs on the movement of goods between EU Member States). However, she added that she wanted to negotiate 'a new, deep and special partnership' between the EU and the UK, explaining her desire to 'find a new framework that allows for a close economic partnership but holds those rights and obligations in a new and different balance'. Mrs May was replaced as prime minister by Boris Johnson in July 2019, but the government's plan remains to negotiate a unique, bespoke deal with the EU. Such a plan is by no means unprecedented: many countries around the world have negotiated bespoke trade deals with the EU, such as the Comprehensive Economic and Trade Agreement (CETA) between the EU and Canada and the EU–Singapore Free Trade Agreement.

But are there other options? The answer is 'yes', with the best known being the so-called 'Norwegian Option'. This could involve the UK leaving the EU as scheduled, but resurrecting its membership of the European Free Trade Association (EFTA), a free trade bloc founded by the UK and six other countries (Austria, Denmark, Norway, Portugal, Sweden, and Switzerland) in 1960. This would enable the UK to remain in the European Economic Area (EEA), along with Norway, Iceland, and Liechtenstein (all EFTA states). The EEA came into existence in 1994 and extended the geographical scope of the EU's 'single market' to any of the member states of EFTA who wished to participate in it. In other words, the EEA allows EFTA states to participate in the EU's 'single market' without being in the EU itself.

In fact, the only EFTA state which is not in the EEA is Switzerland, which brings us to another option, the so-called Swiss Option. Switzerland has had a free trade agreement with the EU since 1973 and has subsequently signed a number of other treaties with the EU, known as 'bilateral agreements', each on a discrete subject area such as the free movement of people, agriculture, road traffic, and so on.

All of the above options could be classified as varieties of a so-called 'soft' Brexit where the UK maintains extensive links with the EU after leaving. However, there is also the possibility that the UK leaves the EU without a deal; a so-called 'hard' Brexit. This would mean severing all existing economic, legal, and political ties with the EU. Any future dealings with the EU would then be subject to World Trade Organization

(WTO) rules. This could well see goods imported into the UK from the EU, and goods exported to the EU from the UK, subject to tariffs, which would make the cost of imports and exports more expensive. On the other hand, the UK would be completely free to negotiate trade deals with other countries around the world (something which is (at the time of writing) not available to the UK as an EU Member State).

6.2 The institutions of the EU

6.2.1 European Council

The European Council comprises all the heads of state or government of the Member States, the Council President, and the President of the European Commission. The European Council began with informal meetings in 1961 but adopted formal 'summits' in 1974. The Council meets in Brussels, four times a year. Although the European Council has no formal executive or legislative powers, it is required to 'provide the Union with the necessary impetus for its development' and to 'define the general political directions and priorities' of the EU (Article 15(1) TEU).

6.2.2 Council of the EU

The Council of the EU, formerly called the Council of Ministers, is usually referred to simply as 'the Council'. It is different from the European Council and should not be confused with it. According to Article 16(2) of the TEU, 'The Council shall consist of a representative of each Member State at ministerial level, who may commit the government of the Member State in question and cast its vote.' When the Council meets, its composition depends on the subject matter under discussion. For example, if the Council were to meet to discuss North Sea fishing stocks, agriculture ministers would attend. Article 16(1) of the TEU stipulates that the Council has the power to 'exercise legislative and budgetary functions'. However, the Council does not operate in isolation in this respect; rather, it interacts with the other institutions as part of the EU's legislative procedures.

6.2.3 European Commission

The Commission is currently headed by twenty-eight Commissioners, one per Member State, regardless of population size or economic strength (thus Germany has one Commissioner, as does Malta), supported by some 25,000 employees. (Assuming that the UK leaves the EU as scheduled at the end of January 2020, the number of Commissioners will be reduced to twenty-seven.) The twenty-eight Commissioners are appointed together for a renewable five-year term. Commissioners are selected (by the Member States) rather than elected. Commissioners must be chosen on the 'ground of their general competence and European commitment from persons whose independence is beyond doubt' (Article 17(3) TEU). Once selected, they must act in the general interests of the EU, rather than in the interests of their Member State (Article 17(3) TEU). Each Commissioner is assigned a portfolio, but the Commission acts as a collegiate body. It is organised into 'directorates general' which correspond with the portfolios. The UK's Commissioner, at least until the end of January 2020, is Julian King, who heads the Security Union directorate general. The Commission's specific functions and powers are found in Article 17(1) of the TEU. Among other things, the Commission:

- is responsible for promoting the 'general interest' of the Union;
- is authorised to take 'appropriate initiatives' to promote the Union. This essentially means the right to propose and draft secondary legislation, which it then passes on to the European Parliament and Council for approval and ultimate adoption. Most of the Commission's legislative proposals take the form of regulations and directives in areas such as consumer protection, health protection, and employment, but the Commission has recently moved into criminal law (for example, criminalising the transportation of toxic waste);
- is empowered to commence 'enforcement' proceedings against Member States if they are not complying with their obligations under EU law. The procedure for doing so is found in Article 258 of the TFEU. Initially, the Commission will issue a 'reasoned opinion' to the state in question, giving it the opportunity to respond. If the Commission is dissatisfied with the response then the state can be brought before the Court of Justice. In the event that it agrees with the Commission, the Court may require the state in question to take whatever 'measures' are deemed 'necessary' (Article 260(1) TFEU). If the state fails to comply with the Court's judgment then the Commission can bring the state back before the Court, which can impose a punishment—either a 'lump sum or penalty payment' (Article 260(2) TFEU);
- is responsible for enforcing EU competition policy. The Commission can prosecute corporations which form illegal cartels (prohibited by Article 101 of the TFEU) or abuse a 'dominant' position in the market (prohibited by Article 102 of the TFEU). The Commission can ultimately issue (very large) fines. In July 2016, a €2.93 billion fine was imposed on several truck manufacturers for forming a cartel and colluding on truck prices, contrary to Article 101 TFEU, over a fourteen-year period. The current record holder is the €4.34 billion fine imposed on Alphabet (Google's parent body) for abusing its dominant position in the internet search market, contrary to Article 102 TFEU, in July 2018.

6.2.4 **European Parliament**

The Parliament (as shown in Image 6.1) was originally called the Common Assembly. In 1962 it began calling itself Parliament, although this was only made official in 1986. The original Members were delegates of Member States' own parliaments. The first

Image 6.1 The Hemicycle, or debating chamber, of the European Parliament
Source: Walencienne/Shutterstock

direct elections were held across Europe in June 1979. Elections are held every five years, with the ninth election taking place in June 2019. There are 751 Members of the European Parliament (MEPs), with the proportions varying per Member State according to size and population. Thus, for example, Germany has ninety-six MEPs, France has seventy-four, the UK (at least until the UK leaves the EU at the end of January 2020) and Italy have seventy-three each, and so on. The four smallest countries have six MEPs each.

The functions of the European Parliament are:

- participation in the legislative process. The Parliament's role here has been, and still is, controversial. Despite being the only directly elected (and hence most democratic) institution in the EU, the Parliament's role in the legislative process is purely reactive. It has the right to be consulted on all draft legislation and, in certain circumstances, can and does veto proposed legislation. But it has no powers to introduce legislation of its own (only the Commission can do this) and the Parliament cannot force through legislation if the Council opposes it;
- supervisory functions (over the Commission);
- budgetary powers.

6.2.5 **Court of Justice of the EU**

The Court of Justice of the EU (CJEU), usually referred to as the Court of Justice, consists of twenty-eight judges, one per Member State (Article 19(2) TEU). (Assuming that the UK leaves the EU as scheduled at the end of January 2020, the number of judges will be reduced to twenty-seven.) Each holds office for a renewable six-year term. Judges are selected from persons 'whose independence is beyond doubt' (Article 19(2) TEU). The judges elect one of themselves as 'President'. The CJEU may sit:

- as the 'full court' comprising all twenty-eight judges;
- in a 'Grand Chamber' comprising fifteen judges;
- in chambers of three or five judges.

The Court sits as a 'full court' only in relatively rare cases, such as those considered of 'exceptional importance'. It sits in a Grand Chamber when a Member State or an EU institution which is a party to the proceedings so requests, and in particularly complex or important cases. Other cases are heard in chambers, which allows for a degree of specialism and greater efficiency. Unlike English courts, the CJEU always gives a single, collegiate judgment; there are no minority judgments (dissenting or otherwise). The CJEU is assisted by nine Advocates-General (A-G), who are legal experts employed to give highly persuasive advisory 'opinions' to the Court before the judges retire to consider their judgment in some (but not all) cases. In most cases where an A-G is used, the CJEU follows the opinion when it gives judgment (often several months later). Thus, once an A-G's opinion is available in a given case, one can predict with some confidence how the CJEU will eventually rule.

6.2.6 **General Court**

The General Court began operations, as the 'Court of First Instance' (CFI), in 1989. Its name was changed in December 2009. There is 'at least' one judge per Member State (Article 19(2) TEU). At present there are twenty-eight judges. Unlike the CJEU, there are no Advocates-General. The General Court mainly handles cases involving EU competition law, and some judicial review cases. Appeals against General Court decisions—on points of law only—are heard by the CJEU.

6.2.7 **European Central Bank**

The European Central Bank, based in Frankfurt, Germany, is the central bank for Europe's single currency, the euro. Its main task is to maintain the euro's purchasing power and thus price stability in the nineteen EU countries that presently make up the 'eurozone'.

6.2.8 **European Economic and Social Committee (EESC)**

The EESC has 350 members, representing three groups: employers, workers, and various others, which include agricultural and consumer interests. Its sole function is to advise the Council, the Commission, and the Parliament (Article 13(4) TEU).

6.2.9 Committee of the Regions (CoR)

The CoR also has 350 members, representing regional and local bodies throughout the EU. Like the EESC, its sole function is also to advise the Council, the Commission, and the Parliament.

6.3 Sources of EU law

6.3.1 The Treaties and the Charter

All of the key provisions of EU law are contained in the TEU and the TFEU.

The Treaty on European Union

The TEU came into effect in November 1993 and has been amended several times since, most recently when the Treaty of Lisbon came into force in December 2009. The TEU contains the fundamental principles relating to the EU and its institutions. It consists of a total of fifty-five articles.

The Treaty on the Functioning of the European Union

The TFEU came into effect in December 2009, replacing the Treaty of Rome. The TFEU elaborates on the fundamental principles in the TEU, seeking (as its name suggests) to ensure that the EU functions smoothly. For example, Article 26 of the TFEU states that '[t]he Union shall adopt measures with the aim of establishing or ensuring the functioning of the internal market', defined as 'an area without internal frontiers in which the free movement of goods, persons, services and capital is ensured'. The TFEU is much bigger than the TEU, containing a total of 358 articles.

The Charter of Fundamental Rights

The Charter of Fundamental Rights was 'adopted' in December 2000, although initially it did not have binding legal force (it did have a persuasive influence, however, especially on the CJEU). That changed in December 2009, when the Charter acquired legal force. The Charter consists of fifty articles on a range of issues, such as human dignity (Article 1), the right to life (Article 2), respect for private and family life (Article 7), freedom of expression (Article 11), right to education (Article 14), right to asylum (Article 18), and equality between men and women (Article 23).

See Chapter 7, 'Human rights in the United Kingdom'.

The Charter is not to be confused with the ECHR, which was signed in November 1950 and which came into effect in September 1953. The Charter and the Convention share a number of common features but are not identical. All twenty-eight Member States of the EU are signatories to the ECHR, along with nineteen non-EU countries including Norway, Russia, Switzerland, and Ukraine. Enforcement of the ECHR is the responsibility of the European Court of Human Rights in Strasbourg.

6.3.2 **Secondary legislation: an introduction**

The TEU and TFEU are framework Treaties, which means that, although they contain the fundamental principles of law upon which the Union is founded and functions, detailed rules are necessary to 'flesh out' those general principles. To facilitate this, law-making powers are conferred upon the EU's institutions (Article 288 TFEU).

6.3.3 **Regulations**

The EU's institutions pass thousands of regulations each year. All regulations are cited by reference to a number followed by the year of enactment. Thus, for example, Regulation 1612/68 was number 1612 to be enacted in 1968. Regulations are described in Article 288 TFEU as having 'general application' and being 'directly applicable'. 'General application' means that regulations, like the Treaties, apply to both the Member States *and* individuals. The term 'directly applicable' means that regulations automatically become part of the domestic legal system of the Member States without the need for any national legislation. 'Direct applicability' is a powerful tool for ensuring legal uniformity throughout the EU. Regulations do *not* allow room for the exercise of any discretion to address national needs. For this reason, regulations tend to be used in highly regulated fields such as agriculture and competition.

6.3.4 **Directives**

Directives are very different from regulations. First, they are not necessarily of general application; instead, they are binding only upon those Member States to which they are addressed. (Having said that, directives usually are addressed to every State.) Second, directives are not binding in their entirety but only as to the 'result to be achieved'. As such, directives instruct Member States to do certain things, but do not specify how this should be done. Member States must 'implement' the provisions of directives into domestic law. All directives are cited by reference to the year of enactment followed by a number. Hence, for example, Directive 2004/38 was number 38 to be enacted in 2004. Here are some other examples:

- Directive 76/207 (the Equal Treatment Directive) established a general principle of equal treatment for men and women in employment throughout the EU.
- Directive 92/85 (the Pregnant Workers Directive) guarantees a minimum maternity leave period throughout the EU of fourteen weeks.
- Directive 93/104 (the first Working Time Directive) guarantees a maximum average working week throughout the EU of forty-eight hours.
- Directive 2000/78 (the Framework Directive) establishes a right of non-discrimination in employment on grounds of age, disability, religion or belief, and sexual orientation, throughout the EU.

Implementation of directives

Member States *must* introduce national legislation to 'implement' each directive. They must do this within a specified time period, stated in the directive itself. The time period varies from one directive to another depending on the difficulty of achieving the required result, but the average time period is approximately two years. Member States must implement directives in a legally certain manner (for example, in the UK by an Act of Parliament or a statutory instrument). For example:

See 3.2.3, 'The origins of legislation'.

- Directive 90/314 was implemented into UK law by the Package Travel, Package Holidays and Package Tours Regulations 1992 (SI 1992/3288);
- Directive 92/85 was implemented into UK law by the Employment Rights Act 1996;
- Directive 93/104 was implemented into UK law by the Working Time Regulations 1998 (SI 1998/1883);
- Directive 2000/78 was initially implemented into UK law by several statutory instruments which were later consolidated in the Equality Act 2010;
- Directive 2005/29 was implemented into UK law by the Consumer Protection from Unfair Trading Regulations 2008 (SI 2008/1277);
- Directive 2011/83 was implemented into UK law by the Consumer Contracts (Information, Cancellation & Additional Charges) Regulations 2013 (SI 2013/3134).

Implications of failing to implement on time

If a Member State fails to implement a directive on time, certain implications may follow:

- The directive itself may be relied upon in litigation in national courts, subject to certain conditions (see 6.6).
- The state may find itself held liable to compensate any individual who has suffered loss as a consequence of this failure, again subject to certain conditions (see 6.7).
- The European Commission may bring an enforcement action under Article 258 of the TFEU, potentially leading to a fine imposed by the CJEU under Article 260 of the TFEU.

6.3.5 **Decisions**

Decisions are legally binding in their entirety upon those to whom they are addressed. Decisions may be addressed to Member States or to individuals.

6.3.6 **Recommendations and opinions**

Recommendations and opinions have, as their names suggest, no binding force. However, they cannot be ignored and have some persuasive authority.

6.3.7 Case law

The case law of the CJEU and the General Court forms an essential source of EU law. Judgments of the two Courts are binding on national courts. The CJEU is not bound by a doctrine of precedent; however, it usually follows its previous decisions. Most of the Courts' workload consists of dealing with enforcement actions under Article 258 of the TFEU or giving 'preliminary rulings' under Article 267 of the TFEU (see 6.4). However, the CJEU has been very active in creating legal principles which underpin the whole of the EU's legal system, including 'supremacy' (see 6.5), 'direct effect' and 'indirect effect' (see 6.6), and 'state liability' (see 6.7).

Every case heard by the CJEU has a reference number. A C-prefix was introduced in 1989, in order to distinguish the CJEU's cases from those of the General Court, which have a T-prefix. Thus, Case C-212/04 *Adeneler and Others* is case number 212 of the year 2004 and was heard in the Court of Justice.

Visit the online resources to watch a video on the fundamental case law of the Court of Justice.

6.4 The preliminary rulings procedure

6.4.1 Introduction

The preliminary rulings procedure is the mechanism by which national courts and tribunals may (or in some cases must) seek definitive 'rulings' from the CJEU on the interpretation of EU legislation.

Key point

The preliminary rulings procedure is *not* an appeal: the relationship between the CJEU and the national courts is not hierarchical, but based on mutual cooperation. Basically, the national courts are responsible for applying EU law and the CJEU is responsible for interpreting it.

6.4.2 Purpose

The procedure exists because of the need to secure the uniform application of EU legislation throughout the Union. After all, if EU law were to be applied differently in different Member States then it would cease to be 'EU law' (it would effectively become national law instead). To ensure uniform application, EU legislation must be interpreted consistently.

6.4.3 **Scope**

Article 267 TFEU stipulates that the CJEU has jurisdiction to give preliminary rulings on:

- the interpretation of 'the Treaties'—both the TEU and the TFEU;
- the interpretation of 'acts of the institutions, bodies, offices or agencies of the Union'—meaning legislative acts, primarily directives and regulations;
- the validity of those 'acts'. (The CJEU cannot rule on the validity of either of the Treaties.)

The CJEU's approach to its task of interpreting a provision of EU legislation was summarised in *Adidas* (Case C-223/98) [1999] ECR I-7081, where the Court stated that:

> it is necessary to consider not only its wording but also the context in which it occurs and the objects of the rules of which it is part . . . where a provision of [EU] law is open to several interpretations, only one of which can ensure that the provision retains its effectiveness, preference must be given to that interpretation.

This is a strong commitment to the 'purposive' approach to interpretation.

See Chapter 4, 'The interpretation of statutes'.

6.4.4 **Who can seek a preliminary ruling?**

Article 267 TFEU provides that 'any court or tribunal' may seek a preliminary ruling if a 'question' relating to the interpretation of EU legislation is raised in a case pending before it.

Whether a body qualifies as a 'court or tribunal' is a question of EU law. The CJEU has adopted a functional test, seeking to identify the characteristics of the body seeking a ruling rather than its formal title, with the ultimate question being whether the body exercises a judicial function. In *Broeckmeulen* (Case C-246/80) [1981] ECR 2311, various factors to be taken into account in deciding this test were identified:

- whether the body is established by law;
- whether it is permanent;
- whether its jurisdiction is compulsory;
- whether its procedure is *inter partes*;
- whether it applies rules of law;
- whether it is independent.

Key point

A body does not necessarily have to have the name 'court' or 'tribunal' in order to be able to invoke the preliminary rulings procedure; the key is whether it carries out judicial functions.

For example, the following bodies have invoked the procedure: Immigration *Adjudicator* (UK); Alien Appeals *Board* (Sweden); Appeals *Committee* (Netherlands); Social Security *Commissioner* (UK); Competition *Council* (Finland).

Subsequent case law has confirmed that independence is critical. The CJEU in *Wilson* (Case C-506/04) [2006] ECR I-8613 identified two forms of independence: external (freedom from outside interference) and internal (lack of bias among the body's members). If either or both of these is missing then a body cannot invoke the procedure (*Schmid* (Case C-516/99) [2002] ECR I-4573). Other cases in which a body was not recognised as a 'court or tribunal' include *Nordsee* (Case 102/81) [1982] ECR 1095 (an arbitrator); *X* (Case C-74/95) [1996] ECR I-6609 (a prosecutor); and *Victoria Film* (Case C-134/97) [1998] ECR I-7023 (a body acting in a purely administrative capacity).

The functional test for deciding whether or not a body is a 'court or tribunal' has attracted criticism. In *Alpe Adria Energia* (Case C-205/08) [2009] ECR I-11525, A-G Ruiz-Jarabo Colomer opined that the CJEU had become too generous with its interpretation of 'court or tribunal', opening up the procedure to what he described as 'quasi-judicial bodies'. He invited the Court to 'lay down a stricter and more consistent body of rules' on admissibility. However, when it gave judgment, the CJEU ignored the invitation.

Thinking point

What is a 'court or tribunal' in the context of the preliminary rulings procedure?

1. Why could the bodies in *Nordsee*, *X*, and *Victoria Film* not seek preliminary rulings? Which factor(s) were missing?
2. Is the functional test for establishing whether or not a body is a 'court or tribunal' too generous, as A-G Ruiz-Jarabo Colomer contends? What are the advantages and disadvantages (if any) of the Court adopting a very wide interpretation?

6.4.5 **Discretionary and mandatory referral**

Article 267 of the TFEU distinguishes between two categories of courts and tribunals—those which 'may' refer a question to the CJEU and those which 'shall' do so. If courts or tribunals fall within the former category then they have complete discretion whether or not to refer. However, courts and tribunals from which there is no 'judicial remedy under national law' must request a ruling. These are often referred to as 'courts of last resort'. Essentially, if there is no right even to seek leave to appeal against the decision of a particular body, then that body is a 'court of last resort'.

The question of which UK courts and tribunals are subject to mandatory referral has attracted debate. The UK Supreme Court (and its predecessor, the Judicial Committee of the House of Lords) is certainly included, but what about, for example, the Court of Appeal in the event that the Supreme Court refuses to give leave to appeal? The answer is that, generally speaking, the Court of Appeal is not a 'court of last resort' because, according to the CJEU in *Lyckeskog* (Case C-99/00) [2002] ECR I-4839, the right to *seek* leave to appeal from the Supreme Court qualifies as a 'judicial remedy' (whether or not leave is given).

In *Bulmer v Bollinger* [1974] Ch 401, Lord Denning commented that mandatory referral applied only to the House of Lords. However, this is too restrictive. As Balcombe LJ noted in *Chiron v Murex* [1995] All ER (EC) 88, there are some situations when there is no right even to seek leave to appeal against a decision of the Court of Appeal, meaning that no 'judicial remedy' would be available, in which case the Court of Appeal should be regarded as a 'court of last resort'.

6.4.6 **Avoiding mandatory referral**

Despite the wording of Article 267 of the TFEU, in *Da Costa* (Cases 28–30/62) [1963] ECR 61 and *CILFIT* (Case 283/81) [1982] ECR 3415 the CJEU has ruled that a 'court of last resort' is under no obligation to refer if:

- the question is not relevant, in the sense that the answer to it cannot affect the outcome of the case;
- a previous decision(s) of the CJEU has already interpreted the provision of EU legislation in question;
- the correct application of the provision of EU legislation is so obvious as to leave no room for any reasonable doubt. This is known as *'acte clair'*. The CJEU has stressed that a national court should not easily reach the conclusion that a provision of EU law is *'acte clair'*. In *CILFIT*, the Court stated that 'the national court or tribunal must be convinced that the matter is equally obvious to the courts of the other Member States and to the Court of Justice'. The Court added that it had to be borne in mind that EU legislation was drafted in several languages and that EU law uses terminology which is 'peculiar to it', emphasising that 'legal concepts do not necessarily have the same meaning' in EU law and in national law.

The *acte clair* doctrine is an important device for cutting out unnecessary, time-consuming requests. However, it can be abused, as happened in *R v Chief Constable of Sussex, ex parte ITF Ltd* [1999] 2 AC 418, where the House of Lords declined to seek rulings on the interpretation of the word 'measures' in Article 35 TFEU and the phrase 'public policy' in Article 36 TFEU—a decision which was criticised by commentators. Estella Baker, for example, said that '[a]t least three moot points lie buried in the case . . . there is a persuasive argument that a reference should have been made' ('Policing, Protest and Free Trade' [2000] Crim LR 95).

The UK Supreme Court also failed to invoke the preliminary rulings procedure—despite its obligation to do so as a 'court of last resort'—in *Abbey National plc v OFT* [2009] UKSC 6, [2009] 3 WLR 1215, concerning the interpretation of a provision in Directive 93/13. Although all five judges decided that the case should not be referred to the CJEU, only Lord Mance paid any attention to the cautionary words in *CILFIT*. He decided that the possibility of the disputed provision having a different meaning in the other language versions of the directive was 'very limited' and that the likelihood of the CJEU or other Member States' courts reaching a different interpretation was 'remote'. In contrast, Lord Walker simply stated that 'we should treat the matter as *acte clair*'. Meanwhile, Lord Phillips said that the matter was not *acte clair*, but should not be referred anyway because 'it would not be appropriate'. This has attracted criticism. Paul Davies described the failure to refer in *Abbey National* as 'dubious', pointing out that the Supreme Court had actually reversed the rulings of the High Court and Court of Appeal ('Bank Charges in the Supreme Court' (2010) 69 CLJ 21).

There are several other recent cases in which the UK Supreme Court decided a case involving a disputed point of EU law but without seeking a preliminary ruling on the basis of *acte clair*. In *Jivraj v Hashwani* [2011] UKSC 40, [2011] 1 WLR 1872, the Supreme Court held (without requesting a preliminary ruling) that the word 'employment' in the Framework Directive 2000/78 did not cover the situation where an arbitrator was appointed to resolve a contractual dispute. Rather, an arbitrator's role was that of an 'independent provider of services who is not in a relationship of subordination with the parties who receive his services' (per Lord Clarke). The *Jivraj* case echoed *Abbey National* insofar as the Supreme Court reached the opposite conclusion to that of the Court of Appeal (in which it had been held—unanimously—that an arbitrator was in 'employment') but did not feel the need to seek a ruling from the CJEU.

Similarly, in *X v Mid-Sussex Citizens Advice Bureau* [2012] UKSC 59, [2013] 1 All ER 1038, the Supreme Court held (again, without requesting a preliminary ruling) that the activities of a volunteer adviser with the Citizens' Advice Bureau fell outside of the scope of the same directive, not being an 'occupation'. *X* is particularly important as it establishes a precedent for the whole of the UK that those in the voluntary sector cannot rely on the directive and/or the UK implementing legislation to challenge alleged discrimination on the grounds listed in the directive. As the UK's 'court of last resort' the Supreme Court was, in principle, obliged to refer to the CJEU a question on the meaning of the word 'occupation', but invoked the *acte clair* doctrine instead. The Supreme Court did at least give serious consideration to one of the *CILFIT* criteria—the possibility that other national courts in the EU might reach a different conclusion—but Lord Mance's judgment was emphatic: 'there is no scope for reasonable doubt about the conclusion that the Framework Directive does not cover voluntary activity.' The decision in *X* not to refer the case to the CJEU was criticised by Clara Rauchegger, in 'European Dimensions' (2014) 3 CJICL 204, who said: 'It can certainly be doubted that it is *acte clair* that voluntary work is not covered by the Framework Directive. A more purposive and less literal interpretation of its Article 3 by the CJEU might have led to a different result.'

Similarly, in *Stott v Thomas Cook* [2014] UKSC 15, [2014] 2 WLR 521 and *Re Olympic Airlines* [2015] UKSC 27, [2015] 1 WLR 2399, the UK Supreme Court again declined to seek a preliminary ruling, despite its theoretical obligation to do so. In the former case, Lord Toulson (with whom the rest of the Court agreed) simply said that 'I would not make a reference to the CJEU . . . I consider the answer to be plain', without even mentioning the *CILFIT* criteria. Similarly, in *Olympic Airlines*, Lord Sumption (with whom the rest of the Court agreed) held that the provision of EU legislation in question was *acte clair* without any reference to the *CILFIT* criteria. In a more recent case, *Magmatic Ltd v PMS International* [2016] UKSC 12, [2016] 4 All ER 1027, better known as the 'Trunki' case, the UK Supreme Court decided that the point of EU law involved was *acte clair* (yet again without even mentioning the *CILFIT* criteria). This attracted criticism from Sara Ashby, 'The UK Supreme Court and the Trunki Case: Missed Opportunities, Mysteries and Misunderstood' (2016) 38 EIPR 527, who said that it was both 'disappointing' and 'surprising' that the Supreme Court did not seek a preliminary ruling.

Thinking points

Why is the UK's court-of-last-resort so reluctant to seek preliminary rulings?

1. Baker commented that the House of Lords in *ITF* had displayed 'palpable reluctance' to seek a ruling. Why would the Lords be reluctant to invoke the procedure?
2. How could the Supreme Court in *Abbey National* and *Jivraj* conclude that the meaning of the disputed provision would be 'equally obvious to the courts of the other Member States and to the Court of Justice' when it was not even obvious to two other courts in England? Does this suggest that the UK Supreme Court has the same 'reluctance' as the House of Lords to seek rulings?

6.4.7 **Docket control**

There are exceptional circumstances in which the CJEU has declined to give a preliminary ruling. One such circumstance is when a ruling is elicited by means of a 'contrived dispute'. This occurred in *Foglia v Novello (No. 1)* (Case 104/79) [1980] ECR 745 and *Foglia v Novello (No. 2)* (Case 244/80) [1981] ECR 3045, where the Court refused to answer requests for preliminary rulings submitted to it by an Italian court on the basis that the dispute between the parties had been fabricated in order to have the Court resolve a disputed point of EU law. The Court stated: 'The duty assigned to the Court by [Article 267 TFEU] is not that of delivering advisory opinions on general or hypothetical questions but of assisting in the administration of justice in the Member States.' Other situations in which a request for a ruling will be rejected include:

- **Lack of factual and/or legal material.** In *Telemarsicabruzzo and Others* (Cases C-320–322/90) [1993] ECR I-393, the Court declared that it was necessary for the national court or tribunal to 'define the factual and legislative context of the questions it is asking or, at the very least, explain the factual circumstances on which those questions are based'.
- **Irrelevance.** In *BP Supergas* (Case C-62/93) [1995] ECR I-1883, the Court stated that a request for a preliminary ruling may be rejected if it was 'quite obvious' that

the ruling sought bore 'no relation to the actual nature of the case or the subject-matter of the main action'.

- **No question of EU law is involved.** In *Vajnai* (Case C-328/04) [2005] ECR I-8577, the CJEU rejected a request for a ruling because there was no question of EU legislation involved. A Hungarian man, Attila Vajnai, had been convicted of publicly displaying a five-point red star during a demonstration in Budapest, a criminal offence under Hungarian law. During his appeal hearing a preliminary ruling was requested but the CJEU declared that it had no jurisdiction to respond, because there was no provision of EU legislation which dealt with the criminal liability of those displaying political symbols.

6.4.8 Preliminary rulings on validity

Under Article 267 of the TFEU, the CJEU can also deal with questions raised about the validity of EU secondary legislation (but not the Treaties). In *Firma Foto-Frost* (Case 314/85) [1987] ECR 4199, the CJEU stated that national courts do not have the power to declare EU secondary legislation invalid—only the CJEU has jurisdiction to do this. Where a question about the validity of secondary legislation is raised in legal proceedings, the national court must, therefore, either declare the legislation valid or make a reference to the CJEU.

6.4.9 The urgent procedure

In 2008, a new urgent procedure (known by its French acronym, PPU) was introduced. It is designed to allow preliminary rulings in exceptional cases to be prioritised. The national court must request that the PPU be applied and the CJEU must agree to the request (otherwise the ruling will be dealt with in the normal way). This allows for potentially enormous time savings. The normal preliminary rulings procedure takes, on average, fifteen months from request to judgment; under the PPU the waiting period can be measured in a matter of weeks. In the first case under the PPU, *Inga Rinau* (Case C-195/08 PPU) [2008] ECR I-5271, a ruling was requested in April 2008. Because the case involved a child custody dispute it was deemed to be urgent and judgment was delivered by the CJEU in July 2008, less than three months later. An ever faster turnaround was achieved in *Santesteban Goicoechea* (Case C-296/08 PPU) [2008] ECR I-6307, in the context of extradition proceedings. A preliminary ruling was requested in July 2008 and judgment was handed down by the CJEU in August, some five weeks later.

The PPU has been cautiously welcomed by commentators. Panis Koutrakos observed that 'there is a balance which must be struck: judges should be given time to reflect on the questions put before them, assess the arguments . . . and consider the wider ramifications of their conclusions . . . Whilst appropriate in certain exceptional circumstances, speed is not the only factor for the organisation of judicial proceedings' ('Speeding up the Preliminary Reference Procedure—Fast But Not too Fast' (2008) 33 EL Rev 617).

6.4.10 **Reform of the preliminary rulings procedure**

The average waiting time for a preliminary ruling is approximately sixteen months, which has in fact come down from a previous record high of more than two years. Even with this reduction in the waiting time, it is clearly unacceptable, for several reasons. First, the case at national level is suspended while the CJEU is preparing its ruling—meaning that the legal dispute which led to the case remains unresolved during that time. Second, national courts may be put off from asking questions because of the delay, meaning that (potentially) a number of very important questions which would otherwise be answered by the CJEU have to be answered by the national courts.

Thinking point

Why does it take such a long time for the Court of Justice to respond to requests for preliminary rulings?

What do you think has caused, or contributed to, this problem? There are in fact several factors—see how many you can identify. A non-exhaustive list of these factors appears at the end of this section.

The solution adopted to deal with this problem is to allow the General Court to handle some of the preliminary rulings workload. Article 256(3) of the TFEU provides that the General Court has jurisdiction to respond to questions referred for a preliminary ruling under Article 267 of the TFEU, but only in 'specific areas', which have not, as yet, been identified. Article 256(3) of the TFEU goes on to state that where the General Court considers that the case requires a 'decision of principle likely to affect the unity or consistency of Union law', it may refer the case to the CJEU for a ruling, and that 'decisions given by the General Court . . . may exceptionally be subject to review' by the CJEU 'where there is a serious risk of the unity or consistency of Union law being affected'.

This solution was agreed by the Member States in 2000, during the negotiations which led to the signing of the Treaty of Nice in 2001. The reform is still not in use nearly twenty years later, however, because no agreement had been reached on what the 'specific areas' should be. Even assuming that some 'specific areas'—or at least one—are eventually identified, there are likely to be teething problems until the new procedure is fully developed. For example:

- The General Court may refer cases onto the CJEU when a 'decision of principle' is involved—but what does 'decision of principle' mean?
- Although the CJEU is only to review General Court rulings 'exceptionally', this arguably undermines the authority of those rulings. For one thing, national courts

will be inhibited from applying a General Court ruling while a possible review is still pending.

As the CJEU's workload has increased over the years, many other reform proposals have been made. Given that the Article 256(3) TFEU solution appears to have stalled, it is worth looking briefly at some of these alternatives.

- **Appoint more judges.** However, this could be counter-productive, as it increases the risk of inconsistent judgments. Anthony Arnull has observed that 'the larger the Court, the less effective it is at delivering prompt and intellectually compelling judgments' ('Refurbishing the Judicial Architecture of the European Community' (1994) 43 ICLQ 296).
- **Abolish mandatory referrals.** However, this would make little practical difference. First, 'courts of last resort' only contribute about 10–15 per cent of the CJEU's workload. Secondly, national supreme courts already have considerable discretion thanks to the CJEU's *Da Costa/CILFIT* jurisprudence.
- **Restrict to national 'courts of last resort' only the right to seek references.** A less drastic version of this reform involves abolishing the rights of first instance national courts and tribunals to seek rulings. This would almost certainly reduce the CJEU's workload, but could threaten the uniformity of EU law and the 'dialogue' that presently exists between the CJEU and all national courts and tribunals. It could create workload problems for national systems, if litigants are encouraged to pursue appeals until they reached a point in the national judicial hierarchy where a ruling could be requested.
- **'Case filtering', whereby the CJEU would be allowed to select cases according to their novelty, complexity, and/or importance.** The advantages are: CJEU workload would be reduced; national courts may become more selective; and it would allow the CJEU to concentrate on those cases which are fundamental to the uniformity and development of EU law. The disadvantages are that it threatens the uniformity of EU law and the open dialogue between the CJEU and national courts.
- **'Decentralisation'.** This would involve renaming the CJEU as the European High Court of Justice (EHCJ), at the apex of a new hierarchy, with four new Regional Courts below it. Under this system, the EU would be divided into four regions, and all the national courts and tribunals in each region would submit ruling requests to the Regional Court for that region. The EHCJ would act as an appeal court, ensuring consistency between the Regional Courts. The idea was proposed by Jean-Paul Jacque and Joseph Weiler in 'On the Road to European Union—A New Judicial Architecture' (1990) 27 CML Rev 185. This system is not dissimilar to that in the USA, where the Supreme Court oversees the Circuit Courts below it, each Circuit consisting of a number of states, so it is workable, but it could be expensive, given the need to set up, equip, and operate four new courts.

- **The creation of new EU courts.** This was suggested by Veerle Heyvaert, Justine Thornton, and Richard Drabble in 'With Reference to the Environment: The Preliminary Reference Procedure, Environmental Decisions and the Domestic Judiciary' (2014) 130 LQR 413. They argued that 'the addition of new EU courts or tribunals could further cut down on delays or, accounting for the continuing rise in proceedings lodged over time, at least keep them on an even keel'. However, the authors acknowledged that '[t]he likely impact on the quality of adjudication is more difficult to predict . . . The introduction of specialised courts may result in better informed rulings, but any beneficial effect might be undercut by greater fragmentation, which risks tainting the coherence and, hence, predictability of EU adjudication.'
- **Abolition of the preliminary rulings procedure, to be replaced by a new system whereby national courts' interpretation of EU legislation would be subject to a review process undertaken by the European Commission.** See further Philip Allott, 'Preliminary Rulings—Another Infant Disease' (2000) 25 EL Rev 538.

Possible causes of the CJEU's workload problem

- The increasing number of Member States, meaning more requests for rulings.
- The increasing number of languages. Initially, the CJEU (and its translators) only had to deal with four language versions of EU legislation. Gradually that has increased as more states joined, so that there are now twenty-three languages (twenty-four if Irish is included).
- The increasing scope and volume of EU secondary legislation. For example, the Framework Directive 2000/78, which prohibits discrimination on various grounds in employment, only came fully into effect in 2006 but has already generated at least seventy-five separate preliminary ruling requests.

6.5 Supremacy of EU law

Given that EU law and national law often deal with the same subjects, such as employment law, consumer protection, and protection of the environment, there is potential conflict between the two. In the event of a dispute, which law is to prevail? There is nothing explicitly in either of the Treaties, although a 'declaration' attached to the Treaty of Lisbon states that 'in accordance with well-settled case law [of the CJEU], the Treaties and the law adopted by the Union on the basis of the Treaties have primacy over the law of the Member States'. The Court touched on the issue of supremacy in *Van Gend en Loos* (Case 26/62) [1963] ECR 1 (see 6.6) but it was first considered in depth in *Costa v ENEL* (Case 6/64) [1964] ECR 585, concerning a conflict between the Treaty of Rome and Italian law. The Court stated that EU law had to prevail, because:

> [b]y creating a [Union] of unlimited duration, having its own institutions, its own personality, its own legal capacity . . . and, more particularly, real powers stemming from

> a limitation of sovereignty or a transfer of powers from the States to the [Union], the Member States have limited their sovereign rights and have thus created a body of law which binds both their nationals and themselves. The integration into the laws of each Member State of provisions which derive from the [Union] . . . make it impossible for the States . . . to accord precedence to a unilateral and subsequent measure over a legal system accepted by them on a basis of reciprocity.

See Chapter 2 on the UK Parliament's view of supremacy.

This decision was not particularly surprising, given that the Member States had signed the Treaty and could be considered to have agreed to bind themselves not to enact legislation contradicting it. In *Internationale Handelsgesellschaft* (Case 11/70) [1970] ECR 1125, however, the Court was asked to consider a much more contentious situation: a conflict between EU secondary legislation and German constitutional law. The CJEU was forthright, stating that '[t]he law stemming from the Treaty . . . cannot because of its very nature be overridden by rules of national law, however framed'. In other words, all forms of EU law, whether primary (the Treaties) or secondary (the 'law stemming from the Treaty'), had to prevail over any conflicting provisions of national law—even national constitutional law. This remains the CJEU's position today.

A practical problem remained: what was a judge in a national court to actually do if faced with a conflict between EU and national law? In *Simmenthal* (Case 106/77) [1978] ECR 629, the CJEU made it clear that:

> [e]very national court must, in a case within its jurisdiction, apply [EU] law in its entirety and protect rights which the latter confers on individuals and must accordingly set aside any provision of national law which may conflict with it, whether prior or subsequent to the [Union] rule . . . It is not necessary for the court to request or await the prior setting aside of such provision by legislative or other constitutional means.

The CJEU reiterated these points in *R v Secretary of State for Transport, ex parte Factortame Ltd* (Case C-213/89) [1990] ECR I-2433, adding that if a national court is prevented by a rule of national law 'from granting interim relief in order to ensure the full effectiveness of the judgment to be given on the existence of the rights claimed under [EU] law' then the court 'is obliged to set aside that rule'.

6.6 **Direct effect**

6.6.1 **Introduction**

The principle of 'direct effect' refers to those provisions of EU legislation which are capable of enforcement by individuals before national courts. The fact that individuals are capable of enforcing EU law in national courts clearly strengthens the impact of EU law. It also means that EU law is more likely to be observed, since the breach of 'directly effective' EU law (either by Member States or by other individuals) can potentially be challenged by individuals before national courts. Whether a particular provision of EU legislation is 'directly effective' depends on its language and purpose.

Some provisions are only binding on, and enforceable by, Member States; others are too vague for enforcement by individuals; others are incomplete and require further implementation. To be directly effective, certain criteria must be satisfied. The key criteria are that the provision in question must be:

- sufficiently clear and precise;
- unconditional.

The question whether or not a particular provision of EU legislation has direct effect is one that can only be answered by a court (not necessarily the CJEU; national courts can make rulings on this question).

6.6.2 **Direct effect and Treaty articles**

The principle of direct effect was first developed in relation to articles of the Treaty of Rome (now the TFEU) in *Van Gend en Loos* (Case 26/62) [1963] ECR 1, involving an alleged breach by the Dutch authorities of what is now Article 30 of the TFEU. The CJEU confirmed that certain provisions of the Treaty were enforceable in national courts, at least in cases where the provision in question was being relied upon by an individual (in this case, a Dutch road haulage company) against one of the Member States. The Court stated:

> [EU] law . . . not only imposes obligations on individuals but is also intended to confer upon them rights which become part of their legal heritage. These rights arise not only where they are expressly granted by the Treaty, but also by reason of obligations which the Treaty imposes in a clearly defined way upon individuals as well as upon the Member States.

The CJEU has subsequently found several Treaty articles to be directly effective. The criteria (set out earlier) have been applied generously, with the result that many provisions which are not *particularly* clear or precise have been found to have direct effect.

Having established the principle of 'direct effect', the next question was whether EU legislation was capable of enforcement in actions brought against individuals, as opposed to the state. This arose in *Defrenne v SABENA* (Case 43/75) [1976] ECR 455, and the CJEU answered in the affirmative.

In *Defrenne v SABENA*, an airline stewardess (Gabrielle Defrenne) brought a claim against her ex-employer (the Belgian airline company SABENA) in the Belgian courts, alleging that she was being paid less than her male colleagues. At the relevant time, there was no Belgian legislation prohibiting pay discrimination. Defrenne therefore relied upon what is now Article 157(1) of the TFEU (which guarantees equal pay for men and women doing the same work). The Labour Court in Brussels, Belgium requested a preliminary ruling from the CJEU under what is now Article 267 of the TFEU. The CJEU held that not only could Article 157(1) be relied upon in national courts, it could be relied upon against private employers. The Court stated: 'Since

[Article 157 TFEU] is mandatory in nature, the prohibition on discrimination between men and women applies not only to the action of public authorities, but also extends to all agreements which are intended to regulate paid labour collectively, as well as to contracts between individuals.'

The idea that EU legislation may be enforced in the context of a dispute between an individual and the state is called 'vertical' direct effect, whereas the notion that EU legislation (or at least Treaty articles) may impose obligations on individuals as well as the state is referred to as 'horizontal' direct effect. More recent examples of horizontal direct effect are:

- *Angonese* (Case C-281/98) [2000] ECR I-4139: an Italian national relied on Article 45(2) of the TFEU in a claim against an Italian bank.
- *Courage Ltd v Crehan* (Case C-453/99) [2001] ECR I-6297: Article 101 of the TFEU was invoked in a dispute between a British brewery/pub chain and a publican.
- *ITWF v Viking Line* (Case C-438/05) [2007] ECR I-10779: Article 49 of the TFEU was relied upon in litigation between the Viking Line ferry company and a trade union.

6.6.3 **Direct effect and the Charter**

As noted above (see 6.3.1), the Charter of Fundamental Rights did not acquire legally binding status until December 2009. However, when that happened, it raised two questions: (a) whether its provisions were capable of direct effect and (b) if so, whether they were horizontally effective. The CJEU has now answered these questions: the answer is 'yes' to both of them.

In *Kücükdeveci v Swedex* (Case C-555/07) [2010] ECR I-365, the CJEU was asked whether Article 21 of the Charter, which provides, inter alia, that '[a]ny discrimination based on any ground such as religion or belief [or] age . . . shall be prohibited', was enforceable horizontally. However, because age discrimination is also prohibited by Directive 2000/78, the Court focused its answer on the directive, which gave 'specific expression' to the principle of non-discrimination on grounds of age, rather than on Article 21 of the Charter. More recently, in *Egenberger v Evangelisches Werk* (Case C-414/16) [2019] 1 CMLR 9, the Court addressed the question head on and stated:

> The prohibition of all discrimination on grounds of religion or belief is mandatory as a general principle of EU law. That prohibition, which is laid down in Article 21(1) of the *Charter*, is sufficient in itself to confer on individuals a right which they may rely on as such in disputes between them in a field covered by EU law. As regards its mandatory effect, Article 21 of the *Charter* is no different, in principle, from the various provisions of the founding Treaties prohibiting discrimination on various grounds, even where the discrimination derives from contracts between individuals.

This was followed in two more cases involving Article 21, *IR v JQ* (Case C-68/17) [2019] 1 CMLR 16 and *Cresco Investigation v Achatzi* (Case C-193/17) [2019] 2 CMLR 20. These developments were welcomed by Aurelia Colombi Ciacchi, 'The Direct

Horizontal Effect of EU Fundamental Rights' (2019) 15 ECL Rev 294, who wrote that 'the *Egenberger* and *IR* v *JQ* decisions are two wonderful pieces of EU constitutional law... These decisions have confirmed and reinforced well-known case law principles on the direct horizontal effect of the prohibition of discrimination in labour relationships.'

Meanwhile, Article 31(2) of the Charter provides that 'every worker has the right to limitation of maximum working hours, to daily and weekly rest periods and to an annual period of paid leave'. In *Bauer and Willmeroth* (Cases C-569, 570/16) [2019] 1 CMLR 36 and *Max-Planck v Shimizu* (Case C-684/16) [2019] 1 CMLR 35, the CJEU confirmed that Article 31(2) was horizontally effective. This development was welcomed by Eleni Frantziou, '(Most of) the Charter of Fundamental Rights is Horizontally Applicable' (2019) 15 ECL Rev 306, who said that, '[a]s most recently reaffirmed in *Bauer*, the constitutional norm now appears to be that the *Charter* is horizontally applicable, at least indirectly and, in many cases, directly as well'.

The *Egenberger* case also addressed the question whether or not Article 47 of the Charter, which provides for 'the right to an effective remedy', was directly effective. The CJEU answered in the affirmative:

> It must be pointed out that Article 47 of the *Charter* on the right to effective judicial protection is sufficient in itself and does not need to be made more specific by provisions of EU or national law to confer on individuals a right which they may rely on as such.

Finally, it must be remembered that any provision of EU legislation can only be given direct effect if it satisfies the key criteria (see 6.6.1). In *Association de Médiation Sociale* (Case C-176/12) [2014] 2 CMLR 41, known as '*AMS*', the CJEU was asked whether Article 27 of the Charter (the right of workers to be informed and consulted) was enforceable horizontally. The Court held not, on the basis that Article 27 lacked sufficient clarity and precision for direct effect.

6.6.4 **Direct effect and regulations**

Provisions within regulations may also be directly effective, both vertically and horizontally, if they satisfy the key criteria. An example of provisions within regulations being relied upon horizontally occurred in *Muñoz v Frumar Ltd* (Case C-253/00) [2002] ECR I-7289.

6.6.5 **Direct effect and directives**

It was originally thought that directives, because they require implementation by Member States, were incapable of direct effect. However, in *Van Duyn v Home Office* (Case 41/74) [1974] ECR 1337, the CJEU ruled that provisions within directives are capable of direct effect, despite the need for implementation, so long as the result to be achieved is clear. However, there is an extra criterion to be met: a directive cannot have direct effect until its implementation date has expired (*Ratti* (Case 148/78) [1979]

ECR 1629). Once a directive has been properly implemented into national legislation, an individual should rely on that legislation rather than on the directive. However, if a Member State fails to implement a directive on time (either at all or properly) then an individual may rely on the directive itself, if its provisions satisfy the criteria for direct effect.

However, this is subject to one final—but very significant—qualification. Having established that directives are capable of direct effect, the CJEU in *Marshall v Southampton Area Health Authority* (Case 152/84) [1986] ECR 723 drew a distinction between vertical and horizontal direct effect. In *Marshall*, the Court held that:

> [i]t must be emphasised that . . . the binding nature of a directive . . . exists only in relation to 'each member state to which it is addressed'. It follows that a directive may not of itself impose obligations on an individual and that a provision of a directive may not be relied upon as such against such a person.

In *Marshall v Southampton AHA*, Helen Marshall was employed by the defendant as a dietician. She was forced to retire at the age of sixty-two on the ground that she had exceeded the authority's compulsory retirement age, which was sixty for women, as opposed to sixty-five for men. This was permissible under the UK's Sex Discrimination Act 1975, which excluded 'provisions relating to death or retirement', but was allegedly in breach of Article 5 of Directive 76/207 (the Equal Treatment Directive), which prohibits discrimination between men and women in terms of 'dismissal' from employment. The Court of Appeal requested a preliminary ruling. The CJEU held that the word 'dismissal' could be interpreted to include compulsory retirement. It then held that provisions in directives were enforceable against the state, but not against private individuals, because directives were addressed to the Member States. However, Ms Marshall was still entitled to enforce Article 5, because the Authority could be regarded as part of the state. This was the case even though the Authority was acting in its capacity as an employer.

Key point

Thus, according to *Marshall*, directives are only capable of 'vertical' direct effect (*Van Duyn* is an example). They are not capable of 'horizontal' direct effect.

The consequences of this are that provisions in an unimplemented directive dealing with some aspect of employment law (for instance) may be invoked by public sector employees against their employer (the state) but the same provisions cannot be invoked by a private sector employee against his/her employer. This particular anomaly led A-G Lenz in *Faccini Dori v Recreb* (Case C-91/92) [1994] ECR I-3325 to invite the Court to reconsider *Marshall*, but it declined to do so. Indeed, the Court has confirmed in several subsequent cases that directives are only enforceable 'vertically'.

However, although directives only have 'vertical' direct effect, in *Marshall* the CJEU held that Southampton Area Health Authority was part of the state, even in its capacity as employer. Indeed, in subsequent cases, the Court has emphasised that directives are potentially enforceable against the state in the sense of central government (as in *Van Duyn*), local government (*Costanzo v Comune di Milano* (Case 103/88) [1989] ECR 1839), and its various 'emanations'. The CJEU has held that the following are capable of being classed as 'emanations' of the state:

- health authorities (*Marshall*);
- the police (*Johnston* (Case 222/84) [1986] ECR 1651);
- the armed forces (*Sirdar* (Case C-273/97) [1999] ECR I-7403);
- nationalised industries (*Foster v British Gas* (Case C-188/89) [1990] ECR I-3133).

The leading case here is *Foster*, where the CJEU stated that directives were enforceable 'against organisations or bodies which were subject to the authority or control of the state or had special powers beyond those which result from the normal rules applicable to relations between individuals'. The continuing validity of this test was recently confirmed by the CJEU in *Farrell v Whitty* (Case C-413/15) [2018] 1 CMLR 46, [2018] 3 WLR 285. This actually gives 'vertical' direct effect a much broader scope than might otherwise have been the case and ameliorates to some extent the decision in *Marshall* to deny 'horizontal' direct effect to directives.

Key point

Although directives are only capable of 'vertical' direct effect, they are enforceable against the state in the sense of central and local government and 'emanations' of the state, such as the police.

Nevertheless, *Marshall* remains one of the CJEU's most controversial decisions and the distinction between vertical and horizontal direct effect of directives generates difficulties. For example, the claimants in *Marshall* and *Foster* were ultimately successful, as their cases were 'vertical', but in a third case, *Doughty v Rolls Royce plc* [1992] 1 CMLR 1045, the claimant was unsuccessful, her case being 'horizontal'. Yet the facts of all three cases were otherwise identical (the claimants were even seeking to enforce the same provision of the same directive).

Application of *Foster v British Gas* in UK courts and tribunals

Strictly speaking, the CJEU in *Foster* could only define in general terms the bodies against which directives were capable of being enforced. Since that judgment, several courts and tribunals in the UK have been called upon to apply *Foster* to various bodies in order to decide whether the provisions of an unimplemented directive could be enforced against them. Generally speaking, the courts have adopted a generous interpretation of *Foster.* The following is a summary of some of the relevant cases:

- *Foster v British Gas (No. 2)* [1991] 2 AC 306. Here, the House of Lords held that British Gas (at least, when it was still a nationalised industry) was an 'emanation of the State'. Lord Templeman said that 'British Gas, which provided a public service, the supply of gas, to citizens of the State generally under the control of the State [and] was equipped with a special monopoly power which was created and could only have been created by the legislature [was] therefore a body against which the relevant provisions of the Equal Treatment Directive may be enforced'.
- *Doughty v Rolls-Royce plc* [1992] 1 CMLR 1045. Here, the Court of Appeal held that the aerospace division of Rolls-Royce was not an 'emanation of the state' because it did not provide a public service and did not possess special powers.
- *Griffin v South West Water Services Ltd* [1995] IRLR 15. In this case, the High Court found that the defendant company was an 'emanation of the state' despite being a private company, largely because it was regulated by OFWAT, the water regulator. Blackburne J held that the question was not 'whether the body in question is under the control of the state, but whether the public service in question is under the control of the State'. He added that it was also 'irrelevant that the body does not carry out any of the traditional functions of the State and is not an agent of the State . . . It is irrelevant too that the State does not possess any day-to-day control over the activities of the body.'
- *NUT v Governors of St Mary's Church of England Junior School* [1997] 3 CMLR 630. Here, the Court of Appeal held that school governors could be regarded as an 'emanation of the state'. Schiemann LJ said that although the governors did not have any 'special powers', they had been made responsible for providing a public service (education) and they were under the control of the state, which was sufficient.
- *Three Rivers District Council v Bank of England (No. 3)* [2003] 2 AC 1, [2000] 2 WLR 1220, in which the House of Lords accepted without dispute that the Bank of England was an 'emanation of the state'.
- *Byrne v Motor Insurers' Bureau and Another* [2007] EWHC 1268 (QB), [2008] 2 WLR 234. Here, the High Court held that the MIB was not an 'emanation of the state', essentially because of the 'complete absence of special powers'.
- *Ministry of Defence v Wallis* [2011] EWCA Civ 231, [2011] 2 CMLR 42. Here, the Court of Appeal described the Ministry as an 'emanation of the state', although strictly speaking a central government department (like the Home Office in *Van Duyn*) *is* the state, as opposed to an 'emanation' of it.
- *NHS Leeds v Larner* [2012] EWCA Civ 1034. Here, the Court of Appeal did not need to decide the issue after NHS Leeds accepted that it was an 'emanation of the state'.

The significance of all of this case law for the English legal system is that it demonstrates that directives are capable of enforcement against a wide variety of British bodies, such as British Gas (at least, when it was a nationalised industry), the Bank of England, and the NHS, even though directives are officially only 'addressed' to the Member States. The effect of this is to enable British claimants to enforce their rights under EU law in UK courts (at least, until the UK leaves the EU at the end of January 2020). Of course, not every claimant is able to do so: the ruling in *Marshall* continues to impose an obstacle to claimants wishing to enforce their legal rights in directives against other individuals. However, there is an alternative solution available for some of those claimants: indirect effect (see 6.6.7).

Several British cases have also involved the much less controversial enforcement of directives against local authorities. These include *Gibson v East Riding of Yorkshire Council* [2000] 3 CMLR 329 (Court of Appeal), *South Tyneside Metropolitan Borough Council v Toulson* [2003] 1 CMLR 28 (Employment Appeal Tribunal), and *Sayers v Cambridgeshire County Council* [2006] EWHC 2029 (High Court). These are less controversial because directives are 'addressed' to the Member States and this clearly includes local as well as central government.

No 'reverse' vertical direct effect of directives

Finally, it should be noted that while directives can be enforced vertically *against* the state, they cannot be enforced vertically *by* the state. In other words, there is no 'reverse' vertical direct effect of directives. This was established in *Kolpinghuis Nijmegen* (Case C-80/86) [1987] ECR 3969, where the Court refused to sanction the Dutch authorities' prosecution of a café for allegedly failing to comply with the provisions of Directive 80/777 relating to the marketing of natural mineral waters—because the directive had not been implemented into Dutch law.

6.6.6 The incidental direct effect of directives

Although it is clear from *Marshall* and *Faccini Dori* that directives cannot be enforced by one individual against another individual, in *CIA Security International* (Case C-194/94) [1996] ECR I-2201 the Court held that a directive could be relied upon by an individual to prevent another individual from enforcing national law which is clearly contrary to it. In other words, directives cannot be used as a 'sword' but can be used as a 'shield'. This precedent was followed in several cases over the subsequent two decades. However, in *Smith v Meade and Others* (Case C-122/17) [2019] 1 WLR 1823, the CJEU appeared to backtrack on itself when it stated that '[a] directive *cannot* be relied on in a dispute between individuals for the purpose of setting aside legislation of a Member State that is contrary to that directive' (emphasis added). Panos Koutrakos, 'Is There More to Say about the Direct Effect of Directives?' (2018) 43 EL

Rev 621 argues that the effect of the *Smith v Meade* case is to confine *CIA* to its very specific facts:

> *Smith* takes us back to the beginning of the development of the direct effect of directives, and explains the various twists along the way: for instance, it clarifies the *narrow* and *exceptional* set of circumstances where the so-called principle of 'incidental effect' would be relevant.

It is also possible to rely on a directive vertically even where this incidentally imposes obligations on another individual. This can be seen in *Wells* (Case C-201/02) [2004] ECR I-723, where Mrs Wells used Directive 85/337 to force the British government to carry out an environmental impact assessment of proposed mining operations at a neighbouring quarry even though that would impact adversely on the quarry's owners. The Court emphasised that the principle of vertical direct effect overrode the 'adverse repercussions' for the quarry's owners.

6.6.7 **Indirect effect**

The lack of 'horizontal' direct effect of directives clearly creates anomalies. However, there is an alternative remedy available to those wishing to enforce directives against other individuals: the 'obligation of interpretation', usually referred to as 'indirect effect'. This obligation was first identified in *Von Colson* (Case 14/83) [1984] ECR 1891, where the Court ruled that, where national legislation has been enacted to implement a directive, national courts are under a duty to interpret that legislation as far as possible in order to achieve the result required by the directive. This duty follows from the obligation placed upon Member States (including the courts) under Article 288 of the TFEU to achieve the results of a directive and their general duty under Article 4(3) of the TEU to take all appropriate measures to ensure fulfilment of their obligations.

An example of the *Von Colson* principle in the UK context is the case of *Litster* [1990] 1 AC 546, where the House of Lords interpreted UK legislation (the Transfer of Undertakings (Protection of Employment) Regulations 1981) in conformity with Directive 77/187, because the 1981 Regulations had been passed specifically in order to implement the 1977 directive.

The scope of the obligation of interpretation was significantly extended in *Marleasing* (Case C-106/89) [1990] ECR I-4135. The CJEU ruled that the obligation applied to all national legislation, including pre-existing legislation, not just legislation specifically implementing a directive. Prior to this ruling, the House of Lords had refused to apply *Von Colson* in a case involving pre-existing UK legislation (*Duke v GEC Reliance Ltd* [1988] AC 618). However, in subsequent cases, the *Marleasing* effect has been deployed between employees and their employers (or ex-employers) involving the interpretation of various sections of the Sex Discrimination Act 1975 (now repealed) in order to achieve results set out in the 1976 Equal Treatment Directive

(Directive 76/207). For example, in *Webb v EMO (Air Cargo) Ltd* [1993] 1 WLR 49, Lord Keith said:

> It is for a UK court to construe domestic legislation in any field covered by a directive so as to accord with the interpretation of the directive as laid down by the [CJEU], if that could be done without distorting the meaning of the domestic legislation . . . This is so whether the domestic legislation came after or, as in this case, preceded the directive.

In *Webb*, the House of Lords felt able to reinterpret a provision of the 1975 Act in a way which brought it into line with the Equal Treatment Directive, which resulted in the House giving judgment to Ms Webb. Other examples of cases in which courts and tribunals in the UK were able to reinterpret the 1975 Act in the light of the Equal Treatment Directive include *Coote v Granada Hospitality Ltd (No. 2)* [1999] IRLR 452 (Employment Appeal Tribunal), *Hardman v Mallon* [2002] 2 CMLR 59 (Employment Appeal Tribunal), and *Relaxion Group v Rhys-Harper* [2003] UKHL 33, [2003] 4 All ER 1113 (House of Lords). You should note that all of these UK cases were 'horizontal', that is, they were disputes between individual employees and their private (non-state) employers, such that direct effect would not have been available (because of the *Marshall* ruling), but indirect effect was available instead.

The obligation of interpretation was further expanded in *Pfeiffer* (Case C-397/01) [2004] ECR I-8835, where the Court indicated that the obligation extended to the 'whole body of rules of national law'—presumably including case law as well as national legislation. In *Impact* (Case C-268/06) [2008] ECR I-2483, the CJEU added that national courts were obliged to do 'whatever lies within their jurisdiction, taking the whole body of domestic law into consideration and applying the interpretative methods recognised by domestic law, with a view to ensuring that the directive in question is fully effective and achieving an outcome consistent with the objective pursued by it'.

In *Adeneler and Others* (Case C-212/04) [2006] ECR I-6057, the CJEU drew a parallel with its case law on direct effect (see *Ratti*) by deciding that the interpretative obligation arises only once the period for implementing the directive has expired. However, there is contradictory case law. *Mangold v Helm* (Case C-144/04) [2005] ECR I-9981 concerned the possible indirect effect of the Framework Directive 2000/78 (which required Member States to introduce legislation to tackle, inter alia, age discrimination), the implementation date of which was still in the future at the time of the dispute. Nevertheless, the Court decided that, because the principle of non-discrimination on grounds of age must 'be regarded as a general principle' of EU law, 'observance of the general principle of equal treatment, in particular in respect of age, cannot as such be conditional upon the expiry of the period allowed the Member States for the transposition' of Directive 2000/78.

The obligation of interpretation is subject to certain limitations. First, national courts are *not* expected to use directives to interpret national legislation in such a way as to create, or exacerbate, criminal liability (*Arcaro* (Case C-168/95) [1996] ECR

I-4705). Second, the obligation on national courts is to interpret domestic legislation 'so far as possible, in the light of the wording and the purpose of the directive' (*Marleasing*). Thus, while indirect effect can be applied to most national legislation (although this may sometimes require a creative approach to interpretation), it will not apply to national legislation the wording of which clearly contradicts the directive (*Pupino* (Case C-105/03) [2005] ECR I-5285), or which is entirely unambiguous and therefore incapable of being interpreted (*QDQ Media v Omedas Lecha* (Case C-235/03) [2005] ECR I-1937).

Critical debate

Professor Michael Dougan has argued for the *Marshall* rule to be scrapped. In 'The "Disguised" Vertical Direct Effect of Directives?' (2000) 59 CLJ 586, he argued that '[t]he "incidental effect" case-law merely joins the unfortunate parade of bizarre nuances which already characterises this particular field . . . Ultimately, the case for toppling this house of cards simply by granting full horizontal direct effect to directives emerges still stronger.' Other academics, such as Professor Paul Craig ('The Legal Effect of Directives: Policy, Rules and Exceptions' (2009) 34 EL Rev 349) and Albertina Albors-Llorens ('Keeping up Appearances: The Court of Justice and the Effects of EU Directives' (2010) 69 CLJ 455), and a number of the CJEU's Advocates-General, have expressed similar views.

On one hand, the Court of Justice has taken the view, based on the wording of the TFEU itself, that because directives are addressed to the Member States they are therefore binding only on the Member States. Hence, while the vertical direct effect of directives is possible (*Van Duyn*), the horizontal direct effect of directives is not (*Marshall*). It can also be argued that it would be unfair to allow an individual to enforce an unimplemented directive against another individual when it was not the fault of the (latter) individual that the directive had not been implemented into national law. Another argument can be made that, when a dispute involves individuals one of whom is seeking to enforce an unimplemented directive, indirect effect provides a more suitable remedy.

On the other hand, academics point out that the *Marshall* rule has been undermined by cases such as *Johnston* and *Foster v British Gas* (which have blurred the boundaries between vertical and horizontal direct effect); *CIA Security International* (which allows for directives to be enforced horizontally, provided the directive is being used as a 'shield' and not a 'sword'); and *Wells* (which allows a directive to be used by one individual to impose an obligation on another individual, provided that this is a side effect of enforcing the directive vertically). They have also pointed out that reliance on indirect effect is not necessarily a perfect solution, as it relies on the national court being able and willing to interpret national law in conformity with EU law.

In the light of this, should the Court of Justice change course and allow horizontal direct effect for directives? What would be the advantages and disadvantages (if any) for doing so? Bear in mind that Treaty articles and provisions in regulations already have horizontal direct effect.

6.7 State liability

6.7.1 Introduction

State liability for breaches of EU law was introduced in *Francovich and Others v Italy* (Cases C-6/90 and C-9/90) [1991] ECR I-5357, when the CJEU declared that the Member States were 'obliged' to compensate individuals for loss and damage caused to them by breaches of EU law. There is nothing explicitly in either of the Treaties to support this, but the Court justified its decision by reference to what is now Article 4(3) of the TEU, according to which Member States have an obligation to ensure the fulfilment of their obligations arising under the Treaties.

6.7.2 The conditions for state liability

Francovich was concerned specifically with the failure of the Italian government to implement a directive. The obligation imposed on states to implement directives is clear (see Articles 4(3) of the TEU and 288 of the TFEU). However, two issues remained unclear:

- what the position might be in relation to other breaches;
- the level of fault required to establish liability.

The CJEU addressed these issues in *Brasserie du Pêcheur SA v Germany; Factortame III* (Cases C-46 and 48/93) [1996] ECR I-1029. The Court made it clear that state liability was a general principle, not restricted to a failure to implement directives, and that three conditions had to be satisfied:

- the rule of EU law infringed must have been intended to confer rights on individuals;
- the breach must be sufficiently serious;
- there must be a direct causal link between the breach of the obligation resting on the state and the damage sustained by the injured parties.

The burden of proof is on the claimant to establish all three conditions. State liability claims are brought in the national court of the defendant state.

An intention to confer rights on individuals

There is a strong link here to direct effect. As A-G Léger noted in *Köbler v Austria* (Case C-224/01) [2003] ECR I-10239, concerning an alleged breach of Article 45 TFEU (which confers the right of free movement on workers): 'The rule of law purportedly infringed . . . is directly effective and its purpose is therefore necessarily to confer rights on individuals.' This first condition has subsequently been held to be satisfied in the case of several directly effective Treaty articles, including Articles 34 and 35

TFEU (which facilitate the free movement of goods) and Article 49 TFEU (which confers the right of 'establishment' on companies and self-employed people). If the first condition is satisfied, the focus shifts to the second condition; if not, then the claim fails. This happened in *Paul and Others v Germany* (Case C-222/02) [2004] ECR I-9425, where the CJEU decided that Article 3(1) of Directive 94/19 was not intended to confer rights on individuals. In *Berlington and Others v Hungary* (Case C-98/14) [2015] 3 CMLR 45, the CJEU held that while Article 56 TFEU (the freedom to provide services) was intended to confer rights on individuals, Directive 98/34 did not do so.

A sufficiently serious breach

The test for determining the second condition, a 'sufficiently serious' breach, is whether the Member State 'manifestly and gravely disregarded the limits on its discretion' (*Brasserie*; *Factortame III*). Although in principle it is national courts who decide this, the CJEU has identified various factors which may be used, as follows:

- the clarity and precision of the rule breached;
- the measure of discretion left by that rule;
- whether the infringement and the damage caused were intentional or involuntary;
- if there was an error of law, whether the error was excusable or not;
- whether the position taken by one of the Union's institutions may have contributed towards the adoption or retention of national measures or practices contrary to EU law.

The first two factors are intrinsically linked. As the CJEU pointed out in *Synthon* (Case C-452/06) [2008] ECR I-7681, the Member State's discretion is 'broadly dependent on the degree of clarity and precision of the rule infringed'.

Many state liability cases involve the failure to properly implement a directive. Such breaches may or may not be sufficiently serious. In *BT* (Case C-392/93) [1996] ECR I-1631 and *Denkavit International v Germany* (Case C-283/94) [1996] ECR I-5063, the failures by (respectively) the UK and Germany were held *not* to be serious, largely because the texts of the directives were unclear, and both states had acted in good faith in trying to implement the directive correctly (suggesting the breach was excusable). Conversely, in *Rechberger and Others v Austria* (Case C-140/97) [1999] ECR I-3499 and *Stockholm Lindöpark v Sweden* (Case C-150/99) [2001] ECR I-493, incorrect implementation was deemed to be serious, because in both cases the relevant directives were clearly worded (suggesting the breach was inexcusable). Meanwhile, in *Dillenkofer v Germany* (Case C-178/94) [1996] ECR I-4845, the CJEU held that failing to implement a directive at all (as opposed to failing to do so properly) would always constitute a sufficiently serious breach, since the obligation to implement directives (under Article 288 of the TFEU) is absolute.

Where a Member State breaches another provision of EU law, typically in the TFEU, the question of liability depends upon the application of these factors to the factual circumstances. Thus the breach of Article 34 TFEU by the German government in *Brasserie du Pêcheur* was deemed to be insufficiently serious because it was an excusable error. However, the breach of Article 35 TFEU by the UK in *Hedley Lomas* (Case C-5/94) [1996] ECR I-2553 was deemed to be serious because of the lack of discretion available. Similarly, the breach of Article 49 TFEU by the UK in *Factortame III* was serious because the government had intentionally breached the provision in question.

Direct causal link

As to the third condition, the CJEU has held that it is, generally speaking, for the national courts to determine whether a direct causal link between breach and damage exists (*Rechberger and Others*).

6.7.3 **What is the 'state'?**

Most state liability cases involve actions against central government or the legislature. In *Berlington and Others*, the CJEU held that the 'principle of Member State liability is applicable, inter alia, where the national legislature was responsible for the infringement'. However, in *Konle v Austria* (Case C-302/97) [1999] ECR I-3099, the CJEU decided that compensation need not necessarily be the responsibility of central government, and in *Haim* (Case C-424/97) [2000] ECR I-5123, the CJEU stated that state liability claims could be brought irrespective of the 'public authority . . . responsible for the breach'. In the UK, the vast majority of state liability actions have been brought against central government, including the cases (mentioned earlier) of *Factortame III*, *Hedley Lomas*, *BT*, and *Synthon*. Usually a specific government minister is named, as in *Negassi v Home Secretary* [2013] EWCA Civ 151, [2013] 2 CMLR 45; *Delaney v Secretary of State for Transport* [2014] EWHC 1785, [2014] 3 CMLR 32; and *Recall Support Services Ltd and Others v Secretary of State for Culture, Media and Sport* [2014] EWCA Civ 1370, [2015] 1 CMLR 38. Local authorities in the UK have also been the subject of state liability actions (*Barco De Vapor BV v Thanet District Council* [2014] EWHC 490; *Ocean Outdoor UK Ltd v Hammersmith and Fulham London Borough Council* [2018] EWHC 2508). State liability cases in the UK have also been brought against various public bodies (*Energy Solutions EU Ltd v Nuclear Decommissioning Authority* [2017] UKSC 34, [2017] 1 WLR 1373; *Allen v HM Treasury and the Revenue & Customs Commissioners* [2019] EWHC 1010).

Even the judiciary may be held liable, according to the CJEU in *Köbler*. Although the claim in that case (against the Austrian Supreme Court) failed, the CJEU expressly ruled that national courts 'adjudicating at last instance' could face liability. This was confirmed in *Traghetti del Mediterraneo v Italy* (Case C-173/03) [2006] ECR I-5177, involving a claim against the Italian Supreme Court. However, the CJEU stressed that 'State liability can be incurred only in the exceptional case where the national court adjudicating at last instance has manifestly infringed the applicable law'.

In *Ferreira da Silva e Brito and Others v Portugal* (Case C-160/14) [2016] 1 CMLR 26, the CJEU held that the non-referral of a question to the Court of Justice under the preliminary rulings procedure by the Portuguese Supreme Court could attract state liability. The Court of Justice pointed out that, in cases such as the present case, which was 'characterised both by conflicting lines of case-law at national level' and by the fact that the provision of EU legislation in question 'frequently gives rise to difficulties of interpretation in the various Member States', a national court of last resort 'must comply with its obligation to make a reference to the Court'. This development had been predicted by Joxerramon Bengoetxea in 'Text and Telos in the European Court of Justice' (2015) 11 ECL Rev 184, where he wrote: 'I would not exclude the possibility of the *Köbler* (or *Traghetti*) jurisprudence being applied to a stubborn national court of last instance abusively declaring *acte clair* in situations that should have been submitted for preliminary ruling.' Now that the Court of Justice has confirmed that this is indeed the case, the UK Supreme Court, as the UK's court of last resort, should perhaps rethink its rather blasé and cavalier approach to its obligation to seek preliminary rulings (see 6.4.6) before it finds itself in a similar situation to its Portuguese equivalent (at least, until the UK leaves the EU at the end of January 2020).

Köbler creates the possibility that a state liability claim brought against a national court could end up being decided in the same court. This actually happened in *Cooper v Attorney General* [2010] EWCA Civ 464, [2010] 3 CMLR 28, when a state liability claim brought against the Court of Appeal had to be decided by the Court of Appeal. The claimant contended that two earlier Court of Appeal decisions (in 1999 and 2000) were in serious breach of EU law. The claim was brought in the High Court and judgment was given to the defendants, but that decision was appealed to the Court of Appeal. The Court (in 2010) decided that the earlier courts had committed a breach of EU law, but not a sufficiently serious breach to justify the imposition of state liability. (Note that in the 1999 and 2000 cases, the Court of Appeal had been 'adjudicating at last instance' because no appeal was available to the House of Lords.)

Finally, in *AGM v Finland* (Case C-470/03) [2007] ECR I-2749, the CJEU introduced a form of vicarious liability when it stated that EU law 'does not preclude an individual other than a Member State from being held liable, in addition to the Member State itself, for damage caused to individuals by measures which that individual has taken' in breach of EU law. Thus liability could, in principle, be imposed on a Member State for breaches of EU law made by individual government employees.

6.7.4 **Limitations**

Member States are allowed to impose conditions on the amount of damages that the claimant can recover in state liability claims. However, any such conditions must not be less favourable than those relating to similar domestic claims (the 'principle of equivalence'), or framed in such a way as to make it in practice 'impossible or excessively difficult' to obtain reparation (the 'principle of effectiveness'). For example, reasonable limitation periods are permissible. In *Danske Slagterier v Germany* (Case C-445/06) [2009] ECR I-2119, the CJEU stated that reasonable time limits for bringing proceedings were justifiable 'in the interests of legal certainty which protects both the taxpayer and the authorities concerned'.

6.8 EU law in the UK post-Brexit: the European Union (Withdrawal) Act 2018

In June 2018, the UK Parliament passed the European Union (Withdrawal) Act 2018 (referred to as the Withdrawal Act in this section). The Withdrawal Act is designed to ensure that, when the UK leaves the EU (currently scheduled for the end of January 2020), the transition is as smooth as possible and no gaps in UK law suddenly appear. This section will explain the key provisions in the Withdrawal Act.

6.8.1 Repeal of the European Communities Act 1972 (the ECA 1972)

The ECA 1972 was the statute that paved the way for the UK to join the EEC, as it was then called, in January 1973. Section 1 of the Withdrawal Act provides that the ECA 1972 will be repealed on the day that the UK leaves the EU, referred to in the Withdrawal Act as 'exit day'.

6.8.2 Saving for EU-derived domestic legislation

Section 2 of the Withdrawal Act provides that UK legislation enacted in order to comply with an EU *directive* will remain in force post-exit day (at least initially). There is a huge amount of this legislation: a House of Commons Briefing Paper, published in January 2017, identifies 'around 7,900 statutory instruments which have implemented EU legislation'. Much of the secondary UK legislation enacted to implement EU directives into UK law since 1973 was passed by government ministers using powers conferred on them by the ECA 1972. Without the 'saving' provision in the Withdrawal Act, all of that secondary UK legislation would cease to exist when the 1972 Act is repealed on 'exit day'. This would create gaps in UK law in many areas, most obviously employment law, consumer protection law, and environmental law.

For example, the Working Time Regulations 1998 (SI 1998/1883) were passed by the Minister for the Department of Trade and Industry, under powers conferred on him by the ECA 1972, in order to implement Directive 93/104. The Regulations confer a range of rights on UK workers, including the right to a maximum working week of forty-eight hours, the right to daily and weekly rest periods, and the right to a minimum of four weeks' paid annual leave. Imagine if all of those rights disappeared overnight! Other examples include the Package Travel, Package Holidays and Package Tours Regulations 1992 (SI 1992/3288), the Consumer Protection from Unfair

Trading Regulations 2008 (SI 2008/1277) and the Consumer Contracts (Information, Cancellation & Additional Charges) Regulations 2013 (SI 2013/3134), all of which were passed under the ECA 1972 in order to implement Directive 90/314, Directive 2005/29, and Directive 2011/83, respectively. All of this legislation will be 'saved' by the Withdrawal Act and will continue to remain in force . . . but not necessarily indefinitely. Section 8(1) of the Withdrawal Act allows for the possibility that the government could amend or repeal such legislation in the future (after exit day).

6.8.3 **Incorporation of 'direct EU legislation'**

Section 3 of the Withdrawal Act provides that 'direct EU legislation' which is 'operative' immediately before exit day will be converted into UK law on exit day. This means that EU *regulations* and *decisions* (which do not require implementation into national law), of which there are thousands, are to be converted into UK law and will remain in force post-Brexit (at least initially). Again, this is not necessarily a permanent state of affairs. Section 8(1) of the Withdrawal Act allows for the possibility that the government could amend or repeal such legislation in the future (after exit day).

6.8.4 **Saving for certain provisions in the Treaties—but not the Charter?**

The provisions of the Withdrawal Act just described deal with *secondary* EU legislation in the form of regulations, directives, and decisions. What about *primary* EU legislation, in the form of the TEU, TFEU, and Charter? Section 4 of the Withdrawal Act provides that all *directly effective* provisions of the Treaties, but *only* those provisions, will remain in force in UK law after Brexit. A good example is Article 157(1) TFEU, which states: 'Each Member State shall ensure that the principle of equal pay for male and female workers for equal work or work of equal value is applied.' This provision was held to be directly effective in *Defrenne v SABENA* (Case 43/75) (1976) and so will remain part of UK law after Brexit. Similarly, the competition law provisions of the TFEU (Articles 101 and 102, which prohibit cartels and the abuse of a dominant position, respectively) were held to be directly effective in *Belgische Radio & Televisie v SV SABAM* (Case 127/73) [1974] ECR 51 and so they will also remain part of UK law post-Brexit. Once again, this is not necessarily a permanent state of affairs, so although all of these provisions will be 'saved' after Brexit, the government will have the power to amend or repeal them after 'exit day'. Meanwhile, all of the non-directly effective provisions of the TEU and TFEU will cease to apply in the UK on 'exit day'.

And what about the Charter? Somewhat controversially, s.5(4) of the Withdrawal Act states that the Charter will *not* be converted into UK law on exit day. However, this perhaps sounds more radical than it actually is, given that most of the provisions of the Charter duplicate provisions found in other international treaties and conventions—most obviously the European Convention of Human Rights (given effect in the UK by the Human Rights Act 1998)—and Brexit has no impact whatsoever on either the ECHR or the HRA 1998.

6.8.5 **Supremacy of EU law post-Brexit**

Section 5 of the Withdrawal Act provides for a (limited) form of the principle of supremacy of EU law to survive, even after Brexit. An example might be where there is an inconsistency between, for example, (a) an Act of Parliament passed *before* exit day, and (b) a provision of UK law which is converted from an EU Regulation *on* exit day. In that situation, the *latter* will take priority. This reflects (and perpetuates) the situation as it is now, that is, before exit day, whereby an EU regulation takes priority over inconsistent national law.

However, this continuation of EU law supremacy post-Brexit is limited. Where, for example, there is an inconsistency between (a) an Act of Parliament passed *on or after* exit day, and (b) a provision of UK law which has been converted from an EU regulation *on* exit day, then the *former* will take priority.

6.8.6 **Interpretation of 'retained EU law'**

The Withdrawal Act contains detailed provisions on the interpretation of 'retained' EU law after exit day. These include the following:

- UK courts and tribunals will lose access to the preliminary rulings procedure (see 6.4) on exit day (s.6(1)(b)).
- Case law of the CJEU delivered *on or after* exit day will be of persuasive precedent only (s.6(1)(a) and (2)).
- Case law of the CJEU delivered *prior* to exit day will continue to be binding precedent in the UK, with the same status as UK Supreme Court case law (s.6(3) and (4)). In other words, CJEU case law on, for example, the interpretation of Regulation 492/2011 or Article 157(1) TFEU (which will be converted into UK law on exit day) will be binding on all UK courts after Brexit. Only the Supreme Court (and the High Court of Justiciary in Scotland) will be able to depart from that case law (s.6(4) and (5)).
- Section 6(3) also retains the obligation on UK courts to interpret UK legislation in conformity with any relevant EU directive (the 'indirect effect' principle, as established in the CJEU cases of *Von Colson* and *Marleasing* (see 6.6.7)) . . . but *only* in relation to UK legislation passed *before* exit day. UK legislation passed *on or after* exit day will not be subject to the 'indirect effect' principle.

Note: 'retained' EU law essentially means (a) all of the UK legislation passed under the ECA since 1973; (b) all of the directly applicable EU law in the form of regulations and decisions which will be converted into UK law on exit day; and (c) those directly effective provisions of the TEU and TFEU which will also be converted into UK law on exit day.

6.8.7 The end of state liability

Schedule 1, para. 4 of the Act provides that there will be no right in domestic law on or after exit day to damages 'in accordance with the rule in *Francovich*'. This means there will no longer be any possibility of seeking compensation against the UK government (or any regional government, UK public body, or the UK Supreme Court) under the principle of state liability (see 6.7) after Brexit.

6.8.8 Dealing with deficiencies arising from withdrawal

Section 8(1) of the Withdrawal Act provides that, after exit day, a government minister may 'make such provision as the Minister considers appropriate to prevent, remedy or mitigate (a) any failure of retained EU law to operate effectively, or (b) any other deficiency in retained EU law, arising from the withdrawal of the UK from the EU'.

This provision is controversial. First, it is an example of a 'Henry VIII' clause whereby government ministers are given powers to amend primary legislation (that is, an Act of Parliament) using secondary legislation. This raises question marks about the level of parliamentary scrutiny involved (see further 3.5.3). Secondly, it has a very wide (and ambiguous) scope—what exactly does 'operate effectively' mean? What does 'any other deficiency' mean? These wide powers will make it very difficult to challenge any statutory instrument passed under the Act on grounds that it was *ultra vires* (see further 3.5.4).

Summary

- The EU was formed in 1993, following the European Coal and Steel Community formed in 1952 and the EEC formed in 1958.
- The EU has twenty-eight Member States (at least, until the UK leaves the Union) with five applicant countries.
- The EU is run by several supranational institutions, including the Council, the European Commission, the European Parliament, and the CJEU.
- There are three main sources of EU law: primary legislation, secondary legislation, and case law of the CJEU.
- Primary legislation consists of the Treaty on European Union, the Treaty on the Functioning of the European Union, and the Charter of Fundamental Rights. These contain the fundamental principles of EU law.
- Secondary legislation includes regulations and directives, which add detail to the fundamental principles. Regulations seek to ensure uniformity throughout the Union. They do not require implementation. Directives are binding only as to the 'result to be achieved'. They require implementation into national law, within a specified time period.

- The CJEU deals with enforcement actions brought by the European Commission against Member States and preliminary rulings. The latter allows national 'courts and tribunals' to seek rulings on the interpretation of EU legislation, which ensures that EU law is interpreted consistently and applied uniformly. The CJEU has a heavy workload, which has led to long delays. Several reforms of the preliminary rulings procedure have been proposed.
- Supremacy: any provision of EU law prevails over any conflicting provision of national law, even national constitutional law.
- Direct effect: sufficiently clear, precise, and unconditional provisions of EU legislation are enforceable by individuals in national courts. Treaty articles, Charter articles, and regulations are enforceable 'vertically' (against the state) and 'horizontally' (against other individuals). Directives are enforceable once the implementation deadline has expired, but only 'vertically'. The state includes central and local government and 'emanations' of the state.
- Indirect effect: the obligation on national courts to interpret national legislation and case law, as far as possible, in conformity with any relevant directive, in order to achieve the result in the directive.
- State liability: Member States are obliged to compensate individuals for loss and damage caused by a failure to comply with EU law, subject to certain conditions.

Questions

1 What are the main functions of the European Commission?
2 What are the key differences between a regulation and a directive?
3 What is a 'court or tribunal' in the context of Article 267 TFEU?
4 What is a 'court of last resort'?
5 Explain the circumstances in which the provisions of a directive could be given direct effect.
6 What is an 'emanation of the state'?
7 How was the principle of 'indirect effect' developed in (a) *Marleasing*; (b) *Pfeiffer*?
8 What are the conditions for state liability?

Sample question and outline answer

Question

In the rare situations when direct effect of EU directives is not available, indirect effect ensures that individuals' rights under EU directives are adequately protected. Critically consider the extent to which you agree with this statement.

Outline answer

Answers to this question should begin by defining 'direct effect'—the concept that provisions of EU law are enforceable in national courts subject to certain prerequisites being satisfied, that is, that the provision in question is sufficiently clear, precise, and unconditional (*Becker*).

Answers should explain that provisions in directives are vertically enforceable—that is, against the state (*Van Duyn, Becker*), but not horizontally—that is, against other individuals (*Marshall*). This situation could usefully be contrasted with that involving provisions in the TFEU, in the Charter, and in regulations, all of which may be enforced horizontally as well as vertically (*Defrenne v SABENA*).

Explain the reasons for the *Marshall* rule—that directives are addressed to Member States, and therefore only binding upon them (the so-called textual argument), who must not be allowed to benefit from their own failure to implement (the so-called estoppel argument); that it would be unfair to impose obligations via unimplemented directives on individuals.

Explain that, despite *Marshall*, directives are enforceable against local authorities and 'emanations of the state' such as the police (*Johnston*), as well as the 'state' in the sense of central government, which significantly ameliorates the strictness of the *Marshall* rule while simultaneously undermining it. After all, the possibility of enforcing directives against the police does not sit comfortably with the textual argument.

In particular, explain that the CJEU in *Foster v British Gas* defined 'emanation of the state' very broadly, that is, as bodies subject to state authority/control or those with special powers, such as nationalised industries and hospitals, which only serves to blur the distinction between vertical and horizontal direct effect.

Explain the possibility of 'incidental' direct effect, that is, where a directive may be used as a 'shield' in order to prevent contradictory national legislation from being enforced (*CIA Security v Signalson*), and 'triangular' direct effect, that is, the situation where a directive is enforced (vertically) against the state even though there is a side-effect whereby obligations are imposed (horizontally) on a third party (*Wells*). Discuss the extent to which the presence of these concepts undermines the *Marshall* decision.

Note other limitations on the enforcement of directives, that is, matters that are only available once the implementation deadline has passed (*Ratti*) or the fact that they cannot be enforced by Member States against individuals, that is, there is no reverse vertical direct effect (*Kolpinghuis*).

Answers should then explain 'indirect effect'—the obligation imposed on national courts to interpret implementing national legislation 'in the light of' EU directives (*Von Colson*). Note the subsequent expansion of indirect effect, in *Marleasing*, to all national legislation whether implementing or not, and in *Pfeiffer* to all national law, that is, case law as well as legislation. Explain the wide scope of indirect effect: in particular, observe that it is available in all cases, including 'horizontal' cases, as in *Marleasing* and *Webb*.

Discuss the limitations of indirect effect: the national legislation must be open to interpretation without 'distortion' (*Marleasing*) and therefore indirect effect will not apply to national legislation, the wording of which clearly contradicts the directive (*Pupino*), or which is entirely unambiguous and therefore incapable of being interpreted (*QDQ Media v Omedas Lecha*); indirect effect is only available once the implementation deadline has passed (*Adeneler*); indirect effect cannot be used to create or exacerbate criminal liability (*Arcaro*).

Reach a conclusion. This will involve assessing whether direct effect of EU directives is or is not available only in 'rare' situations, and whether it is accurate to state that indirect effect ensures that individuals' rights under EU directives are adequately protected, given the various restrictions available on its enforcement. Academic commentary from the likes of Marson (2004) and Craig (2009), both of whom argue that the *Marshall* rule should be scrapped, could be usefully incorporated here.

Further reading

- ***Craig, P.*** *'The Legal Effect of Directives'* (2009) 34 EL Rev 349

  Criticises the rule in *Marshall* that directives cannot be enforced horizontally, in the light of the various exceptions to it that have been identified subsequently.

- ***Davis, R.*** *'Liability in Damages for a Breach of Community Law'* (2006) 31 EL Rev 69

  Discusses the meaning and scope of the 'state' in the context of state liability.

- ***Dougan, M.*** *'When Worlds Collide: Competing Visions of the Relationship between Direct Effect and Supremacy'* (2007) 44 CML Rev 931

- ***Drake, S.*** *'Twenty Years after Von Colson'* (2005) 30 EL Rev 329

  Provides an overview of the CJEU's indirect effect case law, and examines the relationship between indirect effect and incidental direct effect.

- ***Lock, T.*** *Is Private Enforcement of EU Law through State Liability a Myth? An Assessment 20 Years after Francovich* (2012) 49 CML Rev 1675

  Examines the state liability case law in the two decades since the CJEU introduced the concept in 1991.

- ***Marson, J.*** *'Access to Justice: A Deconstructionist Approach to Horizontal Direct Effect'* [2004] 4 Web JCLIIR **www.bailii.org/uk/other/journals/WebJCLI/admin/wjclidex.html**

  Explores the arguments for and against horizontal direct effect of directives.

- ***Rasmussen, H.*** *'Remedying the Crumbling EC Judicial System'* (2000) 37 CML Rev 1071

  Explores the various options for reform of the preliminary rulings procedure (including rewriting of the *CILFIT* criteria to encourage greater use of *acte clair*).

- ***Sif Tynes, D.*** and ***Lian Haugsdal, E.*** *'In, Out or In-between? The UK as a Contracting Party to the Agreement on the European Economic Area'* (2016) 41 EL Rev 753

  Explores the so-called 'Norwegian Option' for the UK post-Brexit.

Online resources

You should now attempt the supporting self-test questions and end-of-chapter questions available at: **www.oup.com/he/wilson-rutherford4e**

Chapter 7

Human rights in the United Kingdom

Learning objectives

By the end of this chapter you should:

- understand the relationship between the law of the United Kingdom and the European Convention on Human Rights (ECHR);
- analyse the impact of the Human Rights Act 1998 upon parliamentary sovereignty;
- consider the consequences of UK law being incompatible with the ECHR;
- understand the significance of s.3 of the Human Rights Act 1998 for the process of statutory interpretation;
- be able to explain the operation of the doctrine of precedent in relation to decisions of the UK courts concerning human rights and the impact of decisions of the European Court of Human Rights;
- appreciate when Convention rights may be directly enforced, that is, when the 1998 Act creates a direct cause of action;
- understand what constitutes a 'public authority';
- be able to explain the remedies available for a contravention of a Convention right.

Talking point

English law has traditionally recognised fundamental freedoms and civil liberties for hundreds of years. These liberties protected individuals from state interference, for example, prevented the state unlawfully entering your home and seizing your private property (see *Entick v Carrington* (1765)). During the eighteenth century, the common law was the main source of developing these liberties but there was some significant legislation too, such as the Habeas Corpus Act 1679 which allowed individuals to challenge the lawfulness of their detention.

However, the peak of the individual's protection against the state came with the enactment of the Human Rights Act 1998. This Act enshrined rights—everything from the right to liberty, to the right to a fair trial, to freedom of expression—and enabled the individual to legally enforce those rights in UK courts if the state failed in its duty and obligation to protect and respect those rights.

Today, the Human Rights Act has come to attract considerable hostility amongst certain sections of the British press. The criticism has often targeted the fact that the Act incorporates the European Convention on Human Rights (ECHR) and enables the European Court of Human Rights to declare that the UK is in breach of its obligations under the Convention. There has been considerable conversation about the enactment of a British Bill of Rights that might replace the Human Rights Act 1998 and, so the argument goes, help to restore parliamentary supremacy in ways that the Act allegedly currently restricts. In 2015, the Conservative government promised to repeal the Human Rights Act 1998 and even possibly withdraw from the ECHR (although the current government has no such immediate plans to do so).

For example, in *Hirst v UK (No. 2)* 205 ECHR 681, a prisoner serving a life sentence successfully challenged s.3 of the Representation of the People Act 1984, which placed a blanket ban on prisoners voting. The European Court of Human Rights held that such a ban was indiscriminate and breached the UK's obligation in respect of the right to vote in free elections. The Court did not say that all prisoners should be given the vote, but simply that a blanket ban was unjustified and thus the UK was in breach. The UK government was given until November 2012 to change its law to comply, but no change occurred. Over a considerable amount of time, politicians in Parliament proved very reluctant to change the law to comply with the ruling. The former Prime Minister David Cameron even referred to the thought of giving prisoners the vote as something that made him 'physically ill'. After further delays, in December 2017, the then Justice Secretary announced a change of rules that would allow offenders on short sentences to vote while on temporary release.

Reflect on the following questions:

- Do you think all human rights are absolute and are based on the inherent dignity of human beings?
- If not, which human rights do you think are conditional? More specifically, which rights and under what circumstances do you think the state should be entitled to restrict?
- Finally, what is your view on the right of prisoners to vote? Do you think the current rules now draw a sensible balance between acknowledging the wrong-doing of those convicted and imprisoned and the principle that all people should be entitled to participate in free elections?

Introduction

The horrors of the Second World War are often cited as the starting point for the development of human rights in the United Kingdom. The war brutally highlighted the human cost of widespread torture, discrimination, forced labour, and religious persecution, most notoriously inflicted by the Nazi regime against the Jewish population in Germany. By the end of the war, the international community, alongside many human rights campaigners, wanted to establish a legal and binding regime that would protect the human rights of all individuals. The establishment of the United Nations was one part of this international effort. Although not binding, the Universal Declaration of Human Rights was proclaimed and adopted by the United Nations on 10 December 1948. The Declaration was intended to declare a common universal benchmark for all nations to protect human rights. It can be found here: **https://www.un.org/en/universal-declaration-human-rights/**. Further international human rights treaties have since followed.

Against this backdrop, there were also European attempts to unite countries that were previously at war, to declare their shared values, and to come together to protect the human rights of their populations. In 1948, Winston Churchill referred to the idea of a 'Charter of Human Rights, guarded by freedom and sustained by law'. In May 1949, the Council of Europe, consisting of ten states, including the UK, was established. Its mission was to protect human rights and promote the rule of law and democracy across Europe. Soon, lawyers across Europe (including those from Britain), and inspired by the Universal Declaration of Human Rights, began drafting a code of legally enforceable human rights. On 4 November 1950, the Convention on the Protection of Human Rights and Fundamental Freedoms (known as the 'European Convention on Human Rights') was signed by the ten member states. The Convention came into force in the United Kingdom in September of 1953.

The aim of the Convention was to establish a common core of human rights and fundamental freedoms and oblige each member state to protect them within their own jurisdictions. The Convention also established the European Court of Human Rights which was to help enforce these obligations. The Court decides and rules on cases that involve the interpretation of rights under the Convention and whether or not a particular state has met their obligations under the Convention. If a state were to be in breach, the Court could make a declaration that the state had breached its obligations and in some cases award 'just satisfaction'—a financial award or remedy to the injured party. Compliance with these judgments and declarations is a matter for each respective state.

Key point

Please don't make the mistake often made by the newspapers and casual observers. The European Convention on Human Rights and the European Court of Human Rights (sitting in France) are completely distinct and separate from the European Union and the Court of Justice of the European Union (sitting in Luxembourg). Do not confuse them and use them interchangeably. The establishment of the Council of Europe and the ECHR pre-dates the economic treaties that were to evolve and later become the European Union.

In light of the UK's withdrawal from the European Union, its membership of the ECHR will be unaffected. However, to slightly confuse matters, the only implication for human rights is that withdrawal from the EU may involve the UK no longer retaining the European Union's own Charter of Fundamental Rights—a position now confirmed by s.5(4) of the EU (Withdrawal) Act 2018. This Charter does contain some rights and protections, particularly in reference to the workplace, that are not found in the ECHR. There has been some criticism that this may leave a gap in the UK's protection of human rights. For an accessible legal analysis of this issue see Professor Mark Elliott's blog entry: **https://publiclawforeveryone.com/2018/02/08/human-rights-post-brexit-the-need-for-legislation/**.

See 4.6, 'Presumptions of statutory intent'.

As an international treaty, the ECHR was not part of the law of the UK and was not directly enforceable by the courts of the UK. Nevertheless, the UK courts did construe domestic legislation, if possible, on the presumption that Parliament intends to legislate in compliance with the UK's treaty obligations. Similarly the ECHR and court rulings remained of considerable persuasive value in the development of the common law.

During the twentieth century, the UK was found to have contravened the Convention on numerous occasions. One such example included the UK's use of interrogation techniques on terrorist suspects in Northern Ireland, including the imposition of hooding, subjection to continuous noise, and sleep deprivation. In the first case brought by one state against another, in *Ireland v United Kingdom* (5310/71) [1978] ECHR 1 the Court held that such interrogation techniques amounted to inhuman and degrading treatment contrary to Article 3 of the Convention. Although already abandoned by the time of the judgment, the UK confirmed that the techniques would not be re-introduced in the course of interrogation of suspects.

The UK only accepted the right of *individuals* to petition the court—based in France—in 1966. This right could only be exercised once all forms of domestic legal redress had been exhausted (e.g. all possible appeals had been made). The judgment of the European Court of Human Rights could lead the UK government to change domestic law.

Example

The UK's contempt of court laws prevented the reporting and publication in the *Sunday Times* of the newspaper's investigation into the thalidomide scandal. Thalidomide was a medicinal sedative given to pregnant mothers but which later resulted in babies being born with severe deformities. The newspaper's application to the European Court of Human Rights on the basis that the contempt laws contravened the Convention right to freedom of expression was successful (*Sunday Times v United Kingdom (No. 1) Ltd* [1979] 2 EHRR 245). The law of the UK was subsequently changed by the Contempt of Court Act 1981.

By the 1990s, there were increasing calls to incorporate the Convention into UK law. These calls found a voice in the Labour Party's 1997 election manifesto pledge to incorporate the Convention and referred to rights being brought home. The fact that public bodies were not strictly obliged to comply with human rights and that taking cases to Strasbourg could take years and cost an excessive amount of money were some of the reasons cited for incorporation. Once Labour were in power, the manifesto pledge was to become the Human Rights Act 1998 (entering into force on 2 October 2000). The Act incorporates the ECHR into domestic law so Convention rights could be directly enforced in domestic courts and the courts themselves could determine whether or not UK law was compliant with the rights in the Convention.

This chapter provides an overview of some of the key features of the Human Rights Act 1998. This is a topic that will be covered in more detail when you study public law (sometimes referred to as 'constitutional and administrative law'). The Act is of considerable constitutional significance and has helped to transform the direction and development of the common law. Some of its provisions have also triggered significant public debate. This includes the relationship between the UK courts and the European Court of Human Rights. In addition, the Act has raised considerable discussion about the role of the judiciary in the UK's unwritten constitution. Specifically, the Act is often said to create a democratic tension between the court's role in interpreting statutes balanced against the court's duty to respect the supremacy of Parliament as the UK's ultimate law-making body. Before turning to the Act, it is useful to begin with the rights found in the Convention and some of the key concepts raised by judges and human rights lawyers.

7.1 The ECHR and the incorporation of Convention rights into UK law

The main rights established under the ECHR are:

- Article 2 Right to life—everyone's right to life shall be protected by law.
- Article 3 Prohibition of torture—no one shall be subjected to torture or to inhuman or degrading treatment or punishment.
- Article 4 Prohibition of slavery and forced labour.
- Article 5 Right to liberty and security.
- Article 6 Right to a fair trial.
- Article 7 No punishment without law—against the retrospective operation of law.
- Article 8 Right to respect for private or family life.
- Article 9 Freedom of thought, conscience, and religion.
- Article 10 Freedom of expression.
- Article 11 Freedom of association and assembly.
- Article 12 Right to marry.
- Article 13 Right to an effective remedy.
- Article 14 Prohibition of discrimination. Article 14 does not create a right in itself but must be linked to discrimination in respect of other Convention rights (see later *A v Secretary of State for the Home Department* [2005] 2 AC 68 and *Ghaidan v Godin-Mendoza* [2004] UKHL 30).

The Convention rights have been complemented by a number of protocols. Under Protocol 1, three rights are created:

- Article 1 Right of natural and legal persons to peaceful enjoyment of their possessions.
- Article 2 Right to education.
- Article 3 The holding at reasonable intervals of free and fair elections in choosing the legislature.

Protocol 13, Article 1 abolishes the death penalty in any circumstances; no derogation is permissible.

Thinking point
Is the Convention outdated?

The ECHR was drafted more than sixty years ago. The European Court of Human Rights sometimes refers to the Convention as a 'living instrument', referring to the flexible approach to interpretation that might be required to ensure that it can apply to situations not contemplated when it was first drafted. Consider whether you think further more radical change is required. Do the rights in the ECHR need to be redrafted in the light of developments since 1949 and, if so, what types of rights should now be protected by the Convention? Should social and economic rights be incorporated such as the right to an adequate standard of living, the right to work, or the right to a healthy environment?

7.1.1 The Human Rights Act 1998 and the incorporation of Convention rights into UK law

Under s.1 of the Human Rights Act 1998, the 'Convention rights' to be incorporated into UK law are specified.

Section 1 provides that the 'Convention rights' are the rights and fundamental freedoms found in:

- Articles 2–12 and 14 of the Convention (note Articles 1 and 13 were not incorporated);
- Articles 1 to 3 of Protocol 1;
- Article 1 of Protocol 13 as read with Articles 16 to 18 of the Convention.

Broadly speaking, there are three types of rights found under the Convention. Some of the rights are *absolute* (which means that the state is not entitled to restrict them). These include the rights in Article 2, 3, 4(1), and 7, although Article 2 sets outs some inherent limitations. There are other rights that are said to be *limited*, for example Article 5 and the right to liberty, principally when an individual is duly convicted in a court of law and is subsequently detained/imprisoned.

Finally, there are *qualified* rights that the state can legitimately restrict when the state has to strike a balance between individual rights and the protection of others and the interests of the wider community. Article 8–11 are all qualified. For example, the right to freedom of expression in Article 10 is qualified for the reasons listed in Article 10(2), including reasons of national security, public safety, prevention of crime, protection of others' reputation, amongst others. Restrictions on these rights need to be lawful, pursue a legitimate aim, and be necessary in a democratic society (often requiring an assessment of whether the state's restriction is proportionate).

Margin of appreciation

The 'margin of appreciation' is an important principle of the Convention and one adopted by the European Court of Human Rights when it interprets the Convention. It recognises that while human rights are universal in the abstract, national courts and authorities are better placed to judge how such rights are to be implemented and better able to arrive at a balance when legitimately restricting those rights (providing the minimum standard is met). Timothy Jones, writing in 1995 in an article entitled 'The Devaluation of Human Rights under the European Convention' [1995] PL 430, said that the margin of appreciation 'refers to the degree of latitude which signatory States are permitted in their observance of the Convention'.

The doctrine affords a measure of discretion to states and acts as a constraint on how far the European Court of Human Rights is able to interfere with, for example, the balance struck between freedom of expression and the right to protect one's reputation. This plainly acknowledges that there is no strict consensus among countries in Europe on many human rights and thus a margin is needed to avoid an onerous and uniform implementation of the Convention.

Handyside v United Kingdom (1976) 1 EHRR 737 provides a good example of the margin in action. In this case, a sexually explicit book directed at school children was seized and destroyed under the Obscene Publications Act 1959. However, the book was freely available in many other states which were bound by the ECHR. Handyside argued that the law was in breach of his right of freedom of expression under Article 10. The European Court of Human Rights decided that there was no breach of Article 10. In its reasoning, the Court determined that it was for individual states to regulate their domestic approach to such matters of morality, having regard 'to the different views prevailing ... about the demands of the protection of morals in a democratic society'.

In Protocol 15 (yet to be ratified by all member states at the time of writing), express reference is made to the principle of subsidiarity. This principle refers to member states having the primary responsibility to secure the rights and freedoms defined in the Convention and Protocols, and that they enjoy a margin of appreciation in doing so.

Proportionality

Another important principle in the Convention is that of proportionality. This principle is adopted by the European Court and it is also adopted by the UK courts when a claimant alleges that a public authority exercising its discretion has breached one of his/her rights under the Convention (see s.6 Human Rights Act 1998). If the defendant alleges that a policy is being adopted to pursue a legitimate aim and thus requires interference with the right, what the courts have to ask is whether the interference is proportionate. Lord Reed of the UK Supreme Court (UKSC) has described this principle as a 'search for a fair balance between the demands of the general interest of the community and the requirement of the protection of the individual's fundamental rights' (*Bank Mellat v HM Treasury (No 2)* [2013] UKSC 39).

In *de Freitas v Permanent Secretary of Agriculture, Fisheries, Lands and Housing* [1999] 1 AC 69, Lord Clyde confirmed that three questions have to be asked in assessing proportionality, namely, whether:

- the legislative objective is sufficiently important to justify limiting a fundamental right;
- the measures designed to meet the legislative objective are rationally connected to it;
- the means used to impair the right or freedom are no more than is necessary to accomplish the objective (per Lord Clyde).

Lord Sumption added in *Bank Mellat v HM Treasury (No. 2)* [2013] UKSC 39 that under requirement three, one could consider whether a less intrusive measure could have been used. However, he confirmed there was a fourth requirement, and, echoing the sentiment of Lord Reed, said that proportionality required considering 'whether, having regard to these matters and to the severity of the consequences, a fair balance has been struck between the rights of the individual and the interest of the community' (see also Huang *v Secretary of State for the Home Department* [2007] UKHL 11).

You will learn more about the UKSC's further refinement and application of proportionality when you study Public Law, and in particular the law on judicial review. The UKSC has discussed the principle variously in recent cases such as *Keyu and Others v Secretary of State for Foreign and Commonwealth Affairs* [2015] UKSC 69, *Pham v Secretary of State for the Home Department* [2015] UKSC 19, and *Kennedy v The Charity Commission* [2014] UKSC 20.

To illustrate with an earlier but no less important example, proportionality was applied in *R (on the application of Daly) v Secretary of State for the Home Department* [2001] 2 AC 532. In this case, a prisoner challenged the legality of the Home Secretary's policy that excluded inmates during searches of their cells by prison officers. The argument focused on the ability of prison officers to access confidential and privileged legal correspondence between the prisoner and their lawyers. The applicant argued that the blanket policy of exclusion infringed his common law right to confidential communication with his legal representative and amounted to a breach of Article 8 of the ECHR. The Home Office argued the search procedure was necessary to maintain prison discipline and prevent criminal activity (e.g. the storage of banned and illegal items etc.) and that the exclusion of prisoners was necessary to avoid prisoners adopting intimidatory or diversionary tactics.

The House of Lords said that the policy was unlawful. The decision was based on the application of common law principles but Lord Bingham said that the same result would be achieved by reliance on the ECHR. Under Article 8(1) of the Convention, the applicant had a right to respect for his correspondence and the policy infringed this right to a greater extent than was necessary for the prevention of crime and maintaining discipline. Put another way, the infringement of the right was greater than was justified by the objectives of the policy. The policy was not proportionate because the *blanket* exclusion could not be justified as the evidence suggested that not *all* prisoners would intimidate. A more nuanced and personalised policy would be more proportionate in light of the importance of respecting privileged legal correspondence.

7.1.2 Derogation from Convention rights

It is possible for the UK government, by Article 15 of the Convention, to *derogate* (i.e. temporarily suspend) the application of Convention rights 'in time of war or other public emergency threatening the life of the nation'. The derogation measures must only be such as are strictly required by the exigencies (demands) of the situation and must not be inconsistent with the state's other obligations under international law. Note that no derogation is permitted from Articles 2, 3, 4(1), and 7, and Protocol 13, Article 1.

By s.1(2) of the Human Rights Act 1998, the articles establishing the 'Convention rights' specified in the 1998 Act have effect subject to any designated derogation. Section14(1) of the Human Rights Act 1998 empowers the Secretary of State to make an order designating any derogation by the UK from an article of the Convention, or of any protocol to the Convention.

 **Example**

One of the most notable examples of the UK's derogation from the ECHR came in the aftermath of the terrorist attacks of September 11, 2001 in the USA. The UK government introduced legislation—the Anti-terrorism, Crime and Security Act 2001—which by s.23 gave the state the power to detain, without trial, suspected foreign terrorists resident in the UK. In order to exercise this power the UK government made a derogation from Article 5, the right to liberty. This derogation was challenged in *A v Secretary of State for the Home Department* [2005] 2 AC 68. The appellants were foreign nationals who were certified by the Secretary of State as suspected foreign terrorists and detained without trial under s.23. It was argued on their behalf that there was not a 'public emergency threatening the life of the nation' which permitted derogation within the meaning of Article 15(1).

The House of Lords, comprising the nine law lords, refused to interfere with the derogation on this basis (although Lord Hoffmann dissented on this point and infamously declared: 'The real threat to the life of the nation, in the sense of a people living in accordance with its traditional laws and political values, comes not from terrorism but from laws such as these'). However, for the majority of eight judges, the issue was largely political and the courts were expected to give great weight to the judgment of the Home Secretary and Parliament on this question, as they were exercising 'a pre-eminently political judgment'.

Nonetheless, in spite of the derogation being unchallenged, the House of Lords declared s.23 to be a disproportionate infringement to liberty under Article 5 and also discriminatory under Article 14 of the Convention (the section applied only to foreign nationals suspected of terrorism and not to UK nationals that were otherwise suspected of the same). In consequence, acting under s.4 of the Human Rights Act 1998 (see later at 7.3), s.23 was incompatible with Articles 5 and 14 of the ECHR.

7.1.3 **Parliamentary sovereignty and the ECHR**

The UK played a major role in establishing and drafting the ECHR. Before the enactment of the Human Rights Act 1998, one of the arguments for resisting the incorporation of the Convention was that it risked disrupting the delicate constitutional balance between Parliament and the courts. Parliament is supreme, able to make and unmake any laws, and the courts cannot challenge the validity of an Act of Parliament. However, by contrast, the criticism often made is that the incorporation of the Convention unduly enhances the power of the judiciary at the expense of preserving the supremacy of Parliament.

The Human Rights Act 1998 avoided this consequence by, first, extending the judicial role in the interpretation of legislation but not empowering the courts to strike down Acts of Parliament that were deemed to be incompatible with the ECHR. In the case of *In Re S (Minors) (Care Order: Implementation of Care Plan)* [2002] 2 AC 291, Lord Nicholls said (at p.313):

> The Human Rights Act reserves the amendment of primary legislation to Parliament. By this means the Act seeks to preserve parliamentary sovereignty. The Act maintains the constitutional boundary. Interpretation of statutes is a matter for the courts; the enactment of statutes, and the amendment of statutes, are matters for Parliament.

The key to understanding the judiciary's relationship with Parliament is located in the operation ss.3 and 4 of the Human Rights Act 1998, as illustrated in Diagram 7.1.

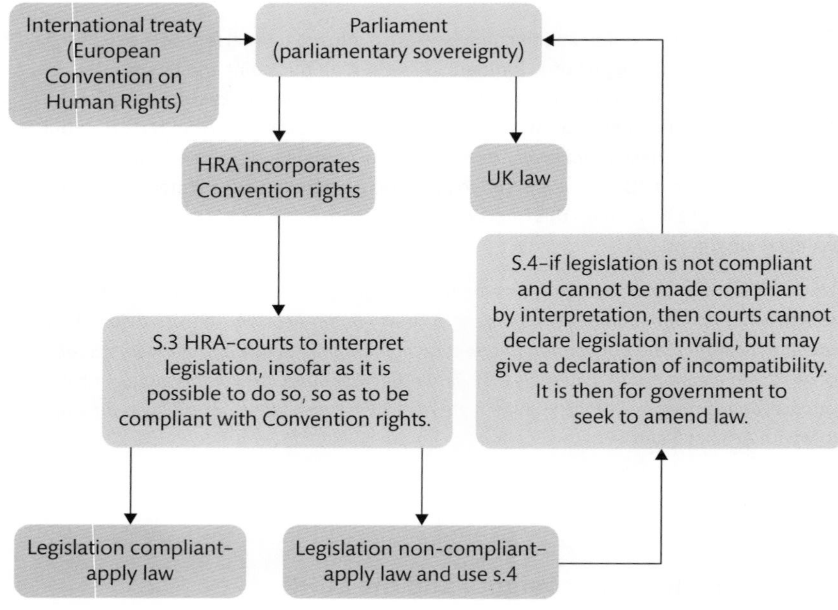

Diagram 7.1 Sections 3 and 4 of the Human Rights Act 1998

7.2 **Interpretation of legislation under section 3**

By s.3(1), the courts are under a duty to read and give effect to primary legislation and subordinate legislation in a way which is compatible with the Convention rights in 'so far as it is possible to do so'.

The duty under s.3(1) applies to primary legislation and subordinate legislation, whether enacted before or after the passing of the Human Rights Act 1998 (see s.3(2)(a)). Also, should the courts be unable to give effect to legislation in a way which is compatible with the Convention rights, this does not affect 'the validity, continuing operation or enforcement' of the legislation (both primary and subordinate: see s.3(2)(b) and (c)). In other words, the incompatible law is still valid and would still apply, pending the intervention of the government and Parliament to change the law.

The question raised by the words 'so far as it is possible to do so' begs the question of how far is permissible? What is the extent to which the courts may stretch the linguistic meaning and/or read words into a statute in the interpretation of domestic legislation? The concern is that when judges go beyond the language used in legislation, judges are not interpreting but are, in fact, *law-making* and thereby usurping Parliament's law-making supremacy.

How, then, have the courts approached this task of interpretation under s.3(1)? Some guidance on this question was given by the House of Lords in *R v A (Complainant's sexual history)* [2002] 1 AC 45. In this case, the House of Lords had to decide whether s.41 of the Youth Justice and Criminal Evidence Act 1999—which restricted the admissibility of evidence relating to a complainant's previous sexual history—infringed the defendant's right to a fair trial under Article 6 of the Convention. The words of an Act of Parliament are the primary source of interpretation but s.3(1) of the Human Rights Act 1998 placed a duty on the courts to interpret an Act so as to ensure compatibility with Convention rights, so far as it is possible to do so. For s.3 to apply, there was no requirement that the provisions had to be ambiguous and have two possible meanings. Indeed, in the view of Lord Steyn, the effect of s.3 may be that it is sometimes necessary to adopt an interpretation which appears linguistically strained. His Lordship concluded that it was permissible under s.3 to read s.41(3)(c) 'as subject to the implied provision that evidence or questioning which is required to ensure a fair trial under Article 6 of the Convention should not be treated as inadmissible'.

Hence, the interpretation of the House of Lords went beyond finding Parliament's meaning from the words used in the Youth Justice and Criminal Evidence Act 1999; instead, the House of Lords introduced a qualification to the operation of s.41 in order to adhere to the obligation in s.3 of the Human Rights Act 1998.

Example

The case of *Ghaidan v Godin-Mendoza* [2004] UKHL 30 concerned the interpretation of the Rent Act 1977. In this case, X, who was the tenant of a dwelling house, had lived with the defendant in a stable homosexual relationship since 1972. On the death of X, the question arose of whether the defendant was entitled to succeed to the tenancy of the deceased. The Rent Act 1977 provided:

> Section 2(1) The surviving spouse (if any) of the original tenant, if residing in the dwelling-house immediately before the death of the original tenant, shall after the death be the statutory tenant if and so long as he or she occupies the dwelling-house as his or her residence.
>
> (2) For the purposes of this paragraph, a person who was living with the original tenant as his or her wife or husband shall be treated as the spouse of the original tenant . . .

A literal interpretation of the words of the statute meant that the survivor of a heterosexual relationship was entitled to a statutory tenancy but not the survivor of a homosexual relationship.

The defendant argued that this difference in treatment was discriminatory in contravention of Article 14 read in conjunction with Article 8, and that this incompatibility could be resolved by s.3 of the Human Rights Act 1998. The House of Lords agreed and interpreted s.2(2) as applying to same-sex partnerships to ensure compatibility. In consequence, the defendant was entitled to succeed to the deceased's statutory tenancy.

As to the process of reading in words, Lord Steyn endorsed the Court of Appeal's approach in interpreting the phrase 'as his or her wife or husband' to mean *'as if they were* his wife or husband'. However, Lord Nicholls took a slightly different approach and said that 'paragraph 2 should be read and given effect to as though the survivor of such a homosexual couple were the surviving spouse of the original tenant'. Of course, one might consider that the precise words to be read into the Act were not significant—what was important was the substantive effect. The claimant was successful and the right to succeed the tenancy protected.

One question to consider is whether there are any limits to the duty under s.3(1)? Clearly, the use in the subsection of the phrase 'so far as it is possible to do so' envisages that there may be situations where the courts cannot achieve compatibility with the Convention. Lord Nicholls, in *Ghaidan v Godin-Mendoza*, explained the operation and limits of s.3(1). His Lordship said (at [32]):

> Section 3 enables language to be interpreted restrictively or expansively. But s.3 goes further than this. It is also apt to require a court to read in words which change the meaning of the enacted legislation, so as to make it Convention-compliant. In other words, the intention of Parliament in enacting s.3 was that, to an extent bounded only by what is 'possible', a court can modify the meaning, and hence the effect, of primary and secondary legislation.
>
> Parliament, however, cannot have intended that in the discharge of this extended interpretative function the courts should adopt a meaning inconsistent with a fundamental feature of legislation. That would be to cross the constitutional boundary s.3 seeks to demarcate and preserve. Parliament has retained the right to enact legislation in terms which are not Convention-compliant. The meaning imported by application of s.3 must be compatible with the underlying thrust of the legislation being construed. Words implied must, in the phrase of my noble and learned friend, Lord Rodger of Earlsferry, 'go with the grain of the legislation'. Nor can Parliament have intended that s.3 should require courts to make decisions for which they are not equipped. There may be several ways of making a provision Convention-compliant, and the choice may involve issues calling for legislative deliberation.

Clearly, the courts are permitted to go beyond the words used by Parliament in seeking to make domestic legislation compliant with the Convention. However, there are limits to the interpretative role of the courts under s.3. A court should not read in words to achieve compliance in the following situations:

- where Parliament has deliberately passed an Act which is intended not to be Convention-compliant then the courts must give effect to Parliament's intention to act in contravention of the Convention;
- where, in the opinion of the court, Parliament, and not the courts, should decide the most appropriate way to make the legislation Convention-compliant.

In these two situations, the court may declare that the legislation is not Convention-compliant and then it becomes an issue for the government and Parliament to resolve.

A recent illustration of the latter situation was seen in *R (on application of T) v Chief Constable of Manchester and Others* [2013] EWCA Civ 25. In this case the Court of Appeal refused to read down legislation on the ground that it would represent a major legislative change from the existing scheme. As there was a legislative choice to resolve the problem, this was to be left to Parliament. In consequence, a declaration of incompatibility was granted in relation to Part V of the Police Act 1997. On appeal, the Supreme Court upheld the declaration of incompatibility ([2014] UKSC 35). Consider the case of *Principal Reporter v K* (Scotland) [2010] UKSC 56 and identify the words that were read into the relevant legislation, in that case the Children (Scotland) Act 1995.

Example

The case of *R (Anderson) v Secretary of State for the Home Department* [2003] 1 AC 837 considered the Home Secretary's power under s.29 of the Crime (Sentences) Act 1997 to determine when mandatory life sentence prisoners may be released. The House of Lords declared the power to be incompatible with Article 6 of the Convention (the right to have a sentence determined by an independent and impartial tribunal). It was not possible to interpret the section using the interpretive obligation under s.3(1) because to do so would effectively remove the Home Secretary's powers which had clearly been intended by Parliament. This, said Lord Bingham, would give an effect to s.29 that would be quite different from that which was intended by Parliament: 'it would not be judicial interpretation but judicial vandalism.' Indeed, if the House of Lords were to have removed such powers, the House would then have to have resolved what to put in place by way of substitution; this would have gone beyond any interpretative function. In consequence, the House of Lords made a declaration of incompatibility under s.4 (see 7.2).

In *Bellinger v Bellinger* [2003] 2 AC 467, the relevant issue was the validity of a marriage between a male and a transsexual female; by s.11(c) of the Matrimonial Causes Act 1973, a marriage is void if the parties are not respectively male and female. It was argued that s.11(c) was incompatible with Articles 8 and 12 of the Convention. The House of Lords refused to use s.3(1) of the Human Rights Act 1998 to interpret the words 'male' and 'female' in the Matrimonial Causes Act 1973 so as to include a transsexual female. Lord Nicholls indicated that interpreting s.11(c) to include transsexuals would have far-reaching ramifications, raising issues that called for broad public consultation and political discussion. Accordingly, such a change was to be left to Parliament, a body that is elected and far better suited to such wide-ranging reform. It happened to be particularly true in this case because the government had already announced an intention to introduce primary legislation on this issue. In consequence, a declaration of incompatibility under s.4 of the Human Rights Act 1998 was made and it was not long before Parliament passed the Gender Recognition Act 2004.

Aileen Kavanagh, in 'Statutory Interpretation and Human Rights after Anderson: A More Contextual Approach' [2004] PL 537, argued that mere linguistic possibility is not the only factor that a court considers in determining whether an interpretation under s.3(1) is possible. Other factors can be taken into account. These factors include whether Parliament will reform the law, how imminent such reform is likely to be, and how radical a change to existing legislation is required to make it Convention-compliant.

Thinking point

What to do? To interpret or to declare?

Section 3 gives the courts considerable latitude in the interpretation of legislation. The courts are willing to read words into legislation, which may expand the scope of a provision, or even read down, that is, limit, the scope of a provision. In certain circumstances, the courts will instead issue a declaration of incompatibility. Consider the case law. Do you consider that the courts have adopted a consistent approach to interpretation under s.3? Does it matter?

7.3 Declaration of incompatibility

Section 4 of the Human Rights Act 1998 sets out the conditions for the making of a declaration of incompatibility. As discussed in the previous section, a declaration of incompatibility is a last resort should the courts be unable to interpret legislation under s.3 to ensure compatibility (see Lord Steyn's comments in *Ghaidan v Godin-Mendoza*). Where a court is satisfied that a provision of primary legislation, for example an Act of Parliament (specifically defined in s.21 of the Human Rights Act 1998), is incompatible with a Convention right, then it may make a declaration of incompatibility. In relation to a provision of subordinate legislation a court may make a declaration of incompatibility if it is satisfied that:

- the provision is incompatible with a Convention right;
- the primary legislation under which the subordinate legislation is made prevents removal of the incompatibility (disregarding any possibility of revocation).

The only English courts that may make such a declaration are the Supreme Court, the Judicial Committee of the Privy Council, the Court Martial Appeal Court, the Court of Appeal, the High Court, and the Court of Protection in certain instances. It is made clear, by s.4(6), that a declaration of incompatibility 'does not affect the validity, continuing operation or enforcement of the provision' of the legislation in question. Rather, the declaration acts as a signal that the incompatibility needs to be addressed by the government and Parliament. One way of understanding this is by way a constitutional and democratic *dialogue* between two core organs of the state—the judiciary and Parliament. The former respects Parliament's supremacy by only informing it of an incompatibility issue.

In *R (on the application of F (by his litigation friend F)) and Thompson (FC) v Secretary of State for the Home Department* [2010] UKSC 17, the Supreme Court had to consider whether s.82 of the Sexual Offences Act 2003 was incompatible with Article 8 of the ECHR (the right to respect for private and family life). Section 82 provides that anyone convicted of a sexual offence and sentenced to thirty months' imprisonment or more is under a lifelong duty to notify the police where they are living and of any intention to travel abroad. Under the legislation there was no right to review the necessity of that duty.

The issue for the Supreme Court was: 'does the absence of any right of review render lifetime notification requirements disproportionate to the legitimate aims that they seek to pursue?' To be clear, the notification provisions themselves were not being challenged; rather, the challenge related to the absence of a right to review the imposition of that duty to notify.

The Supreme Court upheld the decisions of the Divisional Court and the Court of Appeal that the indefinite notification requirements of the Sexual Offences Act 2003 were incompatible with Article 8 and as such, the requirements constituted a disproportionate interference with that article. The declarations of incompatibility originally made were upheld.

This case illustrates the operation of the concept of proportionality: the courts seek to strike a balance between the legitimate aims of legislation (here the protection of the public from convicted sex offenders) and the importance of protecting the offender's Article 8 rights. In doing so, they consider whether the extent of the interference is justified or whether the unreviewable notification requirements of the 2003 Act were proportionate to the legitimate aim. Unsurprisingly, given that it could be demonstrated that some offenders no longer presented a risk of re-offending, the absence of a system of review was disproportionate in its interference with Article 8 rights.

By contrast, in *Hounslow LBC v Powell* [2011] UKSC 8, the Supreme Court refused to make a declaration of incompatibility. Under s.3(1) of the Human Rights Act 1998, the Court refused to read down s.89 of the Housing Act 1980 and similarly refused to make a declaration of incompatibility as there was no evidence that there was incompatibility with the Article 8 Convention right. Ultimately, each case is decided and determined on the precise factual merits.

Example

The following case is a good example of the precise facts being crucial. Due to its moral complexities, *R (on the application of Nicklinson and another) v Ministry of Justice* [2014] UKSC 38 attracted significant media attention. The Supreme Court had to consider whether s.2 of the Suicide Act 1961—outlining the offence of assisting someone to commit suicide—should be subject to a declaration under s.4 due to its incompatibility with Article 8 of the

Convention (the right to respect for private or personal life) The appellants' argument was that s.2 of the Suicide Act 1961 infringed the Article 8 rights of people who have made 'a voluntary, clear, settled and informed decision to commit suicide' but, due to their physical circumstances, require assistance from a third party. In this case, Tony Nicklinson decided that he wanted to end his life because he was paralysed from the neck down and was wholly dependent on others. He had a fully functioning mind but was unable to speak (having to do so via a computer). He described his life as a 'living nightmare'.

The Secretary of State for Justice argued that the courts did not have constitutional competence to decide whether or not s.2 infringes Article 8, and even if the courts did have such competence, a ruling that would essentially create a lawful right to die should be a matter for Parliament to decide, not the courts.

First, the Supreme Court, comprising a panel of nine Justices, were asked to decide whether s.2 of the Suicide Act 1961 was within the UK's margin of appreciation. It held that a 'blanket ban' on assisted suicide was within the margin of appreciation confirmed by the European Court of Human Rights, but in any event s.2 of the Suicide Act 1961 did not constitute a 'blanket ban' (see s.2(4)). It also unanimously held that s.2 of the Suicide Act did engage Article 8 as it prevented people from determining how and when they should die.

In relation to the issue of constitutional competence, the Supreme Court was asked: where the European Court of Human Rights decides that a point is within the margin of appreciation of a member state, is it open to a UK court to declare that a statutory provision which is within that margin nonetheless infringes Convention rights? The Supreme Court, by a majority (Lord Neuberger, Lady Hale, Lord Mance, Lord Wilson, and Lord Kerr), decided that the courts did have constitutional competence and therefore were capable of making a declaration of incompatibility. Lord Neuberger said (at [76]):

> [G]iven that the Strasbourg court has held that it is for each state to consider how to reconcile, or to balance, the Article 8.1 rights of a person who wants assistance in dying with 'the protection of . . . morals' and 'the protection of the rights and freedoms of others', I conclude that, even under our constitutional settlement, which acknowledges parliamentary supremacy and has no written constitution, it is, in principle, open to a domestic court to consider whether section 2 infringes Article 8.

In addressing the issue, the Supreme Court had to consider the constitutional boundaries between Parliament's legislative sovereignty and the courts' power to intervene. The majority decided that it did have discretion to make a declaration of incompatibility under s.4—declaring that s.2 of the Suicide Act 1961 infringed Article 8—provided that the evidence and arguments supported such a declaration. However, even if the arguments and evidence did support a declaration, it was not right to make a declaration at this time, as it was appropriate to first accord Parliament the opportunity to consider whether s.2 ought to be amended. Lord Neuberger identified several reasons for reaching this decision.

First, the amendment of s.2 raised difficult moral and religious questions and should be approached with caution by the courts. Secondly, any incompatibility is not easy to identify and cure (unlike in *Re G (Adoption: Unmarried Couple)* [2009] 1 AC 173) and would give rise to difficult questions of how to amend the legislation; again, this suggests that the courts should not move too quickly. Thirdly, s.2 has been considered on several occasions in Parliament and was due to be debated in the House of Lords, so the issue was still under active consideration by the legislature. Fourthly, less than thirteen years had passed since *Pretty v DPP* [2002] 1 AC 800, in which the House of Lords had not considered it appropriate to make a declaration of incompatibility in relation to s.2, the Supreme Court should, similarly, not now alter its view.

Had the Supreme Court concluded in the circumstances of this case that it would have been institutionally appropriate to consider making a declaration of incompatibility, would the court have done so on the evidence and arguments raised by this appeal?

The majority concluded that no declaration of incompatibility would have been given on the arguments presented to the courts. Lord Neuberger said (at [120]):

> Before we could uphold the contention that section 2 infringed the Article 8 rights of Applicants, we would in my view have to have been satisfied that there was a physically and administratively feasible and robust system whereby Applicants could be assisted to kill themselves, and that the reasonable concerns expressed by the Secretary of State (particularly the concern to protect the weak and vulnerable) were sufficiently met so as to render the absolute ban on suicide disproportionate.

He continued that there were too many uncertainties to justify the making of a declaration of incompatibility.

However, on the issue of making a declaration of incompatibility Lady Hale and Lord Kerr dissented and would have made such a declaration that s.2 was incompatible with Article 8. Lord Kerr emphasised that when courts make a declaration of incompatibility under s.4, they do precisely what Parliament had empowered the courts to do, and remit the issue to Parliament for a political decision informed by the court's view of the law [343]. That declaration did not involve the court making a moral choice which is appropriately left to Parliament who are democratically elected. Lord Kerr would also have held that there was no rational connection between the aim of section 2(1) and the interference with the Article 8 right [350].

You may want to consider the views of four other judges, Lord Sumption, Lord Hughes, Lord Reed and Lord Clarke. These judges shared a subtly different opinion. Although they accepted that the courts had jurisdiction and could declare that s.2 of the Act infringed Article 8 (because the interference was not justified), they were of the view that such an assessment was more institutionally appropriate for Parliament to make (rather than it be left open to judges to weigh up on the evidence presented). Amongst other reasons, they thought that such assessments involved social and moral judgments which involved a choice between two fundamental but often inconsistent moral values, the sanctity of life and the principle of autonomy, and upon which there is no consensus in our society, and that the parliamentary process is a better way of resolving issues arising out of such moral and social dilemmas. For the latest judicial treatment of assisted suicide see *R (on the application of Conway) v Secretary of State for Justice* [2018] EWCA Civ 1431.

Different, but no less morally complex, issues arose in the case of *In the Matter of an Application by the Northern Ireland Human Rights Commission for Judicial Review (Northern Ireland)* [2018] UKSC 27. In this case the Northern Ireland Human Rights Commission sought to challenge the laws that criminalised abortion in Northern Ireland. The Commission argued the laws were not compatible with Article 3 (the prohibition against torture), Article 8 (the right of everyone to respect for their private and family life), and Article 14 (the prohibition of discrimination) in so far as the law prohibited abortion in cases of (a) serious foetus malformation, (b) pregnancy as a result of rape, and (c) pregnancy as a result of incest. Although a challenging read, take a look at the judgment and in particular the judgments of Lady Hale and Lord Kerr. The judgment is available here: **https://www.supremecourt.uk/cases/docs/uksc-2017-0131-judgment.pdf**. Please note the law in Northern Ireland has now changed and abortion was effectively decriminalised on 22 October 2019.

In 2019, the Ministry of Justice's reports on *Responding to Human Rights Judgments: Report to the Joint Committee on Human Rights on the Government's Response to Human Rights judgments* 2018–19 indicated that between the Human Rights Act coming into force and July 2019 there had been forty-two declarations of incompatibility. See **https://assets.publishing.service.gov.uk/government/uploads/system/uploads/attachment_data/file/842553/responding-human-rights-judgments-2019.pdf**.

See 3.3, 'The passage of legislation through Parliament'.

7.4 Statements of compatibility in Parliament

Section 19 of the Human Rights Act 1998 provides that a minister in charge of a bill in either the House of Commons or House of Lords must, before the second reading of the bill, make a statement in writing indicating whether or not the provisions of the bill are compatible, in the minister's view, with the Convention rights. Section 19 recognises the possibility of an Act being passed which is not compatible with Convention rights but it is very unlikely that the UK government would deliberately breach its Convention obligations, and usually a statement of compatibility is issued.

The making of a statement of compatibility indicates to the courts that the legislation is to be interpreted in accordance with s.3 of the 1998 Act. Should a minister state that he is unable to make a statement of compatibility, but nonetheless the government wishes the bill to proceed, it is more difficult to predict the approach of the courts. In relation to the Communications Bill (which became the Communications Act 2003) which banned political advertising on television and radio, the minister did not make a statement of compatibility. The government believed, and had been advised, that the ban on political advertising was compatible with Article 10, but doubt remained about whether the proposed legislation was Convention-compliant following the decision of the European Court of Human Rights in *VgT Verein gegen Tierfabriken v Switzerland* (2001) 10 BHRC 473. In *R (on the application of Animal Defenders International) v Secretary of State for Culture, Media and Sport* [2008] UKHL 15, the House of Lords decided that the restrictions to freedom of expression in ss.319 and 321 of the Communications Act 2003 were necessary to protect the democratic process, given the potentially insidious effect of broadcast media. Parliament had clearly considered the issue in passing the Communications Act 2003 and in the opinion of the House of Lords, the legislation was not incompatible with Article 10. The decision of the European Court of Human Rights in *VgT* was considered but its facts were distinguishable from the present case.

7.5 Remedying incompatibility

7.5.1 Incompatible primary legislation

Section 10 of the Human Rights Act 1998 provides that a minister of the Crown has the power to take remedial action in relation to primary legislation in the following circumstances:

See 3.5.3 for an explanation of Henry VIII clauses.

- either (a) a court has made a declaration of incompatibility and no appeal has been made or there is no appeal possible, or (b) in the light of a finding of the European Court of Human Rights a legislative provision appears to be incompatible with the Convention;
- the minister of the Crown considers that there are compelling reasons for proceeding under s.10;
- then the minister 'may by order make such amendments to the legislation as he considers necessary to remove the incompatibility'.

The power given to the minister is an example of a Henry VIII clause; the minister may repeal or amend the provisions of an Act of Parliament using delegated and secondary legislation.

Thinking point

Ministerial law-making?

Permitting a minister to amend primary legislation by way of relying on a Henry VIII clause is considered to be controversial. Why? Consider all the reasons why such a process might be problematic in a parliamentary democracy. You may want to compare this form of amendment with the normal route of creating and passing and amending primary legislation. See 3.5.3.

7.5.2 Incompatible subordinate legislation

Under s.4 of the Human Rights Act 1998, a court may make a declaration of incompatibility if a provision of subordinate legislation is incompatible with a Convention right *and* the parent Act prevents the removal of the incompatibility. Should such a situation arise then, by s.10(3), a minister of the Crown may by delegated legislation amend the primary legislation in the following circumstances: (i) in order for the incompatibility to be removed, the primary legislation must be amended, and/or (ii) the minister of the Crown considers there are compelling reasons for proceeding under s.10.

However, the Court recently considered the situation where the parent Act did not prevent any attempt at removing the incompatibility. In *RR v Secretary of State for Work and Pensions* [2019] UKSC 52—a case involving a regulation on the 'bedroom tax'—the Supreme Court confirmed that the courts have consistently held that, where it is possible to do so, a provision of subordinate legislation which results in a breach of a Convention right must be disregarded. Lady Hale declared: 'there is nothing unconstitutional about a public authority, court or tribunal disapplying a provision of subordinate legislation which would otherwise result in their acting incompatibly with a Convention right, where this is necessary in order to comply with the HRA.'

7.6 The UK courts and the European Court of Human Rights

The UK courts are not bound by the judgments of the European Court of Human Rights (see Chapter 5, 'The doctrine of judicial precedent'). However, by s.2(1) of the Human Rights Act 1998, a court or tribunal when determining an issue relating to a Convention right 'must take into account' any judgment of the European Court of Human Rights whenever made or given so far as, in the opinion of the Court, it is relevant to the proceedings in which that issue has arisen. A fundamental question naturally arises: what does 'take into account' mean in precise terms. In *R (Alconbury Developments Ltd and Others) v Secretary of State for the Environment, Transport and the Regions* [2003] 2 AC 295, Lord Slynn said (at [26]):

> Although the Human Rights Act 1998 does not provide that a national court is bound by [decisions of the European Court of Human Rights] it is obliged to take account of them so far as they are relevant. In the absence of some special circumstances it seems to me that the court should follow any clear and constant jurisprudence of the European Court of Human Rights. If it does not do so there is at least a possibility that the case will go to that court, which is likely in the ordinary case to follow its own constant jurisprudence.

In *R (Anderson) v Secretary of State for the Home Department* Lord Bingham stated (at p.879) that:

> While the duty of the House under s.2(1)(a) of the Human Rights Act 1998 is to take into account any judgment of the European Court, whose judgments are not strictly

> binding, the House will not without good reason depart from the principles laid down in a carefully considered judgment of the court sitting as a Grand Chamber.

A Grand Chamber of the European Court of Human Rights is a court consisting of seventeen judges.

However, note Lord Hoffmann's comments in *Secretary of State for the Home Department v AF (No. 3)* [2010] 2 AC 269. The case concerned control orders (measures that restrict the liberty of an individual suspected of terrorist activity) under s.2(1) of the Prevention of Terrorism Act 2005 and whether the individual subject to such an order—the controlee—is given a fair trial in compliance with Article 6 of the ECHR. The issue of a fair trial depended upon material which was undisclosed to the controlee on the grounds of national security. The European Court of Human Rights (ECtHR) in *A v United Kingdom* (2009) 49 EHRR 625 determined that a controlee must be given sufficient information about the allegations against him to enable him to give effective legal instructions with regard to his defence of those allegations. As the judgment of the ECtHR was clear and applicable in the *AF* case, Lord Hoffmann said that although the House of Lords was not bound by *A v United Kingdom*, to reject the decision would put the UK in breach of international law obligations under the Convention. In consequence, UK law should be read to ensure compatibility with the ECtHR's interpretation of the Convention. Here the House of Lords not only took the judgment into account but felt compelled to follow it.

In *Manchester City Council v Pinnock* [2010] UKSC 45, Lord Neuberger said (at [48]):

> This court is not bound to follow every decision of the EurCtHR. Not only would it be impractical to do so: it would sometimes be inappropriate, as it would destroy the ability of the court to engage in the constructive dialogue with the EurCtHR which is of value to the development of Convention law (see e.g. *R v Horncastle* [2009] UKSC 14, [2010] 2 All ER 359, [2010] 2 WLR 47). Of course, we should usually follow a clear and constant line of decisions by the EurCtHR: *R (Ullah) v Special Adjudicator* [2004] UKHL 26, [2004] 2 AC 323, [2004] 3 All ER 785. But we are not actually bound to do so or (in theory, at least) to follow a decision of the Grand Chamber . . . Where, however, there is a clear and constant line of decisions whose effect is not inconsistent with some fundamental substantive or procedural aspect of our law, and whose reasoning does not appear to overlook or misunderstand some argument or point of principle, we consider that it would be wrong for this court not to follow that line.

So if the jurisprudence of the European Court is clear and constant then, in effect, the UK courts will be bound. However, if the clear and constant line of decisions is inconsistent with some fundamental substantive or procedural aspect of UK law or has omitted to consider or misunderstood an argument or point of principle then the decisions of the European Court need not be followed by the UK courts. Lord Mance, in *R (on the application of Chester) v Secretary of State for Justice; McGeoch v Lord President of the Council* [2013] UKSC 63, emphasised that where a matter has been considered by a Grand Chamber it would have 'to involve some truly fundamental principle of our law or some most egregious oversight or misunderstanding before it could be appropriate for this court to contemplate an outright refusal to follow Strasbourg authority at the Grand Chamber level'.

It might be said that the Supreme Court's approach is to make the European Court of Human Rights the engine for the development of human rights under both the Convention and under UK law. However, this argument has not found favour in the House of Lords. Lord Bingham, in *R (Ullah) v Special Adjudicator* [2004] 2 AC 323, said (at p.350):

> It is of course open to member states to provide for rights more generous than those guaranteed by the Convention, but such provision should not be the product of interpretation of the Convention by national courts, since the meaning of the Convention should be uniform throughout the states party to it. The duty of national courts is to keep pace with the Strasbourg jurisprudence as it evolves over time: no more, but certainly no less.

This passage from Lord Bingham is often referred to as the mirror principle. See also *R (Al-Skeini) v Secretary of State for Defence* [2007] UKHL 26, [2008] 1 AC 153, [106]. In *R (on the application of Animal Defenders International) v Secretary of State for Culture, Media and Sport* [2008] UKHL 15, Baroness Hale echoed this approach when she said that, in passing ss.3 and 4 of the Human Rights Act 1998, Parliament was certainly not intending to give the courts 'the power to leap ahead of Strasbourg in our interpretation of the Convention Rights'. However, in recent years both Lord Wilson in *Moohan v Lord Advocate* [2014] UKSC 67 and Lady Hale in *Keyu v Secretary of State for Foreign and Commonwealth* Affairs [2015] UKSC 69 have sought to clarify and even modify such a principle with the caveat that if there is no clear and constant line of decisions and reasoning from Strasbourg, the UK courts would work out for themselves, taking into account a range of principles, including from the common law, how to determine the matters at hand.

The courts' approach to s.2 is not without academic criticism. Lord Irvine, the former Lord Chancellor, has argued that the courts have not correctly interpreted s.2(1) of the Human Rights Act 1998 (see 'A British Interpretation of Convention Rights' [2012] PL 237). He contends that Parliament intended by the choice of language in s.2(1) for courts merely to have regard to judgments of the European Court of Human Rights, but ultimately to decide the case themselves. The courts' current approach to judgments of the European Court of Human Rights is to make the decisions effectively binding (or at least give them far greater weight than is necessary). However, the counter-argument would be that if the UK courts did not follow the Strasbourg court's decisions then the UK state would be in breach of its international obligations. Lord Irvine refutes this suggestion and maintains that such a breach would be a matter for the UK government, not the courts. He states (at p.245):

> Parliament contemplated that the domestic courts would not follow Strasbourg in all cases. In doing so it implicitly approved the domestic courts reaching an outcome

which might result in non-compliance with the UK's Treaty obligations. The judges should not abstain from deciding the case for themselves simply because it may cause difficulties for the United Kingdom on the international law plane.

 **Critical debate**

As discussed above, the question of how the UKSC should interpret s.2 of the HRA is open to considerable academic debate. On the one hand, a restrictive interpretation would anchor the UK to the judgments of the European Court of Human Rights and thus may even limit the development of human rights law. Take a close read of Lord Irvine, 'A British Interpretation of Convention Rights' [2012] PL 237. In addition to the points made above, why does Lord Irvine believe that the UK courts have erred in their interpretation of s.2 and what criticisms does he make of the approach?

On the other hand, read Phillip Sales (now a Lord and Justice of the Supreme Court), 'Strasbourg Jurisprudence and the Human Rights Act: A Response to Lord Irvine' [2012] PL 253. Identify the reasons that Sales puts forward to support the Supreme Court's adoption of 'the mirror principle'. Sales refers to 'rule of law values' underpinning 'the mirror principle' approach. What does he mean by this expression, both in principle and practice?

On balance, what do you think the Supreme Court's approach to judgments of the European Court of Human Rights should be? Would a different approach help to deflect criticism of the Human Rights Act 1998 and/or help weaken the case made for a British Bill of Rights?

7.7 Unlawful for a public authority to act incompatibly with Convention rights

By s.6 of the 1998 Act, it is unlawful for a 'public authority' to act in a way which is incompatible with a Convention right. Any breach of a Convention right would be enforceable against the emanations of the state, such as government departments, and other public authorities. Thus, the 1998 Act creates a cause of action against a 'public authority' for contravention of Convention rights. Convention rights under s.6 are not directly enforceable as between two private individuals or companies, that is, in private disputes such as an alleged breach of contract between two parties. Traditionally, Convention rights are only enforceable against public authorities, and this is sometimes referred to as the 'vertical effect' of the HRA or 'vertical rights'.

However, by s.6(3)(b) of the Act, a 'public authority' includes a court or a tribunal and when the courts are applying the law they must not act in a way which is incompatible with a Convention right. In consequence, the courts must develop the common law, including any cause of action in English law, such as in contract, tort, or equity, as well as the interpretation of legislation, consistently with Convention rights. To this extent, an individual or company may enforce Convention rights *indirectly* against another individual or company by claiming under a private cause of action and then raising a supplementary argument that a Convention right has been breached. This is sometimes referred to as the horizontal effect of the HRA or 'horizontal rights'.

It is worth recalling that s.6(1) does not apply where an act by a public authority leading to incompatibility cannot be avoided (a) because of provisions of primary legislation, or (b) where the provisions of primary legislation cannot be read or given effect in a way compatible with the Convention rights and the authority was acting so as to give effect to or enforce those provisions. This is an extension of the legislative supremacy of Parliament. For example, if a court cannot read legislation in such a way as to ensure compatibility with Convention rights, the court would not be in breach of s.6(1). Table 7.1 shows the direct and indirect effects of the Human Rights Act 1998.

7.7.1 Vertical and horizontal rights

As indicated above, you may encounter references to vertical and horizontal rights: vertical rights refer to actions against public authorities, whereas horizontal rights relate to those rights, for example, as between individuals and companies. It appears that the Human Rights Act 1998 has a form of horizontal effect based upon the duty placed on the court as a public authority, by s.6, not to act inconsistently with Convention rights. To illustrate, in *Venables v News Group Newspapers* [2001] 1 All ER 908 the High Court had to consider whether the Convention could be applied against newspapers, these not, of course, being public bodies. Venables and Thompson, who as ten-year-old children had been convicted of murdering a two-year-old boy, were protected by injunctions preventing the publication of information concerning them. Upon reaching eighteen years of age, they sought to have the injunctions extended, so that when they were released any publication of information concerning their new identities would be prohibited. Newspapers argued that such injunctions would interfere with the freedom of expression of the press.

Table 7.1 UK law and Convention rights

	Individual or Company v Public Authority	**Individual or Company v Individual or Company**
Direct effect under s.6	Claim using s.6 as cause of action	No claim under s.6 as no public authority involved (assuming the company is not a public authority)
Indirect effect using existing UK law	Bring a claim under UK law, for example for negligence, and then raise a supplementary argument that a Convention right has been breached	

Dame Butler-Sloss P, in the High Court, relying upon *Douglas v Hello! Ltd* [2001] QB 967 and s.12(4) of the Human Rights Act 1998, held that Article 10 had direct applicability between private parties to litigation. This does not create a free-standing cause of action, but the courts had a duty to 'to act compatibly with Convention rights in adjudicating upon existing common law causes of action'. That being said, in the end, the High Court granted injunctions to prevent the newspapers revealing the whereabouts and identities of the claimants. In doing so, the Court took into account that there was a real and strong possibility that the lives of Venables and Thompson would be at risk if such information was revealed, infringing their rights under Articles 2, 3, and 8. The right to freedom of expression under Article 10 was subject to the restrictions in Article 10(2). By Article 10(2) it is provided that:

> The exercise of these freedoms, since it carries with it duties and responsibilities, may be subject to such formalities, conditions, restrictions or penalties as are prescribed by law and are necessary in a democratic society, in the interests of national security, territorial integrity or public safety, for the prevention of disorder or crime, for the protection of health or morals, for the protection of the reputation or rights of others, for preventing the disclosure of information received in confidence, or for maintaining the authority and impartiality of the judiciary.

Given the potential breaches of Venables' and Thompson's rights under Articles 2, 3, and 8, the High Court decided that the right to freedom of expression of the press should be restricted. The granting of the injunctions to achieve the objective sought was deemed to be proportionate to the legitimate aim, that is, the protection of Venables and Thompson from death or serious harm.

7.7.2 **Meaning of public authority**

Section 6 does not give a complete definition of 'public authority', but s.6(3) provides that the term *includes*: (a) a court or tribunal; and (b) any person certain of whose functions are of a public nature. Under s.6(5) it is confirmed that a person would not be a public authority in relation to a particular function or act 'if the nature of the act is private'.

On the one hand, it is clear and straightforward that 'public authority' would encompass a minister, central government departments, local authorities, health authorities, armed forces, and the police. However, there is some doubt as to which other bodies fall within the term. It will be a question of interpretation and for the courts to decide what constitutes a public authority, taking into account the jurisprudence of the European Court of Human Rights. In *Aston Cantlow and Wilmcote with Billesley Parochial Church Council v Wallbank* [2004] 1 AC 546, the House of Lords said that a 'public authority' is essentially a reference to a body whose nature is governmental in the broadest sense of that expression. It must encompass persons or bodies where all their functions are of a public nature—these are 'core' or 'pure' public authorities.

Nonetheless, other bodies may not be governmental but still perform some functions of a public nature. The key is to concentrate on the nature of the function rather than on the nature of the body. This latter type of body is termed a 'functional' or 'hybrid' authority; it has some functions of a public nature but may in fact be a private body. It is no doubt a grey area for judicial judgments. Certainly, a body may not be a public authority if the nature of a particular act is private. In the *Aston Cantlow* case, a Parochial Church Council (PCC) was considered not to be a public authority as, in seeking to enforce a liability to repair a chancel of a church (the part near the altar and reserved for the clergy, choir, and generally separated from the congregation), the Council's act was deemed to be private in nature; the obligation to repair arose from ownership of land. Lord Hope said (at p.570):

> The nature of the act is to be found in the nature of the obligation which the PCC is seeking to enforce. It is seeking to enforce a civil debt. The function which it is performing has nothing to do with the responsibilities which are owed to the public by the state.

An example of a 'hybrid' authority may include the Financial Conduct Authority as part of its role is to regulate safe financial lending to the public and protect consumers. However, its functions in respect of the financial market and/or dealings with the firms and businesses who pay fees to the authority may be classed as private. To use an old example, the predecessor to Network Rail, Railtrack, was a public authority when exercising a regulatory function in relation to safety on the trains, but would not have been considered a public authority when it acted in a capacity as a commercial property developer.

More acute difficulties have arisen over the status of housing authorities. In *YL v Birmingham City Council and Others (Secretary of State for Constitutional Affairs intervening)* [2008] 1 AC 95, the House of Lords, by a majority of 3 to 2, held that the provision of care and accommodation by a private residential care home did not constitute a 'function of a public nature' within s.6(3)(b), even though Birmingham City Council arranged and paid for such care and accommodation, pursuant to ss.21 to 26 of the National Assistance Act 1948. See further on this case later at 7.7.3. By contrast, in *R (on the application of Weaver) v London and Quadrant Housing Trust* [2009] EWCA Civ 587, [2009] 4 All ER 865, the Court of Appeal held that a housing trust which was a registered social landlord, providing social housing, was a public authority for the purposes of s.6(3)(b) when terminating a tenancy.

Thinking point

How public is public?

What are the characteristics of a 'public authority'? Consider whether the following bodies are public authorities:

- the Law Society;
- the Solicitors Regulation Authority.

Do you think that 'public authority' should be further clarified in the Human Rights Act 1998? If so, in what way? Consider the factors that might need to be taken into account.

The classification of a person or body as a 'core' public authority is important for a further reason: a 'core' public authority cannot have Convention rights. See *Aston Cantlow and Wilmcote with Billesley Parochial Church Council v Wallbank* [2004] 1 AC 546, per Lord Nicholls. In consequence, a public authority cannot make a claim for breach of Convention rights. Diagram 7.2 shows the stages to be considered in determining whether a public authority is in contravention of Convention rights and the effect of such contravention.

Key point

A public authority cannot have Convention rights. It is possible for a hybrid public authority to claim for violation of Convention rights in relation to its private functions.

7.7.3 A case study: determining what is a public authority

To highlight the difficulties that courts might face in determining what a public authority actually is, let's consider the case of *YL v Birmingham City Council and Others (Secretary of State for Constitutional Affairs intervening)* [2008] 1 AC 95 in more detail. In this case, there was a significant difference of opinion in the House of Lords, with a 3 to 2 majority deciding that a care home did not possess functions of a public nature and therefore was not a public authority.

Facts

YL, the appellant, was eighty-four years old and suffered from Alzheimer's disease. She lived in a Southern Cross care home, a privately owned profit-making entity which provided accommodation and care facilities. The accommodation and care were largely paid for by Birmingham City Council and topped up by OL, the daughter of the appellant, under a tripartite agreement among Southern Cross, Birmingham CC, and OL. Birmingham CC entered into the agreement pursuant to its duty under s.21 of the National Assistance Act 1948.

The issue

Southern Cross wanted to terminate YL's residency in the care home and gave notice to this effect. It was argued on behalf of YL that the care home was performing functions of a public nature for the purposes of s.6(3)(b). Thus, Southern Cross was a 'public authority' and by giving notice had acted incompatibly with YL's rights under Article 8 (the right to respect for private or family life) of the Convention and, in consequence, such notice to terminate was unlawful under s.6(1) of the 1998 Act.

In *Aston Cantlow and Wilmcote with Billesley Parochial Church Council v Wallbank* [2004] 1 AC 546, Lord Nicholls said, in determining whether a function

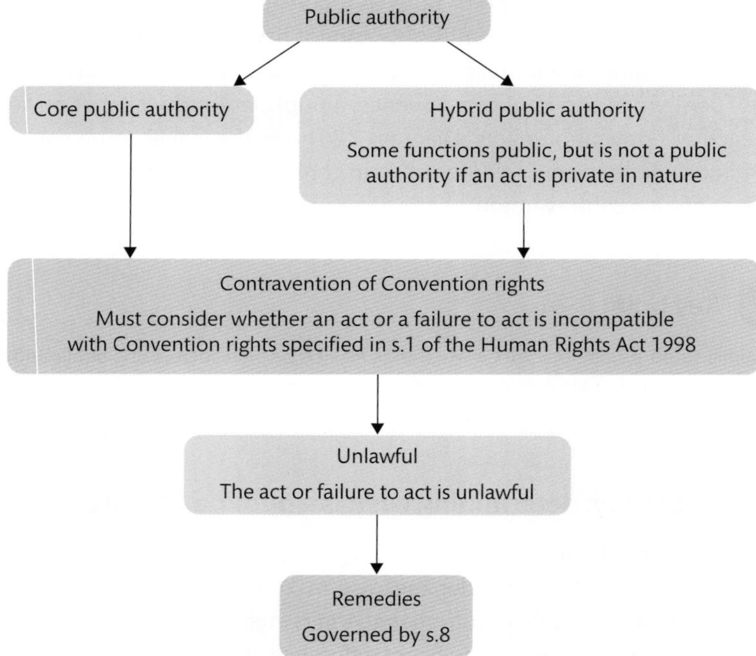

Diagram 7.2 Public authorities

is of a public nature, that there is no single test of universal application; instead, a number of factors must be considered, none of which singly is likely to be determinative and the weighting of the factors will differ from case to case. His Lordship identified a number of relevant factors, but stressed that such a list could not be exhaustive:

- the nature of the function—was it private or public;
- the role and responsibility of the state in relation to the matter in question;
- consideration of the nature and extent of any statutory duty or power with regard to the function;
- the extent to which the performance of the function is regulated, supervised, and inspected by the state and whether any criminal sanctions are imposed for failure to meet set standards;
- the extent to which the state pays for the performance of the function;
- consideration of the risk that failure in performance of the function might impact on an individual's Convention rights.

Lord Bingham

Lord Bingham considered the following points in determining whether Southern Cross was performing a function of a public nature. The function was to provide accommodation and care for those unable to care for themselves; the state had accepted a social welfare responsibility in the last resort.

Sections 21 and 26 of the National Assistance Act 1948 conferred statutory powers and a statutory duty in this regard upon local authorities. A local authority may provide the care directly in a local authority-run care home or arrange for care to be provided by a voluntary organisation or by a private provider.

The provision of accommodation and care was subject to legal control and the application of criminal sanctions in the event of breach of prescribed standards.

Payment for the provision of accommodation and care fell on the state in respect of those, falling within ss.21 and 26 of the National Assistance Act 1948, who are unable to pay for such provision themselves. Lord Bingham said that 'it is indicative of a function being public that the public are, if need be, bound to pay for it to be performed'.

Finally, the risk of infringement of various human rights in care homes was understood by Parliament when passing the Human Rights Act 1998 and the intention must have been to extend the protection to residents of privately run care homes placed in such homes pursuant to the National Assistance Act 1998.

Lord Bingham thus concluded that a private care home was performing a function of a public nature.

Lord Scott

Lord Scott emphasised that Southern Cross was a private company carrying on a business for profit. In providing accommodation and care, Southern Cross did so in pursuance of private law contracts with residents and local authorities. The company itself had no public funding and enjoyed no special statutory powers; it was providing a service for a commercial rate of payment.

In his Lordship's view, the fact that residents were placed by local authorities with Southern Cross care homes pursuant to s.21 of the 1948 Act and paid for by local authorities carried little weight. Southern Cross was paid for a service and in no sense could be said to be subsidised out of public funds. It would be absurd to suggest that a private contractor performing cleaning or catering services at a care home owned by a local authority would be publicly funded and carrying on a function of a public nature, merely because payment was made out of public funds for that service.

In support of YL's contention it was argued that there was no difference in the nature of the function performed in the management of a care home run by a local authority compared with that of a privately run care home. Lord Scott rejected this on the basis that a local authority is under a statutory duty to arrange accommodation and care, the costs of which are met out of public funds, whereas any duties owed by a private care home company are contractual or tortious and within the realms of private law. Merely because a local authority contracts out the performance of a function of a public nature to a private contractor does not mean that the contractor is a public authority under s.6(3)(b) of the HRA 1998.

His Lordship thought it was not enough to consider the activity being performed and that it was necessary to look at the reason why the person in question is carrying on the activity that is being performed. The activity of a local authority running a care home is pursuant to public law obligations, whereas a privately owned care home acts in pursuance of private law contractual obligations.

Finally, Lord Scott said that the argument that vulnerable residents of care homes required the additional protection of s.6 of the 1998 Act added nothing. Other legal remedies already existed.

In consequence, Southern Cross was held not to be carrying on a function of a public nature.

Lord Scott also held that the service of the notice of termination was, in any event, an act relating to the rights and obligations created by the contract between YL and Southern Cross, which was private in nature for the purposes of s.6(5).

In light of the above, Lord Bingham and Lord Scott identified a number of similar factors; however they disagreed on the weight and relevance attached to the factors. In so doing, the respective Lords arrived at different and opposing conclusions. In addition, to fully understand the reasoning in the case, reading the opinions of all the Law Lords (five in the case of YL) is strongly recommended.

The reasoning of the majority is still good law but you may wish to note that the effect of the actual decision in *YL v Birmingham City Council* was changed by s.145 of the Health and Social Care Act 2008 so that a care home, for the purposes of s.6(3)(b), is to be taken to be exercising a function of a public nature. Similarly, under the Care Act 2014, registered providers of care and support under s.73 can also be taken to be exercising a function of a public nature (under s.6(3)(b)).

Thinking point

Public, private, or somewhere in between?

Under s.6(3)(b) and s.6(5) it may not be sufficient for a body to be classed as a public authority in relation to a particular act if the nature of the act is private. What does that mean and how is the nature of an act to be determined? See *R (on the application of Weaver) v London and Quadrant Housing Trust* [2009] EWCA Civ 587, [2009] 4 All ER 865, Elias LJ at [73]–[82]. More generally, do you think the distinction between public and private acts is sustainable in the era of the Human Rights Act 1998? Would there be any consequences if the distinction were to be collapsed and no longer exist?

7.7.4 Enforcement of Convention rights

Under the Human Rights Act 1998, and s.6 specifically, it is an established cause of action to allege that a public authority breached the Convention rights of a claimant. However, in order to enforce these rights, s.7(1) provides that a claimant may:

(a) bring proceedings against the authority under [the Human Rights Act] in the appropriate court or tribunal;

(b) rely on the Convention right or rights concerned in any legal proceedings, but only if he is (or would be) a victim of the unlawful act.

Under s.7(1)(a), proceedings are brought against a public authority by directly relying on s.6, whereas under s.7(1)(b) any legal proceedings are brought against a public authority (e.g. using a cause of action in tort or contract etc.) along with arguments based upon Convention rights.

Under s.7(1), a claimant must satisfy the requirement of being a 'victim' of the unlawful act. In order to be a victim, a person must satisfy the test for being a victim under Article 34 of the Convention for the purposes of bringing proceedings in the European Court of Human Rights (s.7(7)). Article 34 indicates that a victim is 'any person, non-governmental organisation or group of individuals claiming to be the victim of a violation . . . of the rights set forth in the Convention or the protocols thereto'.

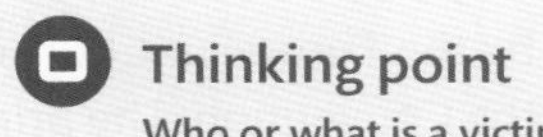

Thinking point

Who or what is a victim?

Does Article 34 adequately indicate what is meant by 'victim'? Are there any areas of uncertainty? Where might one look to find material which will improve our understanding of the meaning of 'victim'?

7.7.5 Remedies

By s.8, where a public authority is found to have acted unlawfully, then a court has a discretion to 'grant such relief or remedy, or make such order, within its powers as it considers just and appropriate'. A court may, for example, give the following relief or remedies, if the court has power to grant such relief or a remedy:

- damages;
- a declaration;
- an injunction;
- a ***quashing order*** (previously called *certiorari*);
- a mandatory order (previously called *mandamus*);
- a prohibiting order (previously called prohibition).

Quashing order *Note that quashing orders, mandatory orders, and prohibiting orders are public law remedies aimed at public bodies:*

- *a quashing order quashes the decision of, for example, an inferior court, a tribunal, or a local authority where the decision-making process exhibits illegality, irrationality, or procedural impropriety;*
- *a mandatory order compels, for example, an inferior court, a tribunal, or a public body to carry out its duty;*
- *a prohibiting order restrains, for example, an inferior court, a tribunal, a local authority, or a government minister from acting in excess of jurisdiction.*

Damages may only be awarded by a court which has power to award damages, or order a compensation payment, in civil proceedings; thus damages are not payable in criminal proceedings. Under s.8(3) of the Human Rights Act 1998, in considering whether an award of damages is appropriate (note that a court has the power to award damages but is not under a duty to do so), account must be taken of all the circumstances of a case, including 'any other relief or remedy granted, or order made', and the consequences of any decision of a court. Damages may be awarded where the court considers that an award is necessary to give just satisfaction. The case law suggests that in many instances, a declaration that Convention rights have been breached will suffice as a remedy.

In determining (a) whether to award damages, or (b) the amount of an award, a court must take into account the principles applied by the European Court of Human Rights in relation to awards under Article 41 of the Convention. The principles of the European Court of Human Rights are not easy to identify. However, the basic principle is that the victim is to be placed in the position they would have occupied had the violation of their rights not occurred. Damages have been given in relation to both pecuniary losses, for example loss of earnings or medical costs, and non-pecuniary losses, for example distress, inconvenience, and humiliation. The basic principle is similar to the tortious measure of damages in English law. The award of damages before the European Court of Human Rights tends to be modest in amount. See generally on this issue *R (on the application of Greenfield) v Secretary of State for the Home Department* [2005] 1 WLR 673, and see also *R (on the application of Faulkner) v Secretary of State for Justice* [2013] UKSC 23.

Summary

- The ECHR is an international treaty. Unless a treaty is incorporated into the law of the UK it is not directly enforceable by the UK courts. Certain articles and protocols of the Convention were incorporated into UK law when the Human Rights Act 1998 came into force on 2 October 2000. The Act is of significant constitutional status.

- Primary legislation cannot be challenged using the Human Rights Act 1998 in the sense of the courts striking down legislation.
- However, by s.3 of the Human Rights Act 1998, both primary and subordinate legislation must be read and given effect in a way which is compatible with the Convention rights, in so far as it is possible to do so.
- By s.4 of the Human Rights Act 1998, the courts can issue a declaration of incompatibility should an Act of Parliament law contravene Convention rights. It is then left to the minister or Parliament to amend UK law.
- By s.2, a court or tribunal determining a question which has arisen in connection with a Convention right must take into account any:

  judgment, decision, declaration or advisory opinion of the European Court of Human Rights . . . whenever made or given, so far as, in the opinion of the court or tribunal, it is relevant to the proceedings in which that question has arisen. But the courts of the UK are not bound to follow the decisions of the European Court of Human Rights.

- The Human Rights Act 1998 does not create a cause of action between individuals or companies for breach of Convention rights. However, an individual or company may sue under UK law and ask the courts to interpret the existing UK law to ensure compliance with the Convention rights in the Human Rights Act 1998. This is achieved because, as a court is a 'public authority', it is under a duty to ensure existing law is in compliance with Convention rights.
- However, it is unlawful for a public authority to act incompatibly with the Convention rights stated in the Human Rights Act 1998. Section 6 creates a direct cause of action against a public authority for contravention of Convention rights.
- Once all domestic avenues for redress of a grievance have been exhausted, a claimant may take a case to the European Court of Human Rights.

Questions

1. Why was the Human Rights Act 1998 introduced into the United Kingdom?
2. How does the Human Rights Act 1998 ensure that the doctrine of parliamentary supremacy is not challenged?
3. What duty is detailed under s.3 of the Human Rights Act 1998? Analyse the extent to which the courts been prepared to go in undertaking this task?
4. Using authority, evaluate the extent to which the UK courts are bound by decisions of the European Court of Human Rights.
5. When does the Human Rights Act 1998 give a direct cause of action?
6. Using authority, explain what is meant by a 'public authority'.
7. Consider the case of *Principal Reporter v K (Scotland)* [2010] UKSC 56 and identify the words that were read into the relevant legislation, in that case the Children (Scotland) Act 1995.

Sample question and outline answer

Question

Under s.3 Human Rights Act 1998, in order to ensure that legislation is Convention-compliant, to what extent may the courts go beyond the words used by Parliament when interpreting a piece of legislation?

Outline answer

This question concerns the meaning and effect of s.3 Human Rights Act 1998. To understand the operation of s.3 it is first necessary to understand the context in which the section operates. After explaining the interpretative obligation that the courts must follow under s.3, the limits of its operation must be explored by reference to relevant case law.

The structure of the 1998 Act indicates that the courts cannot challenge the validity of legislation, even if it is not Convention-compliant. Indeed, if the court decides that legislation is not Convention-compliant, under s.4 a declaration of incompatibility must be made and then it is for the government and Parliament to determine how the matter is to be resolved. The House of Lords has stated in *R v A* [2002] 1 AC 45, in the words of Lord Steyn, 'that a declaration of incompatibility is a measure of last resort. It must be avoided unless it is plainly impossible to do so.'

By s.3 Human Rights Act 1998, so far as it is possible to do so, primary legislation and subordinate legislation must be read and given effect in a way which is compatible with the Convention rights. This places on the courts an interpretative obligation by which Parliament instructs the courts to interpret legislation to ensure it is Convention-compliant, but subject to the important qualification that it is to be 'possible to do so'. However, this does not entitle the courts to make legislation, it is an interpretative process in accordance with the terms of s.3. (See Lord Woolf in *Poplar Housing and Regeneration Community Association Ltd v Donoghue* [2002] QB 48 at pp.72–3: 'When the court interprets legislation usually its primary task is to identify the intention of Parliament. Now, when section 3 applies, the courts have to adjust their traditional role in relation to interpretation so as to give effect to the direction contained in section 3 . . . Section 3 does not entitle the court to legislate (its task is still one of interpretation, but interpretation in accordance with the direction contained in section 3)'.) Kavanagh's argument that, even in relation to interpretation of legislation, judges have a law-making role—but within limits ('The Elusive Divide between Interpretation and Legislation under the Human Rights Act 1998' (2004) 24 OJLS 259)—could be briefly explained here.

The question to be addressed is: when is it possible by the process of interpretation to make legislation Convention-compliant? It is necessary to explore the case law and seek to draw some general conclusions. You can focus on the inter-relationship between s.3 and s.4 too. The courts go beyond the words of an Act by 'reading down'—limiting the extent of words in an Act; see *R v A* [2002] 1 AC 45; or 'reading in'—where the courts 'add' words to alter or expand the meaning of the Act; see *Ghaidan v Godin-Mendoza* [2004] UKHL 30.

In *Ghaidan v Godin-Mendoza*, Lord Nicholls said: 'Parliament, however, cannot have intended that in the discharge of this extended interpretative function the courts should adopt a meaning inconsistent with a fundamental feature of legislation.' So if Parliament intends to pass an Act which is deliberately not Convention-compliant, the courts must give effect to that Act. Also, the intention of s.3 cannot have been to 'require the courts to make decisions for which they are not equipped'. The cases of *R (Anderson) v Secretary of State for the Home Department* [2003] 1 AC 837 and *Bellinger v Bellinger* [2003] 2 AC 467 illustrate these points. In *Anderson*, the role of the Home Secretary in determining life sentences of prisoners contravened Article 6, but as this was a fundamental feature of the legislation, s.3 could not be employed. Equally, in *Bellinger* the ramifications of interpreting legislation to include transsexuals represented a fundamental change to the law. A comprehensive review of the existing law was required, rather than the courts merely dealing with one aspect of the law. Such a review required decisions on issues that Parliament ought to make. In *Anderson* and *Bellinger* the House of Lords refused to use s.3 and instead made a declaration of incompatibility.

In conclusion, a number of points may be made. In following the interpretative obligation imposed by s.3 the courts must interpret, not legislate. It is arguable, however, that the courts will exercise a law-making role, but within limitations. For s.3 to engage, legislation must be incompatible with Convention rights. This may arise even though there is no ambiguity in the wording used by Parliament. The courts may go beyond the words used in legislation by limiting the operation of a provision by the process of 'reading down' or altering the meaning of a provision by 'reading in' words. However, there are limits, and if an interpretation runs counter to a fundamental feature of legislation then a Convention-compliant interpretation under s.3 may not be possible. Also, if a court is in effect asked to legislate, for example by making a wide-ranging change to the law or one which effects only a partial reform to a legal area, again this goes beyond the interpretative obligation in s.3.

Further reading

You will be learning more about human rights during a module on Public Law (sometimes referred to as constitutional and administrative law). I would recommend the relevant chapters in *Le Sueur. A and others. Public Law: Text Cases and Material* 4th edition, Oxford University Press, (2019) and *Elliott. M. and Thomas. R. Public Law* 3rd edition, Oxford University Press (2017). Not only will you find considerably more detail and coverage of the issues, but you will find the books an excellent source for further reading and research. However, in addition to those, I would recommend the following sample of the latest academic debate.

- ***Amos, M.*** *'The Value of the European Court of Human Rights to the United Kingdom'* (2017) 28(3) European Journal of International Law 763

  This article assesses and identifies the benefit of the European Court of Human Rights. The article demonstrates the practical impact of various judgments of the Court on the degree of legal protection of human rights in the UK.

- **Gearty, C.** *On Fantasy Island: Britain, Europe and Human Rights*, Oxford University Press (2016).

  Highly recommended, this excellent book seeks to expose the myths that drive anti-Human Rights Act sentiment in the UK. The book outlines how the Act operates in practice, its everyday impact, and makes a positive argument for the Act's survival and its significance for the UK's future.

- **Fenwick, H.** and **Masterman, R.** *'The Conservative Project to "Break the Link between British Courts and Strasbourg": Rhetoric and Reality?'* (2017) 80(6) MLR 1111

  This article examines the proposal to replace the Human Rights Act with a British Bill of Rights and therefore break the link between the UK and Strasbourg. The article focuses on the relationship with the European Court of Human Rights and the implication of downgrading the status of its judgments to that of an advisory status only.

- **Ferreira, N.** *'The Supreme Court in a Final Push to Go Beyond Strasbourg'* [2015] PL 367.

  This is a concise case comment on the case of *R (on the application of Nicklinson and Another) v Ministry of Justice* [2014] UKSC 38. Its focus is on Lord Bingham's dictum in *Ullah* and whether the courts can or ought to go beyond the jurisprudence of the European Court of Human Rights.

- **Jowell. Sir J.** and **O'Cinneide C.** *The Changing Constitution*, 9th edn, Oxford University Press (2019)

  Recently updated, this is an advanced text that provide wide-ranging, scholarly, and thought-provoking essays on the essential issues surrounding the UK's constitutional developments. There is the latest coverage on the issues posed by Brexit. This new edition of a classic text has been substantively revised to take account of the fast-evolving UK constitutional system, and in particular the challenges posed by Brexit, devolution, and other dramatic recent developments in British constitutional law. Among the chapters, chapter 3 on human rights is particularly recommended.

- **Kavanagh, A.** *'The Elusive Divide between Interpretation and Legislation under the Human Rights Act 1998'* (2004) 24 OJLS 259

  This is a conceptual and theoretical analysis of the judicial role under s.3 Human Rights Act 1998. The author analyses the extent to which s.3 permits the judges to legislate by way of the practice of interpretation. She also provides an examination of judges' own understanding of the distinction between interpretation and legislation.

Visit the online resources to watch a video on the European Court of Human Rights.

Online resources

You should now attempt the supporting self-test questions and end-of-chapter questions available at: **lwww.oup.com/he/wilson-rutherford4e**

Chapter 8

The judiciary

Learning objectives

By the end of this chapter you should:

- be aware of the different types of judicial appointment;
- be able to identify the different types of judge and to discuss their roles and responsibilities;
- appreciate the way in which judicial appointments are made;
- be aware of the arguments concerning diversity of membership of the judiciary;
- be familiar with the importance of the concept of independence of the judiciary, and the laws which safeguard it.

Talking point

'Enemies of the People', screamed the headline in the Daily Mail, beneath photographs of three Supreme Court Justices. It followed the decision of the Supreme Court in *R (on the application of Miller and Dos Santos) v Secretary of State for Exiting the European Union* [2017] UKSC 5, which ruled that Parliament must have a say in the decision to trigger Article 50 to enable Britain to leave the European Union.

The Telegraph front page was headed 'The Judges versus the People', suggesting that the judges had usurped their role and acted against the will of the majority of voters in the referendum.

In light of the Supreme Court ruling, a number of prominent 'Leave' supporters suggested it was time that an American-style political vetting process was introduced to examine the political views of applicants for the Supreme Court bench. At present, Justices of the Supreme Court are chosen by an independent selection commission. The then Lord Chancellor, Liz Truss, defended the freedom of the press to publish such headlines, but was criticised for failing to defend the judges from 'a torrent of abuse'.

The vitriolic attack on the judiciary and the Lord Chancellor's perceived failure to defend their independence led to a great deal of discussion about both the nature of judicial appointments and the role of the Lord Chancellor.

In an interview with the BBC when he stood down as President of the Supreme Court in February 2017, Lord Neuberger referred to these media attacks and the subsequent call for political input in judicial appointments. He counselled against such a move, stating that it would be 'very unfortunate if we had political scrutiny of the appointment of judges in this country'. He emphasised the importance of judicial independence and said: 'if we undermine the judiciary, we are undermining the rule of law. The rule of law together with democracy is one of the two pillars on which our society is based.' In short, political interference would undermine independence.

This chapter on the judiciary includes discussion of the appointment of judges and outlines the role of the Lord Chancellor. Before you read it, consider the following questions:

- Do you think that judges should be examined on their political views before being appointed?
- Do you agree with Lord Neuberger that '[i]f you are a decent judge, your political views will be put on one side when you go into court'?
- What is the role of the judiciary: should judges be political appointees whose job is to uphold the will of the majority?
- Lord Thomas is reported as emphasising: 'An independent judiciary is the cornerstone of the rule of law, and it is the duty of the Lord Chancellor to defend that independence.' Is it important that the Lord Chancellor defends the judiciary?

Introduction

The role of judges is to decide disputes brought before the courts. In so doing, judges exercise a judicial function which involves deciding the facts of the case based upon the evidence presented to the court, establishing relevant law, and then applying the law to the facts in order to reach a decision. It was seen in Chapter 4, in relation to legislation, that judges interpret and apply the law whereas Parliament makes the law. In the common law, the judiciary has a more active role but their law-making power is restricted and the judges generally exercise restraint in this regard.

When considering the judiciary it is important to understand how judges are appointed, what qualifications are required for the various judicial offices, and how judges may be removed. This information is needed when assessing the important and often controversial issues of diversity of the membership of the judiciary, its independence, and its accountability.

8.1 The judicial hierarchy

The structure of the courts is based upon a hierarchy and the same is true of the judges who sit in the courts.

Before the judicial hierarchy is explained, it is important to note that changes were made in the Tribunals, Courts and Enforcement Act 2007 to the qualifications required to become a judge, and therefore any members of the judiciary appointed after the introduction of that Act will have been through a different process from those appointed before the Act came into force. The amendments to the eligibility criteria were made to promote diversity in judicial appointments. See further 8.2.2. Prior to the introduction of this Act, qualification as a judge depended upon rights of audience (permission to appear and present cases) before the courts being held for a minimum period of time. In effect, only barristers and solicitors qualified for at least seven years (or in some cases ten years) were eligible for appointment. It was decided that the criteria for appointment were too narrow and, in order to increase the numbers of people eligible for appointment, changes had to be made.

The role of the judiciary in making law is considered in Chapters 3 and 4, as is the relationship between Parliament and the courts.

By s.50 of the Tribunals, Courts and Enforcement Act 2007, the 'judicial-appointment eligibility condition' must be satisfied for appointment as a judge. The condition is satisfied where:

- a person holds a 'relevant qualification', that is, is a barrister or solicitor or, by s.51, holds a legal qualification specified in an order made by the Lord Chancellor (the Lord Chancellor, under the power given by s.51, has extended eligibility, for a number of judicial posts including district judges to Fellows of the Chartered Institute of Legal Executives and to registered patents agents and trade mark attorneys in relation to certain appointments);

- the total length of the person's 'qualifying period' is N years (N years means the number of years specified in the statute under which the judicial appointment is to be made).

The 'qualifying period' is the period for which a person (a) has a 'relevant qualification' and (b) has gained experience in law. It is not sufficient to simply hold a legal qualification. A person must also accumulate experience in law during the qualifying period: this prevents qualified lawyers who have never practised as lawyers, or been academics in the law, applying for appointment. By s.52, experience in law means being engaged in a law-related activity. By s.52(4), a 'law-related activity' encompasses the following:

- the carrying out of judicial functions of any court or tribunal;
- acting as an arbitrator;
- practice or employment as a lawyer;
- advising (whether or not in the course of practice or employment as a lawyer) on the application of the law;
- assisting (whether or not in the course of such practice) persons involved in proceedings for the resolution of issues arising under the law;
- acting (whether or not in the course of such practice) as mediator in connection with attempts to resolve issues that are, or if not resolved could be, the subject of proceedings;
- drafting (whether or not in the course of such practice) documents intended to affect persons' rights or obligations;
- teaching or researching law;
- any activity of a broadly similar nature to an activity within any of the eight paragraphs in the bullet-point sub-list.

The changes made to the criteria for judicial appointment impact upon the issue of diversity in judicial appointments: see 8.2.2.

Note that another change made by the Tribunals, Courts and Enforcement Act 2007 is to reduce the minimum length of time for which a person must be suitably qualified before appointment to the judiciary. For example, prior to the Act, the qualification to be a Lord Justice of Appeal or to be a High Court judge had to be for a minimum of ten years; this has been reduced to seven years. The requirement that the qualification to be a district judge had to be held for a minimum of seven years was reduced to five years.

8.1.1 **The Lord Chancellor**

Prior to the Constitutional Reform Act 2005, the office of Lord Chancellor carried with it a multiplicity of roles and duties. The Lord Chancellor occupied a unique position as a member of the government (sitting in the Cabinet) and a member of the legislature (Speaker of the House of Lords), and, as well as being head of the judiciary, exercised a judicial role in the Appellate Committee of the House of Lords. This raised issues in relation to the separation of powers—essential to the constitution—and the independence of the judiciary. As a consequence of the disquiet over the overlapping roles of the Lord Chancellor, in 2003 the Labour administration under Tony Blair decided that the office of Lord Chancellor should be abolished. However, after concerns were expressed by the judiciary and others that abolition of the role could not be achieved without an Act of Parliament, and that such a move would have major constitutional implications, the office was retained in a modified form.

As a result of the reforms, the Lord Chancellor no longer acts in a judicial capacity and is not the Speaker of the House of Lords. By s.3 of the Constitutional Reform Act 2005 the Lord Chancellor is under a duty, along with ministers and all others with responsibility for matters relating to the judiciary or otherwise to the administration of justice, to 'uphold the continued independence of the judiciary'. The section further states that 'the Lord Chancellor and other ministers of the Crown must not seek to influence particular judicial decisions through any special access to the judiciary' and that the Lord Chancellor must have regard to:

(a) the need to defend [the independence of the judiciary];

(b) the need for the judiciary to have the support necessary to enable them to exercise their functions;

(c) the need for the public interest in regard to matters relating to the judiciary or otherwise to the administration of justice to be properly represented in decisions affecting those matters.

In relation to the appointment of judges, the Lord Chancellor's role has been curtailed with the establishment of a Judicial Appointments Commission. However, the holder of the office of Lord Chancellor is also the Secretary of State for Justice.

The role of Lord Chancellor is a political appointment made on the recommendation of the prime minister from those 'qualified by experience' as defined by s.2 of the Constitutional Reform Act 2005. The following criteria may be taken into account by the prime minister when making the recommendation: experience as a minister of the Crown; as a member of either House of Parliament; as a qualifying practitioner, for example, a person who has a Senior Courts qualification within the meaning of s.71 of the Courts and Legal Services Act 1990; or as a university teacher of law, or other experience considered relevant by the prime minister. Due to the fact that the appointment is political, the Lord Chancellor has no security of tenure and the Queen, on the advice of the prime minister, may dismiss the Lord Chancellor at any time.

In July 2014 the House of Lords Constitution Committee decided to hold an inquiry into the office of the Lord Chancellor. The committee explored the question as to whether the position of Lord Chancellor should be held by a lawyer or whether the position can be, as it is now, combined with the post of justice secretary. The committee, chaired by Lord Lang of Monkton, explored the following questions:

- What are the current functions of the Lord Chancellor and how are they different from the Secretary of State for Justice?
- To what extent does the Lord Chancellor still have genuine powers?
- How, in practice, does the Lord Chancellor uphold the rule of law and judicial independence?
- Is the combination of the roles of Lord Chancellor and Secretary of State for Justice appropriate? Should the Lord Chancellor be a more independent voice?
- Should there be statutory criteria for appointment as Lord Chancellor?
- Should the Lord Chancellor be a lawyer? Should he or she be a member of the House of Lords?

It has been suggested by commentators that the inquiry was a direct result of disquiet regarding the reforms to legal aid brought about by the then Lord Chancellor, Chris Grayling, and the perception that the 2005 reform of the role has been less than successful due to the incumbent's dual role as justice secretary and Lord Chancellor. (See Chapter 11, 'Access to justice').

The committee's final report was published in December 2014. It recommended that the Lord Chancellor should be identified as the Cabinet minister responsible for oversight of the constitution and it also agreed with those who consider that the dual role of the offices of Lord Chancellor and Secretary of State for Justice could create the risk of a conflict of interest. However, it accepted the evidence it had heard that that the conflicting priorities could be appropriately managed.

The Committee concluded, among a number of observations and recommendations, that in its opinion it is not essential for the Lord Chancellor to be a qualified lawyer, but, unsurprisingly, that a legal or constitutional background is a distinct advantage. Full details of the report can be found at **www.parliament.uk/business/committees/committees-a-z/lords-select/constitution-committee/news/lord-chancellor-report-published/**.

Key point

The reforms resulted in the appointment, in 2012, of Chris Grayling—the first holder of the office of Lord Chancellor since 1673 not to have a legal qualification. The trend of appointing politicians without legal qualifications continued with Michael Gove, Liz Truss, and David Lidington. The appointment in 2018 of David Gauke as Lord Chancellor marked a return to legally qualified appointees. The present Lord Chancellor is a barrister, and former Solicitor General, Robert Buckland.

8.1.2 Justices of the Supreme Court

In October 2009 the constitutional reforms led to the replacement of the Appellate Committee of the House of Lords, the highest court in the United Kingdom (UK), by a Supreme Court. The most senior judges in the UK are the twelve justices of the Supreme Court (see Image 8.1).

Appointment

A selection commission is convened by the Lord Chancellor and when the decision to appoint has been made, the Lord Chancellor, if content with the selection, forwards the name of the person chosen to the prime minister, who then sends details to the Queen, who makes the final appointment. More details can be found at **www.supremecourt.uk/about/appointments-of-justices.htmlQualification**.

By s.25 of the Constitutional Reform Act 2005, to be appointed a justice of the Supreme Court a person must have: (a) held high judicial office for a period of at least two years; or (b) satisfied the judicial-appointment eligibility condition on a fifteen-year basis; or (c) been a qualifying practitioner for a period of at least fifteen years. (A qualifying practitioner means a person who is an advocate in Scotland or a solicitor entitled to appear in the Court of Session and the High Court of Justiciary, or who is a member of the Bar of Northern Ireland or a solicitor of the Court of Judicature of Northern Ireland.)

Image 8.1 The Supreme Court Justices in 2019

Source: UK Supreme Court

House of Lords reform—the creation of the Supreme Court

The Constitutional Reform Act 2005 contained provisions for establishing a Supreme Court for the whole of the UK. Prior to the reform there was criticism of the role of the law lords as the final judges of appeal, because they also had a legislative role as members of the House of Lords in scrutinising, debating, and at times amending government legislation even though, by convention, they did not engage in political debate to preserve the appearance of judicial impartiality. The dual role, both legislative and judicial, is however contrary to a concept of separation of powers and, with the creation of the Supreme Court, the law lords are no longer entitled to sit in the legislative chamber of the House of Lords. Indeed, to emphasise the separation, the Supreme Court sits in a building entirely separate from the Houses of Parliament.

The government announced its intention to create a Supreme Court in June 2003 and the court began operating in October 2009. The law lords already sitting in the House of Lords in October 2009 became the first Supreme Court judges. The senior law lord at that time, Lord Phillips of Worth Matravers, became the President of the Court. In 2017 Lady Hale, Baroness Hale of Richmond, became the first female President of the Supreme Court. The judges who sit in the Court are referred to as justices of the Supreme Court.

8.1.3 Lord Chief Justice of England and Wales

The Lord Chief Justice holds the office of President of the Courts of England and Wales and is head of the judiciary of England and Wales. As President of the Courts of England and Wales, the Lord Chief Justice is responsible for representing the views of the judiciary to government; maintaining appropriate arrangements for the deployment, training, and guidance of the judiciary; and overseeing the allocation of work within the courts. The Lord Chief Justice is president of the Court of Appeal (Criminal Division), and is entitled to sit in any of the following courts: Court of Appeal; High Court; Crown Court; County Court; and magistrates' courts.

8.1.4 Master of the Rolls

The Master of the Rolls is President of the Court of Appeal (Civil Division) and is also the leading judge dealing with civil work in that court. The Master of the Rolls is also responsible for organising the work of the civil division.

8.1.5 Heads of Division

See Chapter 2 for more information on divisions.

The Heads of Division act as judges in the Court of Appeal and, where appropriate, are also responsible for organising the work in their division and sitting as judges in the relevant courts.

To become the Lord Chief Justice, the Master of the Rolls, or a Head of Division, a person must be qualified for appointment as a Lord Justice of Appeal or be a judge in the Court of Appeal: see s.10 of the Senior Courts Act 1981 (prior to 2009 this Act was known as the Supreme Courts Act 1981; however, the name was changed to prevent confusion that could have been caused by the naming of the new Supreme Court). In practice, these senior judges are selected from the Lords Justices of Appeal or Justices of the Supreme Court.

8.1.6 **Judges in the Court of Appeal**

Judges sitting in the Court of Appeal hear both civil and criminal appeals. The judges in the Court of Appeal are the Lords Justices of Appeal and the Heads of Division, that is, the Master of the Rolls, the Presidents of the Queen's Bench Division and of the Family Division, the Chancellor of the High Court, and the Lord Chief Justice of England and Wales. Civil appeal cases are heard by a combination of Lords Justices of Appeal and Heads of Division and the court usually sits with three judges. Although criminal cases are also usually heard by three judges, the composition of the court may be a little different because one High Court Judge and one Senior Circuit Judge (or two High Court judges) may sit alongside either the Lord Chief Justice, the President of the Queen's Bench Division, or one of the Lords Justices of Appeal.

8.1.7 **Lords Justices of Appeal**

The Lords Justices of Appeal are selected from members of the High Court bench and sit in the Court of Appeal. To be appointed as a Lord Justice of Appeal, a person must satisfy the judicial-appointment eligibility condition on a seven-year basis, or be a judge of the High Court: see s.10 of the Senior Courts Act 1981. In practice, only High Court judges are appointed as Lords Justices of Appeal.

8.1.8 **High Court judges**

High Court judges—sometimes known as puisne (literally 'inferior in rank') judges—hear important civil cases and criminal cases, including sitting in the Crown Court and sitting alongside Lord Justices of Appeal for appeals in the Court of Appeal (Criminal Division). These judges sit primarily in London but also travel to the major court centres outside London to hear cases. High Court judges are now selected through a process operated by the JAC. However, to be eligible for appointment they must satisfy the judicial-appointment eligibility condition on a seven-year basis or must have held the office of circuit judge for at least two years as set out in s.10 of the Senior Courts Act 1981.

Visit the online resources to watch a video on a day in the life of a High Court judge.

8.1.9 High Court Masters and Registrars

Masters and Registrars sit in the Chancery and Queen's Bench Divisions to deal with the procedural aspects of civil cases, from commencement of proceedings until trial, if a matter proceeds that far. They are now appointed through the JAC selection process, the statutory qualification being to satisfy the judicial-appointment eligibility condition on a five-year basis. In the Supreme Court, there is a Senior Master, together with nine Queen's Bench Masters (one of whom is the Admiralty Registrar), five Chancery Masters and a Chief Master, and five Bankruptcy Registrars and a Chief Registrar.

8.1.10 Circuit judges

Circuit judges sit in one of seven regions throughout England and Wales and hear cases in the Crown Court and the County Court hearing centres. They often concentrate upon either civil or criminal cases but may hear both. Some judges also deal with very specific specialist areas such as commercial or construction cases. Circuit judges may sometimes be asked to sit in the Court of Appeal (Criminal Division). They are appointed through the selection process operated by the JAC. By s.16 of the Courts Act 1971, to be appointed a circuit judge a person must:

- satisfy the judicial-appointment eligibility condition on a seven-year basis;
- be a recorder; or
- have held as a full-time appointment for at least three years one of the offices listed in Part IA of Sch.2 to the Courts Act 1971. These offices include:
    - President of Social Security Appeal Tribunals and Medical Appeal Tribunals, or chair of such a tribunal;
    - President of the Employment Tribunals (England and Wales) or member of a panel of chairs for employment tribunals for England and Wales;
    - President or member of the Immigration Appeal Tribunal; Master of the Queen's Bench Division;
    - Master of the Chancery Division;
    - District judge;
    - District Judge (Magistrates' Courts).

8.1.11 Recorders

Recorders are part-time judges in the Crown Court. By s.21 of the Courts Act 1971, to be appointed as a recorder a person must satisfy the judicial-appointment eligibility condition on a seven-year basis.

8.1.12 **District judges**

District judges deal with a whole range of civil matters, from divorce and other family proceedings to damages claims. They sit in the County Court in the hearing centre for a particular geographic region (formerly known as a circuit). They may also sit at district registries of the High Court, again dealing with civil business, although in these cases their role will be that of case management rather than acting as trial judge. District judges are appointed through the JAC's application and selection process.

By s.9 of the County Courts Act 1984, for a person to be appointed a district judge or deputy district judge, he or she must satisfy the judicial-appointment eligibility condition on a five-year basis.

The Courts and Tribunals judiciary website has an excellent new section dealing with the work of district judges. This can be found at **www.judiciary.uk/about-the-judiciary/judges-career-paths/videos-district-judges-2018/**.

 Example

A day in the life of a district judge

There is no typical day for a district judge because the work is so varied. Under the Civil Procedure Rules (see Chapter 15) many matters are now dealt with by telephone conference call, rather than requiring attendance in person by the parties. For example, approximately thirty minutes will be allocated to a telephone case management hearing, with fifteen minutes added to this for reading the relevant papers beforehand. An attended appointment in front of a district judge would be the exception. On some days there may be a short appointments list, dealing with case management issues and interim applications, and perhaps short small claims trials. Another day may see a large and complex ancillary relief case (dealing with the allocation of assets in family proceedings) listed to last for three days. Family work would not be dealt with by telephone and a typical family list might see twenty-two hours of contested cases listed for hearing, although many of these would settle beforehand.

This information is based on an interview with an experienced district judge.

8.1.13 **District Judges (Magistrates' Courts)**

District Judges (Magistrates' Courts) used to be known as stipendiary magistrates, and sit in the magistrates' courts to deal with a range of the more complex cases that come before these courts. These cases can be civil or criminal in nature and some District Judges (Magistrates' Courts) are able to hear cases in specialist areas such as family proceedings or extradition proceedings. District Judges (Magistrates' Courts) are appointed through the JAC application and selection process. By s.22 of the Courts Act 2003, the statutory qualification for appointment as a District Judge (Magistrates' Courts) is satisfaction of the judicial-appointment eligibility condition on a five-year basis. The same requirements apply in relation to the appointment as a deputy District Judge (Magistrates' Courts).

8.1.14 **Magistrates—Justices of the Peace (JPs)**

There are approximately 300 magistrates' courts in England and Wales (although the number is decreasing as courts are closed as part of a costs saving exercise), hearing a range of criminal cases and some civil cases, such as family proceedings. However, the overwhelming majority of the work is criminal cases. All criminal cases commence in the magistrates' court and most are dealt with in their entirety in that court (see Chapters 8 and 9). The magistrates' court deals with bail applications as well as trials and sentencing in relation to summary offences and either way offences, where appropriate. Magistrates may also be asked to issue a search warrant.

Magistrates are lay people and generally have no legal qualifications, although having a legal qualification does not prevent a person becoming a magistrate. Magistrates are required to undertake practical training to prepare them for their role, although they are unpaid save for expenses. The system of training, development, and appraisal for magistrates is overseen by the Judicial College and delivered by Magistrates Area Training Committees. More details can be found on the Magistrates' Association website: **www.magistrates-association.org.uk/**. Under this system, all magistrates are appraised on a three- or four-year basis. Appraisal is undertaken by fellow magistrates trained for this purpose. Some magistrates, such as members of family court panels, receive specialist training to enable them to deal with their specific role.

Magistrates sit in panels (known as benches), usually made up of three magistrates, and are supported by a qualified legal adviser (the court clerk). One member of the panel, selected on a random basis, will chair the bench and speak in court to ask questions and give judgments; the other two magistrates are referred to as 'wingers'. All members of the bench have an equal role in making decisions upon the cases that come before them.

At present, magistrates are appointed by the Lord Chancellor following the recommendation of a local advisory committee for the area in question, which will advertise to encourage applications from members of the public. Once the local advisory committee has recommended someone to be a magistrate, approval is requested from the Lord Chief Justice. The aim of the application process is to try to encourage applicants, whatever their gender or age, from a wide range of social and ethnic backgrounds, to ensure that the Bench (the term used for the magistrates as a group, and not to be confused with the use of the term 'bench' to describe a panel of magistrates sitting in court!) is suitably diverse. What was once a secretive and locally politically controlled process has become more inclusive: there was a recent advertising campaign on the back of buses to try to encourage wider participation.

Magistrates are usually asked to sit in court for twenty-six half-days per year and although they will usually sit in the magistrates' court they may also be required to sit in the Crown Court to hear criminal appeals from the magistrates' court. In such appeals two magistrates will hear the case together with a circuit judge. In order to ensure consistency between decisions made in different magistrates' courts throughout the country, magistrates are issued with structured decision-making guidelines to assist the decision-making process. They are also given guidelines in relation to sentencing to try to ensure that sentences for similar crimes are consistent both locally and nationally.

Example

A day in the life of a magistrate

If the court is due to begin sitting at 10 a.m. I usually arrive by 9.30 and sign into the diary. I am given a court list from the clerk and check through it, to get an idea of the nature of cases being dealt with and to ensure that none of the cases involve somebody known to me (in which case I cannot sit to hear that particular case). The list also indicates fellow panel members and will identify the chair of the panel.

Ten minutes before going into court, I meet with the court clerk and discuss the list and any problem cases. The panel Chair is told the name of the prosecutor.

A typical day might involve dealing with bail applications, committals to the Crown Court, adjournments, pre-trial reviews, probation report cases (required to give guidance on sentencing), and road traffic cases. In some of these cases, the panel will retire from the court to consider their decision. Most of these matters are dealt with in the morning session, which usually ends at about 1 p.m. When the afternoon session commences, at 2 p.m., there may be some overspill cases from the morning to deal with and also a half-day trial, for example dealing with an offence of shoplifting. After all the cases have been heard, the panel and the clerk usually have a short discussion about how the day has gone.

This information is based on an interview with an experienced magistrate.

Table 8.1 shows the range of judicial offices, terms of appointment, and tenure.

8.1.15 **Coroners**

Coroners are independent judicial office holders. They occupy a unique position in the English legal system and can trace their lineage back to at least 1194. The coroner's court is inquisitorial rather than adversarial and the coroner's role is to investigate any unexplained or sudden deaths that are reported to them. The coroner's function is governed by Part 1 of the Coroners and Justice Act 2009 and the Coroners (Inquests) Rules 2013. Their main role is to establish who the deceased person was;

Table 8.1 Table of judicial offices and governing legislation

Title	Governing qualification legislation-qualification	Tenure	Court to which assigned
Justice of the Supreme Court	Section 25 Constitutional Reform Act 2005	By s.33 Constitutional Reform Act 2005, office held during good behaviour but may be removed from such office on an address of both Houses of Parliament	Supreme Court
Lord Chief Justice	Section 10 Senior Courts Act 1981	By s.11 Senior Courts Act 1981, office held during good behaviour, subject to a power of removal by Her Majesty on an address presented to her by both Houses of Parliament. Lord Chancellor to recommend exercise of the power of removal	President of Criminal Division of the Court of Appeal
Master of the Rolls	Section 10 Senior Courts Act 1981	As in s.11 Senior Courts Act 1981	President of the Civil Division of the Court of Appeal
Lord Justice of Appeal	Section 10 Senior Courts Act 1981	As in s.11 Senior Courts Act 1981	Court of Appeal
Chancellor of the High Court	Section 10 Senior Courts Act 1981	As in s.11 Senior Courts Act 1981	High Court (Chancery Division)
President of the Queen's Bench Division	Section 10 Senior Courts Act 1981	As in s.11 Senior Courts Act 1981	High Court (Queen's Bench Division)
President of the Family Division	Section 10 Senior Courts Act 1981	As in s.11 Senior Courts Act 1981	High Court (Family Division)
High Court judge (alternatively called a puisne judge)	Section 10 Senior Courts Act 1981	As in s.11 Senior Courts Act 1981	High Court—assigned to a Division by direction given by the Lord Chief Justice after consultation with the Lord Chancellor

Table 8.1 Continued

Title	Governing qualification legislation–qualification	Tenure	Court to which assigned
Circuit judge	Section 16 of the Courts Act 1971	By s.17 Courts Act 1971, a circuit judge may be removed from office on the ground of incapacity or misbehaviour if the Lord Chancellor thinks fit and if the Lord Chief Justice agrees	Crown Court, County Court
Coroners	Section 23 and Schedule 3 Coroners and Justice Act 2009	Schedule 3 paragraph 13 Coroners and Justice Act 2009. The Lord Chancellor may, with the agreement of the Lord Chief Justice, remove a senior coroner, area coroner, or assistant coroner from office for incapacity or misbehaviour.	Coroners Court

when, where, and how the deceased person met their death; and in what circumstances this occurred. The coroner's role is not to apportion blame for a death or to establish criminal or civil liability. An increasingly important part of their role is to produce reports, where appropriate, to make recommendations to prevent future deaths. In addition, they have retained an aspect of their earliest purpose as a collector of taxes and they adjudicate as to whether any treasure discovered buried or hidden is Treasure Trove and therefore declared to be property of the Crown.

There are approximately ninety-seven coroner's areas in England and Wales, each one broadly corresponding to a local authority area. There are thirty-two full-time coroners, known as senior coroners, and a larger number of part-time assistant coroners.

Coroners are appointed by local authorities with the agreement of the Lord Chief Justice and the Chief Coroner. A coroner must be a barrister or solicitor with at least five years' experience. Prior to the implementation of the 2009 Act, medically qualified individuals could be appointed as coroners, but the Act specifies that legal qualifications are now mandatory. The coroner's service is led by a Chief Coroner, whose job it is to standardise and organise what had been a largely unregulated service. The present Chief Coroner is His Honour Judge Mark Lucraft QC. The Courts and Tribunals website has a wealth of material about the Chief Coroner and the coroner's service. This can be found at **www.judiciary.gov.uk/related-offices-and-bodies/office-chief-coroner/**. There is a guide to coroner services at **www.gov.uk/government/uploads/system/uploads/attachment_data/file/363879/guide-to-coroner-service.pdf**.

8.2 Appointment of the judiciary

Historically, the selection and appointment of members of the judiciary was solely in the hands of the Lord Chancellor, a government minister. This resulted in the judiciary being perceived as having a lack of independence from government. The selection requirements and process also led to criticism that members of the judiciary tend to come from a narrow social background and do not reflect diversity in the population in terms of ethnicity, age, and gender.

8.2.1 The Peach Report

Sir Leonard Peach produced a report in 1999 entitled *The Independent Scrutiny of the Appointment Processes of Judges and Queen's Counsel in England and Wales*. In the report he recommended the appointment of a Commissioner for Judicial Appointments and in March 2001, Sir Colin Campbell was appointed to this role. The Commission was established to investigate individual complaints relating to judicial appointments and Queen's Counsel procedures and to review the appointments process for judges (other than law lords and Heads of Division) and Queen's Counsel. This Commission had no role in making or recommending individual appointments. In reports published in 2002, 2003, and 2004 by Campbell's Commission, the appointment of and selection process for members of the judiciary was heavily criticised.

The Law Society also published two consultation papers in 2000 on judicial appointments, recommending the creation of an independent Judicial Appointments Commission with open and transparent selection procedures and a widening of the pool from which candidates for judicial appointment can be drawn, to include all qualified solicitors and barristers, whether or not in private practice.

In 2003 the government announced that it would establish a Judicial Appointments Commission for England and Wales (JAC), and a consultation paper was published in 2003 entitled *A New Way of Appointing Judges*.

This consultation paper put forward a number of proposals concerning the manner in which the Commission would operate. For example, the Commission could have sole power to select and appoint all members of the judiciary; or could operate a selection procedure, but simply recommend appointments to the Queen or a government minister; or could select and appoint members of the judiciary, but only *recommend* appointments to higher office. The paper also dealt with the composition of the Commission, suggesting fifteen members, five of whom would be lawyers, five lay members, and five judges.

Campbell's Commission responded by suggesting that the majority of the JAC should be lay members and all members should be part-time to try to attract high-calibre applicants. The Commission also recommended that the JAC should be able to appoint certain members of the judiciary (up to Circuit Bench level) but only make recommendations for appointment to the High Court and above. It was felt that this approach would strike an appropriate balance between judicial independence and ultimate accountability to Parliament.

Following the consultation paper, and consideration of the responses to it, the Constitutional Reform Bill was introduced in 2004 and the Constitutional Reform Act was passed in 2005, which implemented the introduction of the JAC. From 3 April 2006, the JAC has been responsible for the recruitment and selection of judges. When selection of judges was a matter for the Lord Chancellor, it was increasingly perceived that this was inappropriate, because if the judiciary were selected by a government member it might suggest that the judiciary were not independent from the government. The independence of the judiciary is important in all matters but is particularly vital in situations where the courts are adjudicating on the lawfulness of acts of government.

The creation of the JAC is intended to make the appointment process clear and more accountable, and also to review the way in which judges are appointed to try to broaden diversity among members of the judiciary. As Malleson commented in her article 'Creating a Judicial Appointments Commission: Which Model Works Best':

> [T]he rationale for the establishment of a commission must be that it will guarantee the independence of the system from inappropriate politicisation, strengthen the quality of the appointments made, enhance the fairness of the selection process, promote diversity in the composition of the judiciary and so rebuild public confidence in the system.

Thinking point

The Independence of the Judiciary

It is fundamental that the judiciary must be independent. Equally fundamental is that the judiciary must also appear to be independent so any process for appointment must be transparent. The decision to move the physical location of the Supreme Court from the Houses of Parliament to a separate location, Middlesex Guildhall, is to emphasise the independence of the judiciary from Parliament and the government. What other factors are important in safeguarding the independence, and the appearance of independence, of the judiciary?

The Lord Chancellor will continue to recommend individuals for appointment to the judiciary to the Queen, as the final step in the process, but will no longer be involved in the recruitment and selection process.

The JAC acts independently of government to select candidates for judicial office (those offices set out in Sch.14 to the Constitutional Reform Act 2005 as well as to the offices of Lord Chief Justice, High Court judges, Heads of Division, and Lords Justices of Appeal) on merit where a vacancy arises through fair and open competition and by encouraging a wide range of applicants. There are fifteen members of the JAC, drawn from a range of legal posts and professions, but it also includes lay commissioners with no legal experience. However, the composition is a little different from that put forward in the consultation paper. There are five judges, three of whom are selected by the Judges' Council (see later at 8.5); six lay members; two professional members (one barrister and one solicitor); one magistrate; and one tribunal chair or arbitrator. Other than those members selected by the Judges' Council, there is a competitive application process. The Chairman of the Commission must always be a lay member. The Commission is accountable to Parliament through the Lord Chancellor. The JAC undertook its first selection process in October 2006, advertising in the press for applicants for the post of High Court judge.

The JAC has the role of a recommending body, in that candidates for appointment are recommended to the Lord Chancellor. The process of appointment set out in the Act is broadly similar whatever the nature of the appointment, but, in the case of Supreme Court judges, does involve a symbolic recommendation to the Queen from the prime minister.

Thinking point

The Composition of the Judicial Appointments Commission

In assessing whether the aims of the reform of the judicial appointments have been met it is important to consider the composition and powers of the JAC and to review the nature of the appointments made by the commission. Do you agree with the composition of the JAC and the powers given to it?

The Constitutional Reform Act 2005, as amended by the Crime and Courts Act 2013, sets out various procedures for the selection of judges, as set out in Table 8.2.

For the selection and appointment of (a) the Lord Chief Justice, the Master of the Rolls, the President of the Queen's Bench Division, the President of the Family Division, and the Chancellor of the High Court, and (b) Lords Justices of Appeal, initially the Lord Chancellor must make a recommendation to fill a vacancy in the offices mentioned. A request will be made to the JAC for a person to be selected for recommendation to fill the vacancy. On receipt of the request, the JAC appoints a selection panel, which must consist of four members—of whom one is the chair of the commission or nominee and one is a lay member of the commission—to determine and apply the selection process and make a selection. (Note that senior judges are also included as members of the panel, depending upon the office to be filled; see s.71 in relation to the offices in (a), and s.80 in relation to (b).)

Table 8.2 Selection of judges

Selection of judges	Process
Judges of Supreme Court (s.26)	Sections 27
Lord Chief Justice, Master of the Rolls, and Heads of Division (s.67)	Sections 68–70
Lords Justices of Appeal (s.76)	Sections 77–79
Puisne judges and holders of offices under Sch.14, for example circuit judges, recorders, district judges, tribunal members (s.85)	Sections 86–88

The panel will submit a report to the Lord Chancellor with the name of the person recommended for appointment. Only one person must be selected for recommendation for each request. At this stage, the Lord Chancellor can either accept or reject (if in the Lord Chancellor's opinion the person is not suitable for the office) the person selected, or ask the panel to reconsider their selection if, in the opinion of the Lord Chancellor, there is not enough evidence that the person selected is suitable for the office or there is evidence that the person selected is not the best candidate on merit.

If the Lord Chancellor rejects a selected person, the selection panel may not select that person again. Where the Lord Chancellor requires the panel to reconsider, the panel may select the same person again, or someone else. There are three stages in the Act through which the selection process can progress if the Lord Chancellor rejects a selection or asks the panel to reconsider. At the third stage, the Lord Chancellor must accept the selection. The new process cannot therefore be thwarted by the Lord Chancellor continually asking a panel to reconsider or rejecting their selected candidate. In March 2010, it was reported that a JAC selection panel had been asked by the then Lord Chancellor, Jack Straw, to reconsider their recommendation of Sir Nicholas Wall as preferred candidate for president of the Family Division. Sir Nicholas was subsequently appointed to the post.

Note that for appointment as a justice of the Supreme Court, the Lord Chancellor must convene a selection commission for the selection of a person to be recommended by the prime minister. By Sch.8, the Selection Commission consists of: the President of the Supreme Court; the Deputy President of the Supreme Court; and one member each of the JAC, the Judicial Appointments Board for Scotland, and the Northern Ireland Judicial Appointments Commission.

In October 2007, the government issued a further consultation document on judicial appointments, 'The Governance of Britain, Judicial Appointments'. Examples of further options for change in the consultation document include:

- the JAC itself making all judicial appointments, without the need for the involvement of the Lord Chancellor;
- alternatively, the JAC appointing to more junior judicial posts, the Lord Chancellor retaining a role in relation to the appointment of senior judges;

- the further limiting or removal of the Lord Chancellor's ability to reject a candidate put forward by the JAC or to ask the JAC to reconsider;
- greater involvement of Parliament in judicial appointments.

On 25 March 2008, the prime minister and the Secretary of State for Justice announced a White Paper and Draft Constitutional Renewal Bill to further the constitutional reform process. In the White Paper, the government proposed to reduce the role played by the Lord Chancellor in judicial appointments below the level of the High Court, by removing the Lord Chancellor's power to reject a candidate or to ask the JAC to reconsider their decision. The government also put forward a proposal to remove the prime minister from the process of appointing senior judges and suggested that there should be legislation outlining the key principles representing best practice in making judicial appointments. However, these changes did not become part of the Constitutional Reform and Governance Act 2010. Do you think that the final Act is, accordingly, too timid?

8.2.2 **Diversity in judicial appointments**

The JAC has a statutory duty under the Constitutional Reform Act 2005 to encourage greater diversity among those available for selection as judges: see s.64. The JAC must, however, select solely on merit and ensure that those selected are of good character. The task facing the JAC in encouraging diversity within the judiciary is illustrated in Table 8.3 and Table 8.4.

Traditionally, senior judicial appointments have been made from the ranks of barristers because qualification was based upon the fact of being a barrister or, more recently, experience as an advocate. Clearly, this limited the size and composition of the recruitment pool for the judiciary and impacted upon the types of persons becoming judges. If the recruitment pool is small then the judiciary simply reflect this limited group. Solicitors are now able to attain rights of audience in the higher courts and as a consequence are eligible for appointment as senior judges. The question to be answered, however, is: how many solicitors have been appointed? Equally, the effectiveness of the recent changes made in the Tribunal, Courts and Enforcement Act 2007 to the eligibility criteria for appointment to the judiciary will have to be considered. The statistics on judicial diversity produced since 2012 are presented in a different format from previous years and do not break down the data by gender within the ethnicity and profession categories. The Law Society encourages solicitors to apply for judicial appointment. More information on this can be found at **https://www.lawsociety.org.uk/law-careers/judicial-careers/**.

The JAC has been criticised in the press for failing to create a more diverse judiciary. *The Guardian* newspaper reported (28 January 2008) that the first ten High Court judges appointed under the new rules were all white, male former barristers, six of whom had been privately educated at leading independent schools. The article also

Table 8.3 Gender and ethnicity, statistics as at 1 April 2019

		Gender			Ethnicity							
Appointment name	**Total in post**	**Male**	**Female**	**% Female**	**White**	**Asian or Asian British**	**Black or Black British**	**Mixed**	**Any other back-ground**	**Total BME**	**Unknown**	**% BME of those declaring an ethnicity**
Heads of Division	**5**	5	0	**0.0%**	5	0	0	0	0	0	0	**0**
Court of Appeal Judges	**39**	30	9	**23%**	30	1	0	0	1	2	7	**6%**
High Court Judges	**97**	71	26	**27%**	87	2	0	0	1	3	7	**3%**
Deputy High Court Judges	**87**	65	22	**25%**	54	2	3	2	1	8	25	**13%**
Masters, Registrars, Costs Judges and District Judges (Principal Registry of the Family Division)	**27**	19	8	**30%**	20	1	0	0	0	1	6	**5%**
Deputy Masters, Deputy Registrars, Deputy Costs Judges and Deputy District Judges (PRFD)	**27**	19	8	**30%**	17	0	0	0	0	0	10	**n/k**

(Continued)

Table 8.3 Continued

Appointment name	Total in post	Gender			Ethnicity							
		Male	Female	% Female	White	Asian or Asian British	Black or Black British	Mixed	Any other back-ground	Total BME	Unknown	% BME of those declaring an ethnicity
Circuit Judges	**670**	460	210	**31%**	581	12	3	5	4	24	65	**4%**
Recorders	**873**	687	186	**21%**	651	22	11	21	7	61	161	**9%**
District Judges (County Court)	**424**	247	177	**42%**	364	22	5	7	1	35	25	**9%**
Deputy District Judges (Country Court)	**748**	454	294	**39%**	590	31	7	11	10	59	99	**9%**
District Judges (Magistrates' Courts)	**127**	80	47	**37%**	104	6	0	2	0	8	15	**7%**
Deputy District Judges (Magistrates' Courts)	**80**	54	26	**33%**	55	1	1	1	1	4	21	**7%**
Total	**3210**	2197	1013	**32%**	2564	100	30	49	26	205	441	**7%**

Table 8.4 Judiciary by gender and profession statistics as at 1 April 2019 (as declared)

Appointment name	Gender			Profession				
	Total in post	Male	Female	Barrister	Solicitor	Legal Executive	Unknown	% Non-Barrister
Heads of Division	**5**	5	0	5	0	0	0	**0.0%**
Court of Appeal Judges	**39**	30	9	38	1	0	0	**3%**
High Court Judges	**97**	71	26	93	4	0	0	**4%**
Deputy High Court Judges	**87**	65	22	79	6	0	1	**8%**
Masters, Registrars, Costs Judges, and District Judges (Principal Registry of the Family Division)	**27**	19	8	15	9	0	0	**38%**
Deputy Masters, Deputy Registrars, Deputy Costs Judges, and Deputy District Judges (PRFD)	**27**	19	8	19	8	0	0	**30%**
Circuit Judges	**670**	460	210	580	88	0	2	**13%**
Recorders	**873**	687	186	808	47	0	17	**6%**
District Judges (County Court)	**424**	247	177	117	307	0	0	**72%**
Deputy District Judges (County Court)	**748**	454	294	290	454	2	1	**61%**
District Judges (Magistrates' Courts)	**127**	80	47	49	78	0	0	**61%**
Deputy District Judges (Magistrates' Courts)	**80**	54	26	29	49	0	2	**63%**
Total	**3204**	2191	1013	2,122	1,051	2	26	**33%**

Source: Judicial Statistics 2019

Source: Judicial Diversity Statistics judiciary.gov.uk 2019.

reported that, although at the time there were a further eleven candidates approved for appointment and waiting for a suitable vacancy, only three were women, none of the candidates were from a minority ethnic background, and none of them were solicitors. In a later piece in the same newspaper (19 May 2008) it was reported that, since the inception of the JAC, the percentage of judicial appointments at all levels given to women or members of an ethnic minority had actually decreased.

Thinking point

Should the judiciary reflect society as a whole?

Is it necessary for the judiciary to reflect society as a whole? Is it not ability to do the job on merit, with no regard to race, gender, religion, or ethnicity, that is important? During the debate on the Crime and Courts Bill in 2012, Baroness Butler-Sloss stated:

> I strongly support diversity when—and only when—it equals merit. It will be very important that women—particularly those from ethnic minorities—who may not be able to bear the strain of the judicial process are not placed in a position where they may find themselves failing because there has been too much enthusiasm for diversity and not enough for merit. This is very important. I have a vivid recollection of a woman judge many years ago who was a very fine pianist. She should have remained a pianist.

What do you think of this view?

The then Secretary of State for Justice, Jack Straw, acknowledged that the involvement of the JAC in the judicial appointment process had not fulfilled expectations of creating a more diverse judiciary. It may be suggested however that the situation since 2008 has improved marginally. The Equality and Human Rights Commission, in its report of 2011, *Sex and Power* (see **www.equalityhumanrights.com/key-projects/sexandpower/**), noted that the percentage of women holding senior judicial posts (in the High Court and above) had risen slightly from 9.8 per cent in 2006 to 12.9 per cent in 2011, after a slight dip to 9.6 per cent in 2007–8. The Commission estimated that, at the present rate of progress, it would take forty-five years for women to achieve equality in terms of these judicial appointments—an improvement on the 2008 report, which estimated a period of fifty-five years. Perhaps the appointment process is finally making progress in the right direction, although, as the report points out, the increase in percentages often reflects the appointment of only a small number of candidates in numerical terms.

In July 2010, the JAC reported that the first analysis of the appointment of women and black or minority ethnic candidates to judicial office over ten years (between 1998 and 2009) showed that more of these candidates apply for judicial roles now than before the JAC was set up. It also found that more women candidates are being selected, although the number of successful black or minority ethnic candidates remained constant.

In February 2010, the Advisory Panel on Judicial Diversity, chaired by Lady Neuberger, delivered its report into identifying the barriers to progress on judicial diversity and made recommendations to the Lord Chancellor on how to make progress to a more diverse judiciary at every level and in all courts in England and Wales.

The 2019 judicial statistics demonstrate that there has been a slight increase in the percentage of female judges and black and minority ethnic judges. Only 33 per cent of court judges were non-barristers. The Lord Chief Justice has expressed his concern that these statistics suggest the work carried out by the Judicial Diversity Committee has not yet been successful. The Committee has produced a progress report and an action plan to attempt to improve the situation. See **http://ww.judiciary.uk/judicial-diversity-committee-of-the-judges-council-report-on-progress-and-action-plan-2019/**.

Critical debate

A comparative European study in 2012 reported that only Azerbaijan and Armenia have a lower ratio of women to men in the senior judiciary. The Ministry of Justice has praised its diversity taskforce for implementing '20 of the 53 recommendations' made in Lady Neuberger's report on how to encourage more women to enter the profession. Is it fair to compare England and Wales with other jurisdictions in this respect?

The Panel recommended a 'fundamental shift of approach from a focus on individual judicial appointments to the concept of a judicial career. A judicial career should be able to span roles in the courts and tribunals as one unified judiciary.' In order to deliver this change, the Panel recommended that a Judicial Diversity Taskforce, made up of the Lord Chancellor, the Lord Chief Justice, the Chairman of the JAC, leaders of the legal profession, and the Senior President of Tribunals, should oversee an agreed action plan for change.

The taskforce was set up and produced its first report in May 2011 and its second annual report in September 2012. The report can be accessed at **www.gov.uk/government/publications/improving-judicial-diversity-judicial-diversity-taskforce-annual-report**.

The Crime and Courts Act 2013 includes measures that aim to improve judicial diversity. It is made clear in Sch.13, Part 2, para. 10 that the JAC, while appointing on merit, can appoint the candidate who will increase the diversity of the judiciary. A consultation on the 'equal merit' provision was carried out in 2013 and this consultation, and the replies received, can be found on the JAC website at **consult.justice.gov.uk/digital-communications/equal-merit-provision**.

There is also a section of the judiciary website devoted to diversity; this can be found at **www.judiciary.gov.uk/about-the-judiciary/who-are-the-judiciary/diversity/message-from-lcj-judicial-diversity/**. Twelve High Court judges were appointed in 2019. Half of the appointees were women.

In relation to magistrates, until 2008 the proportion of male and female magistrates appointed was equal. Women now comprise over half of the magistrates in all regions. 12 per cent of magistrates are from black and minority ethnic backgrounds.

There is a report on diversity in public life which was produced in 2019 by the House of Commons Library, *Ethnic Diversity in Politics and Public Life*. It can be found at **https://researchbriefings.parliament.uk/ResearchBriefing/Summary/SN01156#fullreport**. The report looks at ethnicity in relation to positions of power in politics and public life.

In April 2019 a new initiative, the Pre-Application Judicial Education Programme (PAJE), was launched by the Judicial Diversity Forum in a joint initiative from the Judiciary, Ministry of Justice (MoJ), Judicial Appointments Commission (JAC), The Bar Council, The Law Society of England and Wales, and the Chartered Institute of Legal Executives (CILEx). The PAJE is designed to support 'talented lawyers from underrepresented groups to feel more equipped, confident and prepared' when applying for a judicial appointment. It will be interesting to monitor and access how successful this admirable scheme is in opening up the judiciary to diverse talent. More details can be found here: **www.judiciary.uk/diversity/pre-application-judicial-education-programme-paje/**.

Visit the online resources to watch a video on the PAJE initiative.

Thinking point

Composition of the judiciary

It is often stressed that the composition of the judiciary reflects a narrow social base. The criticism levelled at the judiciary is that it is unrepresentative of the general population because its members are predominantly male, white, public school and Oxbridge-educated, and middle class. It is important to keep the judicial statistics under review in order to see who is being appointed to the judiciary, particularly noting the percentage of women, minority ethnic candidates, and solicitors. Of course, the composition of the judiciary may also reflect reluctance in certain groups to apply for judicial appointment. What steps need to be taken to widen the recruitment net and what steps are being taken by the JAC?

8.2.3 Alternative methods of appointment

The judicial appointments process around the world can be very different from that used in England and Wales. In some, rather than having an appointment process, judges are elected or undertake specific training in a judicial career distinct from other branches of the legal profession.

In the United States (US), for example, some judges are elected, or their appointment is subject to confirmation, by the political electorate. Although this system is, arguably, a more democratic process than that used to appoint members of the judiciary in England and Wales, it does not necessarily mean that the best person for the job is the one who is appointed. In fact, it can result in the wealthiest candidates having the most success, due to well-financed promotional campaigns. The American Judicature Society (AJS), an independent body that works to maintain the independence and integrity of the courts and increase public understanding of the justice system, has commented that electing members of the judiciary is only effective if voters can make an informed choice—in some cases, due to the number of candidates this becomes impossible, and in other cases, where only one candidate runs for office, there is no choice at all. The AJS also suggests that in some circumstances, the support of a political party is essential to a candidate's success. This may lead to charges that the independence and impartiality of the office holder may be in doubt, and may result in political credentials being considered more important than aptitude and suitability for the role.

Due to these concerns, some states use commissions to select candidates for judicial appointments. Although the membership of each commission varies, it typically comprises both lay and legally qualified members and is involved in advertising judicial posts, interviewing candidates, and making recommendations to the appropriate appointing authority.

More information about the appointment of judges in the US and the role of the AJS can be found at **www.judicialselection.us/**.

In France, the École Nationale de la Magistrature (ENM) trains French law graduates to be judges. Thus the judiciary includes judges appointed from the legal profession as well as career judges, straight from university, trained for two and a half years by the ENM. This approach means that the average age of judges is lower than in many other countries and has also resulted in the appointment of more female than male judges in France. Of course, this situation can lead to similar criticisms to those levelled in the UK at an overwhelmingly male judiciary. The ENM website is at **www.enm.justice.fr**.

Thinking point

Should academics without professional practical experience be eligible to be appointed as judges?

Academic lawyers can become judges of the Court of Justice of the European Communities in Luxembourg and of the European Court of Human Rights in Strasbourg. Do you think that academics without legal professional qualifications should be appointed to the judiciary in England and Wales?

8.3 Removal and retirement

The age for retirement of judges is usually seventy. However, the Lord Chief Justice has the power to allow certain judges, if appropriate, to carry on until age seventy-five (Judicial Pensions and Retirement Act 1993 s.26). It is possible to remove judges from office but, as has been seen in the Table of Judicial Offices and Governing Legislation (Table 8.1), removal may only take place under very specific circumstances. To summarise the position regarding the removal of judges: only the Queen, on the petition of both Houses of Parliament, can remove judges of the High Court or above. The last occasion on which this happened was in 1830, when Jonah Barrington, a judge of the High Court of Admiralty, was removed for fraudulently taking money that had been paid into court. The Lord Chancellor, with the agreement of the Lord Chief Justice, can dismiss other judges for incapacity, inability, or misbehaviour, depending upon the judicial office held. Bruce Campbell J (a circuit judge) was sacked in 1983 for smuggling spirits, cigarettes, and tobacco into England on his yacht. In April 2009, a district judge was removed from office by the Lord Chancellor and the Lord Chief Justice under s.11 (5) of the County Courts Act 1984. Also in 2009, a district judge, Margaret Short, was removed after a judicial investigation into complaints made about her behaviour towards solicitors appearing before her (this included being 'petulant and rude') and 'a variety of other inappropriate behaviour'. In 2011, a deputy High Court judge was removed from office for 'bringing the judiciary into disrepute' after being convicted of assaulting his wife and in 2015, three judges were removed from office, and a fourth resigned, when they were discovered to have been viewing pornography at work. This was said by one newspaper to be 'an unexpected blow to the reputation of the judiciary, as well as a humiliating public rebuke to the individual ex-judges'. The statement from the Judicial Conduct Investigations Office noted that they were satisfied that 'the material did not include images of children or any other illegal content, but concluded that this was an inexcusable misuse of their judicial IT accounts and wholly unacceptable conduct for a judicial office holder'.

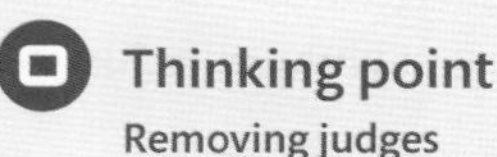

Thinking point

Removing judges

Why do you think it is so difficult to remove judges? Should it be difficult?

8.4 **Judicial independence**

Despite some perceived lack of independence in the judiciary arising as a result of the manner in which they were appointed prior to the Constitutional Reform Act 2005, the independence of judges is in fact protected in a number of ways. As has already been seen, it is difficult to remove judges from office in order to ensure that their decision-making is unaffected by external pressures, political or otherwise. The salaries of judges are substantial (but not as high as salaries for very successful lawyers) to maintain the quality of candidates seeking judicial appointment. Judges are paid from the Consolidated Fund, which was first set up in 1787 as 'one fund into which shall flow every stream of public revenue and from which shall come the supply for every service'. The significance of this is that the Consolidated Fund is not subject to an annual parliamentary vote, so judicial salaries are not a matter of political debate. By s.75 of the Courts and Legal Services Act 1990, certain judges, listed in Sch.11, are barred from private legal practice. The list includes, among others: justice of the Supreme Court, Lord Justice of Appeal, puisne judge of the High Court, circuit judge, district judge, and District Judge (Magistrates' Courts). Under the House of Commons Disqualification Act 1975, full-time judges are disqualified from membership of the House of Commons.

Another aspect of judicial independence is that judges are immune from being sued in connection with the exercise of their jurisdiction. The limits of this immunity were explored in the case of *Sirros v Moore* [1975] QB 118. Magistrates have statutory immunity, under ss.31 and 32 of the Courts Act 2003, for acts or omissions: (a) in the execution of duties as a Justice of the Peace; and (b) in relation to matters within their jurisdiction. The immunity extends to acts or omissions in the purported execution of duty beyond the jurisdiction of a Justice of the Peace so long as there is an absence of bad faith. In relation to defamation, absolute privilege attaches to statements made by judges in the execution of their judicial office.

Thinking point

Should it be possible to sue judges in relation to their decisions?

Can you suggest why judicial immunity from suit (being sued) is important?

Judges are, therefore, mostly independent of government and the legislature and do not become involved in political debate. However, judges may inevitably become involved in hearing, and deciding, cases with political implications. In the 1980s, cases such as *Duport Steel v Sirs* [1980] 1 WLR 142, concerning trade union activities in relation to a strike; *Bromley v Greater London Council* [1982] 1 All ER 129, dealing with pricing policy for the London Underground; and other cases arising from the miners' strike of 1984–5 thrust the courts into areas of political controversy. Indeed, it is said by some that the social and political background of judges predisposes them to favour certain sectional interests in the community and to be unsympathetic to other interests. (See Griffith, *The Politics of the Judiciary*.) However, that is not to say that judges are pro-government. The readiness of the courts to judicially review decisions of the executive and find such decisions unlawful, particularly in the fields of immigration and sentencing, evidences judicial independence. It is also important to have regard to the impact of the Human Rights Act 1998 and the courts' interpretation of UK law in the light of the European Convention on Human Rights (see Chapter 7). You may wish to consider the decision of the Supreme Court in *R (on the application of Miller) (Appellant) v The Prime Minister (Respondent); Cherry and Others (Respondents) v Advocate General for Scotland (Appellant) (Scotland)* [2019] UKSC 41 and the subsequent newspaper coverage and discussion of the role of the Supreme Court and the judges in the constitution. This is the unanimous decision of eleven Supreme Court Justices that the advice given by the Prime Minister to the Queen, that Parliament should be prorogued prior to the United Kingdom's departure from the European Union, was unlawful.

Consider also that judges may be requested to chair royal commissions and tribunals of inquiry. Inevitably such activity places judges in the political arena.

Example

Examples include Lord Denning in relation to the Profumo affair in 1963, Scott LJ's inquiry in the 1990s into the sales of arms to Iraq, and Lord Hutton's report published in January 2004 into the death of the government arms expert Dr David Kelly (HC 247). Judicial independence has been strengthened further, at least ostensibly, in the wake of the Constitutional Reform Act 2005. The Lord Chancellor no longer has a judicial role and, as has been seen, certain functions have been transferred to the Lord Chief Justice. Section 3 of the Constitutional Reform Act also imposes a duty on the Lord Chancellor to uphold judicial independence and not seek to influence judicial decisions through special access to the judiciary. Secondly, Justices of the Supreme Court are disqualified from sitting in the legislative chamber of the House of Lords, and with the establishment of an independent Supreme Court there is a further apparent separation of the judicial and legislative functions. Thirdly, the creation of the independent JAC has largely taken judicial appointments out of the hands of the executive.

On a personal level, to maintain their independence, judges must not engage in activities which might affect, or be thought to affect, their independence. A judge should disqualify him- or herself from sitting in a particular case if an issue of bias arises, for example a financial interest in the outcome of a particular case (*Dimes v The Proprietors of the Grand Junction Canal* (1852) 3 HL Cas 759). The principle of natural justice, which includes the rule against bias, secures the impartiality of decisions made by judges. The other limb of the concept of natural justice is that a hearing must be seen to be fair, and judicial impartiality is an important safeguard for this. Successful appeals have been mounted against the decisions of judges who have interfered in a case by asking too many questions from the bench. These technical rules of natural justice do not however impact upon a perceived prejudice arising out of the social and political background of individual judges. See also the section on judicial conduct at 8.5.2.

Arguably, the leading case on judicial independence is *R v Bow Street Metropolitan Stipendiary Magistrate, ex parte Pinochet Ugarte (No.2)* [2000] 1 AC 119. The House of Lords had ruled, by a 3 to 2 majority, that the former president of Chile, Senator Pinochet, who was accused of various crimes against Spanish nationals resident in Chile in the 1970s, could be extradited to Spain to face trial. However, it subsequently emerged that one of the majority judges, Lord Hoffmann, had links with Amnesty International, a charity which campaigns for justice for political prisoners worldwide. The law lords decided that, because Lord Hoffmann had not declared this interest in advance, his presence in the case created an *impression* of bias sufficient to justify ordering a rehearing. Even the *theoretical possibility* of bias was enough. This was unprecedented, but shows the value placed on judicial independence in this country. At the rehearing, a new panel of judges confirmed that Pinochet could be extradited but the British government then intervened, decided that Pinochet was too ill to face trial in Spain, and allowed him to leave the UK for Chile, where he managed to resist trial on grounds of ill health until his eventual death in December 2006. Lord Browne-Wilkinson said:

> The fundamental principle is that a man may not be a judge in his own cause. This principle has two implications. First . . . if a judge is in fact a party to the litigation or has a financial or proprietary interest in its outcome then he is indeed sitting as a judge in his own cause [and this] is sufficient to cause his automatic disqualification . . . Second . . . where his conduct or behaviour may give rise to a suspicion that he is not impartial, for example because of his friendship with a party . . . In my judgment, this case falls within the first category of case. In such a case, once it is shown that the judge is himself a party to the cause, or has a relevant interest in its subject matter, he is disqualified without any investigation into whether there was a likelihood or suspicion of bias. The mere fact of his interest is sufficient to disqualify him unless he has made sufficient disclosure.

8.5 Governance of the judiciary

The manner in which the judiciary is governed changed following the Constitutional Reform Act 2005. The Lord Chief Justice, rather than the Lord Chancellor, is now responsible for deciding in which court judges sit and what sort of cases they hear. A new structure for the organisation of the judiciary was developed, which includes a new Judicial Executive Board and the existing Judges' Council.

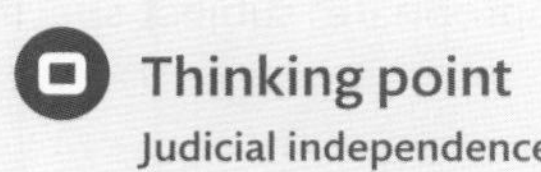

Judicial independence

An independent appointments process; constraints on the removal of judges, as outlined in Table 8.1; and judicial immunity from suit all ensure that judicial independence is safeguarded. Are further safeguards required?

The Judicial Executive Board is made up of the Lord Chief Justice, the Master of the Rolls, the Presidents of both the Queen's Bench and Family Divisions, the Chancellor of the High Court, the Vice-President of the Queen's Bench Division, and the Senior

Presiding Judge. The Board is the vehicle through which the Lord Chief Justice exercises his executive responsibilities relating to issues such as providing leadership, direction, and support to the judiciary and determining roles and responsibilities of the judiciary; considering policies on complaints; developing policy and practice on judicial deployment and appointment to non-judicial roles; and putting forward the requirements for new appointments of certain judges and discussing specific appointments with the JAC. Some aspects of the Board's work will also be undertaken by subcommittees.

The original Judges' Council, dating from 1873, was in place until 1981, when it was wound up by the Supreme Court Act 1981. After much debate as to the pros and cons of having a Council representing the views of judges, the Judges' Council was resurrected in 1988 as a smaller body under the chairmanship of the Lord Chief Justice. The Council is primarily a representative body for the judiciary and advises the Lord Chief Justice on particular issues when requested to do so. The sort of issues upon which the Council presently advises include judicial independence, the development of a judicial code of conduct, and terms and conditions of judges' employment. The Council includes representatives from all areas of the judicial hierarchy, meets a number of times each year, and publishes newsletters and an annual report (see **www.judiciary.gov.uk/how-the-judiciary-is-governed/judges-council/**).

The judiciary is also represented by a number of bodies such as the Association of District Judges and the Magistrates' Association.

8.5.1 Training the judiciary

Responsibility for training the judiciary and magistrates lies with the Judicial College (JC). In April 2011, the College took over the training function that had been undertaken by the Judicial Studies Board since 1973. Membership of the College includes academics, practitioners, judges, and magistrates. The Lord Chief Justice has statutory responsibility for the College. You can find out more about the JC at **www.judiciary.gov.uk/judicial-college/**.

The formal training of judges is now structured and the College has identified three aspects necessary for judicial training:

1. substantive law, evidence, and procedure (and if appropriate, subject-specific expertise);
2. judicial skills;
3. social context.

New appointees have to go through an induction programme and most are assigned a mentor to support them in the first few years of their appointment. The judges are then required to keep up to date by attending continuing education and training sessions. The College training strategy for 2018–20 sets out in detail what the body was trying to achieve over that two-year period and is available at **www.judiciary.uk/wp-content/uploads/2017/12/judicial-college-strategy-2018-2020.pdf**. The College's predecessor, the Judicial Studies Board, published a competence framework for magistrates as part of the revised Magistrates' National Training Initiative. The College has put in place an induction and consolidation training programme to ensure that magistrates are fully trained to discharge their judicial function.

8.5.2 **Judicial conduct**

The Judges' Council, following consultation with the judiciary, drew up a Guide to Judicial Conduct in October 2004. This was fully revised in March 2019 and a standing committee keeps the guide under review. The guide is designed to assist judges in relation to issues of conduct that they might face and is designed to be read alongside their terms and conditions of appointment. The principles and aspirations set out in the guide include judicial independence, impartiality, integrity, propriety, competence, and diligence. These principles having been expressed, the guide goes on to consider a number of specific problems that may be faced by members of the judiciary, such as in respect of personal relationships and perceived bias and activities outside the court, which includes areas such as commercial activities, participation in public debate and gifts, hospitality, and social activities. The guide can be found at **www.judiciary.uk/publications/guide-to-judicial-conduct/**.

There is now a Judicial Conducts and Investigations Office (JCIO). The purpose of this office is to try to ensure the fair and consistent treatment of disciplinary issues involving the judiciary. You can find out more about the JCIO at **judicialconduct.judiciary.gov.uk/index.htm**.

The JCIO deals with complaints about the personal conduct of members of the judiciary, rather than complaints about a judge's decision in a particular case.

Should anyone wish to complain about the JCIO, the complaint may be referred to the Judicial Appointments and Conduct Ombudsman. The role of the Judicial Appointments and Conduct Ombudsman encompasses the investigation of complaints concerning the judicial appointments process and issues arising out of judicial discipline or conduct. You can find out more about the ombudsman at **www.gov.uk/government/organisations/judicial-appointments-and-conduct-ombudsman**.

Summary

- Judges are appointed to work in specific courts and may specialise in hearing particular types of cases, such as civil, criminal, or family. They are governed by the Lord Chief Justice through the Judicial Executive Board.
- The Justices of the Supreme Court are the most senior judges in the UK.
- The system under which members of the judiciary are selected and appointed has changed radically in recent years. This has been fuelled by criticisms of the judiciary's make-up in terms of age, sex, gender, and ethnicity and in terms of their perceived lack of independence from government.

- From April 2006, the JAC has been responsible for operating a selection process for members of the judiciary and recommending appointments to the Lord Chancellor. The JAC is required, under the Constitutional Reform Act 2005, to encourage greater diversity among those selected for appointment and its creation is designed to make the selection process clearer, more accountable, and independent of government. The need for diversity has been underlined by the 'equal merit' provision in the Crime and Courts Act 2013.
- The independence of the judiciary is protected in a number of ways, for example by the process of appointment and by the constraints on the removal of judges.
- The Judges' Council is one of the representative bodies of the judiciary and publishes a Guide to Judicial Conduct. Judges receive training in their role through the Judicial College, which operates an induction process and continuing education.

Questions

1. Why do you think it was considered necessary to change the way in which members of the judiciary were appointed?
2. What is the role and function of the JAC?
3. What are the obstacles to diversification of the composition of the judiciary?
4. Identify the safeguards in place to ensure judicial independence.
5. What sort of training do new members of the judiciary receive?
6. Do you think the PAJE will modernize and open up the appointment process for judges?

Sample question and outline answer

Question

Lord Neuberger, President of the Supreme Court, commented in June 2013 that more had to be done to change the 'monolithic' senior judiciary. Should the judiciary be representative of the population as a whole?

Outline answer

The following guidance will help you to plan and prepare an answer to the above question.

Your introduction should set out what you understand the question to be asking and explain how you will set about answering it. This is a wide question that can be answered in a variety of ways. Provided you set out in your introduction how you intend to answer it, and then go on to do what you set out to do, you cannot go wrong! What follows are a few ideas about how the question could be approached.

The question requires you to discuss whether the make-up of the judiciary is similar to the population of the UK. This requires you to explain what is meant by representative, that is, the contention that in age, social class, gender, ethnicity, and education, the members of the judiciary should represent, in percentage terms, the population of the country.

You might wish to distinguish between the lay judiciary (magistrates) and the professional judiciary (judges). You could set out an overview of the composition of each and explain why that is the present situation.

You could explain the role of judges and why it could be important that they are drawn from a wide section of society, and give an opposing view that the selection process should ensure that judges are able to do the job they are selected for while being drawn from a small pool of applicants. However, you may also wish to investigate a contrary view, as expressed by Baroness Butler-Sloss. You could then go on to explain that the non-representative nature of the judiciary has generally been recognised as a problem and discuss the reforms brought about by the Constitutional Reform Act 2005 and the Tribunals, Courts and Enforcement Act 2007, together with the new procedures for appointment from the JAC.

In your conclusion you should sum up your arguments.

Further reading

Your reading should be directed to making sure you have an overview of the general structure of the judicial hierarchy in England and Wales and a general understanding of the jurisdiction and role played by judges. You should read in more depth about the debate relating to transparency and suitability of the appointment system and you should think about whether the process for removing judges from office is fit for purpose. Finally, the perennial debate about diversity in the ranks of the judiciary is a popular area for assessment. Make sure that you read the broadsheet newspapers: there are often articles and debate about the judiciary that will give you ideas to think about and explore further.

- ***Bradley, A.*** *'Judicial Independence under Attack'* [2003] PL 397

  Considers the attack by David Blunkett against the judiciary arising from a case involving asylum seekers.

- ***Derbyshire, P.*** *Sitting in Judgment: The Working Lives of Judges*, Hart Publishing (2011)

  A discussion of the modern judiciary.

  Democratic Audit of the UK. **www.democraticaudit.com/wp-content/uploads/2013/06/auditing-the-uk-democracy-the-framework-2.pdf**

  Discussion on the independence of the judiciary.

- ***Gerry, F.*** *'Ensuring Gender Equality in the Judiciary'* (2012) 176(48) CL & J 705

  Considers why there are so few women being appointed as judges.

- ***Griffith, J. A. G.*** *The Politics of the Judiciary*, 5th edn reissue, Fontana Press (2010)

  This is an important, and controversial, text. It considers whether the judiciary is able to be neutral or whether they must act politically.

- ***Hale, B.*** *'Equality and the Judiciary: Why Should We Want More Women Judges?'* [2001] PL 489

  This article makes some interesting points about the judicial appointments system which was used to appoint many of the judges currently in post in England and Wales.

- ***Hale, B.*** *Lecture delivered at Constitutional Law Summer School, Belfast: 'Judges, Power and Accountability: Constitutional Implications of Judicial Selection'*, 11 August 2017, **https://www.supremecourt.uk/docs/speech-170811.pdf**

  Judicial Appointments Commission. **jac.judiciary.gov.uk/**

  Includes lots of interesting information, including the application forms and criteria for judicial posts.

- ***Malleson, K.*** *'Creating a Judicial Appointments Commission: Which Model Works Best?'* [2004] PL 102

  A thought-provoking discussion about the alternative ways that a JAC could be dealt with.

- Lord Phillips of Worth-Matravers. *Lecture on the Politics of Judicial Independence delivered at UCI in February 2011*, **www.supremecourt.gov.uk/docs/speech_110208.pdf**

  This speech does exactly what its title suggests—it is an insider's view from the then President of the Supreme Court.

- ***Small, J.*** *'Quis Custodiet Ipsos Custodes?'* (2003) 153 NLJ 624

  In other words, 'who oversees the judges?' A discussion about the best way to appoint High Court judges.

- ***Sumption, J.*** *Law's Expanding Empire. The Reith Lectures 2019—Lecture 1* **www.bbc.co.uk/programmes/m00057m8**

  This is the first of the Reith Lectures given by Lord Sumption in 2019. They are all worth listening to and reflecting upon. In this lecture, Lord Sumption argues that the law is taking over the space once occupied by politics. He argues that the growth of the law, driven by demand for greater personal security and less risk, results in less liberty.

Online resources

You should now attempt the supporting self-test questions and end-of-chapter questions available at: **www.oup.com/he/wilson-rutherford4e**

Chapter 9

The legal profession

Learning objectives

By the end of this chapter you should:

- be able to describe the respective roles of solicitors and barristers in the English legal system;
- be able to identify the basic business models of legal practice and the constraints on such organisations;
- have an understanding of the rules affecting practice as a solicitor or a barrister;
- be able to identify the regulatory organisations overseeing solicitors and barristers and be able to discuss the issues concerning regulation;
- be able to take part in the debate as to whether the two main branches of the legal profession should be fused into one.

Talking point

Is the Uber taxi hire model the future for the legal profession? In Autumn 2017, the Solicitor's Regulation Authority produced a consultation paper which, among a number of proposals for discussion, suggested that individual solicitors should be able to offer legal services to the public on a freelance basis without being part of a firm or recognised legal structure. In other words, an individual solicitor could offer reserved legal services without being employed by a law firm or being registered as a sole practitioner. Under the headline 'SRA ushers in "Uberisation" of legal services', the Law Society Gazette noted: 'The SRA feels solicitors should be able to operate on the same model as barristers, attached to chambers and sharing back-office functions, but essentially working on a freelance basis.' Legal Futures referred to this proposal as the 'new Wild West' of legal regulation.

The Wild West analogy may be a little unfair. The proposal would not be carte blanche to ignore the profession's rules and code of conduct, and freelance solicitors would have to have professional indemnity insurance. As a further safeguard they would not be able to hold client money, except fees and disbursements, nor employ people. The barristers' model would cut overheads and allow individual solicitors to, perhaps, offer a much cheaper service than the traditional model.

The SRA proposals are out for consultation. Consider the following questions—what is your view?

- Do you agree with the Law Society's comment that the proposals put 'vulnerable clients in the hands of inexperienced, unsupervised lawyers' or do you think it would be a healthy step for the profession and would open up competition?
- How would you modernise the profession? What safeguards are necessary for the public?
- What regulation and governance is required for a twenty-first-century legal profession?

Introduction

The past forty years have seen major changes to legal practice and the legal professions. Some changes have been brought about directly by the professions and some have been introduced by Acts of Parliament. Other changes have been necessitated by factors such as the increase in the volume and complexity of laws and increased influence of the internet. A number of Acts of Parliament have sought to make legal services more readily available to members of the public and more responsive to the needs of consumers in order to break down barriers to competition to ensure that legal services are obtainable at the best price for the best service. The legislation includes the Administration of Justice Act 1985, which sanctioned licensed conveyancers and ended the conveyancing monopoly of solicitors, and the Courts and Legal Services Act 1990, which stated in s.17(1) that the objective was

> the development of legal services in England and Wales (and in particular the development of advocacy, litigation, conveyancing, and probate services) by making provision for *new or better ways* of providing such services and *a wider choice of persons providing them*, while maintaining the proper and efficient administration of justice. (emphasis added)

Under this Act, the barristers' monopoly to appear as advocates before the higher courts was ended and solicitors were given the opportunity to gain higher rights of audience.

The Access to Justice Act 1999 continued reforms relating to legal services. In particular, it established the Legal Services Commission, to oversee legal aid via the Community Legal Service and the Criminal Defence Service. The Legal Services Commission was abolished in April 2013, as a result of provisions in the Legal Aid, Sentencing and Punishment of Offenders (LASPO) Act 2012, and replaced by the Legal Aid Agency, which is now responsible for both civil and criminal legal aid and advice in England and Wales. (See Chapter 11, 'Access to justice'.)

In 2007 the Legal Services Act introduced ABS for lawyers, with the aim of providing benefits for consumers by way of more choice, reduced costs, and greater convenience in accessing legal services. Sections of the Act have come into force on a number of different dates. The provisions in respect to ABS came into force in 2011. Under ABS, non-lawyers are permitted to part-own law firms, and it is hoped that the creation of multidisciplinary practices (MDPs) will lead to legal services and non-legal services being offered in combination. The Act has been referred to as 'Tesco law' because of an expectation, not yet fully realised, that supermarkets will provide legal services and compete with law firms.

Approximately 1,000 firms have been licensed to offer legal services since the ABS regime was introduced in 2011. Thus far, the most high-profile firm to be awarded a multidisciplinary licence is the accountancy firm KPMG. The licence, which was granted by the SRA with a number of waivers and exemptions, allows solicitors already employed by KPMG in other capacities to offer their clients more legal services.

The Legal Services Act also seeks to make the legal profession more accountable and transparent in relation to complaints. The self-regulation of the profession has been replaced by a scheme of independent safeguards. Regulation is undertaken by the Legal Services Board, which has as its overriding mandate 'to ensure that regulation in the legal services sector is carried out in the public interest; and that the interests of consumers are placed at the heart of the system'.

The reforms have generated much comment, both positive and negative, and when studying the legal profession the reforms should be considered and evaluated. In essence, the discussion revolves around what is 'in the public interest'. Lawyers view this as meaning that a strong independent profession is required with high ethical standards and a high level of expertise: the price being that there must be restrictions and the cost may be high. The opposing view is that public interest requires competition to improve efficiency, and that control by independent regulation is preferable to self-regulation. To assess the arguments it is necessary to understand the rules governing the work of the legal profession and how they operate.

9.1 The legal profession

In England and Wales, unlike in many other legal systems, the legal profession comprises two distinct branches: barristers and solicitors. In addition there are other personnel providing legal services, such as licensed conveyancers and legal executives. This chapter will look at these different branches of the legal profession.

9.2 Solicitors

The job description of a solicitor has evolved over time but the role has always involved representing individuals and organisations in dealings with the law. The title of solicitor in the present-day sense was first used in the late nineteenth century.

Traditionally solicitors worked in partnerships, based in local communities, and undertook a broad range of work associated with day-to-day legal concerns: divorce, conveyancing, drafting wills, and dealing with criminal and civil litigation. This is still the case with small firms (often referred to as 'high street' firms) but, increasingly, solicitors work in large firms, and as a result individual lawyers have to specialise in specific areas of the law. Large firms of solicitors ('commercial' firms) usually have a number of specialist departments, such as company/commercial, property, private client, and litigation. Many areas of the law are complex and the law can change on a daily basis; it is not possible for an individual solicitor to keep up to date with diverse areas of the law, as they may have done in the past, so solicitors have had to narrow their field of expertise and practice. In large law firms, within broad departments, smaller groups of solicitors will work in specialist units. For example, in the company department there may be sub-departments dealing with intellectual property, pensions, banking and finance, and insolvency. The biggest commercial firms have a huge array of specialist areas of expertise. It is instructive to look at the websites of some of the larger legal firms to find out how their business is organised on a departmental basis.

Example

A typical day for a commercial solicitor in a large specialist department

Work can be for a variety of clients or for one major client. A typical day may involve consideration of contractual documents, such as standard terms of business or contracts relating to intellectual property (for example, computer software). The work often involves drafting, amending, or negotiating contracts on behalf of a client. The day might start with a client meeting to discuss a contract for software provision, followed by a business development lunch with a local accountancy firm. Business development is a very important part of a modern lawyer's work and involves promoting and marketing the firm to local, regional, and often national or international businesses. Part of the afternoon might be spent meeting colleagues, considering business development issues such as how the current work of the firm in a particular commercial area can be expanded. Throughout the day, telephone calls and emails from clients will be dealt with, as well as the post that has arrived in the morning. At the end of the day, post will be checked and signed to be sent out. There is much less paper post than in the past—much work is conducted electronically.

All time spent, both on client matters and on internal administrative tasks, is recorded, whether through a computerised time management clock that runs while working on a particular file (used if working in the office) or through time recording, entered manually on the system, for work undertaken away from the office, such as meeting a client at their premises or going to another firm of solicitors for a meeting. Time recording is an integral part of a modern solicitor's day. The data collected forms part of the billing system and is a vital tool to assess how individual lawyers within a firm are performing. Each solicitor will have a yearly target for billable hours, client development, and fees generated.

This account is based on an interview with an experienced commercial lawyer in private practice.

Solicitors may also work 'in-house', that is, as employees of a business or other organisation—such as the governing body of a sport—or may be employed by local or central government. Many large companies, and local authorities, have their own legal departments and solicitors who, as well as acting for the company in legal matters, may also perform other roles, such as company secretary.

An important issue arises out of the growth in the volume and complexity of the law. This has led to the creation of very large law firms, often with branches in a number of cities or countries; an increasing specialisation in legal practice; and the development of expertise. Sole practitioners and smaller 'high street' firms undertake a wide range of work such as conveyancing, drafting wills, administering estates, and the provision of legal advice on a range of issues, such as boundary disputes, employment matters, and claims arising from the purchase of faulty goods or services. The main income streams of smaller firms will usually be based on fees from conveyancing and litigation, particularly criminal work. If this income is reduced by competition from larger firms offering the savings generated by economies of scale, then smaller firms may be unable to survive. The work required to deal with small, low-value disputes and claims presently dealt with by sole practitioners and 'high street' firms—work which may not be of interest to the larger firms—may therefore be left to pro bono organisations and individuals to deal with.

Thinking point

Will large law firms decrease access to justice?

The presence of law firms on high streets and in local communities is important with regard to access to justice. If large firms, which tend to be based in city centres, prosper at the expense of sole practitioners and smaller, local firms then access to legal advice will be reduced.

9.2.1 **The work of solicitors**

Certain areas of work were once 'reserved' to the solicitors' profession. In other words, some types of legal work could only be undertaken on a commercial basis by qualified solicitors. Reserved areas of work included administering a deceased person's estate (probate), conveyancing, and the conduct of litigation. The solicitors' monopoly on conveyancing work was ended in 1985 by the Administration of Justice Act, which amended the Solicitors Act 1974 and created licensed conveyancers. Following the implementation of the Act, licensed conveyancers became entitled to conduct conveyancing transactions for a fee. Information about licensed conveyancers can be found at **www.clc-uk.org/**.

The Legal Services Act 2007 allows non-solicitors to carry out some types of legal work, subject to authorisation and regulation. By s.12, some areas of legal work, 'reserved legal activity', can only be carried out by 'authorised persons' (see s.18) or otherwise 'exempt persons' (see s.19). 'Reserved legal activity' means:

- the exercise of a right of audience;
- the conduct of litigation (see Sch.2), which means:
  (a) the issuing of proceedings before any court in England and Wales,
  (b) the commencement, prosecution, and defence of such proceedings,
  (c) the performance of any ancillary functions in relation to such proceedings (such as entering appearances to actions). However, advocacy before a court is not part of the conduct of litigation;

- reserved instrument activity (for example, the preparation of any instrument of transfer or charge for the purposes of the Land Registration Act 2002);
- probate activities;
- notarial activities;
- the administration of oaths.

(Note: an 'instrument' is a formal document in writing and 'notarial activity' is work carried out by a notary public. For more information see **www.thenotariessociety.org.uk/**.)

A person may be authorised to carry out a particular 'reserved legal activity' by a relevant approved regulator. As to the meaning of 'approved regulators' see s.20 and Sch.4. 'Approved regulators' include the Law Society, the General Council of the Bar, the Institute of Legal Executives, the Council for Licensed Conveyancers, and the Chartered Institute of Patent Attorneys.

It is an offence for a person to carry on a 'reserved legal activity' where that person is not entitled to carry out that activity.

The impact of Part 3 of the Legal Services Act 2007 is to allow individuals other than solicitors and barristers to undertake 'reserved legal activity' provided that they are authorised to do so under the Act.

See further Chapter 11, 'Access to justice'.

Some legal services have always been available to be provided by non-lawyers. For example, advisers in Law Centres and Citizens' Advice Bureaux may give advice on employment, welfare, housing, or relationship issues. The roles played by these other individuals and bodies providing legal services are an important part of the discussion regarding access to justice. When considering the availability of advice to ordinary citizens it is important to consider the services provided not just by legal professionals but also by charitable organisations, pro bono schemes, and non-lawyers (see later).

9.2.2 **Representation in court**

Solicitors may appear on behalf of a client in certain courts, such as the coroner's court, magistrates' courts, and County Court. Solicitors may also represent clients at tribunals. Traditionally, a barrister had to be instructed where a client required representation in the higher courts. However, solicitors may now be awarded higher rights of audience, allowing them to represent clients in some or all of the following higher courts: the Crown Court, the High Court, the Court of Appeal, and the Supreme Court. Solicitors may be accredited for higher rights following the completion of an advocacy assessment based on the SRA Higher Rights of Audience competence standards. There are separate awards for rights of audience for criminal and civil advocacy. Higher rights of audience were introduced by s.31 of the Courts and Legal Services Act 1990, as amended by the Access to Justice Act 1999. Further information on higher rights of audience can be found at **www.sra.org.uk/solicitors/accreditation/higher-rights-of-audience.page**.

Thinking point

Have higher rights of audience for solicitors increased completion?

In 2019, approximately 6,900 solicitors (out of a total number of solicitors with practising certificates in the region of 146,000) had a higher rights qualification. (There are approximately 16,600 practising barristers.) Has this had an impact on competition in relation to the provision of advocacy services?

9.2.3 **Sole practitioners and partnerships**

The size of a legal firm can vary from one qualified solicitor (a sole practitioner) to firms with a global presence and more than 3,000 solicitors. Some solicitors will be partners in their firm. Partners will be either equity partners, who own a share of the business and therefore are entitled to a share of the profits of the business, or salaried partners who do not own a share of the business and, as the name suggests, are paid a salary. The other solicitors in the firm are referred to as assistant solicitors or associate solicitors (often 'associate' is a title given as a reward after a number of years of service). In a legal partnership formed under the Partnership Act 1890, the partners own the firm: each partner's share of the business will depend on the terms of the partnership agreement. Most firms designate one of the partners to act as managing partner and may also have a partnership committee to deal with the management of the firm.

Other partners may also be given specific roles within the firm, such as being in charge of recruiting trainee solicitors and managing them during their training contract. Assistant or associate solicitors can become partners through selection and promotion by the existing partners of the firm. Sometimes promotion to partnership can involve being asked to contribute capital (money) to the firm. This capital contribution will be reflected in the firms' partnership agreement.

Until 2001, solicitors were only able to practise as sole practitioners or in partnerships. Since the Limited Liability Partnerships Act 2000 was introduced in April 2001, solicitors have been able to form limited liability partnerships (LLPs). An LLP is a legal entity separate from its members. Therefore the LLP can own property, enter into contracts, bring legal proceedings, or have legal proceedings brought against it. In the same way as a partnership under the 1890 Act, the members (partners) of the LLP will usually have an agreement dealing with issues such as management of the business, admission of new members, and so on. Large commercial firms, and some smaller ones, have taken advantage of this opportunity.

Thinking point

Which is best: a partnership or an LLP?

Partnership under the 1890 Act or an LLP? One of the key attractions for adopting the new form of business structure is that the LLP is a separate legal entity from its members (the partners) and, as such, has liability for the debts of the business. If the LLP gets into financial difficulties, the partners are not personally liable for the debts. This position contrasts strongly with that of a partnership under the Partnership Act 1890, where each partner has unlimited liability for the debts of the partnership. However, this also means that it is the LLP, and not the individual partners, which owns the firm.

In his report reviewing legal services, published in December 2004, Sir David Clementi recommended that solicitors (and barristers) should be permitted to enter into 'legal disciplinary practices' (LDPs). The recommendation was enacted under provisions in the Administration of Justice Act 1985 and the Legal Services Act 2007, and, as a consequence, amendments were made to the Solicitors' Code of Conduct (the Code) to permit LDPs. An LDP is defined as 'a form of recognised body providing legal services where the owners and managers are not exclusively:

- solicitors of England and Wales
- registered European lawyers
- registered Foreign Lawyers.'

The change was introduced on 31 March 2009, allowing up to 25 per cent of the partners in a firm to be non-solicitors. This has allowed barristers, legal executives, and other professionals to become partners in law firms.

The Clementi Report is considered in more detail later.

9.2.4 **Qualification**

The process of qualification is set to change. A new qualification process will be introduced in 2021. This will be outlined later in this chapter. At present, qualification as a solicitor is achieved in three stages. Full details can be found on the Law Society website: **www.lawsociety.org.uk/law-careers/becoming-a-solicitor/qualifying-as-a-solicitor/**. The first academic stage is the completion of a qualifying law degree or the graduate diploma in law (GDL), for graduates with non-law degrees, or the Chartered Institute of Legal Executives (CILEX) Professional Qualification in Law. The Law Society and Bar Council prescribe the subjects that must be studied and passed in a qualifying law degree.

Thinking point

Which subjects should be in a qualifying law degree?

At present a qualifying law degree must include the following subjects: constitutional and administrative law, contract law, criminal law, equity and trusts, European Union Law, land law, and tort. Why do you think that study of these particular areas of law is viewed as fundamental for all lawyers? Will Brexit affect the position regarding EU law?

Further detail about the CILEX qualification is included under the heading 'Chartered legal executives'. Following successful completion of the academic stage, a student must enrol for the vocational stage: the legal practice course ('LPC'). This is a one-year course that puts academic legal theory into practice and equips students for their training contract. Following satisfactory completion of the LPC, the practical stage of the training process must be commenced. This is a training contract with a firm of solicitors or local authority. The number of training contracts available is small compared to the number of students successfully completing the LPC and applying for a training contract. Competition is therefore fierce. The training contract is currently regulated by the SRA and lasts two years, during which time the trainee must work in three different areas of practice. For example, a typical training contract at a medium-sized firm could include four 'seats': family law, conveyancing, civil litigation, and crime. A minimum level of salary for trainees was also specified by the SRA until, following a consultation, this was abolished on 1 August 2014. Now the only requirement on employers in terms of trainee salaries is to pay trainees at least the main rate for employees under the National Minimum Wage Regulations. At the end of the successful completion of the two-year training period, a trainee is admitted as a fully qualified solicitor.

Critical debate

The traditional training route to become a solicitor takes at least six years. The introduction of fees for undergraduate courses and the fees charged for GDL and LPC courses mean that prospective trainee solicitors will have accumulated a great deal of debt before seeking a training contract. There is no guarantee of a training place after completion of the academic and vocational stages of training. Numerous studies and reports have suggested that the system discriminates against prospective lawyers from lower socio-economic groups and ensures that the profession remains the preserve of a narrow section of society. Do you agree?
The Legal Services Board 2010 report *Barriers to the Legal Profession* can be accessed at **research.legalservicesboard.org.uk/wp-content/media/2010-Diversity-literature-review.pdf**.

There have been regular proposals over the past two decades to reform the qualification route for solicitors, to increase diversity and opportunities to enter the professions. Consultations include the SRA's Training Framework Reviews in 2001, 2003, and 2005. The initial plans for reform were shelved in 2005. However, discussion and debate continued as to whether legal education was fit for the demands of the professions in the twenty-first century. On 19 November 2010, the SRA, the Bar Standards Board (BSB), and the Institute of Legal Executives professional standards body announced a joint review of legal services education and training, the Legal Education and Training

Review (LETR). As the introduction to its website stated, this 'constitutes a fundamental, evidence-based review of education and training requirements across regulated and non-regulated legal services in England and Wales.'

The review body examined:

- the perceived strengths and weaknesses of the existing systems of legal education and training across the regulated and unregulated sectors in England and Wales;
- the skills, knowledge, and attributes required by a range of legal service providers;
- the potential to move to sector-wide outcomes for legal services education and training;
- the potential extension of regulation of legal services education and training for the currently unregulated sector;
- recommendations as to whether and, if so, how, the system of legal services education and training may be made more responsive to emerging needs;
- suggestions and alternative models to assure (*sic*) that the system will support the delivery of:
  i. high quality, competitive, and ethical legal services;
  ii. flexible education and training options, responsive to the need for different career pathways, and capable of promoting diversity.

The LETR reported in June 2013. Many legal education providers, and the professions in general, had expected radical proposals for overhauling the provision of legal education; however, the final report was generally regarded as a missed opportunity. It was hoped that the review would recommend that a requirement for regular reaccreditation of skills be introduced, as seen in the medical profession, but this was not included. The report did recommend greater emphasis on ethics and client care skills. It also recommended that lawyers should become more reflective practitioners and that continuing professional development (CPD) should provide 'intentional, meaningful learning' and not just be a box-ticking exercise.

Since November 2016 there is no longer a requirement for qualified and practising solicitors to take part in sixteen hours of CPD. After consultation, it was decided that the CPD system was not fit for purpose and did not encourage solicitors to plan appropriate training and relevant CPD. In spring 2015 the SRA published guidance on competency and set out 'what a competent solicitor should look like', which will provide guidance for firms to ensure staff members receive appropriate training. Solicitors' firms will have to make an annual declaration, as part of the application for practising certificates, to confirm that they have considered and dealt with the training needs of staff.

9.2.5 The new qualification route for solicitors

The future of training of solicitors has caused particular difficulty and debate. The overhaul of the academic training of solicitors discussed by the LETR will take place in the academic year 2021–22. The LPC will be discontinued in its present form. The new training system will offer a number of routes into the profession (as a way to widen participation and encourage diversity). The new route will be via a Solicitors Qualifying Examination (SQE).

The SQE will be in two parts. SQE 1 (Functioning Legal Knowledge and Practical Legal Skills Assessments) and SQE 2 (Practical Legal Skills Assessments). At present the intention is that SQE1 will consist of multiple choice tests and SQE2 will include role play and written work. Discussion about the final format is still ongoing.

A prospective solicitor, under the new regime, must have a degree (in any subject) or equivalent qualification or work experience, must pass the SQE; undertake two years of qualifying work experience, and then pass the SRA character and suitability requirements. More details can be found here: **https://www.sra.org.uk/sra/policy/sqe/solicitor-persona/**. If you wish to qualify as a solicitor, it is a good idea to sign up for updates from the SRA site to ensure that you have the latest information. Anyone who has started, completed, or accepted an offer for the CPE, Qualifying Law Degree, or a training contract by the time the SQE is introduced in autumn 2021 can choose to continue to qualify via the existing route.

The legal executive route into the legal profession is becoming increasingly attractive, as is on-the-job training via the development of higher-level apprenticeships. A Trailblazer solicitor apprenticeship allows a student to work in a law firm and study at university at the same time. More details can be found here: **www.lawsociety.org.uk/law-careers/becoming-a-solicitor/qualifying-without-a-degree/apprenticeships/**.

9.2.6 The composition of the solicitors' profession

Statistics are published annually by the Law Society. On 31 July 2019, there were 195,952 solicitors, that is, those listed as being paid-up and qualified members of the profession, on the Roll. This figure has steadily increased over the past decade. Inclusion on the Roll does not mean that the person can practise as a solicitor: a practising certificate is required in order to do this, and 146,913 of the enrolled solicitors had a practising certificate (75 per cent of those on the Roll). Of those solicitors holding practising certificates, for the first time, just over 50 per cent are women and 16.9 per cent overall are from minority ethnic groups.

The statistics show that the majority of law firms are relatively small, with four partners or fewer. However, the statistics show that company structures are increasingly popular. Partnerships, including sole practices, accounted for just over 40 per cent of firms—down from 60 per cent as recently as 2012.

Statistics can be found at **www.lawsociety.org.uk/policy-campaigns/research-trends/annual-statistical-reports/**.

Key point

In seeking to critically appraise any set of circumstances, it is important to have a sound empirical base for your argument. Part of this knowledge might be statistical information. It is worthwhile to look at official statistics to see if trends and patterns can be discerned.

9.2.7 **The Law Society and the SRA**

The Law Society has traditionally both represented the interests of solicitors and regulated their activities in England and Wales. For example, it has dealt with allegations of misconduct and complaints from the public and also represented solicitors' interests, for example in any consultations with central government. Its powers and duties are set out in the Solicitors Act 1974.

The dual roles of enforcer and representative organisation performed by the Law Society were criticised on the basis that there was a potential conflict of interest. Sir David Clementi, in a review of the regulatory framework for legal services (see later at 9.4), recommended that the roles should be split.

In the light of the recommendations, the Law Society established two regulatory bodies: one dealing with consumer complaints, the Legal Complaints Service (LCS); and one governing rule-making and legal education, the SRA. The Legal Complaints Service was superseded by the Legal Ombudsman in 2010 but the SRA still governs the profession.

You can find out more about the SRA at **www.sra.org.uk/**.

The representative function, the voice of solicitors, is still undertaken by the Law Society. Information about the Law Society is found at **www.lawsociety.org.uk/**.

9.2.8 **Complaints about solicitors**

If a complaint is made about the standard of work carried out by a law firm or an individual within the firm, or a sole practitioner, the complaint must first be directed to the firm or practitioner.

All law firms are required to have a designated complaints handler who will try to resolve any client complaints in the first instance. If the client is not satisfied with the outcome of the internal investigation into the complaint they can contact the Legal Ombudsman. The Legal Ombudsman was set up by the Office for Legal Complaints, following the 2007 Legal Services Act. The service is free, independent, and impartial and the Legal Ombudsman will investigate the complaint to try to assist the parties to resolve the matter. If the matter cannot be resolved informally then a report will be produced which can then be accepted by the parties to the dispute or referred to an Ombudsman for a final, binding decision. Details of the Legal Ombudsman can be found at **www.legalombudsman.org.uk/**.

9.2.9 **SRA Standards and Regulations**

All solicitors must act in accordance with a code of conduct that governs their behaviour and sets out the manner in which their work must be conducted.

In November 2019, following a four-year consultation process, the Code of Conduct for Solicitors was replaced by SRA Standards and Regulations. The standards and regulations set out the duties and responsibilities of solicitors towards their clients and dealt with issues such as client confidentiality, conflicts of interest, information to be provided to the client, and complaints procedures. The aim of the new regulations is to simplify the rules. It introduces two codes of conduct: one for firms and one for individual solicitors.

The change in approach from the previous code is designed to remove outdated rules and give solicitors flexibility to ensure that their services are client focused. The SRA Principles 'comprise the fundamental tenets of ethical behaviour that we expect all those that we regulate to uphold'. The Principles underpinning the regulations mandate that solicitors act:

1. in a way that upholds the constitutional principle of the rule of law, and the proper administration of justice.
2. in a way that upholds public trust and confidence in the solicitors' profession and in legal services provided by authorised persons.
3. with independence.
4. with honesty.
5. with integrity.
6. in a way that encourages equality, diversity and inclusion.
7. in the best interests of each client.

The regulations then go on to set out clearly the standards of professional behaviour expected of solicitors. The new regulations are much clearer and easier to follow than the Code they replace:
ww.sra.org.uk/globalassets/documents/sra/standards-regulations.pdf?version=4a1aba.
Failure to comply with the conduct rules may amount to evidence of inadequate professional services in the context of a complaint against a solicitor.

In respect of liability in relation to litigation see 9.3.12.

9.2.10 **Liability of solicitors**

When a solicitor is employed by a client, the relationship between them is contractual and each party may be sued should they fail to meet the obligations set out in the contract. Solicitors may also be sued for negligence if loss has been caused to someone to whom they owed a duty of care, such as a client or beneficiaries under a will (see later). The work undertaken must be carried out with the appropriate standard of care and skill.

 Example

In *White v Jones* [1995] 2 AC 207, a law firm was sued in negligence by the beneficiaries of a will drawn up by a solicitor employed by the firm. The solicitor had failed to make amendments to the will, as instructed by the maker of it, which would have given a legacy to the beneficiaries. A delay on the part of the solicitor meant that the changes had not been made, and attested to, at the time of the maker's death. Despite the lack of a contractual relationship between the solicitor and the beneficiaries, the beneficiaries were able to bring a claim in negligence for the value of the legacies that they would have received had the instructions been correctly carried out.

9.3 **Barristers**

Barristers are popularly portrayed wearing gowns and wigs and arguing their clients' cases in a criminal court, perhaps the most famous depiction being Rumpole of the Bailey in the books by John Mortimer. However, barristers are not just criminal advocates.

Barristers provide specialist legal advice and appear as advocates in both criminal and civil courts on behalf of their clients. Barristers' training focuses on, and reflects, the skills they are required to have to provide this support for clients. Most barristers operate as self-employed individuals, and they work in sets of chambers—essentially a group of barristers sharing premises and administrative facilities. The average set of chambers comprises about thirty barristers, some of whom may be referred to as 'door tenants'. Door tenants are barristers who do not work full time in chambers, and who pay a reduced rent (sometimes a percentage on any cases coming to them through chambers).

Each set of chambers has one or more clerks who are responsible for administering the work that comes to the chambers by negotiating the brief fees and ensuring that the work is given to either the specific barrister instructed or, if no name is specified, to an appropriate advocate. The clerk acts as liaison between the barristers and the instructing solicitors. Part of their job is to organise the diaries of the barristers to ensure that the chamber's work is dealt with efficiently. The chief clerk is usually supported by a number of junior clerks and fees clerks (responsible for billing) and, increasingly, by a manager who deals with marketing and human resource issues.

A barrister who is not a member of a chambers may be employed by a company, carrying out legal work for the company, or, if employed by a law firm, to represent the solicitors' clients. Employed barristers may conduct litigation. Barristers may also be employed by central or local government or by the Crown Prosecution Service.

9.3.1 **'Cab rank' rule**

Barristers are subject to what is called the 'cab rank' rule, which means that a barrister must accept any case referred by a solicitor provided that it is in their area of practice, they are available, and a reasonable fee is payable. The rationale for the 'cab rank' rule is ethical. It is designed to ensure that all defendants, however unpopular, can be represented in court and it also acts to protect barristers from the anger of the community if they are called to represent someone accused of a terrible crime. In *Arthur JS Hall & Co v Simon* [2002] 1 AC 615, Lord Steyn doubted the effectiveness of the rule. His Lordship said:

> It is a valuable professional rule. But its impact on the administration of justice in England is not great. In real life a barrister has a clerk whose enthusiasm for the unwanted brief may not be great, and he is free to raise the fee within limits. It is not likely that the rule often obliges barristers to undertake work which they would not otherwise accept.

The BSB has suggested that any step to remove the cab rank rule would result in a major threat to justice. However, following a consultation process in 2017, the rule does not apply to direct access cases but only when the barrister is instructed by a lawyer.

9.3.2 **Barristers' direct access to clients**

Traditionally, barristers could not accept instructions directly from members of the public and had to be instructed by a solicitor on the client's behalf. This restriction was seen as anti-competitive and unnecessarily expensive because the cost of two lawyers was incurred when one would often be sufficient to do the work required.

A scheme was introduced by the Bar Council to allow some clients to instruct barristers directly. The scheme, known as Licensed Access, allows certain organisations, such as firms of accountants, or specific individuals to apply to the Bar Council to be licensed to instruct barristers directly in an area of law in which those organisations or individuals are thought to have suitable expertise.

In 2004, the Bar Council's Public Access Rules came into force allowing barristers to accept instructions directly from members of the public in mainly civil work. Subject to certain exceptions, barristers may not accept instructions from members of the public in the following areas of law: criminal, family, and immigration. All barristers who want to carry out public access work must now complete a training course. The Bar Standards Board Handbook includes guidance for barristers carrying out direct access work.

9.3.3 **Restrictions on partnerships**

Bar Council regulations used to prevent barristers from forming partnerships with one another. These rules were criticised by the Office of Fair Trading in a report published in March 2001, *Competition in Professions*.

Following the Legal Services Act 2007, and the introduction of LDPs, these rules have now changed. See 9.4.3 for further details.

9.3.4 **Qualification**

The present qualification process for a barrister is similar to the present process for a solicitor. In September 2020, a new qualification pathway will replace the Bar Professional Training Course (BPTC). The academic stage is common to both barristers and solicitors. A qualifying law degree, or a non-law degree and the GDL, must first be successfully completed. Following the completion of the academic stage, the vocational stage must be passed: the BPTC, which is a one-year course that aims to equip students with the skills and substantive knowledge to practise as a barrister. The areas of study are set out in Table 9.1.

Following completion of the BPTC, further work-based training with a set of chambers is undertaken. This is known as pupillage. A trainee barrister is called a pupil. During the one-year pupillage, the first six months are spent by the pupil observing and assisting his or her supervisor, undertaking legal research, becoming familiar with case papers, and attending court and case conferences. The pupil barrister may also shadow other members of chambers in order to see a wide variety of work. The pupillage supervisor will be an experienced member of chambers who has responsibility for supervising pupils and allocating work to them. A supervisor must be a barrister who has been called to the Bar (been qualified as a barrister) for at least seven years and is registered as a pupil supervisor with the Bar Council.

During the second six months of pupillage, the pupil will work as a barrister conducting his or her own cases, which may include making appearances in court on behalf of a client. Although still technically under the supervision of the supervisor, pupil barristers at this stage have a large degree of autonomy in the work that they do, although they are still covered by the professional indemnity insurance of their supervisor. When not practising, a pupil barrister will continue to gain experience through shadowing their supervisor. Some pupillages are split, with the six-month periods being spent in different sets of chambers. Although pupillages used to be unpaid, pupil barristers must now be paid a minimum sum of £15,728 (£18,436 in London) by their set of chambers for the twelve-month period. This is approximately equivalent to the national living wage.

When the new vocational training scheme is introduced in 2020 the BPTC will be replaced by a number of courses, some of which may be split into two parts or may incorporate study for an undergraduate degree to cover the academic component of training. Full details of these new courses have not yet been released. The academic stage, of degree and then the new course, will be followed by pupillage as is the case at present.

Table 9.1 Areas of study

Practical skills	Legal knowledge
casework	criminal and civil litigation
legal research	evidence
general written skills	remedies
interpersonal skills	professional ethics
Advocacy	sentencing
conferencing (leading a meeting with the client and instructing solicitor)	
resolution of disputes	

It is very difficult to secure a pupillage because there are many more students completing the BPTC than there are pupillages available. Competition is therefore intense. Following completion of pupillage, most newly qualified barristers will try to secure a tenancy either with the chambers where the pupillage was undertaken or at another set. Tenancy is also difficult to secure and is not guaranteed, particularly in London. The Law Careers Advice Network estimates that only half of the eligible number of pupils obtains a tenancy with a set of chambers in a given year. Following completion of pupillage, a barrister will be responsible for his or her own case load, although some may also continue to assist more senior members of chambers. All barristers in chambers are self-employed and therefore have no guarantee of regular work or a regular income. Average earnings vary according to location, area of law, and experience.

In the same way that solicitors have to carry out CPD, barristers are required to undertake continuing education. By the end of their first three years in practice they are required to have completed a minimum of forty-five hours' continuing education, which must include at least nine hours of advocacy training and three hours of ethics. After this the requirement is for twelve hours of continuing education per year.

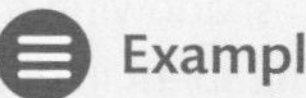

The daily work of a criminal barrister

Perhaps the most exciting element of a criminal barrister's life is its unpredictability. The criminal law is in a state of perpetual flux, and every day is different. There is no such thing as a typical day. The job of a prosecuting barrister is very different from that of defence counsel, and one barrister may be required to act for defendants and for the prosecution, in different cases, on the same day.

Some trials, particularly the most serious ones, are scheduled in the barrister's diary months ahead. Such cases may last several weeks and sometimes several months. On other occasions a barrister will be instructed to prosecute or defend an accused person the night before the trial is to be heard. This might happen if the barrister who had been instructed in the case is delayed in another court in an ongoing case.

On any day a criminal barrister may deal with between one and half a dozen cases. Each set of instructions is known as a brief. Having prepared the papers overnight, or early in the morning, the barrister will have plenty to do at court before any trials or hearings commence. There may be sentencing hearings; concluding cases where the defendant pleaded guilty, or was convicted some weeks before; and meetings with clients and instructing solicitors. If acting for the defence, a barrister will need to explain the likely sentence to the client and the client's family, and take instructions on potential points of mitigation.

Or there may be plea and case management hearings where a defendant will enter a plea of guilty or not guilty. If not guilty, a trial date will be set and the judge will make various orders to 'manage' the case and ensure it is ready for trial at the appropriate time.

On the day of a trial, prosecution counsel will need to check that witnesses are present, ensure all relevant evidence has been served, and then, in court, present the Crown's evidence. Defence counsel may, depending on the circumstances and the weight of the evidence, see if the client wishes to plead guilty to a lesser offence, and if so try to negotiate this with the Crown prosecutor. If a trial is to take place, the client's instructions will need to be confirmed.

The official court day usually runs from 10 a.m. until 4.30 p.m. (although some courts are trialling later sessions) After court, a barrister may have conferences to advise clients before collecting the next day's work from the clerks, and then the whole process begins again.

This information is based on an interview with an experienced criminal barrister.

Barristers undertaking civil work tend to make fewer court appearances than barristers working in criminal law; instead they will carry out more paper-based work to give specialist legal advice in writing (known as an opinion) or at a conference with instructing solicitors (with or without the client). They may represent a client at a public inquiry or tribunal.

9.3.5 The Inns of Court

There are four Inns of Court: Gray's Inn, Lincoln's Inn, Middle Temple, and Inner Temple. The Inns date back to the fourteenth and fifteenth centuries and there used to be more than four of them. They were first established to provide accommodation and training for barristers and they therefore have a long and colourful history. But their chief function as the professional associations for barristers is to ***call men and women to the Bar***.

Called to the Bar *To become a barrister a person must be 'called to the Bar' by one of the four Inns of Court. The prospective barrister attends a 'Call Night' at the Inn and is formally 'called to the Bar' in a ceremony watched by friends and family. The call to the Bar takes place after the successful completion of the BPTC.*

Each Inn is governed by the Masters of the Bench (or Benchers). Benchers are elected from the senior members of the Inn (Queen's Counsel—QCs—or senior members of the judiciary). Students wishing to qualify as barristers must join an Inn before they begin the BPTC and they are required to attend a minimum number of twelve 'qualifying sessions' at their Inn before they can become barristers. Most of these will be completed by a student attending a dinner at the Inn. Each dinner counts as one qualifying session. Dinners are often accompanied by educational events, such as speeches or debates. Dining is also seen as an opportunity for students to meet practising barristers and senior members of the profession. Qualifying sessions can also be accumulated by attendance at other events, such as education days and advocacy training courses.

You can find out more about the Inns of Court on the following websites:

- **www.graysinn.org.uk/**
- **www.innertemple.org.uk/**
- **www.lincolnsinn.org.uk/**
- **www.middletemple.org.uk/**

9.3.6 **Deferral of call**

A student can call him or herself a barrister once called to the Bar, that is, having completed the BPTC and attended the requisite number of qualifying sessions at their Inn. This is the case even though the barrister cannot practise, because pupillage has not been completed. The Bar Council considered that this system should change so that only those who had successfully completed pupillage would be entitled to call themselves barristers. This proposal is known as deferral of call and caused substantial debate among members of the Bar and providers of Bar Professional Training Courses. However, despite wide consultation in 2007, the proposals for reform were not implemented and the situation remains that a person who has passed the BPTC and been called to the Bar can call him- or herself a barrister.

9.3.7 **Queen's Counsel (QCs)**

QCs are the most eminent members of the Bar. QC stands for Queen's Counsel. Appointments to Queen's Counsel are made by the Queen by Letters Patent following recommendation by the Secretary of State (if there is a king on the throne the title is KC or King's Counsel). A QC is often referred to, in colloquial terms, as a 'silk' because they wear silk gowns rather than the basic stuff gown worn by a junior barrister. All barristers, of whatever age or call, are known as juniors if they are not QCs. The purpose of the appointment to the rank of QC is to recognise outstanding ability as an advocate, although the overall legal abilities of an applicant and his or her professional qualities are also important.

The system of appointing Queen's Counsel has been the subject of consultation. In March 2001, the Office of Fair Trading published a report, *Competition in Professions*, which questioned the relevance of the rank of QC as far as consumers were concerned, in part owing to the lack of direct access by members of the public to barristers at that time, the criteria used to award the rank of QC, and whether the award served to distort competition by the effective reservation of certain types of work to QCs and the increase in fees once QCs became involved in cases.

In July 2003, the then Lord Chancellor, Lord Falconer, published a consultation paper, 'Constitutional Reform: The Future of Queen's Counsel'. The paper sought views on the role of QCs, the advantages and disadvantages of the system, and possible changes to the way in which the rank is awarded. Responses to this consultation were published in January 2004.

Prior to 2005, the appointment system required application to the Lord Chancellor by barristers and, after 1994, by solicitors with higher rights of audience. The Lord Chancellor would then recommend suitable applicants be invited to take silk after consultation with fellow members of the Bar, the judiciary, and solicitors. Published criteria were used against which the applicant's abilities were assessed, and applicants were compared with existing QCs and other applicants in their area of practice. Those awarded the rank are regarded as leaders of their profession and all those who meet the necessary thresholds are appointed.

Since 2005, the appointment of QCs has no longer been a governmental recommendation but is carried out by the independent Queen's Counsel Selection Panel, established by the Bar Council and the Law Society with the support of the Department for Constitutional Affairs to administer the application process. A nine-person independent selection panel makes recommendations to the Secretary of State after consideration of individual applications. The Secretary of State cannot remove or add names to those selected by the panel and passes the recommendations to the Queen for approval. Applicants are assessed in relation to seven competences: integrity, understanding the law, using the law, oral advocacy, written advocacy, working with others, and diversity.

The independent nine-member panel includes a lay chair plus two solicitors, two barristers, a judge, and three further lay members.

You can find out more about the appointment of QCs at **www.qcappointments.org**.

9.3.8 **The composition of the barristers' profession**

Statistics are generally published annually by the Bar Council. In the most recent statistics, dated 2019, there were 16,598 practising barristers (self-employed and employed), of which 62 per cent were male and 38 per cent were female. There were 595 sole practitioners and 3,014 employed barristers.

Statistics can be found at **www.barstandardsboard.org.uk/media-centre/research-and-statistics/**.

9.3.9 **The Bar Council**

The General Council of the Bar (Bar Council) represents barristers and 'promote[s] [the role of barristers] at the heart of the justice system in England and Wales'. It was founded in 1894 and represents the interests of barristers on a range of matters. In the same way that the Law Society has been affected by the report of Sir David Clementi on the regulatory review of legal services, the Bar Council has also had to review its regulatory and representative roles. The BSB was set up to oversee the regulatory side of the Bar and has a separate membership from that of the Bar Council. The Board deals with issues such as changes to the barrister's Code of Conduct, as well as education and training and complaints against barristers. It has set up a number of regulatory committees to deal with these matters.

The Bar Council meets approximately seven times a year. Its members are barristers who represent chambers or court circuits in different parts of the country, or who are elected to the Council. More than 100 barristers are members of the Council. The objectives of the Bar Council include protecting the public interest and promoting and maintaining adherence to professional principles.

Details about the Bar Council can be found at **www.barcouncil.org.uk/**.

9.3.10 **Complaints about barristers**

Prior to 2010 the BSB investigated all complaints about barristers. From 6 October 2010, complaints about barristers must be made to the Legal Ombudsman. As with complaints about solicitors, the Legal Ombudsman will deal with complaints about the service received from barristers. Any complaints about conduct, as opposed to professional service, will be referred by the Legal Ombudsman to the BSB because complaints about conduct may amount to professional misconduct. Misconduct could include misleading the court or failing to act in a client's best interests, or acting contrary to instructions. Professional misconduct is a serious issue to be dealt with by the BSB and could result in the barrister concerned being disbarred (prevented from practising as a barrister).

9.3.11 **Barristers' professional Code of Conduct**

The Bar Council of England and Wales publishes the *Bar Standards Board Handbook*, which contains the code of conduct for practising barristers. The code covers issues such as a barrister's duty to the court, rules regarding the acceptance of instructions and confidentiality, and a set of written standards for the conduct of professional work. The latter are intended as a guide to the way in which a barrister should carry out his or her work. The *Handbook* is amended yearly. The *BSB Handbook* can be accessed at **www.barstandardsboard.org.uk/the-bsb-handbook.html**.

9.3.12 **Liability of barristers**

The general common law position was that barristers could not be sued in negligence in relation to anything done by them in preparing a case for court, or for any of their actions in conducting the case in court. This was underlined in *Rondel v Worsley* [1969] 1 AC 191. However, this protection from being sued for negligence was removed in July 2000 following *Arthur JS Hall & Co v Simons* [2002] 1 AC 615. This case involved appeals to the House of Lords by three clients suing their solicitors in negligence. In each case, the solicitors claimed immunity from liability under the common law rule which prevented barristers being sued for negligence, and which had been extended to solicitors in *Rondel v Worsley*, albeit that the rule only related to acts concerned with the conduct of litigation. A majority of the House of Lords panel hearing the case concluded that the arguments relied upon in *Rondel v Worsley* no longer carried sufficient weight to sustain the claimed immunity for either barristers or solicitors, in relation to civil or criminal proceedings.

 **Example**

It is interesting to note the reasons for upholding immunity for advocates in *Rondel v Worsley* and then to compare this with the reasoning in *Arthur JS Hall & Co v Simons*. In the former case, the House of Lords supported the exemption on the following grounds: a barrister owed a duty not only to the client but to the court; a fear of being sued might impact upon the latter duty. The cab rank rule meant that a barrister could not refuse to represent a client and this principle might be under threat if a client appeared to be likely to sue his lawyer. Immunity existed in relation to judges, lawyers, and witnesses in relation to defamation, so immunity in relation to negligence is necessary to enable advocates to conduct litigation properly. Finally, it is against public policy to re-litigate a decided case and a claim for negligence would open up to review the decision in the original case.

In *Arthur JS Hall & Co v Simons* the House of Lords reviewed each reason supporting the advocates' protection from being sued in negligence. It was felt that there was no empirical basis for saying that immunity was needed so that duties owed to the court would be performed. Indeed, performing such duties could not be described as negligent. The cab rank principle, while recognised as valuable, could be circumvented in practice, and in any event had to be balanced against the potential injustice of a litigant suffering financial loss because of an advocate's negligence and being left without a remedy. While it is clear that there are public policy grounds to prevent advocates from being sued for defamation (so that the facts of cases can be fully explored in court without curtailing freedom of speech), there are no such grounds for providing immunity from being sued for negligence.

Tellingly, Lord Steyn commented:

> [P]ublic confidence in the legal system is not enhanced by the existence of the immunity. The appearance is created that the law singles out its own for protection no matter how flagrant the breach of the barrister. The world has changed since 1967.

For information about the Supreme Court and departure from its own previous decisions see Chapter 5.

> The practice of law has become more commercialised: barristers may now advertise. They may now enter into contracts for legal services with their professional clients. They are now obliged to carry insurance. On the other hand, today we live in a consumerist society in which people have a much greater awareness of their rights. If they have suffered a wrong as a result of the provision of negligent professional services, they expect to have the right to claim redress. It tends to erode confidence in the legal system if advocates, alone among professional men, are immune from liability for negligence.

In consequence, the immunity for barristers and solicitor advocates was removed and the House of Lords departed from *Rondel v Worsley*. Although that case was not wrongly decided, the House of Lords held that, due to developments since 1967, the decision no longer reflected public policy.

9.4 **Regulation of the professions and reform: the Clementi Review**

The changes that have come about in the legal professions in the twenty-first century began following a report published in July 2003, *Competition and Regulation in the Legal Services Market* by the Department for Constitutional Affairs. The regulatory framework in place for barristers and solicitors was criticised as outdated and lacking in accountability. Sir David Clementi was asked to review the regulatory system for barristers and solicitors on behalf of the Department for Constitutional Affairs. The terms of reference for the review were to consider:

> what regulatory framework would best promote competition, innovation and the public and consumer interest in an efficient, effective and independent legal sector and to recommend a framework which will be independent in representing the public and consumer interest, comprehensive, accountable, consistent, flexible, transparent and no more restrictive or burdensome than is clearly justified.

Clementi published a consultation paper in March 2004, 'Consultation Paper on the Review of the Regulatory Framework for Legal Services in England and Wales', to which there were 265 written responses.

In the consultation paper, it was argued that the regulatory function and representative functions performed by the Law Society and the Bar Council were in conflict: what is in the best interests of the public might not be in the best interests of lawyers, for example, negotiating fee rates on behalf of their members. Five core functions of regulation were identified in the consultation paper:

(a) ***Entry standards and training***: setting minimum standards of entry qualifications usually linked to educational achievement for candidates wishing to become 'qualified'. It also encompasses matters such as continuing professional development.

(b) ***Rule-making***: formulating rules by which members are expected to work and to which they are expected to adhere.

(c) ***Monitoring and enforcement***: checking the way in which members carry out their work, in the light of the prescribed rules, and enforcing compliance if rules are broken.

(d) ***Complaints***: systems for consumers to bring complaints about providers who have served them poorly, focused on redress to the consumer.

(e) ***Discipline***: powers to discipline members where that person is, for example, professionally negligent, or in breach of the professional rules, focusing on action against that individual.

In December 2004, a final report was published, *Report of the Review of the Regulatory Framework for Legal Services in England and Wales*. Table 9.2 sets out the key issues identified by the review and the three main recommendations made by the review.

The recommendations have been brought into force and are discussed in the following section.

9.4.1 The Legal Services Board

The Board regulates the Law Society and Bar Council (and other professional organisations exercising regulatory functions in relation to legal professionals, such as the Chartered Institute of Legal Executives), and has the power to delegate regulatory functions to such bodies where appropriate. As already discussed, these organisations have been required to alter their governance arrangements so that their regulatory and representative functions are separate. The Board also has statutory objectives including the promotion of the interests of the public and consumers.

Table 9.2 Summary of the report

Issues arising from the review	Recommendations from the review
Concern about the complexity and inconsistency of the regulatory framework and its insufficient regard for consumers' interests	The creation of a new Legal Services Board as part of the establishment of a new regulatory framework
Concern about the complaints system, both in terms of its efficiency and the principle of lawyers handling complaints against other lawyers	The creation of a new complaints system via the Office for Legal Complaints
Concern about the restrictive nature of business structures within the legal profession	ABS for members of the legal professions should be established and LDPs should be permitted

9.4.2 **The Office for Legal Complaints**

The Office for Legal Complaints is an independent body, overseen by the Legal Services Board, dealing with consumer complaints against both barristers and solicitors through the Legal Ombudsman. The Legal Ombudsman website summarises the position as follows: 'The new Legal Ombudsman replaces organisations like the Legal Complaints Service (LCS) and Bar Standards Board (BSB), who used to deal with legal service complaints. If an organisation such as one of these investigated a complaint and the client wasn't happy with the outcome or the service they received from these bodies, they could ask for their complaint to be independently reviewed by the Legal Services Ombudsman (LSO).'

The Legal Ombudsman is concerned primarily with the service offered by a lawyer. Clearly, there will be cases where poor service is linked with misconduct. In these types of cases, the Legal Ombudsman will still look at the service element of the complaint, but will refer the conduct part to the relevant regulatory body, such as the SRA. Discipline remains the province of the SRA and the BSB.

Thinking point

Protecting the independence of the legal profession

The legal profession has consistently asserted that its independence should be protected. This is particularly important where a citizen wishes to challenge the decisions or actions of government. Any attack on the self-regulation of the professions must be seen in this light. The detail of how the Legal Services Board and the Legal Ombudsman are constituted and the nature of their functions must be evaluated to see if the independence of the legal profession is compromised. What balance has been struck by the Legal Services Act 2007?

9.4.3 **Alternative business structures (ABS)**

One of Clementi's main recommendations was to suggest that Legal Disciplinary Practices (LDPs) should be introduced to allow non-lawyers to own and manage law practices and different types of lawyers, such as solicitors and barristers, to work together in law firms for the purpose of providing legal services. An LDP comprises different types of lawyer (for example, barristers and solicitors) with a minority of non-lawyers in management posts.

While in favour of LDPs, the Clementi Report identified and addressed a number of concerns. Of particular concern was the situation where the owners and managers of the firm were different. It was important that regulation ensured that inappropriate owners were not allowed to be part of firms and that conflicts of interest and 'outside owners [bringing] unreasonable commercial pressures to bear on lawyers which might conflict with their professional duties' were avoided.

LDPs have to be regulated using a 'fit to own' test in respect of non-lawyers owning firms and an LDP would not be able to take instructions on a case where the owner had an interest in the matter. Furthermore, protection has had to be put in place, such as qualified lawyers holding key positions and managers adhering to a code of behaviour drawn up by the regulatory body. Qualified lawyers have to be a majority in the management group of the business.

In his report, Sir David Clementi explored the possibility of permitting multidisciplinary practices (MDPs) to be established to bring together lawyers and other professionals to provide a variety of services, both legal and non-legal—for example, a partnership involving solicitors and accountants. MDPs became a reality in 2012, although many believe that LDPs are a more attractive business model.

Thinking point

Advantages and disadvantages of multidisciplinary partnerships

What do you think are the advantages and disadvantages of allowing multidisciplinary partnerships (a form of ABS)? One difficulty is that lawyers are subject to a code of conduct that would not apply to non-lawyers. For example, how can client confidentiality be protected in such an organisation?

The recommendations in the Clementi Report were enacted in the Legal Services Act, which received royal assent on 30 October 2007. Provisions relating to the establishment of the Legal Services Board and the Office for Legal Complaints came into force on 7 March 2008.

ABS were allowed to exist after 6 October 2011. There are now approximately 300 LDPs, including a very small number with barristers as partners. The BSB permits barristers to join LDPs.

Useful information on the Legal Services Act 2007 and its passage through Parliament may be found at **www.publications.parliament.uk/pa/pabills/200607/legal_services.htm**.

The terms ABS, MDP, and LDP can be very confusing. In the Clementi Report, LDPs are classified as ABS; however, the SRA expressly states that its definition of an ABS *excludes* LDPs. The basic definitions are as follows: (more detail can be found on the SRA website at **www.sra.org.uk/home/home.page**):

- Alternative Business Structure (ABS): a firm with more than 25 per cent non-lawyer managers offering legal services and non-legal services;
- Legal Disciplinary Practices (LDP): a firm whose ownership comprises different types of lawyer and a minority of non-lawyers (up to 25 per cent) which carries out legal work. There cannot be any ownership or part ownership of the law firm by non-lawyers who are not managers of the firm;

- Multi-Disciplinary Partnership (MDP): a firm that is also an ABS, which includes ownership or part ownership of the law firm by non-lawyers who are not managers of the firm and which offers a combination of legal and non-legal services.

 **Key point**

When considering the legal profession, much useful information and comment may be found in the weekly journals such as *New Law Journal*, the *Law Society Gazette*, and *Counsel*.

9.5 Should the professions of barrister and solicitor be amalgamated?

In many countries the legal profession is not divided as it is in England and Wales. The question as to whether the two professions should be fused is always topical. The traditional and distinct roles of solicitors and barristers are becoming blurred. For example, the granting of higher rights of audience to solicitors and direct access to barristers on the part of some clients leads many to conclude that the two professions should in fact merge. Nevertheless, both the Bar Council and the Law Society have always argued against the idea of a single legal profession. In a March 2001 report, the Office of Fair Trading suggested that the dual structure of the legal profession added unnecessarily to costs but the Bar Council rejected this suggestion in its response to the report, arguing that there were benefits in a split profession.

Benefits of a split profession:

- Barristers do not conduct litigation (as already seen, this is the province of solicitors), so they are able to attain a much higher level of experience and skill in advocacy than would otherwise be possible.
- The detachment of barristers from clients means that a more objective approach may be adopted and this may lead, ultimately, to the time taken to conclude a case being shortened.
- Independent barristers can perform the advocacy and advisory work in which they specialise more efficiently and cheaply than solicitors because barristers' overheads are lower.
- Members of the public do not know what barristers do and have no idea of the specialisms and services offered, therefore solicitors are needed to act as intermediaries to guide clients to the most suitable barrister. Solicitors will also be able to assess the quality of service provided by barristers and thus promote competition.
- The dual profession also promotes competition among solicitors because small firms of solicitors have access to the specialist legal services provided by barristers and are therefore able to compete with larger firms.

- The public interest lies not only in the promotion of competition but also in 'access to justice and the overriding moral duty of society to pursue the ideal of equality before the law'.

It may be that the reforms made to the professions, together with the organisational changes to the way lawyers work, will inevitably lead to the practical distinction between barristers and solicitors being no longer relevant.

9.6 Other legal professionals

9.6.1 Chartered Legal Executives

Chartered Legal Executives carry out a great deal of the day-to-day work in law firms. Members of the Chartered Institute of Legal Executives qualify as lawyers through a different route from those already discussed. To qualify, the Chartered Institute of Legal Executives (CILEX) Professional Qualification in Law must be attained. CILEX represents legal executives, admits legal executives to the profession, and administers the examination process. Chartered Legal Executives specialise in a specific area of legal practice, such as conveyancing or criminal law and work alongside solicitors. The initial qualification process takes around four years and the academic study is usually undertaken as distance learning or day release while the trainee legal executive is working as a fee earner in a law firm. Legal executives are required to have at least five years' experience working in a legal environment under the supervision of a solicitor before they can become a Chartered Legal Executive (FCILEx).

Chartered Legal Executives may decide to study further to qualify as solicitors by completing the Legal Practice Course. They do not usually have to complete a training contract. The CILEX route is increasingly seen as an attractive route into the legal profession.

You can find out more about Chartered Legal Executives at **www.cilex.org.uk/**.

Test your understanding of this section by answering the following self-test questions.

9.6.2 Licensed conveyancers

A licensed conveyancer is essentially a specialist in property law. Until the 1980s, conveyancing could only be undertaken on a professional basis by solicitors. Since then other people can qualify as licensed conveyancers and undertake conveyancing work. The Council for Licensed Conveyancers is the regulatory body for licensed conveyancers.

You can find out more about licensed conveyancers at **www.conveyancer.org.uk/**.

9.6.3 Paralegals

In the increasingly competitive legal jobs market, the role of paralegal has taken on a growing importance. 'Paralegal' used to refer to an unqualified legal clerk, or secretary, who undertook basic legal tasks to assist the qualified members of staff in a law firm. However, many paralegals now have legal qualifications, such as an LPC, and start their legal careers carrying out legal tasks that can range from assisting qualified lawyers to handling large caseloads. In this way it is hoped that they will eventually secure a training contract. The work is generally very poorly paid. A number of organisations offer paralegal training qualifications for school leavers and there are organisations that paralegals can join, such as the Institute of Paralegals and the National Association of Licensed Paralegals.

A voluntary register for the regulation of paralegals was set up in July 2015 in response to the LETR. The scheme is designed to underline the professional nature of the paralegal role and highlight to prospective clients the 'diversity of high-quality cost-effective legal services'.

Summary

- The legal profession in England and Wales comprises barristers, solicitors, and other legal professionals, such as legal executives and licensed conveyancers.
- Solicitors can operate as sole practitioners; in partnership with other solicitors, either formed under the Partnership Act 1890 or through an LLP; or in LDPs and ABS.
- Solicitors undertake a wide range of legal work, although those working in large firms tend to specialise in a particular area of law. Solicitors may now represent clients in every court, provided they have completed the necessary training or have sufficient experience to be granted higher rights of audience.
- The Law Society is the body that represents solicitors in England and Wales. The regulatory role that it used to have has been split off since the Clementi Report and the SRA now regulates the profession.
- Barristers give clients specialist legal advice and appear in court on their behalf as advocates. They may be self-employed and operate from a set of chambers, be employed barristers in the public or private sector, or be part of an LDP.
- All barristers must be a member of one of the Inns of Court.
- The General Council of the Bar (Bar Council) is the representative body for barristers. It, like the Law Society, has separated its regulatory and representative functions following the Clementi Report and the BSB regulates the profession.
- The Legal Services Act 2007 has changed the way in which solicitors and barristers are regulated and the way in which they practise. The Act establishes the Legal Services Board to oversee both the Law Society and the Bar Council and to establish a new complaints system via the Office for Legal Complaints. The Act also allows solicitors and barristers to operate in ABS which may be owned and managed by non-lawyers.

Questions

1 What do solicitors and barristers do?
2 How would you qualify as a solicitor? Should this process be reformed for the future?
3 Can barristers and solicitors be sued for negligence?
4 What reforms have been introduced to the way in which barristers and solicitors are regulated?
5 What sorts of business structures do barristers and solicitors currently operate under? Which model do you consider to be the most appropriate?
6 Do you consider that the Clementi reforms have gone far enough? What other reforms to the legal professions are necessary or desirable?

Sample question and outline answer

Question

A journalist in the *Economist* noted:

> The original reasons for dividing lawyers into two categories—barristers and solicitors—have long since disappeared, but the distinction remains. In theory the ... barristers are supposed to be the specialists in advocacy or in particular areas of the law. The ... solicitors are, often misleadingly, described as the general practitioners. In fact, some barristers are not specialists, some solicitors are. Some solicitors are better advocates than many barristers.

Is the division in the legal profession between solicitors and barristers still relevant in the twenty-first century, or should the professions be fused?

Outline answer

The following guidance will help you to plan and prepare an answer to the above question.

The introduction should set out what you understand the question to be asking and explain how you will answer it. The question expects you to discuss the differences between solicitors and barristers and the increasingly blurred distinctions between the two professions. You may then want to go on to discuss the advantages and disadvantages of having two branches of the profession, before deciding whether you consider that the present division should remain or that the two professions be joined.

The professions of barrister and solicitor are separate and, traditionally, the work they carry out is different. You could outline the differences.

Fusion, in this context, can be defined as a union resulting from combining or merging different elements or parts. Is this the definition you wish to use?

When this was first investigated, by the Royal Commission on Legal Services in 1979 (the Benson Commission), the result was a strong recommendation to retain the two branches. What has happened since that committee reported? The Law Society view is that the legal profession should be similar to the medical profession. In other words, all lawyers would have a standard training and then those who wished to specialise could apply to become consultants.

Discuss the fact that the granting of higher rights to solicitors and the opening of access to barristers has, perhaps, led to fewer calls for formal change. In terms of advantages/disadvantages, you could discuss, among other issues, the following: lower costs if only one lawyer is needed—however, it may be argued that in practice two lawyers are often required: one to do the day-to-day work on the case and the other to represent a party at trial, for example.

Specialisation—using one lawyer prevents duplication of effort; however, is it always necessary to have a specialist? Perhaps a lower-paid lawyer could do the day-to-day work and call on a specialist for specific, difficult problems (as is the case in the medical profession).

Advocacy—is it an advantage or a disadvantage that one profession specialises in advocacy?

Think about the roles, read widely, and develop your own views on advantages and disadvantages. Refer to the changes that have come about as a result of the Legal Services Act 2007.

Your conclusion will show that you have answered the question asked and will sum up your final view.

Further reading

The business structure of law firms has entered a new phase and the consequences of the advent of ABS, MDPs, and LDPs on the development of the profession is not clear. It is important to read the legal press and quality newspapers to keep up to date with the changes that are taking place. The following list is a starting point for your reading.

- *Clementi Report of the Review of the Regulatory Framework for Legal Services in England and Wales*. **webarchive.nationalarchives.gov.uk/** and **www.legal-services-review.org.uk/content/consult/consult_reviewpaper.pdf**

This is the final report and worth reading to understand the history of regulation of the professions.

- ***Bowyer, R.*** *'Regulatory Threats to the Law Degree: The Solicitors Qualifying Examination and the Purpose of Law Schools'* 30(2) Law and Critique, July 2019, 117–21

  A discussion of the regulatory changes in undergraduate legal education and the role of law schools.

- ***Greene, D.*** *'Time for a New Model'* (2012) 162 NLJ 377

  This very readable article outlines the key provisions of the Legal Services Act 2007 and explains how they are being introduced gradually to allow the legal profession to adapt to the changes to regulation and to prepare for ABS. The author considers how the licensing process may develop and the implications for traditional partnerships, and discusses LDPs and ABS.

- ***The Legal Education and Training Revie*** **w. letr.org.uk/**

  This website includes the report, from June 2013, and a wealth of other information, including the literature review that was carried out in preparation for the report. It is a lengthy document, but the executive summary is clear and easy to read.

- ***Mayson, S.*** *'Something for Everyone'* (2007) 157 NLJ 1073

  This article outlines the provisions of the Legal Services Bill 2006, which was enacted in 2007, allowing for lawyers to take part in ABS. The provisions permit the co-ownership of law firms by non-lawyers. The article highlights the advantages to lawyers of being involved in 'multi-talented practices' and the ways in which the legal services market may change.

- ***Office of Fair Trading.*** *'Competition in Professions'* (2001) **webarchive.nationalarchives.gov.uk/** and **www.oft.gov.uk/shared_oft/reports/professional_bodies/oft328.pdf**

  This report is more than ten years old but it provides an interesting starting point to consider the barriers to competition in the legal professions alongside other professions, such as accountancy.

Online resources

You should now attempt the supporting self-test questions and end-of-chapter questions available at: **www.oup.com/he/wilson-rutherford4e**

Chapter 10

The jury

Learning objectives

By the end of this chapter you should be able to:

- explain the criteria for eligibility for jury service;
- critically consider the merits of the changes to ineligibility, disqualification, and excusal for jury service in the Criminal Justice Act 2003;
- assess the case law and reform proposals in cases where defendants from an ethnic minority seek modification of the ethnic composition of the jury;
- critically consider the arguments for and against (a) the exclusion of jury trials in certain cases and (b) jury waiver;
- explain the policy of jury selection in England and compare it with that in the United States (US).

Talking point

In August 2013, the Ministry of Justice announced that the maximum age limit for jury service was to be raised from seventy to seventy-five, in order to increase the pool of eligible jurors by approximately two million. Section 68 of the Criminal Justice and Courts Act 2015 was duly passed to effect this change and the new age limit of seventy-five came into operation on 1 December 2016. During the passage of the new legislation through Parliament, the government explained that '[r]aising the age limit to 75 will mean that juries better reflect the current demographic make-up of the adult population and will allow juries to benefit from the experience and knowledge of those aged 70 to 75. The existing age limit for jury service was set by the Criminal Justice Act 1988, which raised the upper age limit from 65 to 70. However, that was more than 25 years ago, and it does not reflect the current healthy life expectancy of older people in England and Wales. On that basis, we believe that it is reasonable to expect people aged up to and including 75 to sit as jurors if summoned.'

In many other countries which use jury trials, there is no upper age limit for jurors at all. For example, in Scotland, the upper age limit was abolished in 2011. However, during the passage of the Criminal Justice and Courts bill through Parliament, the government opposed an amendment which would have abolished the upper age limit altogether. The government explained: 'Over the age of 75, there is an increasing risk that people would be unable to perform jury service and as a consequence would seek to be excused for that reason. We do not believe it would be right to put people in those circumstances to the trouble of having to apply for excusal, or indeed to burden the taxpayer with the additional cost of administering those excusals. Our view is that the appropriate age limit is 75.'

In the light of these developments, consider the following questions:

- Who do you think should be eligible to serve on a jury?
- Do you agree with the government's view that an upper age limit is necessary? What are the pros and cons of this limit?
- Excluding age, can you think of any other factors that it could be argued should disqualify a person from jury service?
- Do you think that people who are eligible for jury service should be entitled to seek excusal? In what circumstances?

Introduction

The jury has been called the 'bulwark of the liberties' of the individual against the state and is seen by many as an essential part of the criminal justice system in England and Wales. One of the most distinctive features of the Crown Court trial is, undoubtedly, the input of the jury. However, its role may be more symbolic than most people realise. Crown Court trials represent no more than 2 per cent of all criminal trials, with the vast majority of criminal prosecutions taking place in the magistrates' courts. However, it should be noted that a jury does decide every criminal offence that is triable 'on indictment' (at least, where the accused pleads not guilty). This category includes the most serious offences, such as murder, manslaughter, rape, and robbery. Furthermore, where a criminal offence is one 'triable either way', then the defendant can elect to have trial before a jury. The use of juries in civil proceedings, on the other hand, is very limited (see s.69 (1) of the Senior Courts Act 1981, discussed in 10.1.5).

The composition and operation of the jury have been the subject of much debate in recent years and significant changes have been made to the former. The starting point for an understanding of the jury is a thorough understanding of the basic law relating to it. To that must be added a critical awareness of the current issues relating to the workings of the jury.

10.1 The role of the jury

During a trial, the judge directs the jury as to the relevant principles of law and evidence. The jury's job in a trial is to determine issues of fact, that is, what actually happened, and reach a verdict on that basis. In a civil trial, the jury's function is to determine whether the claimant has established his or her case on the balance of probabilities. As juries in civil trials are now very rare, in the remainder of this chapter all references to juries and jury trials will be to criminal prosecutions in the Crown Court, unless otherwise stated. Image 10.1 shows a typical Crown Court jury.

10.1.1 The jury's function in criminal trials

In a criminal trial, at the close of the case—that is, after the prosecution and defence have presented their version of events and examined and cross-examined the accused, the alleged victim, and any witnesses—the judge sums up the issues and legal principles, and then the jury retires to consider its verdict. This will either be 'guilty' if the prosecuting body, usually the Crown Prosecution Service (CPS), has established its case beyond reasonable doubt, or 'not guilty' if not.

Image 10.1 A jury panel

Source: Alamy

Key point

Although a judge may direct a jury to acquit, the judge may not direct the jury to convict. The decision whether or not the prosecution has proven its case is always a matter for the jury alone.

This principle was confirmed by the House of Lords in *R v Wang* [2005] UKHL 9, [2005] 1 WLR 661. The appellant, Cheong Wang, was indicted on two counts of having an 'article which has a blade or is sharply pointed' in a public place, contrary to s.139(1) of the Criminal Justice Act 1988. He did not deny having the articles—a sword and a knife—with him but argued that he was a Buddhist and liked to stop at 'remote and uninhabited places' to practise a traditional martial art called Shaolin. However, the trial judge directed the jury that, as a matter of law, Wang had no defence and that they were therefore to return guilty verdicts. The jury duly convicted and the Court of Appeal dismissed Wang's appeal. However, on further appeal, the House of Lords quashed the convictions. Delivering a unanimous judgment, Lord Bingham said:

> No matter how inescapable a judge may consider a conclusion to be, in the sense that any other conclusion would be perverse, it remains his duty to leave the decision to the jury and not to dictate what that verdict should be.

Moreover, a judge cannot pressurise a jury into reaching a guilty verdict. Where this happens the Court of Appeal almost inevitably quashes the conviction. In *R v McKenna and Others* [1960] 1 QB 411, Cassells J said:

> It is a cardinal principle of our criminal law that in considering their verdict—concerning, as it does, the liberty of the subject—a jury shall deliberate in complete freedom, uninfluenced by any promise, unintimidated by any threat.

In *R v Watson and Others* [1988] QB 690, Lord Lane CJ said the jury

> must not be made to feel that it is incumbent upon them to express agreement with a view they do not truly hold simply because it might be inconvenient or tiresome or expensive for the prosecution, the defendant, the victim or the public in general if they do not do so.

The principle that juries must not be pressurised into reaching a verdict was emphasised in *R v Buttle* [2006] EWCA Crim 246, the facts of which are given at 10.1.3 (the case also raised issues about the secrecy of jury deliberations). Gage LJ said: 'it is clear that a jury must not be put under undue pressure'. However, 'pressure' should be distinguished from 'exhortation'. In *Shoukatallie v R* [1962] AC 81, Lord Denning said that 'the question . . . is whether the judge went beyond exhortation which is permissible, and exerted some measure of coercion which is not'.

10.1.2 **Jury equity**

One of the supposed strengths of jury trials is that a jury may acquit anyone, regardless of the law or the weight of the evidence. This is known as the principle of 'jury equity'. In *R v Ponting* [1985] Crim LR 318, a jury acquitted the accused of charges brought under the Official Secrets Act 1911. This was despite the fact that there was no argument that the accused had committed all the elements of the offence, and the judge had directed the jury that, as a matter of law, he had no defence.

 Example

***R v Ponting* [1985] Crim LR 318**

In July 1984, Clive Ponting, a departmental head in the Ministry of Defence, sent two documents to Tam Dalyell, a Labour MP. The documents belonged to the ministry and related to parliamentary inquiries about the sinking of the Argentine warship the *General Belgrano*, during the 1982 Falklands conflict. Dalyell was a known critic of the government regarding the *Belgrano* sinking. The first document was unclassified but the second was marked 'Confidential'. Ponting was charged with an offence of disclosing confidential material under the Official Secrets Act 1911, although there was a defence if the disclosure was to 'a person to whom it is in the interest of the State to communicate it'. There was no argument that Ponting had committed all the elements of the offence; his only defence was that Dalyell was a person to whom it was his duty 'in the interest of the State' to communicate the documents. McCowan J directed the jury that, as a matter of law, the 'interest of the State' was synonymous with the 'interest of the government of the day'. However, despite this clear indication from the judge that the defence was unavailable, the jury returned a verdict of 'not guilty'.

According to Feldman's book *Civil Liberties and Human Rights* (1993), at p.641, 'the jury acquitted Mr Ponting, probably reflecting public contempt for the government's attempt to conflate its own narrow political interest with the state's interest'. Birkinshaw, in *Freedom of Information* (1989) at p.81, has suggested that the acquittal 'no doubt related to a jury refusing to be browbeaten by a judge'. Another example of 'jury equity' is the case of Bridget Gilderdale.

Example

***R v Gilderdale, The Times*, 25 January 2010**

In January 2010 Bridget Gilderdale was cleared by a jury at Lewes Crown Court of the attempted murder of her thirty-one-year-old daughter, Lynn. Lynn had been suffering from myalgic encephalomyelitis (ME), otherwise known as chronic fatigue syndrome (CFS)—which causes long-term tiredness which is not relieved by rest or sleep—since she was fourteen years old. Her condition was particularly debilitating and she had previously attempted to take her own life to relieve her suffering. Bridget had cared for Lynn throughout the seventeen years that followed and had tried to persuade her daughter not to take her own life. However, she eventually agreed to help Lynn to die by providing her with morphine and injecting air into her veins after Lynn told her mother that she wanted 'the pain to go'. After Lynn's death, Bridget pleaded guilty to aiding and abetting her daughter's suicide and was given a twelve-month conditional discharge. However, the prosecution proceeded with the attempted murder charge, which eventually led to a not guilty verdict. Given the strength of the prosecution evidence and the guilty plea to the assisted suicide charge, the jury's verdict is widely regarded as an example of jury equity. The trial judge, Bean J, was prompted to comment as follows: 'I do not normally comment on the verdicts of juries but in this case their decision, if I may say so, shows common sense, decency and humanity which makes jury trials so important in a case of this kind.'

Thinking point

Are magistrates more or less likely to acquit than a jury?

In the magistrates' court, the arbiters of fact are not a jury but the magistrates. Would a bench of magistrates have been more or less likely than a jury to acquit the defendants in these cases?

Penny Darbyshire, in 'The Lamp that Shows that Freedom Lives—Is It Worth the Candle?' [1991] Crim LR 740 (at p.748), is very critical of 'jury equity'. She writes:

> Jurors will sometimes acquit, or convict, for a variety of extraneous reasons, which have nothing to do with replacing the law with their own sense of fairness or equity. They include the pressure of incarceration in the jury room and the replacement of the high standard of proof 'beyond reasonable doubt' with a lesser standard . . . Jurors also sometimes base their decisions on sympathy or hostility towards other trial participants, notably counsel and witnesses.

Thinking point

Is jury equity a strength or a weakness?

Is the jury's power to acquit someone in open defiance of the law and/or evidence a strength or a weakness of the jury system?

10.1.3 Appeals against decisions of the jury and the 'confidentiality' principle

Appeals by the prosecution

It is extremely rare for there to be an appeal by the prosecution against an acquittal by a jury. Until quite recently there was no possibility at all; however, s.76 of the Criminal Justice Act 2003 does allow the prosecution to apply to the Court of Appeal to quash an acquittal and order a retrial following a trial on indictment. The first occasion on which this happened was in *R v Dunlop* [2006] EWCA Crim 1354, [2007] 1 WLR 1657. William Dunlop had been charged with the murder of a young woman, Julie Hogg, but pleaded not guilty. At the trial in May 1991 the jury failed to reach a verdict and so a retrial was held in October 1991, with Dunlop again pleading not guilty. The second jury also failed to reach a verdict, at which point the Crown withdrew the case and a verdict of not guilty was entered.

Several years later, while in prison for an unrelated offence, Dunlop admitted his guilt to a prison officer, and in April 2000 he was convicted of perjury for lying to the Crown Court during the 1991 trials. However, after the Criminal Justice Act 2003 came into force in April 2005, the Crown submitted an application to the Court of Appeal to have the 1991 acquittal quashed. The Court agreed and Dunlop was duly tried for Julie's murder for a third time in September 2006. On this occasion he pleaded guilty.

Do not confuse this process and that whereby the Attorney General refers cases to the Court of Appeal following a defendant's acquittal by a Crown Court. Attorney General's References provide an opportunity for the Court of Appeal to state the law on a subject, but do not involve any change to the Crown Court's decision.

Appeals by the defence

Appeals against conviction are much more common. Usually this relates to an alleged misdirection by the judge on a point of law or evidence. However, the Court of Appeal is, in certain circumstances, prepared to hear evidence of events affecting the jury. If it finds an 'irregularity' serious enough to bring the conviction into doubt then it may quash a conviction. An issue that has to be carefully addressed here is s.74(1) of the Criminal Justice and Courts Act 2015 (CJCA 2015), which inserts several new provisions into the Juries Act 1974, effective April 2015. Section 20D(1) of the 1974 Act (as amended) provides that it is an offence for a person 'intentionally

(a) to disclose information about statements made, opinions expressed, arguments advanced or votes cast by members of a jury in the course of their deliberations in proceedings before a court, or (b) to solicit or obtain such information'. There are several exceptions; for example, it is obviously lawful for the jury to deliver their actual verdict (s.20E(1) of the Juries Act 1974 (as amended)). It is also lawful for the trial judge 'to disclose information (a) for the purposes of dealing with the case, or (b) for the purposes of an investigation by a relevant investigator into whether an offence or contempt of court has been committed by or in relation to a juror in the proceedings' (s.20E(2) of the Juries Act 1974 (as amended)).

Section 20F(1) of the Juries Act 1974 (as amended) provides that it is lawful to disclose information about the jury's deliberations if 'the person making the disclosure reasonably believes that (i) an offence or contempt of court has been, or may have been, committed by or in relation to a juror in connection with those proceedings, or (ii) conduct of a juror in connection with those proceedings may provide grounds for an appeal against conviction or sentence'.

Section 20F(7) of the Juries Act 1974 (as amended) then provides that it is not an offence under s.20D(1) for a person to disclose information in evidence in:

(a) contempt of court proceedings brought as a consequence of a juror allegedly breaching s.20D(1);

(b) an appeal where an allegation relating to a juror's conduct forms part of the grounds of appeal.

Section 20F(7)(b) is important, as it means that the Court of Appeal or Supreme Court may be able to hear appeals involving alleged jury misconduct during deliberations without breaching s.20D(1). Section 74(1) of the CJCA 2015 also repealed s.8 of the Contempt of Court Act 1981, which forbade any investigation into things said during the jury's 'deliberations'. Prior to the abolition of s.8, there were a number of cases which examined the extent to which this restricted the appeal courts' ability to hear appeals against alleged irregularities during a jury trial. Some of these cases remain relevant as a guide to the likely scope of s.20D(1).

The classic example is *R v Young* [1995] 2 Cr App R 379, where allegations were made that the jury convicted the defendant of two counts of murder after consulting a makeshift Ouija board while they were sequestered in a hotel overnight. The Court of Appeal first had to decide whether the court itself was bound by s.8. Lord Taylor CJ held that s.8 did, in general terms, bind the court and so, unless s.8 could be avoided, it would be impossible to investigate what may or may not have happened prior to the jury returning their verdict. However, Lord Taylor then held that s.8 did not apply to the facts of the *Young* case, because when the jury was sequestered in the hotel its members were not 'deliberating'. Having decided that s.8 did not apply, the Court held that the use of the Ouija board was 'not merely objectionable but amounted to a material irregularity' and quashed Young's convictions (although it did order a retrial, at which Young was duly reconvicted).

In *R v Qureshi* [2001] EWCA Crim 1807, [2002] 1 WLR 518, the Court of Appeal decided, because of s.8, that it could not give leave to hear an appeal, despite one of the jurors, after conviction, alleging that a range of irregularities had occurred during the jury's deliberations. The allegations included making disparaging remarks about the defendant, bringing newspapers into the jury room, using mobile phones to contact outsiders during the trial, and adopting a bullying attitude. One juror was alleged to have fallen asleep during the evidence; another was alleged to have been deaf and unable to hear all the evidence. Despite all of this, the Court of Appeal felt it had no choice but to refuse leave to appeal because all the allegations related to matters protected by s.8.

In *R v Mirza* [2004] UKHL 2, [2004] 1 AC 1118, the House of Lords heard another case involving post-conviction allegations of irregularities having taken place during the jury's deliberations. One of the jurors alleged that at least some of the other jurors were racist and prejudiced against the defendant, who was from Pakistan but had been living in England since 1998. In a letter sent to the defendant's lawyers, it was alleged that '[t]he bigots [on the jury] had decided that the case brought by the prosecution was not good enough for them, so they embellished it'. This prompted the defendant, who had been convicted of indecent assault, to appeal. The Court of Appeal dismissed his appeal as it considered itself bound by the decision in *Qureshi*. The defendant appealed again. The question for the Lords was whether the juror's letter could be used as a basis for allowing an appeal. The Lords held not, and dismissed the appeal.

However, the Lords actually disagreed with the Court of Appeal in *R v Qureshi* and held that s.8 of the Contempt of Court Act 1981 did *not* apply to the appeal courts (overruling *R v Young* on that point). The Lords decided that there was an even older common law rule to the same effect, preventing appeal judges from investigating appeals relating to alleged irregularities in the course of jury deliberations. The common law rule was designed to ensure the confidentiality of jury deliberations. Several reasons were given for this principle. Lord Hobhouse explained that 'nothing could be more destructive . . . than the juror coming out of court and communicating his or her views about the jury's deliberations to the media or to persons who are likely to disagree with the verdict'. Lord Hope said that 'the law recognises that confidentiality is essential to the proper functioning of the jury process, that there is merit in finality and that jurors must be protected from harassment'.

Thus, it was legally impossible to bring an appeal against conviction based on evidence of allegations of improprieties that may have occurred during the jury's deliberations (the confidentiality principle). However, the confidentiality principle did not apply when appeals were brought against conviction based on evidence of allegations of improprieties caused by or attributable to extraneous matters. The position in both Canadian and English law was summarised by the Supreme Court of Canada in *R v Pan; R v Sawyer* [2001] 2 SCR 344, where Arbour J explained that the law

> seeks to preserve the secrecy of the jury's deliberations, while ensuring that those deliberations remain untainted by contact with information or individuals from outside the jury. As a result, where the evidence establishes that the jury has been exposed to outside information or influences, it will generally be admissible.

A number of English cases have addressed the question of the difference between jury deliberations (which were subject to the confidentiality rule) and extraneous matters which might have influenced those deliberations (which were not):

- An example of the former situation is *R v Buttle* [2006] EWCA Crim 246. Buttle had been convicted of rape and assault by penetration. On appeal, it was contended that one of the jurors had been pressurised by three other jurors to return a guilty verdict. However, the appeal court dismissed Buttle's appeal. Gage LJ simply said that 'this Court cannot enquire into the privacy of what goes on in the jury room'.
- An example of the latter situation is *R v Karakaya* [2005] EWCA Crim 346, [2005] 2 Cr App R 5. Here, the accused had been convicted of rape. After the jury left court, it was discovered that a juror had taken into the jury's deliberating room extraneous documents (academic articles dealing with rape). Karakaya appealed, arguing that the presence of the documents in the jury room amounted to an irregularity. The Court of Appeal quashed the conviction (although a retrial was ordered) because the verdicts were not necessarily based purely on the evidence actually presented at trial. The Court of Appeal distinguished *R v Mirza* on the basis that this case involved consideration of extraneous documents.
- Another example of the latter situation is *R v Pintori* [2007] EWCA Crim 1700, [2007] Crim LR 997, where the defendant had been convicted of possession of heroin but appealed when it emerged, post-verdict, that one of the jurors had been employed by the police force (albeit in a civilian capacity) and knew some of the officers involved in bringing the prosecution. On appeal, it was submitted that this juror—and by extension, the whole jury—may have been biased against the defendant. The Court of Appeal allowed the appeal. *R v Mirza* was again distinguished as this case also involved the question of external influences on the jury's deliberation process.
- Another example of the latter situation is *R v Marshall and Crump* [2007] EWCA Crim 35, [2007] Crim LR 562, although in this case the Court of Appeal upheld the appellants' robbery convictions despite the fact that 'extraneous' material was found in the jury room after the trial had concluded consisting of printouts from three websites: those of the CPS, the Home Office, and a criminal solicitors' practice. Hughes LJ said that although the material was 'wholly extraneous', it was 'largely material which was in the public domain and to which an intelligent member of the public serving on the jury could perfectly legitimately have access'. As a result, the Court concluded that the guilty verdicts were 'safe'.

In *R v Thompson and Others* [2010] EWCA Crim 1623, [2010] 2 Cr App R 27, six appellants appealed against convictions for various offences. In each case the appellant had alleged, inter alia, jury irregularity. The irregularities alleged by each appellant were as follows:

(a) Benjamin Thompson had been convicted at Oxford Crown Court of causing grievous bodily harm with intent. After the trial, several jurors wrote a letter to the trial judge indicating that one of the jurors had used the internet to bring extraneous material 'relating to the case and legal terminology' into the jury room.

(b) Jason Crawford was convicted at Harrow Crown Court of two counts of cocaine possession with intent to supply. After the trial, one of the jurors made a phone call to Crawford's solicitor asserting that, although she had been inclined towards a not guilty verdict, she had been 'put under immense pressure by other jurors to change her decision'.

(c) Ahmed Gomulu was convicted at the Old Bailey of murder and wounding with intent. After his trial, members of Gomulu's family reported that the victim's brother had been seen talking to members of the jury during the trial.

(d) Chris Allen was convicted of rape at Newport Crown Court. After his trial, it was claimed that the jury may have become aware that Allen was facing a second jury trial for an unrelated offence.

(e) David Blake was convicted at Newcastle Crown Court of having an article with a blade or point on school premises. After the trial, evidence emerged that one of the jurors had conducted 'experiments' involving nail clippers.

(f) Kamulete Kasunga was convicted of assault occasioning actual bodily harm at Wood Green Crown Court. After the trial, it emerged that a juror had written to the judge expressing concerns over the verdict.

Only one appeal—Blake's—was successful. The appeals in the other five cases were dismissed. The alleged irregularities in Crawford's and Kasunga's cases were described as 'classic *Mirza* territory'; in other words, they related to allegations protected by the confidentiality principle which were therefore inadmissible. The allegation in Gomulu's case was rejected for lack of evidence. Allen's appeal failed for similar reasons. Thompson's appeal raised more difficulties. Lord Judge CJ said that the use of the internet would have constituted an irregularity. However, the verdict was nevertheless held to be safe on the basis that the jurors' letter to the trial judge 'does not suggest that the juror, or anything he or she said to the other members of the jury, led them, in dereliction of their duty, to do other than follow the directions in law given by the judge, as supplemented by him in answer to the numerous notes in which the jury sought further directions'. On the specific issue of jurors using the internet, Lord Judge CJ offered the following observations:

> The use of the internet has expanded rapidly in recent years and it is to be expected that many, perhaps most, jurors, will be experienced in its use and will make habitual reference to it in daily life . . . [The] use of the internet is so common that some specific guidance must now be given to jurors . . . Jurors need to understand that although the internet is part of their daily lives, the case must not be researched there, or discussed there (for example, on social networking sites), any more than it can be researched with, or discussed amongst friends or family, and for the same reason. The reason is easy for jurors to understand. Research of this kind may affect their decision, whether consciously or unconsciously, yet at the same time, neither side at trial will know what consideration might be entering into their deliberations and will therefore not be able to address arguments about it. This would represent a departure from the basic principle which requires that the defendant be tried on the evidence admitted and heard by them in court. [We] do not purport to lay down a standard form of words; the sense of the message is familiar to all judges. What matters is that it should be explicitly related to the use of the internet. We recommend a direction in which the principle is explained not in terms which imply that the judge is making a polite request, but that he is giving an order necessary for the fair conduct of the trial.

The principles laid down in *R v Mirza*—of the paramount importance of maintaining confidentiality of jury deliberations—can be starkly contrasted with the scenes immediately after the culmination of the Michael Jackson trial (*People of California v Jackson*) in Santa Maria, California, in June 2005. There, members of the jury held an impromptu, televised press conference to discuss the reasons for their not guilty verdicts, which was broadcast around the world. Had that conference taken place immediately after the end of an English criminal trial, the jurors would almost certainly have been prosecuted for contempt of court.

An example of this occurred in *Attorney General v Scotcher* [2004] UKHL 36, [2005] 1 WLR 1867. The defendant, S, who sat as a juror in a trial of two brothers accused of drug dealing in January 2000, was convicted of contempt of court after he wrote a letter to the mother of the accused after the trial telling her that he thought her sons' convictions were unsafe because some of the other jurors had been too keen to get the trial over with and go home. The House of Lords upheld S's conviction, holding that his motives in seeking to overturn a miscarriage of justice provided no defence to a charge of contempt.

Thinking point

Should the principle of jury confidentiality continue to apply?

Should the common law confidentiality principle, as explained by the House of Lords in *Mirza*, continue to apply following the recent amendments to the Juries Act 1974?

Section 18(1) of the Juries Act 1974 is designed to eliminate unnecessary appeals. It states that no judgment after verdict in any trial by jury in any court shall be stayed or reversed by reason:

(a) that the provisions of this Act about the summoning or impanelling of jurors, or the selection of jurors by ballot, have not been complied with; or
(b) that a juror was not qualified in accordance with s.1 of this Act; or
(c) that any juror was misnamed or misdescribed; or
(d) that any juror was unfit to serve.

Examples of this include:

- *R v Chapman and Lauday* (1976) 63 Cr App R 75—evidence emerged after the trial that one of the jurors had such a severe problem with earwax that he could not hear the summing up. The defendants appealed, but the appeal was dismissed.
- *R v Bliss* (1987) 84 Cr App R 1—after conviction, the defendant recognised one of the jurors as being a man with whom he had been involved in a fight in a pub some six months earlier. He appealed, arguing that the juror might have been 'hostile' to him, but this was rejected.
- *R v Richardson* [2004] EWCA Crim 2997—evidence emerged after the defendant's conviction of rape and indecent assault that one of the jurors was actually disqualified because of his own conviction for indecent assault, but had served in any event. However, his appeal was dismissed.

10.1.4 **Majority verdicts**

The concept of majority verdicts was introduced by the Criminal Justice Act 1967 and is now regulated according to s.17 of the Juries Act 1974. This states that a jury's verdict 'need not be unanimous' where at least ten of them agree (s.17(1)(a)) or, in the rare cases where there are ten jurors, at least nine of them agree (s.17(1)(b)). The main advantage of a majority verdict is that it avoids the problem of one juror with extreme and/or intractable views holding out against the rest, and should lessen the need for expensive and time-consuming retrials. Conversely, it has been argued that majority verdicts 'dilute' the concept of proof beyond reasonable doubt—on the ground that if one juror is not satisfied as to guilt, there must be a doubt—and hence gives less protection to the innocent. This, in turn, weakens public confidence in the system.

Thinking points

Are majority verdicts acceptable? Should the jury have to be unanimous?

1. Are majority verdicts acceptable, given the requirement that the prosecution prove its case beyond reasonable doubt?
2. What might be the effect of a requirement to have unanimous verdicts?

10.1.5 **The jury's function in civil trials**

Section 69 of the Senior Courts Act 1981 lists the categories of civil cases that can be heard by a jury in the High Court. The list includes fraud, malicious prosecution, and false imprisonment. For an example of the use of a civil jury in a malicious prosecution case, see *Morrison v Chief Constable of the West Midlands* [2003] EWCA Civ 271; for a case involving a civil jury in a false imprisonment case, see *Lorenzo v Chief Constable of the West Midlands* [2012] EWCA Civ 1863. The list used to include libel and slander (collectively known as defamation) as well, but those actions were deleted by s.11 of the Defamation Act 2013. According to the explanatory notes to s.11, this change does not prevent juries from hearing defamation cases but 'defamation cases will be tried without a jury unless a court orders otherwise'. In *Yeo v Times Newspapers* [2014] EWHC 2853, [2015] 1 WLR 971, the first case involving s.11, the High Court refused to order a jury trial in a defamation case brought by the former Conservative MP Tim Yeo. The Court said that jury trials in defamation cases would now be 'the exception rather than the rule'. In refusing Yeo's request for a jury trial, the Court said that the claimant had failed to 'identify any skills, knowledge, aptitudes or other attributes likely to be possessed by a jury which would make it better equipped than a judge to grapple with the issues'. The Court also pointed out that 'trial by jury invariably takes longer and is more expensive than trial without a jury'. These factors did not preclude jury trial but 'the extra time and cost require justification'. On the basis of *Yeo*, it seems safe to say that jury trials in defamation cases in the future will be very rare.

Even in one of the listed areas, s.69(1) states that 'the action shall be tried with a jury unless the court is of the opinion that the trial requires any prolonged examination of documents or accounts or any scientific or local investigation which cannot conveniently be made with a jury'. In March 1994, nearly twenty years before the Defamation Act 2013, the Court of Appeal denied an application for trial by jury from two environmental campaigners of a libel action (the so-called 'McLibel' case) brought against them by the McDonald's restaurant chain. The Court said that the scientific issues would make it impossible for the case to be heard satisfactorily by a jury. The case duly went to trial before a single judge and lasted over a year—the longest libel action in history.

10.2 **The selection of the jury**

10.2.1 **Liability to serve**

The rules as to eligibility to serve on a jury are contained in s.1 of the Juries Act 1974 (as amended). The requirements can be summarised as follows. The individual must be:

- registered as an elector;
- aged between eighteen and seventy-five. The minimum age is eighteen. As discussed earlier, the maximum age was raised from sixty-five to seventy in 1988 and was raised again to seventy-five in 2016;

- ordinarily resident in the United Kingdom (UK), the Channel Islands, or the Isle of Man for five years from the age of thirteen.

No other eligibility criteria are required. In particular, there is no requirement that jurors be British citizens. This may be contrasted with the position in Canada, for example, where citizenship is a requirement for eligibility for jury service.

Thinking points

Jury eligibility: should citizenship be a criterion? Why is there an upper age limit for jurors?

1. What are the arguments for and against citizenship being a requirement for eligibility to serve on a jury?
2. Although Parliament has now raised the upper age limit for jurors, should the government have gone further and simply abolished the limit?

10.2.2 **Ineligibility**

Major changes were made to this area of law in April 2004, when s.321 of the Criminal Justice Act 2003 came into effect. Previously, Sch.1 to the Juries Act 1974 listed various categories of people as being ineligible for jury service. There were four Groups:

- **The Judiciary (Group A)**: this Group included judges and magistrates, both current and retired.
- **Other Persons Concerned with the Administration of Justice (Group B)**: this was a very large Group. It included the police and barristers and solicitors 'whether or not in actual practice as such'.
- **The Clergy, etc. (Group C)**: this Group included a 'man in holy orders; a regular minister of any religious denomination', and a 'vowed member of any religious order living in a monastery, convent or other religious community'.
- **Mentally Disordered Persons (Group D)**: this Group includes persons 'liable to be detained' under the Mental Health Act 1983 (MHA) or 'resident in a hospital on account of mental disorder' as defined by the MHA (Sch.1 to the Juries Act 1974 as amended by s.2 of the Mental Health (Discrimination) Act 2013).

Section 321 of the 2003 Act abolished Groups A, B, and C. This means that judges, lawyers, the police, and clergy all became eligible for jury service. Only those in Group D remain ineligible.

Key point

The general rule in the English criminal justice system is that all people who are eligible to serve on a jury should do so if summonsed. Only the mentally disordered are ineligible for jury service.

The enactment of s.321 in the 2003 Act was the culmination of a reform proposal advanced by Auld LJ in his Review of the Criminal Courts in England and Wales, commissioned by the government and published in September 2001. Auld LJ had recommended that English law should be brought into line with certain other jurisdictions, including a number of American states, where far fewer restrictions were placed on jury eligibility. The core objective of the reform was to broaden the pool of potential jurors, and to make the jury more representative of society.

Critical debate

Composition of the jury has long been a vexed question. At one time it was said that the English jury was 'middle class, male, middle minded and middle aged'. This was mainly because at one time eligibility for jury service was linked to property ownership. Following the abolition of this requirement in the early 1970s, this criticism is no longer true, but the issue that the jury should be representative of society remains. What were the reasons for excluding from jury service: (a) judges and lawyers; (b) the police; and (c) the clergy? Do you agree with Parliament that these people should now be required to serve on a jury? What are the potential problems with having lawyers and police officers serving as jurors?

The first case involving s.321 to reach the appeal courts was *R v Abdroikov and Others* [2007] UKHL 37, [2007] 1 WLR 2679. The case involved three separate cases which were joined into a single appeal, where it was argued that the presence of certain jurors created a risk of 'apparent' bias, and hence the appellants' entitlement to a fair trial by an 'independent and impartial tribunal', guaranteed by Article 6 of the European Convention on Human Rights (ECHR), was not satisfied. The appellants in the three cases were:

(a) Nurlon Abdroikov, who had been convicted of attempted murder by an Old Bailey jury containing a serving police officer, although he had no connection to the case. The officer's presence on the jury was only revealed at a very late stage in the trial, when the jury had already retired to consider their verdict.

(b) Richard Green, a heroin addict, who had been convicted at Woolwich Crown Court of ABH contrary to s.47 of the Offences Against the Person Act 1861, his jury also containing a police officer, PC Mason. In this case the victim, Sergeant Burgess, was also a police officer (he had pricked his finger on a used syringe in Green's pocket whilst conducting a search). PC Mason and Sergeant Burgess were both serving in the same London borough at the time of the incident and had once served in the same police station at the same time, although the two officers were not known to each other. PC Mason's presence on the jury was only discovered, by chance, after the trial.

(c) Ken Williamson, who had been convicted at Warrington Crown Court on two counts of rape. His jury contained a solicitor, Martin McKay-Smith, who had

> been employed by the CPS since 1986. McKay-Smith had contacted the court in advance to inform them of his occupation and background and defence counsel had sought to challenge his involvement, citing Article 6 of the ECHR. However, the trial judge had rejected this challenge, ruling that he was obliged by s.321 of the Criminal Justice Act 2003 to order McKay-Smith to serve.

The appellants invoked the principle established by Lord Hewart CJ in *R v Sussex Justices, ex parte McCarthy* [1924] 1 KB 256 that 'it is not merely of some importance but is of fundamental importance that justice should not only be done, but should manifestly and undoubtedly be seen to be done', a principle subsequently endorsed by the European Court of Human Rights. The appellants contended that this principle was not met in a case where one of the jurors was employed by a body (the police and the CPS) dedicated to promoting the success of one side in the adversarial trial process. However, the Court of Appeal rejected all of the appeals. Applying the test for 'apparent' bias laid down in earlier case law, namely 'whether the fair-minded and informed observer, having considered the facts, would conclude that there was a real possibility that the tribunal was biased' (*Porter v Magill* [2001] UKHL 67, [2002] 2 AC 357), Lord Woolf CJ held that a fair-minded and informed observer would *not* conclude that there was a real possibility that a juror was biased merely because his occupation was one which meant that he was involved in some capacity or other in the administration of justice.

The three appealed against that decision to the House of Lords, which, albeit by a narrow majority of 3 to 2, allowed the appeals in two of the three cases. Giving the leading judgment, Lord Bingham said:

> It must be accepted that most adult human beings, as a result of their background, education and experience, harbour certain prejudices and predilections of which they may be conscious or unconscious. I would also, for my part, accept that the safeguards established to protect the impartiality of the jury, when properly operated, do all that can reasonably be done to neutralise the ordinary prejudices and predilections to which we are all prone. But this does not meet the central thrust of the case made by [counsel] for the appellants: that these cases do not involve the ordinary prejudices and predilections to which we are all prone but the possibility of bias (possibly unconscious) which, as he submits, inevitably flows from the presence on a jury of persons professionally committed to one side only of an adversarial trial process.

Lord Bingham observed that in the 2001 *Review of the Criminal Courts*, which eventually led to the enactment of s.321, Auld LJ had indicated that police officers and holders of similar occupations should not sit in every case regardless of the circumstances, but that ultimately the trial judge should decide—on a case-by-case basis—whether their presence was compatible with the principle of justice being seen to be done. In Richard Green's case, the majority (Lord Bingham, Baroness Hale, and Lord Mance) pointed out that there was an evidential dispute between Green and Sergeant Burgess (the victim), and the jury had to choose to prefer the evidence of one or the other. As Sergeant Burgess and PC Mason (the juror) shared the same local service background, Lord Bingham held that the 'instinct' of a police officer juror to prefer the evidence of 'a brother officer' to that of the defendant 'would be judged by the fair-minded and informed observer to be a real and possible source of unfairness'. Lord Bingham stated that it 'is not a criticism of the police service, but a tribute to its greatest strength, that officers belong to a disciplined force, bound to each other by strong bonds of loyalty, mutual support, shared danger and responsibility, culture and tradition'. Green was, therefore, 'not tried by a tribunal which was and appeared to be impartial'. His appeal was allowed and the conviction was quashed.

In Ken Williamson's case, Lord Bingham held that it was 'clear that justice was not seen to be done where one of the jurors was a full-time, salaried, long-serving employee of the prosecutor'. His appeal was therefore also allowed and his convictions quashed (although the door was left open for a retrial—presumably without CPS solicitors involved).

The majority did rule that there were situations where police officers and CPS solicitors would meet the tests of impartiality. Indeed, Nurlon Abdroikov's case was one of them and his attempted murder conviction was upheld. Lord Bingham stated that, although it was 'unfortunate' that the police officer's identity was only revealed to the trial judge at such a late stage, 'had the matter been ventilated at the outset of the trial, it is difficult to see what argument defence counsel could have urged other than the general undesirability of police officers serving on juries, a difficult argument to advance in face of the parliamentary enactment' (meaning s.321 of the 2003 Act).

Lords Rodger and Carswell dissented in the appeals of Green and Williamson. Lord Rodger, in a powerful dissent, said that many (if not most) jurors would harbour some prejudices of various kinds. He pointed out that there was a 'risk' in any Crown Court trial that some jurors may (for example) be homophobic, or sexist, or racist. However, he said that the law takes steps to minimise the risk by making jurors take an oath or affirm that they will 'faithfully try the defendant and give a true verdict according to the evidence', and by making the judge give them a direction that they must assess the evidence impartially. Lord Rodger said that it would 'be naïve to suppose that these safeguards will always work with every juror'—but he thought that the presence of the other eleven jurors would 'neutralise any bias on the part of one or more members and so reach an impartial verdict'. He later observed that allowing the appeals in Green's and Williamson's cases would 'drive a coach and horses through Parliament's legislation and will go far to reverse its reform of the law'. He thought that it was the 'rational policy of the legislature' to decide who was eligible to serve as jurors and then to treat them all alike. Applying these principles to the three appeals, Lord Rodger said:

> Like all other jurors, be they clergymen, defence lawyers, butchers, estate agents, prostitutes, petty crooks or judges, police officers and CPS lawyers sit as private individuals. Each brings his or her own particular experience to bear on the case they have to try ... I can see no reason why the fair minded and informed observer should single out juries with police officers and CPS lawyers as being constitutionally incapable

> of following the judge's directions and reaching an impartial verdict... An observer who singled out juries with these two types of members would be applying a different standard from the one that is usually applied.

Referring more specifically to Green's case, Lord Rodger added that Parliament must have known, when passing s.321, that police officers had previously been ineligible for jury service. Nonetheless, Parliament had 'judged it proper in today's world to remove the bar and to rely on the officers' commitment to uphold the law... like any other juror'. Similarly, referring to Williamson's case, Lord Rodger said that 'one of the qualities required of any CPS lawyer is an ability to assess evidence and to take proper decisions based on his assessment of the evidence, regardless of any pressure from the investigating police officers or from the media'. His Lordship concluded that '[a] fair minded and rational observer might just think that such a person would be capable of bringing his realism, objectivity and skills to bear when acting as a juror. Why, at the very least, should the observer assume that they would desert him?'

The guidance provided by the House of Lords has been applied in subsequent cases. *R v I* [2007] EWCA Crim 2999 involved a trial at Carlisle Crown Court. Before the case even began, a potential juror told the judge that he was a police officer and he knew all the officers who were to give evidence. The defence objected to him sitting but the judge disagreed, ruling that the fact of knowledge of particular witnesses in itself was not a bar to an individual being on the panel. He described it as analogous to a barrister sitting on a jury and knowing particular witnesses and the judge. The trial went ahead with the police officer on the jury and the defendant was convicted of a number of offences. However, the Court of Appeal quashed the convictions, holding that 'there was here a real possibility of bias arising from the presence on the jury of a police officer who knew the police witnesses. The possibility that he might be likely to accept the words of his colleagues, irrespective of the dispute between the parties, is one which can only be described as real.'

In *R v Khan and Others* [2008] EWCA Crim 531, [2008] 3 All ER 502, there were five separate cases before the Court of Appeal; this time none of the convictions was quashed. The cases can be summarised as follows:

- Case 1: Bakish Khan and Ilyas Hanif had been convicted at Sheffield Crown Court of conspiracy to supply heroin. During the trial, a juror had informed the judge that he was a police dog-handler and knew one of the witnesses for the prosecution, who was another police officer. The trial judge, however, rejected an application to discharge the juror.
- Case 2: Martin Lewthwaite had been convicted at Bristol Crown Court of causing GBH with intent. At the beginning of the trial, a juror informed the judge that he was a police Detective Chief Inspector but was involved with drugs crimes working outside the Nailsea area where the attack took place, and did not know any of the witnesses. The trial judge also rejected an application to discharge the juror. In both of these cases, the Court of Appeal held that the fact that a juror was

a police officer and might seem likely to favour the evidence of a fellow police officer would not, of itself, lead to an appearance of bias, and therefore did not automatically disqualify the juror.

- Case 3: Michael Khan had been convicted at Hull Crown Court of non-disclosure of property in his bankruptcy, contrary to s.351 of the Insolvency Act 1986. A juror at his trial was employed by the CPS as a media officer. The trial judge rejected an application to discharge the juror. The Court of Appeal upheld the conviction. Here, the Court pointed out that Khan had been prosecuted by the Department of Trade and Industry, not the CPS, and there could be 'no objection' to a member of the CPS being a juror in a case prosecuted by a different authority.
- Case 4: Roy Cross had been convicted of wounding with intent at Worcester Crown Court. After conviction he became aware that one of the jurors was a prison officer at a prison where he had been remanded before and during trial.
- Case 5: Stanley Hill had been convicted of the attempted murder of a woman called Wendy Crooks at Liverpool Crown Court and sentenced to life imprisonment. After conviction, he made essentially the same discovery as Cross. Cross and Hill both argued that there was a risk that the prison officers knew information detrimental to them. This was rejected by the Court of Appeal, which held that the mere suspicion that a juror might, by reason of having been employed as a prison officer, have acquired knowledge of that defendant's bad character could not, of itself, lead an objective observer to conclude that the juror had an appearance of bias.

Thinking point

Should police officers and other people employed in the criminal justice system be able to sit on juries?

Commenting on these case law developments, Nick Taylor ('Jury: Bias—Presence on Jury of Persons Concerned with Administration of Justice' [2008] Crim LR 641) observes that there is now a 'potentially very difficult burden upon the trial judge' to determine suitability. He suggests that Crown Court judges 'may be left wondering whether the clarity of the old exclusionary position was more desirable'. What do you think?

Two of the appellants in Case 1, Bakish Khan and Ilyas Hanif, successfully appealed to the European Court of Human Rights on the basis that the presence of the police officer on the jury in their case had infringed their right to a fair trial under Article 6 of the ECHR. In *Hanif and Khan v UK* (2012) 55 EHRR 16, the Strasbourg court held that, where there was a jury trial (a) involving an 'important conflict' relating to prosecution evidence and (b) where one of the jurors was a police officer who was 'personally acquainted' with the police officer giving that evidence, then 'jury directions and judicial warnings are insufficient to guard against the risk that the juror may, albeit subconsciously, favour the evidence of the police'.

Hence, the *Hanif and Khan* ruling is a relatively narrow one, although there will almost inevitably be further case law exploring the concepts of 'important conflict' and 'personally acquainted', both of which are apparently required for a violation of Article 6. Intriguingly, however, the Strasbourg court stated that it was 'leaving aside the question of whether the presence of a police officer on a jury could *ever* be compatible with Article 6' (emphasis added). This may imply that, had it been required to confront the issue head on, the court would have ruled that the presence of any police officer on a jury (whether 'personally acquainted' with a prosecution witness or not) infringed the defendant's right to a fair trial. In 'Police Officers on Juries' (2012) 71 CLJ 254, John Spencer argues:

> In retrospect it surely was a bad idea to make police officers eligible to serve. In practical terms, the need for judges to question police jurors about their relationships (if any) with witnesses adds a new and needless complication to the trial, and where one does serve and the defendant is convicted, a new and needless ground for possible appeal. And in theoretical terms, however honest the individual officer, in public perception a policeman is a member of the opposing team . . . The government should now make a virtue out of necessity and, taking the initiative, reverse the change its predecessor made before another Strasbourg condemnation forces it to do so.

Meanwhile, the Court of Appeal continues to deal with domestic cases involving challenges to conviction on the basis of allegedly inappropriate jurors. In *R v L* [2011] EWCA Crim 65, [2011] 1 Cr App R 27, the appellant had been convicted of burglary and attempted burglary at the Central Criminal Court (the Old Bailey). He appealed on the basis that the jury had included an employee of the CPS, a serving police officer, and a retired police officer—in other words, three out of the twelve jurors were individuals linked in some way with the prosecuting arm of the criminal justice system. The Court of Appeal emphasised that questions of eligibility or disqualification or excusal were directed to individual potential jurors, not to the jury as a whole, and so the mere fact that a quarter of the jury had connections to the police or the CPS did not of itself render the convictions unsafe. As far as the two police officers were concerned, the Court of Appeal decided that there was no reason why the position of either should cause any concern. Neither had any connection with the police force or the individual officers involved in the trial, nor with the Old Bailey.

However, the position of the CPS employee did cause concern. She had worked for the CPS for nine years, initially as a secretary to the Director of the Service's North East London Sector and subsequently providing administrative support to advocates at Snaresbrook Crown Court. Although stressing that each case had to be considered on its facts, Lord Judge CJ said that her service with the CPS was 'long enough and of sufficient importance' to fall within the ambit of the problem identified by Lord

Bingham in *R v Abdroikov and Others* that 'justice is not seen to be done if one discharging the very important neutral role of juror is a full-time, salaried, long-serving employee of the prosecutor'. As a consequence, the Court allowed L's appeal—but did order a retrial.

10.2.3 **Disqualifications**

Under Sch.1 to the Juries Act 1974, certain persons with a criminal record were disqualified either for life, ten years, or five years, depending on the sentence they received. This category has been preserved by the Criminal Justice Act 2003, although the rules have been simplified. The new position is that the following are disqualified:

- Persons sentenced to imprisonment:
  - those sentenced to five years or more: disqualified for life;
  - those sentenced to up to five years (including suspended sentences): disqualified for ten years;
- Those convicted of an offence under s.20A, s20B, s.20C or s.20D of the Juries Act 1974 (see 10.9 below): disqualified for ten years;
- persons on bail.

Thinking point

Why are some convicted criminals and those on bail prevented from serving as jurors?

Is it fair that someone who has committed a criminal offence could potentially (depending on the sentence imposed) face a lifetime ban from jury service? After all, is imprisonment not meant to serve (at least in part) as a form of rehabilitation into society? What about those on bail—is the disqualification of those on bail not a contradiction of the fundamental legal principle 'innocent until proven guilty'?

10.2.4 **Excusal**

Under the Juries Act 1974, various categories of people were excused as of right from jury service if they did not wish to serve. This included:

- any person who had served on a jury within the preceding two years;
- MPs and MEPs;
- members of the Armed Forces;
- doctors, dentists, nurses, and vets;
- members of religious societies or orders.

Following enactment of the Criminal Justice Act 2003, however, the only people entitled to be excused as of right now are:

- any person who had served on a jury within the preceding two years (s.8 of the 1974 Act);
- members of the Armed Forces (and even here it will require a certificate from the individual's commanding officer that it would 'be prejudicial to the efficiency of the service if that member were to be required to be absent from duty' (s.9 of the 1974 Act)).

Hence, MPs, doctors, dentists, nurses, and vets all lost their entitlement to automatic excusal. Do you agree with Parliament that MPs, doctors, dentists, nurses, and vets should now be required to serve on a jury, with no guarantee of excusal?

Persons may have their jury duty excused or deferred at the discretion of the Jury Central Summoning Bureau (JCSB) if they can show 'good reason'. A Home Office research study in 1999, based on a sample of 50,000 people summoned for jury service, found that 38 per cent of them were excused at the judge's discretion. The study found that the most common reasons were:

- medical (40 per cent);
- care of children and elderly relatives (20 per cent);
- work/financial reasons (20 per cent);
- non-residence (9 per cent);
- being a student (6 per cent);
- transport problems (1 per cent);
- others (4 per cent).

10.2.5 **The process of selection**

Juries are selected from the electoral register. This is designed to ensure a random selection. In *R v Sheffield Crown Court, ex parte Brownlow* [1980] QB 530, Lord Denning MR said:

> Our philosophy is that the jury should be selected at random—from a panel of persons who are nominated at random. We believe that 12 persons selected at random are likely to be a cross-section of the people as a whole—and thus represent the view of the common man . . . The parties must take them as they come.

The case of *R v Salt* [1996] Crim LR 517 provides an interesting illustration of this. The defendant was convicted of burglary but appealed after it emerged that one of the jurors was the son of a court usher, who had been asked by his father to serve on D's jury owing to a shortfall in prospective jurors. D's conviction was quashed. The Court of Appeal actually denied that a random selection policy, as such, existed, but did state that every practicable effort should be made to make the selection random. This was not the case in D's trial.

However, the policy of random selection is not without problems, as certain groups in society (for example young people, students, and members of ethnic minority groups) tend to be under-represented on the electoral register—and hence on juries too. However, some of the problems were alleviated (if not removed) by the introduction in late 2000 of the JCSB computerised system, which now handles all jury summonses.

In his *Review of the Criminal Courts* (2001), Auld LJ recommended that '[q]ualification for jury service should remain the same, save that entitlement to, rather than actual, entry on an electoral role should be a criterion. Potential jurors should be identified from a combination of a number of public registers and lists.' Something similar to this system operates in many American states, whereby driving licence records are used as a means of identifying potential jurors. After all, many people of voting age hold driving licences but are not registered to vote; these potential jurors will never be called for jury service under the present system.

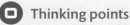

Thinking points

How 'random' is random selection? Could the jury selection process be improved?

1. Is there really 'random' selection of the jury in England?
2. How might the selection process be improved?

10.3 Challenges to jury membership

10.3.1 Challenge 'for cause'

Both prosecution and defence have the right to challenge all or any of the jurors 'for cause'. Challenges 'for cause' are very rare, mainly because the defence has very little information on which to base a challenge and challenges have to be based on a 'foundation of fact' (*R v Chandler* [1964] 2 QB 322). Since 1973, only jurors' names and addresses are known to the defence (prior to that date, jurors' occupations were also known). The only guidance provided by the 1974 Act is s.12 (4), which simply states that '[t]he fact that a person summoned to serve on a jury is not qualified to serve shall be a ground of challenge for cause; but subject to that . . . nothing in this Act affects the law relating to challenge of jurors'.

Useful guidance as to when challenge for cause may exist comes from the Supreme Court of Canada. In *R v Williams* [1998] 1 SCR 1128, McLachlin CJ stated that prejudice might occur in four situations:

- **Interest prejudice:** when jurors may have a direct stake in the trial due to their relationship to the defendant, victim, witnesses, or outcome.

- **Specific prejudice:** when a juror has attitudes and beliefs about the particular case that may render them incapable of deciding guilt or innocence with an impartial mind. These attitudes and beliefs may arise from personal knowledge of the case, publicity through mass media, or public discussion and rumour in the community.
- **Generic prejudice:** when a juror holds stereotypical attitudes about the defendant, victims, witnesses, or the nature of the crime itself. Bias against a racial or ethnic group or against persons charged with sex abuse are examples of this.
- **Conformity prejudice:** when the case is of significant interest to the community, causing a juror to perceive that there is strong community feeling about a case coupled with an expectation as to the outcome.

In the US, by way of contrast, the jury are openly and routinely questioned about a whole range of issues—their occupations, political or religious beliefs, and so on—in order to eliminate bias. This process is known as 'voir dire' and can take hours, days, or even weeks. The examination of the jury in the trial of Jack Ruby for shooting Lee Harvey Oswald, the alleged assassin of President John F. Kennedy in Dallas in 1964, took fifteen days. That was nothing compared to the vetting of the jury for the trial of O. J. Simpson for allegedly stabbing to death his ex-wife and a friend of hers; this vetting took forty days (26 September to 4 November 1994). Both prosecution and defence (in criminal trials) and claimant and defendant (in civil trials) can then employ an unlimited number of challenges for cause to 'strike' unsuitable jurors. Both sides also have a limited number of peremptory challenges (see 10.3.3).

The voir dire is designed to produce juries that are unbiased. However, as well as being very time-consuming (and hence expensive), it has another obvious weakness: it is open to abuse by counsel seeking to secure a favourable jury. Alistair Bonnington ('The Jury: A Suitable Case for Treatment?' (1995) NLJ 847), commenting on the use of voir dire in civil trials in the US, pointed out:

> Now specialised firms have been set up to advise parties on jury selection techniques. They argue strongly that this work . . . will lead to the result desired by their client in virtually every case—in other words, the court process itself doesn't matter at all if you select the right jurors.

The Chief Justice of Canada was moved to speak out against the American voir dire system. In *R v Find* [2001] 1 SCR 863, McLachlin CJ said that voir dire 'treats all members of the jury pool as presumptively suspect'. She observed that 'prospective jurors are frequently subjected to extensive questioning, often of a highly personal nature' and that it was 'unclear that the American system produces better juries' than other systems, including the one in England and Wales.

However, two articles written by British lawyers who witnessed voir dire at first hand were much more positive about the US system. According to Mark George ('Jury Selection, Texas Style' (1988) NLJ 438), jury selection proceeded 'on a rational and logical basis' and the jurors excluded—even those removed peremptorily—would have known that 'there was some reasoning behind their rejection'. Similarly, Richard May ('Jury Selection in the USA: Are there Lessons to be Learned?' [1998] Crim LR 270) commented that the 'care with which the proceedings were undertaken was impressive and leads one to ask whether enough is done in England to ensure that juries are unbiased'. However, in *R v Tracey Andrews* [1999] Crim LR 156, the Court of Appeal came out against introducing voir dire in England and Wales, on the basis that it contradicted the principle of random selection.

Thinking points

Would the American system of 'voir dire' be better than the current English system?

1. Compare and contrast the English system of jury challenges with the American system of voir dire.
2. Are there any arguments in favour of voir dire being introduced into England and Wales?

10.3.2 Challenge by the prosecution

The Crown may ask one or more potential jurors to 'stand by' before they take the juror's oath. Where this happens, the juror is moved to the back of the queue of potential jurors for that trial. No reason need be given, but the situations in which the Attorney General has authorised the use of 'stand-by' are restricted, especially since the defence lost its power of peremptory challenge in 1988 (see later at 10.3.3). Guidelines issued by the Attorney General provide that 'it has been customary' for Crown prosecutors to invoke stand-by only 'sparingly and in exceptional circumstances . . . on the basis of clearly defined and restrictive criteria'. Furthermore, the 'prosecution should not use its right in order to influence the overall composition of a jury or with a view to tactical advantage'.

Two examples of circumstances in which it would be 'proper' for the Crown to exercise its stand-by power are given in the Guidelines. The first is where a prospective juror is revealed to be 'manifestly unsuitable', for example if the case is complex and the juror is illiterate. The second is where a 'jury check' has revealed information justifying exercise of the right to stand by. One such case was *R v McCann and Others* (1991) 92 Cr App R 239, in which three Irish nationals were charged with conspiracy to murder the then Northern Ireland Secretary, Tom King. Because of the national security implications of the case, the Attorney General authorised a jury check and one juror was stood down as a result. The defendants were convicted and appealed, arguing that 'stand-by' was: (a) contrary to the principle of random selection; (b) unconstitutional; and (c) unfair, in that it gave the prosecution an advantage. However, the appeal was dismissed on this ground. Beldam LJ said that the Attorney General's guidelines were both a 'self-imposed restraint on the Attorney General's right of stand-by and in certain circumstances a safeguard for the interests of an accused'.

An example of what could happen if stand-by powers are not restricted occurred in Canada in the case of *R v Biddle* (1995) 96 CCC (3d) 321. The defendant (B) was charged with four counts of assault on women. He was convicted by an all-female jury, which itself is unobjectionable; however, prosecution counsel had set out to empanel an all-female jury and succeeded in doing so by virtue of the standby power given to them under Canadian criminal procedure rules. B successfully appealed to the Supreme Court, albeit on another ground. Interestingly, some of the judges who commented on the stand-by issue did not think that it was necessarily unfair on the defendant. L'Heureux-Dubé J stated that making findings of bias on the basis of 'assumed stereotypical reactions based on gender' was 'dangerous [and] contrary to our concepts of equality and individuality'. She held that there was nothing in the circumstances of the case that lifted the submission that an all-female jury could give rise to a reasonable apprehension of bias 'above the level of unwarranted stereotyping'.

10.3.3 **Abolition of the defence 'peremptory challenge'**

The right of the defence to challenge jurors 'without cause', otherwise known as the 'peremptory challenge', was abolished by s.118 of the Criminal Justice Act 1988. The Committee on Fraud Trials (the Roskill Committee) had recommended the abolition of the peremptory challenge in 1986 on the basis that it was being abused, for example by removing someone who looked like they might understand and/or sympathise with the prosecution and replacing them with someone who looked less likely to understand the case and/or more likely to sympathise with the defence; another ground was that it could upset and/or antagonise rejected jurors. There was also the danger that the peremptory challenge could be abused in cases where the race and/or gender of the accused was a possible factor. As counsel for the defence had little information about prospective jurors when making peremptory challenges, this encouraged the application of stereotypes. The Committee's report concluded that '[t]he public, the press and many legal practitioners now believe that this ancient right is abused cynically and systematically to manipulate cases towards a desired result. We conclude that . . . such manipulation is wholly unacceptable and must be stopped.' This recommendation was duly taken up by the government and then by Parliament when enacting the 1988 Act.

Thinking points

Why was 'peremptory challenge' abolished? And why did the defence lose the right to challenge, but not the Crown?

Up to 1988 it was possible for the defence in a criminal trial to challenge a juror without cause—a 'peremptory challenge'. Was it right to abolish peremptory challenges? Should the Crown's right of 'stand-by' be removed as well?

10.3.4 Challenge to the array

Under s.12 (6) of the Juries Act 1974, the entire jury may be challenged (known as 'challenge to the array') if the official who summoned them was 'biased or acted improperly'. An unsuccessful 'challenge to the array' was brought in *R v Danvers* [1982] Crim LR 680, which is discussed at 10.5.

10.4 Jury vetting

In general terms, jury vetting refers to the covert investigation of potential jurors in order to assess their suitability for a particular trial. More specifically, jury vetting is a two-stage process. First, vetting involves the police checking potential jurors' records for previous criminal convictions (if any). Second, in limited circumstances, a further investigation by the security services may be required.

10.4.1 Police vetting

In *R v Sheffield Crown Court, ex parte Brownlow* [1980] QB 530, the Court of Appeal delivered a damning putdown of jury vetting. Both Lord Denning MR and Shaw LJ were adamant that it should not be introduced into English law, mainly on constitutional grounds. However, the Court of Appeal has subsequently endorsed the practice in *R v Mason* [1981] QB 881. Lawton LJ stated that standard jury vetting by the police was necessary if only to ensure that disqualified persons—essentially those with criminal convictions—are excluded from juries.

He concluded that prosecutors may 'consider that a juror with a conviction for burglary would be unsuitable to sit on a jury trying a burglar; and if he does so he can exercise the Crown's rights [of stand-by]. Many persons, but not burglars, would probably think that he should.'

10.4.2 Further vetting in 'exceptional cases'

In guidelines issued by the Attorney General in 1988, two 'exceptional types of case of public importance' are identified as justifying jury checks going beyond routine police investigation of criminal records. These are stated to be justified 'in the interests of both justice and the public'. They are:

- cases involving national security;
- terrorism cases.

The particular aspects of these cases which may justify 'extra precautions' are: (a) in security cases, a danger that a juror may make an 'improper use' of sensitive evidence; (b) in both security and terrorism cases, the 'danger that a juror's political beliefs are so biased as to go beyond normally reflecting the broad spectrum of views and interests in the community, to reflect the extreme views of sectarian interest or pressure groups to a degree which might interfere with his fair assessment of the facts of the case or lead him to exert improper pressure on his fellow jurors'.

10.5 The ethnic composition of the jury

The Court of Appeal has turned down several claims to a 'right' to a multi-racial jury, stressing the overriding importance of random selection. The leading case is *R v Ford* [1989] QB 868, where Lord Lane CJ said that 'such a principle cannot be correct, for it would depend on an underlying premise that jurors of a particular racial origin or holding particular religious beliefs are incapable of giving an impartial verdict'. This is in line with the majority of earlier authorities on the point, in which ethnic minority defendants were refused permission to have their all-white or predominantly white jury replaced or modified in order to ensure more ethnic minority jurors. In one such case, *R v Danvers* [1982] Crim LR 680, it was argued unsuccessfully that an all-white jury could not comprehend the mental and emotional atmosphere in which black families in England lived.

Two cases took a different view. *R v Binns and Others* [1982] Crim LR 522, 823 involved twelve young, male defendants, all but one of whom was of West Indian origin. The judge and the prosecution accepted the proposition that the jury should contain a reasonable proportion of black people. Eventually, a jury was sworn in containing one young man and two middle-aged women of West Indian origin and one young Asian man. All of the defendants were acquitted. *R v Thomas and Others* (1989) 88 Cr App R 370 involved four defendants of Afro-Caribbean origin charged with murder and wounding with intent. The alleged murder victim was white. The alleged wounding victim was African. When the Old Bailey jury appeared they were all white. At the instigation of the defence, the trial judge ruled that he did have a power to stand by jurors in order to achieve a community balance, but that this power was to be 'used sparingly and in very exceptional circumstances'. He then ruled that the present case was not exceptional; the offences charged were not confined to the black community but could be and frequently were committed by all racial groups. He concluded by saying that he was not persuaded that 'an *à la carte* or specially selected jury' was required. However, both *R v Binns and Others* and *R v Thomas and Others* were disapproved of in *R v Ford*, in the latter case for suggesting that judges had even an 'exceptional' power to interfere with randomly selected juries to ensure a racial balance.

In 1993, the Runciman Commission recommended that in some cases race *should* be taken into account. It suggested that either counsel should be able to apply to the judge for a multi-racial (that is, up to three people from ethnic minorities) jury. The judge would only grant this if the case had some special feature. More recently, in his *Review of the Criminal Courts of England and Wales*, Sir Robin Auld, a senior judge of the Criminal Division of the Court of Appeal, recommended that '[p]rovision should be made to enable ethnic minority representation on juries where race is likely to be relevant to an important issue in the case'. However, in its *Justice for All* White Paper (2002) the government rejected this proposal without explaining why it had done so, other than to say that 'we have concluded that it would be wrong to interfere with the composition of the jury in these cases'. Objections can be advanced against the Runciman/Auld proposals on two grounds: (a) objections in principle; and (b) objections in practice.

10.5.1 **Objections in principle**

On the first point it can be said that the Runciman/Auld proposals seem to presume that an all-white jury would be unable to return an unbiased verdict in a case involving a defendant from a minority ethnic group (see the extract from the judgment in *Ford* earlier). Another objection is based on the 'floodgates' argument. Suppose that the law did allow a black, Asian, or any ethnic minority defendant to request, or even demand, that an all-white jury be modified so as to include some ethnic minority jurors. Would the law then be vulnerable to reform demands that other minority groups should have the same rights?

On this point, in *R v McCalla* [1986] Crim LR 335, the defendant, a young black man, was charged with conspiracy to rob. He applied for the jury to be 'racially balanced' or, alternatively, to have a minimum of two black members. The basis for the application was that only black jurors could fully appreciate the way in which the police treat young black people. Without such appreciation, he argued, he could not expect to receive a fair trial, as the main thrust of his defence amounted to a challenge to the evidence of white police officers. This argument was rejected by the trial judge, who said that it would be wrong in principle to allow a defendant to stipulate the kind of jury to try him. If allowed in this case, the judge argued, it would be capable of 'infinite' extension to other minority groups, such as homosexuals, Freemasons, militant feminists, alcoholics, members of extreme political groups, and even criminals. The trial judge concluded that such a 'fundamental change' in the way juries are made up was not for judicial action but for Parliament.

10.5.2 **Objections in practice**

There are also practical objections to the proposals. Another reason given by the trial judge for rejecting the defendant's request in *R v McCalla* (1986) was that it would be impractical for the jury panel to be artificially enlarged in order to ensure that a 'proper' proportion of its members were black (or indeed from any minority ethnic group). Other practical objections relate to the details of the Auld proposal, which are set out in the questions on the Auld Review proposal next.

The Auld Review proposal

1. What does 'ethnic minority representation' actually mean?
2. Would an Afro-Caribbean defendant (for example) be entitled to Afro-Caribbean jurors, or would jurors of any ethnic minority group (that is, not necessarily the same ethnic minority group as the defendant) suffice?

3. In which cases would it be that 'race is likely to be relevant'?
4. What test could be adopted to establish whether or not an issue is 'important'?

The Court of Appeal confirmed the correctness of the decision in *Ford* in *R v Smith (Lance Percival)* [2003] EWCA Crim 283, [2003] 1 WLR 2229. Smith, who was black, was charged with various offences, including causing grievous bodily harm with intent. The alleged victim was white. The jury at Preston Crown Court was all-white. At trial Smith did not raise any concerns about the jury but, after conviction, he appealed that he had been denied a fair trial, contrary to the guarantee of a fair trial in Article 6 of the ECHR. However, the Court of Appeal found that the trial was nevertheless fair. Giving judgment, Pill LJ said:

> We do not accept that it was unfair for the defendant to be tried by a randomly selected all-white jury or that the fair-minded and informed observer would regard it as unfair. We do not accept that, on the facts of this case, the trial could only be fair if members of the defendant's race were present on the jury. It was not a case where a consideration of the evidence required knowledge of the traditions or social circumstances of a particular racial group. The situation was an all too common one, violence late at night outside a club, and a randomly selected jury was entirely capable of trying the issues fairly and impartially. Public confidence is not impaired by the composition of this jury.

Pill LJ thought that the 'wider the experience of jurors and the deeper their wisdom the greater assistance it will give them in their deliberations', but this was not enough to make Smith's jury unfair.

Thinking point

Should race be a factor in jury selection?

At one point, Pill LJ states: 'It was not a case where a consideration of the evidence required knowledge of the traditions or social circumstances of a particular racial group.' Does this imply that, where a case did require such knowledge, the outcome may be different? If so, in which cases might such knowledge be required?

10.6 Jury intimidation or 'tampering'

10.6.1 Juries in England and Wales

The problem of jury intimidation or tampering (or 'nobbling', as it is sometimes called) led to the suspension of jury trials for terrorist offences in Northern Ireland in 1973 (see 10.6.2). It has caused problems in England too. In 1982, several Old Bailey trials had to be stopped because of attempted 'tampering'—one after seven months. In 1984, jurors in the Brinks-Mat trial had to have police protection to and from the court, and their telephone calls intercepted. In 1994, a four-month fraud trial at Southwark Crown Court was abandoned. Eventually, Parliament acted.

- Section 54 of the Criminal Procedure and Investigations Act 1996 allows for new prosecutions where 'tainted acquittals' are produced (that is, acquittals made by juries that had been intimidated). However, this provision has never been employed.
- Section 44 of the Criminal Justice Act 2003 allows the prosecution to apply to the court for a judge-only trial, which will be granted if two conditions are satisfied:
  - there is 'evidence of a real and present danger that jury tampering would take place' (s.44(4));
  - the 'likelihood that [jury tampering] would take place would be so substantial as to make it necessary in the interests of justice for the trial to be conducted without a jury' (s.44(5)).

Section 44 was invoked for the first time in England in *R v Twomey and Others* [2009] EWCA Crim 1035, [2010] 1 WLR 630. The case started with an armed robbery at Heathrow Airport in February 2004. In 2007, three men stood trial but after more than six months the number of jurors had dwindled to ten, and they were unable to reach a unanimous verdict. They were discharged and a retrial started in the summer of 2008, this time with four defendants. Some six months later, in December 2008, the prosecution informed the trial judge of evidence that approaches had been made to two of the jurors. The jury was again discharged and a second retrial ordered. At this point, the prosecution applied for that trial to be conducted without a jury. The trial judge accepted that a serious attempt at jury tampering had occurred. However, because of the importance of the issues raised, a senior circuit judge, Calvert-Smith J, was brought in to decide whether to invoke s.44. He found that there was a 'real and present danger' that jury tampering would happen again at the retrial. However, he also ruled that a jury protection 'package' involving more than thirty police officers and costing around £1.5million would reduce the risk of jury tampering to an acceptable level. He therefore rejected the application. The prosecution appealed and, in June 2009, the Court of Appeal held that both conditions in s.44 had been met and therefore allowed the appeal. The retrial was ordered to take place without a jury.

The standard of proof

The Court said that, because s.44 applies to criminal proceedings, the criminal standard of proof had to be met for both conditions.

The Human Rights Act 1998 and the right to a fair trial

The Court of Appeal stated very clearly that ordering Crown Court trial by judge alone did not infringe the right to a fair trial by an independent and impartial tribunal that is encapsulated by Article 6 of the ECHR. A judge-only trial ensured all of the necessary procedural safeguards would be met. Lord Judge CJ stated:

> [It] is important to emphasise that . . . the process of dispensing with a jury in a case where it is established that a jury trial is likely to be abused or subverted, the end result is not an unfair trial, but a trial by judge alone, where the necessary procedural safeguards available in a trial by jury are and remain available to the defendant. It therefore does not follow from the hallowed principle of trial by jury that trial by judge alone, when ordered, would be unfair or improperly prejudicial to the defendant. The trial would take place before an independent tribunal and, as it seems to us, for the purposes of article 6 of the European Convention for the Protection of Human Rights and Fundamental Freedoms, it is irrelevant whether the tribunal is judge and jury or judge alone.

The first condition: 'real and present danger'

Lord Judge CJ offered the following guidance on the operation of the first condition in s.44(4), that there must be a 'real and present danger' that jury tampering may take place:

> The first condition addresses the risk that jury tampering may take place at any stage of the trial before the jury has returned their verdict. The real and present danger to be addressed therefore relates to the entire trial process. Where the court is sure that there is a real and present danger that the right to jury trial will be abused or misused by jury tampering, the first condition is established.

Applying these principles, Lord Judge CJ concluded that the first condition was 'emphatically established'.

The second condition: alternative measures to judge-only trial

The second condition in s.44(5) requires that, after making due allowance for any reasonable steps which might minimise the danger of jury tampering, the judge should be sure that there would be a sufficiently high likelihood of jury tampering to make it necessary to have a trial by judge alone. On this issue, Lord Judge CJ referred to a case in the Northern Ireland Court of Appeal *R v Mackle and Others* [2008] NI 183, where s.44 had already been applied. That court had stated that 'the feasibility of measures, the cost of providing them, the logistical difficulties that they may give rise to, and the anticipated duration of any necessary precautions' were all relevant matters to be considered in deciding whether the second condition had been met. The court in *Mackle and Others* had further decided that it was relevant to consider whether the level of police protection required in order to counter the threat of jury tampering might 'affect unfavourably the way in which the jury approached its task. If a misguided perception was created in the minds of the jury by the provision of high level protection this would plainly sound on the reasonableness of such a step.' In *Twomey and Others*, Lord Judge CJ stated:

> We respectfully agree with this approach, and in the course of reaching our own conclusion, we examined some of the possible measures to ensure jury protection. We further examined their likely impact on the ordinary lives of the jurors, performing

> their public responsibilities, and considered whether, in some cases at any rate, even the most intensive protective measures for individual jurors would be sufficient to prevent the improper exercise of pressure on them through members of their families who would not fall within the ambit of the protective measures.

Lord Judge CJ concluded that the protection 'package' identified by Calvert-Smith J would not obviate the risk. A more extensive protection 'package' involving more than eighty police officers and costing around £6 million would be required, but even that did 'not sufficiently address the potential problem of interference with jurors through their families'. Lord Judge CJ stated that even if it were accepted that the more extensive package dealt with 'the dangers posed to the integrity of trial by jury, it would be unreasonable to impose that package with its drain on financial resources and police manpower on the police, and, no less important, it would be totally unfair to impose the additional burdens consequent on the deployment of this package on individual jurors'. Therefore, the second condition was also established.

Defence rights to challenge the trial judge

The Criminal Justice Act 2003 allows the defence to make 'representations' to the trial judge when he or she is considering whether to discharge a jury and/or to proceed to judge-only trial in alleged jury-tampering cases. Lord Judge CJ considered whether this right meant that the Crown had to disclose all of its evidence of jury tampering to the defence. The answer was no, because some of the evidence might be extremely sensitive. In Lord Judge's words, 'Experience suggests that the seriousness of jury tampering problems is usually proportionate to the seriousness of the alleged criminality'—meaning that jury tampering is more likely in cases involving organised crime and/or terrorism. Disclosing all of the Crown's evidence of jury tampering in such cases would be very dangerous for the wider community. Lord Judge CJ said:

> In short, the process [under s.44] could not apply where the actual or potential interference with the jury was of the most serious or sophisticated kind, and where, for example, disclosure of the evidence might imperil life or health or involve the disclosure of police operational evidence or methodology which, if disclosed, would be of considerable interest to the criminal world and damaging to the public interest. In such cases, faced with an order for disclosure, the Crown would be left with no alternative but to discontinue the prosecution. If so, the objective of the jury tampering would have succeeded. In short, therefore, we reject the submission that the evidence relied on by the Crown, or the bulk of it, must always be disclosed.

The implications for the trial judge

Lord Judge CJ also considered what a trial judge should do after having identified jury tampering, deciding that the provisions of s.44 are satisfied, and therefore discharging the jury. There were two options: (a) proceed directly to a judge-only trial with the same judge, or (b) terminate the trial (effectively forcing the CPS to bring a retrial, possibly in front of a different judge). Lord Judge CJ stated that the former option was preferable:

> [Given] that one of the purposes of [s.44] is to discourage jury tampering, and given also the huge inconvenience and expense for everyone involved in a re-trial, and simultaneously to reduce any possible advantage accruing to those who are responsible for jury tampering or for whose perceived benefit it has been arranged by others, and to ensure that trials should proceed to verdict rather than end abruptly in the discharge of the jury, save in unusual circumstances, the judge faced with this problem should order not only the discharge of the jury but that he should continue the trial.

This very issue arose subsequently in *R v S* [2009] EWCA Crim 2377, [2010] 1 All ER 1084. The trial judge in that case had decided that, following evidence of jury tampering, the s.44 conditions were satisfied. He had discharged the jury but decided to continue as the judge in a judge-only trial. The appellant, S, had challenged that decision. The Court of Appeal in *S* allowed the appeal, but it did point out that the case was 'unusual' and 'indeed an extreme case'.

Twomey and Others: the aftermath

Following the Court of Appeal's ruling, the first Crown Court criminal trial in England and Wales without jurors for more than 350 years duly took place at the Old Bailey in March 2010. At the end of the trial, Treacy J convicted all four defendants of robbery, and three were also convicted of possession of a firearm with intent to commit robbery. Appeals against conviction were subsequently dismissed by the Court of Appeal (*R v Twomey and Others* [2011] EWCA Crim 8, [2011] 1 WLR 1681) and the European Court of Human Rights (*Twomey and Others v UK* (2013) 57 EHRR SE15). The Strasbourg court noted that although 'several' signatory states to the ECHR provided for jury trials, not all did so, and that 'there is no right under Article 6 of the Convention to be tried before a jury'. The Court stated that trial with a judge and jury and trial with a judge alone were 'two forms of trial which are in principle equally acceptable under Article 6'. For an excellent summary and discussion of the issues raised in *Twomey and Others* see Nick Taylor's case note in *Criminal Law Review* ([2010] Crim LR 82).

In *R v J and Others* [2010] EWCA Crim 1755, [2011] 1 Cr App R 5, the Court of Appeal held that a trial judge's decision to order a judge-only trial was wrong, on the basis that the condition in s.44(5) had not been met. The appeal court decided that, because the trial (for conspiracy to pervert the course of justice) was only estimated to last for two weeks, any protective measures needed to safeguard the jury against tampering would not 'impose an unacceptable burden on the jurors by intruding for a prolonged period on their ordinary lives'. Lord Judge CJ emphasised that judge-only trial must remain the 'decision of last resort' and hence that a trial judge had to be 'sure' that the conditions in the Act had been met.

In *R v Guthrie and Others* [2011] EWCA Crim 1338, [2011] 2 Cr App R 20, the four appellants were facing charges of six counts of conspiracy to defraud, at Wood Green Crown Court in London. During deliberations, it emerged that jury tampering had taken place, albeit involving tampering carried out by a third party. Nevertheless, the trial judge decided to discharge the jury and to continue the trial on her own. The appellants appealed, unsuccessfully, against that decision. In the Court of Appeal, Lord Judge CJ began by pointing out that the issues in a case such as *R v Twomey* (2009) (where the trial judge has to decide whether a trial can *start* without a jury) and those in cases such as *R v S* (2009) and the present case (where a jury has been discharged and the question was whether to *continue* without a jury) were 'not identical'. In the latter type of case, s.46(3) of the Criminal Justice Act 2003 applied. This states that:

> [w]here the judge, after considering any such representations, discharges the jury, he may make an order that the trial is to continue without a jury if, but only if, he is satisfied (a) that jury tampering has taken place, and (b) that to continue the trial without a jury would be fair to the defendant or defendants.

Lord Judge CJ stated:

> Nothing in the legislation suggests that the trial judge who has made findings that the pre-conditions to the discharge of the jury and the continuation of the trial are satisfied must then recuse himself. Such a proposition would effectively extinguish the power created by s.46 (3). It would be strange if it were possible for a criminal or group of criminals to take extreme steps to undermine the process of trial by jury, and then to argue that judge who had made the necessary findings should not continue the trial.

Lord Judge CJ added that, although there were situations (for example where the trial judge had considered material on public interest immunity grounds which bore on the entire conduct of the prosecution) in which it might be right for the trial judge to disqualify him- or herself, the 'normal approach' was that the case should continue with the same judge. The Court of Appeal also decided that the provisions in the 2003 Act were not limited to 'serious' criminal activity, nor were they confined to cases involving 'serious' intimidation. Finally, there was no need to ascribe responsibility for jury tampering to each, or indeed any, of the defendants in any given trial. The 2003 Act was concerned with the trial process, not the behaviour of the defendant(s). Applying these principles in *Guthrie and Others*, it was therefore irrelevant that:

- the charges faced by the appellants were not especially serious;
- the tampering did not involve 'serious' intimidation;
- the tampering had been carried out by a third party (in any case, a 'personal link' between the third party and one of the appellants was 'amply established').

Section 46(3) was invoked again in *R v McManaman* [2016] EWCA Crim 3, [2016] 1 WLR 1096. M was on trial for rape at Liverpool Crown Court. During the trial, M's nephew, B, who had been in the public gallery, sent a Facebook friend request to one of the jurors (Miss D). She informed the court. Although B told police that he had contacted Miss D simply because he found her attractive, the trial judge, Hatton J, dismissed that explanation as 'fanciful'. Instead, Hatton J decided that B's motivation had been either to intimidate Miss D or to develop a relationship with her to interfere with the judicial process. Hatton J concluded that (a) there had been jury tampering and (b) it had been with M's knowledge or at least his acquiescence. He therefore discharged the jury but exercised his powers under s.46(3) to continue the trial without a jury. M was convicted and appealed, contending that (a) Hatton J could not have been sure to the criminal standard of proof that B's approach to Miss D had been a deliberate attempt to frighten or otherwise influence her; (b) it was unfair to remove M's right to a jury trial unless *his* involvement in the tampering was proved. The appeal was dismissed: (a) on the evidence, Hatton J had been entitled to decide that the explanation given by B was 'fanciful' and that he had deliberately sought out Miss D; (b) it was not necessary to prove that M was involved in the jury tampering. Lord Thomas CJ said that the 2003 Act only 'requires proof of jury *tampering*; it does not require proof of tampering *by the defendant*' (emphasis added). Indeed, jury tampering would 'ordinarily' be conducted by someone other than the defendant. Lord Thomas said that 'in such cases, the objective of the legislation is to prevent the tampering, it matters not that the defendant is not involved or not proved to be involved'.

10.6.2 **Criminal juries in Northern Ireland**

Between 1973 and 2007, all cases in Northern Ireland involving (or potentially involving) terrorism were heard by a single Crown Court judge without a jury. These were called 'Diplock courts' after Lord Diplock, who chaired the Commission that recommended this form of trial. The Northern Ireland (Emergency Provisions) Act 1973 (subsequently replaced by the Northern Ireland (Emergency Provisions) Act 1991 and most recently s.75 of the Terrorism Act 2000) created a presumption against jury trial in respect of various offences, including murder. Diplock courts were designed to deal primarily with the problems caused by sectarian 'troubles' involving Republican and Loyalist terrorism offences. Diplock courts were justified for two reasons:

- the threat of intimidation—not just of individual jurors but members of their family;
- the danger of perverse verdicts by partisan jurors—for example, if a Catholic defendant was to be tried by a jury consisting predominantly of Protestant jurors (or vice versa).

Although designed as a means of allowing—as far as possible—unbiased trials involving, or potentially involving, crimes allegedly committed by organisations such as the IRA (Irish Republican Army) or the UDF (Ulster Defence Force), Diplock courts were used in other cases. In 2005, Abbas Boutrab, an Algerian national, was convicted by a single judge at Belfast Crown Court of possessing and collecting information 'for a purpose connected with the commission, preparation or instigation of an act of terrorism', contrary to s.57 of the Terrorism Act 2000. Boutrab had downloaded information from the internet on how to blow up a passenger jet. According to *The Times* newspaper, Boutrab's case was a landmark because he was the first 'Islamist terrorist' to be tried and convicted using the Diplock system.

In August 2006, however, the British government announced that Diplock courts were to be abolished for the majority of Crown Court trials in Northern Ireland, effective July 2007. According to the *Belfast Telegraph* in an article published in July 2007:

> [T]housands of cases have been tried using the [Diplock] system including the loyalist paramilitary gang, the Shankill Butchers, who were sentenced to life imprisonment in the 1970s for murdering Catholics in north and west Belfast. The number of trials being carried out at the courts has dropped dramatically over the last few years with just 61 cases last year and 49 in 2005.

These reforms were implemented by the Justice and Security (Northern Ireland) Act 2007, effectively bringing Crown Court trials in Northern Ireland into line with England and Wales. However, the Director of Public Prosecutors (DPP) is authorised to order a judge-only trial in Northern Ireland if 'satisfied that there is a risk that the administration of justice might be impaired if the trial were to be conducted with a jury' (s.1(2) of the 2007 Act). In 2016, the DPP ordered a judge-only trial for a former British soldier accused of the attempted murder of an unarmed civilian in County Tyrone, Northern Ireland, in June 1974. The defendant challenged the DPP's decision but it was upheld by the UK Supreme Court (*Re Hutchings' Application for Judicial Review* [2019] UKSC 26). Giving the unanimous judgment of the Supreme Court, Lord Kerr said that:

> [t]aking effective precautions against jury bias presents formidable difficulties. These difficulties are particularly acute in cases which involve attacks on the security forces or where members of the security forces have fired on individuals. Such cases are almost invariably highly charged, and they give rise to strong feelings in both sides of the community. Apprehension that jury trial in such cases might put the goal of a fair trial in peril is unavoidable . . . It is important to focus on the need for a fair trial. Trial by jury is, of course, the traditional mode of trial for serious criminal offences in the United Kingdom. It should not be assumed, however, that this is the unique means of achieving fairness in the criminal process.

10.7 **Juries in serious fraud trials**

One area of jury trials that has attracted considerable attention in recent years is cases of serious fraud. By their very nature, allegations of fraud imply secrecy and deception. The issues involved in such cases tend to be very complex, with much accounting and financial information to be examined. There may also be several defendants. This all means that serious fraud trials are very time-consuming. The

Roskill Committee (1986), the Home Office (1998), and Auld LJ (2001) all examined the use of the jury in these cases, and all broadly concluded (the exact recommendations differed) that jury trials should be at least modified, if not entirely abolished, in serious fraud cases. The Home Office's 1998 consultation paper (*Juries in Serious Fraud Trials*) stated that a single judge offered a 'simple, viable alternative to jury trial' in 'long and complex fraud trials'. However, it also acknowledged that 'jurors could do a good job in complex fraud trials if they were selected in a special way'.

The Home Office proposed two such special selection processes: (a) 'some sort of screening procedure' for jurors; and (b) an 'entirely separate pool of jurors to be summoned exclusively to sit on serious fraud trials'. The latter proposal was acknowledged to be 'more radical and much more difficult'. The government observed that there was 'no lack of precedent for this'. It was observed that District Judges (Magistrates' Court) dealt with summary cases alone and that 'trial by judge alone is the general rule in civil cases in England'. Moreover, the government noted that 'the Northern Ireland experience'—meaning Diplock courts—'provides an example of how such an arrangement can work . . . in relation to serious criminal offences'.

Auld LJ's Review was more radical. It suggested that:

> in serious and complex frauds the nominated trial judge should have the power to direct trial by himself and two lay members drawn from a panel established by the Lord Chancellor for the purpose (or, if the defendant requests, by himself alone).

The panel would comprise people identified as having expertise in financial matters—accountants, auditors, bankers, stockbrokers, and so on. Although this proposal retained some lay involvement in the trial process, it was a significant reduction from twelve randomly selected members of the public to only two people. Perhaps more significantly, this panel would not be deciding guilt or innocence alone (as the present jury does) but would operate alongside the judge.

The Labour government's response, in the *Justice for All* White Paper (2002), accepted the principle of this idea but not the specific proposal. The government stated that 'identifying and recruiting suitable people raises considerable difficulties . . . we propose such cases are tried by a judge sitting alone'. Section 43 of the Criminal Justice Act 2003 implemented this latter proposal. It provided for judge-only trials where

> [t]he complexity of the trial or the length of the trial (or both) is likely to make the trial so burdensome to the members of a jury hearing the trial that the interests of justice require that serious consideration should be given to the question of whether the trial should be conducted without a jury.

However, so controversial were the proposals that the Labour government only secured the approval of Parliament by agreeing not to implement s.43 unless Parliament was given a further opportunity to debate the issue. In the end s.43 was never brought into effect, and it has now been repealed by s.113 of the Protection of Freedoms Act 2012. The Coalition government's explanatory notes accompanying the 2012 Act indicate that this repeal gave effect to their pledge to 'protect historic freedoms through the defence of trial by jury' ('Programme for Government', section 3: civil liberties).

10.7.1 Exclusion of juries from serious fraud trials: summary of the arguments

- Advantages: judge-alone trial saves time at trial because the judge does not have to explain so many matters to the jury. In theory, it should also lessen the risk of bias or outside influence. Judges are expected to explain and justify their decisions, unlike juries, who simply return a verdict of 'guilty' or 'not guilty'. Thus, where a judge reaches a guilty verdict, he or she must justify this decision with reasons; this provides greater transparency to the decision-making process and may give the defence an opportunity to consider an appeal which would not otherwise be possible.
- Disadvantages: judge-alone trial reduces the amount of lay participation in the legal system. There is the possibility that judges sitting alone would become 'case-hardened' or 'prosecution-minded'. The extra burden on the judge may be too onerous. Although he or she would no longer have to direct the jury, the judge would now have to assimilate all the issues of fact *and* reach a verdict. The fact that judges are required to justify their decisions may open up new possibilities for expensive, time-consuming appeals.

10.8 Jury waiver

In his *Review of the Criminal Courts* (2001), Auld LJ proposed that 'defendants in the Crown Court . . . should be entitled with the court's consent to opt for trial by judge alone'. This recommendation is known as 'jury waiver'. In many common law jurisdictions—Australia, Canada, New Zealand, and the US—where trial by jury exists, the defendant may nevertheless waive their 'right' to jury trial and instead opt for trial by a single judge. In *R v Turpin and Siddiqui* [1989] 1 SCR 1296, for example, Wilson J in the Supreme Court of Canada stated that a 'jury trial may not be a benefit and may even be a burden on the accused'. The obvious question to raise in response to this is: why would a defendant entitled to jury trial waive that right? According to the commentators Doran and Jackson ('The Case for Jury Waiver' [1997] Crim LR 155), there are three reasons:

- The notion of a jury as 'defence friendly' is outdated. Although juries may acquit against the evidence, there is a 'worrying phenomenon' of doubtful convictions.
- Judges may be better equipped to analyse certain kinds of evidence. In particular, juries are 'in awe' of scientific evidence and are 'neither willing nor qualified' to be critical of such evidence.

- Judges may be better equipped to handle certain types of issues than juries. A 'common view' among defence counsel was that sexual cases were 'difficult' to defend in front of a jury; they would prefer the case to be dealt with in a 'colder, unemotional fashion'.

Other possibilities involve cases where the defendant could appear unsympathetic or where the evidence was potentially inflammatory (for example, child abuse) or gruesome, where the jury might be shocked into a guilty verdict. Jury waiver may also be appropriate in cases that have attracted pre-trial publicity (especially publicity that was adverse to the accused). Recent examples in England and Wales of such cases include:

- Rosemary West, convicted of the 'Cromwell Street' murders of ten young women and girls, including her own sixteen-year-old daughter Heather;
- Tracie Andrews, convicted of her boyfriend's murder after publicly claiming he had been murdered in a 'road rage' incident by a stranger;
- Dr Harold Shipman, Britain's most prolific serial killer (now deceased).

In many of these cases—including West and Andrews—the defendants appealed against their convictions arguing that the adverse pre-trial publicity prejudiced the jury against them and therefore denied them a fair trial. In all such cases the appeals were dismissed, the Court of Appeal taking the view that warnings given to the respective juries by the trial judges had ensured that justice had been done. In *R v West* [1996] 2 Cr App R 374, for example, Lord Taylor CJ stated that it would be 'absurd' if allegations of murder were 'sufficiently horrendous so as inevitably to shock the nation' that the accused could not be given a fair trial. Of course, no one argues that the defendants should not be tried at all purely because the case has attracted publicity—but does it follow that jury trials will be fair?

A more recent Court of Appeal case dealing with pre-trial publicity is *R v Abu Hamza* [2006] EWCA Crim 2918, [2007] 2 WLR 226. The case involved Abu Hamza, the imam of Finsbury Park Mosque in north London, who was convicted in February 2006 of six counts of soliciting murder (in addition to a number of other offences). On appeal, it was argued that Abu Hamza had not received a fair trial because of 'changes in attitude and public perception in relation to terrorism' following the attacks on New York on 11 September 2001 and London on 7 July 2005. It was contended that the adverse pre-trial media publicity meant that Abu Hamza's trial was unfair. It was argued that the media had led a 'sustained campaign' which was 'almost entirely hostile' and 'couched in particularly crude terms'. However, the appeal was dismissed. Lord Phillips CJ acknowledged that there had been a 'prolonged barrage' of adverse publicity, some of which treated the defendant as 'an ogre'. However, the Lord Chief Justice accepted the trial judge's conclusion that a properly directed jury would be able to return an impartial verdict. Abu Hamza had received a fair trial.

The government agreed with Auld LJ's proposal to introduce jury waiver into English law. The government's *Justice for All* White Paper (2002) stated that 'defendants in the Crown Court should in future have the right to apply to the court for trial by a judge sitting alone. The judge will have discretion whether to grant the application and will have to give reasons for this decision.' The subsequent Criminal Justice Bill, when introduced into Parliament in 2002, stated that if defendants were to apply for waiver, the judge 'must' grant it, subject to a proviso. The judge would be entitled to refuse if 'satisfied that exceptional circumstances exist which make it necessary in the public interest for the trial to be conducted with a jury'. However, by the time the Criminal Justice Act 2003 was passed, the jury waiver reform had been dropped following opposition from Parliament, primarily in the House of Lords. At the time of writing, there seems little political incentive for another attempt at implementing jury waiver.

Thinking points

Should the accused be entitled to 'waive' their right to jury trial?

1. Should the defendant faced with the prospect of trial by jury in the Crown Court be allowed to 'waive' that right? If so, should this be with the consent of the court, the prosecution, both, or neither (in which case it would effectively be 'waiver on demand')?
2. Can you think of any circumstances where the prosecution may object to a defendant seeking to 'waive' trial by jury?
3. When might the judge decide that 'exceptional circumstances . . . in the public interest' (to use the terminology from the Criminal Justice Bill 2002/03) would justify rejecting a plea for jury waiver and, effectively, forcing a reluctant defendant to face a jury?

10.9 Jurors, social media, and the internet

A number of recent cases have highlighted the problems created for the proper administration of justice if jurors succumb to the temptation to either discuss a case on social media or conduct their own online research into the case. In so doing, the jurors risk breaching their obligation to decide the case based solely on the evidence that they see and hear in the courtroom. These cases have now prompted Parliament to intervene, in the form of the creation of a number of new criminal offences in the CJCA 2015, which came into effect in April 2015.

10.9.1 Power of judge to order jurors to surrender electronic communications devices: s.15A, Juries Act 1974 (as amended)

Section 69 of the CJCA 2015 inserted a new provision, s.15A, into the Juries Act 1974. The new provision empowers a trial judge to order members of jury to surrender 'electronic communications devices' such as smartphones or tablets. The power is exercisable at the judge's discretion, and will be available if the judge considers that to do so 'is necessary or expedient in the interests of justice' and that such an order would be 'a proportionate means of safeguarding those interests' (s.15A(2)). Failure to comply would amount to a criminal offence (s.15A(5)). 'Electronic communications device' is defined as 'a device that is designed or adapted for a use which consists of or includes the sending or receiving of signals that are transmitted by means of an electronic communications network' (s.15A(7)).

10.9.2 **New offence of conducting research into a live case: s.20A, Juries Act 1974 (as amended)**

Section 71(1) of the CJCA 2015 inserted a new provision, s.20A, into the Juries Act 1974. The new provision creates an offence of conducting 'research' into a case during the trial period by a member of the jury. The offence will only be committed if the juror 'intentionally seeks information' and 'when doing so, knows or ought reasonably to know that the information is or may be relevant to the case' (s.20A(2)). The ways in which a person may be regarded as having sought information in contravention of s.20A(1) include (but are not limited to) asking a question; searching an electronic database, including by means of the internet; visiting or inspecting a place or object; conducting an experiment; or asking another person to seek the information (s.20A(3)). It would *not* be an offence to seek information 'if the person needs the information for a reason which is not connected with the case' (s.20A(6)), or to seek information from the judge (s.20A(7)(b)), or to seek information 'from another member of the jury, unless the person knows or ought reasonably to know that the other member of the jury contravened this section in the process of obtaining the information' (s.20A(7)(d)). 'Information' which is 'relevant to the case' for the purposes of the offence includes (but is not limited to) information about any of the following: a person involved in events relevant to the case; the trial judge; any other person involved in the trial, whether as a 'lawyer, a witness or otherwise'; the law relating to the case; the law of evidence; or court procedure (s.20A(4)).

The new offence is designed to deal with situations such as that which arose in *Attorney General v Dallas* [2012] EWHC 156 (Admin), [2012] 1 WLR 991. In that case, a juror conducted her own research into the case and, when discovered, was charged with—and convicted of—contempt of court, under s.8(1) of the Contempt of Court Act 1981 (since repealed). This conduct would now be prosecuted under s.20A. In *Dallas*, Lord Judge CJ explained why this conduct attracted criminal liability. He said the juror 'did not merely risk prejudice to the due administration of justice, but she caused prejudice to it . . . The damage to the administration of justice is obvious.' This 'damage' manifested itself in at least five different ways, according to Lord Judge. First, the information which the juror found online, although not adduced in evidence, might have played its part in her verdict. Secondly, she disclosed some or all of that information to her fellow jurors. Thirdly, the complainant had to give evidence of his ordeal again, at the retrial. Fourthly, the time of the other members of the jury was wasted. Finally, the public was put to additional unnecessary expense in paying for the retrial.

10.9.3 New offence of sharing information obtained during prohibited research with other jurors: s.20B, Juries Act 1974 (as amended)

Section 72(1) of the CJCA 2015 inserted a new provision, s.20B, into the Juries Act 1974. Section 20B(1) creates a new offence of intentionally disclosing information obtained during prohibited research (that is, in contravention of the new offence under s.20A, discussed earlier) with other jurors.

The new offence is designed to deal with situations such as that which arose in *Attorney General v Beard* [2013] EWHC 2317 (Admin), [2014] 1 Cr App R 1. In that case, a juror conducted research into the case and then disclosed his findings to another juror. He was charged with, and convicted of, contempt of court, contrary to s.8(1) of the Contempt of Court Act 1981. This conduct would now be prosecuted under s.20B.

10.9.4 New offence of engaging in 'prohibited conduct': s.20C, Juries Act 1974 (as amended)

Section 73(1) of the CJCA 2015 inserted a new provision, s.20C, into the Juries Act 1974. Section 20C(1) creates a new offence of intentionally engaging in 'prohibited conduct', defined as 'conduct from which it may reasonably be concluded that the person intends to try the issue otherwise than on the basis of the evidence presented in the proceedings on the issue' (s.20C(2)). An offence under s.20C(1) is committed whether or not the person knows that the conduct is prohibited conduct (s.20C(3)).

The new offence is designed to deal with situations such as that which arose in the cases of *Attorney General v Fraill and Sewart* [2011] EWHC 1629, [2011] 2 Cr App R 21 and *Attorney General v Davey* [2013] EWHC 2317 (Admin), [2014] 1 Cr App R 1. In the former case, a juror contacted one of the defendants via Facebook and they discussed the case (while it was still ongoing); in the latter case a juror posted a comment on Facebook about how he was going to be able to decide the fate of the accused (who had been accused of sexual activity with a child), whom the juror described as a 'paedophile', even though the case was still ongoing. In both cases the jurors were charged with, and convicted of, contempt of court, contrary to s.8(1) of the Contempt of Court Act 1981. This conduct would now be prosecuted under s.20C.

In *Fraill and Sewart*, Lord Judge CJ explained the underlying principles involved when he said:

> If jurors make their own inquiries into aspects of the trials with which they are concerned, the jury system as we know it, so precious to the administration of criminal justice in this country, will be seriously undermined, and what is more, the public confidence on which it depends will be shaken. The jury's deliberations, and ultimately

> their verdict, must be based—and exclusively based—on the evidence given in court . . . The revolution in methods of communication cannot change these essential principles . . . Information provided by the internet (or any other modern method of communication) is not evidence. Even assuming the accuracy and completeness of this information (which, in reality, would be an unwise assumption) its use by a juror exposes him to the risk of being influenced, even unconsciously, by whatever emerges from the internet. This offends our long-held belief that justice requires that both sides in a criminal trial should know and be able to address or answer any material (particularly material which appears adverse to them) which may influence the verdict.

10.10 **Advantages of jury trials**

10.10.1 **Public participation**

Juries allow the ordinary citizen to take part in the administration of justice, so that verdicts are seen to be those of society rather than the judicial system. Lord Denning has described jury service as giving 'ordinary folk their finest lesson in citizenship'. According to W. R. Cornish, in *The Jury* (1968 at p.255):

> The system has the intrinsic advantage that in drawing upon a steady stream of ordinary citizens it is not only educating them in the work of the courts, but also, since they are generally satisfied with their own performance, sending them back to their ordinary lives with a sense of the fairness and propriety of the judicial process in this country.

A Home Office consultation paper entitled *Juries in Serious Fraud Trials* (1998) postulated that the presence of members of the public on juries offered 'reassurance that the defendant's guilt or innocence is not being determined by the State . . . public involvement in the justice system is the sign of a healthy and democratic society'. Perhaps slightly optimistically—one might even say naively—it was asserted that '[n] ot only is the quality of justice improved by the participation of the public but the community is enriched by it . . . jury trials keep the law in touch with the public and encourage the lawmakers to take account of their wishes'.

The alternative viewpoint has been put forward very forcefully by Darbyshire (1991 at p.746). She argued that this 'romanticism' about juries is 'quite devoid of constitutional or jurisprudential support'. She suggested that 'most of those who justify the jury as the quintessence of lay participation in a lawyer's paradise ignore the massive involvement of lay people'—meaning magistrates—in decision-making in the English legal system.

10.10.2 **Juries are the best judges of facts**

There is an argument that jurors (being, in the main, ordinary members of the public) are better equipped than judges or magistrates to assess issues such as the credibility of witnesses and whether the defendant in a theft trial is dishonest. Many defences in criminal law involve a 'reasonable man' test—diminished responsibility, duress, self-defence . . . who better to undertake this task than jurors? As most jurors only serve once, they should approach their cases relatively fresh and with an open mind, unlike judges and magistrates, who are vulnerable to the argument that they can become 'case hardened'—meaning that they can become cynical, having heard similar arguments in similar cases perhaps over many years. Furthermore, there is a 'strength in numbers' argument, or, put another way, twelve heads are better than three (magistrates) or one (judge). Weight of numbers arguably helps to minimise the possible risks of prejudicial views influencing the verdict.

10.10.3 **Clear separation of responsibility**

It has been argued that juries provide a better balance to proceedings in the trial courts, dividing the responsibilities of the trial into those who determine the law (the judge) and those who determine the facts (the jury).

10.10.4 **Encourages openness and intelligibility**

Because a jury is composed of randomly selected members of the public, the lawyers (especially those acting for the prosecution) have to present their evidence in a manner which the jury can understand. After all, the burden of proof in most matters of criminal law is on the prosecution (the main exceptions being the insanity and diminished responsibility defences), and to get a conviction the Crown needs to persuade the jury of the defendant's guilt 'beyond reasonable doubt'. In other words, if the jury members are confused and do not understand the prosecution case, how can the jury be convinced of the defendant's guilt? Because of this, it should follow that the general public—who may be watching the trial from the public gallery or hearing about the trial on the TV or reading about it in the newspapers—are better able to understand what is going on. There is a risk that replacing the jury either with a single judge, a panel of judges, or some other alternative will encourage the lawyers to present their case in a more specialised, technical way with more legal jargon. This would in turn mean that trials may no longer be readily comprehensible to the public.

10.11 **Disadvantages**

10.11.1 **Cost and time**

Jury trials are much more expensive than trial by magistrates. It has been estimated that an uncontested case in the Crown Court costs five times more than one in the magistrates' court, while a contested Crown Court case costs around eight times as much. Why is there such a dramatic cost disparity? The main reason is time: jury trials are much lengthier than trial by magistrates. The time factor leads to other disadvantages: defendants may spend months on remand awaiting a Crown Court trial, and it can also lead to witnesses' recollection of the events getting weaker. Not everyone agrees that the extra cost and time is a disadvantage, however. According to Heather Hallett QC (*Counsel*, October 1998, p.3), '[a] jury trial is superior to a trial before magistrates and there is a greater chance of seeing justice done at the Crown Court than at the magistrates' court, if only because greater time, trouble and money are spent on jury trials.'

10.11.2 **Risk of perverse verdicts**

Excessive damages awards in civil actions

There are numerous examples of juries in civil trials in the High Court awarding large sums of money in compensation which are often contested and, sometimes, reversed on appeal. The leading cases all involve defamation, where the claimant seeks compensation for damage to their reputation caused by the publication of an untrue statement about them. The leading cases are:

- *Sutcliffe v Pressdram Ltd* [1990] 1 All ER 269—in which Sonia Sutcliffe, the wife of Peter Sutcliffe, the Yorkshire Ripper, was awarded £600,000 against the publishers of *Private Eye* magazine which had published an article suggesting that she had been paid £250,000 by the *Daily Mail* for her story. She denied this claim and sought compensation. The jury's award was overturned on appeal; subsequently, Mrs Sutcliffe accepted £60,000 in out-of-court settlement.
- *Rantzen v Mirror Group Newspapers* [1993] 4 All ER 975—in which Esther Rantzen, the erstwhile TV presenter and founder of the Childline charity, was awarded £250,000 against the publishers of *The People* newspaper for a series of articles which alleged that, despite her knowing that a boys' schoolteacher in Kent was guilty of sexually abusing children, she had nevertheless protected him because of his past services to her in assisting in the preparation of a TV programme about the sexual abuse of children. The award was overturned on appeal, with the Court of Appeal substituting an award of £110,000. Neill LJ said: 'Judged by any objective standards of reasonable compensation or necessity or proportionality the award of £250,000 was excessive.'
- *John v Mirror Group Newspapers* [1996] 2 All ER 35—in which Elton John was awarded £350,000 against the publishers of the *Sunday Mirror* newspaper. He had sued in respect of allegations made in the *Sunday Mirror*, under the headline 'Elton's diet of death', that he was on a fad diet called 'Don't swallow and get thin', whereby he chewed food but spat it out instead of swallowing it. In particular, there were specific allegations that he had been spotted spitting food into a napkin at a dinner in Los Angeles. The jury's award was overturned on appeal, with the Court of Appeal awarding £75,000. The Court described the jury's awards as 'manifestly excessive'. Lord Bingham MR said that it was 'offensive to public opinion,

> and rightly so, that a defamation plaintiff should recover damages for injury to reputation greater, perhaps by a significant factor, than if that same plaintiff had been rendered a helpless cripple or an insensate vegetable'. He added that the time had come 'when judges, and counsel, should be free to draw the attention of juries to these comparisons'.

In *Grobbelaar v News Group Newspapers* [2002] UKHL 40, [2002] 1 WLR 3024, the Court of Appeal took the apparently unprecedented step of reversing a High Court jury's verdict in a defamation case as to liability—not just on the amount of damages. *The Sun* newspaper had published a series of articles in which it claimed that Bruce Grobbelaar, the former Liverpool FC goalkeeper, had fixed football matches for money. The allegations were based on covert video recordings in which Grobbelaar appeared to have confessed to having taken money to 'throw' matches. Grobbelaar was subsequently prosecuted on two counts of corruptly attempting to influence the outcomes of matches. He admitted the comments captured on video were true, but claimed that he had done so as a ruse to help bring those paying the bribes to justice. The Crown Court jury could not agree on a verdict. A retrial was ordered; this time the jury acquitted on one count and failed to agree on the other, whereby a second not guilty verdict was entered.

Grobbelaar then began defamation proceedings against the publishers of *The Sun*. At the end of the trial, the High Court jury found for the claimant and awarded £85,000 damages. *The Sun*'s publishers appealed, inter alia, on the ground that the verdict was perverse. Simon Brown LJ said that the Court of Appeal 'must inevitably be reluctant to find a jury's verdict perverse and anxious not to usurp their function' but that it was 'the experience of all of us that juries from time to time do arrive at perverse verdicts'. He went on to hold that the decision of the High Court jury was 'not merely surprising but unacceptable'; the result was 'an affront to justice'. Thorpe LJ agreed, saying that 'it would be an injustice' to allow the jury's verdict to stand.

On Grobbelaar's appeal to the House of Lords, the Court of Appeal judgment was reversed, and that of the jury reinstated (mostly). The Lords ruled that the task of an appellate court was to seek to interpret the jury's decision and not to take upon itself the determination of factual issues. In the case, there was no justification for concluding that the jury must have acted 'perversely' in making its finding and so the jury's verdict that Grobbelaar had been defamed was reinstated. However, the Lords also ruled that the jury had fallen into serious error in its approach to the amount of damages. Grobbelaar had in fact acted in a way in which no decent or honest footballer would act and which could, if not exposed and stamped on, undermine the integrity of the game. It would be an affront to justice if a court of law were to award substantial damages to a man shown to have acted in such flagrant breach of his legal and moral obligations. Accordingly, the jury's award of damages was quashed and an award of £1 nominal damages substituted.

Criminal trials

Juries can, and do, return verdicts against the evidence (*R v Ponting* [1985] Crim LR 318, discussed earlier, is an example). A 1972 study by McCabe and Purves, *The Jury at Work*, looked at 173 acquittals, and concluded that only fifteen (9 per cent) defied the evidence (the rest being down to a weak prosecution case and/or a credible defence). In 1979, however, a study by Baldwin and McConville—*Jury Trials*, which examined 500 cases (both convictions and acquittals)—found that 25 per cent of the acquittals were questionable. They described jury trial as 'an arbitrary and unpredictable business'.

Darbyshire ('The Lamp that Shows Freedom Lives' [1991] Crim LR 740) is very critical of this facet of the jury system, and in particular the way that it is held up by defenders of the jury as an advantage. She asks (at p.750): 'What business have the jury to be rewriting the law? . . . The jury is an anti-democratic, irrational and haphazard legislator, whose erratic and secret decisions run counter to the rule of law.' She is particularly scathing about other commentators' reaction to a case in which a hot-dog seller was acquitted by a 'sympathetic' jury on a charge of wounding on the ground of provocation—which is, as a matter of law, not a defence to that crime. One such commentator had suggested that the jury 'were saying . . . that provocation ought to be a defence' to wounding, 'and in saying this they would have the support of the bulk of the nation' (M. D. A. Freedman, 'The Jury on Trial' (1981) 34 *Current Legal Problems* 65 at p.93). Darbyshire retorted by asking how the jury, or anyone else for that matter, could know what the 'bulk of the nation' wants. Instead, she supported the following assessment by Duff and Findlay ('The Jury in England: Practice and Ideology' (1982) 10 IJLS 253 at p.258): 'The jury, so irrationally selected, would appear to be a crude engine for the job of checking unpopular laws . . . The jury then may even be counterproductive in such situations, as the legislature may not feel constrained to intervene if they know that harsh or outdated laws are not being strictly applied.' If a jury can acquit despite the evidence, Darbyshire points out, then what is to stop them convicting despite the evidence? The answer is, of course, nothing.

Thinking point

Should 'jury equity' be abolished by Parliament?

In his *Review of the Criminal Courts* (2001), Sir Robin Auld recommended that '[t]he law should be declared, by statute if need be, that juries have no right to acquit defendants in defiance of the law or in disregard of the evidence'. The government, in its response, did not adopt this recommendation. Should juries be required, as Auld LJ suggested, to comply with the law? In other words, should 'jury equity' be abolished by Parliament?

10.11.3 **Racist jurors in criminal trials**

Article 6 of the ECHR confers the right to a fair trial by an impartial tribunal. This provision has been invoked in two cases before the European Court of Human Rights in Strasbourg where at least one juror has faced an accusation of racism: *Gregory v UK* (1998) 25 EHRR 577 and *Sander v UK* (2001) 31 EHRR 44. In *Gregory*, where one juror alleged during the course of the trial that other jurors had been making racist comments and jokes—which was collectively denied by the others—the trial judge allowed the trial to continue albeit after warning the jurors to remember their oath to try the case according to the evidence. The Strasbourg court held that the applicant's Article 6 rights had not been infringed. However, there was a very different result in *Sander*. Here, after similar allegations, one juror admitted he may have made racist comments but denied actually *being* racist. The judge allowed the trial—albeit again after reminding the jurors of their oath—to continue and Sander was convicted. But his appeal to the Strasbourg court was successful (albeit by a majority verdict). The Court held that the trial judge should have discharged the jury and held a retrial. The difference in the two cases appears to be that in *Gregory* there was only an unsubstantiated allegation of racism, whereas in *Sander* one juror did admit making racist comments.

It seems that the timing of allegations of racism is critical. In both *Gregory* and *Sander*, the juror involved raised the allegations during the trial and the appeals related to the judge's response to them. However, when allegations of racism are made after a verdict, it is much more difficult to investigate. You should refer back to the cases of *R v Qureshi* [2001] EWCA Crim 1807, [2002] 1 WLR 518 and *R v Mirza* [2004] UKHL 2, [2004] 2 WLR 201, in which the Court of Appeal and House of Lords, respectively, declared themselves unable to investigate post-verdict allegations of jury impropriety, including allegations of racism. The guilty verdicts in both cases were upheld.

 **Thinking point**

How should the courts deal with evidence of juror prejudice?

Is the decision in *Sander* compatible with the outcomes in the cases of *Qureshi* and *Mirza*, discussed earlier? If there is evidence of jury prejudice, should it matter whether the evidence was raised during the trial (as in *Sander*) or afterwards (as in *Qureshi* and *Mirza*)?

10.11.4 **Compulsory jury service**

While research has shown that many people find jury service a rewarding experience, others may have a negative attitude towards it. This may be because some people see jury service as an obligation rather than a privilege. It may be regarded by some jurors as time-consuming, inconvenient, and even financially disadvantageous. These attitudes may lead to people seeking excusal or deferral. Those who are unsuccessful in getting their jury service excused or deferred may then be resentful and not take their responsibility seriously enough, or try to get the deliberations over with as quickly as possible. For an example of a case where this may have happened, refer back to *Attorney General v Scotcher* [2004] UKHL 36, [2005] 1 WLR 1867, discussed earlier.

10.11.5 **Distress caused to jury members**

Especially in murder, rape, and child abuse cases, the jury has to hear and, sometimes, see very graphic and potentially distressing evidence. After Rosemary West's murder trial in 1995, some jury members were offered professional counselling. In *R v Wagner and Bunting*, the notorious Australian 'Snowtown' murders case in 2002—otherwise known as the 'Bodies in Barrels' murders—the evidence was so gruesome that three of the original jury dropped out, unable to cope with the evidence of sadistic torture and killing. Some of the jurors in South Australia's Supreme Court who did make it through to the end (and delivered guilty verdicts) had to receive counselling afterwards.

During his summing up at the end of the trial of the 'M25' rapist, Antoni Imiela, at Maidstone Crown Court in 2004, the trial judge told the jury to put aside feelings of 'revulsion, distress or dismay' and to decide their verdict in a 'calm and dispassionate manner'. He concluded that it was 'essential that you come to your decision based on the facts with your judgment unclouded and not distorted by emotions'. After deliberating, the jury returned seven guilty verdicts of rape.

More recently, at the start of the January 2007 murder trial of Canadian pig-farmer Robert William Pickton, accused of abducting and murdering six prostitutes and then feeding their remains to his pigs, the trial judge in British Columbia's Supreme Court had to warn the jury that their task would be grisly. He said that 'where evidence is particularly distressing, there is a concern that it may arise feelings of revulsion and hostility, and that can overwhelm the objective and impartial approach jurors are expected to bring to their task. You should be aware of that possibility and make sure it does not happen to you.' Pickton was eventually convicted of six counts of second-degree murder in December 2007.

10.11.6 **Lacking skill?**

Lord Denning MR once suggested that jurors should not be selected at random but should be selected in much the same way that magistrates are, with interviews and references required. This would, he thought, improve the decision-making skills of the jury as a whole. However, such a system would obviously be more time-consuming and expensive than the present system. There is also the danger that a jury capable of satisfying such a selection process would be self-selecting—more intelligent, better educated people are likely to be drawn from a narrower socio-economic group than the population as a whole. Introducing a selection process would also appear to run counter to the government's policy, in recent years, to widen the pool of jurors as much as possible.

Summary

- The main use of the jury in the English legal system is for trial on indictment in the Crown Court. Civil juries are rare.
- The role of juries in criminal trials is to determine issues of fact and deliver a verdict. Juries cannot be directed to convict, nor must they be pressurised into returning a verdict. Juries are entitled to return a not guilty verdict, even if this appears to be in defiance of the law and/or evidence—this is 'jury equity'.
- The deliberations of the jury are secret and alleged irregularities which occur during them cannot form the basis of an appeal against conviction (*R v Mirza*). However, the situation is different if extraneous matters may have influenced the jury's verdict.
- The jury's verdict does not have to be unanimous—majority verdicts are allowed.
- The rules as to eligibility are contained in s.1 of the Juries Act 1974, but these rules were significantly amended by s.321 of the Criminal Justice Act 2003. Previously, the judiciary (including magistrates), lawyers, the police, and clergy (among others) were ineligible. Now, only the mentally disordered are ineligible. The fact that lawyers and police officers can serve on juries has been challenged in litigation which has reached the House of Lords (*R v Abdroikov and Others* (2007)) and the European Court of Human Rights (*Hanif and Khan v UK* (2012)).
- Various people are disqualified from jury service (for example, people in prison) and others are entitled to be excused (for example, members of the armed forces).
- Juries are selected from the electoral register. Both prosecution and defence have the right to challenge all or any of the jurors 'for cause', but the core principle in England and Wales is of random selection. This may be contrasted with the 'voir dire' system used in the US.
- There is no 'right' to have the ethnic composition of a jury modified, although the introduction of such a 'right' has been proposed as a possible reform of jury trials.
- In cases of jury 'tampering' it is possible for a trial involving an indictable offence to be heard in a Crown Court by a judge acting alone, under s.44 of the Criminal Justice Act 2003, subject to stringent conditions being satisfied. 'Judge-only' trials do not infringe the right to a fair trial in Article 6 of the ECHR (*Twomey and Others v UK* (2013)).
- Section 43 of the Criminal Justice Act 2003 provided that serious fraud trials should be heard by a judge alone, not by a jury. However, this option was never brought into effect and it has now been repealed by the Protection of Freedoms Act 2012.
- One option which exists in other countries is 'jury waiver', where the accused may opt out of jury trial. However, this is not an option in England and Wales.
- Jurors who discuss an ongoing case using social media and/or who conduct their own internet research into an ongoing case face criminal liability for contempt of court. The core principle here is that jurors must reach their verdict based only on the evidence heard in court.

Questions

1 What are the eligibility criteria for jury membership under the Juries Act 1974?

2 Following the reforms introduced in the Criminal Justice Act 2003, which people are disqualified from jury service, and which people are entitled to be excused from jury service?

3 What rights do the prosecution and defence have, at the outset of a Crown Court trial, to challenge prospective jurors, either with or without cause?

4 In which circumstances may the prosecution apply for a Crown Court trial without a jury?

5 In which circumstances may a trial judge modify the ethnic composition of a Crown Courty jury?

6 What is meant by 'jury vetting'?

Sample question and outline answer

Question

In passing the Criminal Justice Act 2003, Parliament abolished most of the categories of persons either ineligible for, disqualified from, or entitled to be excused from jury service. It was quite right to do this: after all, juries are supposed to reflect the public's involvement in the criminal justice system. Discuss.

Outline answer

Answers should briefly explain what 'jury service' means, especially in the context of the 'criminal justice system': twelve members of the public, randomly selected to decide guilt or innocence in a Crown Court trial.

Describe the basic eligibility rules (as set out in the Juries Act 1974): minimum/maximum age limits; five-year residency in the UK (but not necessarily nationality); registration on the electoral roll.

Describe the ineligibility/disqualification/excusal rules prior to the CJA 2003: judges, magistrates, lawyers, police, clergy, mentally ill, and so on ineligible; certain criminals and people on bail disqualified; MPs, MEPs, peers, doctors, dentists, vets, armed forces, those with previous jury service, and those aged over sixty-five entitled to automatic excusal. Comment on the reasons for these rules: important jobs, possible bias, ability to influence other jurors, etc.

Explain the post-CJA 2003 legal landscape: only the mentally ill are ineligible; little change to disqualification; only those with previous jury service and armed forces entitled to be excused. Comment on the reasons for the changes: to produce a more representative jury by getting more middle-class professionals (judges, lawyers, police, doctors, and so on) involved; to reduce the likelihood of the same people being selected more than once because of a larger 'pool' of potential jurors, etc.

Discuss the post-CJA case law involving police officers, prison officers, and CPS employees on juries: *R v Abdroikov and Others* (2007), House of Lords; *R v I* (2007), Court of Appeal; *R v Khan and Others* (2008), Court of Appeal; *R v L* (2011), Court of Appeal; *Hanif and Khan v UK* (2012), European Court of Human Rights. Observe, for example, that in *Hanif and Khan* the ECHR stated that the defendant's right to a fair trial would be violated where a police officer on the jury was 'personally acquainted' with a police officer giving evidence on behalf of the prosecution, at least where there was an 'important conflict' about this evidence, which is ostensibly a narrow ruling. However, the Court seems to imply that the presence of any police officer on a jury might violate Article 6 of the ECHR.

Reach a conclusion as to whether or not the UK Parliament was 'quite right' to change the eligibility/disqualification rules.

Further reading

- ***Corker, D*** *'Trying Fraud Cases Without Juries'* [2002] Crim LR 283

  This article explores a number of issues around the idea of 'judge-only' trials in fraud cases, such as the complex safeguards that would be required, and might help the reader to understand why s.43 of the Criminal Justice Act 2003 was never brought into force (and has now been repealed).

- ***Crosby, K.*** *'Controlling Devlin's Jury: What the Jury Thinks, and What the Jury Sees Online'* [2012] Crim LR 15

  Analyses the ability of the criminal justice system to 'control' jurors (that is, stop them from conducting their own research into a case) in a society where internet use is so prevalent.

- ***Darbyshire, P.*** *'The Lamp that Shows that Freedom Lives—Is It Worth the Candle?'* [1991] Crim LR 740

  In which the author offers a powerful critique of 'jury equity'.

- ***Doran, S.*** and ***Jackson, J.*** *'The Case for Jury Waiver'* [1997] Crim LR 155

  Presents arguments in favour of introducing into the English legal system an option for defendants to 'waive' their 'right' to jury trial in the Crown Court.

- ***Hungerford-Welch, P.*** *'Police Officers as Jurors'* [2012] Crim LR 320

  Analyses the background to the Criminal Justice Act 2003 reforms on eligibility and the leading cases since, including *Abdroikov and Others* and *Hanif and Khan*.

- ***Quinn, K.*** *'Jury Bias and the European Convention on Human Rights: A Well-Kept Secret?'* [2004] Crim LR 998

  Assesses the principle of 'confidentiality' of jury deliberations and its compatibility with Article 6 of the ECHR, the right to a fair trial, as seen in cases such as *Mirza*, *Gregory*, and *Sander.*

- ***Thornton, P.*** *'Trial by Jury: 50 Years of Change'* [2004] Crim LR 683

  Provides a valuable summary and analysis of the major changes to the system of jury trials from 1953 to 2003 (including the reforms introduced by the Juries Act 1974, the Contempt of Court Act 1981, and the Criminal Justice Act 2003).

Online resources

You should now attempt the supporting self-test questions and end-of-chapter questions available at: **www.oup.com/he/wilson-rutherford4e**

Chapter 11

Access to justice

Learning objectives

By the end of this chapter you should:

- be aware of the issues and arguments surrounding access to justice;
- be able to discuss the impact of the recent changes to legal aid provision;
- be able to outline the basic principles relating to public funding in civil and criminal cases;
- be able to describe the differences between a conditional fee agreement (CFA) and a contingency fee agreement;
- appreciate the difficulties in evaluating whether there is 'access to justice' in the English legal system.

Talking point

Legal aid was introduced in 1949 and was viewed by many as the fourth pillar of the welfare state. Over the past seventy years its scope has gradually been eroded, although it is claimed that the annual £2 billion legal aid budget is 'one of the most generous in the world'. In September 2017 the Bach Commission (commissioned by the Labour Party) reported following a two-year investigation into access to justice. The report is published by the Fabian Society and is called *The Right to Justice*. The Commission found that cuts to legal aid have created a two-tier justice system in which the poorest go without representation or advice. Nicola Mackintosh QC, a member of the Commission, summed up the conclusions:

> The combination of legal aid cuts, court closures, and unaffordable court fees has resulted in the vast majority of people being unable to access the legal help they need. Justice has therefore been reserved only for the privileged few. This undermines the rule of law and risks the breakdown of society . . . People are left to represent themselves in court or just give up because they do not have the legal help they need. This . . . is unacceptable in a civilised society.

In 2015, the then Lord Chancellor, the Conservative Michael Gove emphasised the importance of the rule of law in a speech that gave hope to the legal profession. However, cuts to the number of legal aid contracts for criminal work caused many to be concerned, in the words of Law Society president Andrew Caplan, that 'vulnerable people may not be able to obtain legal representation if they are accused of wrongdoing'. Although the reforms are presently on hold, the issue of the affordability of legal aid has not gone away.

Consider the following questions:

- How do you think the government should save money on legal aid and what impact do you think reforms will have on access to justice? Is the rule of law at risk?
- Should all citizens have access to legal aid and who should pay?
- Is your view in respect to civil legal aid the same or different from your view in respect to criminal legal aid?

Introduction

This chapter is entitled 'Access to justice', but what is meant by this phrase? Generally, access to justice can be taken to refer to the fact that the advice necessary to obtain legal redress should be available to all and not be exclusive to any section of society. Justice should not be a commodity beyond the means of all but the wealthiest in society. Professor Richard Moorhead has emphasised that access to justice does not simply equate to legal aid. Access to justice means being 'treated fairly according to the law and if you are not treated fairly being able to get appropriate redress'. Over the course of the twentieth century, and into the twenty-first century, the English legal system has arguably become more difficult to navigate as a result of the growth in the volume and complexity of the law. It is instructive to visit a law library and compare the size of the yearly statute books from the beginning of the twentieth century with those of recent years. The labyrinthine legal system comprises a complex and detailed set of rights and responsibilities in areas such as welfare, housing, and employment law. Accessing legal assistance when something goes wrong can be a difficult and costly process. Rights are only of use if an individual is aware of those rights and has the resources and ability to enforce them.

When discussing access to justice it is therefore important to consider whether those citizens who want to access legal remedies or assistance are able to do so, or whether they are prevented from doing so by a combination of lack of awareness of their rights, an inability to pay for legal assistance or perhaps a lack of access to appropriate legal assistance. It is also important, as in all aspects of the English legal system, to separate discussion of the availability of help and advice in criminal cases from consideration of the assistance available in civil matters. Access to justice can refer to the right to have representation if accused of a crime but can also refer to the obtaining of legal help in a divorce case or employment matter, or in relation to civil litigation.

The creation of the Legal Aid scheme in 1949 was intended to provide publicly funded advice, assistance, and representation in criminal and civil cases. The scheme was regarded by many as the fourth pillar of the welfare state. The costs of legal aid have increased beyond what had been envisaged by the designers of the scheme. Additionally, it is difficult to control costs, due to the scheme being demand-led. Anyone requiring legal services, who is eligible under the rules, will receive financial assistance to obtain legal advice. From year to year costs have been impossible to predict as it cannot be known, for example, how many people might be arrested and require representation, or how many individuals would require advice on marital breakdown.

The story of legal aid since the 1980s is one of governments trying to control legal aid expenditure in the face of escalating demand. Despite a number of initiatives and the lowering of financial eligibility thresholds, legal aid costs rose from approximately

£1.5bn in 1997 to more than £2bn in 2012. The LAA net expenditure for 2018–19 was £1.8bn. In relation to civil legal aid alone, the Legal Aid Agency spent £623.4m in 2018–19. This was an increase of £434m from the preceding year. However, criminal legal aid spending fell by £15.9m to £910.5m. The annual report can be found here: **https://assets.publishing.service.gov.uk/government/uploads/system/uploads/attachment_data/file/814457/6.5273_-_LAA_-_Annual_Report_and_Accounts_2018-19_WEB.pdf**.

Within the legal aid budget, two areas of expenditure in particular increased considerably, leading to the need to control the legal aid budget as part of government austerity measures: criminal defence expenditure in the Crown Court and the costs of childcare proceedings. Government schemes and plans to control expenditure have given rise to the related problem of how to allocate finite resources to meet potentially infinite needs. In recent years, the allocation of funds for civil legal aid has fallen while spending on criminal legal aid has increased. The government, in *Implementing Legal Aid Reform: Government Response to the Constitutional Affairs Select Committee Report*, Cmnd 7158 (June 2007), said of its proposals to reform the legal aid programme:

> Controlling expenditure is not, in and of itself, the goal of the reform programme. The aim of improved efficiency and better control over spending is, ultimately, to ensure that more people can be helped by legal aid within the resources available, without any reduction in quality, and in a way that contributes to, and benefits from, improved efficiency in the wider justice systems. (para. 33)

Major changes to the civil legal aid system in England and Wales were announced in November 2010. The proposals aimed to cut the legal aid bill by £350m a year by 2015. More detail on these changes will be given throughout the chapter. As well as the changes to civil legal aid, changes were also announced to the general funding of civil cases as a result of the report of Jackson LJ, who published his findings in January 2010.

See Chapter 9, 'The legal profession'.

When investigating and discussing access to justice it is important to consider the whole of the legal system and the wider picture. The issue is not simply that individuals cannot obtain funding for legal advice and representation, but that even if money is available, the funding arrangements may influence the legal profession's willingness to undertake certain types of legal work. For example, as a result of the withdrawal of legal aid for most divorce cases, some firms of solicitors no longer carry out low-value matrimonial work, preferring to specialise in company and commercial work where fees are more lucrative. Many large firms have closed their matrimonial departments, which has resulted in a lack of lawyers carrying out this work in some areas of the country or, more positively, niche practices being set up by the lawyers who have been made redundant. The issue of funding directly impacts upon the way in which the legal profession operates and the provision of legal services.

Furthermore, a number of schemes to try to solve disputes without recourse to the courts have been established, such as mediation and arbitration services. The question may then arise as to whether the quality of justice being provided by the alternative forms of dispute resolution is equal to that of the courts.

The purpose of this chapter is to consider the ways in which access to legal advice and representation is funded in both civil and criminal cases, alternative methods of paying legal costs, and reform of the way in which the state funds legal advice and representation. Throughout the chapter consideration will be given to evaluating the effectiveness of funding for legal services. Deciding how to fund legal advice and assistance is a major issue for governments. Reforms to the criminal legal aid provision are ongoing and civil legal aid is also in a state of flux.

Thinking point

Is equality before the law more apparent than real?

If a lack of funds means that many cannot pursue a remedy for a legitimate grievance, it may be argued that the rule of law, and the principle that all citizens are equal before the law, is more apparent than real.

11.1 **Legal Aid Agency**

The current system of funding legal advice and assistance is based on the Access to Justice Act 1999 and associated legislation, including the Legal Aid, Sentencing and Punishment of Offenders Act (LASPO) 2012, which came into force in April 2013. The 1999 Act introduced major changes to the way in which legal aid was delivered, but many of the changes introduced by the Act were swept away by the 2012 Act. Legal aid is now administered by the Legal Aid Agency (LAA), which was established in April 2013. The strategic objectives of the LAA are expressed to be to:

- Provide simple, timely, and reliable access to legal aid;
- Build strong relationships across government and the justice system;
- Secure value for money for the taxpayer in all that [they] do;
- Achieve [their] full potential through being fair, proud, and supportive.

The LAA includes the Public Defender Service (PDS), which provides independent advice, assistance, and representation on criminal matters, and the Civil Legal Advice Service.

Further details about the LAA can be found at **www.justice.gov.uk/about/laa**.

11.2 **Civil Legal Advice Service**

The Civil Legal Advice Service is the scheme under which advice and representation are provided in civil cases. The scheme is administered by the LAA, either through direct funding to firms of solicitors and other advice agencies or through coordination and partnership with other funders of legal services such as local authorities. Civil legal aid is provided for:

- debt, if the applicant's home is at risk;
- housing, if the applicant is homeless or at risk of being evicted;
- domestic abuse;
- family, if the applicant has been in an abusive relationship;
- special educational needs;
- discrimination;
- issues around a child being taken into care;
- some child abduction cases.

Representation for benefit appeals is no longer supported via legal aid.

11.2.1 **Availability of funding**

 **Thinking point**

Availability of Legal Aid

The geographical location of firms of solicitors is important for access to justice. Not all solicitors have a contract to provide services under the Legal Aid scheme and therefore access will be difficult for many people. This is particularly true in small towns and in the countryside, as the greatest concentration of firms of solicitors tends to be in the major urban areas.

There is a range of levels of service funded by the LAA in civil cases:

- **Legal help.** This is a service which offers advice on rights and options and help with negotiations and paperwork. This could include writing letters, negotiation, preparing a written case, and getting a barrister's opinion on the legally aided person's behalf. The eligibility for legal help is means-tested.
- **Help at court.** If legal aid is granted for help at court, a legal representative is appointed to help and speak for the assisted person in a civil court. This does not include formal representation. Again, eligibility depends upon a means test.

- **Family mediation.** Family mediation is used to help parties to a marriage come to an agreement without going to court. Under family mediation, an independent mediator seeks to aid the parties in reaching an agreed settlement in relation to issues surrounding children, money, and the family home.
- **Legal representation.** This is available in very limited circumstances. Under the legal representation scheme, funding may be limited to investigative help, which will only cover investigating the strengths of the proceedings and is used in cases where the chances of the case being successful are not clear and the investigation is likely to be expensive. Alternatively, funding under this scheme can be for full representation. Representation is subject to a means and a merits test; if both tests are fulfilled, a solicitor or barrister can be paid to prepare and handle the legal work required to prepare a case for court and to provide representation at any court hearings.

Certain types of legal case are excluded from the Legal Aid scheme. These include personal injury cases, including, from April 2013, those involving clinical negligence (excepting children with brain injuries resulting in severe disability, which have arisen in the womb, during birth, or in the eight-week postnatal period); claims of negligence causing damage to property; boundary disputes; will writing; the creation of lasting powers of attorney under the Mental Capacity Act 2005; conveyancing; matters of trust law; matters of company or partnership law; cases arising in the course of carrying on a business or concerning libel or slander; and private family law cases such as divorce, or disputes about children and finances unless the case involves domestic violence or abuse.

In certain exceptional cases legal aid may be available if the applicant can show that being refused legal aid would infringe:

- rights under the European Convention on Human Rights (ECHR);
- European Union rights to legal representation.

Thus in certain circumstances legal aid is available for representation of a party in a coroner's court, where it is necessary to carry out an effective investigation into a death, as required by Article 2 of the ECHR ('the right to life'), or where there is a significant wider public interest in the individual being represented.

Critical debate

A method of controlling the legal aid budget is to reduce eligibility. At first sight it may appear strange that personal injury cases, which constitute a large proportion of civil claims, should not be eligible for legal aid. Personal injury cases were covered by legal aid until 2000; however, the cost of supporting such claims was very high, and therefore the government introduced legislation to remove legal aid from such cases and instead allow the claims to be funded by CFAs. The cost of bringing personal injury claims was therefore transferred from the public purse to the parties involved and the claimants' lawyers. Lawyers undertaking work on a conditional fee basis take the risk of not receiving payment should a claim be lost. Is there a risk inherent to access to justice in adopting such an approach to the funding of litigation?

See 11.2.7, 'Conditional fee agreements'.

The changes made to legal aid in 2000 did not affect clinical negligence claims because it was considered that lawyers might not be prepared to take the risk of medical negligence cases under a CFA. However, in April 2013 legal aid was withdrawn from all but a small number of clinical negligence cases as a result of provisions in LASPO 2012.

Thinking point

The link between legal aid and access to justice

The legal aid reforms have removed legal aid funding from a wide range of civil cases, including divorce, welfare benefits, school admissions and exclusions, employment, immigration (where the individual is not detained), consumer, and clinical negligence claims. When the proposals to remove legal aid in these areas were first put forward they were criticised by the Law Society, which expressed severe doubts that those who need help the most would still be protected, despite the fact that the government's stated aim was to make certain that the legal aid reforms ensured that the resources available were targeted at those in most need of help. The cuts to legal aid funding are likely to affect small legal aid providers the most. What potential impact may this have on access to justice?

Official investigation of legal aid reform

The *Public Accounts Committee—Thirty-sixth Report Implementing Reforms to Civil Legal Aid* was published in January 2015. The report, as set out in the executive summary, states that the Ministry of Justice is 'on track to make a significant and rapid reduction to the amount that it spends on civil legal aid'. But the report went on to warn that the major changes had been introduced 'on the basis of no evidence in many areas, and without making good use of the evidence that it did have in other areas', and that the government 'does not understand the link between the price it pays for legal aid and the quality of advice being given . . . [and] the knock-on costs of its reforms across the public sector [and] whether the projected £300 million spending reduction . . . is outweighed by additional costs elsewhere'.

This report can be found at **https://publications.parliament.uk/pa/cm201415/cmselect/cmpubacc/808/808.pdf**.

Eligibility for funding for civil legal aid

Assessing eligibility for funding is complicated, with different thresholds of earnings, capital, and disposable income depending upon the level of service involved. The solicitor or adviser dealing with the case will give advice as to whether the person asking for help will be eligible for legal aid funding. There is also an online legal aid calculator which can be used to work out eligibility, at **www.gov.uk/check-legal-aid**.

As a general guide, in most cases, if disposable monthly income exceeds £733 or disposable capital exceeds £8,000 then the individual concerned will not be eligible. Contributions are required if disposable capital is more than £3,000 or monthly disposable income is more than £315. The thresholds can alter depending, for example, on the number of dependent children in the family, or for pensioners on low incomes, but the levels are set at very low sums. Where legal representation is provided, a contribution towards the cost of this service may be payable out of an applicant's capital or income. The level of contribution depends upon various financial thresholds. In some cases, a statutory charge is levied if money or property is recovered. For example, under the Legal Help scheme, if money or property is recovered, the solicitor or adviser concerned must use this towards paying the legal costs incurred.

11.2.2 **Community legal service partnerships**

In 1999 the Legal Services Commission, the forerunner of the LAA, set up community legal service partnerships to coordinate legal services on a regional level. These partnerships involved the Commission, the relevant local authority, and other funders of legal services in the area in question and were designed to allow monitoring of the needs of the area, with the provision of legal services planned and coordinated. However, the partnerships are no longer facilitated and those local partnerships that still exist have been asked to evaluate the effectiveness of their work and to continue to meet only if they consider it appropriate to do so.

11.2.3 **Citizens Advice Bureaux**

Citizens Advice is a national charity that sets and monitors standards, gives support and guidance, and provides services to Citizens Advice Bureaux (CABs) throughout England, Wales, and Northern Ireland. All CABs are members of Citizens Advice. The Citizens Advice service helps people resolve a range of legal, financial, and welfare benefit-related problems. The advice is free. Advisers in many bureaux have contracts with the LAA to provide legal help. Collectively, CABs help with more than five million problems each year. The majority of advisers in the CAB are volunteers trained by the CAB and although some volunteers have legal qualifications, many do not. In some CABs solicitors are employed directly, or local solicitors provide services linked with the bureau. The CAB website is **www.citizensadvice.org.uk/**.

11.2.4 Law Centres

Law Centres were first established in the 1970s to address the legal advice needs of the poor and disadvantaged in their local communities. Today there are approximately forty-two Centres in England and Wales, employing solicitors, barristers, and other legal advisers. This number has decreased from around sixty. The Centres specialise in areas of social law such as housing, employment, and welfare rights. Law Centres do more than simply take on individual cases; they provide training and information about legal rights to local groups and organisations and may work with local authorities to address issues relevant to a particular section of the community, such as problems associated with inadequate social housing. Law Centres are independent non-profit-making organisations and depend upon funding from central and local government, including from the LAA, and from trusts and charities. recent reforms have cut funding to Law Centres and a number have had to close. Local Law Centres may have their own websites but a great deal of information can be found at the Law Centres Network website: **www.lawcentres.org.uk/**.

11.2.5 Student law clinics

A number of universities offer pro bono (free) legal services to members of the public through student law clinics. These schemes are set up to assist clients while giving students experience of legal work as part of their academic and professional development. The students may offer a full legal service to clients, like firms of solicitors, or may offer a basic advice-only service. Practising lawyers closely supervise the students' work and have overall responsibility for ensuring that clients receive a professional service. An example of a very successful law office at Northumbria University can be found at **www.northumbria.ac.uk/about-us/academic-departments/northumbria-law-school/study/student-law-office/**.

In March 2015 the University of Law became the first university to be granted an alternative business structure (ABS) licence by the Solicitors Regulation Authority (SRA), to enable trainee solicitors undertaking their training at firms or businesses unable to offer dispute resolution experience to undertake that part of their training at the university.

11.2.6 Pro bono schemes

Pro bono—shortened from the Latin phrase *pro bono publico*, 'for the public good'—services are sometimes offered by barristers or solicitors' firms to provide legal advice and assistance to clients without payment or for reduced fees. For example, a scheme to draft simple wills for free runs once a year under the banner of 'Will Aid'. More details of pro bono work can be found on the website of the legal charity LawWorks: **www.lawworks.org.uk/**.

11.2.7 **Conditional fee agreements**

At common law, it was long held that contracts for the conduct of litigation where payment was related to results were void as being contrary to public policy. Section 58 of the Courts and Legal Services Act 1990 changed this rule in relation to certain types of litigation. The Access to Justice Act 1999 allowed a number of different forms of agreement relating to the payment of fees. The most common, and the one which will be considered here, is the conditional fee arrangement (CFA), popularly known as 'no win, no fee'. The Access to Justice Act, and the general relaxation of the rules relating to the advertisement of legal services, led to an explosion in no win, no fee litigation firms. Sections 44 and 46 of the LASPO Act 2012 changed the rules yet again regarding CFAs.

A CFA arises where a solicitor agrees with the client that the firm's legal fees will only be paid if the client wins the case. If the client wins the case then the solicitor will be paid an 'uplift' on the normal fees that would have been charged. This is known as a success fee and could include a percentage increase in the bill. However, until the law changed in April 2013 following LASPO, a solicitor carrying out contentious work was not allowed to be paid a fee which was a percentage of any damages that the successful client might be awarded. This type of arrangement—a 'contingency fee agreement'—is not allowed at common law and was not permitted by legislation, and therefore was not legal in England, although it is commonly used in the United States (US). However, LASPO introduced damages-based agreements (DBA), which are a form of contingency fee agreement. Since April 2013, DBAs have been lawful for contentious work and a lawyer can agree to take a percentage of any damages awarded at the end of a successful case. In practice, DBAs, governed by the DBA Regulations 2013, have been generally shunned due to the complexity and lack of clarity in the Regulations and, perhaps, a feeling that taking part of a successful party's damages is too difficult to sell to a litigating party. There was a hope that the Regulations would be amended to allow hybrid agreements, known as 'no win, low fee' contingency agreements, instead of the 'all-or-nothing' approach, but this hope was quashed in November 2014 when the government stated that it would not allow such agreements.

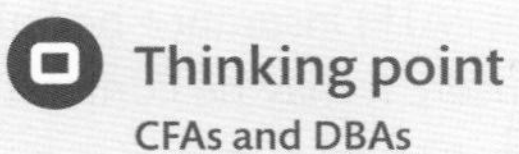

CFAs and DBAs

CFAs allow a percentage increase in the fee payable should a claimant be successful. A DBA, on the other hand, allows a lawyer to claim a percentage of the damages recovered. Thus the additional fee payable in a CFA is linked to costs, while in a DBA it is linked to the damages awarded. In the past it was suggested that contingency fee agreements might encourage lawyers who have a financial interest in the outcome of a case to employ dubious professional practices, such as inflating the claim for damages, coaching witnesses, and so on, and might encourage the pursuit of unmeritorious claims. What evidence is there to suggest that this will be the outcome of such agreements? Why did the government decide to allow DBAs? What regulation of such agreements is needed?

The reform of civil litigation funding and costs includes DBAs being permitted in civil litigation. The changes came about as a result of the Jackson Report's recommendation that both solicitors and barristers should be able to enter into contingency fee agreements with their clients in contentious civil cases, subject to controls on costs recovery and regulation but always subject to a client receiving independent advice on the arrangement.

The rules governing CFAs are found in the Courts and Legal Services Act 1990 s.58 (as amended by the Access to Justice Act 1999 and LASPO 2012). Clients must be given specific information to enable them to decide whether a CFA is appropriate. It is important for solicitors to ensure that clients understand the risks and consequences of this type of agreement. CFAs are now permitted in all proceedings other than certain types of family proceedings and criminal proceedings.

 **Example**

A solicitor enters into a CFA with a client injured as a result of tripping on a damaged paving stone. The case is straightforward and the client seems likely to be successful. The solicitor therefore includes a relatively small uplift of 10 per cent. The client wins the case and is awarded damages of £10,000. The legal fee for dealing with the case, if a CFA had not been entered into, would be £4,000. However, as a result of the CFA, the final bill is increased by 10 per cent, bringing the total to £4,400. The defendant will pay the costs of the case (the general principle is that the loser pays), including the £4,000 costs charged by the claimant's solicitor, and the claimant will pay his solicitor the £400 success fee.

A CFA covers liability for the costs of the claimant's solicitor but does not absolve liability for the costs of the other side if the claim is not successful (although there are special rules for personal injury cases that are outside the scope of this book). This may have a deterrent effect upon a claimant pursuing a claim. A claimant bears the risk of being ordered to pay the costs of the winning party if the claim is unsuccessful, and therefore insurance to cover the risk is commonly taken out either at the start of the case or when it appears likely that the case is going to be decided by a court hearing. This type of insurance is known as 'after the event' (ATE) insurance because insurance cover is bought after the cause of action has arisen. It may be contrasted with 'before the event' (BTE) insurance, which is explained at 11.2.8.

Ever since their introduction, CFAs have been subject to criticism. It has been argued that there is no incentive for lawyers to take on difficult cases, because they will do so at their own risk; instead, the tendency is to accept only clearly winnable or straightforward cases. There is also the issue of some lawyers having disproportionately increased fees under CFAs. As far back as September 2008, Jack Straw expressed concern that CFAs were not working as had been hoped. He said:

> It's claimed they have provided greater access to justice, but the behaviour of some lawyers in ramping up their fees in these cases is nothing short of scandalous. So I am

going to address this and consider whether to cap more tightly the level of success fees that lawyers can charge.

When Sir Rupert Jackson produced his final report on the costs of civil litigation in January 2010, the recommendations made in the report formed part of the reform of civil litigation funding and costs. The reform includes changing the system of conditional fees so that success fees and ATE insurance premiums are no longer recoverable from the losing party. This is because claimants under CFAs have no incentive to keep their costs down because they do not have to pay them, and these recoverable costs represent a significant burden for the losing party, who can end up paying more than the reasonable costs of litigating the case because the level of the success fee might have been set too high. Since April 2013, any success fee has had to be borne by the client in a successful case and not the losing defendant.

11.2.8 Before the event insurance (BTE)

BTE insurance is an alternative way of funding legal fees, avoiding the need for a CFA or a DBA. This type of insurance is commonly available in motor insurance policies as 'legal expenses cover' and insures the policy holder against the costs of litigation arising out of a road traffic accident where the policy holder is the claimant. A solicitor advising a client on paying for legal advice must always check to find out whether BTE exists before advising the use of any other form of funding.

11.3 Criminal legal aid

The LAA provides advice and representation to the accused person in criminal cases. The service is available for people who have been arrested, questioned, or charged by the police. There is free legal advice available to all those questioned in a police station.

The scheme is administered by the LAA either through direct funding to firms of solicitors and other advice agencies or through coordination and partnership with other funders of legal services, such as local authorities.

11.3.1 Direct funding

The LAA only funds advice or representation directly where the firm of solicitors concerned has a contract with the Agency.

See Chapter 7, 'Human rights and fundamental freedoms'.

There is a range of levels of service funded by legal aid in criminal cases:

- **Advice and assistance**. This covers general legal advice, letter writing, and negotiation; preparing a written case; and getting a barrister's opinion.
- **Police station advice and assistance**. This provides individuals being questioned by the police about an offence with free legal advice from a solicitor with an LAA

contract. There will be a duty solicitor on call, or one can be chosen from a list of local firms kept by the police.

There is also a duty solicitor scheme operating in the magistrates' courts, giving free advice and advocacy assistance on a first appearance in court, subject to some exceptions.

The right to advice and assistance can be seen in the light of the protection of basic human rights. By Article 6 of the ECHR, a defendant has the right to a fair trial. Where a person is charged with having committed a criminal offence, as a minimum, that person has a right:

> (b) to have adequate time and facilities for the preparation of his defence; (c) to defend himself in person or through legal assistance of his own choosing or, if he has not sufficient means to pay for legal assistance, to be given it free when the interests of justice so require.

- **Advocacy assistance**. Advocacy assistance covers the cost of case preparation and initial representation in certain proceedings in both magistrates' courts and the Crown Court but does not include full representation before a court.
- **Representation**. This covers the cost of preparation of a defence and representation in court, including, if the case is to be heard in the Crown Court, the cost of a barrister.

Representation under this scheme will only be granted if it is in the interests of justice to do so. Examples of instances where it is likely to be in the interests of justice for representation to be granted include the likelihood, if convicted, of a prison sentence or loss of employment, or where there are substantial questions of law in issue. The decision to grant legal representation is made by the magistrates' court where the case will be heard. If the court decides not to allow representation it must give reasons for doing so and a further application may be made to the court to review the case, or, if the case is going to the Crown Court, an application may be made to that court.

Eligibility for funding

There is a means test for advice and assistance. Accused children—persons under eighteen—automatically get free legal aid, as do those in receipt of the following:

- Income Support;
- income-based Jobseeker's Allowance;
- Universal Credit;
- State Pension Guarantee Credit;
- income-based Employment and Support Allowance (then there is a 'passporting' right to qualify under the means test). The level of income/capital above which funding for advice and assistance is not available is generally above £99 disposable

income per week and above £1,000 disposable capital. The methods of calculating disposable income/capital take account of a number of factors, including the income of a partner and the number of children in the household.

NOTE: Universal Credit replaced Income Support and Jobseekers Allowance. All claimants will be moved to the new benefit by 2023.

As already seen, advice at a police station under the duty solicitor scheme is free.

Under the provisions of the Criminal Defence Service Act 2006, from 2 October 2006, eligibility for free legal representation in the magistrates' court involves passing both a merits test (or interests of justice test) and a means test. Some applicants qualify automatically, such as those receiving income support. Others may qualify by meeting a simple means test, which involves applying a formula used to assess adjusted gross annual income and applying financial eligibility criteria. Applicants who fail to qualify automatically must pass a full means test. The full means test involves assessing an applicant's disposable income. To qualify under the full means test, an individual's annual disposable income must be less than £3,398. Means testing in the magistrates' courts, combined with the 'interests of justice' test, results in around a third of all defendants being granted legal aid.

In January 2010 means testing to assess eligibility for free representation in the Crown Court was introduced and this scheme has now been rolled out across the whole of England and Wales. Eligibility is based upon assessing the financial position of the applicant via examination of their household income, outgoings, capital and equity. If the defendant has an annual household disposable income of £37,500 or more they will not be eligible for legal aid in a Crown Court trial. If their disposable income is above £3,398 but less than £37,500, they will have to make an income contribution towards the costs. If the defendant has £30,000 in capital and equity and is convicted they may have to contribute towards their final defence costs.

A calculator for eligibility for criminal legal aid can be found at **www.justice.gov.uk/legal-aid/assess-your-clients-eligibility/crime-eligibility/criminal-eligibility-calculator**.

11.3.2 **Public Defender Service**

The public defender has long been a feature of the courts system in the United States but was not adopted in England and Wales until May 2001. The LLA directly employs solicitors, accredited representatives, and administrators to undertake criminal defence work. The aims of the PDS are to provide independent, high-quality, and value-for-money criminal advice, assistance, and representation to defendants in criminal cases. The PDS lawyers are available twenty-four hours a day, seven days a week to give advice to people in custody and represent clients in magistrates' courts, the Crown Court, and higher courts if necessary.

The service is very unpopular with private firms contracted by the LAA. Public defenders effectively compete with private firms for work and are paid by the LAA, and therefore it is considered by some that they constitute unfair competition. Research carried out to assess the cost of the PDS concluded that it was between 40 and 90 per cent more expensive than an equivalent service provided by contracted firms. There are currently four PDS offices in England and Wales. In 2014 a specialist Advocacy Unit was opened which employs twenty-one barristers and higher courts advocates, including five QCs. The unit was set up to provide a country-wide service with particular emphasis on serious and complex Crown Court cases.

The PDS website can be found at **www.publicdefenderservice.org.uk/**.

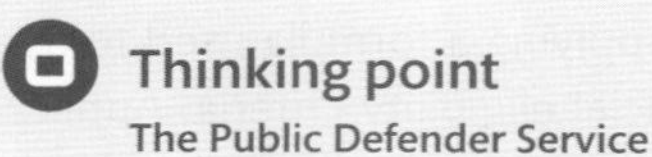

Given the higher costs of the PDS, what advantages of the service may be identified?

11.4 Recent history of legal aid reform

Legal aid has been an increasing burden on the public purse and the degree to which there should be state provision of legal advice and assistance has presented a difficult problem for politicians to solve. Proposals for reform lead to debate in relation to access to justice, the fees charged by lawyers, the merits of individual cases, and the income levels that should allow access to paid assistance in civil and criminal matters. The system has been subject to much tinkering and many changes in the seventy years of its existence. Kenneth Clarke commented in the 2010 report *Proposals for the Reform of Legal Aid in England and Wales* that '[s]ince 2006, there have been over thirty separate consultation exercises on legal aid'. Some of the history of past consultations and proposals are included in this section, including a summary of the 2013 reforms.

In July 2005, the Department for Constitutional Affairs published a command paper, *A Fairer Deal for Legal Aid*. This paper set out the need to improve the way in which the legal aid system worked, especially in relation to criminal defence services.

In July 2006, Lord Carter published a review of legal aid procurement, *Legal Aid: A Market-Based Approach to Reform*. The review recommended moving to a market-based approach to legal aid, focusing on quality and value for money. Among the recommendations in the report were:

- best-value tendering for legal aid contracts based on quality, capacity, and price;
- fixed fees per case for legal aid work carried out in police stations, including travelling and waiting time;

- tighter controls on very high-cost criminal cases;
- new graduated fees for litigators in Crown Court matters.

Following Lord Carter's review, the Department for Constitutional Affairs and the Legal Services Commission published a joint consultation paper in July 2006 called 'Legal Aid: A Sustainable Future'. The paper set out proposals for the ways in which Lord Carter's recommendations would be implemented and included proposals to introduce a unified Legal Services Commission contract covering both civil and criminal work and both solicitors and not-for-profit providers of legal advice and assistance. Following this consultation, further proposals were made by the Department for Constitutional Affairs and the Legal Services Commission in November 2006, in *Legal Aid Reform: The Way Ahead*, Cmnd 6993. The paper included some changes to the original implementation proposals and changes in the proposed start date for implementation of some schemes.

Many of the proposals were not favourably received by solicitors, particularly those relating to best-value tendering for legal aid contracts. For example, the Law Society lobbied the Ministry of Justice (previously the Department for Constitutional Affairs) regarding proposals to give judges powers to deal with delay in very high-cost cases (including the power to order the withdrawal of representation). The plans were changed so that the Legal Services Commission would have the ultimate responsibility for terminating representation in a particular case. The Law Society also commenced judicial review proceedings against the Legal Services Commission in relation to aspects of the civil legal aid contract. These proceedings were discontinued in April 2008 following an agreement reached between the Law Society, the Legal Services Commission, and the Ministry of Justice.

The government proposals were also criticised by the Constitutional Affairs Select Committee in *The Implementation of the Carter Review of Legal Aid* (May 2007), HC 223. Concerns expressed by the Committee included:

- the transitional arrangements based on fixed and graduated fees might drive providers of legal aid-funded services out of the sector due to lack of profitability;
- fixed fees with little graduation may be a disincentive to the undertaking of difficult cases and may lead to cherry-picking of cases, to the detriment of needy clients;
- the inclusion of travel costs in fixed fees raises problems in relation to rural areas and small towns where specialist legal provision is uneven;
- the inclusion of waiting time, for example at police stations or at court, in fixed fees places the risk of such delay with the provider when waiting time is largely outside the control of providers;
- the problem of maintaining quality of service in the face of reduced fees.

The transitional arrangements were seen as potentially damaging to the stability of the existing providers of legal services, which would ultimately impact upon the operation of the proposed market-based best-value competitive tendering for legally aided work. The Constitutional Affairs Select Committee, in its conclusions, said:

> The reform package is being implemented at too fast a speed. There has been no time for proper business planning by practitioners or even for them to understand the raft of proposals, counterproposals and consultations which have been emanating from the Legal Services Commission. Although it is clear that there is an urgent problem with Legal Aid expenditure, it is no solution to try to introduce changes in an atmosphere of panic.
>
> A major part of the proposals involves the introduction of transitional arrangements which are over complex and too rigid. We think that the Government should reconsider whether they are necessary. We doubt whether the risk to the supplier base which they pose justifies their introduction. We would prefer to see competitive tendering—insofar as that is a solution to the problem—implemented directly, once there has been adequate piloting.
>
> We are extremely concerned that the Department is trying to engage in such a far reaching change to the structure of Legal Aid on the basis of little or no evidence about which cost drivers have caused the problem or how its plans for a solution are likely to affect both suppliers and clients. We fear that if the reforms go ahead there is a serious risk to access to justice among the most vulnerable in society. It is clear that the Government has been unwise in attempting to reform the entire system rather than in concentrating on those areas which cause the problem: Crown Court and public law children cases.

In June 2007, the government responded to the report of the Constitutional Affairs Select Committee in a report entitled *Implementing Legal Aid Reform: Government Response to Constitutional Affairs Select Committee Report*, Cmnd 7158. This report rejected the criticisms of the Committee.

Thinking point

Legal aid deserts

The concern is that legally aided work will be so poorly funded that lawyers will decide to switch resources to other areas of legal work, leaving a gap in provision or causing the quality of the service supplied by the remaining providers to diminish. Either way, access to justice suffers. What evidence would you have to collect to investigate these issues?

The reform agenda moved on under the Conservative/Liberal Democrat Coalition government, which held two consultations on reforming civil litigation funding and costs and reforming legal aid. The latter consultation included further changes to reform criminal legal aid fees.

LASPO, which came into force in April 2013, reversed the position where legal aid had been available for all civil cases, except those specifically excluded by the Access to Justice Act 1999. The Act removed some types of case from the scope of legal aid funding, as discussed previously, and ensures that other cases will only qualify when they meet certain criteria. The legislation had a very difficult progression through Parliament and the bill was defeated fourteen times in the House of Lords before being passed by the narrowest of margins. Despite concerns from many quarters that the legislation would impact on the most vulnerable in society, who would no longer be able to access legal assistance, the Ministry of Justice made clear that while it considered legal aid an 'essential part of the justice system', resources provided by taxpayers are nevertheless limited.

One of the major concerns voiced by opponents to the reforms was that the lack of access to lawyers would result in individuals having to act in person, which will result in the court system becoming even more slow and inefficient.

The changes brought into force in April 2013 are not the end of legal aid reform. At the same time as LASPO came into force, a consultation entitled 'Transforming Legal Aid: Delivering a More Credible and Efficient System' was opened. The proposals for further changes included in the consultation document included:

1. The aim of improving public confidence in the Legal Aid scheme by ensuring that legal aid is not available for prisoners for matters that 'do not justify the use of public funds', and the introduction of a household disposable income threshold above which defendants would no longer receive criminal legal aid.
2. In relation to civil legal aid, the reduction of the use of legal aid to fund 'weak' judicial reviews.
3. The introduction of price competition in the criminal legal aid market, initially for the full range of litigation services and magistrates' court representation. In other words, providers of legal aid services would have to tender for work, with the contracts going to the lowest bidder.
4. The reform of fees in criminal legal aid to reduce the cost of criminal legal aid fees for Crown Court advocacy and very high-cost cases (both litigation and advocacy).
5. The reform of fees in civil legal aid to include reducing solicitor representation fees in family public law cases by 10 per cent, to align the fees for barristers and other advocates in non-family cases, and to remove the 35 per cent uplift in provider legal aid fees in immigration and asylum appeals.
6. The reduction of fees paid to experts in civil, family, and criminal cases by 20 per cent.

These proposals can be read at **https://consult.justice.gov.uk/digital-communications/transforming-legal-aid**. There was general agreement in the legal profession and the press that the proposals would narrow access to justice and could lead to miscarriages of justice and leave individuals without representation in critical cases. A total of 16,000 responses were received and the Ministry of Justice held fourteen 'stakeholder events' during the consultation period to listen to opinions on the proposals and to decide how to proceed.

In September 2013, the then Lord Chancellor, Chris Grayling, announced that the proposals to introduce competitive tendering and the proposed reforms to criminal advocacy fees were to be withdrawn, and it was decided to undertake a second phase of consultation entitled 'Transforming Legal Aid: Next Steps'.

As a result of the consultation, the government announced that it intended to make the required savings by reducing the sums paid to barristers and solicitors and 'restructuring' the legal aid market. The reduction to fees was to be phased in to allow lawyers to adjust and plan for the new regime. An initial reduction of 8.75 per cent applied to new cases starting on or after 20 March 2014, and the next reduction was to take place in July 2015. In addition, a new model of tendering for duty provider work was introduced 'to achieve value for money and make sure there is always help available for people questioned or charged with a crime'; 525 contracts were awarded in October 2015.

The proposals met with unprecedented opposition from the legal profession and days of action by barristers (see Image 11.1), which had a profound effect on the conduct of trials. In May 2014, a serious fraud trial at Southwark Crown Court was halted because the defendants were unable to obtain legal representation. The judge, Anthony Leonard QC, explained that 'very substantial . . . but unsuccessful'

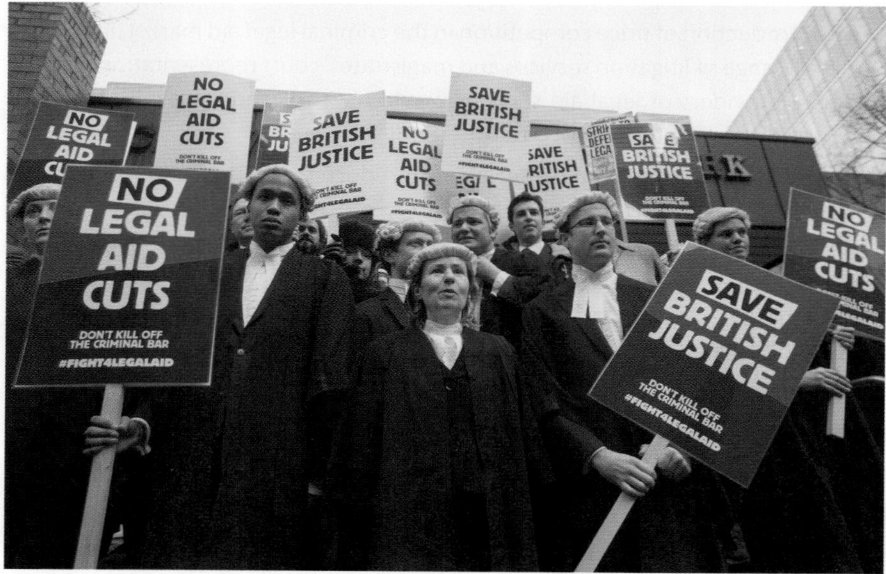

Image 11.1 Barristers protesting against legal aid cuts

Source: London News Pictures/Shutterstock

efforts had been made to find barristers to accept instructions but that none could be found willing to take on the complex matter at the legal aid rates being offered. The decision to halt the trial was later overturned by the Court of Appeal and the trial restarted after a ruling that the defendants would be able to receive a fair trial with legal representation from the PDS.

On 8 July 2014, the House of Commons Justice Committee, chaired by Alan Beith MP, began to hear evidence on the impact of the civil legal aid cuts under LASPO 2012. The *Law Society Gazette* reported that MPs on the Committee expressed 'concern over the "cult of the amateur" lawyer as they heard that thousands of vulnerable people are falling through the net of legal aid funding following cuts'. Evidence was given to the Committee about the rise in the use of 'untrained, uninsured and unregulated professional "***McKenzie friends***", who have emerged to fill the gap as people are left without access to proper legal advice and representation'. The Committee reported in March 2015 and concluded that the government had achieved its aim of substantially reducing the civil legal aid budget. However, it emphasised that this did not mean the new scheme was delivering better overall value for money for the taxpayer. The reforms had failed to ensure that legal aid was available and provided to those who needed it most; equally worryingly, the Committee noted that the legislation had not discouraged unnecessary litigation at public expense.

McKenzie friend
A person who assists a litigant in person but does not act for them. A McKenzie friend is not required to be legally qualified.

The general election of 2015 ushered in a further period of review and reform of the civil and criminal courts and associated issues regarding access to justice. The then Lord Chancellor, Michael Gove, in his first major speech in the role, emphasised the 'case for the rule of law as an institution which safeguards progressive values'. He went on to state that he would 'strive to make the justice system work for everyone' in the country. The speech can be accessed at **www.gov.uk/government/speeches/what-does-a-one-nation-justice-policy-look-like**.

One of Michael Gove's first actions, following his consideration of the position, was to shelve the ongoing major reform of the legal aid system in England and Wales.

In September 2016, the Lord Chancellor, the Lord Chief Justice, and the Senior President of Tribunals released a joint statement titled 'Transforming Our Justice System', setting out the vision for the future of the justice system in England and Wales. The report stated: 'This will be a justice system with people's needs and expectations at its heart. The transformation of the courts and tribunals across the country will be based on three core principles that build on its established strengths:

- Just
- Proportionate
- Accessible.'

The report is widely drafted and precise details will need be developed and discussed over time. The statement can be found at **www.gov.uk/government/uploads/system/uploads/attachment_data/file/553261/joint-vision-statement.pdf**.

The Law Society is also campaigning to improve access to justice. Further information can be found at **www.lawsociety.org.uk/policy-campaigns/campaigns/access-to-justice/**.

The Labour Shadow Justice Secretary, Lord Falconer, said the government's plans had 'descended into utter chaos'. However, there appeared to be a willingness to reassess the proposed changes and try to come up with a more sustainable and acceptable model. Of course, the problem of the unaffordable costs of legal aid has not gone away. There will still need to be reform. The Bach Report in September 2017, commissioned by Jeremy Corbyn, focused criticism on LASPO, and the Ministry of Justice commissioned a review of the impact of LASPO. Part 1 of the Review of LASPO was published in February 2019 subtitled 'an action plan to deliver better support to people experiencing legal problems'. A Legal Support Action Plan was produced as part of the review process and noted that 'Justice is at the centre of a safe, fair and prosperous society and this Government is committed to protecting and guaranteeing access to justice for future generations'. The plan for future legal support included extending legal aid in some family cases. It also included a commitment to a review of eligibility criteria and thresholds for legal aid. The focus of the report seems to have retreated from simply attempting to cut costs, but rather encouraging people to be aware of their right to support and to seek early legal advice. An extra £1.5m a year was committed to enhancing support for litigants in person via Personal Support Units at court centres. The actual reforms will depend upon the political situation once the Brexit situation has been concluded.

The Bach Report can be accessed at **www.fabians.org.uk/wp-content/uploads/2017/09/Bach-Commission_Right-to-Justice-Report-WEB.pdf**. The Ministry of Justice Report is here: **assets.publishing.service.gov.uk/government/uploads/system/uploads/attachment_data/file/777038/post-implementation-review-of-part-1-of-laspo.pdf**.

Key point

Reform of the legal aid system in order to try to balance the competing demands of the public purse and the needs of citizens who need legal advice is a complex conundrum for both politicians and the organisations that represent lawyers. The fundamental reforms that took place in 2013 are not the end of the changes but the beginning. The government has to decide how best to secure an adequately funded legal aid system. The hope of the Law Society, and other bodies that represent lawyers, is that the result of the reviews, proposals, reforms, and discussions will be a system that offers quality representation and access to justice for all.

Summary

- The Access to Justice Act 1999 introduced major changes to the way in which the state funds advice and representation in both civil and criminal cases.
- LASPO 2012 continued the reform of the legal aid system.
- The LAA contracts directly with firms of solicitors and other advice agencies to provide advice and representation in both civil and criminal cases, where a range of levels of service are funded.
- Eligibility for funding depends on the level of service, whether civil or criminal work is involved, and whether a means test and/or merits test is satisfied. In some civil cases, a statutory charge is levied if money or property is recovered.
- Organisations involved in giving legal advice include CABs and Law Centres.
- Methods of funding legal advice and representation include CFAs, DBAs, and BTE insurance.
- Reform of the legal aid system is ongoing.

Questions

1 Does the entitlement to free legal advice of a suspect at the police station depend upon means testing?
2 Can a person accused of a crime receive funding for legal representation: (a) in a magistrates' court; and (b) in the Crown Court?
3 Apart from funding via legal aid, in what other ways may civil litigation be funded?
4 Does the legal aid system cost too much?
5 Do you consider that the legal aid reforms have gone far enough?
6 Have the legal aid reforms gone too far and adversely affected access to justice for individuals?
7 What does access to justice mean?

Sample question and outline answer

Question

In 2011, when introducing proposals to reform legal aid, Kenneth Clarke, the then Justice Secretary, declared: 'I genuinely believe access to justice is the hallmark of a civilised society.' Do you agree? Have the recent changes to legal aid affected that access?

Outline answer

The following guidance will help you to plan and prepare an answer to the above question.

The introduction should set out what you understand the question to be asking and explain how you will answer it. It would be advisable to explain what you understand by 'access to justice'. Read widely and find some quotations and definitions that you can use to support your definition.

You may want to outline the purpose of legal aid, and perhaps distinguish between civil and criminal legal aid, and then explain why legal aid was introduced as the 'fourth pillar' of the welfare state.

Try to put the question in context. Explain why changes to the system are necessary. For example, you could quote the Ministry of Justice, which has stated: 'At around £2bn a year we have one of the most expensive legal aid systems in the world. At a time when everyone is having to tighten their belts we cannot close our eyes to the fact legal aid is costing too much and has mushroomed into something far bigger than it was intended to be.'

Set out your understanding of the changes proposed and suggest what effect you think they will have. You could refer to any of the case studies in *The Guardian* article at **www.theguardian.com/society/2013/jul/02/legal-aid-cuts-widespread-miscarriages-justice** or find your own examples. You can agree with the proposition made or disagree, so long as you support your view with evidence and sources.

Decide whether you think that access to justice, as you have defined it, has been affected by the changes and conclude accordingly.

Further reading

This is not a settled area of the law, due to the ongoing consultations on legal aid. Your reading should ensure that you can come to an informed decision about what access to justice means. Questions in this area will often ask you to decide whether you agree or disagree with the proposals for reform of legal aid, or to discuss whether the various methods of paying for legal advice ensure justice for all. The newspapers are an excellent source of articles and examples to use in support of your arguments and, because this is such a topical issue, legal journals will have articles and discussion pieces dealing with the most recent proposals and changes. You will have to keep up to date with the reform proposals.

- ***Bevan, C.*** *'Self-represented Litigants: The Overlooked and Unintended Consequence of Legal Aid Reform'* (2013) 35(1) J Soc Wel & Fam L 43–54

  This article is a thoughtful piece reviewing the research on the demographics, motivations, and case outcomes for litigants in person (people who represent themselves in front of courts and tribunals). In particular, the author examines the concerns of family lawyers about the consequences of the expected increase in litigants in person participating in family proceedings due to legal aid reforms.

- ***MacDonald, M.*** *'Jackson Reforms: First Impressions'* (2013) Post Mag, 6 June, 22–5

  This is a report giving an overview of a roundtable discussion of specialists from the insurance and legal sectors on whether the Jackson reforms are producing the intended results. It is an interesting and readable discussion giving the views of those dealing with litigation under the reformed system.

- ***Ministry of Justice.*** *'Proposals for the Reform of Legal Aid in England and Wales'* CP12/10 (November 2010)

  This is the consultation document that formed the basis of the Conservative-Liberal Democrat Coalition government's proposals for the legal aid system. It is long but it is worth reading the executive summary, the introduction, and the background sections.

- ***Ministry of Justice.*** *'Transforming Legal Aid—Next Steps'* (September 2013)

  The website **https://consult.justice.gov.uk/digital-communications/transforming-legal-aid-next-steps** provides lots of information about the 2013 consultation.

- ***Moorhead, R.*** *'An American Future? Contingency Fees, Claims Explosions and Evidence from Employment Tribunals'* (2010) 73 MLR 752

  This article considers whether England and Wales will experience similar problems to America in relation to the use of contingency fees for litigation. The author discusses the link between contingency fees and a perceived increase in the number of civil claims commenced. The article also examines the inequalities in access to justice experienced by claimants and considers how far contingency fees address those concerns. Particular reference is made to the experience of lawyers in employment tribunals.

- ***Lord Neuberger.*** *Access to Justice, Welcome address to Australian Bar Association Biennial Conference, 3 July 2017*, **www.supremecourt.uk/docs/speech-170703.pdf**

  The text of a wide-ranging speech that tackles the topic of access to justice by the then President of the Supreme Court.

- ***Organ, J.*** and ***Sigafoos, J.*** *The Impact of LASPO on Routes to Justice*, Equality and Human Rights Commission 2018 **https://www.equalityhumanrights.com/sites/default/files/the-impact-of-laspo-on-routes-to-justice-september-2018.pdf**

  A report on research into the impact on individuals of those who have attempted to resolve legal problems without access to legal aid.

- ***So, W.*** *'A Brief History of the Law of Costs—Lessons for the Jackson Reforms and Beyond'* (2013) 32(3) CJQ 333–48

  If you are interested in the history and development of the law of costs, this is the article for you. The author comments on the Jackson reforms in the light of previous efforts to develop a system that is just, predictable, and efficient.

Online resources

You should now attempt the supporting self-test questions and end-of-chapter questions available at: **www.oup.com/he/wilson-rutherford4e**

Chapter 12

The criminal process: the suspect and the police

Learning objectives

By the end of this chapter you should:

- have a basic knowledge of police powers of search, seizure, and arrest;
- have an understanding of police powers and duties when a suspect is at the police station;
- understand the law relating to confession evidence;
- understand the extent to which an accused person has a right to silence in the police station;
- appreciate the factors that must be taken into account in deciding whether to prosecute someone for a criminal offence.

Talking point

On 9 September 2010, Ann Juliette Roberts had been travelling on a bus in London without a valid ticket. She gave a false name and address to a ticket inspector and (falsely) claimed that she did not have any proof of her identity. A police officer arrived and thought that Ms Roberts was holding her bag in a suspicious manner. She therefore decided to search Ms Roberts using powers under s.60 of the Criminal Justice and Public Order Act (CJPOA) 1994. Ms Roberts, a special needs assistant working with children and young people, was reluctant to be searched in public. She resisted the search and was taken to the ground and handcuffed for the search to take place. Only bank cards in the name of Ms Roberts and her son were discovered.

This chapter will explain some of the key powers the police have to investigate crime, including powers to stop and search members of the public. For example, s.60 of the CJPOA 1994 allows the police to search for offensive weapons or other dangerous instruments. A police officer of the rank of inspector or above may authorise searches under s.60 in a locality if violence is anticipated. Section 60 is controversial because an officer does not need to have reasonable grounds to suspect that a person is carrying a weapon or dangerous instrument before searching them. The Equality and Human Rights Commission has published research showing that s.60 searches have been carried out disproportionately against black people. Ms Roberts was from African-Caribbean heritage.

Ms Roberts claimed that she had been unlawfully searched and that the power to search without reasonable suspicion violated Article 8 of the European Convention on Human Rights (ECHR). In October 2015, the Supreme Court heard Ms Roberts' case and decided that the search of Ms Roberts was lawful (*R (on the application of Roberts) v Commissioner of Police of the Metropolis and Another* [2015] UKSC 79). The Court concluded that s.60 is compatible with the ECHR because there are sufficient safeguards to ensure that searches are carried out in accordance with the law. For example, Code A to the Police and Criminal Evidence Act provides that stop and search powers must be exercised without unlawful discrimination.

As you read this chapter, ensure you understand the scope of each police power that is discussed, as well as any safeguards that accompany that power.

Before you start, reflect on the following questions:

- Do you think the police officer should have been able to search Ms Roberts and, if so, should the officer have been allowed to use force to carry out the search?
- Should there be any restrictions on the ability to search members of the public and, if so, what restrictions would strike an appropriate balance between the prevention of crime and individual liberty?

Introduction

A number of publicly funded local and national bodies have the power to investigate and prosecute offences. For example, the Health and Safety Executive can investigate and prosecute those suspected of breaching health and safety legislation. Private individuals can also bring prosecutions. However, the vast majority of criminal offences are investigated by the police and prosecuted by the Crown Prosecution Service (CPS).

In order to investigate an offence, the police may need to exercise certain powers. They may wish, for example, to search a person or a building for evidence in connection with the offence, or to detain and question a suspect. The exercise of such powers will often involve infringing the rights and freedoms of individuals. The search of a house interferes with an occupier's right to respect for their home and private life. The detention of a suspect interferes with their right to liberty. The law, therefore, aims to balance the public interest in ensuring that the police can investigate offences effectively, on the one hand, against the rights and liberties of individuals, on the other. This balance is achieved by giving the police powers, while laying down rules that control and limit those powers and the circumstances in which they may be exercised.

This chapter is concerned in particular with police powers to search, arrest, detain, and question suspects. We will also look at the consequences that may follow when the police misuse their powers or break the rules. In relation to police interviews, we will consider both the rules that protect suspects and the extent to which the right to silence has been eroded.

Finally, not all investigations result in prosecution. We will examine who decides whether to bring a prosecution against a particular suspect and the criteria that are taken into account in making that decision.

12.1 The structure and organisation of the police

England and Wales has forty-three local police forces, rather than a single national police force. In a 2018 report, the House of Commons Public Accounts Committee noted that funding for police forces had fallen by 19 per cent since 2010–11. As at 31 March 2019, there were 123,171 full-time equivalent police officers in the forty-three police forces of England and Wales, a reduction of 14 per cent since numbers peaked in 2009. The Public Accounts Committee concluded that the Home Office 'is not showing strategic leadership of the policing system and has acted too slowly in response to known financial sustainability problems'. The Home Affairs Committee published a report the same year warning that 'without additional funding for policing . . . there will be dire consequences for public safety, criminal justice, community cohesion and public confidence'.

Police officers are supported by civilian staff, police community support officers (PCSOs), and special constables. Introduced in 2002, PCSOs are uniformed civilians employed in a 'highly visible, patrolling role' (Home Office, *Police Service Strength*, SN00634, 25 July 2013)—see Image 12.1. PCSOs have a number of standard powers, such as the power to issue a fixed penalty notice for littering, limited powers to search detained persons and seize items, and, in certain circumstances, the power to require the name and address of a person who has committed an offence. Chief constables also have the authority to grant PCSOs a range of discretionary additional powers. Special constables are volunteers who are trained by their local police force to work with, and offer support to, police officers. The Home Affairs Committee observed that one of the consequences of the reduction in funding has been cuts to the number of PCSOs, with one force planning to remove them altogether.

Thinking point

How important is a visible police presence?

What do you think the consequences of removing, or reducing the number of, PCSOs might be? Remember that more PCSOs means more visible foot patrols, sometimes referred to as 'bobbies on the beat'. Opinion polls have consistently shown high levels of public support for foot patrols. There is no evidence that they reduce crime rates, but could they reduce fears of crime and/or improve community relations? (See *Policing for the Future*, HC 515, 2018, available at **https://publications.parliament.uk/pa/cm201719/cmselect/cmhaff/515/515.pdf**.)

Image 12.1 Two Police Community Support Officers on foot patrol

Source: Photofusion/Shutterstock

The Crime and Courts Act 2013 created the National Crime Agency (NCA), which works with local and international police forces to address certain types of crime. The NCA focuses on tackling organised crime, strengthening United Kingdom (UK) borders, fighting fraud and cybercrime, and protecting children and young people. NCA officers may be designated with the combined powers of police constables, immigration officers, and customs officers.

12.1.1 **Police and Crime Commissioners**

The Police Reform and Social Responsibility Act 2011 provided that Police and Crime Commissioners (PCCs) were to be appointed for each force outside London. PCCs are elected officials responsible for securing the maintenance of their police force and ensuring that it is efficient and effective. They have powers to decide local policing priorities, set policing budgets, and hire and fire chief constables.

The first PCCs were elected in November 2012 by an average of just 15 per cent of voters. In its 2014 Report, *Police and Crime Commissioners: Progress to Date* (HC 757, 2014), the Home Affairs Select Committee acknowledged that the exceptionally low turnout for the PCC elections was problematic, as it 'raised a legitimate concern as to whether the commissioners have a sufficient mandate on which to set policing priorities for their areas' (para. 3). In 2016, the Home Affairs Committee published a new Report, *Police and Crime Commissioners: Here to Stay* (HC 844, 2016), which recommended PCCs engage with the public as a matter of priority. When the second round of PCC elections took place in 2016, turnout rose to 26 per cent, although it is likely this rise can be attributed to PCC elections taking place alongside local council elections on this occasion.

12.1.2 **The Independent Office of Police Conduct (IOPC)**

The IOPC replaced the Independent Police Complaints Commission (IPCC), which was established in response to concerns about the system for investigating police complaints. Like its predecessor, the IOPC is an independent body responsible for overseeing the police complaints system. Although the majority of complaints are still investigated by the professional standards department of the relevant local force, the IOPC carries out investigations in specified serious cases, including those where police conduct has caused death or serious injury. In addition, a person who is unhappy with the way a local force has handled their complaint may be able to appeal to the IOPC. The IOPC also identifies and shares best practice and works to ensure this is reflected in police guidance and training. When in force, provisions of the Policing and Crime Act 2017 will give the IOPC enhanced powers, to initiate its own investigations, determine appeals, and recommend remedies.

A key aim of the IOPC is to improve public trust and confidence in policing. The IPCC was criticised because many of its staff were former employees of police forces and it was suggested that this compromised its independence. In October 2019, 17 per cent of IOPC Operations staff (i.e. caseworkers and investigators) were ex-police officers, 9 per cent were formerly civilian employees with the police service, and 2 per cent had previously been employed by the police in both capacities.

Thinking point

Should the IOPC be prohibited from hiring former police officers?

What are the advantages and disadvantages to the IOPC in employing former police staff? Could it be argued that a former police officer is well placed to investigate a complaint as he or she will have knowledge of the relevant rules, procedures, and systems? Or should the IOPC be prevented from employing former police officers in order to improve public confidence in the independence of its investigations?

12.2 **PACE and the Codes of Practice**

Police officers have a range of statutory and common law powers, the most significant of which are considered in this chapter. Some police powers are exercisable only on the authority of senior officers of specified ranks. Diagram 12.1 sets out the rank structure for forces outside London. (The Metropolitan Police and City of London Police have different titles for senior ranks and the head of these forces holds the rank of Commissioner.)

Prior to 1984, police powers derived from a mixture of common law, statute, and byelaws. In 1977, a Royal Commission on Criminal Procedure (RCCP) was established to examine the powers and duties of the police in respect of the investigation of criminal offences, and the rights and duties of suspects and accused persons. The RCCP, chaired by Sir Cyril Philips, was set up partly as a result of the miscarriage of justice that occurred in the *Maxwell Confait* case.

Example

In 1972 three youths, the eldest of whom was eighteen but had a mental age of eight, were convicted of offences of murder, manslaughter, and arson, arising out of the killing of Maxwell Confait. Each of them had confessed during police questioning to some degree of involvement in the crimes. It was later discovered that none of the three could possibly have committed the offences and their convictions were overturned by the Court of Appeal (*R v Lattimore, Salih and Leighton* (1976) 62 Cr App R 53). The *Confait* case fuelled concerns about police interrogation procedures and techniques.

Following the report of the RCCP (Cmnd 8092, 1981), the Police and Criminal Evidence Act 1984 (PACE) was introduced. Police powers today are mostly to be found in PACE

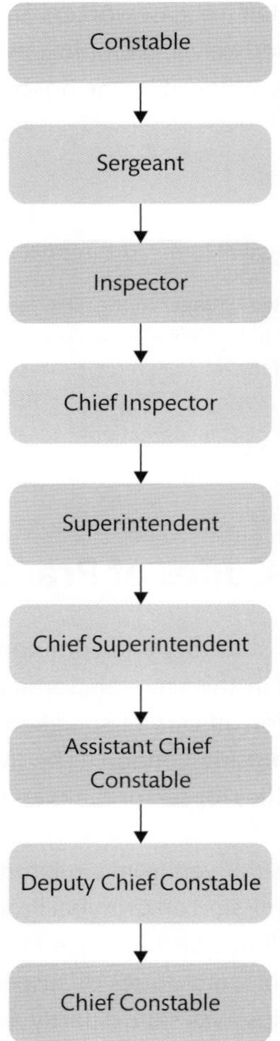

Diagram 12.1 The rank structure for police forces outside London

and in the Codes of Practice (Codes A to H) made under PACE. Among other things, PACE and the Codes of Practice govern the powers of the police to:

- stop and search persons and vehicles;
- enter and search premises;
- arrest, detain, and question people;
- take samples, photographs, and impressions; and
- conduct identification procedures.

PACE was designed to strike a balance between police powers and civil liberties. Since 1984, successive governments have sought to adjust that balance and

PACE has been supplemented and amended by various Acts of Parliament. The Codes of Practice have also been amended on a number of occasions. The latest versions of PACE Codes A to H may be found at **www.gov.uk/guidance/police-and-criminal-evidence-act-1984-pace-codes-of-practice**.

PACE is a statute and, as such, is binding upon the police. The Codes of Practice are made under PACE but are not part of the statute itself. PACE s.67, clarifies the legal status of the Codes of Practice by providing that they are admissible in evidence and that the court may take account of relevant provisions of the Codes when determining any issues that arise in criminal proceedings. However, although the police are required to comply with PACE and the Codes of Practice, failure to do so will not necessarily mean that any evidence obtained as a result is inadmissible.

Key point

Where evidence is admissible in a criminal trial, this means that the jury may hear about it. Where a judge rules that a piece of evidence is *in*admissible, the jury will not be made aware of it. In the context of a summary trial, the magistrates or district judge must decide whether a piece of evidence is admissible or not. If they decide that it is inadmissible, they must ignore it when deciding the case.

For examples of cases in which the courts have excluded evidence because of breaches of PACE or the Codes of Practice, see 12.4.4.

Even where evidence is obtained by the police unlawfully or improperly, it can often still be used by the prosecution at trial (*Kuruma v R* [1955] AC 197). Breaches of PACE or the Codes of Practice could, however, lead to various other adverse consequences for the prosecution and/or the police, such as:

- the giving of an appropriate warning to the jury where evidence is admitted in the context of such a breach;
- a stay of criminal proceedings for abuse of process (that is, bringing the criminal proceedings against the accused to an end);
- the instigation of police disciplinary proceedings and/or
- the bringing of civil or criminal proceedings against the police (for example, if a police officer is alleged to have assaulted a suspect).

Thinking point

Should the prosecution be allowed to use unlawfully obtained evidence at trial?

In some countries, whenever the police break the law (for example, by conducting an illegal search), any evidence obtained as a result is automatically inadmissible. Such evidence is sometimes referred to as 'the fruit of the poisonous tree'. What do you think this metaphor means? Is excluding unlawfully obtained evidence a good way of ensuring that the police always obey the laws or rules that govern the exercise of their powers? What if it means that a guilty person is acquitted because a police officer simply made a mistake?

12.3 **Police powers to search, seize property, and make arrests**

The principles that govern the powers of the police to search, seize property, and make arrests are mostly to be found in PACE and in the following Codes of Practice:

- Code A (the Revised Code of Practice for the Exercise by: Police Officers of Statutory Powers of Stop and Search; Police Officers and Police Staff of Requirements to Record Public Encounters, 2015);
- Code B (the Revised Code of Practice for Searches of Premises by Police Officers and the Seizure of Property Found by Police Officers on Persons or Premises, 2013);
- Code G (the Revised Code of Practice for the Statutory Power of Arrest by Police Officers, 2012).

12.3.1 **Powers to stop and search and seize articles**

PACE s.1 gives police officers the power to search any person or vehicle for stolen or prohibited articles, bladed articles, or fireworks carried in contravention of fireworks regulations. 'Prohibited articles' are offensive weapons or articles made, adapted, or intended for use in connection with one of the offences listed in s.1(8) (which include burglary, theft, or criminal damage). In order to exercise this power, the officer must have reasonable grounds for suspecting they will find a stolen or prohibited article, bladed article, or firework. This means that the police cannot normally carry out random, speculative searches.

The power to stop and search may only be exercised in a place to which the public have access and the person being searched may not be required to remove clothing, other than a coat, jacket, or gloves, in public (s.2(9)). If the officer does find a relevant article, s.1(6) gives them the power to seize it.

Unlike the power to search contained in s.60 of the CJPOA 1994, which is discussed in the Talking Point at the start of this chapter, s.1 is an example of a police power that can only be exercised if a police officer has reasonable grounds for suspicion. As explained in the Talking Point, there are some stop and search powers that do not require reasonable suspicion, but these are controversial.

'Reasonable suspicion' is not defined in PACE. Code A provides that a two-part test should be applied. First, the officer must have 'formed a genuine suspicion in their own mind that they will find the object for which the search power being exercised allows them to search' (para. 2.2). Second, the suspicion must be reasonable, which means that it must have an 'objective basis . . . based on facts, information and/or intelligence which are relevant to the likelihood that the object in question will be found' (para. 2.2). Code A contains a reminder that the Equality Act 2010 makes it unlawful to discriminate against any person on the grounds of any of the 'protected characteristics' set out in the Act, which are: age; disability; gender reassignment; pregnancy and maternity; race, religion, or belief; sex; and sexual orientation. A person's appearance, including any of the protected characteristics, or the fact that a person is known to have a previous conviction, cannot form the basis of reasonable suspicion. Furthermore, reasonable suspicion cannot be based upon stereotypes that certain groups or categories of people are more likely to be involved in crime.

Example

PC O'Connell is on mobile patrol at 11 p.m. in a part of London in which a series of burglaries has been reported in the past week. All of the burglaries have taken place in the early hours of the morning and entry to each of the properties was gained using a screwdriver. One homeowner saw the burglar and described him as a black man.

At 11:30 p.m., PC O'Connell sees Omar, a young black man, walking down a street. Upon seeing PC O'Connell's marked police car, Omar pulls his hood over his head and hunches his shoulders. He puts his right hand in his pocket, removes something, and places it under his jumper. PC O'Connell thinks that Omar must be concealing a screwdriver or similar implement and decides to stop and search him.

PC O'Connell clearly personally suspects that he will find a screwdriver when he searches Omar. A screwdriver would be a prohibited article if it was intended for use in connection with an offence of burglary. PC O'Connell's suspicion also appears to be objectively reasonable. The fact that Omar is black, or that he is young, cannot form the basis of reasonable suspicion but his furtive behaviour and the fact that he is seen to conceal something could give rise to reasonable suspicion.

Code A identifies certain information that must be given to a person prior to a search taking place, including a clear explanation by the officer of the purpose of the search. Code A indicates that it will generally be desirable for a brief conversation to take place prior to a search to avoid unsuccessful searches, to gain cooperation, and to reduce tension. This is necessary because the exercise of stop and search powers by the police has, at times, caused controversy—it has been alleged that the police use their powers to target particular categories or groups of people. For example, a 2016 Report by the Equality and Human Rights Commission highlighted that 'if you are a black person, you are at least six times as likely to be stopped and searched by the police in England and Wales as a white person. If you are Asian, you are around twice as likely to be stopped and searched as a white person' (*Stop and Think: A Critical Review of the Use of Stop and Search powers in England and Wales*, EHRC, 2016).

In an effort to ensure that stop and search powers are not used disproportionately against specific sections of the community, Code A lays down procedures for the recording, monitoring, and supervision of stop and search powers. These procedures require an electronic or paper record to be made of every search, which must include the object of the search, the grounds for reasonable suspicion, and the self-defined ethnicity of the person searched. Senior officers are expected to monitor these records and to address any trends or patterns that give cause for concern.

A 2013 report by Her Majesty's Inspectorate of Constabulary (HMIC) found 'disturbingly low levels' of supervision by senior officers of the conduct of stop and search encounters. A total of 27 per cent of stop and search records did not contain reasonable grounds to search people. The report concluded that there were low levels of understanding of the term 'reasonable suspicion', poor supervision, and lack of oversight by senior officers (*Stop and Search Powers: Are the Police Using Them Effectively and Fairly?* HMIC, 2013).

Further, it could be argued that records do not paint a complete picture because there is no requirement to make a record of a 'stop and account'. When an officer requests a person in a public place to account for themselves by asking what the person is doing, why they are in the area, where they are going, or what they are carrying, there is no national requirement for a record to be made. It is only if a stop and account results in a search that the encounter must be recorded.

In the year ending March 2019, 370,454 stops and searches were carried out under s.1 of PACE, an increase of 32 per cent compared to the previous year. Approximately 16 per cent of these stop and search encounters led to an arrest. Table 12.1 sets out the ethnicity of persons searched under s.1 of PACE.

Although PACE s.1 is the main stop and search power that the police possess, there are various other stop and search powers. For example, see: s.23 of the Misuse of Drugs Act 1971 (which permits an officer to stop and search persons and vehicles if the officer has reasonable grounds to suspect that the person is in possession of controlled drugs); s.60 of the CJPOA 1994 (which gives officers the power to stop and search in anticipation of violence without reasonable suspicion being required); and s.47A of the Terrorism Act 2000 (which contains a power to search in specified locations to prevent acts of terrorism). Section 47A of the Terrorism Act 2000 was inserted by the Protection of Freedoms Act 2012 to replace the power contained in s.44 of the Terrorism Act 2000. Under s.44, senior officers could authorise random searches of persons and/or vehicles. Such searches did not require the police to have reasonable suspicion.

In *Gillan and Quinton v United Kingdom* [2009] ECHR 28, the European Court of Human Rights ruled that the use of s.44 constituted an interference with the right to respect for private life. Article 8 of the ECHR provides that there shall be no interference by a public authority with the right to private life except such as is in accordance with the law and is necessary to protect certain specified interests. The Court ruled

Table 12.1 Proportion of stops and searches under s.1 of PACE by self-defined ethnicity, 2015/16 and 2016/17

	2017/18							2018/19						
	White	Black (or Black British)	Asian (or Asian British)	Chinese or Other	Mixed	Not stated	Total	White	Black (or Black British)	Asian (or Asian British)	Chinese or Other	Mixed	Not stated	Total
E&W* excl. MPS	71	8	7	1	3	10	100	68	7	7	1	3	13	100
MPS**	34	32	14	3	4	13	100	32	30	15	3	4	16	100
England & Wales	53	19	10	2	4	11	100	51	18	11	2	3	15	100

*excludes South Wales

**MPS = Metropolitan Police Service.

Note: We assume that these figures have been rounded.

Source: Police powers and procedures England and Wales statistics, Home Office.

that the interference created by s.44 was not in accordance with the law because it was not 'sufficiently circumscribed' and there were no 'adequate legal safeguards' to prevent misuse of the s.44 powers. The Court noted that the available statistics showed that the power was used disproportionately against black and Asian persons. As a result, the Court found that there had been a violation of Article 8 of the ECHR.

On 8 July 2010, then Home Secretary Theresa May announced the government's intention to amend the law so that s.44 powers to stop and search were compliant with the ECHR. As a result, the Protection of Freedoms Act 2012 repealed s.44 and inserted a new s.47A in its place. Section 47A provides that a senior police officer may only give an authorisation to stop and search under the Terrorism Act if they reasonably suspect that an act of terrorism will take place. The senior officer must also consider both that the authorisation is necessary and that the geographical extent of the authorisation and its duration are necessary. Once a s.47A order is in place, an officer conducting a search in the specified area does not require reasonable suspicion. A Code of Practice for the authorisation and use of stop and search powers under the Terrorism Act was introduced. It contains a reminder that the Equality Act 2010 prohibits unlawful discrimination and states that officers must take care to avoid any form of racial or religious profiling when selecting people to search under a Terrorism Act authorisation.

A similar issue has arisen in relation to s.60 of the CJPOA 1994, which gives police officers additional powers to stop and search without reasonable suspicion being required. Section 60 of the CJPOA 1994 provides that an officer of the rank of inspector or above may authorise officers to stop and search persons and vehicles for offensive weapons or dangerous implements. The inspector must reasonably believe that:

- incidents involving serious violence may take place;
- an incident involving serious violence has occurred and an offensive weapon or dangerous instrument used in the incident is being carried by someone in the area; or
- persons are carrying offensive weapons or dangerous instruments in the area without good reason.

An authorisation under s.60 must be limited to a specific area and must be for a specified period of no more than twenty-four hours. In other words, officers do not have a general power to conduct speculative searches for weapons. An officer of the rank of superintendent or above may extend the period for a further twenty-four hours. As discussed in the Talking Point at the start of this chapter, it has been suggested that s.60 is used disproportionately to search black people, particularly in London (see *R v (Roberts) v Commissioner of Police of the Metropolis and Others* [2014] EWCA Civ 69). Research conducted by the Equality and Human Rights Commission into the use of stop and search powers under s.60 found 'evidence that people from some ethnicities are stopped significantly more often than other people' (*Race Disproportionality in Stops and Searches under Section 60 of the Criminal Justice and Public Order Act 1994*, EHRC, 2012).

In October 2015, the case of *Roberts* reached the Supreme Court, which held that there are sufficient safeguards and restrictions to ensure that s.60 is compatible with the ECHR (*R (on the application of Roberts) v Commissioner of Police of the Metropolis and Another* [2015] UKSC 79). In particular, s.60 powers must be exercised in accordance with Code A, which specifically states that police officers must use their powers to stop and search without unlawful discrimination (Code A, para. 1.1). The current version of Code A adds that s.60 powers must not be used for purposes unconnected with the s.60 authorisation that is in place at the time (Code A, para. 2.14A). The Supreme Court observed that although a 'suspicionless' power to stop and search, such as that found in s.60, 'carries with it the risk that it will be used in an arbitrary or discriminatory manner in individual cases', there are also 'great benefits to the public in such a power' ([2015] UKSC 79, [41]). The Court suggested that the power to conduct random searches has a deterrent effect and increases the chance that weapons will be found. In the case of *Roberts* itself, the s.60 authorisation was issued following gang violence in a London borough. Although the Court acknowledged concerns that black and ethnic minority people were being disproportionately targeted for searches, they added that 'it is members of these groups who will benefit most from the reduction in violence, serious injury and death that may result from the use of such powers. Put bluntly, it is mostly young black lives that will be saved if there is less gang violence in London and some other cities' ([2015] UKSC 79, [41]).

Critical debate

In March 2015, Her Majesty's Inspectorate of Constabulary published an updated report on the use of stop and search (*Stop and Search Powers 2: Are the Police Using Them Effectively and Fairly?* HMIC, 2015). The report concluded that, although good progress had been made with regard to utilising technology to record stop and search encounters, there remained a need to 'improv[e] officers' understanding of the impact that stop and search encounters can have on community confidence and trust in the police'.

What impact do you think stop and search can have on an individual who is subject to these powers? How do you think the use (or misuse) of stop and search powers might affect the way communities view the police?

In 2015, a revised Code A was introduced with the aim, in particular, of clarifying the meaning of 'reasonable grounds for suspicion'. In addition, all forty-three police forces in England and Wales voluntarily signed up to the Home Secretary's 'Better Use of Stop and Search Scheme' (BUSSS), requiring them to record stop and search outcomes in more detail to 'show the link, or lack of one, between the object of the search and its outcome' (**https://assets.publishing.service.gov.uk/government/uploads/system/uploads/attachment_data/file/346922/Best_Use_of_Stop_and_Search_Scheme_v3.0_v2.pdf**). The BUSSS also provided more stringent requirements for a s.60 search.

Table 12.2 Key features of s.60 CJPOA and the BUSS Scheme compared

s.60 CJPOA 1994	BUSSS (2014)
Authorisation may be given by an officer of or above the rank of inspector.	Raised the level of authorisation to an officer of at least the rank of Assistant Chief Constable.
Authorising officer must reasonably believe that incidents involving serious violence *may* take place.	Authorising officer must reasonably believe that incidents involving serious violence ***will*** take place.
A s.60 authorisation can be for a specified period not exceeding 24 hours.	A s.60 authorisation can be for a specified period not exceeding 24 hours.
An officer of the rank of superintendent or above may direct that the authorisation shall continue for a further 24 hours. (Maximum overall time for a s.60 authorisation = 48 hours.)	An officer of at least the rank of Assistant Chief Constable may direct that the authorisation shall continue for a further 24 hours. (Maximum overall time for an authorisation = 39 hours.)

A comparison between the legislative framework and the more restrictive approach under the BUSSS is set out in Table 12.2, above.

In August 2019, in response to growing concerns about knife crime, the Home Secretary announced that a pilot scheme to remove the above BUSSS conditions would be extended to all police forces. A Home Office Equality Impact Statement dated the same month noted that available data suggests a disparity in the use of s.60 search powers on individuals from Black and Minority Ethnic communities, 'especially black men compared with white men. It is possible that this disparity is at least in part a result of discrimination/stereotyping on the part of officers and forces carrying out searches under s.60.' The authors warned that an increase in stop and search might have a 'potentially negative impact on trust in the police', adding that trust and cooperation with the police is 'often necessary for effective community police, [so] such changes may create broader issues'.

12.3.2 **Powers to make arrests**

A person is under arrest when they are no longer at liberty to go where they please. An arrest is usually carried out by physically seizing or touching a person with a view to detaining them, although a person can be arrested by words alone (that is, by being told that they are under arrest). Where PACE confers powers (such as the power of arrest), an officer may use reasonable force if necessary when exercising those powers (PACE s.117).

A magistrates' court may, in certain circumstances, issue a warrant for a person's arrest. A warrant is a written document which authorises the police to arrest a person in order to bring them before the court. The police may arrest a person who is the subject of a warrant at any time and take them into custody before bringing them before the court at the earliest opportunity. This is known as 'executing' the warrant. A warrant of arrest may be endorsed or 'backed' for bail. This means that, once arrested, the person is to be released on bail subject to a duty to appear before a magistrates' court on a specified date and at a specified time (Magistrates' Courts Act 1980 s.117).

Bail is defined later in the section.

However, a police officer will not always have time to go before the magistrates' court to apply for a warrant of arrest. An officer may need to arrest someone immediately in order to prevent an offence being committed. For this reason the police also possess a variety of powers to arrest *without* a warrant, the most notable of which is contained in PACE s.24.

Under PACE s.24, a police officer may arrest without a warrant:

- anyone who is in the act of committing, or about to commit, an offence;
- anyone whom the officer has reasonable grounds to suspect is in the act of committing, or about to commit, an offence;
- anyone who is guilty of an offence that has already been committed (or whom the officer has reasonable grounds to suspect is guilty of such an offence); or
- anyone whom the officer has reasonable grounds to suspect is guilty of an offence that the officer has reasonable grounds to suspect has been committed.

Thus, an officer does not have to wait until an offence has actually been committed before arresting someone. Nor do they have to be *sure* that the person they are arresting has committed (or was in the act of committing, or was about to commit) an offence; they merely have to have *'reasonable grounds to suspect'*. In this context, the courts have held that 'reasonable suspicion' is partly subjective and partly objective. The officer must personally suspect that the person was, for example, about to commit an offence (the subjective element) but the grounds for that suspicion must be grounds that an ordinary person would regard as reasonable (the objective element) (*O'Hara v Chief Constable of the Royal Ulster Constabulary* [1997] AC 286).

Example

In *Alanov v Chief Constable of Sussex* [2012] EWCA Civ 234, the appellant (A) had been arrested when the police conducted house to house enquiries in an area where a particularly violent rape had occurred. The arresting officer suspected A of the offence because, when he knocked on A's door:

1. A's partner initially lied and said that A was not at home;
2. A's partner was nervous;
3. A remained in the bathroom and continued showering after his partner allowed the police into the house;
4. A became aggressive and was uncooperative;

5. although the description of the rapist did not match A's appearance, that description might have been inaccurate.

The Court of Appeal held that these factors 'do not pass even the low threshold for establishing, objectively speaking . . . *"reasonable suspicion"*'.

In addition, the power of arrest under s.24 may only be exercised if the officer has reasonable grounds to believe that an arrest is *necessary* for one of the reasons specified in s.24(5), such as:

- to enable the person's name or address to be ascertained;
- to prevent the person causing injury to himself or another, or loss or damage to property;
- to protect a child or vulnerable person;
- to allow the prompt and effective investigation of the offence; or
- to prevent prosecution for the offence from being hindered by the person's disappearance.

Thinking point

Why is it important for powers of arrest to be restricted?

Why do you think the law requires police officers to have 'reasonable grounds for suspicion' before they can make an arrest? And why must an arrest be 'necessary' if it is to be carried out without a warrant? Remember that an arrest is a serious infringement of personal liberty.

Bail
Bail means the release from custody of an accused or convicted person. Bail may be granted either unconditionally or subject to conditions, such as a condition that the person resides at a particular address or reports to a police station at a particular time. 'Street bail' is the power that police officers now have to grant bail to persons who have been arrested without having to take them first to a police station. The only condition that an officer can impose on street bail is a condition that the person attends a named police station at a specified time.

Code G emphasises that it is for the individual officer to decide whether to arrest, report for summons (for a definition of a summons see 13.2.4), grant 'street ***bail***', issue a fixed penalty notice, or take any other action that is open to them. However, an officer who chooses to arrest is required to examine and justify the need to arrest the person and take them to a police station. This is because arrest and detention deprive a person of their liberty, which is a fundamental human right.

An officer must personally believe that arrest is necessary and that belief must be objectively reasonable (*Hayes v Chief Constable of Merseyside* [2011] EWCA Civ 911). In *Richardson v Chief Constable of Essex* [2011] EWHC 773 (QBD), the High Court held that the word 'necessary' is an ordinary English word and there is no need to paraphrase it. Before arresting a suspect, an officer must consider whether it is necessary to do so. If they conclude that it is necessary, they must be able to give reasons to support that conclusion. The officer should consider whether having the suspect attend the police station voluntarily is a practicable alternative to arrest.

 Example

In *Richardson v Chief Constable of Essex* [2011] EWHC 773 (QBD), R was a schoolteacher with no previous criminal convictions or cautions. He was alleged to have assaulted a pupil and was asked to attend a police station for interview. When R arrived at the police station, the custody area was closed and he agreed to travel to an alternative police station. Upon arrival at the second police station, R was arrested.

The arresting officer maintained that she had arrested R because, as a voluntary attender, he would be entitled to leave at will, which could disrupt the interview. She claimed that R's arrest was therefore necessary to allow the prompt and effective investigation of the offence. R was interviewed while under arrest but was released without charge. He was later informed that no further action would be taken against him.

R successfully challenged the lawfulness of his arrest. The High Court held that R's status as a voluntary attender, meaning that he could leave during the interview, did not mean that his arrest was necessary. There was no basis for thinking that R would disrupt the interview by leaving, particularly given that he had voluntarily travelled to two different police stations for interview.

In *Lord Hanningfield of Chelmsford v Chief Constable of Essex* [2013] EWHC 243 (QB), the High Court reiterated the need for police officers to give consideration to alternatives to arrest. Lord Hanningfield had been arrested at his home at 6:45 a.m. on suspicion of fraud. His home was searched without a warrant having first been obtained from a magistrates' court. The police argued that Lord Hanningfield's arrest was necessary under s.24 of PACE because, if they attempted to question him without first arresting him, he might become uncooperative and might hide or destroy evidence, or alert others who were suspected of participating in the fraud.

The High Court ruled that Lord Hanningfield's arrest had not been necessary (*Lord Hanningfield of Chelmsford v The Chief Constable of Essex Police* [2013] EWHC 243 (QB)). There was nothing to suggest that he would not cooperate with the investigation; the idea that he might conceal or destroy evidence was pure speculation; and, although he had known of the investigation for some time, there was nothing to suggest that he had colluded with others or intended to do so.

Eady J stated that '[t]his process of addressing alternatives [to arrest] is not a matter of box-ticking. The record must show that genuine consideration was given to practicable options.' His Lordship added that s.24 of PACE should not be used to bypass the statutory safeguards that apply when an application is made for a warrant of arrest. In accordance with the jurisprudence on the necessity condition for arrest, Code G now provides that an officer 'must consider whether the suspect's voluntary attendance is a practicable alternative for carrying out the interview. If it is, then arrest would not be necessary.'

Article 5 of the ECHR guarantees the right to liberty and security of the person. Article 5 provides a definitive list of the circumstances in which a person may lawfully be deprived of their liberty. This includes the arrest or detention of a person on reasonable suspicion of having committed an offence, or where it is reasonably necessary to prevent them committing an offence, or to prevent them from escaping after having done so. Any such arrest must be carried out in accordance with procedures prescribed by national law and must be for the purpose of bringing the person before a competent legal authority. Thus, although arrest inevitably deprives a person of their liberty, it will not constitute a breach of the ECHR if it is necessary and is carried out in accordance with PACE and the Codes of Practice.

Under Article 5(2) of the ECHR, an arrested person must be informed promptly, in a language that they understand, of the reasons for the arrest and of any charges. The arrestee must be brought promptly before a court and is entitled to trial within a reasonable time or to release pending trial. They are entitled to have the lawfulness of their detention determined speedily by a court and their release must be ordered if the detention is unlawful.

In accordance with Article 5(2), PACE s.28 provides that at the time of arrest, or as soon as practicable thereafter, the arrested person must be informed both that they are under arrest and of the ground for the arrest. Failure to comply with these requirements renders the arrest unlawful. Code G provides that an arrested person must also be ***cautioned***.

Cautioned
The term caution can be used to mean two different things in criminal law. In this context a person is cautioned when they are given a warning about the implications of anything they might say (or not say) when asked questions about a criminal offence.

The wording of the caution is set out at 12.4.3. The alternative meaning of the term 'caution' is considered at 12.4.7.

Code C provides that once a decision to arrest a suspect has been made, the suspect must not be questioned concerning the offence except at a police station or other authorised place of detention. To question a suspect prior to their arrival at a police station would deprive them of various rights and entitlements under PACE and the Codes of Practice, such as the right to free legal advice. However, an exception may be made, and a suspect may be questioned immediately upon arrest, if delay would be likely to:

- lead to interference with, or harm to, evidence or people;
- lead to serious loss of, or damage to, property;
- lead to the alerting of other suspects; or
- hinder the recovery of property.

12.3.3 **Power to enter and search premises and seize articles**

Where the requirements of PACE s.8 are satisfied, a Justice of the Peace may issue a search warrant (that is, a warrant authorising the police to enter and search premises). Section 8 applies when there are reasonable grounds to believe that an indictable offence has been committed and that there is material on the premises that is likely to be of substantial value to the investigation of that offence. Certain other criteria must also be met. For example, there must be one of a number of specified reasons for needing the warrant, such as that entry to the premises will not be granted without one. Further consideration of s.8 is outside the scope of this work.

The police also possess a variety of powers to search premises *without* a warrant. Under PACE s.17, a police officer may enter and search premises for one of the purposes specified in s.17(1), which include:

- to execute a warrant of arrest;
- to arrest a person for an ***indictable offence***;
- to arrest a person for one of a number of specified summary offences, such as driving while under the influence of drink or drugs; or
- to save life and limb or prevent serious damage to property.

Indictable offence
An indictable offence is an offence that either may or must be tried in the Crown Court. Conversely, a summary offence can only be tried in the magistrates' court. Thus, trial on indictment takes place in the Crown Court and summary trial takes place in a magistrates' court. For further details see 13.1.

Other than in relation to saving life or limb, or preventing serious damage to property, s.17 powers may only be exercised if the officer has reasonable grounds for believing that the person they seek is on the premises.

Alternatively, under PACE s.18, a police officer may enter and search premises occupied or controlled by a person who is under arrest for an indictable offence. However, this power may only be exercised if the officer has reasonable grounds for suspecting that there is evidence on the premises that relates to that offence or to a connected or similar indictable offence. Furthermore, the power to search under s.18 usually requires the written authorisation of an officer of the rank of inspector or above.

All searches must be limited to the extent necessary to achieve the object of the search. Reasonable and proportionate force may be used to enter premises if necessary. Both s.17 and s.18 of PACE contain powers to seize relevant material discovered in the course of a search.

12.3.4 **Power to search a person following arrest**

Section 32 of PACE empowers a police officer to search an arrested person if there are reasonable grounds to believe that the person may present a danger to himself or others. An officer may also search an arrested person for anything which might be used in order to escape, or for evidence relating to an offence (if there are reasonable grounds for believing that such items may be concealed on the arrested person). Additionally, where the arrest was for an indictable offence, the officer may enter and search premises in which the arrested person was at the time of arrest or immediately before the time of arrest. This power may only be exercised if the officer has reasonable grounds to believe that there is evidence on the premises relating to the offence. This is different from the power in s.18 as it can be exercised even where the arrested person does not own or control the premises. Again, a search under s.32 must be limited to the extent that is reasonably required to achieve the object of the search.

In accordance with Article 8 of the ECHR, Code B emphasises that the exercise of powers of entry, search, and seizure must be fully and clearly justified because the exercise of such powers may significantly interfere with the privacy of the occupier.

12.3.5 **Policing protestors**

Section 60 of the CJPOA 1994 is considered at 12.3.1.

The police may exercise their usual powers under PACE in relation to demonstrators, such as the power to stop and search under s.1 of PACE. In addition, s.60 of the CJPOA 1994 may be used to stop and search protestors without reasonable suspicion in certain circumstances, provided an officer of at least the rank of inspector has authorised the use of s.60 powers.

In 2012, a statutory stop and search authorisation under s.60 of the CJPOA 1994 was issued in relation to the royal wedding of Prince William to Kate Middleton on the basis of police intelligence that demonstrators intended to disrupt the wedding. However, some officers continued to use their powers under s.1 of PACE when searching for items other than offensive weapons or dangerous implements (*R (on the application of Hicks) v Commissioner of Police for the Metropolis* [2012] EWHC 1947 (Admin)).

The death of Ian Tomlinson during the protests at the G20 summit in London in 2009 called attention to police tactics at demonstrations. Mr Tomlinson was a newspaper vendor who was on his way home when he found himself inside a cordon that the police had set up to contain protestors. When he tried to leave, a police officer (PC Harwood) hit him with a baton and pushed him to the ground. Mr Tomlinson got up and began to walk away but collapsed and died a short time later. The police at first denied that excessive force had been used, and an initial police post-mortem examination suggested that Mr Tomlinson had died of natural causes. However, video footage came to light showing Mr Tomlinson being pushed to the ground from behind by PC Harwood. A second post-mortem examination established that Mr Tomlinson died as a result of internal bleeding caused by a blow.

PC Harwood was eventually charged with manslaughter but acquitted after trial. He was, nevertheless, sacked after a Metropolitan Police disciplinary panel found him guilty of gross misconduct. Despite the jury's verdict, the Metropolitan Police agreed to pay damages to Mr Tomlinson's family and, in July 2013, Deputy Assistant Commissioner Maxine de Brunner apologised for PC Harwood's use of 'excessive and unlawful force'.

The assault on Ian Tomlinson occurred as the police were setting up a cordon around demonstrators: a practice known as 'kettling'. Opponents of kettling argue that it amounts to a deprivation of the liberty of anyone caught inside the police cordon and is therefore unlawful under Article 5 of the ECHR (the right to liberty and security of the person).

In *Austin v UK* (2012) 55 EHRR 14, the European Court of Human Rights considered a case in which the police cordoned off Oxford Circus on 1 May 2001 while protests against capitalism were taking place. For seven hours a crowd consisting of protestors and members of the public was contained inside the cordon, where conditions were uncomfortable. Although those inside the cordon were able to move about, it was cold and wet, there was no access to shelter or toilet facilities, and no food or water was provided. The European Court of Human Rights declined to rule that the kettling of protestors violated Article 5. The Court accepted that kettling might be the least intrusive and most effective means 'to isolate and contain a large crowd in volatile and dangerous conditions' so as to 'avert a real risk of serious injury or damage'. There is a distinction between a restriction on freedom of movement and the deprivation of liberty and the Court was unable to say that, in the instant case, a deprivation of liberty had occurred. However, if the police maintained a cordon after it was necessary for crowd control and in order to punish or 'teach a lesson to' demonstrators, it is likely that Article 5 would be engaged and the detention of those inside the cordon would become unlawful.

12.4 The suspect at the police station

The principles that govern the treatment of a person who has been arrested and taken into custody by the police are to be found in PACE and in the following Codes of Practice:

- Code C (the Revised Code of Practice for the Detention, Treatment and Questioning of Persons by Police Officers, 2019);
- Code E (the Revised Code of Practice on Audio Recording Interviews with Suspects, 2018);
- Code F (the Revised Code of Practice on Visual Recording with Sound of Interviews with Suspects, 2018).

12.4.1 Arrival at the police station

When a person attends a police station voluntarily (that is, without having been arrested), PACE s.29 provides that they may leave at will unless placed under arrest.

When a person is under arrest, Code C requires them to be brought before the custody officer as soon as practicable. Section 36 of PACE provides that each designated police station must appoint one or more custody officers of at least the rank of sergeant. A custody officer must be independent and cannot be an officer who is involved in investigating the offence for which a person is in police detention.

The custody officer must open a custody record in which information relating to the person's detention is recorded. This information includes: the offence for which the detainee has been arrested, the grounds for detaining them, whether legal advice was requested, details of periodic checks carried out, and all reviews of detention. The detainee's solicitor is entitled to consult the custody record.

Where an arrested person is brought before the custody officer, it is the custody officer's duty under PACE s.37 to make the decisions shown in Diagram 12.2.

If there is insufficient evidence to charge an arrested person then and there, they may be detained if there are reasonable grounds to believe that detention is necessary to secure or preserve evidence relating to the offence or to obtain such evidence

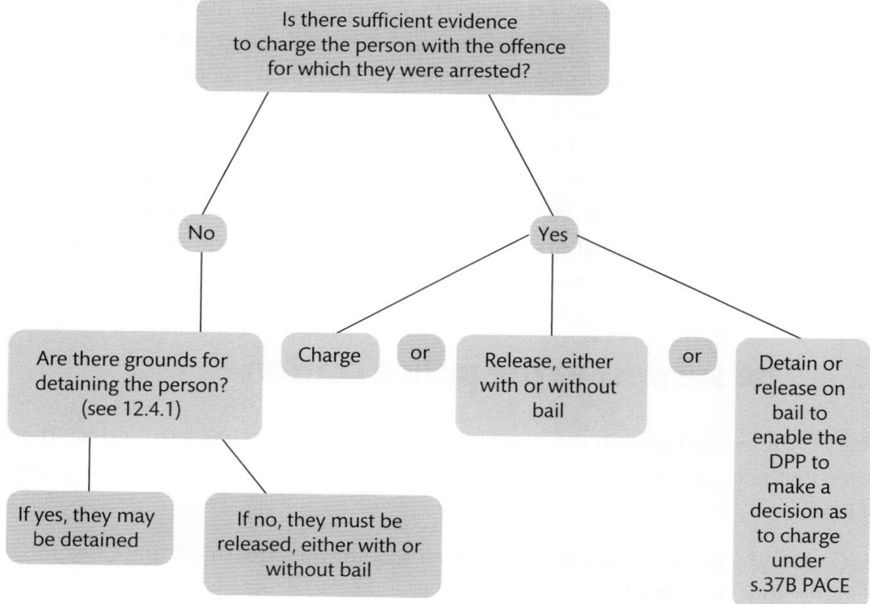

Diagram 12.2 A custody officer's decision-making process under PACE s.37

by questioning. It is the latter that gives the police the power to detain a suspect in order to interview them.

A detainee has the right not to be held incommunicado. Under PACE s.56, they have the right to have someone informed of their whereabouts as soon as practicable. Under Code C, the detainee must also be given writing materials on request and be allowed to telephone one person for a reasonable time. However, what they say or write (other than in a communication to a solicitor) is not private as it may be read or listened to and used in evidence.

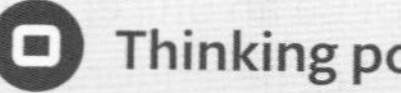

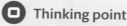

Thinking point

Why should communications between solicitor and client be private?

The Notes for Guidance to Code C state that a detainee's right to consult or communicate with a legal representative in private is 'fundamental'. Why should any communications between detainee and solicitor remain private? Is access to confidential legal advice an essential corollary of the right to a fair trial?

Under PACE s.58, a detainee has the right to consult a solicitor in private at any time, personally, in writing, or by telephone. Free independent legal advice is available from the duty solicitor. Code C provides that the custody officer must inform the detainee of the right to legal advice and a detainee who requests legal advice should not be interviewed until that advice has been received. A detainee is entitled to have a solicitor present in interview, and the solicitor may properly intervene during the interview, for example:

- to seek clarification;
- to challenge an improper question or the manner in which a question is put;
- to advise the detainee not to answer a question; or
- if the solicitor wishes to give further advice to the detainee.

Thinking point

Why do detainees have a right to legal advice?

Why is it important for a detainee to be allowed to see or speak to a solicitor? Why should they be allowed to have a solicitor present during an interview? Consider whether their rights would necessarily be adequately protected without a solicitor.

Under PACE ss.56 and 58 and Annex B to Code C, the detainee's right to have someone informed of their detention may be delayed on the authorisation of an officer of at least the rank of inspector, and the right to legal advice may be delayed on the authorisation of an officer of superintendent rank or above. These rights may only be delayed where a person is detained in connection with an indictable offence and there are reasonable grounds for believing that notifying someone will lead to interference with (or harm to) evidence or persons or the alerting of other suspects, or will hinder the recovery of property obtained in connection with the offence.

If a suspect is either a juvenile (that is, aged under eighteen) or a person who is vulnerable, Code C requires the custody officer to ask an 'appropriate adult' to come to the police station to give the suspect advice and assistance. The term 'vulnerable' is defined in Code C 1.13(d) to include persons who may have difficulties understanding or communicating due to a mental health condition or mental disorder. An appropriate adult is a responsible adult who is not a police officer or anyone employed by the police. The appropriate adult could be a parent, guardian, or social worker in the case of a juvenile. In the case of a person who is vulnerable, the appropriate adult could be a relative, guardian, or someone experienced in dealing with those who have mental health difficulties. The right to an appropriate adult is in addition to the detainee's right to legal advice. Code C also imposes special requirements where a suspect appears to be unable to speak or understand English or has a hearing or speech impediment (in which case an interpreter must be provided) or where the suspect is blind or seriously visually impaired.

12.4.2 Detention conditions and care and treatment of detainees

Sections 8 and 9 of Code C set out minimum standards for the care and treatment of those detained in police custody. Where practicable, there should be one detainee to a cell, which should be adequately heated, cleaned, ventilated, and lit. There should be clean bedding and access to toilet and washing facilities. At least two light meals and a main meal must be offered every twenty-four hours, with drinks at mealtimes and on reasonable request. Normally, a detainee should be allowed a continuous eight-hour period every twenty-four hours, normally at night, which is free from interruption. Detainees should be checked at least every hour and the custody officer is responsible for ensuring that a detainee receives appropriate clinical attention if they are injured or appear to be ill, suffering from a mental disorder, or in need of clinical attention.

Thinking point

Why are a suspect's basic human rights important?

The existence of minimum standards for the care and treatment of detainees ensures that a suspect's basic human rights are respected. Why is this important? Think about Article 3 of the ECHR, which provides that no one should be subjected to torture or to inhuman or degrading treatment.

12.4.3 The police station interview

Code C 11.1A states that any questioning of a person regarding their involvement or suspected involvement in an offence constitutes an 'interview'. Following arrest, a suspect may usually only be interviewed at a police station or other authorised place of detention.

Before a detainee can be interviewed, Code C provides that the custody officer must assess whether they are fit enough to be interviewed or whether they are 'at risk' (see Code C, Annex G). This assessment may involve consulting a healthcare professional. A detainee may be at risk if interviewing them could cause significant harm to their physical or mental state or if anything they say *might* be considered unreliable in subsequent court proceedings as a result of their physical or mental state. In some circumstances, it may not be appropriate to interview a detainee at all. In other cases, safeguards, such as having an appropriate healthcare professional present, may enable the interview to take place.

» The right to silence and the circumstances in which inferences can be drawn from a suspect's failure to answer questions are dealt with at 12.4.5.

The custody officer may have authorised detention on the basis that it was necessary in order to obtain evidence by questioning the detainee. However, the detainee cannot be compelled to answer questions and may choose to remain silent in interview. The police can interview a detainee even if they will not answer questions. If a detainee refuses to cooperate, for example by refusing to leave their cell, the interview may take place there.

Usually, however, interviews will take place in designated interview rooms. Code C provides that these should be adequately heated, lit, and ventilated and interviewees must not be required to stand. Breaks should take place at recognised mealtimes and there should also be short refreshment breaks roughly every two hours. Before questioning commences, Code C requires the interviewee to be cautioned.

The caution normally takes the following form:

> You do not have to say anything. But it may harm your defence if you do not mention when questioned something which you later rely on in court. Anything you do say may be given in evidence.

The first part of the caution is straightforward: it informs the person being interviewed that it is their right to refuse to answer questions. The second part of the caution is designed to alert the suspect to the fact that inferences (that is, common-sense conclusions) may be drawn if they rely at trial on any fact they could reasonably have been expected to mention in interview but did not so mention. The final part of the caution is to advise a suspect that anything that they do say may be introduced in evidence at trial, usually by the provision to the jury or magistrates of a transcript or summary of the interview.

Code C 11.7 requires an accurate record to be made of all interviews. In relation to summary offences, this can be a written record, an audio recording, or a visual recording with sound. Where, however, a suspect has been cautioned in respect of an indictable offence, the police must make either an audio recording (to which Code E applies) or a visual recording with sound (to which Code F applies).

Requirements imposed by Code E concerning the conduct of audio-recorded interviews include:

- the recording media must be unwrapped in the suspect's presence;
- once the recording has commenced, the police officers must identify themselves and must ask any others present to do so;
- the suspect must be cautioned and reminded of their right to free legal advice; and
- at the end of the interview, the master tape must be sealed in the suspect's presence.

These provisions are designed to instil confidence in the reliability of the recording as an impartial and accurate record of the interview. In addition to protecting suspects, the requirements imposed by PACE and the Codes of Practice may also protect interviewing officers from allegations of misconduct.

Code C provides that an interview must cease as soon as the officer in charge of the investigation is satisfied that all relevant questions have been put to the suspect and, taking into account any other available evidence, there is sufficient evidence to provide a realistic prospect of conviction.

12.4.4 Confessions made by the accused

Under PACE s.82(3), a confession is any statement that is either wholly or partly adverse to the person who made it. The term 'confession' is not confined to statements in which the suspect admits the offence.

 Example

Roger is shot and killed at his place of work. An eyewitness identifies Bryan, an employee, as the murderer. Bryan is arrested and interviewed by the police. Consider the following alternative scenarios:

(a) Bryan admits that he shot Roger;
(b) Bryan denies shooting Roger but admits being present at the time of the shooting;
(c) Bryan says that he was at home watching television at the time of the shooting.

Bryan's statement in scenario (a) is clearly a confession, as it is wholly adverse to Bryan. In scenario (b), Bryan's statement is a 'mixed statement' because his admission that he was present at the scene of the offence makes the statement partly adverse to him. Thus, the statement in scenario (b) is also a confession within the meaning of s.76, even though Bryan denied the shooting. Scenario (c) involves a wholly exculpatory statement. This statement is not adverse to Bryan in any way and is, therefore, not a confession.

The effect of PACE s.76(1) is that a confession is admissible in evidence against the person who made it, provided it is relevant and is not excluded by the court under s.76(2).

Under PACE s.76(2) a confession will be inadmissible in either of two circumstances:

- if it was obtained by oppression (s.76(2)(a)); or
- if it was obtained in consequence of anything said or done which was likely, in the circumstances, to render any confession unreliable (s.76(2)(b)).

Section 76(2)(a)

Oppression is only partially defined in s.76(8) as including torture, inhuman or degrading treatment, and the use or threat of violence. The courts have held that oppression should be given its ordinary dictionary definition and that it includes the exercise of authority or power in a burdensome, harsh, or wrongful manner; unjust or cruel treatment; or the imposition of unreasonable or unjust burdens (*R v Fulling* [1987] QB 426). In *R v Miller* (1993) 97 Cr App R 99, the appellant was arrested on suspicion of murder. He was interviewed on a number of occasions for a total of thirteen hours. The police bullied and hectored him, shouting what they wanted him to say. After denying the offence 300 times, the appellant eventually confessed. The Court of Appeal held that the conduct of the interviewing officers constituted oppression and the conviction was quashed. *R v Fulling* [1987] QB 426 suggests that there must be impropriety on the part of the interrogator for conduct to amount to oppression.

Section 76(2)(b)

In contrast, it appears that the court may be required to exclude a confession for unreliability even if there is no suggestion of improper conduct on the part of the police. In *R v Barry* (1992) 95 Cr App R 384, police officers made statements that may have led the appellant to believe that he was more likely to be given bail if he confessed. The appellant had particularly strong reasons for wanting bail because he was the sole carer of his nine-year-old son. The statements made by the officers were 'something said' under s.76(2)(b). In the circumstances existing at the time (namely the appellant's concern for his son), the Court of Appeal found that his resulting confession was unreliable. The Court of Appeal held that this would be so whether or not the police officers' statements were 'flagrant or cynical or even deliberate'.

If the defendant asserts that the confession may have been obtained in either of the ways set out in s.76(2)(a) or s.76(2)(b), the prosecution must prove beyond reasonable doubt that the confession was not so obtained.

Thinking point

Should the prosecution have to prove that a confession was obtained lawfully?

Why should the prosecution bear the legal burden of proving that the accused's confession was not obtained by oppression and was not unreliable in consequence of something said or done? Is this an example of what might be regarded as the 'weighting' of the criminal process in favour of the accused? When looking at the criminal process, note other rules that weight the system in favour of the accused. Consider whether this is an inevitable consequence of a system in which the accused is 'innocent until proven guilty' and in which prosecuting authorities have access to investigative and financial resources that are not available to the accused.

The question of the admissibility of a confession will be decided at a 'trial within a trial', known as a voir dire. In the Crown Court, the judge will hold the voir dire in the absence of the jury. If the prosecution is able to prove beyond reasonable doubt that the confession was not obtained by oppression or in consequence of something said or done which was likely to render it unreliable, the confession will be admissible. If the prosecution is not able to prove these things, then the judge must exclude evidence of the confession and the jury will never hear of it.

In a summary trial, the magistrates or district judge will make the decision as to the admissibility or otherwise of the confession. If they decide that it is inadmissible, they will be required to put it out of their minds for the remainder of the trial.

Thinking point

Can magistrates disregard prejudicial information when hearing a trial?

In the magistrates' court, questions of admissibility can be determined by the same magistrates who go on to hear the trial. If they determine that evidence is inadmissible, they will be required to ignore it when deciding whether the defendant is guilty of the offence charged. Is it realistic to expect magistrates to 'forget' evidence in this way? Could this procedure unfairly prejudice the defendant?

Even if a confession upon which the prosecution seeks to rely is not excluded under PACE s.76(2), the court may still exercise its exclusionary discretion under PACE s.78. The s.78 discretion enables the court to exclude any evidence tendered by the prosecution. The test to be applied is whether, having regard to all the circumstances, including those in which the evidence was obtained, its admission would have such an adverse effect on the fairness of the proceedings that the court ought not to admit it. The court is likely to exercise the s.78 discretion so as to exclude a confession where there have been breaches by the police of requirements imposed either by PACE or by Code C that were significant or substantial.

In *R v Walsh* (1990) 91 Cr App R 161, the appellant confessed in interview to robbery with a firearm. He had been denied access to a solicitor. The police also breached Code C by failing to make a record of the interview. The Court of Appeal held that these were significant and substantial breaches of PACE and the Codes of Practice. The conviction was quashed on the grounds that the admission of the confession in those circumstances had such an adverse effect on the fairness of the proceedings that the judge ought to have excluded it under s.78.

Key point

Unlike PACE s.76, the operation of PACE s.78 is not restricted to the exclusion of confessions. Section 78 may be used to exclude any prosecution evidence which it would be unfair to admit. Consequently, s.78 is a provision that is of fundamental importance in the context of criminal evidence.

12.4.5 **The accused's silence at the police station**

It is a fundamental principle of the criminal justice system that an accused person has a right to silence. However, where a person exercises that right, the court may be entitled to draw an appropriate inference against them under s.34, s.35, or s.36 of the CJPOA 1994. Section 34, which relates to the accused's silence in the police station, is the most important of these three sections and the only one that will be considered in detail in this chapter.

Under s.34 of the 1994 Act, the court may draw an adverse inference where the accused relies at trial upon a fact that they failed to mention when questioned or charged, provided the fact was one they could reasonably have been expected to mention in the circumstances. An 'adverse inference' means the jury or magistrates may conclude that the defendant remained silent either because they had no answer to give, or no answer that would stand up to questioning.

Section 35 of the 1994 Act, which concerns the silence of the accused in court, is considered at 13.11.4.

Thinking point

Why might a suspect refuse to answer police questions?

Is it always reasonable to infer that a defendant remained silent in interview because they had no answer to give, or no answer that would stand up to questioning? What other reasons could there be for a person in police custody not wanting to answer questions?

Adverse inferences can only be drawn where the accused relies at trial upon a fact they *failed to mention* when questioned or charged. If the accused gave an account in interview and gives the same account at trial, no inference can be drawn.

Example

William witnesses a burglary and recognises the burglar as Daniel, someone he used to go to school with. Daniel is arrested and interviewed on suspicion of burglary. He says that at the time of the burglary he was at home watching television with his girlfriend and that William must be mistaken. He then refuses to answer any further questions. Consider the following two alternative scenarios:

(a) At trial, Daniel gives evidence that he was at home with his girlfriend at the time of the burglary and that this is a case of mistaken identification.

(b) At trial, Daniel gives evidence that he was at home with his girlfriend at the time of the burglary. He adds that William has held a grudge against him ever since Daniel had an affair with William's wife. He suggests that William is implicating him as an act of revenge.

In scenario (a), Daniel has not relied at trial on any fact that he failed to mention in interview. Even though he failed to answer questions, the jury would not be able to draw an adverse inference from his silence.

In scenario (b), Daniel relies on new facts that he could have been expected to mention in interview, namely that Daniel had an affair with William's wife and that William has held a grudge against him ever since. The jury could infer that he did not give that explanation in interview either because it is something that he has made up between interview and trial, or, although Daniel had thought of it prior to his interview, he knew it would not stand up to investigation.

Even where the accused relies at trial on a fact they failed to mention in interview, an adverse inference cannot be drawn unless the fact is one they could *reasonably have been expected to mention in the circumstances* existing at the time of interview. The courts have held that the expression 'in the circumstances' should be interpreted widely and might include matters such as the time of day and the accused's age, experience, mental capacity, state of health, sobriety, tiredness, and personality (*R v Argent* [1997] Cr App R 27).

The vast majority of cases on this issue, however, concern the relevance of legal advice. Can adverse inferences be drawn where the accused makes no reply in interview because a solicitor advised them to remain silent? Or can the accused argue they could not reasonably have been expected to mention anything in those circumstances?

In *Condron v UK* (2001) 31 EHRR 1, the applicants were heroin addicts who were arrested and interviewed on suspicion of offences involving the supply of heroin. The Force Medical Examiner concluded that both were fit for interview but their solicitor disagreed. He formed the view that they were suffering from heroin withdrawal symptoms and advised them not to answer any questions at that time. The judge should have directed the jury that it could only draw an adverse inference if satisfied that the applicants remained silent because they had no answer to give, or none that would stand up to examination. The judge's direction left it open to the jury to draw an adverse inference even if the jury was satisfied that the applicants remained silent because of their solicitor's advice. The European Court of Human Rights ruled that the fact that a solicitor has advised the client to remain silent is a factor that should be given appropriate weight.

The Court of Appeal has subsequently emphasised that the decision in *Condron* does not mean that defendants can use their solicitor's advice as a convenient shield behind which to hide. In order for legal advice to be a valid reason for failing to mention a fact in interview, the defendant's reliance on that advice must be both genuine and reasonable (*R v Hoare* [2004] EWCA Crim 784).

Thinking point

Is it fair to allow adverse inferences from a suspect's silence in interview?

Can the modifications to the right to silence introduced by the CJPOA 1994 be regarded as part of a process of reducing the traditional weighting of the criminal process in favour of the accused?

Article 6 of the ECHR, which guarantees the accused the right to a fair trial, does not expressly guarantee the accused a right to silence. However, the European Court of Human Rights has indicated that the right to silence is an aspect of an Article 6 fair trial. While the right to silence is not an absolute right, the denial of access to legal advice at the police station may give rise to a violation of Article 6. The court cannot draw an inference if the accused was not allowed an opportunity to consult a solicitor prior to being questioned. Even if the accused was allowed to consult a solicitor, the nature of the judge's directions to the jury concerning the drawing of inferences from silence may be crucial when determining whether there has been an Article 6 violation (*Murray v UK* (1996) 22 EHRR 29; *Condron v UK* (2001) 31 EHRR 1; and *Beckles v UK* (2003) 36 EHRR 13). Finally, the European Court of Human Rights has held that the jury must not convict wholly or mainly on the basis of an inference from silence.

12.4.6 **Review and extension of detention**

PACE sets out the maximum period for which a person can be detained without charge. PACE s.40 also provides that detention should be reviewed at regular intervals by the review officer to ensure that it is still necessary. If the detainee has been arrested and charged, the review officer is the custody officer. If the detainee has not been charged, the review officer must be an officer of the rank of inspector or above who has not been directly involved in the investigation.

The first review of detention should take place no later than six hours after detention was first authorised. The second and subsequent reviews should take place at intervals of no more than nine hours. In some circumstances a review may be postponed, for example, where the detainee is being questioned and the review officer is satisfied that interrupting the interview would prejudice the investigation.

Section 41 of PACE provides that a person should not normally be kept in police detention for more than twenty-four hours in total without being charged. This is either twenty-four hours from the person's arrival at the police station or twenty-four hours after arrest, whichever is earlier. Where the detainee is under arrest for an indictable offence, PACE s.42 permits an officer of the rank of superintendent or above to authorise further detention for up to an additional twelve hours. To authorise such an extension, the superintendent must have reasonable grounds to believe that further detention is necessary to secure or preserve evidence relating to the offence or to obtain such evidence by questioning. They must also be satisfied that the investigation is being conducted diligently and expeditiously.

Thus, the police have the power to authorise the detention of a suspect for up to thirty-six hours. Before this period expires, a magistrates' court may issue a warrant of further detention under PACE s.43, authorising the police to keep a person in detention for a further period not exceeding an additional thirty-six hours. The court may only issue a warrant of further detention if satisfied there are reasonable grounds for believing that further detention is justified on the same grounds as those mentioned earlier in relation to s.42. Before that period expires, PACE s.44 provides that a magistrates' court may extend the warrant of further detention by a maximum of an additional thirty-six hours (up to a maximum overall period of detention of ninety-six hours) if satisfied there are reasonable grounds for believing that further detention is justified.

Parliament has deemed it appropriate to modify the safeguards provided by PACE and the Codes of Practice in the context of investigations into terrorist offences so as to permit additional periods of detention without charge. The Terrorism Act 2006 increased the maximum period for which a terror suspect can be held without charge from fourteen days to twenty-eight days. This controversial measure was originally intended to be only temporary; the Act provided that the maximum period of pre-charge detention would revert to fourteen days after one year unless renewed by an affirmative order. However, the twenty-eight-day period was renewed annually until July 2010, when it was renewed for six months. On 24 January 2011, no renewal was sought and the maximum pre-charge detention period reverted to fourteen days. The Protection of Freedoms Act 2012 permanently reduced the maximum period of pre-charge detention to fourteen days in terrorism cases and removed the power to increase the period to twenty-eight days by affirmative order. Whether the power to detain for fourteen days prior to charge is an appropriate response to the threat of terrorism is an issue that has been hotly debated.

12.4.7 Photographs, fingerprints, and samples

Caution
Where an offence has been committed, the police or the CPS may be prepared to deal with the matter without instituting a criminal prosecution. Instead they may decide to caution the offender. A caution can only be given where the evidence is sufficient to have warranted prosecution. The offender must both admit guilt and agree to accept the formal caution. A caution will usually be administered at a police station by an inspector. Although it does not have the same status as a conviction, a caution will be recorded on the Police National Computer. Cautions cannot be given for indictable-only offences or for certain specified either way offences (s.17 of the Criminal Justice and Courts Act 2015).

PACE s.64A empowers the police to take photographs of suspects in a variety of situations. For example, photographs may be taken of a detainee at a police station even if they do not consent. Code D provides that photographs obtained under s.64A may only be used or disclosed for purposes related to the prevention or detection of crime, the investigation of offences, the conduct of prosecutions, or the enforcement of sentences. After being so used or disclosed, photographs may be retained but can only be used or disclosed again for the same purposes.

Under s.61 of PACE, the police can take fingerprints without consent in a variety of situations, most notably where a person detained at a police station has been arrested for, or charged with, a recordable offence. A recordable offence is one for which a conviction, ***caution***, reprimand, or warning may be recorded in national police records (basically, offences which carry a sentence of imprisonment, plus certain offences that do not).

PACE s.61A empowers the police to take footwear impressions without consent from a person detained at a police station who has been arrested for, or charged with, a recordable offence.

Under PACE s.62, an intimate sample (which includes a sample of blood, semen, or urine, or a dental impression) may be taken from a detainee if authorised by an officer of the rank of inspector or above. The officer must have reasonable grounds both for suspecting the person's involvement in a recordable offence and for believing that the sample will tend to confirm or disprove the person's involvement in the offence. Where a person refuses consent to the taking of an intimate sample without good cause, the court or jury may draw an appropriate inference.

Under PACE s.63, a non-intimate sample (which includes a hair sample or a sample from, or under, a nail) may be taken from a person *without consent* in various circumstances. For example, a non-intimate sample may be taken without consent from a detainee who is under arrest for a recordable offence or from a person who has been charged with such an offence.

Code D governs the information that must be provided to a suspect before a photograph, fingerprint, footwear impression, or sample is taken; this includes the reason it is being taken. The suspect must also be informed that it may be retained and may be the subject of a speculative search (that is, the fingerprint, footwear mark, or DNA profile derived from the sample may be checked against records held by the police and other law enforcement authorities inside and outside the UK).

In 2001, PACE s.64 was amended to enable the police to retain DNA samples, fingerprints, and footwear impressions regardless of whether the person from whom they were taken was ultimately charged with, or convicted of, an offence. In *S and Marper v United Kingdom* [2008] ECHR 1581, the European Court of Human Rights held that this was a breach of the Article 8 right to respect for private life. The Protection of Freedoms Act 2012 introduced a legislative scheme for the retention of biometric data. The 2012 Act inserted ss.63D–63U into PACE, creating an extremely complex statutory framework for the retention or destruction of fingerprints, footwear impressions, DNA samples, and DNA profiles obtained from such samples.

Under s.63S, footwear impressions may be retained for as long as is necessary for purposes related to the prevention or detection of crime, the investigation of an offence, or the conduct of a prosecution, but must otherwise be destroyed within six months. The remainder of the new provisions focus on 's.63D material', which consists of fingerprints and DNA profiles derived from samples obtained under PACE. (Section 63R provides that the DNA sample itself must usually be destroyed as soon as a DNA profile has been obtained from it.)

Where s.63D material was taken unlawfully, or following an unlawful arrest, or where the arrest was a result of mistaken identity, it must be destroyed (s.63D(2)). Otherwise, where a person is convicted, warned, reprimanded, or cautioned, their fingerprints or DNA profile can be retained indefinitely. If they are not convicted, warned, reprimanded, or cautioned, the general rule is that s.63D material must be destroyed at the conclusion of the proceedings, or at the conclusion of the investigation if charges were never actually brought. However, this general rule is abrogated, and the police will be permitted to retain s.63D material in many cases, depending upon the offence with which the person was charged, their age, and the nature of any previous convictions. Thus, there remains a power to retain biometric data obtained from unconvicted persons and, as Professor Ed Cape has suggested, '[i]t might be that the complexity of the new regime will make effective challenge on human rights grounds difficult' ('The Protection of Freedoms Act 2012: The Retention and Use of Biometric Data Provisions' [2013] Crim LR 23).

12.5 **Release under investigation, bail, or charge**

As we have seen, PACE s.37 provides that the custody officer is required to determine whether there is sufficient evidence to charge an arrested person with an offence.

12.5.1 **Release under investigation (RUI)**

Following a person's arrest, the police may need to carry out further investigations before a charging decision can be made. In this situation, the suspect may be released under investigation or released on pre-charge bail (also known as 'police bail'). A suspect on pre-charge bail is under a legal obligation to attend the police station again at a future date and time. Conditions can also be placed on pre-charge bail, such as: a requirement to reside at a different address, a prohibition on contacting a named person or persons, a curfew, and/or a requirement to report to a police station on a regular basis. Such conditions might seriously restrict the suspect's liberty in circumstances where they have not been charged with any criminal offence. This issue came to the attention of the mainstream media in 2017, when high profile suspects in the phone hacking and Operation Yewtree investigations challenged the use of pre-charge bail for extended periods.

 **Example**

Radio DJ Paul Gambaccini was arrested in 2013 as part of the Operation Yewtree investigation into historic sexual abuse. He was kept on bail for almost a year. Between January 2014 and October 2014, when he was finally told that he would not be charged with any offence, he was re-bailed on six occasions. The Chair of the Home Affairs Select Committee observed that he had been 'left in limbo for what he described as "twelve months of trauma", his life was put on hold, his employer stopped his contract and his costs from lost earnings and legal fees totalled £200,000' (**www.parliament.uk/business/committees/committees-a-z/commons-select/home-affairs-committee/news/150320-police-bail-rpt-pubn/**).

The Policing and Crime Act 2017 changed the law and the police can now bail a suspect for a maximum of just twenty-eight days. This period can be extended by a superintendent by up to three months. A further extension may be granted by a magistrates' court if the judge or magistrates have reasonable grounds to believe that further time is needed to make a charging decision and the investigation is being conducted diligently and expeditiously. The court also has to be satisfied that bail is necessary and proportionate in all the circumstances, having regard in particular to any conditions that are attached to the person's bail.

An unforeseen consequence of these 2017 reforms is that, in many cases, the police are opting to release suspects under investigation (RUI) instead of bailing them. There is no time limit for RUI and the suspect is not subject to any conditions. In a 2019 briefing paper, the Law Society observed that 'this impacts on victims, who may be targeted again by the same perpetrator, as well as on the public in general' (*Release Under Investigation*, Law Society 2019, available at **www.lawsociety.org.uk/policy-campaigns/campaigns/criminal-justice/release-under-investigation/**). Data obtained for *The Times* newspaper suggests that an average of 6,228 people were released under investigation by each police force in 2017/18, with just 1,416 being released on bail. The average length of release under investigation is an average of forty-nine days longer than the average pre-charge bail period prior to the 2017 reforms (Jenny Wiltshire, 'Reform to Bail Rules Has Proved Bad News for Suspects' *The Times*, 8 April 2019).

The use of RUI in domestic abuse cases is particularly controversial. In a recent report, Her Majesty's Inspectorate of Constabulary and Fire & Rescue Services found that the number of people being released on bail for this type of offence had fallen by 65 per cent. The authors expressed concern that, 'in more and more cases of domestic abuse, bail conditions are not being used to safeguard victims' (Report, *The Police Response to Domestic Abuse*, HMICFRS 2019). In May 2019, the National Police Chief's Council issued new guidance emphasising that, when deciding whether to impose pre-charge bail or RUI, 'a key consideration must always be the need to protect victims and witnesses, and ensure public safety'. The guidance requires documented decision-making if a suspect is to be released under investigation in a domestic abuse case.

Thinking point

What impact might RUI have on suspects and victims?

What are the advantages and disadvantages of the increased use of RUI? Consider the impact on both suspects and victims. Should different considerations apply where there is an allegation of domestic abuse and, if so, why? Are bail conditions more likely to be needed in this type of case?

12.5.2 **Charging a detainee**

In determining whether to charge and, if so, with which offence, PACE s.37A requires the custody officer to have regard to guidance issued by the Director of Public Prosecutions (DPP) (see **www.cps.gov.uk/publications/directors_guidance/dpp_guidance_5.html**). The guidance explains that the police may make charging decisions in relation to summary-only offences, offences of retail theft (that is, shoplifting), and most either way offences provided it is anticipated that the defendant will plead guilty and the case is suitable for sentence in the magistrates' court. More serious either way offences, or any either way offence to which a not guilty plea is anticipated, must be referred to a Crown Prosecutor for a charging decision.

Crown Prosecution Service (CPS)
The CPS is the main public prosecuting authority for England and Wales, its head being the DPP. The CPS is divided into 14 regional teams, each headed by a Chief Crown Prosecutor. It also operates a 'virtual' 15th team, known as CPS Direct, which provides out-of-hours charging decisions. The CPS works with, but is independent of, the police. The Attorney General is accountable to Parliament for the CPS.

Crown Prosecutors are lawyers employed by the ***Crown Prosecution Service***. A Crown Prosecutor may also provide guidance to the police throughout the process of investigating and prosecuting an offence (for example, advising on the evidence that will be required to support a prosecution).

Both police and Crown Prosecutors should apply the Code for Crown Prosecutors (issued under s.10 of the Prosecution of Offences Act 1985) when determining whether to charge and, if so, what the charge(s) should be. The Code sets out the tests to be applied in deciding whether to prosecute a person for an offence.

The 'Full Code Test' has two stages: the 'evidential stage' and the 'public interest stage'. At the 'evidential stage', the Crown Prosecutor must decide whether there is enough admissible and reliable evidence to provide a realistic prospect of conviction. If there is sufficient evidence to justify a prosecution, the next question is whether a prosecution is required in the public interest (the 'public interest stage'). The Prosecutor should take into account factors including:

- the seriousness of the offence;
- the impact of the offence on the community; and
- the suspect's level of culpability, age, and maturity.

The Code also provides that the circumstances of the victim must be considered, including any views expressed by the victim as to the impact the offence(s) have had. 'However, the CPS does not act for victims or their families in the same way as solicitors act for their clients, and prosecutors must form an overall view of the public interest' (Code for Crown Prosecutors, para. 4.14(c)).

Where all of the evidence in relation to an offence is not yet available and the Full Code Test cannot be applied at the time when the Crown Prosecutor is required to make the charging decision, the suspect should be released on police bail pending further enquiries. Alternatively, if the seriousness or the circumstances of the case justifies making an immediate charging decision and there are substantial grounds to object to bail, the Crown Prosecutor should decide whether to charge the suspect by applying the 'Threshold Test'. The Threshold Test is satisfied if there is a reasonable suspicion that the person committed an offence, further evidence can be obtained to provide a realistic prospect of conviction, and it is in the public interest to charge the suspect. In such a case, the decision to charge must be kept under review and the Full Code Test must be applied as soon as the anticipated further evidence is available. For the Code for Crown Prosecutors go to **www.cps.gov.uk/publication/code-crown-prosecutors**.

A decision not to prosecute a suspect may be distressing for the victim. A European Directive establishing minimum standards on the rights, support, and protection of victims (2012/29/EU) was adopted on 25 October 2012. Subsequently, in June 2013, the DPP introduced the Victims' Right to Review (VRR) Scheme. The VRR Scheme provides that whenever a prosecutor decides not to bring charges against a suspect, or to stop a case that has already commenced, the victim of the offence must be notified of their right to request a review of that decision. The reviewing prosecutor will reconsider the evidence and the public interest before making a fresh decision as to whether a prosecution should take place. Details of the scheme can be found at **www.cps.gov.uk/victims_witnesses/victims_right_to_review/index.html**.

12.5.3 After charge

Except in terrorism cases, a detainee who has been charged may not be questioned further about the offence unless it is necessary: (a) to prevent or minimise harm or loss to a person or the public; (b) to clear up ambiguity in a previous answer or a previous statement; or (c), in the interests of justice, to put information concerning the offence which has subsequently come to light to the accused for comment (Code C 16.5). Before such an interview takes place, the accused must be reminded of the right to legal advice and cautioned by being told 'you do not have to say anything, but anything you do say may be given in evidence'. Thus, no inferences can be drawn from a person's failure to answer questions after they have been charged.

Once a person has been charged, PACE s.38 requires the custody officer to order the person's release unless certain specified circumstances apply. Examples of such circumstances are where:

- the person's name and address cannot be ascertained or there are reasonable grounds for believing that the person will fail to appear in court to answer bail;
- (if the person was arrested for an imprisonable offence) there are reasonable grounds for believing that detention is necessary to prevent the person from committing another offence;
- (if the offence is not an imprisonable offence) there are reasonable grounds for believing that detention is necessary to prevent the person from causing physical injury to another person or loss or damage to property;
- the charge is one of murder.

Where a person is kept in police detention following charge, PACE s.46 requires that the person be brought before a magistrates' court as soon as is practicable and no later than the first sitting after being charged.

Summary

- Police powers are regulated by provisions of PACE and the Codes of Practice made under PACE.
- The police possess a variety of powers to search premises, to seize property, and to make arrests.

- The treatment of the suspect at the police station is subject to detailed requirements imposed by PACE and Code C.
- The admissibility of confessions is subject to the operation of PACE ss.76 and 78.
- Where the accused gave a no-comment interview at the police station, the jury may be entitled to draw inferences from their silence.
- PACE imposes limits upon the maximum period for which a suspect may be detained at the police station.
- PACE permits the taking of fingerprints, footwear impressions, intimate samples, and non-intimate samples from a detainee. The regime governing the retention of fingerprints and DNA profiles obtained from such samples is extremely complex but, in general, material must be destroyed if the detainee is not charged or is ultimately acquitted of the offence.
- It is normally a CPS lawyer, rather than the police, who decides whether a suspect should be prosecuted.

? Questions

1. Do the police require a warrant: (a) in order to search a suspect's house; or (b) in order to search a suspect?
2. Identify three rights that an arrested person has upon arrival at a police station.
3. What are the potential consequences for a suspect who refuses to answer police questions?
4. What is a confession?
5. How long can a person be kept in police custody before being charged or released?
6. If a person is acquitted of an offence, can the police retain their fingerprints?

Sample question and outline answer

Question

Seema is a twenty-three-year-old classroom assistant. One morning, on her way to work, Seema passes the site of a demonstration about the refusal of planning permission to build a new mosque in the area. Some of the protestors have drawn slogans on the surrounding walls and pavements. As she is walking by, PC Odell approaches Seema and tells her that she is going to search her under s.1 of PACE. PC

Odell tells Seema that she must take off her coat and hijab. PC Odell then searches the pockets of Seema's coat and finds two marker pens. PC Odell takes the pens and decides that she needs to interview Seema about them. She tells Seema that she is under arrest on suspicion of possessing items with intent to damage property.

Seema is taken to the police station where she is placed in a cold, damp cell and left unattended for seven hours. She is then taken to an interview room, where she is interviewed by PC Thomas. Seema tells PC Thomas that she was taking the marker pens to work. PC Thomas says that he does not believe her. He shouts at her more than 100 times that she must admit that she was going to use the pens to write slogans. Seema eventually says that she intended to use the marker pens to damage property by writing on walls.

Advise Seema whether the police officers acted lawfully and explain whether the evidence of the marker pens and her confession would be admissible at any subsequent trial.

Outline answer

There are two main types of question in law examinations: the discursive, essay-type question and the problem-based question, which requires students to apply the law to the facts of a given scenario. This is an example of the latter. When answering a problem question, you should work through the scenario in chronological order. At each stage, you should explain what the relevant law is and then apply the law to the facts set out in the question. You may find it helpful to use headings to structure your answer and to ensure that all of the problems in the scenario are covered.

Stop and search

Section 1 of PACE allows an officer to search a person if they have reasonable grounds to suspect they will find a stolen or prohibited article, bladed article, or firework. Although prohibited articles include articles intended for use in connection with criminal damage (PACE s.1(8)), it does not appear that PC Odell had reasonable grounds for suspecting Seema. Seema was simply passing the site of a demonstration. Although the demonstration concerned the building of a mosque and may therefore have been attended by Muslim protestors, the fact that Seema is Muslim cannot form the basis of a reasonable suspicion (PACE Code A).

PC Odell ought to have had a conversation with Seema before searching her (PACE Code A). If she had asked Seema where she was going, she might have realised that there was no need to search her. Before searching Seema, PC Odell should have clearly explained the purpose of the search (PACE Code A). A person can only be required to remove an outer coat in public and not any other clothing (PACE Code A). Seema should not have been asked to remove the hijab.

Having discovered the marker pens, PC Odell was entitled to seize them (PACE s.1(6)). The fact that the search was not carried out in accordance with s.1 of PACE and Code A does not mean that evidence of the discovery of the marker pens will be inadmissible at Seema's trial (*Kuruma v R* (1955)).

Arrest

A police officer can arrest a person without a warrant under s.24 of PACE if there are reasonable grounds to suspect they are in the act of committing, or are about to commit, an offence. The officer must also have reasonable grounds to believe the arrest is necessary. Here the possession of the marker pens may well give PC Odell reasonable grounds to suspect that Seema intended to cause criminal damage.

However, it is not clear why her immediate arrest was necessary. An officer who believes it is necessary to interview someone should consider whether the suspect's voluntary attendance at the police station would be a practicable alternative (Code G). PC Odell does not appear to have considered any alternatives to arrest (*Richardson v CC of West Midlands* (2011); *Hanningfield v CC of Essex* (2013)).

Detention

It is not clear whether Seema was brought before the custody officer immediately upon her arrival at the police station, as she ought to have been. She should have been informed that she had the right to have someone informed of her whereabouts (PACE s.56) and that she had the right to consult a solicitor (PACE s.58). The custody record will show whether she was informed of these rights.

Seema should not have been placed in a damp, cold cell. Cells should be adequately heated, cleaned, ventilated, and lit (PACE Code C). Seema should have been checked every hour (PACE Code C) and her detention should have been reviewed by the custody officer after six hours (PACE s.40). She should not have been left unattended for seven hours.

Interview

It is not clear whether the custody officer assessed whether Seema was fit for interview as required by Code C. Even if she was, the conduct of the interview was certainly unlawful. Seema should have been cautioned and informed of her right to have a solicitor present (PACE Code C). Shouting repeatedly at a suspect constitutes oppression within the meaning of s.76(2)(a) of PACE (*R v Miller* (1993)). Unless the prosecution can prove that Seema's confession was not obtained by oppression, it will not be admissible at her trial (PACE s.76(2)(a)). The interview should have been recorded (PACE Code C), so there should be no difficulty in establishing what took place.

Further reading

When reading articles and reports on the role of the police and the rights of suspects, your primary aim should be to grasp the nature and scope of the power or right that is being discussed. Consider also any criticisms of the way in which the power or right is exercised and note any problems that have arisen in practice.

- **Ashworth, A.** *'Stop and Search Realigned?'* [2013] Crim LR 947

  Summarises the findings of Her Majesty's Inspectorate of Constabulary's 2013 report on police use of stop and search powers.

- **Cape, E.** *'The Protection of Freedoms Act 2012: The Retention and Use of Biometric Data Provisions'* [2013] Crim LR 23

  Explains the complex regime governing the retention of fingerprints, footwear impressions, and DNA profiles.

- **Colman, S.** *'A Comparison of the Implementation of the Victims' Right to Review in England and Wales, Scotland and Northern Ireland'* [2018] Crim LR 365

  Analyses the strengths and weaknesses of the different victims' right to review schemes in the four jurisdictions of the UK.

- **Dennis, I.** *'Silence in the Police Station: The Marginalization of Section 34'* [2002] Crim LR 25

  Analyses the circumstances in which inferences may be drawn from a suspect's silence in response to questioning in the police station.

- **Her Majesty's Inspectorate of Constabulary.** *'Stop and Search Powers: Are the Police Using Them Effectively and Fairly'* (HMIC 2013) and *'Stop and Search Powers 2'* (HMIC 2015)

  Official reports based upon the inspection of stop and search records, exploring whether stop and search powers are used appropriately.

- **Home Office.** *'Equality Impact Assessment: Relaxation of Section 60 Conditions in the Best Use of Stop and Search Scheme'* (Home Office 2019)

  Looks at the potential effects of relaxing the requirements for authorisations under s.60 CJPOA, including racial disparities and the potential negative impact on trust in the police.

- **Leng, R.** *'Silence Pre-trial, Reasonable Expectations and the Normative Distortion of Fact-finding'* (2001) 5(4) E & P 240

  Explores whether the power to draw adverse inferences from silence in response to police questioning is necessary and whether it promotes the interests of justice.

- **Malkani, B.** *'Article 8 of the European Convention on Human Rights and the Decision to Prosecute'* [2011] Crim LR 943

  Discusses the relationship between Article 8 of the ECHR (right to respect for private life) and the decision to prosecute an individual for an offence.

- ***Purshouse, J.*** *'Article 8 and the Retention of Non-conviction DNA and Fingerprint Data in England and Wales'* [2017] Crim LR 253

  Discusses whether police retention of DNA and fingerprints of non-convicted persons violates Article 8 of the ECHR.

- ***Smith, J.C.*** *'Exculpatory Statements and Confessions'* [1995] Crim LR 280

  Explains the meaning of the term 'confession'.

Online resources

You should now attempt the supporting self-test questions and end-of-chapter questions available at: **www.oup.com/he/wilson-rutherford4e**

Chapter 13

The criminal process: pre-trial and trial

Learning objectives

By the end of this chapter you should:

- be aware of the process by which a person may end up before a criminal court;
- appreciate the differences between the Crown Court and magistrates' courts;
- be aware of the distinctions between summary trial and trial on indictment;
- be aware of the major pre-trial stages that occur in criminal proceedings;
- be familiar with the process of a criminal trial;
- have a basic understanding of some of the key rules of criminal evidence.

Talking point

In 2014, footballer Ched Evans was convicted of rape. His conviction was quashed by the Court of Appeal in 2016 after that court heard fresh evidence from witnesses who had consensual sexual interactions with the complainant in similar circumstances (*R v Evans* [2016] EWCA Crim 452). Evans was acquitted following a retrial.

As a general rule, evidence of a complainant's sexual behaviour with other people, or their previous sexual history with the defendant, is irrelevant, as it does not mean they consented on the occasion that is the subject of the charge. Under s.41 of the Youth Justice and Criminal Evidence Act 1999, questioning about such matters is usually impermissible and will only be allowed where it is deemed necessary because otherwise the defendant could not have a fair trial. Following the Evans case, some politicians and sections of the media called for the introduction of a 'rape shield', which would completely prohibit any questions about a person's previous sexual behaviour.

Section 41, which will usually prevent a complainant from being cross-examined in this manner, is one of a number of provisions that have been introduced in recent years to protect the rights of witnesses (including complainants) and make it less unpleasant for them to give evidence in court. As you read this chapter, try to identify any other rules or procedures that may benefit either witnesses or defendants and consider whether they go far enough.

Before you start, consider the following questions:

- Should there be a complete prohibition on cross-examination about a person's previous sexual history?
- Are the rights of defendants more important than the rights of victims, or is it the other way round?
- Is it possible for the courts to strike a fair balance between the rights and interests of defendants and victims, and what might be the consequences of failing to do so?

Introduction

This chapter will examine how cases progress through the criminal justice system. Not every person in respect of whom proceedings are instituted will necessarily appear in court. For example, a driver who is caught speeding may be able to plead guilty by post and be sentenced in their absence. In the majority of cases, however, a person who is charged with a criminal offence will have to attend court and their first appearance will be before a magistrates' court.

Most cases will remain in a magistrates' court, while more serious cases will be transferred to the Crown Court. The circumstances in which a case will be 'sent' to the Crown Court, and the procedures involved, depend upon the offence alleged. 'Summary only' offences, which are relatively minor offences, will remain in a magistrates' court. Very serious offences are 'indictable only', and must be sent to the Crown Court to be tried on indictment. In between are a range of offences that are 'triable either way' and may be tried and/or sentenced in either court.

The Crown Court and magistrates' courts each have their own rules and procedures. It is useful to have an understanding of the types of hearing that take place in each venue and the steps that need to be taken to prepare a case for trial. You may be surprised to discover that, in the vast majority of cases, defendants plead guilty and no trial takes place. Where a defendant maintains a not guilty plea, the major difference between Crown Court trial and summary trial is that the former takes place before a jury, whereas the latter takes place before either magistrates or a district judge. In both courts the format of a trial is very similar. The same evidential issues can also arise in the context of both summary trial and trial on indictment. This chapter will examine some of these evidential issues, such as the right to silence and the extent to which this has been eroded by statutory provisions that enable inferences to be drawn against a defendant who chooses not to testify.

13.1 **The criminal courts of trial and the classification of offences**

For further information about the composition of magistrates' courts, see 2.5.2.

Criminal trials may take place in the Crown Court, magistrates' court, or youth court. Consideration of the constitution and operation of the youth court is outside the scope of this book. An adult defendant will be tried in either a magistrates' court or the Crown Court.

A magistrates' court comprises either a district judge or a bench of lay magistrates. Lay magistrates are not legally qualified and are advised on the law by a legal adviser (formerly known as a magistrates' court clerk). District judges and magistrates are the sole arbiters of proceedings in magistrates' courts. They decide both questions of law and questions of fact. As the tribunal of law, they are responsible for deciding all of the legal issues that arise in the proceedings, including issues as to the admissibility of evidence. For example, if a defendant confesses to the crime and later claims that they only did so as a result of police oppression, the magistrates or district judge will have to decide whether, as a matter of law, the confession is admissible. As the tribunal of fact, a district judge, or a bench of lay magistrates, is also responsible for

See 12.4.4 for further consideration of the difficulties that may arise where a district judge or magistrates are required to decide whether a confession is admissible.

hearing the evidence, making findings of fact and deciding whether the defendant is guilty or not guilty.

In contrast, in a jury trial the judge decides questions of law and the jury decides the facts of the case. The dual role of the tribunal in magistrates' courts has been criticised as having the potential to lead to unfairness because, where the district judge or magistrates make a ruling that evidence is inadmissible, they are nevertheless aware of its existence. If, for example, a defendant made a confession to the police, which was ruled inadmissible by a bench of magistrates under s.76 of the Police and Criminal Evidence Act 1984 (PACE), the same bench of magistrates would go on to determine whether or not the defendant was guilty of the offence. Critics of this system argue that it is unrealistic to expect magistrates to put evidence, such as an inadmissible confession, from their minds when reaching a verdict.

For further information in relation to juries see Chapter 10.

The Crown Court comprises a judge and a jury of twelve randomly selected members of the public. In a Crown Court trial, the judge decides all questions of law, such as whether or not certain evidence is admissible. However, it is the jury that decides the facts of the case. On the basis of those facts, and applying any directions of law that the judge has given them, the jury decides whether the defendant is guilty or not guilty.

Whether a defendant is tried in a magistrates' court or the Crown Court depends upon the classification of the offence(s) with which they are charged. For these purposes, all criminal offences fall into one of three categories:

- summary only offences;
- indictable only offences; or
- offences that are triable either way.

Summary only offences can usually only be tried in a magistrates' court. The sentencing powers of the magistrates/district judge are restricted. For this reason, summary only offences tend to be less serious offences, such as speeding, being drunk and disorderly, and common assault. In limited circumstances, summary offences may be tried in the Crown Court. For example, s.40 of the Criminal Justice Act 1988 provides that certain specified summary offences, including common assault or driving a motor vehicle while disqualified, may be included in an indictment if they are founded on the same facts or evidence as an indictable offence.

Example

John is charged with dangerous driving and is to be tried on indictment in the Crown Court. The evidence shows that he was disqualified from driving at the time of the offence. Section 40 of the Criminal Justice Act 1988 allows a charge of driving whilst disqualified to be added to the indictment even though driving whilst disqualified is a summary only offence.

Indictable only offences can only be tried 'on ***indictment***' in the Crown Court. They include the most serious criminal offences, such as murder, robbery, and rape.

> ***Indictment*** *An indictment is a formal document that must be prepared for Crown Court proceedings. It sets out the charge or charges against the defendant and must include the name of the court, a statement of each offence, and brief particulars (that is, details) of each offence.*

Either way offences, as the name suggests, may be tried in either a magistrates' court or on indictment in the Crown Court. Either way offences include theft, assault occasioning actual bodily harm, and affray. If a defendant is charged with an either way offence and intends to plead not guilty, an allocation hearing must take place to determine the appropriate venue for the trial. The procedure at an allocation hearing is considered at 13.4.4.

Key point

It is important not to confuse the terms 'indictable' and 'indictable only'. An indictable offence is any offence that is capable of being tried on indictment in the Crown Court. There are, therefore, two types of indictable offence: those that are indictable only and *must* be tried in the Crown Court and those that are triable either way, which *may* be tried in the Crown Court.

All common law offences are indictable offences. A statutory offence will only be indictable if either the offence is listed in Sch.1 to the Magistrates' Courts Act 1980, or the statute specifies a penalty to be imposed if the offence is tried on indictment. Note that the classification of an offence is determined by the offence itself and not by the facts of the case. Thus, handling stolen goods is always an either way offence, whether the defendant is found in possession of a stolen DVD or valuable diamond jewellery.

13.2 **Instituting criminal proceedings**

A variety of public bodies, as well as individuals, have the power to institute criminal proceedings. However, most prosecutions for both summary and indictable offences are brought by the Crown Prosecution Service (CPS).

13.2.1 **The Crown Prosecution Service (CPS)**

In 1981, the Royal Commission on Criminal Procedure (referred to at 12.2) recommended that an independent state agency should be set up to institute and oversee the prosecution of offences. As a result, the CPS was created by the Prosecution of

Offences Act 1985. The CPS is a national prosecution service headed by the Director of Public Prosecutions (the DPP).

Section 3 of the 1985 Act gives the DPP the power to institute criminal proceedings. In practice, decisions as to whether to institute proceedings are taken by local Crown Prosecutors on behalf of the DPP. Where a prosecution is brought by another agency or by a private individual, s.6 of the 1985 Act gives the DPP the power to take over the conduct of the proceedings. The DPP even has the power to take over a case and then discontinue it in appropriate circumstances.

Thinking point

Should the police be responsible for both investigations and prosecutions?

Prior to 1986, most prosecutions were brought by the police. What criticisms could be made of a system in which the police both investigated and prosecuted offences? Is the CPS, as an independent body, more likely to be able to assess evidence objectively and conduct cases fairly at court?

Even after the 1985 Act was passed, the police retained the power to prosecute adults for certain specified low-level offences, such as minor road traffic violations. In 2012, further offences were added to this list, including careless driving and criminal damage where the value of the property damaged is less than £5,000. In 2014, the police were additionally given the power to prosecute cases involving theft from a shop of goods worth £200 or less. However, the police can only prosecute cases if the defendant does not attend court and has not objected to any of the evidence against them. If the defendant pleads not guilty, the case must be conducted by the CPS.

13.2.2 **Commencing criminal proceedings**

Although an indictable offence may eventually be tried in the Crown Court, criminal proceedings against adult defendants for both summary and indictable offences always begin in a magistrates' court. Perhaps the most obvious way in which criminal proceedings commence is when a person is arrested and charged with an offence. They will then be either detained and produced before a magistrates' court, or released by the police on bail with a condition of attendance before a magistrates' court on a specified day.

Alternatively, proceedings may be instituted by the issuing of a written charge and requisition, or the laying of an information and the issue of a summons.

13.2.3 **Written charge and requisition**

Where a defendant is not charged at the police station, a prosecutor may institute criminal proceedings by issuing a 'written charge' (which charges the defendant with an offence) and a 'requisition' (which requires them to appear before a magistrates' court to answer the written charge). The written charge and requisition must be served on the defendant and copies must be served on the court. This is now the only procedure available to public prosecutors (such as CPS prosecutors), who can no longer lay an information to obtain a summons or warrant of arrest.

13.2.4 **Information and summons**

The procedure for laying an information to obtain a summons is still available to private prosecutors. An 'information' is a statement alleging that a person has committed an offence and providing brief details about that offence. An information may be laid (that is, put before a magistrates' court) either orally or in writing. The court may then issue a summons requiring the defendant to appear before a magistrates' court (Magistrates' Courts Act 1980 s.1). A summons is a formal document calling upon a named person to present themselves before the court on a given date.

13.2.5 **Time limits**

Proceedings for a summary only offence must normally be brought within six months of the offence being committed (Magistrates' Courts Act 1980 s.127). There is no time limit for commencing proceedings for an either way or an indictable only offence.

Thinking point

Should Parliament introduce time limits for prosecuting all criminal offences?

Some countries have a 'statute of limitations' preventing criminal proceedings from being instituted after a specified period of time. What reasons might there be for imposing time limits on prosecutions? Do they encourage the police to investigate offences promptly and efficiently?

Why do you think we only have time limits in relation to summary only offences in this country? Bear in mind that it may take time to investigate an offence and the absence of a time limit for indictable offences means that more serious offences can always be prosecuted.

A further time limit is applicable to some road traffic offences. Under ss.1 and 2 of the Road Traffic Offenders Act 1988, a conviction cannot be obtained in respect of certain offences, such as speeding, unless the driver was given notice of intended prosecution within fourteen days of the commission of the offence.

13.2.6 **Fixed penalty notices for road traffic offences and penalty notices for disorder**

In relation to some minor road traffic offences, such as speeding, the police may decide to issue a motorist with a fixed penalty notice. In this case, unless the motorist denies the offence, or requests a hearing for some other reason, they will pay a specified sum and, if appropriate, their licence will be automatically endorsed with a fixed number of penalty points; they do not need to appear in court.

Under s.2 of the Criminal Justice and Police Act 2001, the police can issue an adult with a penalty notice for disorderly behaviour (PND) in relation to offences such as theft, littering, being drunk in a public place, and possession of cannabis. PNDs are often referred to as 'on the spot fines', and a person who receives such a notice can request a hearing or can pay the specified penalty. In the year ending March 2019, 20,800 PNDs were issued. The most common offences resulting in PNDs were: theft; possession of cannabis; being drunk and disorderly; and causing harassment, alarm or distress. These offences accounted for 91 per cent of all PNDs. (See **https://assets.publishing.service.gov.uk/government/uploads/system/uploads/attachment_data/file/825364/criminal-justice-statistics-quarterly-march-2019.pdf**).

Thinking point

What are the advantages of fixed penalty notices?

What advantages do fixed penalty notices have for both the offender and the police? Note that a person who pays a fixed penalty for disorderly behaviour does not receive a conviction for the relevant offence. Consider the implications for police resources if every minor offender had to be charged or requisitioned to attend court.

13.3 Reform of the criminal justice system

In 1999, the Lord Chancellor, the Home Secretary, and the Attorney General appointed Auld LJ to conduct a review into the working of the criminal courts. In announcing the appointment, the Lord Chancellor stated:

The Government's aim is to provide criminal courts which are, and are seen to be:

- modern and in touch with the communities they serve;
- efficient;
- fair and responsive to the needs of all their users;
- cooperative in their relations with other criminal justice agencies; and
- with modern and effective case management to remove unnecessary delays from the system. (Auld LJ, Review of the Criminal Courts of England and Wales, 2001, Foreword, para. 2)

A study carried out by the Law Commission for the Auld Review in 2000 found that there were 207 Acts of Parliament containing provisions relating to criminal procedure and/or evidence, one of which dated back to 1795. There were also sixty-four pieces of secondary legislation containing rules that differed in application according to whether they governed summary trials or trial on indictment. These statutory provisions were supplemented by guidance issued by both the Lord Chief Justice and the Attorney General (*Auld Review*, Chapter 10, para. 272). Auld LJ stated:

> Fairness, efficiency and effectiveness of the criminal justice system demand that its procedures should be simple, accessible and, so far as practicable, the same for every level and type of criminal jurisdiction. There are many features of criminal procedure that are common to summary proceedings and those on indictment, yet at present they are separately provided for in each jurisdiction and in a multiplicity of instruments and, often, in quite different language. Such a mix of different provisions providing for common procedural needs is an impediment to understanding by courts, legal practitioners, parties and others of the workings of the courts, and thus to the accessibility of the law. (*Auld Review*, Chapter 10, para. 271)

The Auld Review recommended that there should be a unified criminal court with a single procedural code. A unified court came into being in 2005 when Her Majesty's Courts Service was created. HM Courts Service amalgamated with the Tribunals Service in 2010. HM Courts and Tribunals Service is now a single, integrated agency of the Ministry of Justice, which is responsible for the administration of the criminal, civil, and family courts and tribunals in England and Wales (see **www.justice.gov.uk/about/hmcts**). A single procedural code was created by the Criminal Procedure Rules 2005. The approach for the Criminal Procedure Rules was based on the Civil Procedure Rules, which had been introduced seven years earlier (see Chapter 15).

In February 2014, Sir Brian Leveson was asked to conduct a review into the efficiency of criminal proceedings. The review took place against a background of cuts to legal aid and decreasing funding for HM Courts and Tribunals Service, the police, the CPS, and the National Offender Management Service. Sir Brian's final report, which was published in January 2015, made a number of recommendations for improving the efficiency of the criminal process, including the development of a common IT platform and greater use of video conferencing technology in order to reduce the number of preliminary hearings that take place before the courts. (See **www.judiciary.gov.uk/wp-content/uploads/2015/01/review-of-efficiency-in-criminal-proceedings-20151.pdf**).

13.3.1 **The Criminal Procedure Rules 2015**

Procedure in the criminal courts is now governed by the Criminal Procedure Rules 2015 (CrimPR) (see **www.justice.gov.uk/courts/procedure-rules/criminal/rulesmenu-2015**). CrimPR Part 1 states that the 'overriding objective' of the criminal justice system is to ensure that cases are dealt with justly, which includes:

- acquitting innocent defendants and convicting the guilty;
- dealing with the parties fairly;

- recognising the defendant's rights (and, in particular, the right to a fair trial under Article 6 of the European Convention on Human Rights (ECHR));
- respecting the interests of witnesses, victims, and jurors;
- dealing with cases efficiently and expeditiously; and
- dealing with cases in ways that take into account the gravity of offences, the complexity of issues, the severity of the consequences, and the needs of other cases.

The court is required to further the overriding objective and the parties are also required to prepare and conduct the case in accordance with it.

Key point

The overriding objective seeks to balance the interests of the prosecution and the defence. Throughout the remainder of this chapter, consider the extent to which the criminal justice system as a whole achieves this aim.

The CrimPR are divided into eleven sections that correspond with the different stages of a criminal case, from 'preliminary hearings' to 'appeals'. The CrimPR are supplemented by the Criminal Practice Directions (CPD), which include directions about practice and procedure in the criminal courts.

13.4 **First hearings**

As previously discussed, a person who is offered, and pays, a fixed penalty will not need to appear before the court. In all other cases involving adult defendants, whether proceedings are instituted by arrest or by the issuing of a written charge and requisition, the defendant's first hearing will take place in a magistrates' court.

Visit the online resources to watch a video on the magistrates' court.

In 2015, a new criminal justice initiative called Transforming Summary Justice (TSJ) was introduced. The aim of TSJ is to reduce delays, in part by reducing the number of hearings that take place in magistrates' courts. In the past, it was common for only limited information about a case to be available when a defendant first appeared before a magistrates' court, and many cases would simply be adjourned for a further hearing. CrimPR Part 8 now requires the prosecutor to provide the defendant and the court with key information prior to the first hearing, namely: a summary of the circumstances of the relevant offence(s); a summary of any account given by the defendant in interview; any written witness statement or exhibit that is available and is material to plea or to the allocation of the case for trial or sentence; the defendant's criminal record, if any; and any available statement of the effect of the offence on the victim. The aim is to ensure that the court can make progress at the first hearing as a defendant has enough information to consider whether they wish to plead guilty or not guilty.

13.4.1 **First hearings: summary only offences**

A defendant charged with a summary only offence may wish to plead guilty. This can usually be done at the first appearance before a magistrates' court and the court will either proceed straight to sentence or adjourn for pre-sentence reports to be prepared (see Chapter 14). If the defendant pleads not guilty, steps will be taken to prepare for trial. These steps include setting the trial date and dealing with pre-trial issues, such as disclosure.

For further information about disclosure, see 13.8.

13.4.2 **First hearings: either way offences**

Where the defendant is charged with an either way offence, a formal 'allocation' procedure must take place to determine the trial venue. If the case is allocated to the Crown Court for trial, the defendant is forthwith sent to the Crown Court under s.51 of the Crime and Disorder Act 1998. This means that a defendant will be given a date on which they must attend the Crown Court for a hearing.

The main consideration for both the court and the defendant at allocation is the appropriate sentence for the offence(s) if the defendant is convicted. The sentencing powers of a magistrates' court are limited to six months' imprisonment (or twelve months where the defendant is charged with two or more offences that are triable either way), whereas the Crown Court will usually have the power to impose a longer sentence up to the statutory or common law maximum for the offence in question.

13.4.3 **Plea before venue**

Before the allocation procedure commences, a defendant must be given an opportunity to indicate whether, if the offence were to proceed to trial, they would plead guilty or not guilty (Magistrates' Courts Act 1980 s.17A). This is known as the 'plea before venue' procedure. If the defendant indicates that they would plead guilty to the offence, the magistrates' court should record a conviction without hearing any evidence. The magistrates (or district judge) must then decide whether their sentencing powers are adequate or whether the defendant should be committed (that is, transferred) to the Crown Court for sentence. If the defendant indicates that they would plead not guilty, or declines to indicate what their plea would be, the court must follow the allocation procedure laid down by ss.19 to 23 of the 1980 Act (as amended by s.41 and Sch.3 of the Criminal Justice Act 2003 (CJA 2003)). Diagram 13.1 illustrates the plea before venue procedure.

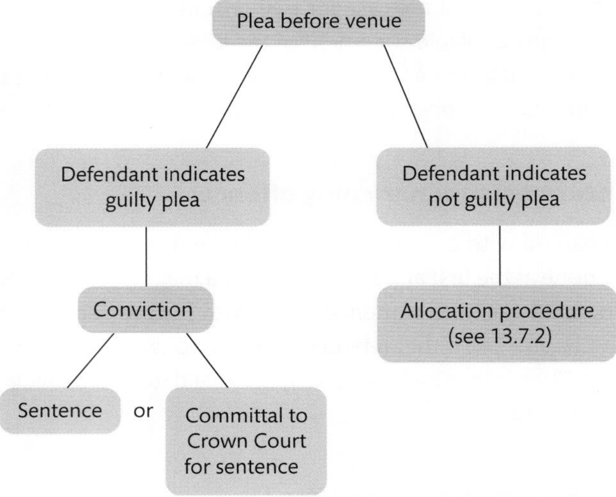

Diagram 13.1 Plea before venue

A defendant obviously cannot be expected to indicate their likely plea unless they know the substance of the charges they face. As explained at 13.4, CrimPR Part 8 provides that the prosecution must serve initial details of the prosecution case prior to the first hearing.

13.4.4 **Allocation procedure**

If the defendant either indicates a not guilty plea or declines to indicate a plea at all, allocation proceedings will take place. At the allocation hearing, the magistrates/district judge must first decide whether the case is suitable for summary trial or whether it is not suitable for summary trial, for example because it is too serious. If the court decides that the case is *not* suitable for summary trial, the defendant will be sent to the Crown Court and will have no choice in the matter. However, if the court decides that the case *is* suitable for summary trial, the defendant can either accept summary trial or elect trial by jury in the Crown Court. Before making a decision, the defendant may ask the court for an indication as to whether they would receive a custodial or a non-custodial sentence if they were to plead guilty. The court does not have to give an indication but may do so if asked. Diagram 13.2 shows the procedure that will be followed at an allocation hearing.

There are a number of factors that a magistrates' court must take into account in deciding whether a case is suitable for summary trial. The parties are entitled to make representations as to the suitability of the case for summary trial or trial on indictment. The court must also consider the nature of the case, the seriousness of the offence, the adequacy of the magistrates' court's sentencing powers, and any other relevant circumstances. The court should be informed of the defendant's

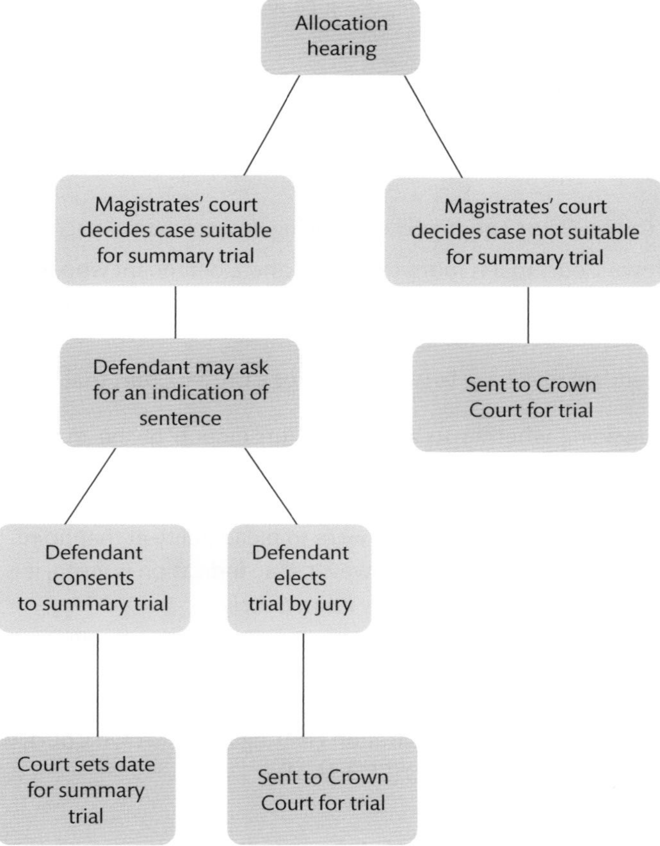

Diagram 13.2 Allocation procedure

previous convictions, as these may affect the likely sentence (Magistrates' Courts Act 1980 s.19).

An Allocation Guideline has been issued by the Sentencing Council to provide guidance to magistrates when determining whether summary trial or trial on indictment is more suitable. The Guideline provides that, in general, either way offences should be tried summarily unless the magistrates' court's sentencing powers will clearly be insufficient (**www.sentencingcouncil.org.uk/overarching-guides/magistrates-court/item/allocation/**).

If the magistrates or district judge decide that summary trial would be more suitable, the defendant must be told that they may either consent to summary trial or may choose to be tried on indictment in the Crown Court. The following factors may influence their decision:

- Statistically, there is a greater chance of acquittal before a jury.
- A jury, unlike magistrates, will not hear potentially prejudicial evidence that has been excluded by the judge in their absence (for example, if a judge rules that

a confession is inadmissible, the jury will never get to hear of it: see 13.1 and 12.4.4).

- A Crown Court judge may be better equipped to deal with issues of law than lay magistrates.

Conversely:

- The Crown Court has greater sentencing powers than a magistrates' court.
- A Crown Court trial is more expensive and a defendant who is convicted may be ordered to pay a proportion of the costs incurred by the prosecution in bringing the case.
- A defendant may have to wait longer for a Crown Court trial.

Before deciding whether to accept the jurisdiction of the magistrates' court, the defendant may ask for an indication of sentence. Any indication that is given should be limited to an indication as to whether a custodial or a non-custodial sentence would be passed if the defendant were to plead guilty at that point. The court does not have to give an indication. However, if an indication is given, it is binding on the court if the defendant pleads guilty immediately.

If the magistrates' court does not consider the case suitable for summary trial, or if the defendant chooses trial by jury, the case must be sent forthwith to the Crown Court under s.51 of the Crime and Disorder Act 1998. The magistrates' court must set a date for a Plea and Trial Preparation Hearing in the Crown Court, which must take place within twenty-eight days (CPD 3A.11).

13.4.5 **Abolition of committal proceedings**

Before s.41 and Sch.3 of the CJA 2003 came into force on 28 May 2013, either way offences had to be 'committed' to the Crown Court if a magistrates' court declined jurisdiction or the defendant elected trial on indictment. The purpose of committal proceedings was to ensure that a defendant was only committed to the Crown Court if there was sufficient evidence against them. When asked to commit a case to the Crown Court for trial, the role of the magistrates was to inquire into the case as 'examining justices'. This meant that the court had to decide whether the case was strong enough to put the defendant on trial before a jury.

Prior to the committal taking place, the prosecution had to serve a 'committal bundle' on the defence, consisting of the evidence relied upon by the prosecution. Where the defence accepted that there was sufficient evidence to put the defendant on trial, the proceedings took the form of a committal without consideration of the evidence under s.6(2) of the Magistrates' Courts Act 1980, and the magistrates simply agreed to commit the defendant to the Crown Court for trial.

However, if the defendant's legal representative submitted that there was insufficient evidence to put the defendant on trial in the Crown Court for the offence, s.6(1) of the 1980 Act required the magistrates to consider the evidence. The prosecutor had to read out the evidence contained in the committal bundle and the court could only commit the defendant for trial if of the opinion that there was sufficient evidence to put the defendant on trial for an indictable offence.

Committal proceedings were abolished by s.41 and Sch.3 of the CJA 2003, which came fully into force on 28 May 2013. The aim of the allocation provisions is to ensure that, where Crown Court trial is more appropriate, the case arrives at the Crown Court as soon as possible. Although the magistrates' court no longer considers the evidence in a case, the defendant is entitled to make an application to the Crown Court for the charges in the case to be dismissed. A Crown Court judge must then consider the evidence and must dismiss a charge if it appears that the evidence would not be sufficient for the defendant to be properly convicted (Sch.3 para. 2 to the Crime and Disorder Act 1998).

13.4.6 **First hearings: indictable only offences**

Where an adult appears before a magistrates' court charged with an offence triable only on indictment, s.51 of the Crime and Disorder Act 1998 requires the magistrates' court to send them to the Crown Court forthwith. (Under s.51B and s.51C of the 1998 Act, complex or serious fraud cases, and certain cases involving child witnesses or child complainants, may also be transferred to the Crown Court without an allocation hearing. Further consideration of these types of case falls outside the scope of this work.) As with either way offences that are sent to the Crown Court, the magistrates' court must set a date for the Plea and Trial Preparation Hearing, which must be held within twenty-eight days (CPD 3A.11).

13.4.7 **First appearance in the Crown Court**

In order to promote the overriding objective of the CrimPR, courts are required to actively manage cases, for example by setting time limits for the various steps that need to be taken in preparation for a trial. This is the purpose of the Plea and Trial Preparation Hearing (PTPH). A PTPH always takes place in the context of trial on indictment, regardless of whether any other form of pre-trial hearing takes place.

At the PTPH the defendant will be arraigned. This means that the indictment will be read out and the defendant will be asked whether they plead guilty or not guilty to the charges contained therein.

If the defendant pleads guilty to the indictment, there will obviously be no need for a trial. The judge may sentence the defendant then and there. Before passing sentence, the judge may require a pre-sentence report to be prepared, the purpose of which is to assist in determining the appropriate sentence (see Chapter 14). Pre-sentence reports can often now be prepared immediately by a probation officer at court (known as a 'stand down report'), enabling the sentencing hearing to take place the same day.

For further consideration of indictments, see 13.5.

If the defendant pleads not guilty, the judge will require information from the parties in order to set a timetable for trial. The advocates in the case are therefore required to complete a questionnaire concerning various matters, including:

- the issues in the case;
- which prosecution witnesses the defence requires to attend;
- whether the prosecution intends to rely on expert evidence; and
- whether there are to be any bad character or other applications (see 13.11.2).

In straightforward cases, the judge will set a date for trial at the PTPH. In complex cases, or if the judge decides the interests of justice require a further hearing, a Further Case Management Hearing (FCMH) may take place. However, the CPD indicates that a further hearing should only be held in one of the circumstances listed at CPD 3A.21, such as: the offence is particularly serious, the case involves a vulnerable witness, the defendant is a child, the defendant is unrepresented, or the trial is likely to be lengthy.

Under s.40 of the Criminal Procedure and Investigations Act 1996, the judge at a pre-trial hearing (such as the PTPH) may make rulings concerning the admissibility of evidence or other questions of law. Such rulings are binding until the case is disposed of, although a judge may subsequently discharge or vary a ruling made under s.40 in the interests of justice. In practice, however, issues concerning the admissibility of evidence are often deferred in order to be determined by the trial judge either prior to, or on the day of, the trial.

13.5 **Indictments**

Crown Court trial is known as 'trial on indictment' because the document that contains the charges against the defendant is called an indictment. An indictment may contain one or more ***counts***.

> ***Count*** *A count charges the defendant with an offence. A count must contain both a statement of the offence with which the defendant is charged and particulars (that is, brief details) of the offence (CrimPR Part 14.2). The statement of the offence should describe the offence in ordinary language and identify any legislation that creates the offence. The particulars of the offence should make clear what the prosecutor alleges against the defendant.*

The following is an example of an indictment.

INDICTMENT

IN THE CROWN COURT AT NEWCASTLE UPON TYNE
THE QUEEN—v—JOHN ROBERT PARKER
JOHN ROBERT PARKER is charged as follows:

Count 1

STATEMENT OF OFFENCE

BURGLARY, contrary to section 9(1)(b) of the Theft Act 1968

PARTICULARS OF OFFENCE

JOHN ROBERT PARKER, on the 9th day of August 2019, having entered as a trespasser a building, being a dwelling known as 31 Seaview Road, Newcastle upon Tyne, stole therein a television set, DVD player and twelve DVDs.

Count 2

STATEMENT OF OFFENCE

BURGLARY, contrary to section 9(1)(b) of the Theft Act 1968

PARTICULARS OF OFFENCE

JOHN ROBERT PARKER on the 12th day of August 2019, having entered as a trespasser a building, being a dwelling known as 82 Regent Road, Newcastle upon Tyne, stole therein a laptop computer and £120 in money.

Normally, a single count should charge the defendant with a single offence. A count that charges the defendant with more than one offence is said to be 'duplicitous'. Where a defendant is alleged to have committed more than one offence, there should normally be one count on the indictment for each offence. In order for a number of counts to be contained (or 'joined') in the same indictment, they must either be founded on the same facts, or must form, or be part of, a series of offences of the same or a similar character (CrimPR Part 3.21).

More than one defendant may appear on the same indictment and more than one defendant may be charged in a single count. This would be the usual course where two or more defendants have committed an offence together.

Where a number of counts have been properly joined in an indictment, the Crown Court may still order that a count or counts be tried separately (Indictments Act 1915 s.5). This is known as 'severing' the indictment. The court may order severance if, for example, the defendant would be prejudiced if two or more offences were tried together. This might be the case where trying several counts together would result in a very complicated case or might make the jury hostile to the defendant (*Ludlow v Metropolitan Police Commissioner* [1971] AC 29). Equally, the court has the power to order separate trials of co-defendants charged in the same indictment (*R v Grondkowski* [1946] KB 369).

13.6 **Plea bargaining**

As discussed earlier, not all cases result in trials being held, because many defendants plead guilty at some stage of the court process. Indeed, if all cases were to result in trials, there would be too much work for the courts and the criminal justice system would inevitably grind to a halt. The courts therefore offer certain incentives to defendants to plead guilty and have begun to move towards establishing a plea-bargaining system.

A 'plea bargain' is an agreement under which a defendant enters a guilty plea to an offence in return for an undertaking that they will receive a specified sentence. Plea bargaining is common practice in some countries but was not an acceptable practice in England and Wales until relatively recently.

One of the difficulties with plea bargaining is that a defendant could feel pressurised into pleading guilty to something that they have not done in order to benefit from a concession in relation to their sentence. For example, if a defendant were told that they would receive a custodial sentence if convicted after trial but would not be sent to prison following a guilty plea, they might feel that, realistically, there was little choice but to plead guilty.

Prior to 2005, the only form of 'bargaining' that was acceptable in this country was what is sometimes known as 'charge bargaining'. Charge bargaining occurs where the defendant is charged with an offence, but offers to plead guilty to a lesser offence. In some cases the prosecution may agree that if the defendant pleads guilty to that offence, they will not prosecute the more serious charge.

 **Example**

A defendant charged with wounding with intent to cause grievous bodily harm contrary to s.18 of the Offences Against the Person Act 1861 may be prepared to admit wounding the victim intending to cause some harm, but may deny intending to cause grievous bodily harm. The defendant may therefore offer a guilty plea to the lesser offence of wounding contrary to s.20 of the 1861 Act. The prosecution may accept the lesser plea if, for example, the evidence as to the defendant's intent is not strong. Even if there is some evidence of intent, the prosecution might be persuaded to accept the lesser plea because a judge would still have significant sentencing powers (the maximum sentence for s.20 wounding being five years' imprisonment). The acceptance of the plea also avoids potential further trauma to the victim by having to give evidence in court.

Similarly, the courts have long followed the practice of awarding a discount in sentence to a person who pleaded guilty. In most cases, a defendant who pleaded guilty could be expected to receive a discount of up to one third (see 14.2.2).

However, prior to 2005, a judge was not permitted to indicate the type or length of sentence they would pass in advance of a guilty plea. In particular, a judge was not allowed to indicate that on a plea of guilty they would impose one sentence but on conviction following a trial they would impose another, more severe, sentence (*R v Turner* [1970] 2 WLR 1093). Thus, although charge bargaining was relatively commonplace, plea bargaining in the strict sense was not allowed.

Thinking point

Might an innocent defendant be pressured to plead guilty to obtain a reduced sentence?

A defendant would always know that they were entitled to a discount in sentence if they pleaded guilty and judges were permitted to remind defendants of this. Why do you think judges were nevertheless restricted from indicating the exact sentence they were prepared to impose in order to encourage defendants to plead guilty? Was there a danger that defendants would feel that they were being unfairly pressurised into admitting offences whether or not they were actually guilty?

In *R v Goodyear* [2005] 3 All ER 117, the Court of Appeal relaxed the rules, and a defendant is now permitted to formally seek an 'indication' as to the sentence they will receive. An indication is essentially a promise that the defendant will receive a particular sentence, or type of sentence, if they plead guilty at the point at which the indication is given. The nature of the *Goodyear* indication procedure is summarised in CPD VII, at paras C.1–8.

The Court of Appeal anticipated that a '*Goodyear* indication' would normally be sought at the Plea and Case Management Hearing (which has now been replaced by the PTPH, discussed earlier), although agreed that a defendant could seek an indication at any time after that. In practice, indications are often sought on the day of trial before the jury is sworn.

The judge is entitled to refuse to give an indication. However, if an indication is given and the defendant pleads guilty immediately, the court is bound by the indication and must pass the promised sentence. If the defendant declines to plead guilty following an indication, the indication ceases to have effect. If the defendant pleads guilty at a later stage, the judge will not be bound by the indication given on the earlier occasion and may pass a more severe sentence.

13.7 **Bail**

At most court appearances, the issue of bail will be considered and the court will decide whether to ***remand*** the defendant in custody, or 'on bail' in the community, until the next court hearing.

Remand
A remand is an order that the defendant be kept in custody or granted bail between court appearances.

13.7.1 Remand in custody

The decision to remand a defendant in custody prior to trial is a serious matter. Article 5 of the ECHR recognises that the right to liberty is a fundamental human right. Consequently, there is normally a presumption in favour of granting bail to a defendant who has not yet been convicted of an offence. If bail is refused, there are strict time limits that apply to the period for which a defendant can be remanded in custody pending trial, although these may be extended if there is good cause and the prosecution can show that they have acted with diligence and expedition.

Under s.128 of the Magistrates' Courts Act 1980, the court may remand a defendant in custody for a maximum of eight clear days. In practice, defendants do not always have to be brought back before the court before the expiry of this period, as s.128 provides that a defendant who is legally represented may consent to being remanded in their absence on up to three consecutive occasions before they have to be brought back before the court. Furthermore, s.128A provides that where a court fixes a date for the next stage in the proceedings to take place, a defendant who has already been remanded once may be remanded for a maximum period of twenty-eight clear days for the next stage of the proceedings to take place (s.128A).

To ensure that defendants awaiting trial are not imprisoned indefinitely, regulations made under s.22 of the Prosecution of Offences Act 1985 set down maximum periods for which a defendant may be kept in custody pending trial. The maximum period between first appearance and summary trial is usually fifty-six days. Where a defendant appears before the magistrates' court for an indictable only offence, or is sent to the Crown Court for trial for an either way offence, the maximum period for which they may be remanded in custody by the Crown Court before the start of the trial is usually 182 days, less any period during which they have been in the custody of the magistrates' court.

Thinking point

Is it acceptable for defendants facing Crown Court trial to be remanded in custody for longer?

The regulations allow the courts to remand a defendant in custody for a longer period if they are to be tried in the Crown Court. Do you think this is justifiable? Bear in mind that the Crown Court has the power to try more serious cases, which may take longer to prepare.

13.7.2 Remand on bail

Bail is the release of a defendant subject to a duty to surrender to custody (Bail Act 1976 s.3). This simply means that the defendant has a duty to return to court on a specified date.

Under s.4 of the 1976 Act, a defendant appearing before either a magistrates' court or the Crown Court has a general right to bail. However, Sch.1 to the Act provides that this right does not apply in certain circumstances, such as where the instant offence is an indictable offence and was committed while the defendant was on bail in respect of another offence, or if the court is satisfied that the defendant should be kept in custody for their own protection. A defendant may also be refused bail if they have tested positive for a Class A drug and the conditions in Sch.1, para. 6B to the 1976 Act are established.

Section 25 of the Criminal Justice and Public Order Act 1994 provides that where a defendant is charged with a specified offence, such as murder or rape, and has a previous conviction for such an offence, they will only be granted bail in exceptional circumstances. Section 114(2) of the Coroners and Justice Act 2009 adds that, where a defendant is charged with murder, they may not be granted bail unless there is no significant risk of them committing an offence that would be likely to cause physical or mental injury to another person.

More generally, Sch.1 to the 1976 Act allows a court to refuse bail in relation to an indictable offence where there are substantial grounds to believe that, if released on bail, the defendant would fail to surrender to custody, commit further offences, or interfere with prosecution witnesses or otherwise obstruct the course of justice. In taking its decision, the court should take into account:

- the nature and seriousness of the offence;
- the strength of the evidence;
- the defendant's character, antecedents, associates, and community ties;
- the defendant's record in relation to fulfilling obligations under previous grants of bail;
- where there are substantial grounds to believe the defendant will commit further offences if granted bail, the risk of such conduct being likely to cause physical/mental injury to another person; and
- any other factors that appear to be relevant.

Thinking point

What factors are relevant to bail decisions?

Community ties may be relevant because, for example, a person with family ties and a job has strong connections to the area and is therefore less likely to abscond if granted bail. Consider how the other factors set out in Sch.1 may be relevant to the decision to grant bail.

Under s.3 of the 1976 Act, the court may require a defendant to provide a ***surety or a security*** before releasing them on bail.

Surety/Security
A surety is a person who agrees to forfeit a sum of money if the defendant fails to surrender. A security is a sum of money or assets that the defendant may forfeit themselves if they fail to surrender.

Section 3 also allows the court to set such other conditions of bail as appear to be necessary, for example, to ensure that the defendant surrenders to custody, does not commit further offences, or does not interfere with witnesses. Such bail conditions might require the defendant to live at a specified address, to report regularly to a police station, to stay out of a particular area, or not to contact specified persons. A defendant who fails to comply with the bail conditions may have their bail revoked and be remanded in custody. A defendant who is released on bail and fails to surrender without reasonable cause commits an offence under s.6 of the 1976 Act which is punishable by imprisonment.

Where an offence is not punishable with imprisonment, or where there is no real prospect of a custodial sentence, the circumstances in which bail can be refused are much more limited.

Thinking point

Should a court be allowed to remand in custody if there is no real prospect of a prison sentence?

Do you think a court should always be required to grant bail if there is no real prospect of a custodial sentence being imposed for the offence in the end? Consider how serious an offence is likely to be if there is no real prospect of a custodial sentence. Would it be disproportionate to remand someone in custody for such an offence?

In an effort to tackle domestic abuse, the Legal Aid, Sentencing and Punishment of Offenders Act 2012 provided that a defendant charged with an imprisonable offence need not be granted bail if the court is satisfied that there are substantial grounds to believe they will commit further offences by engaging in conduct that would be likely to cause physical or mental injury to an 'associated person'. An associated person is defined to include: a current or former spouse, civil partner, or cohabitee; anyone who has had an intimate personal relationship with the defendant which was of a significant duration; a relative; or a person who lives or has lived with the defendant (other than as an employee, tenant, lodger, or boarder). Even where an offence is non-imprisonable, if the defendant has previously been remanded on conditional bail in the proceedings and has breached any of the conditions, the court may remand the defendant in custody if satisfied there are substantial grounds to believe they would commit a further offence that is likely to cause physical or mental injury to an associated person.

13.8 **Pre-trial issues: disclosure**

Before a trial can take place, the parties need to be in possession of the relevant material to enable them to properly prepare and present their case. A defendant is entitled to copies of the evidence upon which the prosecution proposes to rely. This may include, for example, witness statements, transcripts of interviews, and documentary exhibits. The defendant is also entitled to copies of certain types of material that the prosecution do not intend to use. The provision of this other material is known as 'disclosure'.

13.8.1 Section 9 of the Criminal Justice Act 1967

If the prosecution wishes to rely upon the evidence of a witness at trial, a copy of the witness' statement must be supplied to the defence. A witness statement must comply with the requirements of s.9 of the Criminal Justice Act 1967. A defendant who receives a section 9 statement has seven days to object to it being used in evidence. If no objection is received, the statement will simply be read out at trial as agreed evidence, thus removing the necessity of calling the witness. This can be an important device to save court time and costs.

A defendant is not obliged to serve copies of the statements of defence witnesses, although they may do so if they wish.

13.8.2 Unused material

Material that the prosecution has that is relevant, but which it does not intend to rely upon, is known as 'unused material'. In addition to giving the defendant the evidence upon which it proposes to rely, the prosecution is also required to review all of the unused material in a case to assess whether there is anything that ought to be ***disclosed*** to the defence. The prosecution is not required to disclose material that is neutral or damages the defence case. However, s.3 of the Criminal Procedure and Investigations Act 1996 imposes a duty on a prosecutor to disclose any material in their possession, or which they have inspected, that 'might reasonably be considered capable of undermining the case for the prosecution against the defendant or of assisting the case for the defendant'. The Attorney General has issued Guidelines on Disclosure, which can be found at **www.cps.gov.uk/legal/a_to_c/attorney_generals_guidelines_on_disclosure/**.

Disclosed
Material is disclosed when the prosecutor either provides the defendant with a copy of it or allows the defendant to inspect it.

Following this 'initial disclosure' by the prosecution, s.5 of the 1996 Act requires the defendant to provide a 'defence statement'. Section 6A sets out the matters that a defence statement must address and provides that it must include the nature and particulars of the defendant's defence, particulars of any alibi, and details of any issues of law which the defendant wishes to raise. Under s.6C, the defendant must also provide the name, address, and date of birth of any witnesses they propose to call to give evidence. In the past, there was no obligation upon defendants to disclose their defence. It was suggested that some defendants took advantage of this by raising new issues at trial and thereby 'ambushing' the prosecution. The courts have emphasised that a criminal trial is a search for the truth and not a 'game' (*R v Gleeson* [2003] EWCA Crim 3357; *R (on the application of Firth) v Epping Magistrates' Court* [2011] EWHC 388 (Admin)). It is therefore important that a defence statement now highlights the real issues in the case. (In the context of summary trial, s.6 of the 1996 Act continues to provide that the giving of a defence statement by the defendant is voluntary.)

Following initial disclosure, the prosecution is under a continuing duty to keep the question of disclosure under review (s.7A of the 1996 Act). The prosecutor is also required to specifically review the position in light of the defence statement and provide any material that might reasonably be expected to undermine the prosecution case or assist the defence.

A defendant who has given a defence statement can apply for disclosure under s.8 of the Act if they have reasonable cause to believe that there is prosecution material that is required to be disclosed but has not been so disclosed. This may include material that is in the hands of third parties to which the prosecutor has access. This is one reason for giving a defence statement in the magistrates' court, where it would otherwise be optional.

In summary, the prosecution is obliged to supply the defence with copies of all of the evidence it intends to present at trial. There are also strict duties to disclose material the prosecution does not intend to use where such disclosure is necessary to ensure a fair trial. There is no corresponding duty on the defence to disclose material in the defendant's possession that might undermine the defence case or assist the prosecution. In fact, defendants are not even required to serve the statements of defence witnesses on the prosecution. However, under s.6C of the Criminal Procedure and Investigations Act 1996, defendants are now required to notify the prosecution and the court of the names and addresses of all defence witnesses. This enables the prosecution to investigate these witnesses in advance of trial.

Thinking point

Should the defence be required to disclose material that undermines their case?

Why do you think the defence is not under a duty to disclose material that is adverse to the defendant's case? Is this another example of the weighting of the criminal justice system in favour of the defendant? Or is it simply a facet of the principle that the defendant is innocent until proven guilty?

Problems with the current regime were highlighted in late 2017 and early 2018, when several high-profile cases collapsed due to disclosure failures.

Example

In December 2017, Liam Allan, a student, was on trial facing twelve counts of rape and sexual assault. A download from the complainant's mobile telephone was in the possession of the police but the officer in charge of the case maintained that it did not contain anything of relevance. The download was finally disclosed after Mr Allan had given evidence at his trial. Defence counsel discovered material that undermined the prosecution case to such an extent that the CPS ultimately decided to stop the case.

In 2018, the House of Commons Justice Committee considered the disclosure of unused material in criminal cases. They concluded that not all police officers 'recognise their duty as a search for the truth'. They did not recommend any fundamental changes to the 1996 Act but concluded that there needs to be a 'shift in culture towards viewing disclosure as a core justice duty, and not an administrative add-on'. They also stressed the need for enhanced skills and technology in light of the volume and complexity of material that is now routinely collected by investigators.

13.9 **Trial on indictment**

Where the defendant has pleaded not guilty to a count, or counts, it will be necessary for a jury to be sworn. The defendant will then be 'given in charge' to the jury. This is the point at which the jurors will be informed of the charges and told that it is for them, having heard the evidence, to determine whether the defendant is guilty or not. Under s.44 of the CJA 2003, the prosecution may apply to have a trial conducted by a judge without a jury where there is a real and present danger of jury tampering. This is an exceptional course, which happens very rarely in practice.

Normally the defendant will be present at trial, but the court does possess discretion to try the defendant in their absence, for example where the defendant deliberately absconds from the trial or disrupts the trial (*R v Jones* [2003] 1 AC 1).

Criminal trials normally take place in public, but there are exceptions to this general rule. For example, where a person is charged with an offence under the Official Secrets Acts of 1911 or 1920, the public may be excluded if holding the trial in public would be prejudicial to national safety. Similarly, there are restrictions on the information that the press may publish. For example, under s.1 of the Sexual Offences (Amendment) Act 1992, information identifying a sexual offence complainant may not be published.

Legislation preventing the publication of the identity of rape complainants was first introduced in 1976 (Sexual Offences (Amendment) Act 1976 s.4). The rationale underpinning the legislation was that 'public knowledge of the indignity which [the complainant] has suffered in being raped may be extremely distressing and even positively harmful, and the risk of such public knowledge can operate as a severe deterrent to bringing proceedings' (*Report of the Advisory Group on the Law of Rape*, Cmnd 6352, 1975).

The 1992 Act extended this protection to victims of all types of sexual offence. The aim of the Act was to encourage victims of all types of sexual crimes to come forward and report offences, in the knowledge that their identities would not be publicised. Whether an offence is classified as a sexual offence is therefore of critical importance. In 2015 Parliament created a new offence of disclosing private sexual photographs and films with intent to cause distress (known as 'revenge porn'). Unfortunately, this offence is not currently classified as a sexual offence, so victims' identities are not protected by the provisions of the 1992 Act. This is clearly an anomaly and campaigners have called for it to be rectified.

In 2010, the government announced its intention to extend anonymity in rape cases to defendants (HM Government, *The Coalition: Our Programme for Government*, 2010, para. 20). Proponents of the view that those who are accused of rape ought to remain anonymous unless and until they are convicted argue that a special stigma attaches to a rape allegation, which does not go away even if the defendant is ultimately acquitted. Those in favour of maintaining the status quo suggest that publishing the name of a man accused of rape may encourage other of his victims to come forward. The government's proposal to grant anonymity was ultimately abandoned on the ground that there was insufficient empirical evidence on which to base a decision to afford anonymity to those accused of rape. See David Wolchover's articles 'Rape Defendant Anonymity' (2012) 176 JPN 5 and (2012) 176 JPN 24 for further discussion of this issue.

13.9.1 **The case for the prosecution**

Once the jury has been sworn, the prosecution advocate makes an 'opening speech'. In this speech, the advocate will outline the case against the defendant so as to enable the jurors to more easily understand the evidence they will hear. Following the opening speech, the prosecution advocate 'calls' the prosecution evidence. This will involve bringing witnesses into court to give evidence that will prove the elements of the offence. When the prosecution calls a witness, the witness is first examined in chief by the prosecution advocate. They may then be cross-examined by the defence advocate. If there are several co-defendants, the witness will be cross-examined by the advocate for each of them in the order in which the defendants' names appear on the indictment. Following all cross-examination, the witness may be re-examined by the prosecution advocate.

In general, where the prosecution serves a witness statement on the defence, the prosecution should call the witness to give live evidence. However, if the defence agrees, the prosecution may read the witness' statement instead (Criminal Justice Act 1967 s.9, see 13.8.1).

A party is only likely to serve the statement of a witness whose evidence will support their own case. The advocate will have a witness statement, or 'proof of evidence', which will contain the evidence that the witness is expected to give. The advocate will hope that the witness will 'come up to proof', that is, gives evidence in accordance with their statement. Even if the witness fails to come up to proof when giving evidence, the advocate who called the witness is not normally permitted to cross-examine the witness by asking leading questions.

As a general rule, advocates may not ask their own witness 'leading questions' in order to elicit evidence, unless the evidence to which the question is directed is not in dispute. A leading question is one that either suggests the answer to the witness or assumes the existence of facts about which the witness has not yet given evidence.

Example

If one of the issues in the case is whether a car was blue, the question 'was the car blue?' would be a leading question as the advocate has suggested the colour 'blue' to the witness. Leading questions may not be asked in examination in chief. Instead the advocate should ask: 'What colour was the car?'

Unlike examination in chief, leading questions may be asked during cross-examination (*Ex parte Bottomley* [1909] 2 KB 14). The key rule in cross-examination is that the advocate must put their case to the witness to give the witness the opportunity to respond to it. However, cross-examination of a sexual offence complainant relating to his or her sexual behaviour on other occasions will require leave of the trial judge under s.41 of the Youth Justice and Criminal Evidence Act 1999.

Leave is not normally required before asking particular questions of a witness. Section 41 of the 1999 Act was passed to address concerns that sexual offence complainants were being questioned inappropriately about their previous sexual behaviour. These types of question could be designed to unsettle the witness, to scandalise, and to attack the victim's character, rather than to elicit the truth about what happened at the time of the alleged offence. The law now prevents such questioning unless it is relevant to the case.

Where the defendant has not appointed a defence advocate, the provisions of Chapter 2 of Part 2 of the Youth Justice and Criminal Evidence Act 1999 prohibit the defendant from personally cross-examining sexual offence complainants and certain child witnesses. The court also possesses discretion to prevent a defendant from personally cross-examining witnesses in other types of case. If the defendant declines to appoint an advocate to cross-examine the relevant witness, the court can appoint a qualified legal representative to cross-examine the witness on the defendant's behalf.

The provisions of the 1999 Act concerning cross-examination by the defendant in person provide another example of recent legislation intended to make the process of giving evidence as a witness in a criminal trial less unpleasant. The provisions were enacted in response to two widely publicised cases, in which defendants acting in person cross-examined at great length complainants who had made allegations of rape against them.

Following cross-examination, the advocate for the party who called a witness is entitled to re-examine the witness. Essentially, the rules that govern examination in chief also govern re-examination and leading questions should not be asked. In addition, re-examination should normally only relate to matters that were raised in cross-examination (*Prince v Samo* (1838) 7 Ad & El 627).

13.9.2 **Defence submissions of no case to answer**

At the close of the prosecution case, the defence may make a submission of 'no case to answer'. This is a submission that no jury, properly directed, could convict on the prosecution evidence. The judge will hear submissions from both defence and prosecution advocates in the absence of the jury and will direct an acquittal if either:

- there is no evidence that a defendant committed the offence with which they are charged; or
- the evidence is so inherently weak or tenuous that, even taken at its highest, a properly directed jury could not properly convict (*R v Galbraith* [1981] 1 WLR 1039).

Example

Bob is charged with theft of a watch. One of the elements of theft which the prosecution must prove is that the property in question belonged to another person. In Bob's case, the prosecution calls no evidence to prove that the watch that was found in Bob's possession belonged to someone else. The jury should be directed to acquit Bob following a defence submission of no case to answer because there is no evidence in relation to an element of the offence with which he is charged.

13.9.3 **The case for the defence**

If the defendant intends to give evidence and call other witnesses of fact, the defence advocate may make an opening speech outlining the defence case and the evidence that will be called on the defendant's behalf (under s.2 of the Criminal Evidence Act 1898). In practice, defence opening speeches are rare. Indeed, if a defendant is to be the only defence witness, or if they do not intend to give evidence, the defence advocate is not entitled to make an opening speech.

Where a defendant does testify, s.79 of the Police and Criminal Evidence Act 1984 provides that they must be called before any other defence witnesses unless the court orders otherwise. Defence witnesses (including the defendant) are examined in chief by the defendant's advocate. They may be cross-examined by the advocate for the prosecution, and may then be cross-examined by advocates for any co-defendants, before being re-examined by the defence advocate. Where written statements are admissible on behalf of the defendant because their contents are agreed, the defence advocate will read them to the jury.

For the admissibility of bad character evidence see 13.11.2.

If there are several co-defendants, their defence cases will be presented in the order in which the defendants' names appear on the indictment.

The prosecution should not normally be permitted to call further evidence following the close of the prosecution case. In an appropriate case, however, the prosecution may be entitled to call rebuttal evidence (that is, evidence to contradict or nullify defence evidence). For example, if the defendant gives evidence that wrongly suggests that they are of good character, the prosecution may be entitled to call bad character evidence in rebuttal.

13.9.4 **Closing speeches by prosecution and defence advocates**

Following the close of the case for the defence, the prosecution advocate is usually entitled to make a closing speech. (The prosecution advocate is not entitled to make a closing speech where the defendant is not legally represented and has called no witnesses other than themselves.) Finally, the defence advocate is entitled to make a closing speech. Section 1 of the Criminal Procedure (Right of Reply) Act 1964 provides that the making of a closing speech by the prosecution must take place prior to the making of a speech by or on behalf of the defendant. This means the defence is entitled to the last word before the judge sums up the case.

13.9.5 **The trial judge's summing up**

Before the jury retires to consider its verdict, the judge sums up the case for the jury. In the course of summing up, the judge will remind the jury of the evidence and give the jury directions on the relevant law, including explaining the elements of the offence and the burden and standard of proof. The judge may also be required to direct the jury concerning a variety of other matters, such as the drawing of inferences from silence (see 12.4.5 and 13.11.4) and the significance of evidence of the defendant's good or bad character (see 13.11.2 and 13.11.3).

To assist judges in formulating their directions to the jury, the Judicial Studies Board provides guidance and examples of appropriate directions. These can be found at **www.judiciary.gov.uk/publications/crown-court-bench-book-directing-the-jury-2/**. Finally, the judge should direct the jury to retire to the jury room to reach a unanimous verdict.

13.10 **Summary trial**

The tribunal in a magistrates' court normally consists of either three lay magistrates sitting with a legal adviser, or a legally qualified district judge. Sections 46–50 of the Criminal Justice and Courts Act 2015 enable certain types of case to be heard by a single lay magistrate sitting with a legal adviser. This 'single justice procedure' only applies where a case is uncontested and the defendant is an adult who is charged with a non-imprisonable, summary only offence. It is designed to apply to cases in which the defendant fails to engage with the court process and does not respond to correspondence or attend hearings. In such cases a single magistrate can decide the case on the basis of written documents, without the prosecutor or defendant needing to attend court.

When a defendant appears before a magistrates' court and pleads not guilty, then unless the matter is to be sent to the Crown Court for trial, a date will be set for summary trial (i.e. magistrates' court trial) (see 13.4.1). The defendant will then be tried by either lay magistrates or by a district judge, who will act as both the tribunal of law and the tribunal of fact. Thus, the magistrates or district judge decide both whether evidence is admissible and whether the defendant is guilty. The procedure at a summary trial is otherwise similar to trial on indictment.

Where the tribunal in the magistrates' court consists of lay magistrates, their legal adviser will advise the magistrates on any issues of law that have arisen during the case before they retire to consider their verdict. This advice should be given in the presence of both the prosecution and the defence advocate so that the advocates may make submissions if the legal adviser says anything with which they disagree.

13.11 **Evidential issues**

The law of evidence is a complex subject. A course on the English Legal System cannot hope to cover all relevant areas. This section outlines a few of the key evidential issues that are likely to arise in the context of both summary trial and trial on indictment.

13.11.1 **Burden and standard of proof**

Where the defendant pleads not guilty to an offence, the prosecution will bear the legal burden of proving the defendant's guilt to the criminal standard of proof. In general, the prosecution bears the legal burden both of proving the elements of the offence with which the defendant is charged and of disproving any defences raised by the defendant (*Woolmington v DPP* [1935] AC 462).

 Example

In *Woolmington v DPP* (earlier), the defendant was charged with the murder of his wife by shooting her. He claimed that the gun had gone off by accident. The trial judge directed the jury that it was for the prosecution to prove that the defendant killed his wife, but the defendant had to show that her death was an accident. The defendant was convicted of murder. The House of Lords allowed his appeal against his conviction, saying:

> Throughout the web of the English Criminal Law one golden thread is always to be seen, that it is the duty of the prosecution to prove the prisoner's guilt.

Accordingly, it was for the prosecution to prove both that the defendant killed his wife and that her death was not an accident.

Consequently, where the defendant relies upon a defence such as self-defence, provided that there is some evidence before the court to raise the defence, the prosecution bears the legal burden of disproving the defence to the criminal standard of proof (*Mancini v DPP* [1942] AC 1).

Thinking point

Why does the prosecution bear the burden of proof in a criminal case?

The '*Woolmington* principle' imposes the legal burden of proof in criminal proceedings upon the prosecution, subject to limited exceptions. Is this an example of the weighting of the criminal justice system in favour of the defendant?

At common law there is only one exception to the general rule that the prosecution bears the burden of proof in a criminal case. Where the defendant relies upon the common law defence of insanity, the defendant bears the legal burden of proving this defence (*M'Naghten's case* (1843) 10 Cl & Fin 200). Some statutes also impose the legal burden of proving a defence upon the defendant, either expressly or by implication. Thus, for example, s.2 of the Homicide Act 1957 states that the defendant bears the legal burden of proving the defence of diminished responsibility.

The criminal standard of proof is proof beyond reasonable doubt. This means that the jury must not find the defendant guilty unless they are 'satisfied so they feel sure' of the defendant's guilt (*R v Summers* [1952] 1 All ER 1059). Where, exceptionally, the defendant bears the legal burden of proving a defence, the requisite standard of proof is merely proof on the balance of probabilities (*R v Carr-Briant* [1943] KB 607).

Article 6(2) of the ECHR guarantees the defendant the right to be 'presumed innocent until proved guilty according to law'. Consequently, the courts have held that the statutory imposition of a legal burden of proof upon the defendant may violate Article 6, although it will not necessarily do so (*Salabiaku v France* (1988) 13 EHRR 379). Whether or not imposing a legal burden of proof on the defendant violates Article 6 will depend upon factors such as the reason for imposing a legal burden of proof upon the defendant, how difficult it would be for the defendant to discharge that burden, and the potential consequences for the defendant if they fail to discharge the burden (*Sheldrake v DPP* [2004] 3 WLR 976).

In *Sheldrake v DPP* (earlier), the defendant was charged with being in charge of a motor vehicle while the proportion of alcohol in his breath exceeded the prescribed limit, contrary to the Road Traffic Act 1988 s.5(1)(b). Under s.5(2) of the 1988 Act, it is a defence for a person to prove that there was no likelihood of them actually driving the vehicle. The defendant in *Sheldrake* argued that this was a violation of the presumption of innocence and that, rather than having to prove he was not likely to drive his car, the prosecution should have had to prove that he *was* likely to drive it. The House of Lords ruled that whether the defendant was likely to drive his vehicle was a matter within his own knowledge, making it appropriate for the defence to bear the burden of proof in relation to this issue.

In relation to limiting the meaning of statutory provisions, see Chapter 4.

In circumstances in which imposing a legal burden of proof upon the defendant would violate Article 6, the court may be able to 'read down' the relevant statutory provision (under s.3(1) of the Human Rights Act 1998) as merely imposing an 'evidential burden' upon the defendant (*Attorney General's Reference (No. 4 of 2002)* [2004] 3 WLR 976). The effect of reading down a provision in this way is that, provided there is evidence before the court to raise the relevant defence, the legal burden of disproving the defence to the criminal standard of proof is borne by the prosecution.

13.11.2 **Bad character**

Section 98 of the CJA 2003 defines bad character as evidence of misconduct, namely criminal offences or other reprehensible behaviour. Evidence which has to do with the facts of the offence with which the defendant is charged, or which concerns the investigation or prosecution of that offence, does not constitute evidence of bad character. The most common form of evidence of bad character will be a person's previous convictions.

Prior to 2003, evidence of a defendant's bad character could not be adduced at trial save in very limited circumstances. The circumstances in which such evidence can be used were expanded significantly by the CJA 2003. Critics have argued that this is another example of the rebalancing of the criminal process to favour the prosecution. However, it is important to note that a defendant remains entitled to adduce bad character evidence under the 2003 Act. For example, the defendant may wish to introduce the previous convictions of a prosecution witness or a co-defendant to undermine that person's evidence.

The bad character of the defendant

Evidence of the defendant's bad character will only be admissible under the CJA 2003 if one of what the Court of Appeal in *R v Hanson* [2005] 1 WLR 3169 described as the 'gateways' created by s.101(1)(a) to (g) of the CJA 2003 is applicable.

- Under gateway (a), evidence of the defendant's bad character is admissible by agreement between the parties.
- Gateway (b) permits the defendant to adduce evidence of his or her own bad character.
- Gateway (c) renders evidence of the defendant's bad character admissible if it relates to the background history of the offence with which the defendant is charged.
- Under gateway (d), which is the most important gateway, evidence of the defendant's bad character is admissible if it is relevant to an important matter in issue

between the defendant and the prosecution. This can include evidence that the defendant has the propensity to commit offences of the kind with which they are charged, or evidence that they have a propensity to be untruthful.

- Under gateway (e) one co-defendant may adduce evidence of another co-defendant's bad character if it has substantial probative value in relation to an important matter in issue between them.
- Under gateway (f), evidence of the defendant's bad character may be adduced to correct a false impression that the defendant has given, either at the police station or in court. This gateway may be used, for example, where the defendant wrongly suggests when giving evidence that they have no previous convictions.
- Under gateway (g), evidence of the defendant's bad character is admissible where the defendant has attacked another person's character, either at the police station or in court.

Where evidence is tendered under gateway (d) or (g), the defence may object under s.101(3), in which case the court must not admit the evidence if to do so would have such an adverse effect on the fairness of the proceedings that the court ought not to admit it.

Where evidence of the defendant's bad character is admitted in criminal proceedings, it will be necessary for the judge to give the jury careful directions concerning matters such as the relevance of the previous convictions and the fact that the jury should not assume that the defendant is guilty merely because they have previous convictions (*R v Hanson* [2005] 1 WLR 3169; *R v Highton* [2005] 1 WLR 3472).

Traditionally, English courts were reluctant to admit evidence of a defendant's previous convictions due to the danger that the jury might find them guilty because of their previous convictions rather than on the basis of the evidence. Although evidence of the defendant's bad character was admissible in exceptional circumstances, the provisions of the CJA 2003 now make it much easier for the prosecution to introduce such evidence.

Critical debate

Under the CJA 2003, the prosecution may be allowed to adduce evidence of a defendant's bad character to show that they have a 'propensity' to commit offences of the type with which they are charged. What do you think 'propensity' means in this context? Do you agree that a jury ought to be made aware that a defendant has previous convictions for the type of offence they are considering? What arguments might there be for suggesting that evidence of a person's propensity to commit offences is prejudicial? Is there a danger that the jury may make assumptions about a defendant on the basis of their previous behaviour, rather than focusing on the evidence specific to the offence with which they are now charged?

The bad character of non-defendants

Evidence of the bad character of persons other than the defendant (such as witnesses) will only be admissible under the CJA 2003 if a s.100 gateway is applicable. The main example is s.100(1)(b), under which evidence of the bad character of a person other than the defendant is admissible if it has substantial probative value in relation to an issue of substantial importance in the case. Traditionally, evidence of a witness's bad character was admissible in order to discredit the witness. Section 100 of the CJA 2003 now restricts the ability of parties to criminal proceedings to adduce evidence of the bad character of a witness other than the defendant.

 **Key point**

Section 100 forms one of a number of provisions in recent years that, potentially, make it less unpleasant for witnesses to give evidence in criminal proceedings.

13.11.3 **Good character**

At common law the defence was entitled to adduce evidence of the defendant's good character in the form of evidence as to their general good reputation (*R v Rowton* (1865) Le & Ca 520). This common law rule was preserved by s.118 of the CJA 2003. Where the defence adduces evidence of the defendant's good character, the jury should be directed that a person of good character is both less likely to be guilty and more likely to be truthful (*R v Vye* [1993] 1 WLR 471).

13.11.4 **Silence: failure of the defendant to testify**

The options available to a defendant in a criminal trial have changed significantly since the late nineteenth century. Prior to the Criminal Evidence Act 1898, the law did not permit a defendant to give evidence on oath on their own behalf, although it had become common practice for defendants to make unsworn statements from the dock. Section 1 of the 1898 Act amended the position to make defendants competent to give sworn evidence.

The 1898 Act faced opposition from those who felt that it would effectively require a defendant to prove their innocence. Supporters of the Act argued that defendants were entitled to decline to give evidence and therefore retained the right to silence. The prosecution was not permitted to make any adverse comment concerning a defendant's failure to give evidence and the trial judge's ability to comment was limited.

By the latter part of the twentieth century, criticisms of the law in this area were mounting. It was felt by many that the ability to choose whether or not to give evidence gave defendants an unfair advantage. It was suggested that defendants should not be allowed to remain silent with impunity. Eventually, Parliament enacted the

Criminal Justice and Public Order Act 1994. Section 35 of this Act provides that a jury is entitled to draw an inference in respect of a defendant's silence at trial, unless the physical or mental condition of the defendant makes it undesirable for them to testify (Criminal Justice and Public Order Act 1994 s.35). This means that the jury is now entitled to conclude that a defendant did not give evidence because they had no answer to the prosecution's case, or none that would stand up to cross-examination.

The judge must direct the jury that they may only draw an inference against the defendant if satisfied that the prosecution's case is so strong that it calls for an answer. As in the case of s.34, the jury must also be directed that a conviction cannot be based wholly or mainly on a s.35 inference.

For inferences from the defendant's silence at the police station under s.34 of the 1994 Act, see 12.4.5.

Thinking point

Should defendants have an absolute right to silence?

Section 35 of the 1994 Act makes it dangerous for the defendant to offer no defence and simply require the prosecution to prove guilt. Is this unfair to the defendant or is it an example of the rebalancing of the criminal process?

13.12 Verdicts

Following trial on indictment, the jury decides whether the defendant is guilty or not guilty. If the defendant is tried summarily, it is the magistrates (or the district judge) who determine whether the defendant is guilty or not guilty.

13.12.1 Trial on indictment

If a jury decides that the defendant is not guilty of the offence with which they are charged, the jury may be entitled to find the defendant guilty of a lesser offence. Thus, for example, where the jury finds a defendant not guilty of murder, it may find them guilty of the lesser offence of manslaughter (Criminal Law Act 1967 s.6(2)). Generally, the jury may find a defendant guilty of a lesser offence if the allegation in the indictment amounts to or includes an allegation of the lesser offence (Criminal Law Act 1967 s.6(3)).

Example

Joe is charged with burglary contrary to s.9(1)(b) of the Theft Act 1968. It is alleged that Joe entered 12 Elmfield Park as a trespasser and stole therein a television set and DVD player. If the jury is not satisfied that Joe was a trespasser, he cannot be guilty of burglary. However, if the jury is satisfied that Joe stole the items, he may be convicted of theft instead, because burglary of this type includes an allegation of theft (*R v Lillis* [1972] 2 QB 236).

Initially, the judge must require the jury to reach a unanimous verdict. Sometimes, however, a jury may be unable to reach a unanimous verdict. After at least two hours and ten minutes have elapsed from the time the jurors retired to consider their verdict, the judge is entitled to accept a majority verdict (Juries Act 1974 s.17; Practice Direction (Criminal Proceedings: Consolidation), para. IV.46). A majority verdict is a verdict on which at least ten of twelve jurors agree. If the jury has been reduced to eleven jurors (for example, due to a juror falling ill during the trial), a majority verdict still requires at least ten jurors to agree. In exceptional cases where there are ten jurors, a majority verdict requires nine jurors to agree. Where a guilty verdict is returned by a majority, the foreman must state in open court the number of jurors who agreed with the verdict and the number who dissented from it. The ability to accept a majority verdict is necessary because of the risk that, otherwise, it might be impossible for a jury to reach a verdict as a result of a single juror having particularly extreme and intransigent views.

If the jury cannot reach a majority verdict, the judge will discharge the jury, in which case a retrial may follow.

13.12.2 **Summary trial**

Where a case is tried by lay magistrates, a unanimous verdict is not required. Magistrates may reach a verdict upon which two of them agree. Subject to limited statutory exceptions, if a magistrates' court finds a defendant not guilty of the offence with which they are charged, the defendant may not be convicted of a lesser offence (*Lawrence v Same* [1968] 2 QB 93).

13.12.3 **Retrials**

A guilty verdict is final, subject to any right of appeal (see Chapter 18). A not guilty verdict is also usually final, as the prosecution generally has no power to appeal against a not guilty verdict. The rule against 'double jeopardy' means that a defendant who has been acquitted of an offence may not subsequently be charged with the same offence again, even if new evidence is discovered.

The double jeopardy principle was called into question by the Macpherson Inquiry into the case of Stephen Lawrence, a black teenager who was stabbed to death in a racist attack by a gang of white youths in 1993. After failings in the police investigation into the murder, in 1996 Stephen Lawrence's parents brought a private prosecution against three of the youths alleged to have killed their son. The private prosecution failed and the youths were acquitted. The investigation continued and it was hoped that new evidence against the killers might be discovered. The Macpherson Report recommended that consideration be given to permitting a person to be prosecuted after an acquittal where fresh and viable evidence was discovered.

In 2001, the Law Commission also recommended a limited exception to the double jeopardy principle. The Commission proposed that, in cases of murder only, the Court of Appeal should have the power to quash an acquittal where there was reliable and compelling new evidence of the defendant's guilt. In response, Parliament introduced Part 10 of the CJA 2003, which is wider than the Law Commission's proposals. Under s.76 of the 2003 Act, where a person has been acquitted of a 'qualifying offence', a prosecutor may apply to the Court of Appeal for an order quashing the acquittal and ordering a retrial. Qualifying offences include murder, manslaughter, rape, arson endangering life, and certain serious drugs offences. The Court of Appeal must order a retrial if there is new and compelling evidence against the acquitted person (s.78). Compelling evidence means evidence that is reliable, substantial, and highly probative in the context of the case. An order under s.76 may only be sought with the consent of the DPP, who must be satisfied that it is in the public interest to seek a retrial.

In 2010, new scientific evidence was discovered in relation to the Stephen Lawrence case. Two men were charged with murder, including Gary Dobson, who had been acquitted in 1996. The Court of Appeal quashed his acquittal and ordered a retrial. Both defendants were subsequently convicted of the murder of Stephen Lawrence.

Summary

- The criminal courts of trial are the Crown Court and magistrates' courts. Trial on indictment (that is, trial by jury) takes place in the Crown Court whereas summary trial takes place in magistrates' courts.
- Criminal proceedings are usually instituted by arresting and charging the defendant or by issuing a written charge and requisition. Some cases will then remain in the magistrates' court, while others will be 'sent' to the Crown Court.
- At a criminal trial on indictment, the basic procedure is that the prosecution case is heard first. The defence may then (where appropriate) submit that there is no case to answer. If this submission is unsuccessful, the defence case follows. Closing speeches are then made, followed by the judge's summing up. At the end of the trial the jurors retire to reach their verdict. The summary trial procedure is very similar.
- The prosecution bears the burden of proving the case against the defendant beyond reasonable doubt.
- A variety of other evidential issues may arise at trial, such as the admissibility of character evidence and the implications of a defendant's failure to testify.

Questions

1 (a) How are criminal offences categorised?
  (b) What sort of offences are summary only?
  (c) What is meant by trial on indictment?
2 What factors are taken into account when deciding whether an either way offence should be tried in the magistrates' court or in the Crown Court?
3 Is plea bargaining allowed in the courts of England and Wales?
4 Who bears the burden of proof in criminal proceedings and what is the standard of proof?
5 Which party to criminal proceedings is entitled to cross-examine a witness?
6 In what circumstances might a defendant's previous convictions be used against them in a criminal case?

Sample question and outline answer

Question

Suraya, who is twenty-two years old and works as a care assistant, has been charged with theft of a bicycle (an offence that is triable either way). She has a previous conviction for handling stolen goods. Suraya admitted to the police that she stole the bicycle but now says that she only confessed because the police bullied her. Suraya intends to plead not guilty. She is frightened about attending court and says that she is too scared to testify. Advise Suraya about the following matters:

(a) What procedure will be used to determine whether her case is tried in the magistrates' court or in the Crown Court?

(b) If Suraya is given the choice, should she opt for a magistrates' court trial or elect Crown Court trial?

(c) If Suraya does not testify in her own defence, will this mean she will be convicted?

Outline answer

Theft is triable either way. The first part of the question requires you to demonstrate your knowledge of the procedure that applies to all either way offences. Part (b) requires you to discuss the relative advantages and disadvantages of summary trial and trial on indictment and to give your opinion as to which venue would be preferable. Part (c) tests your knowledge of one of the fundamental rules of evidence applicable to criminal trials, namely the right to silence.

(a) Theft is an either way offence, so is subject to the plea before venue (PBV) and allocation procedures. Suraya must attend the magistrates' court for the PBV hearing. Under s.17A of the Magistrates' Courts Act 1980, Suraya should be informed of the PBV procedure and warned that she could be committed for sentence if the sentencing powers of the magistrates' court are insufficient. Suraya will then be asked whether she intends to plead guilty. If she indicates a not guilty plea, the court must determine whether the offence appears more suitable for summary trial or trial on indictment (Magistrates' Courts Act 1980 s.19). The prosecution and defence advocates will make representations and the court will be informed about Suraya's previous conviction. The court must also consider the Sentencing Council's Allocation Guideline, which states that either way offences should generally be tried summarily unless the court's sentencing powers will clearly be insufficient. If the court decides that the case is not suitable for summary trial, Suraya will clearly be sent to the Crown Court (Crime and Disorder Act 1998 s.51(1)). If the court decides that summary trial would be more suitable, Suraya may consent to be tried summarily or may elect Crown Court trial. Before making this decision, Suraya is entitled to ask for an indication as to whether, if she pleaded guilty, she would receive a community sentence or a custodial sentence.

(b) A Crown Court trial is more expensive and the Crown Court has greater sentencing powers than a magistrates' court. However, acquittal rates are higher in the Crown Court. A Crown Court judge decides questions of law, including questions about the admissibility of evidence. This means that, if the judge decides that Suraya's confession is inadmissible, the jury will never hear it. Conversely, in the magistrates' court, the magistrates or district judge decide questions of law and fact, and will therefore have heard a confession even if they subsequently rule it inadmissible. Given that Suraya's case involves an argument about the admissibility of a confession, a Crown Court trial would probably be in her best interests.

(c) If Suraya does not give evidence, an inference can be drawn from her silence unless her physical or mental condition makes it undesirable for her to testify (Criminal Justice and Public Order Act 1994 s.35). The fact that Suraya is frightened about attending court would not be enough to preclude the drawing of an adverse inference. Thus, if Suraya chose not to testify, the magistrates or jury would be entitled to conclude that her silence was due to her having no answer to the charge against her, or none that would stand up to cross-examination.

Further reading

Your reading should be directed to understanding the process by which a criminal case comes before the courts. Because the criminal justice system is about balancing the rights of the accused against the rights of victims and the public at large, you should consider whether the particular procedure or rule you are reading about favours the prosecution or the defence and whether, if it does favour either party, this is justifiable.

- ***Buxton, R.*** *'The Private Prosecutor as a Minister of Justice'* [2009] Crim LR 427

  Explores some of the practical and ethical difficulties of private prosecutions.

- ***Dennis, I.*** *'Prosecution Disclosure: Are the Problems Insoluble?'* [2018] Crim LR 829

  Explores the problems with the current disclosure regime. Discusses recommendations for reform and concludes that more radical measures are required to prevent miscarriages of justice.

- ***Dent, N.*** and ***Paul, S.*** *'In Defence of Section 41'* [2017] Crim LR 613.

  Analyses responses to the *Ched Evans* case and considers proposals to prevent any questioning of a complainant about their previous sexual behaviour in sexual offence cases.

- ***Garland, F.*** and ***McEwan, J.*** *'Embracing the Overriding Objective: Difficulties and Dilemmas in the New Criminal Climate'* (2012) 16(3) E&P 233

  Describes a study into the practical effect of the case management provisions of the Criminal Procedure Rules.

- ***Hamer, D.*** *'The Presumption of Innocence and Reverse Burdens: A Balancing Act'* (2007) 66(1) CLJ 142

  Explains the circumstances in which placing the burden of proof on the defendant has been deemed to be compatible with the presumption of innocence enshrined in Article 6 of the ECHR.

- ***Law Commission.*** *'Double Jeopardy and Prosecution Appeals'* (Part IV, Law Com No. 267, 2001)

  Explains why there was a need for reform to the rule that a person who had been acquitted could not subsequently be charged with the same offence.

- ***Padfield, N.*** *'Efficiency in Criminal Proceedings'* [2015] Crim LR 249

  Summarises the key recommendations made by Sir Brian Leveson's Review of Efficiency in Criminal Proceedings.

- ***The Secret Barrister,*** *Stories of the Law and How It's Broken* (Picador 2018)

  An entertaining, accessible, and powerful first-hand account of the fundamental problems that plague the criminal justice system. This book is essential reading for anyone interested in learning about the criminal process. You can also follow the Secret Barrister on Twitter @BarristerSecret #TheLawIsBroken

- ***Vamos, N.*** *'Please Don't Call It "Plea Bargaining"'* [2009] Crim LR 617

  Examines the advantages and disadvantages of plea bargaining in the United States (US) and contrasts the US approach with the approach taken in England and Wales.

- ***Ward, J.*** *'Transforming "Summary Justice" through Police-led Prosecution and "Virtual Courts": Is "Procedural Due Process" Being Undermined?'* (2015) 55(2) Br J Criminol 341

  Discusses whether police-led prosecutions and the use of video link technology may undermine principles of due process.

- ***Wolchover, D.*** *'Rape Defendant Anonymity'* (2012) 176 JPN 5 and *'Rape Defendant Anonymity Part 2'* (2012) 176 JPN 24

  Highlights the arguments for and against protecting the identities of those accused of rape.

Online resources

You should now attempt the supporting self-test questions and end-of-chapter questions available at: **www.oup.com/he/wilson-rutherford4e**

Chapter 14

Sentencing

Learning objectives

By the end of this chapter you should:

- be familiar with the aims of sentencing;
- be aware that the maximum sentence available varies from one offence to another;
- appreciate the factors that the court must take into account in determining the appropriate sentence to impose on an offender;
- understand the role of sentencing guidelines and be familiar with how guidelines are structured;
- have a basic knowledge of the types of sentence that may be imposed upon an adult;
- have a basic knowledge of the types of sentence that may be imposed upon a child or young person.

 Talking point

On 13 July 2017, two people on mopeds carried out five acid attacks in the space of ninety minutes in central London. Recent years have seen an alarming rise in such incidents, which involve the throwing of corrosive substances, often causing life-changing injuries to victims. One victim, describing her own injuries as a 'life sentence', called for tougher punishment for those convicted of assaults involving acid throwing. Announcing a review of the law in this area, then Home Secretary Amber Rudd stated that 'life sentences must not be reserved for acid attack survivors'. Although an offence of this kind may result in a sentence of life imprisonment being imposed upon the offender, it will not automatically do so at present. So how do judges decide upon the appropriate sentence to pass in this type of case and generally?

There are five main purposes of sentencing:

1. to punish the offender;
2. to reduce crime;
3. to reform and rehabilitate the offender;
4. to protect the public;
5. to make the offender give something back, such as compensation, or through engaging in restorative justice processes, which enable a victim to tell the offender about the impact the crime had on them.

The judge or magistrates will have these overarching aims in mind, but the type and length of any sentence will depend on the facts of the individual case. The sentence that is chosen will take into account the seriousness of the offence, any harm that was caused (or was intended to be caused), and the offender's level of culpability. The judge or magistrates must have regard to the maximum sentence that is available for the offence and to sentencing guidelines, which set out various factors to be considered when determining the appropriate sentence, such as whether the offender demonstrated remorse by pleading guilty and saving their victim the trauma of giving evidence at a trial.

For some offences there is a minimum sentence that the judge or magistrates must impose. For example, there is a minimum sentence of five years' imprisonment for certain firearms offences, and a court must impose a life sentence if an offender is convicted of murder.

As you read this chapter, consider whether you agree with the general aims of sentencing and think about what factors you might consider to be important when sentencing someone for an offence.

Before you start, consider any views you may already have on the following questions:

- Is acid throwing an offence that should attract a minimum sentence? If so, what should that sentence be?
- When passing sentence on someone who has caused serious injury in an acid attack, what should a judge take into account and why?
- Is it right that a defendant who pleads guilty should receive a lesser sentence?

The following chapter will help you to decide whether the current sentencing system functions well or is in need of reform.

Introduction

The final stage of the criminal process is the sentencing of a convicted offender. There are various sentencing options available to the courts, ranging from an absolute discharge to a custodial sentence.

The Powers of Criminal Courts (Sentencing) Act 2000 (PCC(S)A 2000) and the Criminal Justice Act 2003 (CJA 2003) are the main statutes governing the imposition of custodial sentences, including life imprisonment and extended sentences for dangerous offenders. The CJA 2003 also empowers the courts to make community orders, enabling offenders to serve their sentences in the community. Requirements that are commonly attached to such orders include rehabilitation activity requirements (involving attending appointments and participating in certain activities as directed), unpaid work in the community, and curfews.

Successive governments have struggled to strike the appropriate balance between the different aims of sentencing, which include punishment, rehabilitation, and reparation. The primary purpose of a prison sentence is to punish an offender, whereas a community sentence may be directed towards rehabilitation. This chapter will explore the purposes of sentencing before considering different types of sentence in more detail. The separate regime governing the sentencing of youths is dealt with at the end of the chapter.

14.1 **Statutory provisions governing the sentencing of offenders**

The sentencing regime in England and Wales is largely governed by the PCC(S)A 2000 and the CJA 2003. However, there has been a recent flurry of legislation amending and supplementing these statutes, including the Legal Aid, Sentencing and Punishment of Offenders Act 2012 (LASPO 2012), the Crime and Courts Act 2013, the Offender Rehabilitation Act 2014, the Criminal Justice and Courts Act 2015, and the Policing and Crime Act 2017. Sentencing practice is complicated by the fact that not all of the provisions of all of these statutes are in force. Sentencing legislation is, therefore, extremely difficult to navigate. In 2018 the Law Commission published a report recommending consolidating the law of sentencing by introducing a single sentencing statute (Law Com. No. 382). The Commission's proposed 'Sentencing Code' has been welcomed by academics, practitioners, and the judiciary because the complexity of the current sentencing regime frequently causes confusion and errors.

Thinking point

Would it be easier if all sentencing laws were in one place?

In 2013, barrister and sentencing expert Robert Banks published a study of a sample of appeals against sentence that were heard by the Court of Appeal in 2012. Banks found that, of 262 cases studied, unlawful sentences had been passed in 95 cases. He concluded: 'we can no longer say the sentencing system is working properly' (R. Banks, *Banks on Sentence*, 8th edn 2013; Law Commission, *Sentencing Procedure: Issues Paper 1—Transition*, July 2015, para. 1.9). What do you think would be the advantages to having all sentencing provisions in a single Act of Parliament? Would this solve the problems Banks identified?

Sentencing is also a complicated exercise because, when Parliament changes the law, the new provisions are rarely retrospective. A person will usually fall to be sentenced in accordance with the law that was in force at the time the relevant offence was committed (*R v H* [2011] EWCA Crim 2753). As the number of historic offences being prosecuted increases, practitioners must be familiar not only with the current law, but also with sentencing provisions that have been in force at various points in the past.

It is simply not possible, or necessary, to cover all of the sentencing provisions that have ever been in force during an English Legal System course. This chapter will therefore outline the main sentencing principles and provisions that would be applicable in the case of an offender who committed an offence at the time of writing in November 2019.

The purposes of youth sentencing are discussed at 14.4.1.

14.1.1 **The purposes of sentencing**

When passing sentence a court must bear in mind the purposes of sentencing, which are set out in s.142 of the CJA 2003, namely:

- punishing offenders;
- reducing crime (including by deterring others from committing similar offences);
- reforming and rehabilitating offenders;
- protecting the public; and
- reparation by defendants to those affected by their offences.

Key point

The aims listed in s.142 are not necessarily compatible with one another. For example, a community order involving an unpaid work requirement has punishment as its primary aim, rather than rehabilitation.

One advantage of having a 'menu' of purposes is that it is flexible, enabling courts to promote a particular aim when the interests of justice so dictate. A disadvantage of having a non-hierarchical list of aims is that different judges may pass different types of sentence in similar cases.

Thinking point

Can the aims of sentencing conflict?

How might the aims of sentencing set out in s.142 of the CJA 2003 conflict with one another? Do you think the statute should state which aim(s) is/are the most important?

Governments have, at various times, elevated certain sentencing aims above others. A government wanting to be seen as 'tough on crime' will tend to promote the aims of punishment and deterrence above reform and rehabilitation. In 1993, at the Conservative Party conference, Michael Howard famously declared that 'prison works'. However, government policy on sentencing has fluctuated. In 2010, Kenneth Clarke became Justice Secretary and publicly acknowledged that credible community sentences were often preferable to short custodial sentences. In a bid to reduce the burgeoning prison population, Mr Clarke indicated a preference for expanding the use of community penalties.

The policies of Mr Clarke's successor, Chris Grayling, focused on punishment rather than rehabilitation. In early 2013, the government introduced legislation to ensure that all community sentences have a punitive element, such as a curfew, or unpaid work. Mr Grayling also planned to increase the length of time that certain offenders spend in prison by amending the early release provisions that allow prisoners to be released part-way through serving custodial sentences.

At the Conservative Party conference in 2015, Michael Gove (then Justice Secretary) indicated a move away from the 'prison works' orthodoxy. Against a background of concerns about prison overcrowding, Mr Gove acknowledged that the prison system imposes 'pointless enforced idleness' and suggested there needs to be a 'new and unremitting emphasis in our prisons on reform, rehabilitation and redemption'. He concluded that 'the best criminal justice policies are good welfare, social work and child protection policies'. In subsequent years there were even proposals to abolish short prison sentences on the basis that they are ineffective in reducing reoffending rates. The current Justice Secretary, Robert Buckland QC, abandoned this plan and has instead promised to increase the period spent in prison by those convicted of serious violent and sexual offences. Image 14.1 shows a single cell in one of the largest prisons in the UK.

Thinking point

Should the size of the prison population have any impact on sentencing?

Do you think that the number and length of custodial sentences that are imposed should be curbed in order to reduce the prison population?

Image 14.1 A single cell in HM Wandsworth Prison

Source: Peter Dazeley/Getty Images

Sentencing at large
When sentencing is at large, the Crown Court can impose any sentence up to and including life imprisonment.

14.1.2 Maximum sentences

Before sentencing an offender, the first thing the court needs to know is what its sentencing powers are in relation to the relevant offence(s). Where a defendant has been convicted of a common law offence, such as kidnapping, sentencing is said to be ***'at large'***.

Where a defendant has been convicted of a statutory offence, the maximum penalty that the court may impose for the offence will be set out in the Act of Parliament that creates the offence. If the offence is triable either way, the Act will specify the maximum sentence that can be imposed if a defendant is either convicted on indictment or committed to the Crown Court for sentence.

If a defendant is convicted following summary trial, or pleads guilty before a magistrates' court and is not committed for sentence, the maximum penalty the magistrates' court can impose is never more than six months' imprisonment for a single offence (PCC(S)A 2000 s.78). However, if a defendant falls to be sentenced for two or more either way matters, the magistrates' court may impose up to twelve months' imprisonment (Magistrates' Courts Act 1980 s.133(2)).

 **Key point**

A statute may specify a maximum penalty of less than six months' imprisonment following summary conviction. For example, s.5 of the Public Order Act 1986 provides that the maximum sentence for the offence of disorderly behaviour is a fine. However, a statute cannot currently permit a magistrates' court to impose more than six months' imprisonment for a single offence.

 **Example**

Theft is an offence that is triable either way (that is, it can be tried in either the magistrates' court or the Crown Court). Section 7 of the Theft Act 1968 provides: 'A person guilty of theft shall on conviction on indictment be liable to imprisonment for a term not exceeding seven years.' If a defendant is convicted of theft in the Crown Court, or if they are committed to the Crown Court for sentence, they may receive a sentence of up to seven years in prison. If a defendant is convicted of theft in the magistrates' court and is not committed for sentence, the maximum penalty the magistrates' court can impose is six months' imprisonment. (See 13.4.3 for further information about committal for sentence.)

Section 154 of the CJA 2003, which has not been brought into force, would increase magistrates' courts' sentencing powers to twelve months' imprisonment for any one offence. In 2013, Justice Minister Damian Green MP stated that the government did not intend to bring s.154 into force because of the risk that this would lead to a rise in the prison population. However, the Magistrates' Association, which represents lay magistrates, has lobbied for greater sentencing powers, arguing that it would be cheaper to process more cases in the magistrates' courts. In 2019, the House of Commons Justice Committee recommended that the government should introduce a presumption against short custodial sentences but added that, where custody is unavoidable, magistrates (and district judges) should have the power to impose custodial sentences of up to 12 months (*The role of the magistracy: follow -up*, HC 1654, 2019).

Thinking point

Should magistrates be able to pass longer sentences?

What other arguments could be made for and against increasing the sentencing powers of magistrates' courts? Remember that anyone who is sentenced by a magistrates' court has an automatic right of appeal to the Crown Court. Could the commencement of s.154 result in a greater number of appeals?

The Court of Appeal has consistently held that the maximum sentence for an offence should normally be reserved for the most serious examples of that offence. The following section will explore how the courts decide precisely what sentence to impose within the available sentencing range.

14.2 Determining the appropriate sentence

In addition to the factors set out in s.142 of the CJA 2003 (see 14.1.1), the seriousness of the offence is a key consideration in passing sentence.

Example

Lewis burgles a house while the occupier is asleep in bed. He smashes a window to gain entry, then ransacks the downstairs rooms and takes a laptop, an Xbox, and a stack of video games. He also steals a piece of jewellery of sentimental value to the homeowner.

Donna burgles a house during the daytime while the homeowner is out. She gains entry via an open window and does not cause any damage. She takes a purse that had been left on the table but does not steal anything else.

The burglary committed by Lewis is more serious than the burglary committed by Donna and will attract a higher sentence.

In determining the appropriate sentence, the court must follow any sentencing guidelines that are relevant to the case (Coroners and Justice Act 2009 s.125).

14.2.1 Sentencing guidelines

Section 118 of the Coroners and Justice Act 2009 created a Sentencing Council for England and Wales. Section 120 of the 2009 Act empowers the Sentencing Council to issue sentencing guidelines relating to the sentencing of offenders.

Key point

The Sentencing Council is an independent body, whose role is to issue guidelines to be used by all courts with a view to achieving transparency and consistency in sentencing (see **www.sentencingcouncil.org.uk**).

Section 125 of the Coroners and Justice Act 2009 provides that a court 'must follow' any applicable sentencing guidelines, unless it would be contrary to the interests of justice to do so. This is an important change from the previous legislation, which provided only that the court had to 'have regard to' any sentencing guidelines (CJA 2003 s.172).

Critical debate

Read s.121 of the Coroners and Justice Act 2009, then read the Sentencing Council's definitive guideline for burglary offences (available at **https://www.sentencingcouncil.org.uk/offences/crown-court/item/domestic-burglary/**). What is an offence 'category' and what is a 'category range'? What is the starting point for a Category 3 domestic burglary, and what is the category range? What factors should result in a court imposing a sentence *below* the starting point for a Category 3 domestic burglary? Do you think it is a good idea to require judges to follow sentencing guidelines in most cases, or should judges always be able to use their discretion to pass any sentence up to the maximum for the offence?

It has often been said that guidelines are not 'tramlines' and that 'slavish adherence' to guidelines is not required (see *R v Blackshaw and Others* [2011] EWCA Crim 2312). Nevertheless, where a judge does not follow an applicable sentencing guideline, they must explain why they are of the opinion that it would be contrary to the interests of justice to do so.

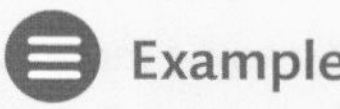

Between 6 and 10 August 2011, riots occurred in towns and cities across England. In *R v Blackshaw and Others*, the Court of Appeal heard the appeals against sentence of ten defendants who were convicted of offences committed during the riots.

Jordan Blackshaw had created a public event on Facebook entitled 'Smash down in Northwich Town'. He referred to the ongoing riots, adding 'we'll need to get on this, kicking off all over'. The police were notified of the event and closed the webpage down.

Blackshaw was subsequently arrested and charged with doing an act capable of encouraging riot, burglary, and criminal damage. He pleaded guilty and was sentenced to four years' imprisonment, even though the event that he had encouraged never actually took place.

Blackshaw appealed on the ground that his sentence was beyond the range set out in the relevant sentencing guidelines. The Court of Appeal dismissed his appeal. Section 125(1) of the Coroners and Justice Act 2009 provides that sentencing guidelines do not have to be followed if the court is satisfied that it is not in the interests of justice to do so. In Blackshaw's case, the Lord Chief Justice pointed out that none of the guidelines contemplated offences taking place within the context of nationwide public disorder. Accordingly, having regard to the courts' duty to protect the public, 'the imposition of severe sentences, intended to provide both punishment and deterrence, must follow'.

Visit the online resources to watch a video on sentencing guidelines.

14.2.2 **Offence seriousness; aggravating and mitigating factors**

In determining the seriousness of an offence, the court must have regard to both the culpability of the offender and the harm the offence caused (or was intended to cause, or might foreseeably have caused) (CJA 2003 s.143). For detailed guidance on offence seriousness, including important ***aggravating and mitigating factors***, see the sentencing guideline *Overarching Principles: Seriousness* (available at **https://www.sentencingcouncil.org.uk/overarching-guides/magistrates-court/item/general-guideline-overarching-principles/**).

Examples of aggravating factors identified in the guideline include use or threat of a weapon, abuse of trust, where the victim is vulnerable, and established evidence of community/wider impact. Mitigating factors may include a lesser or subordinate role in the offence, the fact that a defendant has a mental disorder or a learning disability, the defendant's age or lack of maturity, and personal mitigation such as remorse and cooperation with the investigation.

Under s.143 of the CJA 2003, the court must treat a previous conviction as an aggravating feature if it is reasonable to do so, having regard to the nature, relevance,

Aggravating factors
Aggravating factors are features which indicate a higher than usual level of culpability on the part of the defendant, or a higher than usual degree of harm, or both.

Mitigating factors
Mitigating factors are features that indicate that the defendant's culpability is unusually low, or that the harm caused by the offence is less serious than would be usual for an offence of that type.

and age of the earlier offence. Similarly, where a defendant commits an offence on bail, this will be an aggravating factor (s.143(3)). A sentence should also be increased where an offence was racially or religiously aggravated, or aggravated in relation to the victim's disability, sexual orientation, or transgender identity (ss.145 and 146).

The sentencing court is entitled to take into account any matters that appear to the court to be relevant in mitigation of a defendant's sentence (s.166). For example, a guilty plea is normally regarded as a mitigating feature. Section 144 of the CJA 2003 requires the court to take into account the stage in the proceedings at which the offender indicated their intention to plead guilty. The sentencing guideline entitled *Reduction in Sentence for a Guilty Plea* provides that courts should discount sentences by up to one-third where a defendant pleads guilty: see **https://www.sentencingcouncil.org.uk/overarching-guides/magistrates-court/item/reduction-in-sentence-for-a-guilty-plea-first-hearing-on-or-after-1-june-2017/**. There is a sliding scale for discounting the sentence, ranging from a one-third discount where a guilty plea is entered at the earliest opportunity, to a discount of one-tenth or less where a plea is entered at the last minute, for example, on the first day of trial.

Thinking point

Should a defendant receive credit for pleading guilty?

What are the advantages and disadvantages of allowing the courts to impose lesser sentences on those who plead guilty? If there were no discount at all, and therefore no incentive for a defendant to plead guilty, would this result in more trials?

In deciding upon the appropriate sentence, a court will often be assisted by a pre-sentence report.

14.2.3 Pre-sentence reports

Pre-sentence report
A pre-sentence report will be written by a probation officer after meeting the defendant. The report will explore the reasons for the defendant's offending behaviour, assess the risk of future offending, and make recommendations as to the defendant's suitability for various types of sentence.

When a defendant is convicted, either following a trial or by pleading guilty, the court may either sentence them immediately or require a ***pre-sentence report*** to be prepared prior to passing sentence.

Section 156 of the CJA 2003 provides that the court must normally obtain a pre-sentence report when considering a custodial sentence or certain community sentences. A pre-sentence report will address the aggravating and mitigating features of the case, including any mitigation relating to the offender's personal circumstances. The writer of the report will make recommendations as to the type(s) of sentence that might be appropriate, although the final decision is always that of the judge or magistrates.

14.2.4 *Newton* hearings

Sometimes a defendant pleads guilty to an offence but does not accept all the facts alleged by the prosecution. If the differing versions would attract different sentences, the court must either accept the defence version of the facts and sentence on that basis or hold a trial of the issue, also known as a '*Newton* hearing' (see *R v Newton* (1983) 77 Cr App R 13). At a *Newton* hearing, the judge (or magistrates) will hear evidence and must decide whether the prosecution has proved beyond reasonable doubt that its version of the facts is correct.

Example

Steve is charged with robbery. Robbery involves the use or threat of force in order to steal. The prosecution case is that Steve held a knife to John's throat, then punched him in the face and stole his wallet. Steve admits punching John and stealing his wallet but denies having a knife. Steve thus admits the offence of robbery. However, the presence of a knife is an aggravating feature, since if it were proved that Steve had a knife, he would receive a longer prison sentence. A judge would, therefore, be likely to require a *Newton* hearing to determine whether Steve did have a knife before proceeding to sentence.

During the *Newton* hearing John, and any other witnesses on this point, would be called by the prosecution to give evidence to establish the presence of the knife at the time of the robbery. Steve would then be entitled to give evidence in his own defence, to say that he did not have a knife, and also to call any other witnesses to support his version of events. Unless the judge is sure that Steve had a knife, he or she must sentence on the basis that Steve did not have a knife.

14.2.5 Offences taken into consideration

A defendant who is being sentenced in respect of an offence may wish to have other offences 'taken into consideration', even though they have not been charged with those offences. Such offences are referred to as 'TICs'. If the court is prepared to take offences into consideration, the defendant is not convicted of the TICs but the court will take them into account and must pass a total sentence that reflects all of the offending behaviour. The sentence imposed will usually be increased to reflect the fact that other offences have been taken into consideration, although this will depend upon the number and seriousness of the offences in question. The advantage to the defendant is that TICs may not add greatly to their sentence, and he or she cannot later be separately prosecuted and punished for them (*R v Miles* [2006] EWCA Crim 256).

14.3 Types of sentence

The criminal courts have a range of sentences open to them. The types of sentences available will now be considered in ascending order of seriousness.

14.3.1 **Absolute and conditional discharges**

At the bottom of the scale, under s.12 of the PCC(S)A 2000, come the 'absolute discharge' and the 'conditional discharge'. To impose an absolute or conditional discharge the court must be of the opinion that it would be inexpedient to inflict punishment for the offence. In the case of an absolute discharge, the defendant remains convicted but is not punished at all. In the case of a conditional discharge, the defendant will not be punished unless they commit another offence within a specified period. If they do commit a further offence, they may be sentenced both for the new offence and the offence for which they received the conditional discharge. The maximum period of a conditional discharge is three years; there is no minimum period.

14.3.2 **Fines**

Fines are the most common penalty imposed by the criminal courts. In 2018, 77 per cent of offenders were fined. There is no limit to the amount of fine that the Crown Court may impose (CJA 2003 s.163). The maximum fine that a magistrates' court can impose for an offence used to be £5,000 but this cap was removed for most offences in 2015 (Legal Aid, Sentencing and Punishment of Offenders Act 2012 s.85). However, the maximum that can be imposed for a particular offence may be limited by the statute that creates the offence.

 Example

Using threatening, abusive, or insulting words or behaviour likely to cause harassment, alarm, or distress is an offence contrary to s.5 of the Public Order Act 1986. Section 5(6) states that a person who is guilty of this offence is liable to 'a fine not exceeding level 3 on the standard scale' (s.5(6)). The standard scale of fines is set out in s.37 of the Criminal Justice Act 1982. Under s.37(3), there are five levels of fine and a level 3 fine is £1,000. Thus, the maximum sentence that can be imposed on a person who is convicted of an offence contrary to s.5 of the Public Order Act 1986 is a fine of £1,000.

Section 164 of the CJA 2003 provides that a fine must reflect the seriousness of the offence but that the court must also take into account the circumstances of the case, including the financial circumstances of the defendant. Any financial penalty imposed should be an amount that, having regard to the defendant's means, can be paid in full within a year.

14.3.3 **Community orders**

The sentencing court may impose a community order (CJA 2003 s.177), which is an order that the defendant abide by one or more specified requirements. In 2018, the courts imposed community orders on 21 per cent of offenders who were sentenced for indictable offences. The requirements that may currently be imposed upon a defendant under a community order are:

- unpaid work for between 40 and 300 hours (formerly known as 'community service');
- a rehabilitation activity requirement (attending appointments with a probation officer and participating in activities as instructed);
- a prohibited activity requirement (preventing the offender from participating in specified activities) during a specified period;
- a curfew, for between two and sixteen hours a day, for a maximum of twelve months;
- an exclusion requirement (preventing the offender from entering a specified area for up to two years);
- a residence requirement (ordering the offender to live at a specified address);
- a foreign travel prohibition requirement (preventing the offender from travelling outside Britain for up to twelve months);
- a mental health treatment requirement;
- an alcohol treatment or drug rehabilitation requirement; and/or
- an electronic monitoring requirement.

Under s.148 of the CJA 2003, the court may only impose a community order if it is of the opinion that the particular offence is serious enough to warrant it. Indeed, even where this s.148 'threshold' for making a community order has been passed, the court may decide that a financial penalty or a conditional discharge is appropriate.

Under s.148, the requirement(s) imposed under a community order must be those which, in the opinion of the court, are the most suitable for the offender, and any restrictions on liberty must be commensurate with the seriousness of the offence. Since 2013, it has been mandatory to include at least one requirement for the purposes of punishment (such as unpaid work, an exclusion requirement, a curfew, or a fine) as part of every community order.

A defendant who fails to comply with the requirements of a community order may be returned to court. Where a court finds the defendant to be in breach of the order, it must either impose more onerous conditions or re-sentence the offender for the original offence. If the offender has wilfully and persistently failed to comply with the order, they may be sentenced to imprisonment even if the offence is not so serious that it originally merited a custodial sentence.

14.3.4 **Custodial sentences**

In 2018, 7 per cent of all those sentenced received prison sentences and the average custodial sentence length was 17.3 months. Unsurprisingly, the proportion of offenders who received custodial sentences was highest for those convicted of indictable offences, which are more serious criminal offences, with 33 per cent of such offenders receiving an immediate custodial sentence.

Key point

Where a custodial sentence is an available option, s.152 of the CJA 2003 provides that the court must not pass such a sentence unless of the opinion that the offence (or the combination of the offence and associated offence(s)) is so serious that neither a fine nor a community order can be justified.

Determinate custodial sentences

The factors that will influence the court's decision as to the length of sentence to impose are considered at 14.2. Where the court does pass a custodial sentence, it must normally be for the shortest term that is commensurate with the seriousness of the offending (CJA 2003 s.153). Moreover, the fact that the s.152 'custody threshold' has been passed does not automatically mean that the court should impose a custodial sentence. Circumstances such as mitigation relating to the offender's personal circumstances may enable the court to impose a community sentence instead (see CJA 2003 s.166 and see the Sentencing Council's *Overarching Principles* guideline).

Thinking point

Can the context of an offence be relevant to the sentencing decision?

The sentences imposed upon defendants for offences committed during the riots of 2011 were criticised by many as being too harsh. For example, in addition to the case of Jordan Blackshaw (discussed in the earlier example), the media reported that a twenty-three-year-old man had been imprisoned for six months for stealing bottled water worth £3.50. To what extent were these sentences commensurate with the seriousness of the offences committed?

As we have already seen, the maximum custodial sentence that the magistrates' court can impose on a defendant is six months for a single offence. Where the defendant is charged with two or more 'either way' offences, the magistrates' court may aggregate the terms of imprisonment imposed in respect of each offence up to a maximum of twelve months. In the case of either way offences, if the magistrates' court considers that this is insufficient, it can, of course, commit the defendant to the Crown Court for sentence.

Offenders do not commonly serve the full period of imprisonment to which they are sentenced. Instead, they will normally be released on licence after serving half of their sentence and will remain on licence until the expiry of the sentence. Since 2015, offenders serving sentences of less than two years have been subject to additional supervision following the expiry of their licence. The aim of introducing additional 'post-sentence supervision' was to address the high rate of reoffending by prisoners who are released after serving short custodial sentences.

Prisoners who are serving a sentence of between three months, and four years and twelve weeks, may be eligible to be released before the halfway point under the home detention curfew scheme. A prisoner on home detention curfew will be confined to their home for a specified period (usually 7 p.m.–7 a.m.) and will have to wear an electronic tag, usually around their ankle.

Minimum terms of imprisonment

In certain circumstances, statutes lay down the *minimum* custodial sentence that the court must impose. For example, s.111 of the PCC(S)A 2000 provides that, subject to certain conditions, where a person is convicted of a domestic burglary and has previously been convicted of two other domestic burglaries, the court must impose a sentence of imprisonment for a term of at least three years. This is sometimes known as the 'three strikes' rule.

More recently, s.28 of the Criminal Justice and Courts Act 2015 introduced a minimum sentence of six months' imprisonment for those who are convicted of a second offence of possessing a knife or offensive weapon.

Consecutive or concurrent prison sentences

Where an offender is convicted of more than one offence and custodial sentences are imposed, the sentences may be consecutive or concurrent. For example, where the court intends to impose a period of imprisonment of three months for one offence and nine months for another offence, these may either be ordered to be served consecutively, making a total sentence of twelve months, or served at the same time, making a total sentence of nine months. The judge or magistrates should state, in the presence of the defendant, whether the terms of imprisonment are consecutive or concurrent (see the Criminal Practice Directions 2015, VII E). Concurrent sentences will normally be appropriate where the offences of which the defendant was convicted arose out of the same incident (*R v Noble* [2003] 1 Cr App R (S) 65). Where consecutive sentences are imposed, the court may mitigate the sentence by considering its totality (CJA 2003 s.166). In other words, the appropriate overall sentence may be less than the aggregate of the sentences that would otherwise be imposed for each of the individual offences.

Suspended sentence orders

Perhaps in recognition of the fact that there may be a limit to what can be achieved during a short prison sentence, the courts have long had the power to suspend sentences in certain circumstances. Under s.189 of the CJA 2003, where the court imposes a sentence of imprisonment of between fourteen days and two years, the court may suspend the sentence for between six months and two years (known as the 'operational period'). If the offender commits another offence within the operational period specified, a future court may, and usually will, order that the custodial sentence be served. This is intended to ensure a defendant's good behaviour for the period of the suspension.

A court imposing a suspended sentence may also order the offender to comply with one or more of the requirements of a community order (see 14.3.3). A failure to comply with these requirements would place the offender in jeopardy of being ordered to serve the custodial sentence.

Thinking point

When, if ever, should a prison sentence be suspended?

Consider why the courts have the power to suspend prison sentences. Do you think the imposition of a suspended sentence, coupled with the requirements of a community order, is likely to act as a greater incentive to good behaviour than the imposition of a community order alone?

Deferred sentences

Either a magistrates' court or the Crown Court may defer sentencing an offender for up to six months. The court may impose requirements on the offender during the deferral period, such as a residence requirement or a supervision requirement. Deferring sentence enables the court to have regard to the offender's conduct between the date of the offence and the date on which they are finally sentenced. For example, where an offender is already subject to other court orders, deferring sentence enables the court to give the offender an opportunity to comply with those orders before sentence is passed. If the offender does comply with existing orders during the deferral period, the court may impose a community sentence where it would otherwise have imposed a period of imprisonment.

Under s.44 and Sch.16 of the Crime and Courts Act 2013, courts also have the power to defer sentence where the offender and victim agree to take part in the restorative justice (RJ) process. The court may then have regard to the offender's engagement, or lack of engagement, in the RJ process when passing sentence. RJ is considered further at 14.4.4.

The Sentencing Council has issued explanatory materials in relation to community sentences, deferred sentences, custodial sentences, and suspended sentences. These materials explain the criteria for imposing each type of sentence and the requirements of each (see **https://www.sentencingcouncil.org.uk/explanatory-material/**).

Extended determinate sentences

The controversial indeterminate sentence of imprisonment for public protection (IPP) was abolished by LASPO 2012. Sentences of IPP were imposed on offenders who were deemed to be 'dangerous'. When sentencing an offender to IPP, the judge had to specify the minimum term of imprisonment to be served. However, the offender did not have the right to be released after serving the minimum term and could only be released if the parole board was satisfied that they were no longer dangerous. Thus, an offender sentenced to IPP did not know when, or if, they would be released. Furthermore, in order to demonstrate that they were no longer dangerous, an offender had to complete certain courses or training programmes in prison, yet funding difficulties meant that places on such courses were very often unavailable. The IPP provisions were ultimately abolished in response to heavy criticism from the judiciary, the legal profession, and academics.

Under the current law, where an offender is deemed to be 'dangerous', in accordance with the provisions of s.225 of the CJA 2003, the court may impose an extended licence period (known as an 'extended sentence'). An offender will be regarded as 'dangerous' if they have been convicted of an offence specified in Sch.15 to the CJA 2003 and the court considers that there is a significant risk that the offender will cause serious harm to the public by committing further specified offences. The court must also be satisfied that either the offence would normally attract a custodial sentence of at least four years or the offender has a previous conviction for one of the serious offences listed in Sch.15B to the CJA 2003. If so satisfied, the court may impose an additional licence period of up to five years for a specified violent offence, or up to eight years for a specified sexual offence.

Sentencing offenders of particular concern

Section 6 and Sch.1 of the Criminal Justice and Courts Act 2015 created a new type of custodial sentence for certain offenders who are of 'particular concern'. Under these provisions, if an adult is convicted of an offence listed in Sch.18A to the CJA 2003 and the court does not pass either a life sentence or an extended determinate sentence, the court must impose a custodial sentence to be followed by an additional licence period of one year. The offences listed in Sch.18A include various terrorism offences and sexual offences against children under thirteen years.

Life sentences

At the top end of the scale of prison sentences comes the life sentence for murder, which is 'fixed by law' (Murder (Abolition of Death Penalty) Act 1965 s.1). Although called a 'life sentence', the court is required to order that the 'early release provisions' will apply unless the offence is so serious that, in the court's opinion, such an order should not be made (CJA 2003 s.269). This means that the trial judge will usually order a 'minimum term' that the offender must serve before being considered for release. On rare occasions where the seriousness of the offence(s) is exceptionally high, the court may make a 'whole life order' and life will actually mean life. At the end of December 2018, there were 7,038 prisoners serving life sentences in England and Wales, of whom only sixty-six were subject to whole life orders.

Example

On 23 November 2016, Thomas Mair was sentenced to life imprisonment after being convicted of the murder of MP Jo Cox. Ms Cox had recently been elected to Parliament and was on her way to a constituency surgery when she was killed by Mair, who was armed with a handgun and a knife. In passing sentence, Wilkie J observed that there was 'no doubt that this murder was done for the purpose of advancing a political, racial and ideological cause, namely that of violent white supremacism and exclusive nationalism most associated with Nazism and its modern forms'. His Lordship concluded that the killing was 'of such a high level of exceptional seriousness that it can only properly be marked by a whole life sentence'.

Under Sch.21 to the CJA 2003, the 'minimum term' for an offence of murder will usually be at least fifteen years, although it can be significantly more (see also Division VII M of the Criminal Practice Directions 2015). If and when an offender is released from such a sentence, they remain on licence for life. This means they will be released subject to certain conditions, such as residence requirements, a curfew, or maintaining contact with a probation officer. If they breach the conditions of the licence, for example by committing an offence or by failing to comply with other conditions, their licence may be revoked and they will be recalled to prison.

Certain other serious offences have a maximum sentence of life imprisonment, and these include manslaughter, wounding with intent to cause grievous bodily harm, robbery, and rape. The court retains the discretion to impose a life sentence in such cases (*R v Saunders and Others* [2013] EWCA Crim 1027). However, the court will usually only impose a life sentence if the conditions in s.224A or s.225 of the CJA 2003 are satisfied. Section 224A deals with those who are convicted of a second serious offence, and s.225 deals with offenders who are deemed to be dangerous.

Under s.224A, the court may be required to impose a life sentence if the offender falls to be sentenced for an offence listed in Sch.15B to the CJA 2003 and has a previous conviction for such an offence. Offences listed in Sch.15B include manslaughter, wounding with intent to cause grievous bodily harm, robbery with a firearm, and certain serious sexual offences.

Under s.225, the court must impose a life sentence if the offender has been convicted of a 'serious offence' and there is a significant risk that they would cause ***'serious harm'*** to members of the public by committing further specified offences. The court must also be satisfied that the seriousness of the offence justifies the imposition of a life sentence. 'Specified offences' are those offences that are listed in Sch.15 to the CJA 2003. In addition to the serious offences listed in Sch.15B (discussed earlier), Sch.15 includes a number of less serious offences, such as malicious wounding, assault occasioning actual bodily harm, and sexual assault.

Serious harm
Serious harm means death or serious physical or psychological injury (CJA 2003 s.224(3)).

Thinking point

What are the effects of the different types of sentence?

Imposing a sentence upon an offender may potentially have a variety of consequences. For example, it may prevent the offender from committing other offences by keeping them out of circulation; it may assist in reforming the offender; it may deter others from committing similar offences; it may punish the offender; or it may satisfy the need for retribution felt by the victim, the victim's family, or the public at large. Which types of sentence discussed in the preceding sections do you think may have any or all of these consequences?

14.3.5 **Other sentences and orders upon sentence**

Examples of other orders that a criminal court might make or sentences that it might impose include:

- An offender may be bound over to keep the peace and be of good behaviour (Justices of the Peace Act 1968 s.1(7)), whereby a person agrees to forfeit a sum of money if they fail to behave themselves.
- An offender may be disqualified from driving (PCC(S)A 2000 s.146). In addition to the courts' powers to disqualify those convicted of certain road traffic offences, s.146 of the 2000 Act gives any court the power to disqualify an offender from driving on conviction for any offence, even if the offence is not connected with the use of a motor vehicle.
- Banning orders under the Football Spectators Act 1989 can be used to prohibit a person from attending football matches.
- A criminal behaviour order (CBO) can be imposed upon conviction if it would help to prevent the offender from engaging in behaviour that is likely to cause harassment, alarm, or distress (Anti-social Behaviour, Crime and Policing Act 2014 s.22). CBOs replaced anti-social behaviour orders (ASBOs). A CBO may impose specific

requirements on an offender, or may prohibit them from doing certain things described in the order. A CBO is not a sentence in itself but may be imposed in addition to the sentence that is passed for an offence.

- Notification requirements may be imposed under the Sexual Offences Act 2003, under which a person convicted of a sexual offence must notify the police of a variety of matters, including their home address.
- Compensation orders can be made, which require an offender to pay compensation for personal injury, loss, or damage resulting from an offence (PCC(S)A 2000 s.130). The imposition of a compensation order must be considered in any case where the court has the power to do so. A compensation order may be the only sentence imposed for an offence or it may be imposed in addition to most other types of sentence.
- Confiscation orders may be made, under which the amount by which an offender has benefited from criminal conduct may be confiscated (Proceeds of Crime Act 2002).

14.3.6 **Costs and surcharges**

When a defendant has been convicted of an offence, s.18 of the Prosecution of Offences Act 1985 provides that a sentencing court has discretion to make such order as to costs as it considers just and reasonable. Before imposing an order as to costs, the court must have regard to the defendant's means and ability to pay (*R v Northallerton Magistrates' Court, ex parte Dove* [2000] 1 Cr App R (S) 136).

Since 2007, courts have also been required to impose a victim surcharge when sentencing offenders. See Table 14.1 for details of the amount that an offender aged

Table 14.1 Criminal Justice Act 2003 (Surcharge) (Amendment) Order 2016/985

Disposal type	Victim surcharge
Conditional discharge	£21
Fine	10 per cent of value of fine (but minimum £32 and maximum £181)
Community order	£90
Suspended sentence order (six months or less)	£122
Suspended sentence order (more than six months)	£149
Imprisonment (six months or less)	£122 (six months or less)
Imprisonment (six months–two years)	£149
Imprisonment (more than two years)	£181

eighteen or over must pay, which is dependent upon the sentence imposed. Revenue raised by the victim surcharge is used to fund services that support victims' recovery from the effects of crime.

14.4 Sentencing children and young people

A different sentencing regime applies to those under the age of eighteen. (Note that a child under the age of ten is deemed to be incapable of committing a criminal offence and cannot appear before a criminal court.) The vast majority of offenders under the age of eighteen are dealt with before youth courts. A youth court tribunal consists of three specially trained magistrates or a district judge. Its procedures and atmosphere are less formal than those of an adult magistrates' court. In certain circumstances, such as where a child or young person is charged alongside an adult, they may appear before a magistrates' court. In exceptional circumstances, where the offence is particularly serious, they may be sent to the Crown Court.

14.4.1 Aims of youth sentencing

Under s.37(1) of the Crime and Disorder Act 1998, the principal aim of the youth justice system is to prevent re-offending. The court must also have regard to the welfare of the child or young person (Children and Young Persons Act 1933 s.44(1)). The Sentencing Council's overarching guideline, *Sentencing Children and Young People*, explains in detail the importance of taking into account a child or young person's age, background, and circumstances in order to identify the sentence that is most likely to stop them committing any more offences.

Thinking point

How do the aims of adult and youth sentencing differ?

Consider the purposes of sentencing set out in s.142 of the CJA 2003, outlined at 14.1.1. How do the aims of youth sentencing differ from the aims of adult sentencing?

The types of sentence available for youths are considered next, in ascending order of severity.

For absolute and conditional discharges in relation to adult offenders, see 14.3.1.

14.4.2 Absolute and conditional discharges

Absolute and conditional discharges under s.12 of the PCC(S)A 2000 are available for children and young people as they are for adults.

14.4.3 **Fines**

A child or young person may be fined. As with an adult offender, any fine that is imposed should reflect both the seriousness of the offence and the offender's ability to pay. In the case of a child under the age of sixteen, it is the parent or guardian who is legally responsible for paying the fine and it is their ability to pay that must be taken into account.

14.4.4 **Referral orders**

When a youth court or magistrates' court does not intend to impose an absolute or a conditional discharge, the court must normally make a referral order if the offender is under the age of eighteen, has no previous convictions, and has pleaded guilty to an offence that is punishable with imprisonment. The court also has the power to make a referral order where the offender has previous convictions, but is not required to do so.

A referral order requires the child or young person to attend a youth offender panel and to agree a contract with the panel. Such a contract may require them to make restitution or reparation to the victim of the offence, for example, by repairing any damage caused by the offence. The child or young person may also be required to undertake a programme of interventions and activities aimed at addressing their offending behaviour.

Referral orders commonly utilise 'restorative justice' (RJ) approaches. RJ enables a victim to tell an offender what impact the crime has had on them. Victims are able to ask the offender questions and obtain an apology. The majority of victims who agree to RJ choose to attend a face-to-face meeting with the offender. A study commissioned by the Ministry of Justice, which began in 2001, suggested that RJ is likely to result in a 27 per cent reduction in the frequency of re-offending (J. Shapland et al., *Restorative Justice: Does Restorative Justice Affect Reconviction? The Fourth Report from the Evaluation of Three Schemes*, Ministry of Justice, 2008).

14.4.5 **Youth rehabilitation orders**

Where the circumstances do not make a referral order mandatory, a youth rehabilitation order may be made if the offence is serious enough to warrant it (Criminal Justice and Immigration Act 2008 s.1). The requirement(s) imposed under a youth rehabilitation order must be those which, in the opinion of the court, are most suitable for the child or young person, and any restrictions on liberty must be commensurate with the seriousness of the offence.

The court must specify a period no more than three years from the date of sentence within which the requirements imposed under the order must be completed. The following requirements may be imposed under a youth rehabilitation order:

- an activity requirement for no more than ninety days in total;
- supervision;

- unpaid work for between 40 and 240 hours (which can only be imposed on an offender aged sixteen or seventeen);
- a programme requirement;
- an attendance centre requirement;
- a prohibited activity requirement;
- a curfew for between two and sixteen hours a day for up to twelve months;
- an exclusion requirement;
- residence with a specified person or at a specified address;
- a fostering requirement;
- mental health treatment;
- intoxicating substance treatment or drug treatment (with or without drug testing);
- an education requirement; and/or
- intensive supervision and surveillance.

An electronic monitoring requirement may also be imposed to monitor compliance with other requirements of the order.

For adult community orders see 14.3.3.

14.4.6 **Custodial sentences**

Detention and training orders

A detention and training order (DTO) may only be made in respect of an offence that is punishable by imprisonment. A DTO is a custodial sentence for children and young people and must only be imposed as a 'measure of last resort' (United Nations Convention on the Rights of the Child, Art. 37(b)). Where a child is under the age of fifteen, a DTO may only be made if they are a 'persistent offender'. A DTO cannot be imposed upon a child under the age of twelve.

A DTO may be imposed for a period of four, six, eight, ten, twelve, eighteen, or twenty-four months. An offender who is sentenced to a DTO will be detained in a secure children's home, a secure training centre, or a young offender institution for half of the term of the order, after which they will be released into the community, where they will be supervised and will undergo appropriate training and education until the expiry of the DTO.

Detention under s.91 of the PCC(S)A 2000

When a child or young person is charged with an offence punishable by at least fourteen years' imprisonment, the case may be sent to the Crown Court under s.51A of the Crime and Disorder Act 1998 and s.91 of the PCC(S)A 2000. These provisions also apply to children and young people charged with certain sexual offences and those aged sixteen to eighteen who are charged with certain firearms offences. If the child or young person is subsequently convicted before the Crown Court and the judge is of the opinion that neither a youth rehabilitation order nor a DTO is suitable, they may be sentenced to detention for any period up to the maximum for the offence in question. In an appropriate case, the court may pass a sentence of detention for life. The term 'detention' is used instead of the term 'imprisonment' because a youth will be detained in secure accommodation or, more commonly, a young offender institution, rather than an adult prison.

Life imprisonment

A person who is convicted of murder and was under the age of eighteen on the date the offence was committed must be detained 'during Her Majesty's pleasure'. This is effectively a life sentence and the judge will set a minimum term that the child or young person must serve before being considered for parole. The starting point for the minimum term is usually twelve years, as opposed to fifteen years for an adult (see Life sentences at 14.3.4).

Summary

- There are a number of different aims of sentencing, which may conflict with one another.
- Sentencing is governed by a complex statutory regime and the courts have a variety of sentencing options available to them, ranging from absolute discharges to custodial sentences.
- There is a maximum sentence that can be imposed in relation to each offence. For some serious offences, the maximum sentence will be life imprisonment. For some minor offences, the maximum sentence is merely a fine.
- In determining the appropriate sentence to impose, the court will take into account the seriousness of the offence and any aggravating and mitigating factors. The court must also follow any sentencing guidelines unless it would be contrary to the interests of justice to do so.
- The court may find it necessary to adjourn in order to obtain pre-sentence reports before sentencing.
- If a defendant disputes the prosecution's account of the facts of the case, the magistrates or judge may be required to hold a *Newton* hearing to determine the appropriate basis upon which to sentence.
- Youth sentencing is subject to different considerations and different types of sentence are available.

Questions

1 What are the aims of sentencing adult offenders?

2 Can the court take a defendant's previous convictions into account when sentencing him or her?

3 What is the 'custody threshold'?

4 What sort of requirements may be attached to a community order?

5 What types of order may be available in addition to a sentence?

6 How do the sentencing options for a court dealing with a child or young person differ from the sentencing options for a court dealing with an adult offender?

Sample question and outline answer

Question

Monique, who is twenty-one years old and has no previous convictions, has been charged with a single offence of theft. Monique works in a photography shop and the prosecution allege that she stole a sum of money from the shop's safe. Monique's first appearance before the magistrates' court will take place next week. She intends to plead guilty.

Discuss the factors the court will consider in deciding whether to sentence Monique to a period of imprisonment.

(Note that theft is an either way offence carrying a maximum sentence of seven years' imprisonment.)

Outline answer

The question is deliberately vague about the facts of the offence and so requires you to discuss general sentencing principles. Because theft is an either way offence, you will need to discuss the position in both the magistrates' court and the Crown Court.

Introduction

Monique could be sentenced in the magistrates' court or her case could be committed to the Crown Court for sentence if the magistrates/district judge consider their powers to be insufficient.

Maximum sentences

If Monique is sentenced in the magistrates' court, the maximum sentence would be six months' imprisonment. If she is committed to the Crown Court, the judge could pass a sentence up to the seven-year maximum for the offence.

Determining the appropriate sentence

Either court must have regard to the purposes of sentencing, which include punishment and deterrence but also the rehabilitation of offenders (CJA 2003 s.142). Before imposing a custodial sentence, a pre-sentence report should normally be obtained (CJA 2003 s.156). The court must consider the seriousness of the offence and any aggravating and mitigating factors (CJA 2003 s.143). The sum of money stolen will be important in determining offence seriousness. The fact that Monique is an employee is an aggravating feature, as an employee is in a position of trust. Her exact position in the company and the degree of trust invested in her will therefore be relevant. However, Monique is young, which is a mitigating feature. Monique's guilty plea is also a mitigating factor. In accordance with sentencing guidelines, Monique will be entitled to a discount of one-third for her early guilty plea.

The court may only pass a custodial sentence if the offence is so serious that neither a fine nor a community order can be justified (CJA 2003 s.152). It must pass the shortest term that is commensurate with the seriousness of the offence (CJA 2003 s.153).

The court must follow any applicable sentencing guidelines unless it would be contrary to the interests of justice to do so (Coroners and Justice Act 2009 s.125). If the court chooses to depart from the guidelines it must explain the reasons why.

If the proposed sentence is between fourteen days' and two years' imprisonment, the court may suspend the sentence. The court may order Monique to comply with requirements, such as a rehabilitation activity requirement, unpaid work, or a curfew, during the period of suspension.

Further reading

- **Ashworth, A.** *'The Evolution of English Sentencing Guidance in 2016'* [2017] Crim LR 507

  Discusses the relationship between guidelines issued by the Sentencing Council and guidance contained in case law from the Court of Appeal.

- **Ashworth, A.** *'Prisons, Proportionality and Recent Penal History'* (2017) 80(3) MLR 473

  Explores the changes in policy and practice that resulted in a steep rise in the prison population between 1993 and 2012.

- **Ashworth, A.** *'The Common Sense and Complications of General Deterrent Sentencing'* [2019] Crim LR 564

  Discusses the role of deterrence in sentencing and analyses the approach taken to deterrence by politicians, the Sentencing Council, and judges.

- ***Kelly, R.*** *'Reforming Maximum Sentences and Respecting Ordinal Proportionality'* [2018] Crim LR 450

  Discusses how maximum sentences are fixed and explains how the statutory maximum period of imprisonment for an offence may affect the length of sentences imposed.

- ***Law Commission***. *The Sentencing Code: Volume 1* (Law Com No. 382, 2018)

  Outlines the problems with the current law of sentencing and proposes a new Sentencing Code.

- ***Leverick, F.*** *'Sentence Discounting for Guilty Pleas: An Argument for Certainty over Discretion'* [2014] Crim LR 338

  Analyses and critiques the principle of sentence discounting for guilty pleas, comparing the process in England and Wales with the position in Scotland.

- ***Roberts, J.V.*** *'Sentencing Riot-related Offending'* (2013) 53(2) Br J Criminol 234

  Examines public attitudes to the sentencing of those involved in the 2011 riots and discusses the divergence of perspectives between the community and the courts.

- ***Shapland, J., Robinson, G.***, and ***Sorsby, A.*** *Restorative Justice in Practice*, Routledge (2011)

  Evaluates the work of three RJ projects and considers the effect of RJ on the frequency of re-offending.

Online resources

You should now attempt the supporting self-test questions and end-of-chapter questions available at: **www.oup.com/he/wilson-rutherford4e**

Chapter 15

The civil process

Learning objectives

By the end of this chapter you should:

- be able to describe the process by which a civil claim will be dealt with in the County Court or in the High Court;
- be aware of the major case management powers possessed by the civil courts and appreciate how these powers should be exercised so as to further the overriding objective of the Civil Procedure Rules 1998 (as amended);
- be able to list the major differences between civil and criminal trials;
- have a basic understanding of some of the major principles of civil evidence;
- be familiar with the procedures and principles which govern the award of costs in civil proceedings;
- be able to describe how civil judgments can be enforced.

Talking point

Following an in-depth review of the civil process and civil courts, Lord Briggs produced his recommendations, *Civil Courts Structure: Final Report*, in July 2016. Perhaps the most headline-worthy recommendation was the proposal to establish an Online Court for Civil Disputes. The news prompted Professor Richard Susskind to declare: 'I am the happiest man in England.' Not everyone was as enthusiastic as Professor Susskind, who is a well-known advocate of information technology and has for many years prophesied the replacement of many legal services by automated systems. The Young Bar was more pessimistic and stated that 'it will just be an expensive disaster'. However, there seems to be general agreement that the Civil Court System needs to modernise and 'paperless' web-based access is most likely the way forward.

The Online Court would be designed for the issue and conduct of civil claims by citizens with minimal assistance from lawyers. The Briggs Report suggests that such a court would, at first, be for 'straightforward money claims valued at up to £25,000' and would have its own set of user-friendly rules which would replace the CPR. The Online Court would be accessible from smartphones and tablets and could be introduced by 2020.

As the report concludes: 'The Online Court project offers a radically new and different procedural and cultural approach to the resolution of civil disputes which, if successful, may pave the way for fundamental changes in the conduct of civil litigation.'

What do you think? Is online justice the way forward? Consider the following questions:

- How does this proposal to change the civil dispute process link with the issues raised in the chapters on access to justice and the legal profession? Will it lead to a two-tier justice system with the full civil process being used only by those who can pay for it?
- How will people access justice who do not have the skills or desire to use a computer? Will this unfairly prejudice certain sections of the population?
- Can the rules be simplified without compromising justice?
- Lord Briggs has indicated that he is unhappy with the term 'Online Court'—what alternative name could you suggest?

Introduction

The civil court process is the means by which the state enables individuals to settle disputes. It is clearly in the public interest to ensure that those disputes that are incapable of informal resolution and must go to court are dealt with as quickly and efficiently as possible. In the latter half of the twentieth century it was acknowledged by judges, lawyers, and court users alike that the civil justice system was too slow, too expensive, too complicated, and inaccessible. In 1994, Lord Woolf, then Master of the Rolls, was commissioned to investigate the civil justice system and produce a report to recommend reforms to the system to improve access to justice. Lord Woolf's final report, *Access to Justice*, published in July 1996, recommended a complete overhaul of the system, including a new set of rules and procedures and a change in the courts' attitude towards case management. As a result, the Civil Procedure Rules (CPR) came into force in 1999.

This chapter will consider the major changes introduced by the CPR and by the practice directions, protocols, and guides that accompany them. Although the CPR have largely been welcomed by practitioners, the judiciary, and academics, the extent to which they have actually improved access to justice has been a matter of some debate. Indeed, the problem of spiralling civil litigation costs led to a second major review of the system by Jackson LJ, whose final report was published in January 2010.

This chapter will look at five stages of the civil process:

- the civil process prior to the commencement of proceedings;
- the civil process between the commencement of proceedings and trial;
- the civil trial itself;
- the awarding of costs in civil proceedings;
- the enforcement of civil judgments.

In the context of the civil trial, some basic principles of civil evidence will be highlighted.

This is a dynamic topic. The rules are constantly updated and there are court decisions every day about their interpretation and application. Mastery of the CPR will ensure that you can best serve your litigation client's interests and perhaps outwit, legitimately, your opponent.

15.1 The nature of civil proceedings

A criminal case is usually brought by the state (in the name of the Queen) against an individual. Conversely, a civil case is commenced by an individual or organisation against another individual or organisation: in other words, a civil case is a lawsuit instigated to settle a private dispute. Sometimes a particular event may give rise to both criminal and civil liability. Criminal law governs an individual's obligations to the state in general (that is, contrary to the Queen's Peace) and civil law oversees specific relationships.

 Example

After drinking a few pints of beer, Joe decides to see how fast his new Porsche Turbo sports car can go. He drives it at high speed around a blind bend and crashes into an oncoming car driven by Anne. Anne is injured in the collision and her car is written off.

Joe could be prosecuted in the criminal courts for offences such as driving under the influence of alcohol above the prescribed limit and dangerous driving. The criminal charges would be determined in either the magistrates' court or the Crown Court.

Anne could also bring a claim against Joe in the civil courts for negligence (a tort). Anne's aim would be to recover damages from Joe to compensate her for her personal injuries and the damage to her car. Her civil claim would be heard in either the County Court or the High Court.

15.2 **Pre-civil justice reform**

The CPR have been in force for twenty years. In order to appreciate the present debates and discussions regarding civil procedure, in particular those sparked by the Briggs Report, it is important to appreciate the historical development of the rules that govern the civil courts. It is appropriate to mention briefly the state of the system prior to 1994 and to be aware of the magnitude of the task set for Lord Woolf when he was appointed to conduct the comprehensive review of the civil justice system—and why it was necessary to have a root-and-branch reform of the civil legal system that still resonates today.

The system that Lord Woolf was asked to reform was complex and costly. As now, civil claims were dealt with in either the High Court or in a County Court; however, each court had separate procedural rules, which were often unnecessarily convoluted. Even the basic terminology was confusing: for example, a person bringing a claim was referred to as 'the plaintiff' and proceedings were commenced in the County Court by a 'summons' and in the High Court by a 'writ'. Time limits were different in each court and often rules were disregarded or ignored, and local County Courts had their own idiosyncrasies. Lawyers had to carry two huge books to court—the White Book for the High Court rules and the Green Book for the County Court rules. It was not only students and newly qualified lawyers who found this confusing.

The court system struggled to deal with the volume of plaintiffs and defendants and there was no recognised alternative to court proceedings to settle disputes.

There had been a number of reviews of the civil court system in the twentieth century prior to the Woolf Report (the Evershed Committee in 1953, the Winn Committee in 1968, and the Cantley Committee in 1979) but despite widespread agreement that change and reform were required, no proposals for change were implemented.

In 1988 the Civil Justice Review carried out a far-ranging examination of the civil justice system: one of its findings was that, in the county courts, costs often equalled or outweighed damages awarded. The 1988 report was largely ignored, save for acknowledgement that the delays in the system were not acceptable, and the county court jurisdiction was extended in the hope that this would go some way to speeding up the process of justice by dealing with lower-value cases more quickly. However, the inefficiencies and delays continued and, despite a report commissioned by the Bar Council and the Law Society (the Heilbron-Hodge Report) that came to the same conclusion as all of the preceding reports—that the system was slow, expensive, and unnecessarily complex—there was seemingly no political appetite for wholesale reform. The English court system was creaking at the seams and satisfying no one. It was outdated and cumbersome, leading inevitably to tortuous and expensive litigation and inadequate access to justice.

Finally, in 1994, Lord Woolf was appointed not just to report on the failures of civil justice but also to suggest reform to make the system fit for the twenty-first century rather than the nineteenth.

15.3 **The Woolf reforms**

Following an extensive programme of consultation with individuals and interest groups, Lord Woolf concluded, as had his predecessors, that the civil justice system was too slow, too expensive, and too complicated. In particular:

- the cost of litigation often exceeded the value of the claim;
- the system favoured wealthy litigants over those who lacked resources;
- there were difficulties in predicting how long litigation might last and how much it would cost, which created uncertainty;
- the system lacked a coherent structure;
- there was a general lack of openness and cooperation between opposing parties;
- rules and court orders were too often ignored.

One of the major aims of the Woolf Review was to improve access to justice for individuals and small businesses. Those who want to bring cases in the civil courts will often have to fund the litigation themselves and may be unable to afford legal advice or representation. Lord Woolf recommended that the system should therefore be clear and accessible to ordinary people. You may wish to consider whether, twenty years after the introduction of the rules, this desire has been achieved.

Unlike the preceding reports, in *Access to Justice* Lord Woolf made extensive recommendations for reform that were accepted. He suggested root-and-branch reform and a sweeping aside of the old rules which would be replaced by a unified set of rules for both the High Court and the County Courts. There should be incentives to parties to prepare cases at an early stage and to attempt to settle before the commencement of court proceedings. In order to ensure compliance and uniformity, Woolf proposed that the courts should have wide and comprehensive case-management powers to ensure that the parties to claims were encouraged to litigate efficiently and effectively. The majority of his recommendations were implemented through the CPR, which came into force on 26 April 1999.

15.3.1 **The Civil Procedure Rules**

Other than in relation to certain specialised forms of proceedings (for example, family proceedings and insolvency proceedings), the CPR now govern all proceedings in the County Court, the High Court, and the Civil Division of the Court of Appeal.

The CPR are divided into 'parts', with each part containing the basic rules to be followed in relation to a particular aspect of procedure, and more detailed guidance in accompanying ***practice directions***. The procedures to be followed before proceedings commence are contained in the pre-action protocols. At present there are sixteen pre-action protocols. The number of protocols is always under review. For example, a new protocol for Media and Communications claims came into force on 1 October 2019.

Practice directions
Practice directions are sets of rules and procedures which supplement and support parts of the CPR. They tell parties what the courts expect of them and also what may happen if they do not comply with rules or court orders.

Throughout the remainder of this chapter, CPR means the Civil Procedure Rules 1998. Thus, for example, CPR 26 means Part 26 of the Civil Procedure Rules 1998 and CPR 7 PD refers to the practice direction that supplements CPR Part 7. The CPR can be found at **www.justice.gov.uk/civil/procrules_fin/menus/rules.htm**.

The aim of the CPR draftsmen was to create a set of rules for modern litigation that are more user-friendly and intelligible than the rules they replaced. When they were introduced they were designed to be a completely new start to bring coherence and clarity to the England and Wales civil courts system by using plain English, in the place of Latin and technical language, in order to make the rules accessible to all. For example, a party bringing a claim is referred to as a 'claimant' rather than plaintiff, which you will see used in pre-1999 law reports.

Thinking point

Have the CPR simplified the civil litigation process?

Critics have suggested that the CPR have not simplified the civil process as intended. As well as being supplemented by numerous practice directions, pre-action protocols, and court 'guides', the CPR have been updated ninety-two times (as of October 2017) since 1999. Is this consistent with a system that is supposed to be easy to use and intelligible to non-lawyers?

The overriding objective of the CPR, expressed in CPR 1.1, is to deal with cases justly and, following the changes to the rules in 2013, at proportionate cost. This is the governing purpose of the CPR and is to be borne in mind by the parties and the court when conducting litigation. In order to achieve the overriding objective, major changes were introduced to streamline the processes and allocate resources appropriately. The main processes and procedures prescribed in the CPR, designed to simplify and streamline civil claims, are set out in Table 15.1.

Expert evidence in civil proceedings is considered further at 15.15.4.

The CPR increase the powers of the civil courts. Judges and court staff can manage cases so as to reduce the extent to which the conduct of the parties might affect the progress of a case. The CPR also seek to restrict the adversarial nature of civil proceedings by encouraging cooperation and openness.

A good example of the reforms introduced by the CPR is provided by the civil courts' ability to limit the admissibility and nature of expert evidence. Under the pre-CPR regime, the duration and cost of civil trials was often increased by disproportionate reliance upon expensive expert evidence. Now the courts now possess the power to restrict expert evidence to that which is reasonably required, to direct that expert evidence be given by a single joint expert (that is, one expert instructed

Table 15.1 Overview of the purpose of the Civil Procedure Rules

General overview of the way claims must be handled under the CPR	Purpose—to further the overriding objective
Claims are allocated to one of three 'tracks' according to the value of the claim	To ensure appropriate resources are allocated according to the value and complexity of claims
The courts are responsible for setting timetables and ensuring that rules and procedures are complied with. Sanctions may be imposed upon a party who does not comply	To ensure appropriate resources are allocated according to the value and complexity of claims and to enforce compliance with the rules, practice directions, and orders
Costs in many cases are fixed or the court has wide powers to control costs	To manage the cost of cases and save expense
Any party to the proceedings can make offers to settle the whole or part of a dispute, with sanctions for those who turn down appropriate and reasonable offers	To encourage the parties to deal with case cost-effectively
An expectation of cooperation and openness between parties both prior to commencement of proceedings, in the hope that litigation will be avoided, and once the case has been ***issued*** at court	To encourage the parties to deal with cases cost-effectively
Encouragement to use ADR and to issue proceedings as a last resort	To deal with the case in ways which are proportionate

by the parties jointly), and to limit such evidence to written reports rather than oral testimony, thereby ensuring speedier, less expensive, and less complex trials.

 **Critical debate**

Is the emphasis on the need for cooperation and openness in civil proceedings consistent with the maintenance of an adversarial system?

The Civil Procedure Rules emphasise the importance of using court as a last resort and encourage parties in dispute to try alternative dispute resolution (ADR) methods, such as mediation, before issuing court proceedings. Indeed, a party who fails to try ADR may be penalised in costs: see the cases of *Dunnett v Railtrack* [2002] EWCA Civ 302, *Halsey v Milton Keynes General NHS Trust* [2004] EWCA 3006 Civ 576, and *Burchell v Bullard* [2005] EWCA Civ 358.

However, this encouragement to cooperate before litigation commences and during the preparation for trial is very different from what happens in a courtroom if the parties finally end up there. Is it perhaps time to get rid of the adversarial process in civil cases completely? Are there any circumstances, do you think, in which an adversarial process is more appropriate to settle a dispute than a conciliatory approach? Does the fact that many more cases are now settled without recourse to trial, in private, and without reference to formal legal rules and procedure, mean that the whole basis of the common law system (based on judicial precedent) is undermined?

15.3.2 The overriding objective and the court's duty to manage cases

The CPR has an 'overriding objective' of dealing with cases justly at proportionate cost. The court must have regard to the overriding objective when exercising its powers under the CPR and when interpreting the CPR. CPR 1 provides that dealing with a case justly and at proportionate cost includes:

- ensuring that the parties are on an equal footing;
- saving expense;
- dealing with the case in ways which are proportionate—
  - (a) to the amount of money involved;
  - (b) to the importance of the case;
  - (c) to the complexity of the issues;
  - (d) to the financial position of each party;
- ensuring that it is dealt with expeditiously and fairly;
- allotting to it an appropriate share of the court's resources, while taking into account the need to allot resources to other cases;
- enforcing compliance with rules, practice directions, and orders.

The parties must help the court to further the overriding objective and the court itself must further the overriding objective by active case management. CPR 1 explains that active case management includes:

- encouraging cooperation between the parties;
- identifying the issues at an early stage;
- deciding promptly which issues need full investigation and trial and accordingly disposing summarily of the others;
- deciding the order in which issues are to be resolved;
- encouraging the parties to use an ADR procedure if the court considers that appropriate, and facilitating the use of such procedure;
- helping the parties to settle the whole or part of the case;
- fixing timetables or otherwise controlling the progress of the case;
- considering whether the likely benefits of taking a particular step justify the cost of taking it;
- dealing with as many aspects of the case as it can on the same occasion;
- dealing with the case without the parties needing to attend at court;
- making use of technology;
- giving directions to ensure that the trial of a case proceeds quickly and efficiently.

A change to the CPR that came into force on 1 October 2015 has further underlined the court's role in actively managing cases. An amendment to CPR Rule 3.1 sets out the courts' management powers to include carrying out an ***Early Neutral Evaluation (ENE)*** of a case.

Early Neutral Evaluation (ENE) *A form of ADR whereby a neutral party (or the judge) gives an opinion at an early stage on the merits of the case in hand as a whole, or in respect to a specific issue. The ENE is not binding on the parties but will be very persuasive.*

Thinking point

Is the overriding objective easy to interpret?

Professor Michael Zander has argued that the multiple considerations of the overriding objective are potentially conflicting. This leads to a risk of inconsistent decisions, as different judges can come to different decisions in similar cases. Can you foresee a situation in which the different aspects of the overriding objective conflict? Are some of the terms used by the overriding objective, such as 'fairness', easy to define or are they open to interpretation?

15.3.3 **Proportionate cost**

The key to understanding the aim of the CPR is the concept of proportionality. In the major update to the rules in April 2013, proportionality, which had always been central to the spirit of the rules, was elevated to an integral part of the overriding objective when the stated overarching purpose of the CPR—to deal with cases justly—was amended to expressly include the phrase 'at proportionate cost'. Thus it is incumbent on all parties, and the court, to consider the cost of each and every step in the litigation process to ensure that any action taken is necessary and carried out in the most efficient and cost-effective manner.

When considering the proportionality of costs it is important to be aware that 'costs' include not only the sums charged by the lawyers but also court fees—every form, application, and hearing comes with an associated fee (see leaflet EX50 **hmctsformfinder.justice.gov.uk/HMCTS/GetLeaflet.do?court_leaflets_id=264**); payments to experts for reports; charges by the police for accident reports; and payments for medical notes.

Thinking point

What costs can be incurred in a personal injury case?

Remember it is not just the solicitors' costs that have to be paid.

For example:

Lilian, aged thirty, is very badly injured in a road traffic accident when the car she is travelling in is hit by a lorry driven by Bert. Lilian loses a leg, has a head injury (and may develop epilepsy), and is unable to care for herself. Liability is denied on the basis that Bert lost control of his vehicle when he was stung by a wasp. The costs of this case for the claimant could include:

- Medical report—orthopaedic surgeon £800
- Medical report—prosthetics expert £800
- Medical report—neurologist £800
- Medical report—plastic surgeon £800
- Psychiatrist's report—£1,250
- Medical notes from hospital and GP—£150
- Rehabilitation expert (occupational therapist)—£800
- Architect's report for reconfiguring claimant's house—£2,000
- Care expert—£2,250
- Accident reconstruction expert—£2,000
- Police report—£100
- Police photographs—£200
- Tachograph report—£500
- Mediator (failed mediation)—£2,000
- Solicitors' costs—£50,000-£100,000

- Barrister's fee—£10,000–£15,000
- Court fees—issue fee, directions questionnaire fee, set-down fee, and fees for interim applications.

Clearly, if this case was worth £4m then the costs would not be disproportionate. Would they be disproportionate if the case was worth £50,000?

Even in a simple case, it is easy to incur fees of £3,000. For example: Ahmed trips and cuts his leg on a broken paving slab. The claim is worth more than £1,000 for the injury. Court fees, solicitors' costs, and medical report fees will all have to be incurred.

15.3.4 The Jackson Review

Supporters of the Woolf reforms claim that the CPR introduced greater efficiency and reduced delays. Unfortunately, however, the costs of civil litigation have increased. The lack of proportionality between the value of claims and the cost of litigating them remains a major concern. For example, in 2009 it was reported that a defendant in a boundary dispute between neighbours had been ordered to pay £70,000 in costs to the claimant. The area of land involved in the dispute was approximately six square metres. Although this may be an extreme example, excessive and disproportionate costs are a problem. In 2008, Jackson LJ was appointed by the Master of the Rolls to undertake a review of the rules and principles governing costs in civil litigation. His final report, published in January 2010, made a number of recommendations designed to control costs. Key recommendations included:

- legal expenses must reflect the nature and complexity of the case and must be proportionate;
- qualified one-way costs-shifting (that is, a claimant who is unsuccessful should not be ordered to pay the defendant's costs);
- fixed costs in fast track cases.

There are also a number of major recommendations concerning the funding of civil litigation, which are considered in Chapter 11. These recommendations and the subsequent implementation of the recommendations will be considered later.

15.4 The civil courts

The main civil courts are the County Court and the High Court, although magistrates' courts have a limited civil jurisdiction in relation to family law cases. A magistrates' court in its civil jurisdiction is known as the Family Proceedings Court. Magistrates have the power to decide family matters such as adoption, residence, contact, and maintenance. Further consideration of the civil jurisdiction of magistrates is outside the scope of this chapter.

Image 15.1 The Civil Justice Centre in Manchester

Source: Daniel Hopkinson/Alamy

15.4.1 **The County Court**

On 22 April 2014, s.17 and Sch.9 of the Crime and Courts Act 2013 repealed s.1 and s.2 of the County Courts Act 1984 and inserted a new s.1A. The individual county courts were abolished as individual courts of record and a single County Court was put in place with its own seal, in the same way that the High Court is a unitary court with its own seal. In every Act of Parliament where the court is referred to as 'a county court' this must now be read as 'the County Court'. A typical County Court is shown in Image 15.1.

The new County Court is designed to be a costs-saving measure, and follows a recommendation made by Sir Henry Brooke in his 2008 report *Should the Civil Courts Be Unified?* The unitary court follows implementation of a programme of court closures to save money. The reorganisation has been backed up by the introduction of an increased emphasis on online and electronic handling of cases. The remaining individual county court buildings, of which there are approximately 160, are now known as hearing centres and there are now two national business centres that have been established to centralise the issue of claims and the early management of cases. The County Court Money Claims Centre in Salford deals with the issue of any claims involving money, and in addition to issuing paper claims has a process that can be accessed online for claims for fixed amounts under £100,000. This can be found at **www.gov.uk/make-money-claim-online**. The second centralised service is the County Court Business Centre in Northampton. The Business Centre states that it provides 'an excellent service . . . [using] modern, streamlined systems to facilitate the removal of repetitive staff-intensive work from local courts to a central, computer-supported office'. Most of the judicial work of the County Court is carried out by district judges and deputy district judges. Circuit judges and recorders deal with the more complex matters. This includes pre-trial case management decisions, the trial of cases that are allocated to the small claims ***track*** and, in some hearing centres, the trial of cases that are allocated to the fast track. A district judge may also try a multi-track case with the consent of the Designated Civil Judge (that is, the senior civil judge at the relevant trial centre). However, the County Court trial of most cases that are allocated to the multi-track or the fast track takes place before a circuit judge or a recorder.

Tracks
Each civil case is allocated to one of three tracks, namely the 'small claims track', the 'fast track', or the 'multi-track'. The appropriate track depends upon the value and complexity of the case. In essence, the lowest-value cases are allocated to the small claims track, the medium-value cases to the fast track, and the high-value cases to the multi-track. Value of a case is the starting point for allocation but issues of complexity, importance, and numbers of witnesses are also taken into account. Each track has its own rules that govern the conduct of a case.

In some civil cases, liability will not be in issue and the court only needs to determine the amount of damages to be paid. For example, a defendant may admit breaching a contract but dispute the amount that he should have to pay to the claimant. Depending upon the value involved, and the complexity of the issues, a district judge may conduct the hearing to determine the amount of damages regardless of the track to which the case has been allocated. CPR 7 and CPR 7A PD provide that certain proceedings must be commenced in the County Court. These include proceedings where the value of the claim does not exceed £100,000 or, if the case involves personal injuries, where the value of the personal injuries claim is less than £50,000.

Thus, the vast majority of civil claims commence in the County Court. The court statistics are produced quarterly and can be found at **www.gov.uk/government/collections/civil-justice-statistics-quarterly**. The latest statistics available at the time of writing, for April to June 2019, show that a total of 465,000 claims were issued. The trend until 2012 was for a decrease in claims. Since 2012 the trend has been upwards although there has been a decrease since 2018. The trend, up or down, is driven by money claims. Non-money claims have continued to decrease. Perhaps the increase in litigants in person has increased the number of people issuing claims? There are, however, some limitations upon the County Court jurisdiction. For example, in accordance with s.15(2) of the County Courts Act 1984, the County Court does not normally possess jurisdiction to hear defamation proceedings. Before issuing a claim it is important to check CPR 7 and the associated practice directions to ensure that the procedure for issuing proceedings is correctly followed.

Note: In addition to the new County Court, the Crime and Courts Act 2013 s.17(3) established a dedicated family court that came into being on 22 April 2014.

Visit the online resources to watch a video on how a County Court trial works.

15.4.2 **The High Court**

The High Court is made up of three divisions: the Queen's Bench Division, the Chancery Division, and the Family Division.

The Queen's Bench Division (QBD) deals predominantly with claims in contract and ***tort***, although it can deal with a variety of other matters. The QBD has specialist subdivisions which include the Commercial Court and the Admiralty Court, where judges with specific expertise determine matters of commercial law and shipping, respectively. There is also the Divisional Court of the QBD (as distinct from the QBD itself). The Divisional Court of the QBD has appellate jurisdiction (that is, it determines appeals from decisions of lower courts) and can determine appeals by way of case stated (an appeal decided on an agreed set of facts) and applications for judicial review. When it is hearing a judicial review, the Divisional Court of the Queen's Bench Division is called the Administrative Court.

Tort
A tort is a civil wrong for which the injured party is entitled to some form of redress. Examples of torts include negligence, nuisance, and defamation.

In October 2000 a separate Administrative Court was established to deal with applications for judicial review. This Administrative Court forms part of the Queen's Bench Division of the High Court.

The Chancery Division deals with matters such as the sale of land, mortgages, trusts, bankruptcy, and patents, and encompasses the Bankruptcy Court and the Companies Court. Cases dealt with by the Family Division include matrimonial matters and proceedings under the Children Act 1989.

Many types of claim may be brought before more than one division (for example, professional negligence claims may be brought in either the Queen's Bench Division or the Chancery Division). However, certain types of claim must be brought before a particular division (for example, cases concerning the execution of trusts must be brought in the Chancery Division).

The High Court is based at the Royal Courts of Justice on the Strand in London. There are also approximately fifty district registries in England and Wales at which a claimant may commence High Court proceedings.

More information about High Court judges, district judges, and masters can be found in Chapter 8.

At the Royal Courts of Justice, pre-trial case management is mainly undertaken by masters (they have a similar jurisdiction to that of a judge sitting in chambers, or in other words, not in open court). At district registries, such work is generally undertaken by district judges (who will be appointed both as County Court district judges and as High Court district judges). Trials are conducted by a High Court judge or a deputy High Court judge. Certain other functions must also be performed by a High Court judge or a deputy High Court judge, such as making a 'freezing order' (which prevents a person from disposing of assets) or a search order (CPR 25A PD).

For some types of case, the CPR do not specify where the case should commence. Where proceedings may be commenced either in the High Court or in the County Court, it will be for the claimant to decide where to commence the proceedings. The claimant should commence proceedings in the High Court rather than in the County Court if it is the case that a High Court judge should deal with the matter in view of:

- the financial value of the claim;
- its complexity; or
- the importance of its outcome to the public (CPR 7A PD).

Where a party chooses to commence proceedings in the High Court, the High Court may order the proceedings to be transferred to the County Court if appropriate (s.40 of the County Courts Act 1984). Similarly, where a party chooses to commence proceedings in the County Court, either the County Court or the High Court may order the proceedings to be transferred to the High Court (ss.41–42 of the County Courts Act 1984).

15.5 **Case management powers**

Prior to the Woolf reforms, there were two distinct sets of rules that set out the procedural steps to be taken by litigants and the time limits within which those steps were to be taken: one set of rules for the county courts and one set for the High Court. However, the rules were often ignored by litigating parties or applied in a piecemeal fashion. One of Lord Woolf's main objectives was to ensure that the courts took a decisive role to effectively control and manage proceedings to ensure that the court process was efficient and effective. In order to achieve this aim, CPR 3 confers a variety of general case management powers upon the civil courts. Control of the proceedings is achieved by instructions to the parties by the issuing of court orders. An order is the method by which a court directs the parties and tells them what to do to progress the claim.

For example, a court may make an order to:

- extend or shorten time limits laid down by the CPR;
- adjourn a hearing or bring it forward;
- require a party or a legal representative to attend court;
- hold a hearing by telephone conference call;
- stay (that is, suspend) the proceedings;
- determine the order in which issues are to be dealt with at trial; or
- exclude an issue from consideration at trial.

A party to litigation may apply to the court for an order but the court may also make an order of its own volition without application by either of the parties, if this is required to manage the proceedings efficiently. Thus, the conduct of litigation is not simply left to the parties to the litigation: the court takes an active role. A court order may set out what steps the parties must take to progress the claim and may specify the consequences of a party's failure to comply. For example, an 'unless order' may specify that 'unless' a party complies with the order, the ***statement of case*** will be struck out. Even where no 'unless order' has been made, the court may strike out a statement of case if there has been a failure to comply with a rule, a practice direction, or some other court order. As a result of the Jackson reforms, judges have been requested, and trained accordingly, to be much tougher on default than they have been in the past. Parties to litigation are advised to have their case in first-class order at all times. There is no guarantee that a court will grant an extension of time to carry out a step in the process, or to make amendments to the case or replace an expert.

Statements of case
A statement of case is a document in which a party sets out concisely the facts and basis of their case. Statements of case, pre-CPR, were known as 'pleadings' and are still commonly referred to as such by practitioners, although the term is not used in the CPR. Examples of statements of case are particulars of claim, defences, counterclaims, and replies (see 15.6.3 and 15.7.1).

The case management powers of judges were thrown into sharp focus by the decision in *Andrew Mitchell MP v News Group Newspapers Limited* [2013] EWCA Civ 1537 (the judgment was upheld by the Court of Appeal, leading to general panic among civil litigators who realised that there was to be no leniency for missing deadlines and often no guarantee of an extension of time for any steps in the litigation process, leading, in some cases, to a return to aggressive point scoring and pre-Woolf reforms levels of distrust between parties, and a breakdown in cooperation).

The *Mitchell* case came about as a result of the failure by Mitchell's solicitors to file a costs budget seven days before the case management conference, as required by a court order. At the costs management hearing, the Master held that the claimant (Mitchell) was to be treated as having filed a costs budget comprising only the applicable court fees and the balance of the costs were to be disregarded.

Mitchell's solicitors were understandably concerned that if this judgment stood, even if the client won the case, he would not be entitled to be paid his costs, and therefore they applied for relief from sanctions. The application was dismissed and an appeal was lodged against both decisions. The appeals were dismissed.

As a result of this decision it was clear to all parties to litigation that court orders and the CPR must be followed to the letter, to ensure that all deadlines were complied with. Failure to do so, even if no prejudice was caused to either side, would expose the party in default to the risk of sanctions being imposed, which would seriously disadvantage their position, or indeed mean that the case could not proceed.

The dismissal of the appeal was not, of course, the end of the matter and the case has had major repercussions for the conduct of civil litigation. Detailed discussion of the difficulties and problems resulting from the decision in *Mitchell* is outside the scope of this textbook, although an excellent discussion and overview of the issue, and its importance to all civil litigators, can be found on Gordon Exall's blog, *Civil Litigation Brief*, at **civillitigationbrief.wordpress.com/2013/12/12/mitchell-case-watch/**.

On 4 July 2014, the Court of Appeal took the opportunity to clarify the position post-*Mitchell* via their judgments in a trio of joined appeals: *Denton v T H White; Decadent Vapours v Bevan and Utilise v Davies* [2014] EWCA Civ 906. In an eagerly awaited judgment, the Court of Appeal panel, which included Jackson LJ and the

Master of the Rolls, Lord Dyson, gave guidance that they hope will reduce satellite litigation (court proceedings linked to the original case but dealing with a separate matter, such as a dispute about costs or interpretation of the court rules) and introduce a consistent approach to CPR 3.9. They also noted that it should no longer be necessary to refer to earlier decisions relating to sanctions. The judgment introduced a three-stage test to allow judges to decide whether there should be relief from sanctions. In short, if the breach is neither serious nor significant, or where there is good reason for the breach, relief is likely to be given.

The decision in *Denton* should ensure that litigation is conducted in a cooperative environment and encourage sensible case management decisions to further the overriding objective. It does however warn parties to litigation that they must comply with the CPR, and failure to do so may have far-reaching, and expensive, consequences for the defaulting party. Of course, the best way to ensure that there is no risk of a sanction being imposed is to comply with all rules, orders, and directions at the appropriate time and, if there is a risk that a deadline cannot be met, to make an application to the court in good time to request an extension. This underlines the importance to civil litigators of a comprehensive and reliable case management or diary system.

Thinking point

Is striking out a proportionate sanction?

Striking out means that the court will order a document, or part of a document, to be deleted so that it may no longer be relied upon. Striking out a party's statement of case will often effectively mean that proceedings are decided in favour of the opposing party. Should the court be allowed to impose such a severe sanction for the breach of a procedural rule?

Instead of exercising the power to strike out a party's statement of case, the court may impose other sanctions where a party fails to comply with a rule, a practice direction, or a court order. Alternative sanctions include ordering the party at fault to pay costs, or refusing to give that party permission to rely on evidence to which the rule or order related.

The Jackson reforms have simplified the rules to introduce a much stricter approach to default. As well as considering 'all the circumstances of the case so as to enable it to deal justly' with an application for relief, the court must also now take into account the need:

(a) for litigation to be conducted efficiently and at proportionate cost;
(b) to enforce compliance with rules, practice directions, and orders.

The system of sanctions introduced by the CPR was said to be an integral part of case management. Lord Woolf stated that the threat of punishment was necessary to ensure compliance with court orders and procedural rules. However, he acknowledged that the judiciary would need to take a much more robust approach if sanctions were to have any real effect. Critics of the Woolf reforms have suggested that, in practice, judges have been too willing to exercise mercy and grant relief from sanctions (see for example A. Zuckerman, 'Litigation Management under the CPR' in Dwyer (ed.), *The Civil Procedure Rules Ten Years On*, Oxford University Press (2009)). Jackson LJ clearly took this view on board and, as a result, failure to comply with orders, and the resultant increases in costs, will no longer be tolerated. After the hiatus caused by the *Mitchell* decision, and the clarification in *Denton* which indicated that the *Mitchell* decision had been misunderstood, it appears that the position is as expressed by Etherton LJ in *Ryder Plc v Beever* [2012] EWCA Civ 1737, where it was emphasised that the CPR are 'intended to make solicitors comply with orders or face the consequences with their eyes open. They are not intended to create traps for the unwary or slightly incompetent.'

15.6 **Commencing civil proceedings**

Starting a civil claim is fairly straightforward. A claim form must be completed and delivered to the court to be ***issued***. Proceedings formally start when the claim form is issued by the court. The person issuing the claim form is referred to as the claimant and the person against whom the claim is made is the defendant. A single case may involve more than one claimant and/or more than one defendant. Remember that the aim of the CPR is to enable the parties to a civil dispute to prepare their case for court and to ensure that only the issues that cannot be agreed are tried. Settlement is encouraged before trial if possible. The relevant forms can be found on the Courts and Tribunals website at **hmctsformfinder.justice.gov.uk/HMCTS/FormFinder.do**.

Issued
A claim form is issued when it is dated by the court and stamped with the court seal.

15.6.1 **Preliminary matters**

Prior to commencing proceedings (that is, prior to issuing the claim form) there is a variety of matters that a party and/or his solicitor must consider. In the first instance, the solicitor and client will need to discuss the various methods by which civil litigation may be funded. (This is discussed in more detail in Chapter 11.) The primary considerations in relation to the claim itself are the nature of the claim and the remedy being sought. For example, it may be that a person seeks damages (compensation) for personal injuries or for breach of contract. Alternatively, the claimant may be seeking a remedy, such as an injunction to prevent a nuisance from continuing. Diagram 15.1 is a flow chart which illustrates the complete process of a civil dispute. Follow this flow chart as you learn about the process.

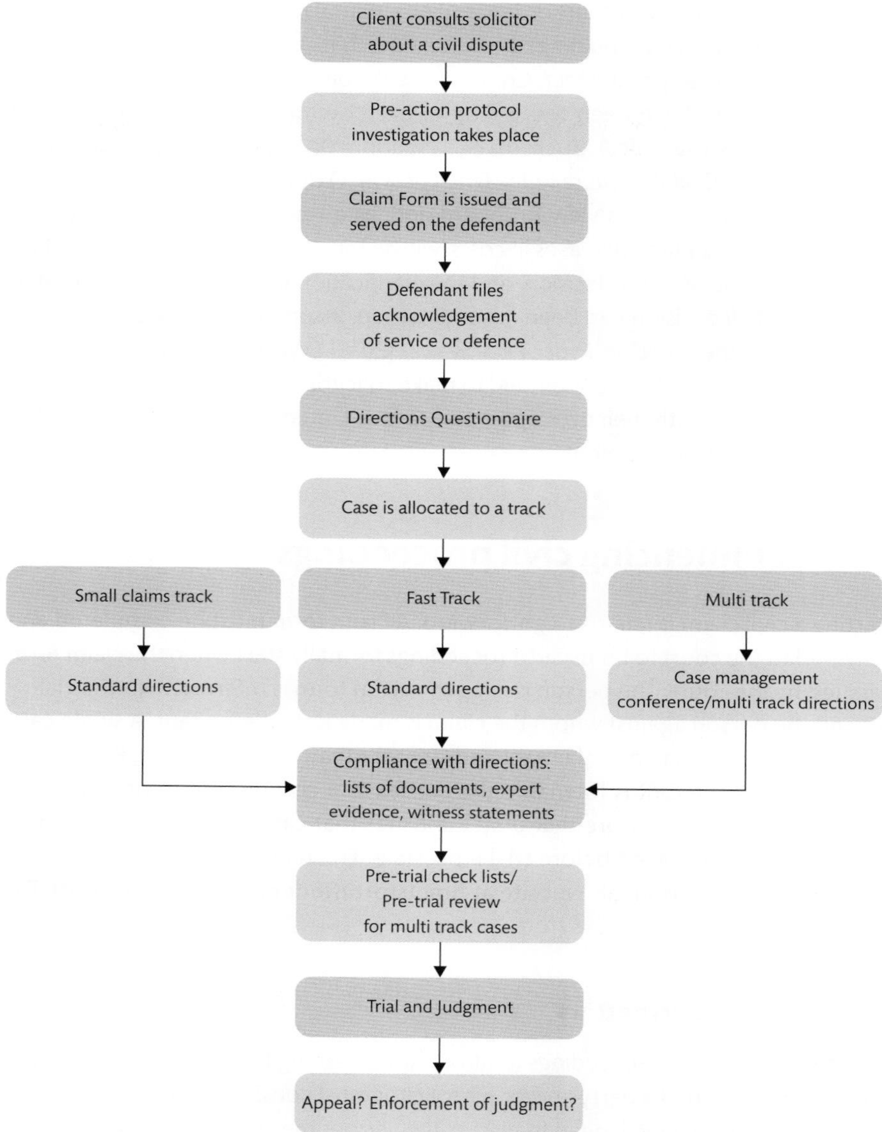

Diagram 15.1 Simplified diagram of the civil process

The legal basis for the claim is particularly important because there are time limits imposed by statute within which specific claim forms must be issued. If proceedings are not commenced within the applicable limitation period, the defendant will be able to argue that the claim is statute barred and should be discontinued, whatever the merits of the case.

Example

Under the Limitation Act 1980, in relation to a claim for breach of contract, the claimant must issue the claim form within six years from the date of the breach. In relation to a personal injury claim, the claimant must usually issue the claim form within three years of the date on which the personal injury was suffered. In disease cases, where the precise date of the injury is difficult to identify, the general rule is that proceedings must be issued within three years of the claimant's date of knowledge (see s.14 of the Limitation Act 1980).

Prior to commencing proceedings, the solicitor for the claimant will begin to collect evidence to support the claim. The solicitor will take statements from the client and from other witnesses of fact, such as a person who saw the accident take place (that is, not expert witnesses). Decisions will also be made about what other evidence, such as expert reports, should be obtained. Evidence to support the case might include: copies of written records, such as accident reports from the police or from an employer; photographs of the scene of an accident; and medical notes and records and evidence from an expert in a particular field, such as a consultant surgeon or an engineer. The solicitor and client must also consider whether some form of ADR may be more appropriate than litigation.

Alternative dispute resolution is considered in Chapter 16.

15.6.2 **Pre-action protocols**

One of the aims of the CPR is to encourage the early resolution of cases. For this reason, the CPR are supplemented by 'pre-action protocols'. Each protocol is applicable to a particular type of action, such as personal injury claims, defamation claims, housing disrepair cases, and judicial review. There is also now a practice direction on pre-action conduct (PDPAC), which contains a protocol that is applicable to *all* claims even if a specific protocol does not exist for the type of claim in hand. In his final report on the costs of civil litigation, published in January 2010, Jackson LJ recommended the retention of pre-action protocols but suggested that they should be reviewed and amended. The protocols have been revised and are regularly updated.

There is a section of the Courts and Tribunals Judiciary website which includes lots of interesting material dealing with the review, available at **www.judiciary.gov.uk/publications/review-of-civil-litigation-costs/**.

The funding of civil cases is considered in Chapter 11.

The pre-action protocols and the PDPAC protocol lay down rules and procedures to be followed before a claim form may be issued. They are the 'recipe' to get the case ready for issue or settlement. The main aim of the protocols is to encourage the exchange of early and full information, which is known as the 'cards on the table' approach. It is hoped that this will enable the parties to avoid litigation by settling the claim without recourse to court proceedings. Where litigation is unavoidable, early disclosure should support the efficient management of the case and the opportunity to narrow the issues that have to be decided at trial. To encourage the parties to abide by the protocols, the court may take account of any failure to comply when determining costs. The pre-action protocols can be found at **www.justice.gov.uk/civil/procrules_fin/menus/protocol.htm/**.

Most of the protocols require the claimant to notify the defendant of an intention to make a claim by sending a letter of claim. The defendant then has a period of time to investigate the claim and reply to the letter of claim before the claimant can commence court proceedings. For example, under the pre-action protocol for personal injury claims, the claimant should send two copies of a letter of claim to the defendant before proceedings are issued (one copy being for the defendant's insurer, if there is one). The letter of claim should summarise the facts and indicate the nature of any injuries and any financial loss. If neither the defendant nor the insurer replies within twenty-one days, the claimant is entitled to issue proceedings. If the defendant and/or the insurer reply to acknowledge the letter of claim, they then have up to three months to fully investigate the claim to ensure that a detailed letter of reply can be sent to the claimant to explain whether liability is admitted or denied and, if so, why it is denied. This process is designed to enable appropriate cases to be settled at an early stage and to afford time for defendants to investigate claims and make offers to settle, if appropriate, in the hope that very few cases will remain to be decided by the courts.

An exception to the letter of claim approach applies to low-value personal injury claims in road traffic cases, where the accident occurred on or after 30 April 2010, and low-value personal injury claims (public liability and employer's liability claims) after July 2013, where the protocols prescribe the use of an electronic portal to notify claims, file documents, and deal with the cases. The protocol, which came into force on 6 April 2015, can be found at **www.justice.gov.uk/courts/procedure-rules/civil/protocol/pre-action-protocol-for-low-value-personal-injury-employers-liability-and-public-liability-claims** and the portal can be found at: **www.claimsportal.org.uk**. The aim of the electronic handling of claims is to reduce costs and streamline the process. Cases that are dealt with through the portal are subject to fixed costs.

In addition to requiring the early notification of a potential claim, the pre-action protocols contain rules relating to expert evidence. This is because the expense of expert witnesses was a major reason for the high cost of civil litigation. For example, in a personal injury case, a medical expert will usually be required to provide evidence as to the nature and extent of the claimant's injuries and a prognosis for the future. Before the CPR, both parties would instruct expert witnesses and the fees of both experts would usually, ultimately, be borne by the losing party. Most CPR pre-action protocols now provide that before instructing an expert witness, a party should give the other party a list of suitable experts and agreement should be reached as to which expert should be instructed. The expectation is that opposing parties will then share the same expert, who is referred to in the CPR as a single joint expert. Expert evidence cannot be used at court unless the court has agreed that it can be adduced. Thus the court can decide whether an issue requires expert evidence to assist the decision-making process. For example, a judge may decide that she can come to her own decision regarding disability on the labour market from the medical evidence and does not require a report from an employment expert to explain the position.

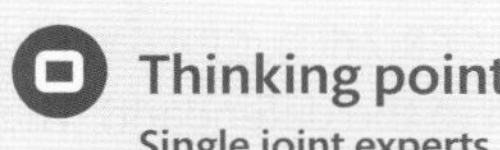

Thinking point
Single joint experts

Is the introduction of single joint experts consistent with the adversarial nature of the English legal system? If there is more than one valid point of view that an expert could hold on an issue, might the requirement for a single expert effectively pre-judge the case?

Finally, the pre-action protocols encourage the parties to settle claims rather than commence court proceedings. For example, under the pre-action protocol for personal injury claims, the parties are required to consider whether it is appropriate to make a pre-proceedings offer to settle the claim under CPR 36. If such an offer is made, the party making the offer must provide sufficient evidence or information to enable it to be properly considered. Part 36 offers can be made by both claimants and defendants. The protocol also provides that the parties should consider whether some other form of ADR, such as mediation, is appropriate.

CPR 36 offers, which may be made before or after proceedings commence, are considered at 15.10.

The Pre-Action Protocol for Low Value Injuries in Road Traffic Claims applies to claims where the value of personal injuries is between £1,000 and £10,000. It was introduced because these cases form a high proportion of all civil claims but were often subject to delays and disproportionate costs. The aim of the protocol is to ensure that claimants receive fair compensation in a timely manner and at a proportionate cost. It introduces strict timetables and fixed costs, which vary in amount depending upon the stage at which a case is settled.

15.6.3 **Claim forms**

Civil proceedings commence when a claim form is issued by the court at the claimant's request (CPR 7).

In accordance with CPR 16, the claim form must state the nature of the claim, specify the remedy sought, and, where money is sought, contain a statement of value. The claim form should confirm whether the claimant expects to recover:

- not more than £10,000;
- more than £10,000 but not more than £25,000;
- more than £25,000.

If the value of the claim is unknown, the claim form should state that the claimant cannot say how much is expected to be recovered.

The requirement for claimants to specify the broad value of the claim is set to enable the court to assign the case to the appropriate track and thus ensure that appropriate resources are allocated to the management of the case. The claimant must complete the necessary steps to serve the claim form on the defendant within four months of the claim form being issued by the court, although the court may extend this period in certain very limited circumstances set out in CPR 7.6(3). CPR 6 sets out the ways in which documents may be served (that is, given to the defendant). These include: personal service (by leaving the document with the relevant person); posting the document by first-class post or via a document exchange service (DX); or sending the document by fax or by other electronic communication. If the ***particulars of claim*** are not written on the claim form, these must either be served with the claim form in a separate document or served as a separate document within fourteen days of the service of the claim form. See **www.justice.gov.uk/courts/procedure-rules/civil/forms** for the claim form templates.

All statements of case have to be verified by a 'statement of truth'. The significance of this requirement is considered at 15.15.2.

Particulars of claim
The particulars of claim is the document in which the claimant sets out the basis of the case against the defendant. It will set out the allegations being made and the facts relied upon in support of those allegations. It must contain the matters specified in CPR 16 and the associated practice direction.

15.7 Responding to particulars of claim, acknowledgement of service, admissions, and default judgments

Once particulars of claim are served on a defendant under CPR 7, the defendant may, in accordance with CPR 9, respond by:

- filing or serving an admission i.e. accepting the responsibility to compensate the claimant (under CPR 14);
- filing a defence (under CPR 15);
- doing both of these if part of the claim is admitted; or
- filing an acknowledgement of service (under CPR 10).

15.7.1 Filing a defence or a reply

Filing
Where a party is required to file a document this means that the party is required to deliver the document to the court.

Where a defendant wishes to defend all or part of the claim, a defence should be ***filed***. CPR 16 provides that, among other matters, the defence must state which of the allegations in the particulars of claim the defendant denies, which of the allegations are admitted, and which allegations the defendant is unable to admit or deny but requires the claimant to prove. In relation to an allegation that is denied, it is not sufficient to simply deny the allegation being made; the defendant must set out the reasons why it is denied and set out his own version of events. Under CPR 15, the general rule is that a defence should be filed within fourteen days of service of particulars of claim.

When a defence is filed, copies are served on all other parties to the proceedings. On receipt of the defence, the claimant may then file a reply to the defence, although this is not compulsory. The claimant may file a reply if, for example, he wishes to allege further facts in response to the defence. Sometimes a defendant may make a counterclaim under CPR 20. A counterclaim means that the defendant makes his own claim against the claimant.

Example

Assume that a road traffic accident took place between cars driven by Clare and Dave. Both Clare's car and Dave's car were damaged. Clare brings civil proceedings against Dave. Clare alleges in the claim form and particulars of claim that the accident was caused by Dave's negligence. She seeks damages to compensate her for the cost of repairs to her vehicle. In response, Dave files a defence denying liability for the accident and putting forward his version of the accident circumstances. His defence includes a counterclaim in which he claims that the accident was caused by Clare's negligence and in which *he* seeks damages from *Clare*.

Where a defendant makes a counterclaim under CPR 20, the claimant should file a defence to it, just as a defendant must file a defence if he wishes to defend a claim.

15.7.2 Filing an acknowledgement of service

Where a defendant needs to have more time to file a defence, he may file an acknowledgement of service within fourteen days of service of the particulars of claim (CPR 10). He then has a further fourteen days in which to file his fully pleaded defence. The effect of these provisions is to give the defendant twenty-eight days in total in which to file a defence, instead of the basic fourteen days. The claimant and defendant can also agree in writing to allow the defendant a further twenty-eight days to file and serve the defence, giving the defendant a possible fifty-six days in total (CPR 15).

Default judgment
A default judgment is a judgment without trial against the party who has 'defaulted' by failing to file an acknowledgement of service or a defence as required.

15.7.3 Default judgments

Where a defendant files neither a defence nor an acknowledgement of service within the time periods laid down by the CPR, the claimant may be able to obtain judgment against the defendant. This is known as a ***default judgment*** (CPR 12).

Equally, the defendant may be able to obtain a default judgment against the claimant in the context of a counterclaim under CPR 20 where the claimant fails to file a defence within the time limit allowed by the rules.

CPR 23, which governs the making of applications for court orders, is considered at 15.12.

The claimant may obtain a default judgment by simply filing a *request* if the claim is either for a sum of money or for delivery of goods where the claim form gives the defendant the alternative of paying the value of the goods. In certain circumstances the claimant must *apply* for a default judgment—see CPR 12.

CPR 12 therefore provides an incentive to defendants to respond promptly when particulars of claim are served upon them. A defendant who fails to respond within the time limits prescribed by the CPR may find that the case is concluded by way of a default judgment. However, even if the claimant obtains a default judgment, that is not necessarily the end of the matter. CPR 13 gives the court discretion to set aside or vary a default judgment upon application by the defendant. The court may set aside or vary a default judgment if the defendant has a real prospect of successfully defending the claim, if there is some other good reason why it should be set aside or varied, or if there is some other good reason why the defendant should be allowed to defend the claim. The matters which the court should consider in exercising this discretion include whether the defendant applied to have the judgment set aside promptly.

15.7.4 **Formal admissions**

A party to civil proceedings does not have to contest the whole, or part, of the claim. A formal admission may be made whereby the truth of all or part of the other party's case is admitted. CPR 14 provides that an admission must be made in writing, such as in a statement of case or in a letter. The basic rule is that an admission should be made within fourteen days following service of the claim form, or within fourteen days of service of the particulars of claim. Where a party makes a formal admission, the other party may apply to the court for judgment on the admission.

The court's permission is usually required for a party to amend or withdraw a formal admission. Special rules concerning the making of formal admissions apply when the claimant only seeks the payment of money.

15.7.5 **Stay of proceedings**

What happens if the defendant has not served or filed an admission, a defence, or a counterclaim and the claimant has not entered or applied for a default judgment? CPR Part 15 provides that in these circumstances, once six months have expired from the deadline for filing a defence, the claim will be stayed. This means that the proceedings are formally suspended unless and until the stay is lifted. In effect, the proceedings sit on the court file and nothing happens. Either party may apply to have the stay lifted.

Under Part 20, a defendant who wishes to make a counterclaim against the claimant must file particulars of the counterclaim. If the defendant wishes to counterclaim against a party other than the claimant, an application must be made to the court for permission to have the other person added to the counterclaim as an additional party.

15.8 **Allocation and case management tracks**

Civil proceedings are allocated to one of three case management tracks, namely the small claims track, the fast track, or the multi-track. When deciding to which track the claim should be allocated the court will consider the value and complexity of the claim as well as the remedy sought and the views of the parties. Table 15.2 sets out the broad scope of the tracks.

The financial boundaries of the fast track have not been changed, even though the ceiling for the small claims track was increased from £5,000 to £10,000 in April 2013. There has been an expectation, since the Jackson Report, that further changes will be made to the boundaries, but currently they remain as set out in Table 15.2.

Some claims (for example, rent possession and mortgage possession) are not allocated to a track but the court may allocate them if they become defended. Otherwise, the parties will simply be given a date for a short hearing.

When a defence is filed by the defendant, a court officer will provisionally decide to which track the claim should be allocated and then notify the parties of this, along with some preliminary directions (CPR 26). The aim is to streamline the allocation process and ensure that, if possible, the administrative tasks required at the beginning of the case are centralised. Many steps, such as initial allocation and taking steps when parties do not return documents, are carried out by court staff rather than judges. The parties are required to complete a directions questionnaire (formerly called an allocation questionnaire) and file it by a specified date. The directions questionnaire asks the parties to answer questions about a variety of matters, such as:

- Has the solicitor explained to the client the importance of trying to settle the claim without court proceedings, the use of ADR, and the costs consequences of failing to do so?
- Do the parties require a stay (that is, a suspension of proceedings) for one month to attempt to settle the claim by informal discussion or ADR?
- Has there been compliance with the applicable pre-action protocol?
- What witnesses of fact will be called to give evidence?
- Is a single joint expert witness suitable for the case?
- What are the names of any experts/single joint experts relied upon?
- Do the parties want their experts to give oral evidence?
- Which track is most suitable for the claim?
- How long will the trial take?
- What case management directions are appropriate and required at this stage?
- What do the parties estimate their costs to be?

Table 15.2 Summary of CPR tracks

Name of Track	CPR	Financial value of case	Other considerations	Example of type of legal case dealt with in track
Small claims track	Part 27	Less than £10,000 (personal injury cases—damages for the injury must be less than £1,000).		Claim against hotel for compensation for an unsatisfactory holiday. Claim against a garage regarding incomplete repairs to a car
Fast track	Part 28	More than £10,000 but less than £25,000	The trial is not likely to last for more than one day. Oral expert evidence limited to two expert fields and to one expert per party in each expert field (provided the court has allowed the parties to instruct separate experts rather than a single joint expert)	Personal injury claim following a car crash—minor injury. Claim by a business for breach of contract by a supplier
Multi-track	Part 29	More than £25,000	Complex cases. Cases where remedies other than damages are sought. Cases where there is a wider public interest	Claim for damages against a health trust arising from clinical negligence. Commercial dispute involving multiple parties

Thinking point—-
Should ADR be compulsory?

The directions questionnaire specifically invites the parties to consider whether proceedings should be suspended to enable them to take part in ADR. The court also provides a free mediation service in cases on the small claims track. Should ADR, such as mediation, be a compulsory prerequisite to bringing a claim before the civil courts?

The purpose of the directions questionnaire is to assist the court in exercising its case management powers.

Usually the court will allocate the claim to a track when every defendant has filed a directions questionnaire or upon the expiry of the period for filing the questionnaires. The court may order a party to provide further information and/or may decide that it is necessary to hold an allocation hearing to determine the appropriate track in the presence of the parties.

The court does not have to allocate a case to the track to which it appears to belong by virtue of the monetary value of the claim. When deciding whether to allocate a claim to its normal track, CPR 26 requires the court to consider:

- the financial value of the claim;
- the nature of the remedy sought by the claimant;
- the complexity of the case;
- the number of parties;
- the value and complexity of any Part 20 claim (generally a counterclaim);
- the number of witnesses required to give oral evidence that may be required;
- the importance of the claim to anyone who is not a party;
- the views of the parties and their circumstances.

Where a claim has no financial value, that is, a remedy is sought, the court will allocate it to the track which it considers most suitable, taking into account the remainder of the matters referred to earlier.

15.8.1 **The small claims track**

Simplified procedures apply on the small claims track. This track was initially designed for parties to deal with low-value cases quickly and efficiently without the need for lawyers. Consequently, various parts of the CPR do not apply. The limit for small claims is now £10,000; arguably, this financial limit now means that more cases fall to be dealt with on the small claims track than were envisioned when the small claims process was set up. CPR 27 provides that where a claim is allocated to the small claims track:

- hearings will be informal;
- the strict rules of evidence will not apply;
- evidence need not be given under oath;
- the court may limit cross-examination;
- expert evidence, written or oral, may only be given at a hearing with the court's permission.

When a case is allocated to the small claims track, the court will generally fix a date for the trial and give standard directions to tell the parties when the formal steps in the case have to be taken (CPR 27). These include requiring the parties to file and serve copies of all documents on which they intend to rely at least fourteen days prior to trial. The parties will be given at least twenty-one days' notice of the trial date, unless they agree to accept less, and will be informed of the length of time allowed for the trial.

In appropriate circumstances, the court may find it necessary to give special directions as well as, or instead of, standard directions. A non-standard direction would be a direction that expert evidence is required in relation to a specific issue and that such evidence should be given by a single joint expert. For example, a report from an expert on interpreting tachographs might be required in a road traffic case involving a delivery lorry.

A small claims track case will usually have no pre-trial hearings. The first time the parties or their representatives appear before the court will therefore be the day of trial. However, the court may hold a preliminary hearing before the trial if it considers it necessary to ensure that the case is progressing satisfactorily. A preliminary hearing may be held, for example, to give special directions to the parties; to enable the court to dispose with the claim on the basis that a party has no real prospect of success at trial; or to enable the court to strike out a statement of case on the basis that it discloses no reasonable grounds for bringing or defending the claim.

The expectation is that the parties will attend trial in person. However, under CPR 27, where a party gives the court and the other parties at least seven days' written notice that he will *not* attend the trial and requests that the court decide the claim in his absence, the court will do so, taking into account both the party's statement of case and any documents that the party has filed and served, such as witness statements. If a claimant fails to attend the trial without giving such written notice the court may strike out the claim. If a defendant fails to attend the trial without giving written notice, the court may decide the claim solely on the basis of the claimant's evidence.

If neither party attends the trial and both parties fail to give written notice, the court may strike out both the claim and any defence or counterclaim. The conduct of the hearing, bearing in mind the more informal nature of the track, will depend upon the approach of the district judge. The final hearing may be conducted like a trial or the district judge may simply question the parties to establish the facts: this is more likely if the parties are acting in person.

Finally, it should be noted that CPR 27 imposes limits upon the costs that a party may recover where a claim is allocated to the small claims track. The basic position (under CPR 27 and CPR 27 PD) is that unless the party who is ordered to pay costs has acted unreasonably, the costs that may be recoverable from him essentially comprise:

- fixed costs in respect of issuing the claim;
- costs for legal advice and assistance (not exceeding £260) if the proceedings involve a claim for an injunction or an order for specific performance;
- court fees and expenses incurred by the other party or a witness in travelling or staying away from home (limited to £95 per day per person);
- a sum for loss of earnings by the other party or a witness;
- a sum not exceeding £750 in respect of an expert's report.

15.8.2 **The fast track**

If a case is allocated to the fast track, the court will give case management directions and will set a timetable for the steps that are to be taken prior to the trial (CPR 28). The parties will be required to file a directions questionnaire; the questionnaire is in the same format for fast track and multi-track cases. The proposed directions should be agreed between the parties if possible. In fast track cases the directions should follow those set out in CPR 28.

When the case is allocated, the court will either fix the trial date or fix a period of up to three weeks within which the trial will take place (the 'trial window'). There will usually be a period of no more than thirty weeks between the giving of directions and the trial. Case management directions given at this time will relate to matters such as disclosure of documents (see 15.9), service of witness statements (see 15.15.2), and expert evidence (see 15.15.4). A typical timetable for preparing a fast track case, running from the date of the notice of allocation, would be as set out in Table 15.3.

A pre-trial checklist (listing questionnaire) deals with matters such as confirming that the party has complied with directions, how many witnesses the party intends to call, questions relating to expert evidence, and whether the estimate of the time needed for the trial has changed since the directions questionnaires were filed. This is, in effect, the court checking to make sure that the parties have done their homework!

Table 15.3 Timeline for directions

	Time frame: Calculated from date of allocation	Four weeks	Ten weeks	Fourteen weeks	Twenty weeks	Twenty-two weeks	Thirty weeks
Allocation	Action required	Disclosure of documents	Exchange witness statements	Exchange expert reports	Pre-trial checklists sent by court	Parties return checklists to court	Trial

Following the date for filing pre-trial checklists, the court will confirm the trial date, give any directions for the trial which it considers appropriate (including a trial timetable), and specify any further steps that must be taken before the trial, such as agreeing a core bundle of documents for use at trial.

The expectation is that directions at both allocation and listing stages will be given without a hearing (CPR 28 PD). Thus, as in small claims cases, the first time the parties or their representatives appear before the court will usually be at trial. However, the court does have the power to hold pre-trial hearings in fast track cases if necessary. A hearing may be necessary, for example, to discuss any non-standard directions that may be required to ensure proper preparation of the case, or where a party has failed to comply with directions that have already been given.

Fast track costs will normally be assessed summarily by the judge at the end of the trial. Under CPR 45.38, the fast track trial costs which the court may award are as follows:

- £485 where the value of the claim does not exceed £3,000;
- £690 where the value of the claim is more than £3,000 but does not exceed £10,000;

Key point

Trial costs are, essentially, the advocate's fee. All other reasonable costs are also recoverable. In his report on the costs of civil litigation, Jackson LJ proposed that all costs on the fast track should be fixed for certain types of case, including personal injury cases. In other types of fast track case, he suggested that costs should be limited. The report argued that this would promote certainty and ensure that costs are always proportionate. Fixed costs have been introduced in personal injury cases.

- £1,035 where the value of the claim is more than £10,000 but does not exceed £15,000;
- £1,650 where the value of the claim exceeds £15,000.

CPR 45 also sets out what fixed costs can be awarded in a variety of other claims such as road traffic accidents and low-value personal injury claims.

15.8.3 **The multi-track**

When a case is allocated to the multi-track, the court will either give case management directions and set a timetable for the steps to be taken prior to the trial, or will arrange a case management conference or a pre-trial review (CPR 29). It will also deal with costs management, or budgeting. Budgeting now applies to all multi-track cases unless the case is worth more than £10m or the court orders otherwise. The parties have to submit a budget, in form 'H', for the projected costs of the continued conduct of the case, for the court's approval.

As soon as is practicable the court will fix the trial date or the trial period. When the court does so, the parties will be notified and a date will be specified for filing a pre-trial checklist. If the parties agree case management proposals and the court considers that they are suitable, the court may approve the proposals without holding a case management hearing and may give appropriate directions. If a party wishes to vary the trial date, the trial period, or the date fixed by the court for a case management conference, a pre-trial review, or the return of a pre-trial checklist, the permission of the court will be required. Other directions may be varied by agreement between the parties, provided that the trial date is not moved.

The matters considered at a case management hearing might include the disclosure and inspection of documents and what expert evidence is required (CPR 29 PD). The *Queen's Bench Guide* and the *Chancery Guide* indicate that at a pre-trial review, the court will review the state of preparation of the respective parties, will deal with outstanding matters, and will give any necessary directions (such as directions concerning the order in which witnesses will be called). The *Guides* are on the CPR website at **www.justice.gov.uk/courts/procedure-rules/civil/court_guides**. In multi-track cases, the parties will be required to complete pre-trial checklists within time limits specified by the court. These checklists deal with matters such as whether trial bundles (the agreed set of documents to be used in court at the trial) have been completed and which witnesses of fact and expert witnesses are to be called, as well as asking the parties to provide estimates of the minimum and maximum length of the trial.

After the parties have filed completed pre-trial checklists, or after the court has held a listing hearing or a pre-trial review, the court will set a trial timetable. In accordance with CPR 39, the court should consult with the parties when setting a trial timetable.

If the successful party has completed the case within the stated budget, it is likely that the trial judge will simply allow the costs without further process. If the party has overstepped the budget then it is likely that costs will subsequently be assessed by a costs judge via a detailed assessment of costs under CPR 47.

15.9 The disclosure and inspection of documents

Documentation to support the claim being made is vital. One of the main aims of the CPR is to encourage openness and cooperation between parties. The key to this includes ensuring that all parties to civil proceedings have access to relevant documents enabling them to make informed decisions about the merits of their case. Some of the documents may be in the hands of an opponent. The requirement to disclose documents is a long-standing feature of the civil justice system in England and Wales and, arguably, the Woolf reforms refined this requirement rather than extended it.

Documents
Under CPR 31, documents does not refer only to paper hardcopy documents but also anything in which information is recorded, including, for example, information stored on a computer.

CPR 31 concerns the disclosure and inspection of ***documents*** and applies to claims that are allocated either to the fast track or to the multi-track.

Previously, where the court ordered disclosure under CPR 31, this meant standard disclosure. Standard disclosure required a party to disclose:

- the documents upon which he relies;
- any documents which adversely affect his case;
- any documents which adversely affect the case of another party;
- any documents which support the case of another party.

A party was under a *duty* to make a reasonable search for documents of the latter three descriptions. However, under the Jackson reformed rules standard disclosure no longer applies in multi-track cases, except in personal injury cases. The idea is to prevent pointless lists of copious documents being disclosed and to make sure that the parties concentrate on the issues in the case that are disputed. A list of options will be considered by the court to ensure that relevant documents only need to be disclosed, dealing with the substantial issues in dispute.

Disclosure of a document means stating that the document either exists or has existed. A party gives disclosure by serving a list on the other parties which identifies the relevant documents. In most cases, CPR 31 also provides that the other party then has the right to inspect the document (that is, to have a copy and read it).

A party may claim that it is his right to withhold inspection of a document, for example, as a result of legal professional privilege. Legal professional privilege applies to confidential communications between a party and his legal representatives which were made for the purpose of giving or obtaining legal advice. It also extends to confidential communications with third parties which were made in connection with litigation or in contemplation of litigation. A party does not have to allow inspection of privileged documents, although they will have been disclosed. It is important not to confuse 'disclosure', the process of informing the other side that a document exists, with 'inspection', which is the process by which a party can have a copy of the document or inspect the original. Where a party believes that the documents disclosed by another party do not fulfil that party's duty to give the appropriate disclosure, application can be made to the court for an order for specific disclosure, requiring the other party to disclose specified documents, to carry out a search for specified documents, and to disclose any documents located in consequence of the search. CPR 31.7 makes it clear that the duty to search for a document is subject to a reasonableness test based on a number of factors, such as the location of the documents and the number involved. The court will consider whether it is proportionate to order a party to make a search. The duty to give the appropriate agreed disclosure continues throughout the proceedings and, consequently, where documents to which the duty applies come to a party's attention following service of the list of documents, the other parties must be notified.

Thinking point

Which documents should be disclosed?

Why do you think a party does not have to disclose documents containing communications with his solicitor for the purpose of seeking advice about his case? Is it in the public interest for clients to be able to speak freely to their lawyers without risk of disclosure?

15.9.1 **Without prejudice communications**

Negotiations with a view to settlement in the context of civil proceedings may be subject to 'without prejudice privilege'. The without prejudice privilege arises where the purpose of the negotiations is to resolve a dispute between the parties. Where it applies, the content of the negotiations is not admissible in evidence unless both parties agree to waive the privilege. Thus, where there are negotiations on a without prejudice basis aimed at settling a dispute but no settlement is reached, the trial judge cannot be told of any admissions or concessions that were made by any party during the course of the negotiations. The reason for this rule is to encourage the parties to enter into correspondence with a view to settling their dispute without fear that anything that is said could later be used against them.

The privilege may arise whether or not correspondence is headed 'without prejudice', although it is good practice to use this heading when parties intend to negotiate on a without prejudice basis (*Rush and Tompkins v Greater London Council* [1988] 3 WLR 939—a case arising from a construction dispute). Conversely, the privilege will not arise where a party makes clear that negotiations are taking place on an 'open' basis (*Dixon's Stores Group Ltd v Thames Television plc* [1993] 1 All ER 349. In this case the correspondence was not marked as being without prejudice.) There are also a number of exceptions to the privilege. For example, where a negotiating party makes an offer which is expressed to be without prejudice except as to costs, the privilege does not prevent the judge from considering the content of the negotiations in relation to the issue of costs (*Cutts v Head* [1984] Ch 290).

15.10 **Part 36 offers**

Parties to civil litigation should try to settle claims without recourse to the court. It is likely that negotiations, both formal and informal, will take place throughout the currency of a case. Part 36 is a formal process to make an offer to settle.

Either the claimant or the defendant may make an offer to settle the claim under CPR 36. Such an offer is referred to as a 'Part 36 offer'. If the offer is accepted, the defendant must pay the agreed sum to the claimant within fourteen days. In order to encourage parties to settle disputes, CPR 36 provides that there may be costs consequences where either party unreasonably refuses to accept an offer.

A Part 36 offer must comply with the strict requirements laid down by CPR 36. For example, it must be made in writing, must state that it is intended to have the consequences set out in Part 36, and must specify a period of at least twenty-one days within which the other party may accept the offer. Failure to comply exactly with the requirements will result in the defective Part 36 offer having no Part 36 effect. A form is available, although its use is not compulsory, to ensure that all formalities are complied with. This can be found at **hmctsformfinder.justice.gov.uk/courtfinder/forms/n242a-eng.pdf**.

Example

Carrie claims damages for breach of contract. Daniel denies that there has been a breach of contract but is nevertheless prepared to settle the case to avoid the time and expense of going to court. He makes a Part 36 offer in the sum of £30,000. Carrie does not accept this offer and the case proceeds to trial. At trial, the judge finds that there has been a breach of contract and awards Carrie damages in the sum of £22,000.

The general rule is that the successful party is entitled to his costs (see 15.16). However, although Carrie has succeeded in proving her claim for breach of contract, the outcome is less advantageous for her than it would have been if she had accepted the Part 36 offer. This means that she must pay Daniel's costs from the date that his offer expired.

If the defendant makes a Part 36 offer which is not accepted by the claimant, the case will proceed to trial in the usual way. If after trial the claimant fails to obtain a judgment that is more advantageous than the Part 36 offer, the general rule is that the defendant is entitled to costs and interest upon those costs, from the date when the ***relevant period*** expired. CPR 36.17 specifies an additional amount to be paid by defendants who do not accept a claimant's Part 36 offer and then fail to beat that offer at trial. The uplift can be substantial. For awards up to half a million pounds an extra 10 per cent is added and for sums between £500,000 and £1m pounds an extra 5 per cent is added, up to a limit of £75,000. Clearly this provision is designed to ensure that defendants consider claimants' offers very carefully and that claimants pitch their offers at an appropriate level.

Relevant period
The relevant period is the period of at least twenty-one days, specified in the Part 36 offer, within which the offer may be accepted.

The claimant may also make a Part 36 offer. If this is not accepted by the defendant and the judgment after trial is equal to, or less than, the sum specified in the claimant's offer, the general rule is that the claimant is entitled to interest on the whole or part of the money awarded for some or all of the period following expiry of the relevant period. The claimant will also be entitled to costs on an ***indemnity basis*** (and interest on those costs) from the date on which the relevant period expired.

Indemnity basis
Where costs are assessed on a standard basis, the court will only allow costs that have been reasonably incurred, are reasonable in amount, and are proportionate to the matters in issue. Where costs are assessed on an indemnity basis, the court will still only allow costs that are reasonably incurred but will give the benefit of the doubt to the receiving party if any items are in dispute. Furthermore, the proportionality test does not apply.

CPR 36 provides that a Part 36 offer is made without prejudice except as to costs. Thus, subject to exceptions, for example where the proceedings have been stayed following acceptance of the offer, the fact that the offer has been made should not be communicated to the trial judge until the case has been decided.

The Part 36 procedures are designed to provide a strong incentive to parties to settle their disputes. However, Jackson LJ was of the view that Part 36 does not go far enough. In order to provide an even greater incentive to defendants to settle cases, his report recommended that, where a defendant fails to beat a claimant's Part 36 offer, the amount that the claimant recovers should be enhanced by 10 per cent. This measure was implemented in CPR 36.14. In many cases this will have a significant impact and concentrate the minds of the lawyers during the conduct of the case. Opponents of this measure argue that it places defendants under too much pressure to settle cases even though their defence may have merit. It is another indication of the courts' intention to control and limit litigation to the most contentious matters.

15.11 **Qualified one-way costs shifting**

In April 2013, under CPR 44.13 to CPR 44.17 qualified one-way costs shifting (QOCS) was introduced for personal injury cases. The rule is that the claimant will not be required to pay the defendant's costs if the claim fails, but if the claim succeeds the defendant must pay the claimant's costs in the usual way.

The aim of QOCS is to avoid the need for the claimant to take out after-the-event insurance. The Legal Aid, Sentencing and Punishment of Offenders Act 2012, which came into force in relation to insurance policies taken out after 31 March 2013, made the premiums non-recoverable from the defendant. It is argued that the disadvantage to defendant insurers of not recovering costs in cases that they win is outweighed by not having to pay after-the-event insurance premiums when they lose.

The aim of the reform is to ensure that claimants in personal injury cases can proceed in the knowledge that they will not be liable for defendants' costs and therefore it is no longer necessary to take out after-the-event insurance.

However, QOCS does not sit comfortably alongside Part 36. A claimant who is successful at trial but fails to beat a defendant's Part 36 offer will be ordered to pay all of the defendant's costs from the date of expiry of the time for accepting the offer, although the order is only enforceable, without leave of the court, up to the level of damages awarded by the court. Thus the claimant may actually receive no payment of damages because the awarded sum has to be used to pay the defendant's costs. The effect of QOCS is to ensure that claimants and defendants will be extra careful to consider all aspects and consequences of Part 36 offers.

15.12 **Applying for court orders**

CPR 23 deals with the process for applying for court orders. The CPR and the directions and timetables imposed by the court are designed to cover most eventualities that arise in the course of proceedings. However, any party to the proceedings has the option of applying to the court for a specific order should it become necessary. In other words, if a party wants something done as part of the litigation process, and agreement cannot be reached with the opponent, an application can be made to ask the court to make an order.

Default judgment was considered at 15.7.3. Summary judgment will be considered at 15.13.

For example, where a party has failed to comply with a standard rule or direction, the opponent may apply under CPR 23 for an order that *unless* the respondent complies with the relevant rule or order, his claim will be struck out or judgment will be entered. This is known as an 'unless order' (see 15.5). The CPR 23 procedures must also be used to make an application for default judgment or summary judgment. Application may also be made for an extension of time to take a step in the proceedings, to ask for permission to instruct an expert, or to instruct an alternative expert. Under the new, tough court regime, an application for the latter may well be refused. It is important not to confuse default judgment and summary judgment.

A party may also apply for an order for an interim remedy. The court may grant a variety of interim remedies, such as:

- ***interim injunctions;***
- ***freezing injunctions;***
- ***search orders.***

Interim injunctions *An injunction is an order that a person does something or refrains from doing something. An example would be an injunction restraining a party from causing a nuisance. An interim injunction, as the name suggests, is a temporary injunction which takes effect pending the final decision in a case.*

Freezing injunctions *Sometimes a party may fear that his opponent will dispose of assets prior to the final decision in a case and thereby evade justice. In such a case the concerned party may apply to the court for a freezing injunction to prevent his opponent from removing his assets from the jurisdiction or from dealing with assets either within or outside the jurisdiction. Freezing injunctions were formerly known as* Mareva *injunctions, after* Mareva Compania Naviera SA v International Bulk Carriers SA *[1975] 2 Lloyd's Rep 509.*

Search orders *A party may also apply for a search order, which allows him to enter premises for the purposes of preserving evidence. Search orders were formerly known as Anton Piller orders due to the case in which civil search warrants were first established,* Anton Piller K.G. v Manufacturing Processes Ltd *[1976] Ch 55 (CA).*

A party seeking any of these types of interim remedy must abide by the rules in both CPR 23 and 25.

CPR 23 provides that, whatever the nature of the court order that is applied for, an application notice must be served by the party seeking the order (the applicant) on the person against whom the order is sought (the respondent). Service should take place as soon as possible after the application notice is filed and, unless the CPR or a practice direction or court order provide otherwise, must take place at least three days before the court deals with the application. Thus, the opposing party will usually be aware of the application at least three days before it is heard. An application notice must state both the order that the applicant seeks and why the order is sought. When served, it should be accompanied by a copy of any supporting witness statement(s).

In limited circumstances, an application may be made without notice being given to the other party. Applications without notice were formerly known as *'ex parte'* applications.

Thinking point

Search orders and freezing orders

Consider the reasons why a party might apply for a search order or a freezing order. Why might it be desirable to make such an application on a without notice basis? If the opposing party was aware in advance that a certain order might be made, might he frustrate the purpose of the order, for example by disposing of evidence that might be found if a search order was executed?

The court may also make an order on its own initiative without an application. In such circumstances, any party affected by the order may apply for it to be varied or set aside.

An application for an order may be dealt with by the court without a hearing if the parties agree the terms of the order, if the parties agree that there should not be a hearing, or if the court does not consider that a hearing would be appropriate. Moreover, where a party fails to attend the hearing of an application, the court may proceed in the absence of that party. Often hearings for interim orders will be dealt with by telephone conference call, which saves the costs of the parties attending court in person.

15.13 **Summary judgment**

Under CPR 24, the court may be able to dispose of a claim or an issue without holding a trial by entering judgment on a claim or dismissing the claim. This is known as summary judgment. The court may grant summary judgment against a claimant or a defendant where the claim or defence has no real prospect of success, provided that there is no other compelling reason for holding a trial. Do not confuse summary judgment with default judgment: see 15.7.3.

15.14 **Civil trial**

If attempts to settle a case are unsuccessful, the ultimate conclusion to resolve outstanding issues in civil proceedings is a trial. Under CPR 39, the general rule is that civil trials and other hearings (for example, applications for interim remedies) will be held in public. There are exceptions where, for example, the hearing involves confidential information. The court also possesses a general discretion to hold a hearing in private in the interests of justice.

Under CPR 39, the court is entitled to conduct a trial in the absence of a party. Alternatively, if neither party attends, the court may strike out the proceedings. If the claimant does not attend, the court may strike out both the claim and the claimant's defence to any counterclaim; if the defendant does not attend, the court may strike out the defence and/or any counterclaim. Where the court gives judgment or makes an order against a party who failed to attend the trial, the party may make an application to the court to have the judgment or court order set aside. The application must be supported by evidence. The court may only grant such an application if the party made the application promptly, had a good reason for failing to attend, and had a reasonable prospect of succeeding at the trial.

Thinking point

Hearings in public

Why do you think that court hearings are held in public? Is it important that justice is not just done but seen to be done? It would assist your understanding of the court process if you could find time to attend your local court to see justice in action. You do not have to make an appointment—just turn up and go in. Lists of the cases being heard will be posted on the wall in the foyer or waiting room, although the lists will only mention the name of the case and the nature of the hearing, not the detail or subject matter of the case. Speak to the court usher, who will be able to help you. You can find your local court at **hmctscourtfinder.justice.gov.uk/hmcts/**.

A civil trial which is allocated to the fast track or the multi-track will usually start with an opening speech on behalf of the claimant, although where the judge has read the papers he may decide to dispense with an opening speech (CPR 28 PD and 29 PD).

The claimant's witnesses will give evidence first. The rules provide that a witness statement will usually stand as the witness's evidence in chief; in other words, the witness will not be required to repeat the contents of the statement but will be cross-examined on it. However, a witness may be permitted to expand upon the witness statement or to give evidence in chief about matters that have arisen since the witness statement was served (CPR 32). The witness may be cross-examined on behalf of the defendant and may then be re-examined on behalf of the claimant. The same procedure is then followed in relation to any defence witnesses.

The trial will conclude with closing speeches, first on behalf of the defendant and then on behalf of the claimant. Finally, judgment will be given by the judge. Usually this will be given immediately but in complex cases the judge may reserve judgment to a later date. In the context of a fast track trial, judgment will often be followed immediately by the summary assessment of costs by the trial judge. Where the trial is long or complex, however, the judge may decide to give judgment on costs at a later date. Under CPR 40, a judgment takes effect either on the day it is given or on a later date specified by the court. A party is usually required to comply with a judgment or order for the payment of money within fourteen days.

In general, civil trials take place without a jury, but an application for jury trial may be made within twenty-eight days of the defence being served in the context of claims of fraud, libel, slander, malicious prosecution, and false imprisonment (Senior Courts Act 1981 s.69; County Courts Act 1984 s.66; CPR 28). Where trial by jury takes place in the County Court, the jury consists of eight jurors, rather than the usual twelve (County Courts Act 1984 s.67).

15.14.1 **Burden and standard of proof in civil proceedings**

In civil proceedings, a party who raises a fact in issue bears the legal burden of proving it (*Wakelin v London and South Western Railway* [1886] 12 AC 41). Thus, for example, in the context of a civil claim for battery, the claimant bears the burden of proving the elements of battery. If the defendant merely asserts in his defence that the battery did not take place, the defendant does not bear the legal burden of proving this defence, as it merely amounts to a denial of the claimant's assertion. If, however, the defendant raises new facts in issue, such as alleging that he acted in self-defence, the defendant bears the burden of proving the defence (*Ashley v Chief Constable of Sussex Police* [2007] 1 WLR 398).

The *standard* of proof in civil proceedings is 'on the balance of probabilities'. This means that a party discharges the legal burden of proof if he persuades the court that the facts asserted are more probably true than not (*Miller v Minister of Pensions* [1947]

2 All ER 372). This is a lower standard of proof than the criminal standard of 'beyond reasonable doubt'. Do not confuse the *burden* of proof and the *standard* of proof (even the BBC does this sometimes).

This does not necessarily mean that the court must decide in favour of one party and against the other, as it may be that neither party's version of events is credible. In *Rhesa Shipping v Edmunds* [1985] 1 WLR 948, a ship sank in the Mediterranean. The cause of the sinking was unknown. Its owner was insured against 'the perils of the sea', but the insurance did not cover loss due to wear and tear. The insurers refused to pay the insurance claim and the owner issued proceedings in the civil courts. At trial, the owner put forward the theory that the ship had struck a submerged submarine (a peril of the sea). The insurers suggested that prolonged wear and tear caused the hull of the ship to open up.

The trial judge found that the claimant's and the defendant's versions of events were both improbable. However, he preferred the claimant's evidence, so gave judgment for the claimant. On appeal, the House of Lords held that the judge did not have to decide between the two explanations. The burden of proving that the loss was caused by a peril of the sea was on the claimant. If the trial judge, having heard all of the evidence, was not satisfied that the claimant's version of events was more probably true than not, then the claim should have been dismissed.

Some criminal offences are also capable of being tried as civil wrongs. For example, a battery is both a criminal offence and a tort. (See also the example given at 15.1.) Where a *serious* allegation of a criminal nature, such as fraud or rape, is alleged in the context of civil proceedings, questions have arisen as to what the standard of proof should be. The courts have held that, in a civil case, the standard of proof remains proof on the balance of probabilities. It has been suggested that, given the rarity of such conduct compared to that of an ordinary civil wrong, it would take strong evidence to persuade the court that the facts alleged were more probably true than not (*Re H and Others (Minors) (Sexual Abuse: Standard of Proof)* [1996] 2 WLR 8). However, in *Re B (Children)* [2008] UKHL 35, the House of Lords again emphasised that the standard of proof remains proof on the balance of probabilities.

In certain exceptional circumstances, the criminal standard of proof (that is, proof beyond reasonable doubt) is applicable in civil proceedings. The best known example of this is provided by proceedings for civil ***contempt of court***.

Contempt of court
Contempt of court means conduct which interferes with the administration of justice. Contempt may arise in the context of civil or criminal proceedings.

In *Re Bramblevale* [1970] Ch 128, a civil case, the appellant's company went into liquidation. The liquidator asked the appellant for copies of the company's books and papers. The appellant at first admitted that he had these but later claimed that they had been destroyed in a road traffic accident. He was ordered on several occasions to produce the papers but only produced some of them. He was eventually committed to prison by a judge for contempt of court. In this case the contempt proceedings were in the context of a civil case and were determined by a civil court. However, it was held that proceedings for contempt were always criminal in nature because the liberty of the individual is at stake.

15.15 **Evidence in civil proceedings**

CPR 32 to 35 contain rules concerning a variety of other aspects of civil evidence, the major examples of which are considered below.

15.15.1 **Exclusionary discretion**

CPR 32.1 empowers the civil court to control the evidence that it receives by giving directions as to the issues on which it requires evidence, the nature of the evidence required, and the way in which the evidence should be given. Rule 32.1 also allows a judge to exclude evidence and to limit cross-examination. This rule is therefore an important example of the court's power to manage its cases. The court should, of course, exercise this discretion so as to further the overriding objective.

15.15.2 **The evidence of witnesses in civil proceedings**

Under CPR 32, the general rule is that the evidence of witnesses will be proved at trial by their oral testimony. At a hearing other than a trial, the general rule is that evidence will be given by written statements. A party may also rely upon matters set out in a statement of case or an application notice if verified by a statement of truth (see the following Key Point). At a hearing other than a trial, a party may apply to the court for permission to cross-examine the person whose written evidence is relied upon.

 **Key point**

CPR 22 requires that various documents (including statements of case, witness statements, and experts' reports) be verified by a statement of truth. A statement of truth is essentially a sentence stating that the party believes the facts stated to be true. The statement of truth must be signed by the person making it. Where a *statement of case* is not verified by a statement of truth, CPR 22 provides that the court may strike it out and, until struck out, it may not be relied upon as evidence of the matters in it. Where a *witness statement* is not verified by a statement of truth, CPR 22 provides that the court may direct that it is not admissible in evidence. The wording of the statement of truth will be different when a solicitor is signing on behalf of a client, instead of the client himself.

Where a witness is called to give evidence in civil proceedings, the general position, under CPR 32, is that the witness' written statement will stand as his evidence in chief. See 15.14 for more detail.

Although a witness statement will often be drafted by a solicitor, it should be in the witness's own words and be written in the first person. An excellent checklist and guide to drafting witness statements can be found at **civillitigationbrief.wordpress.com/2014/01/10/drafting-witness-statements-that-comply-with-the-rules-a-checklist-too-important-to-ignore/**.

The court will give the parties directions about the service of witness statements on the other parties. Where a party fails to comply with such directions as to service, the witness may only be called to give evidence with the court's permission.

Where a party who wishes to call a witness is unable to obtain a statement from that witness, the court may permit him to serve a witness summary. This is a summary of the evidence that would be in the witness statement or a summary of the matters about which the witness is to be questioned.

The provisions concerning the service of witness statements and witness summaries are necessary to ensure openness in civil proceedings. The parties should be aware of what evidence will be called. A party to litigation will not be permitted to ambush their opponent by failing to disclose the nature and detail of a witness' evidence in advance. Part 32 of the CPR allows the court to define and limit the scope and extent of the factual evidence that may be called, taking into account the overriding objective. This is another area in which the court's case management powers will be demonstrated.

15.15.3 **Witness summonses and the competence and compellability of witnesses**

There may sometimes be doubt as to the capacity of a witness to give evidence. A decision must then be made as to whether the witness in question is 'competent' to give evidence. Alternatively, a witness may be reluctant to testify and the issue may arise as to whether such a witness can be compelled to give evidence.

In civil proceedings the test of competence is the common law test of whether the witness can understand the nature and significance of the oath (*R v Hayes* [1977] 1 WLR 234). Consequently, an adult witness who is unable to satisfy this test, such as a witness who has a very low IQ, will not be competent to testify.

Conversely, a child witness in civil proceedings (someone aged under eighteen) may still be competent to give unsworn evidence, even if he is incapable of understanding the nature and significance of the oath (s.96 of the Children Act 1989). A child may give unsworn evidence provided that he understands that he has a duty to speak the truth and has sufficient understanding to justify his evidence being heard.

The court may issue a witness summons to secure the attendance of a witness at court (CPR 34). A witness summons may require the witness to attend to give evidence or to produce documents. Thus, a reluctant witness may be compelled to attend court, although whether this is desirable will have to considered by the party compelling the witness. A reluctant witness may be worse than no witness at all.

Where a witness fails to attend a High Court hearing in compliance with a witness summons, he may be liable to be punished for contempt of court, which may include a prison sentence (CPR Sch.1 RSC Order 52). Where a witness fails to attend the County Court hearing in compliance with a witness summons, ness may be liable to a fine (s.55 of the County Courts Act 1984 and CPR CR Order 34).

15.15.4 **Expert evidence in civil proceedings**

The admissibility of expert evidence in civil proceedings is governed by s.3 of the Civil Evidence Act 1972. Expert evidence will be admissible to provide the court with information that falls outside the court's experience and knowledge, provided that the witness possesses the requisite skill that the court lacks. For example, in a personal injury case an orthopaedic surgeon may be called to give evidence about the nature and extent of a claimant's leg injury.

However, both CPR 35 and CPR 32.1 (which was considered at 15.15.1) confer broad case management powers upon the civil courts, enabling the judge to exclude or limit expert evidence and to determine the means by which such evidence will be given. CPR 35 provides that expert evidence should be restricted to that which is reasonably required. The parties must also provide the court with an estimate of the cost of the proposed expert evidence. In line with the overriding objective of proportionality, the court will then consider whether the costs are reasonable and proportionate to the matters in issue. The general rule is that expert evidence will be given by written report and the court's permission is required if an expert is to be called to give oral evidence. The court may also set out precisely what issues the expert evidence should address: this may be limited to one narrow point. The court is also empowered to limit the amount of the expert's fees and expenses that the instructing party can recover from other parties.

Further, the court may direct that expert evidence in relation to an issue must be given by a single joint expert (that is, an expert who is instructed by all of the parties). Where the parties cannot agree upon a single joint expert, the court may select one from a list prepared or identified by the parties or may direct some other manner of selecting the single joint expert. As well as identifying the name and area of expertise of an expert that a party wants to instruct, the cost of the expert must also be disclosed before permission is given to rely upon that expert.

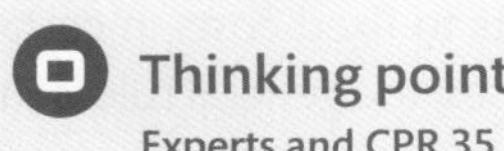

Thinking point

Experts and CPR 35

The power of the courts to direct that the parties instruct a single joint expert was a major change introduced by the CPR. Critics argued that to force opposing parties to use the same witness was to usurp the adversarial process. However, there are many who regard the single joint expert as one of the successes of the CPR. There has even been support for the suggestion that court-appointed experts should be introduced. Court-appointed experts are common in civil law jurisdictions.

Under CPR 35, a party is entitled to put written questions either to expert witnesses instructed by other parties or to a single joint expert within twenty-eight days of receiving the expert's report. The expert's answers form part of the report. Where each party is permitted to instruct his own expert, the court may direct that a discussion between experts take place in order to identify and discuss the issues and, where possible, to reach an agreed opinion.

Thinking point

'Hot tubbing'

In Australia, a practice known as 'hot tubbing', or concurrent evidence, takes place between experts. Instead of giving evidence sequentially, experts sit in the witness box together at trial and the judge chairs a discussion between them. Therefore the experts help the court to reach a conclusion together, rather than being pitted against one another. Concurrent expert evidence may be directed under PD 35.11. Is this another way in which the civil justice system is becoming less adversarial?

CPR 35 makes provision concerning the contents of experts' reports and also makes it clear that the overriding duty of an expert witness is to the court and not to the party who instructed him. Thus, for example, CPR 35 PD makes clear that an expert should consider all material facts, including those which detract from his opinion.

The court will give directions concerning the disclosure of experts' reports and simultaneous disclosure will normally be required. Under CPR 35, where a party fails to disclose an expert's report, the expert evidence will only be admissible with the court's permission.

15.16 **Costs**

All parties to civil litigation inevitably face costs in relation to the conduct of the proceedings, such as court fees and legal expenses. CPR 44 gives the court discretion as to whether costs are payable by one party to another, the amount of those costs, and when they are to be paid.

As was indicated at 15.6.2 and 15.8.1, the CPR limits costs to fixed costs in certain types of case, unless the court orders otherwise. In other cases, the general rule is that 'costs follow the event'. This means that the unsuccessful party pays both his own costs and the costs of the successful party. However, in deciding what order to make in relation to costs, the court also consider matters such as the conduct of the parties, whether a party whose case was not wholly successful was partially successful, and any payment into court or offer to settle (including a CPR 36 offer). CPR 44 provides that costs which have been unreasonably incurred or which are unreasonable in amount will not be allowed.

Costs

Would it be better if costs did not 'follow the event' and instead, as in the United States, each party was responsible for their own costs? One obvious advantage of this approach would be to encourage the parties to keep costs to a minimum. What might be the disadvantages of this approach? Might a person be dissuaded from seeking justice by the thought that she would have to pay her own legal expenses?

Under the reforms following the Jackson Report, a defendant will be required to pay the claimant's costs if the claimant is successful, but the claimant will not be required to pay the defendant's costs if the claim is unsuccessful. This is known as 'qualified one-way costs shifting' (see 15.11). There will be an exception to this general rule if the claimant has behaved unreasonably.

15.16.1 **Costs-only proceedings**

Sometimes a dispute may be settled before proceedings are commenced but the parties, having agreed which party is to pay the costs, may fail to agree the amount of the costs to be paid. CPR 44 provides that either party may start 'costs-only proceedings' under CPR 8. The effect of this is that the court will either order costs in an amount to be determined by detailed assessment or dismiss the claim.

15.17 **Enforcement of judgments and orders**

Parties do not always comply with judgments or orders made at the conclusion of civil proceedings. It is therefore essential that mechanisms are in place to enable remedies awarded by the courts to be properly enforced.

CPR 70 to 74 provide a number of methods by which a *judgment creditor* may enforce a judgment or order against a *judgment debtor*.

> ***Judgment creditor/judgment debtor*** *A judgment creditor is a person who has obtained a judgment or order. A judgment debtor is a person against whom a judgment was given or an order was made.*

CPR 70 PD indicates that a judgment or order for the payment of money (including a judgment or order for the payment of costs) may be enforced by a *writ of control* (the law changed in April 2014; this was formerly known as a writ of *fieri facias*), a *warrant of control* (formerly a warrant of execution), a *third party debt order*, a *charging order*, or an *attachment of earnings order*.

> ***Writ of control*** *A writ of control may be obtained in the High Court to enforce a judgment for the payment of money (see CPR Sch.1 RSC Orders 45 and 46). Under a writ of*

control, goods belonging to the person against whom the judgment was entered or the order was made are seized and sold by a High Court enforcement officer in order to satisfy the judgment debt, interest, and costs.

Warrant of control *The County Court equivalent to a writ of control is a warrant of control. A warrant of control will be executed by a bailiff rather than by a High Court enforcement officer (see CPR Sch.2 CCR Order 26).*

Third party debt order *Sometimes a third party may owe money to a judgment debtor. For example, the judgment debtor may have an account with a bank or building society which is in credit. In such cases CPR 72 provides that a third party debt order may be made, requiring the third party, such as the bank or building society, to pay the judgment creditor directly.*

Charging order *CPR 73 and the Charging Orders Act 1979 enable a judgment creditor to obtain a charge on specified property belonging to the judgment debtor in order to secure the payment of money due under a judgment or court order. A charge on a property means that if the property is sold, the charge usually has to be paid first before any of the proceeds of the sale can be given to the judgment debtor. The charging order itself does not compel the judgment debtor to sell the property. However, once a charging order has been made, the judgment creditor can apply for an order for sale of the property to satisfy the debt.*

Attachment of earnings order *The County Court may make an attachment of earnings order to satisfy a judgment debt under CPR Sch.2 CCR Order 27 and the Attachment of Earnings Act 1971. This is an order requiring a judgment debtor's employer to deduct sums from the judgment debtor's earnings and pay them to the court.*

Where a judgment creditor requires information in order to enforce a judgment, application may be made for an order requiring the judgment debtor to attend court to provide information concerning his means and any other matters in relation to which information is required, such as details concerning the judgment debtor's bank accounts (CPR 71). When the judgment debtor attends the hearing he will be questioned by a court officer under oath, but not normally in the presence of a judge.

Summary

- The main civil courts are the County Court and the High Court.
- Procedure in relation to most civil proceedings is governed by the Civil Procedure Rules 1998 (as amended).
- The civil courts must seek to give effect to the 'overriding objective' of the CPR.
- The CPR confers extensive case management powers upon the civil courts.
- Civil claims are allocated to the small claims track, the fast track, or the multi-track.
- The civil courts possess discretion to restrict or exclude evidence in civil proceedings.

- The court possesses discretion concerning the payment of costs, but in general costs 'follow the event' and in certain types of case, costs are limited to fixed costs.
- Civil judgments may be enforced by a variety of methods.
- The CPR sets out the steps required to settle a case or, if settlement is not possible, to prepare the case for trial.

Questions

1. What is meant by 'the overriding objective'?
2. What are directions?
3. What is meant by a Part 36 offer?
4. How does the standard of proof in civil proceedings differ from that in criminal proceedings?
5. Where a civil court awards a claimant damages, how can the claimant enforce the judgment against the defendant?

Sample question and outline answer

Question

In his article 'The Civil Justice System and the Legal Profession—The Challenges Ahead' (2003) 22 *Civil Justice Quarterly* 235, Lightman J stated:

> [O]n the whole the defects inherent in the adversary system have been aggravated rather than remedied by recent developments. The inflated expectations and returns of members of the legal profession and the parasitic costs of our case law system have made access to civil justice increasingly a luxury few can afford. The legal landscape has changed, but in my view we are today even further from our goal of a system delivering justice to all than we were 40 years ago.

Have the reforms to the civil litigation process brought about by Lord Woolf's reforms resulted in increased access to justice and an improved civil justice system? Is it time, twenty years after the introduction of the CPR, for a change?

Outline answer

The following guidance will help you to plan and prepare an answer to the above question.

This question requires you to have understood and thought about the Woolf reforms and the later Jackson reforms, and the reasons for the changes to the process and procedures of civil justice.

The answer should include reference to the problems that led to the need for reform and a critical discussion of the changes made. This may be broad or focused depending upon how you interpret the question. In order to achieve a good mark you should set out in your introduction the parameters of your response.

There should be a definition of, and consideration of, what 'adversary system' means. What problems were identified by Lord Woolf in the previous system?

What did the CPR set out to do? How do the CPR seek to make justice quicker, fairer, and more open—what is the overriding objective?

In what ways has it been successful? What is justice for all?

Why was it necessary for the Jackson Report to be commissioned? Have the latest changes broadened access (or is it too early to tell)? Is the civil system, based on precedent, too complex? Remember that the CPR were designed as a code for civil justice but are now, arguably, just as unwieldy as the rules that they replaced. The White Book (the main bound version of the CPR and the book that you will see solicitors and barristers carry into court) is full of precedent and complex argument after each 'straightforward' rule.

Is the system cheaper? Make reference to no win, no fee and the contraction of civil legal aid.

If this question was set as coursework you would be advised to read the article from which the quotation was taken. Consider the recommendations in the Briggs Report. You must quote from your own reading and develop an argument to either agree or disagree with Lightman J's conclusion.

Further reading

Your reading should be directed to making sure you appreciate the changes that have been made to the civil justice system, not only as a result of the Woolf reforms but also more recently following the Jackson Review. The effects of the changes introduced by Jackson LJ's proposals are still settling. This is a fast-moving area and you should keep an eye on the legal press to find what other changes are proposed. The upper limit for the small claims track and the upper limit for personal injury claims in the small claims track are both under review.

The promised tougher attitude expected of judges will be shown as cases make their way through the system. Watch for Court of Appeal decisions dealing with the new rules. You should study in more depth the debate about costs savings and dealing with cases justly and proportionately. Think about whether you consider the CPR to have had the effect of encouraging early settlement and more efficient and cheaper access to justice.

- ***Briggs, Lord Justice.*** *'Civil Courts Structure: Final Report'* (2016) **www.judiciary.gov.uk/wp-content/uploads/2016/07/civil-courts-structure-review-final-report-jul-16-final-1.pdf**

  Lord Briggs was asked to analyse the existing civil court structure. This is his report.

- ***Brooks, A.*** *'Expert Meetings and Joint Reports'* (2002) 2 JPI Law 180

  A general practical guide to the process of meetings between experts and how joint reports are compiled.

- ***Brown S.*** *'Teaching Old Dogs New Tricks'* NLJ 28 March 2013, Part Two 12 April 2013

  An interesting discussion and overview of the budgeting provisions discussed in section 15.8.3.

- ***Dwyer, D. (ed.)*** *The Civil Procedure Rules Ten Years On*, Oxford University Press (2009)

  This is a book resulting from a conference discussing ten years of the CPR. It is useful to gain a historical perspective and to consider some of the chapters in the light of the 2010 Jackson Report. In particular, the first part (the book includes twenty-four chapters divided into seven sections), comprising reflections on the historical basis of and comparative background to the CPR, is a thought-provoking read.

- ***Peysner, Professor J.*** *'Impact of the Jackson Reforms: Some Emerging Themes'* **www.judiciary.gov.uk/wp-content/uploads/2014/05/impact-of-the-jackson-reforms.pdf**

  This report was prepared by Professor Peysner of Lincoln University for the Civil Justice Council Cost Forum in 2014 and provides a very useful and concise overview and discussion of the effect of the Jackson reforms. The report is compiled from qualitative research gleaned from semi-structured interviews with lawyers and a review of reports in the legal press.

- ***Sime, S.*** *A Practical Approach to Civil Procedure*, 22nd edn, Oxford University Press (2019)

  This is a standard textbook on civil procedure. It is comprehensive and includes access to an online updating service.

- ***Sorabji, J.*** *'Late Amendment and Jackson's Commitment to Woolf: Another Attempt to Implement a New Approach to Civil Justice'* (2012) 31(4) CJQ 393–412

  This article, written by Professor Sorabji, Barrister and Legal Secretary to the Master of the Rolls, considers the approach of the civil courts towards the late amendment of claims and the effect of the civil justice reforms advocated by Lord Woolf in the 1990s that developed into the CPR. It looks at the likely impact of the proposals of Jackson LJ's report and is a good starting point to think about the CPR changes introduced in 2013.

- ***Sorabji, J.*** *'Prospects for Proportionality: Jackson Implementation'* (2013) 32(2) CJQ 213–30

  This article considers whether the implementation of the civil procedure reforms put forward in the Jackson Report is likely to achieve the aim of ensuring that litigation is conducted at no more than proportionate cost. The author discusses the causes of the costs crisis that the Jackson reforms seek to address and considers whether proportionality is an appropriate aim for the civil litigation process.

- **Taylor, P.** *'Proportionality and Legal Costs'* Law Society Gazette (12 March 2014) **www.lawgazette.co.uk/practice/proportionality-and-legal-costs/5040225.fullarticle**

  Taylor discusses the meaning of proportionality under the Court Rules and the fact that under the new rules reasonableness and necessity are no longer to be considered when deciding whether costs are proportionate.

- **Zander, M.** *'The Government's Plans on Civil Justice'* (1998) 3 MLR 61

  Although this article is now of historical interest only, it is a helpful criticism of the Woolf reforms and discusses the expectation that the reforms will not do what they set out to do. It is a useful article to read as a starting point to consider the effect of the changes to the civil justice system.

Blogs

There are a number of very helpful blogs by practitioners covering developments and comment on civil procedure. Of particular note are 'Civil Litigation Brief' by Gordon Exall, barrister of Zenith Chambers in Leeds, and 'Jackson in Practice' by Kerry Underwood, solicitor of Underwoods Solicitors in Hemel Hempstead. See **civillitigationbrief.wordpress.com/** and **kerryunderwood.wordpress.com/.**

Online resources

You should now attempt the supporting self-test questions and end-of-chapter questions available at: **www.oup.com/he/wilson-rutherford4e**

Chapter 16

Alternative dispute resolution

Learning objectives

By the end of this chapter you should be able to:

- understand the reasons for the existence of alternative methods of dispute resolution (ADR), such as arbitration and mediation;
- describe the different forms of ADR;
- compare and contrast the different forms of ADR;
- assess the relative advantages and disadvantages of different forms of ADR compared to civil litigation.

Talking point

The law and courts of England and Wales have long attracted international parties to use the English legal system for the purpose of resolving disputes. Often this dispute resolution is achieved through the courts, but it could also be achieved through an Alternative Dispute Resolution (ADR) method, such as arbitration (where the parties to a contract agree in that contract to have a dispute resolved by an arbitrator) or mediation (where the parties attempt to negotiate an agreed settlement with a mediator helping to facilitate that agreement). One issue, following the June 2016 referendum decision on European Union (EU) membership, is to ensure that this legal work is protected once the UK leaves the EU at the end of March 2019 (Brexit). The Chancery Bar Association have produced a booklet entitled 'English Law, UK Courts and UK Legal Service after Brexit: The View beyond 2019' (available at **www.chba.org.uk/news/brexit-memo**) which sets out the case for maintaining the ability of international parties to access the courts and ADR in the UK. On the latter, the booklet states:

Arbitrators: London is renowned for its choice of specialist and experienced arbitrators. Many will be members of, or trained by, the Chartered Institute of Arbitrators, an internationally recognised body that provides high quality training for arbitrators. Many arbitrators will be highly skilled members of the legal profession. Others will be technical or industry experts. High Court judges can also be appointed as arbitrators, thus providing the benefit of their knowledge and experience in adjudicating disputes, without the need to go through a formal court process.

Mediators: The UK has a well-established body of high quality mediators. The majority of mediators have been accredited by at least one of the main mediation providers, who also offer training. A mediator who is a member of a regulated professional body, such as the Law Society or Bar Council, will be subject to their professional codes of conduct, which ensure that they have indemnity insurance and observe high standards of conduct.

This chapter will examine the role of both arbitration and mediation, along with other forms of ADR such as conciliation and 'med-arb' (a hybrid of mediation and arbitration), as methods of resolving legal disputes without going to court. Before you read this chapter, consider the following questions:

When you're reading through this chapter, ensure you understand why these forms of dispute resolution exist and what their advantages and disadvantages are. While you are reading, consider whether you think ADR should remain as a voluntary 'alternative' to litigation—or could it be made compulsory?

Introduction

'Alternative dispute resolution' (ADR) is an umbrella term which describes a range of methods of resolving legal disputes without recourse to litigation in the courts. ADR covers arbitration, conciliation, mediation, and 'med-arb', among others. There are certain similarities between all of these methods—there is no judge and there need not be any lawyers present either. They tend to be less formal than going to court, and have more flexibility in terms of where and when the parties to the dispute meet. Arbitration is the most formal of the various forms of ADR, and is typically used for resolving contractual disputes. An arbitrator will listen to the arguments presented by both sides and then give a binding decision. With mediation, a mediator will try to help the parties to the dispute to negotiate a compromise agreement—but, unlike arbitration, the mediator has no power to impose a solution on the parties. Conciliation is similar, but a conciliator has more scope to suggest possible solutions to the parties. Again, however, the conciliator has no power to impose a solution on the parties. 'Med-arb', as the name might suggest, is a combination of mediation and arbitration. The remainder of this chapter will look at the different forms of ADR in more detail, and will seek to explain why ADR exists in the first place.

16.1 **Arbitration**

16.1.1 **Commercial arbitration—general principles**

Arbitrators typically aim to resolve disputes as to a contract, having been nominated in advance by the parties themselves for that very reason. Commercial arbitration is governed by the Arbitration Act 1996. Section 1(a) states that 'the object of arbitration is to obtain the fair resolution of disputes by an impartial tribunal without unnecessary delay or expense'. Section 33(1) provides that the tribunal shall (a) 'act fairly and impartially as between the parties, giving each party a reasonable opportunity of putting his case and dealing with that of his opponent', and (b) 'adopt procedures suitable to the circumstances of the particular case, avoiding unnecessary delay or expense, so as to provide a fair means for the resolution of the matters falling to be determined'.

16.1.2 **Arbitrators**

An arbitrator will typically be an expert in the particular field of commerce to which the contract relates. There is no rule preventing legally qualified persons from being arbitrators, and judges can and do sit as arbitrators. Once appointed, the arbitrator is obliged to act in an impartial manner (like a judge), but he will have been appointed because of his specialist knowledge, thus avoiding the need to have technical points explained to him by expert witnesses (unlike a judge). Section 15 of the 1996 Act provides that, in any arbitration, the parties are free to agree on the number of arbitrators; if there is no agreement as to the number of arbitrators, then the tribunal shall consist of a sole arbitrator.

16.1.3 Appeals and judicial review

Section 68(1) of the Arbitration Act 1996 states: 'A party to arbitral proceedings may . . . apply to the court challenging an award in the proceedings on the ground of serious irregularity affecting the tribunal, the proceedings or the award.' Section 69(1) states that 'unless otherwise agreed by the parties, a party to arbitral proceedings may . . . appeal to the court on a question of law'. Appeals require either the agreement of all the other parties to the proceedings, or leave of the court. Appeals on findings of fact were abolished by the Arbitration Act 1979, primarily for the reason that the possibility of lengthy and expensive appeals to the High Court subverted the whole point of having the case heard by an arbitrator in the first place. There is also the possibility of judicial review. If the proceedings were allegedly not conducted in a 'judicial manner', the case may be reviewed in the High Court.

Thinking point

What are the problems with litigation that led to arbitration (and other forms of ADR) becoming more widespread?

For many years arbitration was the main alternative to litigating a case before the courts. In recent times, arbitration has been seen as beset by similar problems to those associated with litigation before the courts. What do you think these problems are?

16.2 Mediation

Mediation can be defined as the process whereby a neutral third party, the mediator, helps both sides to a dispute to come to a mutually acceptable agreement. If an agreement is reached it can be written down and form a binding contract which, if necessary, is enforceable in court. If not, traditional civil litigation is still open to the parties.

Key point

Mediation is a process which depends on the voluntary participation of both parties to the dispute. The aim is to establish a mutually acceptable compromise through negotiation and, eventually, agreement. The outcome can therefore be very flexible: it is whatever the parties agree upon. However, there is no guarantee that any agreement will be forthcoming, which is one of the drawbacks of mediation.

16.2.1 The scope of mediation

Mediation is a form of ADR which had, until relatively recently, been associated primarily with the resolution of matrimonial disputes. Indeed, this is still an area where mediation has a key role, as its informality and privacy are ideally suited to such disputes. Until relatively recently, mediation was regarded as a novelty and of little importance (see Michael Lind, 'ADR and Mediation—Boom or Bust?' (2001)151 NLJ 1238). However, the situation has changed dramatically since then. The landmark cases of *Dunnett v Railtrack* and *Cowl v Plymouth City Council* led to a massive increase in the profile of ADR in general and mediation in particular. The following section explores the areas of dispute resolution in which mediation is now firmly established.

Divorce and subsequent disputes

A court may be a particularly inappropriate place for divorce and subsequent disputes over property and custody, since the adversarial nature of the system can aggravate the differences between the parties. This is likely to be especially harmful where children are involved, since the couple will normally have to maintain some kind of contact after divorce. Hence, mediation has been available to divorcing couples for some time—not necessarily to try to get them back together, but to try to ensure that any arrangements between them are made as amicably as possible. Part II of the Family Law Act 1996 aimed to make mediation for divorcing couples compulsory, as opposed to voluntary. However, there were various objections to this reform, and in February 2001 the then Lord Chancellor, Lord Irvine, announced that Part II was to be repealed. The Court of Appeal subsequently decided (in *Halsey v Milton Keynes NHS Trust* [2004] EWCA Civ 576, [2004] 1 WLR 3002, a medical negligence case) that mediation in all circumstances must be voluntary and that, although courts can strongly encourage mediation, it is going too far for any outside party—whether government, Parliament, or the courts—to insist that parties with a dispute try mediation. This was confirmed by the High Court in the context of matrimonial disputes in *Mann v Mann* [2014] EWHC 537, [2014] 1 WLR 2807. Here, Mostyn J in the High Court said: 'As things stand, the court cannot impose a mandatory order on the parties that they must participate in ADR . . . I cannot compel the parties to engage in the mediation. But I can robustly encourage them.'

Negligence actions

Mediation is now well established in the context of negligence claims, covering personal injury (*McCook v Lobo* [2002] EWCA Civ 1760), claims for property loss (*Dunnett v Railtrack* [2002] 1 WLR 2434), and professional negligence (*Hurst v Leeming* [2002] EWHC 1051).

Judicial review

In *Cowl v Plymouth City Council* [2001] EWCA Civ 1935, [2002] 1 WLR 803, a judicial review action, Lord Woolf CJ was adamant that mediation had a role to play in such cases:

> Even in disputes between public authorities and the members of the public for whom they are responsible, insufficient attention is paid to the paramount importance of avoiding litigation whenever this is possible . . . both sides must now be acutely aware of the contribution [ADR] can make to resolving disputes in a manner which both meets the needs of the parties and the public and saves expense and stress.

For a more recent example of a case involving the role of mediation in the context of judicial review, see *Crawford v Newcastle University* [2014] EWHC 1197, discussed later at 16.2.2.

Trust and probate disputes

Mediation has a potentially invaluable role to play in the context of trust and probate disputes. The privacy and confidentiality, flexibility, and informality of the process may well help to avoid, or at least minimise, conflicts between family members over the distribution of assets.

Property disputes

The same arguments can be made in support of the use of mediation in property disputes between neighbours. In *Valentine v Allen* [2003] EWCA Civ 915, involving a complicated dispute between neighbours over rights of way, the trial judge encouraged the parties to consider mediation. Although it was unsuccessful in that case, it nevertheless illustrates that the judge considered the dispute could potentially have been resolved outside of court.

Landlord and tenant disputes

The case of *Shirayama Shokusan v Danovo Ltd* [2003] EWHC 3306 (Ch) involved a dispute between a landlord and tenant in a commercial tenancy. Blackburne J in the Chancery Division ordered the parties to attempt mediation. (Note: the notion that judges had a power to compel parties into mediation was disapproved of in *Halsey*; see further later at 16.2.2.) A more recent example of a dispute involving a commercial tenancy is *PGF II SA v OMFS Co 1 Ltd* [2013] EWCA Civ 1288, [2014] 1 WLR 1386, discussed later at 16.2.2.

Contractual disputes

Although it was noted earlier (see 16.1.1) that contractual disputes often lend themselves to resolution by way of arbitration, such cases are also eminently suitable for resolution by way of mediation. Four such cases are discussed later at 16.2.2: *Burchell v Bullard* [2005] EWCA Civ 358; *Garritt-Critchley v Ronnan and Solarpower Ltd* [2014] EWHC 1774; *Northrop Grumman Mission Systems Europe Ltd v BAE Systems (Al Diriyah C4I) Ltd* [2014] EWHC 3148, [2015] 3 All ER 782; and *ICI Ltd v Merit Merrell Technology Ltd* [2018] EWHC 177.

Commercial disputes

Cable & Wireless PLC v IBM (UK) Ltd [2002] EWHC 2059 and *Leicester Circuits v Coates Brothers* [2003] EWCA Civ 333 are examples of cases where mediation has been used (albeit not necessarily successfully) in the context of commercial disputes.

Medical disputes

In *Great Ormond Street Hospital for Children NHS Foundation Trust v Yates and Others (No. 2)* [2017] EWHC 1909 (Fam), [2017] 4 WLR 131, involving a dispute between a hospital and the parents of a young child over whether it was in his best interests that he be taken off the artificial ventilation that was keeping him alive and allowed to die, or instead to receive experimental medical treatment, Francis J in the High Court said:

> It is my clear view that mediation should be attempted in all cases such as this one even if all that it does is achieve a greater understanding by the parties of each other's positions. Few users of the court system will be in a greater state of turmoil and grief than parents in the position that these parents have been in and anything which helps them to understand the process and the viewpoint of the other side, even if they profoundly disagree with it, would in my judgment be of benefit and I hope that some lessons can therefore be taken from this tragic case which it has been my duty to oversee.

 Example

***Great Ormond Street Hospital for Children NHS Foundation Trust v Yates and Others (No. 2)* [2017] EWHC 1909 (Fam), [2017] 4 WLR 131**

In the summer of 2017, the tragic case of Charlie Gard attracted international attention. Charlie had been born in August 2016 with Mitochondrial DNA Depletion Syndrome (MDDS), a rare genetic disorder for which there was no known treatment and which usually causes death in infancy. From October 2016, he was looked after at Great Ormond Street Hospital in London, where he was placed on an artificial ventilation system to help him breathe. Soon afterwards, Michio Hirano, a neurologist in New York, was contacted and invited to visit Charlie in London. He had been working on an experimental treatment for MDDS known as nucleoside supplementation. However, in January 2017, before Dr Hirano could travel to the UK, Charlie suffered seizures which caused brain damage. The hospital took the view that further treatment would be futile and could even prolong Charlie's suffering. They contacted Charlie's parents, Chris Gard and Constance Yates, about withdrawing his life support and providing only palliative care. The parents, who wanted to pursue the option of Dr Hirano's experimental treatment, objected, and began to raise funds to send Charlie to New York. The hospital went to court to seek an order preventing this. Over the spring and summer of 2017 the case was heard in the High Court and the Court of Appeal, both of which agreed with the hospital that it would be lawful for Charlie's artificial ventilation to be withdrawn and that he should not undergo the experimental treatment. The UK Supreme Court and European Court of Human Rights both rejected applications from Charlie's parents to challenge those rulings. Eventually, in July 2017, the case returned to the High Court. By this stage, Charlie's parents accepted that their son was 'beyond any help even from experimental treatment and that it is in his best interests for him to be allowed to die'. Charlie was transferred to a hospice and died on 28 July 2017.

Other areas

Other areas where mediation should, in principle, be able to provide a solution include defamation (see R. Shillito, 'Mediation in Libel Actions' (2000) 150 NLJ 122) and housing disputes (see R. Mahendra, 'Popular but no Panacea' (2004) 154 NLJ 1398).

16.2.2 The 'cost consequences' of a failure to mediate

In *Dunnett v Railtrack plc* [2002] 1 WLR 2434, the Court of Appeal controversially ordered that the successful party in negligence litigation should pay the losing side's costs—because of the former's failure to respond positively to the Court's suggestion that they should enter into mediation. This was despite the fact that mediation was first proposed after the defendant had already won in the County Court. Brooke LJ said:

> Skilled mediators are now able to achieve results satisfactory to both parties in many cases which are quite beyond the power of lawyers and courts to achieve. This court has knowledge of cases where intense feelings have arisen, for instance in relation to clinical negligence claims. But when the parties are brought together on neutral soil with a skilled mediator to help them resolve their differences, it may very well be that the mediator is able to achieve a result by which the parties shake hands at the end and feel that they have gone away having settled the dispute on terms with which they are happy to live. A mediator may be able to provide solutions which are beyond the powers of the court to provide . . . It is to be hoped that any publicity given to this part of the judgment of the court will draw the attention of lawyers to their duties to further the overriding objective . . . and to the possibility that, if they turn down out of hand the chance of ADR when suggested by the court . . . they may have to face uncomfortable costs consequences.

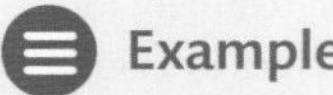

***Dunnett v Railtrack plc* [2002] 1 WLR 2434**

Facts: Susan Dunnett brought a claim against Railtrack plc seeking damages for negligence arising out of the deaths, in July 1996, of three of her horses which had been struck by an express train on the Swansea-to-London mainline. The judge in the County Court dismissed her claim, but she was given leave to appeal to the Court of Appeal. Pending the appeal, Dunnett suggested ADR to Railtrack, but they flatly rejected it. Accordingly, the appeal proceeded. At the Court of Appeal in London, the appeal was dismissed, and Railtrack sought its costs from Dunnett. However, the Court ordered Railtrack to pay its own costs. This decision was highly controversial, as it created an exception to the 'normal' rule which is that the losing party in any litigation pays the winning party's costs. The Court of Appeal took the view that the advantages of mediation over litigation were so obvious that Railtrack had to be 'punished' for not responding more positively to the suggestion of mediation.

The Court of Appeal followed and applied *Dunnett* in *Leicester Circuits v Coates Brothers* [2003] EWCA Civ 333. Here, after both sides had agreed to mediate in an attempt to resolve their dispute, Coates withdrew, forcing the case to proceed to litigation. Judge LJ regarded this as unreasonable. He said that the

> unexplained withdrawal from an agreed mediation process was of significance to the continuation of this litigation . . . We take the view that having agreed to mediation it hardly lies in the mouths of those who agree to it to assert that there was no realistic prospect of success.

However, *Dunnett* has been distinguished in several subsequent cases, on the basis that a party to litigation will be entitled to reject a mediation proposal when it is 'justified' in doing so. This is when mediation would have no 'realistic prospect of resolution of dispute'. In *Hurst v Leeming* [2002] EWHC 1051 (Ch), Lightman J held that:

> Mediation is not in law compulsory . . . but [ADR] is at the heart of today's civil justice system, and any unjustified failure to give proper attention to the opportunities afforded by mediation, and in particular in any case where mediation affords a realistic prospect of resolution of dispute, there must be anticipated as a real possibility that adverse consequences may be attracted . . . If mediation can have no real prospect of success a party may, with impunity, refuse to proceed to mediation. But refusal is a high-risk course to take . . . Further, the hurdle in the way of a party refusing to proceed to mediation on this ground is high . . . the starting point must surely be the fact that the mediation process itself can and does often bring about a more sensible and more conciliatory attitude on the part of the parties than might otherwise be expected to prevail before the mediation, and may produce a recognition of the strengths and weaknesses by each party of his own case and of that of his opponent, and a willingness to accept the give & take essential to a successful mediation.

In *Société Internationale de Télécommunications Aeronautiques SC (SITA) v Wyatt Co (UK) Ltd* [2002] EWHC 2401 (Ch), Park J also refused to penalise a litigant as to costs despite refusing to mediate. He explained that this was because of the attitude of the other party in trying to instigate mediation, which he variously described as 'self-serving', 'disagreeable', 'off-putting', and 'bullying'. In *McCook v Lobo* [2002] EWCA Civ 1760,

Pill LJ said that 'this was not a case where there was scope for mediation' and hence there was no order to deprive the winning litigant of his costs. Similarly, in *Valentine v Allen* [2003] EWCA Civ 915, Arden LJ decided not to penalise either of the parties for their failure to respond to the judge's entreaties to mediate: 'it is not clear that [they] could by mediation have come to any agreement. The failure to go to mediation is of no cause or effect.' In *Halsey v Milton Keynes General NHS Trust* [2004] EWCA Civ 576, [2004] 1 WLR 3002, the Court of Appeal confirmed these developments. Dyson LJ said:

> In deciding whether to deprive a successful party of some or all of his costs on the grounds that he has refused to agree to ADR, it must be borne in mind that such an order is an exception to the general rule that costs should follow the event. In our view, the burden is on the unsuccessful party to show why there should be a departure from the general rule. The fundamental principle is that such departure is not justified unless it is shown (the burden being on the unsuccessful party) that the successful party acted unreasonably in refusing to agree to ADR . . . We accept that mediation and other ADR processes do not offer a panacea, and can have disadvantages as well as advantages: they are not appropriate for every case. We do not, therefore accept that there should be a presumption in favour of mediation. The question whether a party has acted unreasonably in refusing ADR must be determined having regard to all the circumstances of the particular case.

The Court of Appeal significantly reduced the scope of the *Dunnett* rule by emphasising that, when a court was deciding whether to impose cost sanctions for a failure to mediate, the burden of proof fell on the losing party to prove that there was a realistic prospect of mediation being a success. Dyson LJ stated that the losing party had to prove that a refusal to mediate was unreasonable; there was no burden on the winning party to prove that their refusal to mediate was reasonable. He stated that 'it would not be right to stigmatise as unreasonable a refusal by the successful party to agree to a mediation unless he showed that a mediation had no realistic prospect of success'. According to Dyson LJ, there were at least six factors which may be relevant to the question of whether a party has unreasonably refused mediation:

(a) the nature of the dispute;

(b) the merits of the case;

(c) the extent to which other settlement methods had been attempted;

(d) whether the costs of ADR would be disproportionately high;

(e) whether any delay in setting up and attending the ADR would have been prejudicial;

(f) whether the ADR had a reasonable prospect of success.

He did emphasise that 'in many cases no single factor will be decisive, and that these factors should not be regarded as an exhaustive checklist'. Reaction to the decision in *Halsey* has generally been positive (see, for example, M. Supperstone, D. Stilitz, and C. Sheldon, 'ADR and Public Law' [2006] PL 299).

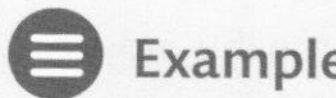

Example

Halsey v Milton Keynes General NHS Trust [2004] EWCA Civ 576, [2004] 1 WLR 3002

Lillian Halsey brought an action against the Milton Keynes NHS Trust alleging negligent treatment of her late husband, Bert. He had been admitted to hospital in June 1999 with serious health problems. A 'nasogastric' feeding tube was fitted—allegedly negligently, so that, instead of directing liquid food into Bert's stomach, it went instead into his left lung, resulting in his death. This was denied. Mrs Halsey (via her solicitors) contacted the trust in January 2000, indicating that she would accept £7,500 damages. The trust (through its solicitors) replied in February indicating that they would 'take all necessary steps to resist a claim'.

A few days later, Mrs Halsey contacted the trust again proposing mediation. In March, the trust again insisted there was no claim to mediate about. In April 2001, Mrs Halsey indicated that she would settle for £12,500.

The trust refused to settle or mediate. In May 2002, Mrs Halsey issued her claim, although she again proposed mediation. This was rejected in September 2002. In April 2003, Mrs Halsey again proposed both settlement and/or mediation. After this was rejected, she wrote another letter to the trust pointing out the decisions in *Dunnett* and *Hurst v Leeming*. In May 2003, the trust replied that mediation would have 'little chance' of success and that the mediation (being doomed to failure) would be a waste of money. Trial took place in June 2003, and judgment was given to the trust. The trial judge also held that the trust should not be deprived of any of its costs. Mrs Halsey appealed. The Court of Appeal dismissed the appeal.

The *Halsey* factors were considered in detail by the Court of Appeal in *Burchell v Bullard* [2005] EWCA Civ 358.

Example

Burchell v Bullard [2005] EWCA Civ 358

Nick Burchell, a builder, had agreed to build two large extensions to the Bullards' home in Bournemouth, with payment in stages. The Bullards refused to make the third payment as they were unhappy with the work. Burchell's solicitor wrote to the Bullards, suggesting the case be referred to 'a qualified construction mediator'. The Bullards (on advice from their surveyor) rejected this on the basis that the issues were technically too complex. Burchell duly made a claim for more than £18,000; the Bullards counterclaimed for more than £100,000. In court, the judge awarded Burchell his £18,000 but also awarded the Burrells £14,000 of their counterclaim. Thus, the Bullards had to pay Burchell the difference of some £5,000 once VAT and interest had been added on. On costs, the parties were ordered to pay each other's costs. Burchell appealed against the costs order. The Court of Appeal was scathing of the Bullards, in particular their gross exaggeration of their counterclaim and their dismissive attitude towards Burchell's offer to mediate. The Court said that 'the defendants cannot rely on their own obstinacy to assert that the mediation had no reasonable prospect of success'. The Court thought that the nature of the dispute was suitable for ADR, the merits of the case also favoured mediation, and the costs of ADR would have been relatively small. However, because the offer to mediate was made before the decision in *Dunnett*, the Court thought that the defendants' decision not to mediate had to be judged against the prevailing legal circumstances at the time, and hence ordered that no costs sanction be imposed against the Bullards. However, the Court of Appeal did modify the trial judge's costs order by ordering the Bullards to pay 60 per cent of all of the costs (on both sides) and hence leaving Burchell with only 40 per cent to pay.

The next two cases examined whether or not a complete failure to respond to an invitation of ADR might be regarded as unreasonable. The answer is: generally speaking, yes, but it all depends on the individual circumstances of the case. As a result, in the first case, silence in the face of a mediation offer was unreasonable, but in the second case the opposite was true.

In the first of the two cases, *PGF II SA v OMFS Co 1 Ltd* [2013] EWCA Civ 1288, [2014] 1 WLR 1386, a commercial property dispute, the Court of Appeal held that, as a general rule, silence in the face of an invitation to participate in ADR was 'of itself unreasonable', regardless of whether a refusal to engage in ADR might have been justified. However, the Court added that it was possible that there might be 'rare cases' where ADR was 'so obviously inappropriate' that to characterise silence as unreasonable would be 'pure formalism', or where the failure to respond was the result of a mistake, in which case the onus would be on the recipient of the invitation to provide an explanation.

The Court stated that there were 'sound practical and policy reasons' for this extension to the *Halsey* guidelines: (a) an investigation of the reasons for refusing to mediate posed 'forensic difficulties' for the court concerning whether those reasons were 'genuine'; (b) a failure to provide reasons for a refusal was 'destructive of the real objective' of encouraging parties to consider and discuss ADR. Any difficulties or reasonable objection to a particular ADR proposal should be discussed, so that the parties could narrow their differences; (c) it would also serve the policy of proportionality.

Accordingly, the defendant's silence in the face of two requests to mediate from the claimant was unreasonable conduct, sufficient to warrant a costs sanction. In the case, it would be 'perverse' not to regard silence in the face of repeated requests for mediation as 'anything other than a refusal to mediate'. That was all the more so because the claimant's first request was 'couched in such detailed and sensible terms that it could not reasonably have been regarded as a mere tactic'.

In the second case, *Crawford v Newcastle University* [2014] EWHC 1197, a dispute between a medical student and the university, the High Court concluded that the university had *not* acted unreasonably in refusing to enter into mediation and was therefore entitled to its costs. In June 2010, the claimant (C) had failed his fifth and final year exams. He repeated the year but, in June 2011, failed again. C instigated an internal appeal, but this was rejected in August 2011. While that was ongoing, he repeated his complaint to the Independent Adjudicator for Higher Education. In November 2011, the Adjudicator provisionally rejected his complaint, at which point C launched a judicial review action against the university. This litigation automatically terminated that adjudication process. In May 2012, C contacted the university and proposed mediation. The university's lawyers agreed in principle, but the university itself never actually responded to the mediation proposal. In July 2012, the judicial review was temporarily stayed while C reopened the complaint to the Adjudicator. In January 2013, the Adjudicator gave a final ruling, dismissing the complaint. The judicial review then resumed but, in January 2014, the High Court rejected the application. The only remaining issue was costs. The university applied for its costs, being the winning party; C contended that the university had unreasonably refused to engage in mediation and should pay its own costs, despite winning the judicial review. Grubb J applied the six *Halsey* factors in order to determine this issue:

(a) **The nature of the dispute:** Although the university's lawyers had agreed 'in principle' to mediation, this was not 'an unqualified acceptance that mediation was appropriate'. There had been nothing further to mediate beyond the substance of C's claim that he was entitled to his degree because his final paper had been wrongly marked. He had already been allowed to re-sit his final year. It was not in dispute that the university could, in exceptional circumstances, allow a further re-sit, but C had not raised any exceptional circumstances.

(b) **The merits of the case:** The university was entitled to take the view that it could resist C's challenge to its decision. It already had the Independent Adjudicator's provisional decision.

(c) **The extent to which other settlement methods had been attempted:** At the time that C proposed mediation, the adjudication process was already underway. The university was fully engaged with that process. The reality of the situation was that adjudication was a form of ADR, and it was difficult to see how the university was being unreasonable in not engaging in a different and further form of ADR (that is, the mediation). The fact that the university's solicitors had agreed in principle to ADR did not amount to an unqualified acceptance that it was appropriate, especially as there had been no proposal from C as to what mediation might achieve.

(d) **Whether the costs of mediation would be disproportionately high:** It was unlikely that they would be.

(e) **Whether any delay in setting up ADR would be prejudicial:** This did not have 'particular weight' in the present case.

(f) **Whether the ADR had a realistic prospect of success:** On this point the burden of proof was on the losing party, that is, C. Grubb J decided that there had

> been no reasonable prospect of the mediation succeeding. He said that the university had been 'discourteous' in not responding to C's mediation invitation, and that silence *might* be unreasonable and lead to costs sanctions even if an outright refusal to participate would have been justified on reasonable grounds. However, that was *not* an invariable rule; the burden remained on the claimant to show that the failure to respond had been unreasonable. Moreover, it could not be said that the university had refused to engage in *any* form of ADR, because it had engaged with the adjudication process.

In two recent cases involving contractual disputes which ended up in the High Court, after one side proposed mediation and the other rejected it, the respective judges again used the *Halsey* factors in order to decide whether the refusal to engage in mediation was reasonable in order to determine the award of costs.

In the first case, *Garritt-Critchley v Ronnan and Solarpower Ltd* [2014] EWHC 1774, the claimant, Philip Garritt-Critchley, had proposed mediation but the defendants rejected it on the basis that the parties were, in their opinion, 'too far apart'. Lawyers for the defendants had also written to the claimant telling him that they were aware of the consequences of such a refusal being deemed unreasonable, but did not think that such an outcome was likely in their case, because 'our clients are extremely confident of their position and do not consider there is any realistic prospect that your client will succeed'. After several further, unsuccessful, attempts by the claimant to persuade the defendants to mediate, the case went to trial, after four days of which the defendants agreed to settle the case. When it came to awarding costs, the trial judge held that the defendants' failure to engage in mediation was unreasonable, rejecting the defendants' suggestion that mediation would have been pointless because of 'considerable dislike and mistrust between the parties'. He said:

> This case by its very nature was eminently suitable for ADR as the claimants appreciated . . . it is precisely where there may be distrust or emotion between the parties, which it might be thought is pushing them down the road to an expensive trial, where the skills of a mediator come in most usefully. They are well trained to diffuse emotion, feelings of distrust and other matters in order that the parties can see their way to a commercial settlement.

He also rejected the defendants' suggestion that mediation would have been a waste of time given the distance between the parties. He pointed out that in civil litigation, the parties themselves 'don't know whether in truth they are too far apart unless they sit down and explore settlement. If they are irreconcilably too far apart, then the mediator will say as much within the first hour of mediation.'

In the second case, *Northrop Grumman Mission Systems Europe Ltd v BAE Systems (Al Diriyah C4I) Ltd* [2014] EWHC 3148, [2015] 3 All ER 782, the defendants, BAE Systems, won the case but, when it came to awarding costs, Ramsey J held that BAE had unreasonably rejected a mediation proposal from the claimant (Northrop). Ramsey J went through the *Halsey* factors:

(a) **The nature of the dispute:** The case centred on a technical issue of contractual interpretation.

(b) **The merits of the case:** BAE had 'reasonably considered that it had a strong case'. Where a party faced a claim which they regarded as unmeritorious and wished to contest, the court should be 'slow to characterise that conduct as unreasonable'. The fact that a party 'reasonably believes that it had a watertight case might well be sufficient justification for a refusal to mediate'. Having said that, mediation could have a positive effect, even if the claim had no merit. A mediator could bring a 'new independent perspective'. On balance, BAE's reasonably held view that it had a strong case provided 'some limited justification' for its refusal to mediate.

(c) **The extent to which other settlement methods had been attempted:** Before the case had gone to trial, BAE had made a settlement offer which Northrop had rejected. Had Northrop accepted that offer, they would have been in a better position than they were as a result of the trial (given that BAE won the case). That was a factor that was 'marginally' in BAE's favour when it came to assessing its refusal to mediate.

(d) **Whether the costs of ADR would be disproportionately high:** Mediation would have cost around £40,000. That cost was not disproportionately high, given that Northrop's claim was for £3 million in compensation and the legal costs actually incurred totalled some £500,000.

(e) **Whether any delay in setting up and attending the ADR would have been prejudicial:** This was not a factor. Mediation could have taken place without affecting the litigation.

(f) **Whether the ADR had a reasonable prospect of success:** It was likely that there would have been a mediated settlement. Mediation, was, in general, successful. Moreover, the court had to look beyond the polarised positions of the parties. A skilled mediator could find 'middle ground' by analysing the parties' positions and making each 'reflect' on its own and the other's position. The mediator's 'necessary skills of evaluation and facilitation' could have found solutions that the parties had not even considered. Thus, even though BAE reasonably considered that it had a strong case, it had acted unreasonably in rejecting Northrop's offer to mediate.

The *Northrop v BAE* case is discussed by Erich Suter in 'Unreasonable Refusal to Mediate and Costs' (2015) 81 Arbitration 2.

The six *Halsey* factors were applied again in *Laporte and Christian v Metropolitan Police Commissioner* [2015] EWHC 371, in the context of a claim against the police for damages for assault and battery, false imprisonment, and malicious prosecution, demonstrating once more that mediation is suitable for virtually any type of legal action.

 Example

***Laporte and Christian v Metropolitan Police Commissioner* [2015] EWHC 371**

The claimants had brought unsuccessful claims for damages against the defendant Commissioner for, inter alia, assault and battery, false imprisonment, and malicious prosecution. The claims arose following the claimants' ejection from Haringey Civic Centre in north London and subsequent arrest by Metropolitan Police officers following a protest during which many people, including the claimants, had gained access to restricted areas of the building in order to protest against proposed cuts to Haringey Council's budget. Although the High Court rejected all of the claimants' allegations, Turner J agreed with the claimants that the defendant Commissioner had unreasonably refused to engage in mediation (which the claimants had proposed) prior to the case coming to trial. Turner J went through the *Halsey* factors:

(a) **The nature of the dispute:** The case was *not* unsuitable for mediation. There were issues of fact to be resolved 'upon which both sides ran the risk of adverse findings'. Moreover, there was 'no continuing commercial relationship between the parties and it is unrealistic to suggest that a settlement by way of ADR would have been inappropriate for this type of dispute'.

(b) **The merits of the case:** Although the Commissioner successfully defended the case at trial, 'the merits of the defence were not perceived to be so strong in themselves to have justified a refusal to engage in ADR'.

(c) **The extent to which other settlement methods had been attempted:** The defendant had 'made no offers to settle the case before ADR was suggested'. The defendant could not, therefore, say that he had 'exhausted other opportunities of resolving the case which would have obviated the need to go to court'.

(d) **Whether the costs of ADR would be disproportionately high:** Even the defendant conceded that 'the costs of mediation would not have been disproportionately high'.

(e) **Whether any delay in setting up and attending the ADR would have been prejudicial:** There was no reason why mediation would have had the effect of delaying the trial. The first offer of ADR was made in September 2013, some nine months before the trial began in June 2014.

(f) **Whether the ADR had a reasonable prospect of success:** There was a 'reasonable chance' that ADR would have been successful, either 'in whole or in part'.

Turner J considered an argument from the defendant based on public policy, 'that it may be reasonable for a defendant who routinely faces wholly unfounded claims to take a stand even where the costs of so doing are likely to be disproportionate to the alleged value of the claim'. However, Turner J rejected the argument, saying that this was not a case 'which was so self-evidently unfounded that it should be fought regardless of the risk of incurring disproportionately high costs'. He added that 'there was no real risk here of any settlement having a potential impact on police powers or policing tactics'.

The *Laporte and Christian* case is discussed by Sidoli del Ceno and Fionda in 'The Cost of Failing to Mediate' (2015) 81(3) Arbitration 343. More recently, in *Primeview Developments Ltd v Ahmed and Others* [2017] UKUT 57, the Upper Tribunal (Lands Chamber) decided that a refusal to enter into mediation in a property dispute was not unreasonable. The Upper Tribunal (UT) held that the First-tier Tribunal (FTT) had adopted the guidance in *Halsey* and 'applied it in an appropriate manner when deciding that the two most relevant factors in this case were cost and the prospects of success'. The FTT had been 'entitled to conclude from the evidence before it that the prospects of success were slight and that the costs of mediation were likely to be disproportionately high. It follows that the FTT was entitled to determine that [the] refusal to mediate should not be sanctioned.'

Three more recent cases demonstrate yet again that whether or not a refusal to mediate is unreasonable depends on all of the facts in each case. In *Gore v Naheed and Ahmed* [2017] EWCA Civ 369, the Court of Appeal refused to penalise the claimant, Graham Gore, even though he had not responded to the defendants' offer to mediate their property dispute. The Court noted that Gore's solicitor had advised him that mediation had 'no realistic prospect of succeeding' and 'would only add to the costs'. The case also raised 'quite complex questions of law' which 'made it unsuitable for mediation'. By way of contrast, in another property dispute, the High Court penalised the defendants after they 'dragged their feet and delayed for so long' that the claimants withdrew an offer to mediate, in a decision which was upheld on appeal. In that case, *Thakkar v Patel* [2017] EWCA Civ 117, the Court of Appeal said that the case was 'plainly' suitable for mediation and 'there was a real chance of achieving a settlement', which meant that the defendants' conduct in response to the claimants' offer was unreasonable. Similarly, the claimant in a contractual dispute was also penalised for failing to respond to the defendant's offer to mediate in *ICI Ltd v Merit Merrell Technology Ltd* [2018] EWHC 177. Fraser J in the High Court said that the claimant's failure to engage in mediation was 'wholly unreasonable'. He added that the defendant's willingness to engage in mediation 'was in stark contrast to the claimant's approach, which throughout had been to engage in litigation by attrition'. It should be noted that the decision in *Gore v Naheed and Ahmed* has been criticised for failing to follow the precedents established in the earlier cases. Masood Ahmed ('Mediation: The Need for a United, Clear and Consistent Judicial Voice' (2018) 37 CJQ 13) pointed out that the complexity of a case was *not* a justification for failing to engage in mediation, citing the case of *Burchell v Bullard* (2005), discussed earlier, as an example of a complex case which was suitable for mediation.

Table 16.1 shows the timeline of the key 'cost consequences' case law.

16.2.3 **The importance of the voluntary nature of mediation**

It is important to emphasise that mediation, at least in England, is a voluntary process. There are two main reasons for this: first, if mediation was compulsory or participants were forced to participate, it could create barriers between the parties and

Table 16.1 Timeline of the key 'cost consequences' case law

Case	Year	Points to note
Dunnett v Railtrack plc	2002	Parties refusing to mediate may face 'uncomfortable costs consequences' even if later successful in court
Hurst v Leeming	2002	***Dunnett*** principle held to be inapplicable in cases where there is 'no realistic prospect' of mediation being successful
Halsey v Milton Keynes General NHS Trust	2004	***Dunnett*** principle restricted to cases where the party refusing to mediate had 'acted unreasonably'. Burden of proof placed on the party alleging that the refusal was unreasonable
PGF II SA v OMFS Co 1 Ltd	2013	Silence in the face of an offer to mediate will, generally speaking, be unreasonable, being tantamount to a refusal to mediate

the mediator and inhibit the negotiation process. Secondly, the typical outcome in a successful mediation process is a compromise solution to which both parties have agreed. As both can be satisfied with the outcome (sometimes referred to as a 'win/win' outcome), there is therefore a greater chance that the agreement will continue. Conversely, forcing one, or even both, unwilling parties into mediation would probably achieve nothing in terms of a settlement, and would just prolong the dispute as it would have to go to court to be litigated anyway, wasting both parties' time as well as that of the mediator.

In *Halsey*, the Court of Appeal identified another reason for keeping mediation voluntary: that ordering mediation could involve denying litigants access to court and could therefore contravene Article 6(1) of the European Convention on Human Rights (ECHR) (the right to a fair trial). However, when the Court of Justice of the European Union (CJEU) considered this issue in *Alassini v Telecom Italia SpA* (C-317/08) [2010] 3 CMLR 17, involving a provision of Italian legislation which precluded court proceedings for certain disputes until a mandatory attempt to settle the dispute using ADR had been undertaken, the Court held that the Italian law did *not* infringe the parties' Article 6(1) right to a fair trial. The CJEU stated:

> Fundamental rights do not constitute unfettered prerogatives and may be restricted, provided that the restrictions in fact correspond to objectives of general interest [and] do not involve . . . a disproportionate and intolerable interference which infringes upon the very substance of the rights guaranteed . . . The aim of the national provisions at issue is the quicker and less expensive settlement of disputes and a lightening of the burden on the court system, and they thus pursue legitimate objectives in the general interest . . . The imposition of an out-of-court settlement procedure does

> not seem disproportionate [because] no less restrictive alternative to the implementation of a mandatory procedure exists, since the introduction of an out-of-court settlement procedure which is merely optional is not as efficient a means of achieving those objectives.

This decision was recently confirmed by the same court in *Menini and Rampanelli v Banco Popolare Società Cooperativa* (Case C-75/16) [2018] 1 CMLR 15, another case involving a requirement under Italian legislation that parties must participate in pre-trial mediation in certain types of dispute. The CJEU did impose certain conditions that must be met in order for compulsory mediation to be compatible with the right to a fair trial. The Court stated that 'the requirement for a mediation procedure as a condition for the admissibility of proceedings before the courts may prove compatible with the principle of effective judicial protection, provided that that procedure does not result in a decision which is binding on the parties'. This would seem to decide that compulsory pre-trial *arbitration* (as opposed to conciliation or mediation), which does lead to a binding decision, would be incompatible with Article 6(1) ECHR. Other conditions were that the compulsory mediation 'does not cause a substantial delay for the purposes of bringing legal proceedings, that it suspends the period for the time-barring of claims and that it does not give rise to costs—or gives rise to very low costs—for the parties'.

Tronson ('Mediation Orders: Do the Arguments against Them Make Sense' (2006) 25 CJQ 412) has observed that *Halsey* is a 'paradox', in that the Court of Appeal is (on one hand) denying that the courts have the power to order mediation but is also (on the other hand) threatening to penalise parties that do not mediate (if that refusal is unreasonable). Tronson concludes that, in reality, the Court of Appeal probably has made mediation compulsory because the financial risks of not mediating are simply too great. Ahmed ('Implied Compulsory Mediation' (2012) 31 CJQ 151) shares this view. He writes:

> Despite the express rejection of the concept of court compelled mediation . . . the powers of the courts and judicial attitudes towards Alternative Dispute Resolution processes (in particular mediation) have the inevitable consequence of compelling parties to engage in Alternative Dispute Resolution processes. This compulsion is largely driven by existing court powers which allow it to punish a party in costs for failing to participate in settlement processes.

In March 2011, the Ministry of Justice published a Consultation Paper entitled 'Solving Disputes in the County Court: Creating a Simpler, Quicker and More Proportionate System'. Among other reform ideas, the government proposed making mediation compulsory in some small claims cases, while also raising the ceiling for small claims cases. In April 2013, the ceiling for small claims cases was duly raised from £5,000 to £10,000 (refer back to 15.8), but the government has not (yet) made mediation compulsory.

Critical debate

Lind has noted that '[i]n certain US states, mediation is ordered automatically in many cases. However, a call for mediation to become mandatory in the UK would conflict directly with the voluntary nature of mediation' ('ADR and Mediation—Boom or Bust?' (2001) 151 NLJ 1238). Three years later, Mahendra ('Popular but no Panacea' (2004) 154 1398) pointed out that:

> *Halsey* brought home the reality to those advocating greater use of ADR. The court explained that to oblige unwilling parties to refer their disputes to mediation would be to impose an unacceptable obstruction on the right of access to the court, and that if the court were to compel parties to enter into mediation when unwilling, that would achieve nothing except to add to the costs, possibly delay matters and damage the perceived effectiveness of ADR.

Compulsory mediation exists in a number of jurisdictions (including Australia and parts of Canada, as well as the US), raising the question: if it can work there, why not here? The answer, according to commentators such as Lind and Mahendra, is that non-voluntary mediation could be perceived to be an infringement of the litigants' right, enshrined in Article 6(1) of the ECHR, to 'a fair and public hearing . . . by an independent and impartial tribunal established by law'. Conversely, jurisprudence at the level of the Court of Justice of the European Union suggests that compulsory mediation does not breach Article 6(1) provided certain conditions are met. Compulsory mediation could also be a waste of time and resources—after all, mediation is predicated on the parties' willingness to negotiate their way to a mutually acceptable compromise solution to their dispute, so forcing parties unwillingly into the process is unlikely to lead to a productive outcome.

The counter-arguments were neatly presented by Dreadon in 'Mediation Order' (2005) 149 SJ 12, who argued:

> The judgment in *Halsey* is at odds with the accepted view in Australia and the United States and, probably, the view of most experienced mediators in England. Even where a party is initially unwilling to participate, surprising results can be achieved with the aid of a skilful and experienced mediator. Further, mediations can be set up very quickly and parties are free to leave at any time, so concerns about the obstruction of a party's right of access to the court would appear to be misconceived.

De Girolamo ('Rhetoric and Civil Justice: A Commentary on the Promotion of Mediation without Conviction in England and Wales' (2016) 35 CJQ 162) has argued that the UK government should do more to clarify the legal position, given the various judicial pronouncements that mediation is not compulsory on one hand, and the threat of financial sanctions that await those who unreasonably fail to engage with mediation on the other. She writes:

> Government needs to redress the current schism between talk and action . . . There seems to be a desire by the English courts and government to continue under a façade which holds to the view that compulsory mediation is not appropriate for England and Wales. However, the rules and pre-action protocols of their civil justice system, the statements made by the judiciary in cases and speeches, and the actions of government all point to a regime that seeks to do indirectly what it feels it should not do directly. Furthermore, it

supports a system which is *ad hoc*, opaque and burdensome on litigants. There is a need for clear articulation about the expectations of the civil justice system.

In the light of this, identify the advantages and disadvantages of making mediation compulsory. Are there some areas of dispute resolution that would be more suitable than others for compulsory mediation?

16.3 Other forms of ADR

16.3.1 Adjudication

The construction industry has long been bedevilled by disputes. Arbitration is widely used but to some extent suffers from many of the drawbacks of litigation. Disputes during lengthy construction projects have been particularly problematic, as delays to the project were inevitably caused. Section 108(1) of the Housing Grants, Construction and Regeneration Act 1996 introduced another form of ADR: adjudication. The section states that a 'party to a construction contract has the right to refer a dispute arising under the contract for adjudication under a procedure complying with this section'. Adjudication is designed to be quick and to take place during the continuation of the construction contract, rather than leaving resolution of the dispute until after completion of the project. Adjudication, however, does not necessarily finally resolve a dispute. The parties may contractually agree that a dispute adjudicated upon is determined for the remainder of the duration of the construction contract only, and thereafter will be finally resolved by arbitration. In this sense, adjudication can be seen as an interim measure.

16.3.2 Conciliation

This is similar to mediation, except that the conciliator plays a more interventionist role. The Advisory, Conciliation and Arbitration Service (ACAS; **www.acas.org.uk/**) administers a statutory conciliation scheme in collective employment disputes.

In May 2014, following the enactment of the Enterprise & Regulatory Reform Act 2013, which introduced s.18A into the Employment Tribunals Act 1996, an 'early conciliation' scheme was introduced for most forms of employment dispute, including allegations of unfair dismissal, workplace discrimination, unlawful wage deduction, unpaid notice or holiday pay, breach of the right to equal pay for men and women, and so on. The scheme was launched on a voluntary basis in April 2014 but became mandatory a month later. Under the scheme, employees or ex-employees who would otherwise have pursued a case before an employment tribunal (ET) (see Chapter 17) are instead *required* (that is, not just encouraged) to inform ACAS of the claim. ACAS will then seek to discover whether or not the dispute could be settled through discussion between employee and employer, with the help of ACAS (if the dispute is in an area of employment law to which the scheme applies). If so, the parties will then proceed to conciliation; if not, the case can then be taken to an ET in the usual way.

This new scheme, which is free, has been very popular, with ACAS itself reporting that more than 17,000 people used the service during its first three months of operation. As a result, there has been a steep drop in the number of people taking cases to ETs (a decline which has been accelerated by the introduction in July 2013 of fees for taking a case to an ET), with some reports suggesting that ETs are dealing with 70 per cent fewer cases in 2015 compared to 2013. It is important to note, however, that the new scheme does not make conciliation itself mandatory. Although the employee or ex-employee is obliged to inform ACAS about their claim, there is no suggestion that anyone would be compelled to enter unwillingly into conciliation, nor is there any suggestion that either party will suffer any adverse consequences should they be unwilling to enter into and/or proceed with conciliation.

16.3.3 **Med-arb**

This is a hybrid of mediation and arbitration. One weakness of mediation is that there is no guarantee of a successful resolution of the dispute, whereas with arbitration a solution will be reached when the arbitrator imposes his or her decision. 'Med-arb' therefore begins with mediation, and the parties try to reach a compromise agreement. If this is achieved then the dispute is resolved. But if mediation is unsuccessful, then the process shifts to arbitration, because that will produce a solution. Med-arb is well established in the US and may be set for expansion in this country following its recommendation by the Court of Appeal in the case of *IDA Ltd and Metcalf v Southampton University and Howse* [2006] EWCA Civ 145. The case involved a dispute over who was entitled to a patent for a cockroach trap, originally invented by Professor Philip Howse of Southampton University but subsequently modified following a suggestion made by Colin Metcalfe of IDA Ltd. In that case, Jacob LJ said (emphasis added):

> Parties to these disputes should realise, that if fully fought, they can be protracted, very very expensive and emotionally draining. On top of that, very often development or exploitation of the invention under dispute will be stultified by the dead hand of unresolved litigation . . . It will often be better to settle early for a smaller share than you think you are entitled to—a small share of large exploitation is better than a large share of none or little. This sort of dispute is particularly apt for early mediation. Such mediation could well go beyond conventional mediation (where the mediator facilitates a consensual agreement). *I have in mind the process called 'medarb' where a 'mediator' trusted by both sides is given the authority to decide the terms of a binding settlement agreement.*

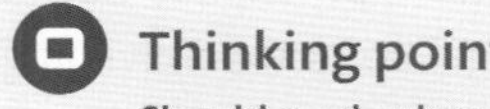

Thinking point

Should med-arb replace mediation?

It was noted earlier that one of the problems with mediation is that, because it involves two parties trying to reach a compromise through negotiation, it does not necessarily follow that any agreement will be reached. Where this happens, the parties are really back to square one. Med-arb avoids this frustrating (non)-outcome by starting with mediation but then switching to arbitration if no agreement can be reached through negotiation. Given this, do you think med-arb should replace mediation? Are there any disadvantages with med-arb?

16.3.4 **Early neutral evaluation/expert determination**

According to the Centre for Effective Dispute Resolution (CEDR) website (**www.cedr.co.uk/**), early neutral evaluation is 'a preliminary assessment of facts, evidence or legal merits. This process is designed to serve as a basis for further and fuller negotiations or, at the very least, help parties avoid further unnecessary stages in litigation.' Meanwhile, expert determination is

> a process in which an independent third party, acting as an expert rather than judge or arbitrator, is appointed to decide the dispute. There is no right of appeal and the expert's determination is final and binding on the parties. It is particularly suited to disputes of valuation or a purely technical nature across a range of sectors.

16.3.5 **Industry codes of conduct**

A number of industries have their own codes of conduct, the aim of which is to provide protection for consumers. The best-known example is probably the travel industry scheme set up by ABTA, the Association of British Travel Agents (**abta.com/help-and-complaints/customer-support/resolving-disputes**). Their scheme encourages resolution of any dispute between holidaymakers and travel companies through independent arbitration and/or conciliation.

ABTA's scheme was recently discussed in the High Court in *Briggs and Others v First Choice Holidays* [2017] EWHC 2012. The claimants were seeking compensation from the defendant travel company following holidays to Turkey where the standards of food and accommodation were alleged to be of very poor quality. Some, but not all, of the claimants had become ill with 'acute gastric symptoms'. The claimants had all issued legal proceedings rather than using ABTA's scheme. A question arose during the litigation as to whether the failure, on the part of those claimants who had not become ill, to use ABTA's scheme was 'unreasonable' in the light of the case law on the costs consequences of failing to mediate, in particular *Halsey v Milton Keynes NHS Trust* (discussed above at 16.2.2). At first instance, the trial judge held that '[w]here there is an established and cheap method of ADR, the non-illness claimants did not in my view act reasonably by resorting to group litigation', principally because ABTA's scheme would have involved significantly lower legal costs than civil litigation. However, on appeal, Singh J in the High Court said that the trial judge's ruling that it was *automatically* unreasonable to eschew ABTA's scheme in favour of litigation was 'plainly wrong'. He said: 'I do not consider that the position has yet been reached where the mere availability of an arbitration scheme will suffice to make it unreasonable *in itself* to embark on litigation instead . . . Rather, the true principle is that *all the circumstances* have to be considered' (emphasis added).

16.4 Court's powers to 'stay' litigation

In many areas of dispute, one party may be more willing to try an alternative form of resolution than the other. In some cases, however, both parties to a commercial contract agree to incorporate a provision into their contract committing themselves to a form of ADR (arbitration, adjudication, mediation, etc.) in the event of a dispute. Are such contractual clauses legally binding? Generally speaking, the answer is 'yes', and the courts will grant a 'stay' of litigation until the prescribed form of ADR has been attempted.

Section 9(1) of the Arbitration Act 1996 expressly states:

> A party to an arbitration agreement against whom legal proceedings are brought . . . in respect of a matter which under the agreement is to be referred to arbitration may . . . apply to the court in which the proceedings have been brought to stay the proceedings so far as they concern that matter.

This provision is important as it serves to emphasise that if parties have agreed to arbitrate in advance of any dispute arising, and it does subsequently arise, they cannot renege on that agreement. Section 9(1) was applied by the Court of Appeal in *Inco Europe v First Choice Distribution and Others* [1999] 1 WLR 270. Inco had brought an action against the four defendants claiming a breach of contract. This was despite the fact that Inco had earlier agreed to refer such a dispute to arbitration. One of the defendant companies, Steinweg, applied for a stay under s.9(1). The judge hearing the application ruled that the arbitration agreement was 'null and void or inoperative' and refused the application. On appeal, however, the Court of Appeal reversed this decision and granted the stay.

In *Cable & Wireless plc v IBM (UK) Ltd* [2002] EWHC 2059, the High Court held that a contractual agreement to go to ADR is analogous to a contractual agreement to arbitrate, and so the same principles applied. A contract between Cable & Wireless and IBM stated:

> [T]he Parties shall attempt in good faith to resolve any dispute or claim arising out of or relating to this Agreement . . . through negotiations . . . If the matter is not resolved through negotiation, the Parties shall attempt in good faith to resolve the dispute or claim through an Alternative Dispute Resolution (ADR) procedure as recommended to the Parties by the Centre for Dispute Resolution.

Subsequently, a dispute did arise, and a question was then raised regarding the enforceability of the ADR clause. The High Court held that the clause was enforceable, provided that it was sufficiently certain. In this case, it was, because of the reference to the Centre for Dispute Resolution being able to recommend a particular procedure. The effect of this ruling is that one of the parties to a contract containing an ADR clause can injunct the other party from pursuing litigation until ADR has at least been attempted—provided the ADR clause is sufficiently certain.

In *DGT Steel & Cladding Ltd v Cubitt Building & Interiors Ltd* [2007] EWHC 1584 (TCC), a case in which the parties had agreed in their contract to refer any future dispute to adjudication, the Court again ruled that it had the power to grant a temporary stay to restrain litigation until an adjudication of the underlying dispute had taken place. In another contractual dispute, *Ohpen Operations UK Ltd v Invesco Fund Managers Ltd* [2019] EWHC 2246, the High Court again ordered a stay to legal proceedings until the parties had attempted mediation because the contract contained a clause in which they had agreed to pursue mediation in the event of a dispute arising.

16.5 Problems with court hearings

Lord Woolf's report *Access to Justice: Final Report* (July 1996) identified numerous problems with civil litigation, which have arguably contributed to the growth of ADR ever since. In his report Lord Woolf stated:

> The defects I identified in our present system were that it is too expensive in that the costs often exceed the value of the claim; too slow in bringing cases to a conclusion and too unequal: there is a lack of equality between the powerful, wealthy litigant and the under-resourced litigant. It is too uncertain: the difficulty of forecasting what litigation will cost and how long it will last induces the fear of the unknown; and it is incomprehensible to many litigants. Above all, it is too fragmented in the way it is organised since there is no-one with clear overall responsibility for the administration of civil justice; and too adversarial as cases are run by the parties, not by the courts and the rules of court, all too often, are ignored by the parties and not enforced by the court.

16.5.1 High cost

Legal costs can be exorbitant, meaning that those individuals with neither private means nor access to legal aid have little prospect of taking a case to court or, if they do get to court, of taking it to appeal should they lose. For example, it has been estimated that the amount of damages likely to be awarded at a 'typical' libel trial might constitute 'between 2 and 4 per cent of the total costs, or less' (see Shillito, 'Mediation in Libel Actions' (2000) 150 NLJ 122; see also Webber, 'Mediate!' (2000) 144 SJ 654).

16.5.2 Adversarial procedure

A trial necessarily involves a winner and a loser, and the adversarial process may divide the parties, making them enemies even when they did not start out like that.

This is particularly problematic where there is some reason for the parties to maintain a relationship afterwards—for example, child custody cases. In 1999, the Lord Chancellor's Department (now the Ministry of Justice) published a consultation document, *ADR—A Discussion Paper*, in which the government argued:

> Typically, a claim for damages proceeds by establishing liability, and then determining an award. It is therefore a process focused on finding the fault; not just adversarial, but antagonistic, with an inherent risk of entrenching positions, and encouraging the nursing of grievances. Characteristically, too, in litigation one side 'wins' and one side 'loses'.

16.5.3 **Inaccessible**

Courts do not sit on weekends or in the evenings, making access very difficult for employed people. The nearest court may also be a considerable distance away, making access very difficult for everybody.

16.5.4 **Inflexible**

Despite the revolution in civil litigation under the Civil Procedure Rules, discussed in Chapter 15, courts nevertheless still have to apply rules—both of procedure and of evidence. This may be inappropriate for some cases.

16.5.5 **Publicity**

The majority of court hearings are public. This may be undesirable in some business disputes, where one or both of the parties may prefer not to make public the details of their financial situation or business practices because of potentially damaging publicity. Nor do they want sensitive information becoming available to the public at large, including their competitors. Publicity can also portray celebrity claimants in a less than flattering light, even if they are successful in litigation, especially where the defendant is a newspaper or magazine publisher.

16.5.6 **Imposed solutions**

Court judgments impose a solution on the parties which, since it does not involve their consent, may need to be enforced.

16.6 **Advantages of ADR**

The advantages of ADR in general, and mediation in particular, are well known. We can list them as follows:

- it is quick and cost-effective;
- the parties retain control of their dispute;

- its informality and the lack of adversarial procedure help to preserve the parties' existing relationship;
- it is confidential.

16.6.1 **Low cost**

With mediation and conciliation, the theory is that neither party will be represented (although in practice this is not always the case). This helps to keep costs down. The lack of specialised facilities—in terms of courtrooms and so on—also saves cost.

16.6.2 **Speed**

Given its flexibility, ADR is generally much faster. Of course, there are exceptions. If mediation fails to produce a compromise solution, then litigation may be necessary and the time spent in fruitless negotiation has been wasted. Similarly, if one party challenges the award of an arbitrator and the case then has to go to the High Court, the advantages of time-saving are lost.

16.6.3 **Informality**

ADR procedures and locations are usually much less formal, less adversarial, and less stressful as a result. This affords a greater chance of preserving an ongoing relationship than litigation does. This has benefits in just about every possible dispute, from contractual disputes between business partners or corporate organisations, to disputes between neighbours, to matrimonial disputes, particularly where there are children involved. In other words, ADR means that disputes can be more quickly and easily resolved and (as a bonus) the parties have a better chance of maintaining a relationship afterwards. By contrast, litigation, which is formal and adversarial, will eventually produce an outcome to the dispute, but it will take longer and may perhaps come at a much higher cost in terms of the parties' relationship.

16.6.4 **Accessibility**

Arbitrators and mediators will usually be able to sit on a pre-arranged date and time to suit both parties, so minimising time-wasting for all concerned. Virtually all forms of ADR are much more accessible than courts, in that they do not have to sit at a specific venue and have been known to sit in places as diverse as local authority buildings, solicitors' offices, church halls, hotels, and so on. It has been argued that 'it must be preferable to take the justice to the people rather than expecting the people to come to the judgment seat' (see MacMillan, 'Employment Tribunals: Philosophies and Practicalities' (1999) 28 ILJ 33).

16.6.5 **Expertise**

Arbitrators and mediators will usually be specialists in their particular field. For example, disputes in shipping contracts could be referred to specialists in shipping, and disputes between the various parties to a construction contract could be arbitrated by a surveyor or an architect. The arbitrator or mediator's expertise will allow him or her to grasp the issues in dispute much more quickly, consequently saving time and therefore cost.

16.6.6 **Privacy**

With ADR the proceedings are in private, so that the individuals are not obliged to have their personal circumstances or confidential business secrets broadcast to the general public. This also prevents the taint that disputes can have on reputations. Moreover, the losing party (in arbitration) is not faced with the public ignominy of defeat.

16.6.7 **Agreed solutions (mediation)**

Mediation helps the parties to explore mutually agreeable options for the resolution of their dispute. An agreement reached with the consent of all parties to the dispute is more likely to be adhered to than if it had been imposed by a judge or an arbitrator.

16.6.8 **Eases pressure on the courts**

Sir John Donaldson, in his book *Arbitration for Contractors* (1987), wrote that arbitration was

> a vitally important alternative to resorting to the courts for the settlement of disputes. If it did not exist, it would have to be invented, because the courts could not possibly handle the sheer volume of disputes which arise in a complex modern society.

These comments also apply, perhaps even more strongly, to other forms of ADR, such as mediation. Similarly, in her article 'The Rise of Mediation in Administrative Law Disputes: Experiences from England, France and Germany' [2006] PL 320, Sophie Boyron writes (about the French legal system, but the arguments do apply to England):

> There are three main reasons why . . . courts aspire to pre-trial mediation. First, the caseload is growing at an alarming pace; the workload of many [administrative courts] seems to have reached critical levels and the issue needs to be addressed. Until now the answer had always been to create more courts, to increase the number of chambers in each court and to recruit an ever larger number of judicial personnel. However, it is felt that it is not possible to resort to such solutions forever.

16.7 Disadvantages of ADR

16.7.1 Non-availability of legal aid

Full civil legal aid is available for mediation only in certain cases. Of course, ADR is designed to dispense with the need for representation—but the hard facts are that in many cases an individual would be faced with a well-resourced and consequently well-represented opponent. This obviously puts the individual at a disadvantage.

16.7.2 Lack of legal expertise

Where a dispute hinges on difficult points of law, an arbitrator or mediator may not have the required legal expertise to judge. This might generate appeals (bear in mind that the Arbitration Act 1996 specifically allows for appeals to the courts on points of law), generating delays and costs.

16.7.3 Imbalance of power

One weakness regarding mediation is its assumption that the parties freely negotiate the terms of their final agreement from a position of equal bargaining strength. This is not necessarily the case and a more powerful party (whether employer; business rival; or ex-partner, husband, or wife) may be able to exploit the weaker party and distort the mediation process to their advantage. Unless the mediator is sufficiently aware of these dangers, the weaker party may find the dispute resolved but on very disadvantageous terms to themselves. Arguably, those in a weaker bargaining position should seek the protection of legal representation before the courts rather than risk being exploited in mediation.

Similarly, two-thirds of cases brought to ACAS are either settled by it or withdrawn. This is sometimes taken as an indication of its success; however, this is to ignore the imbalance of power between employer and employee—just because a case has been settled does not mean it was done fairly.

16.7.4 No system of precedent

Because each case is judged on its merits and there is no doctrine of precedent, there may be no guidelines for future cases. There is no reason, however, why ADR should not be allowed to create precedents while at the same time preserving the hallmarks of privacy and confidentiality that make ADR so attractive in the first place. This could be done by publicising anonymised decisions, which could be referred to in future cases.

Thinking point

What are the pros and cons of litigation compared with ADR?

Sum up the advantages and disadvantages of litigation when compared to ADR.

16.7.5 'Legalism' in arbitration

One area of ADR in which there have been accusations of 'legalism' is commercial arbitration. John Flood and Andrew Caiger put forward an argument that 'lawyers have been engaged in a struggle to shift the procedures and style of arbitration from the informal to the formal end of the spectrum. That is, their aim is to reproduce the court within the arbitral forum' ('Lawyers and Arbitration: The Juridification of Construction Disputes' (1993) 56 MLR 412). In support of this theory, they quoted an anonymous 'senior construction solicitor' who commented that 'lawyers tend to overjudicialise the arbitration process', while an engineer observed that 'the lawyers have hijacked arbitration; it's no different from going to court'.

More significantly, they also quote a senior barrister, John Uff QC, who says: 'The whole process of arbitration has become far too legal and complicated.' The reason given for this was that many arbitrators in construction disputes were engineers or architects, with little knowledge of building issues. This encouraged both sides to call witnesses, and adopt what he called 'the formal High Court procedure' of examination followed by cross-examination.

More recently, Uff returned to this topic in 'What Has History Taught Us in ADR? Is Arbitration Costly and Pedestrian?' (2015) 81 Arbitration 180. He acknowledges that while tribunals can 'sometimes' be costly and pedestrian, such problems were the fault 'of the professionals and not the system'. He contends that the situation has improved significantly in recent years, driven by developments in other jurisdictions (he cites Dubai, France, and Singapore) whereby arbitrators are incentivised to reach a decision on the case more quickly. In the UK, Uff argues that there is potential for much greater time-saving if more arbitrators were to make use of their power in s.39 of the Arbitration Act 1996 to make 'provisional awards'. He sums up the position as follows:

> The best system of dispute resolution is to avoid the dispute. Otherwise it depends upon the skill of all the professionals involved to avoid the pitfalls of excessive time and disproportionate expenditure while still achieving proper consideration of the issues in accordance with the rules of fairness. That will always remain so . . . Arbitration practice in any country, including our own, is regularly compared and assessed against performance elsewhere in terms of speed and cost, and adjustments and refinements called for where needed. But arbitration will always remain as the bedrock of dispute resolution.

Summary

- There are several different forms of ADR:
  - **arbitration**, which is relatively formal and in which the arbitrator conducts proceedings like a judge and gives a binding decision;

  - **mediation**, which is much more informal, negotiations with the mediator facilitating a mutually acceptable compromise solution (although this is not guaranteed);
  - **conciliation**, which is as described earlier, but the conciliator is more proactive/ interventionist;
  - **med-arb**, a process which starts with mediation but, if no compromise agreement is forthcoming, changes to arbitration, which guarantees a solution.
- Reasons why ADR exists are essentially the converse of the problems with litigation:
  - cost and time-consuming nature of litigation;
  - accessibility issues;
  - lack of flexibility in courts' procedure/range of outcomes;
  - publicity;
  - formality;
  - adversarial nature of litigation.
- There is a growing body of case law on 'adverse costs consequences', which was designed to promote mediation/ADR by penalising litigants who failed to respond positively to a suggestion from the other party to enter into mediation (*Cowl, Dunnett v Railtrack*). However, this hardline approach has since softened and the courts now require the losing party to litigation to prove that the winner's failure to mediate was unreasonable (*Hurst v Leeming* and *Halsey v Milton Keynes NHS Trust*).
- Silence in the face of an invitation to mediate will, as a general rule, be deemed unreasonable (*PGF II SA v OMFS Co 1 Ltd*). However, it is not an absolute rule and there may be circumstances where silence may be categorised as 'discourteous' but not necessarily unreasonable (*Crawford v Newcastle University*).
- The courts have no powers to compel mediation or indeed any other form of ADR (*Halsey*), as to do so would create barriers and could even infringe the human rights of the litigants (Article 6 ECHR: right to a fair trial). However, courts can and do strongly encourage alternatives to litigation.

Questions

1 Why is ADR so much cheaper than going to court?
2 Why is ADR so much quicker than going to court?
3 What are the other advantages of ADR?
4 Why is lack of precedent, a typical feature of ADR, a possible disadvantage?
5 What are the other disadvantages of ADR?

Sample question and outline answer

Question

The problems inherent in civil litigation make it imperative that parties are shown the benefit of alternatives to litigation, such as arbitration and mediation. It is therefore regrettable that the Court of Appeal has taken the step of curtailing courts' power to penalise parties for not pursuing ADR in *Halsey v Milton Keynes Trust*. A return to the firm line taken by the Court in *Dunnet v Railtrack* is required. Discuss.

Outline answer

Begin your answer by explaining the inherent problems of civil litigation—cost, delays, publicity, formality, inaccessibility (in terms of location and restricted 'opening hours'), how the involvement of lawyers and the adversarial nature of court-based litigation creates antagonism, the limited range of solutions available to the courts, and so on.

Explain the alternatives—mediation, arbitration, conciliation, med-arb, etc. Make sure that you differentiate these different forms of ADR from each other. Point out, for example, that arbitration is relatively formal and not necessarily cheaper than litigation, but leads to a definite solution. Also point out, for example, that mediation is relatively informal but is dependent on the parties' willingness to negotiate a compromise solution. Perhaps comment that this is a weakness of mediation (the fact that there is no guarantee of an outcome to the dispute) and that med-arb arguably provides a better solution (that is, if mediation fails, the process switches to arbitration).

Explain how the courts have tried to promote alternatives to litigation in cases such as *Dunnett v Railtrack* (2002) (promotion of mediation) and *IDA* (2006) (promotion of med-arb). In particular, explain how the Court of Appeal in *Dunnett* indicated that a failure by a litigant to respond with sufficient enthusiasm to an offer from the other party to mediate might lead to 'uncomfortable costs consequences', that is, that even if they were to succeed in court, the winning litigant may be penalised by having to pay the other party's costs.

Then explain how *Dunnett* has been distinguished in subsequent cases such as *Hurst v Leeming* (which decided that costs penalties will only follow where mediation has a realistic prospect of success), effectively limiting *Dunnett* to cases where it was unreasonable to refuse to consider mediation. Explain how, in *Halsey v Milton Keynes NHS Trust* (2004), the Court of Appeal clearly placed the burden of proof on the party asserting that a failure by the other side to respond to an offer to mediate was unreasonable.

Explain the factors which Dyson LJ (as he then was) identified as being relevant in determining this issue, that is, the nature of the dispute, the merits of the case, the extent to which other settlement methods had been attempted, whether the costs of ADR would be disproportionately high, whether any delay in setting up and attending the ADR would have been prejudicial, and whether the ADR had a reasonable prospect of success.

Explain the extension of *Halsey* in *PGF II SA v OMFS Co 1 Ltd* (2013) whereby silence in the face of a mediation invitation will—generally speaking—be regarded as unreasonable, but note that this is not an absolute rule (*Crawford v Newcastle University* (2014)).

Consider the application of the factors in subsequent cases such as *Burchell v Bullard* (2005), *Garritt-Critchley v Ronnan and Solarpower Ltd* (2014), *Northrop v BAE Systems* (2014), and *Laporte and Christian v Metropolitan Police Commissioner* (2015).

Reach a conclusion. Your conclusion will depend on whether you agree with the hardline approach of the Court of Appeal in *Dunnett* or the more flexible approach of the same court in *Halsey*.

Further reading

- ***Ali, S.*** and ***Lee, F.*** *'Lessons Learned From a Comparative Examination of Global Civil Justice Reforms'* (2011) 53 Int JLM 262

  Examines the legal developments in five jurisdictions (Canada, Hong Kong, Malaysia, Singapore, and the UK) involving legislative and judicial reforms to encourage (or, in some cases, compel) the use of mediation.

- ***Boyron, S.*** *'The Rise of Mediation in Administrative Law Disputes: Experiences from England, France and Germany'* [2006] PL 320

  Examines the use of mediation in the resolution of public law disputes (that is, those involving public bodies) in three different jurisdictions.

- *Civil Justice Council Final Report.* 'ADR and Civil Justice' (2018) available at **https://www.judiciary.uk/wp-content/uploads/2018/12/CJC-ADR-Report-FINAL-Dec-2018.pdf**

  The Civil Justice Council make a strong case for the various forms of ADR to be better publicised, in order to make citizens 'aware that when civil disputes arise there are alternatives to the present choice of capitulation or litigation'. The Council also calls upon the government and the courts to continue to encourage its use.

- ***De Girolamo, D.*** *'Rhetoric and Civil Justice: A Commentary on the Promotion of Mediation without Conviction in England and Wales'* (2016) 35 CJQ 162

  Examines the case law since *Halsey* (2004) and various pronouncements from government over the years in order to ascertain whether mediation is in fact compulsory in England and Wales.

- ***Flood, J.*** and ***Caiger, A.*** *'Lawyers and Arbitration: The Juridification of Construction Disputes'* (1993) 56 MLR 412

  Examines the differences between arbitration proceedings in the construction industry conducted with the involvement of lawyers and similar proceedings conducted using subject specialists, for example architects, surveyors, etc.

- ***Koo, A.*** *'Ten Years after Halsey'* (2015) 34 CJQ 77

  Examines the English case law on the cost consequences of a failure to mediate in the decade since the landmark *Halsey* judgment, and compares developments in England with those in Hong Kong.

- ***Shipman, S.*** *'Court Approaches to ADR in the Civil Justice System'* (2006) 25 CJQ 181

  Examines the Court of Appeal's case law (including *Dunnett* and *Halsey*) on the cost consequences of failure to mediate.

- ***Tronson, B.*** *'Mediation Orders: Do the Arguments against them Make Sense?'* (2006) 25 CJQ 412

  Compares and contrasts the situation in the English legal system (whereby mediation can only be encouraged by the courts) with other jurisdictions, in particular New South Wales in Australia (where the courts have the power to order mediation).

Online resources

You should now attempt the supporting self-test questions and end-of-chapter questions available at: **www.oup.com/he/wilson-rutherford4e**

Chapter 17

Tribunals

Learning objectives

By the end of this chapter you should be able to:

- understand the reasons for the existence of tribunals;
- explain the nature and types of tribunal and understand the problems associated with tribunals;
- assess the relative advantages and disadvantages of tribunals, compared to civil litigation in the ordinary courts.

Talking point

In July 2017, the UK Supreme Court gave judgment in the case of *Unison v Lord Chancellor* [2017] UKSC 51, [2017] 3 WLR 409. The case involved an allegation by the trade union Unison (supported by the Independent Workers Union of Great Britain (IWUGB) and the Equality and Human Rights Commission) that the government had acted unlawfully when, in 2013, it introduced fees for claimants (employees or ex-employees) wishing to bring cases before an employment tribunal (ET) or the Employment Appeal Tribunal (EAT). Unison argued that the fees were set at such a level that they were unaffordable to many potential claimants. The government argued that the imposition of fees was necessary to shift the cost of paying for employment tribunal cases from the taxpayer to those that actually used the tribunals, to encourage settlement of cases, and to discourage weak or vexatious claims. Consider the following questions:

- What do you think were the strengths and weaknesses of the competing arguments in this case?
- Do you think that people wishing to bring claims in the ET or EAT should have to pay any fees at all, or are some fees justifiable?
- If the payment of a fee is justifiable, do you think that the courts should have the power to intervene and declare fees to be unlawful if they are set at a level which is too high?
- Under the government's rules, some of the highest fees were charged for people wishing to bring claims alleging discrimination in the workplace. Why do you think that was, and who do you think would be most likely to bring such claims?
- Do you think that the charging of higher fees for discrimination cases strengthens the government's case, or Unison's?

The *Unison v Lord Chancellor* case is discussed at 17.6.

Introduction

There is no accepted definition of a 'tribunal'. Essentially, they are like courts in that they are dedicated places where people can go to try to resolve legal disputes. However, there are key differences. Whereas courts—especially civil courts—often have a very broad jurisdiction, tribunals specialise in specific subject areas such as employment or social security. Another notable difference is the presence in many tribunals of lay members—non-legally qualified people who sit alongside a legally qualified chair and contribute fully to the decision-making process.

17.1 **Background**

The earliest tribunals date back over 200 years. For example, the General and Special Commissioners of Income Tax were established in 1799 and 1805, respectively. The Railway and Canal Commission, established in 1873, subsequently evolved into the Transport Tribunal (and is now part of the General Regulatory Chamber of the First-tier Tribunal—see 17.3). However, the present system has grown up since the 1940s. The main reason has been the expansion of legislation in many areas previously regarded as outside of the control of the state, such as education, employment, housing, social security, and town and country planning. This legislation gave people rights—to a school place, to benefits, to protection from eviction, to keeping a job—and imposed obligations on government departments, local authorities, and employers. Naturally, this led to disputes. Given the vast number of disputes, it was recognised that the ordinary courts could not cope with the workload: the Royal Commission on Legal Services discovered (in 1979) that the number of cases being dealt with by tribunals was six times that of the number of contested cases in the county and High Courts *combined*. In 2010, the Administrative Justice and Tribunals Council (AJTC) reported that tribunals dealt with 650,000 cases annually, compared to 223,000 criminal cases and 63,000 civil cases that were heard in the courts. According to the website of the Judicial Office (**www.judiciary.uk**), tribunals 'hear about a million cases each year, more than any other part of the justice system'. As Elliott and Thomas put it in 'Tribunal Justice and Proportionate Dispute Resolution' (2012) 71 CLJ 297, 'tribunals are big business'.

Nor would the ordinary courts have been the best forums for resolution of many of these disputes: given the detailed nature of the legislation, and the complexity of some of the issues raised in the disputes, it was perhaps inevitable that specialised tribunals would be needed. Indeed, new tribunals are still created, usually by statute, to deal with increased demand for a means of resolving legal disputes in a specialised area. For example, the Charity Tribunal and the Consumer Credit Appeals Tribunal were both created by statute in 2006 and began work in 2008. (Note: both of these tribunals have already been abolished and their functions transferred to the General Regulatory Chamber of the First-tier Tribunal. See 17.3.)

17.2 **What is a tribunal?**

What distinguishes a tribunal from a court? As already indicated, tribunals are specialist and (compared to courts) relatively informal bodies, designed for resolving legal disputes within their area of expertise quickly and relatively cheaply. A particular feature of most (but not necessarily all) tribunals is the presence of non-legally qualified (lay) members alongside a legally qualified judge, to provide an extra level of specialist expertise. According to the Franks Committee Report on Tribunals (1957, p.9), the defining qualities of tribunals are 'cheapness, accessibility, freedom from technicality, expedition and expert knowledge of their particular subject'. However, there has been an increasing trend for some tribunals, at least, to become more like courts—with greater use of legal representation, greater reporting of decisions and reliance on them as precedents, and more procedural rules—such that it is getting harder to distinguish them from courts. There are, however, two distinct types of tribunal:

- those established by the state, generally described as 'administrative tribunals' to perform judicial functions, typically reviewing decisions made by some government department;
- those established by non-state institutions such as professional and sporting associations and trade unions as part of their disciplinary procedures.

Thinking point

Would more specialised courts be better than tribunals?

Do the advantages of tribunals over courts justify having this extra tier of dispute resolution? Would the English legal system be better served by having more specialised courts?

17.3 The organisation of tribunals: the Tribunals Service

Until quite recently, there was very little coherence or structure to the administrative tribunal system. Individual tribunals had been set up by different Acts of Parliament with little or no consistency when it came to procedures and related matters such as the availability of appeals. In May 2000, Lord Irvine, the then Lord Chancellor, appointed Sir Andrew Leggatt, a former Court of Appeal judge, to undertake a review of the administrative tribunal system. Sir Andrew published his report, entitled *Tribunals for Users—One System, One Service*, in 2001. Sir Andrew identified a number of serious problems with the system.

17.3.1 Problems with the old tribunal system

Lack of independence

Many tribunals dealt with disputes between citizens and government departments. When looking at these tribunals, Sir Andrew found that there was an 'uneasy relationship' between most tribunals and the government departments whose decisions were being challenged. He found that many tribunal members did not feel that they had sufficient independence from those departments. Sir Andrew concluded that 'plainly they are not independent'. This was especially the case with tribunals funded by government departments but, even where that was not the case, Sir Andrew thought that 'there can be an unhealthy closeness'.

Lack of coherence

Sir Andrew found that most tribunals were 'entirely self-contained' and operated separately from other tribunals, which meant that they were all using different practices and standards. This meant confusion—not just for ordinary members of the public who are the users of tribunals, but also for solicitors and other advisers.

Inconsistency of appeals

Lord Justice Woolf, in 'A Hotch-Potch of Appeals—The Need for a Blender' [1988] CJQ 44, wrote that the various appeal routes available from different tribunals' decisions were a 'hotch-potch'. Sir Andrew agreed that the structure of appeal routes was 'haphazard, having developed alongside the unstructured growth of the tribunals themselves'. He noted that, while some tribunals had a two-tier structure (for example, appeals from the ET were (and indeed still are) heard by the EAT), most did not. Sir Andrew was particularly concerned that people wishing to challenge decisions in 'important areas', such as decisions of the Mental Health Review Tribunal, were 'effectively left with no recourse apart from judicial review'. His conclusion was that the inconsistent appeal system was 'not satisfactory'. The solution was obvious: 'to simplify, to ensure that appeal routes are rational and clearly defined. There should be a single route for all appeals from tribunals.'

The key recommendation of Sir Andrew's 2001 report was the creation of a Tribunals Service, designed to provide a common administrative service for all tribunals and streamline the appeal structure. The new Service would provide:

- **Independence:** a Tribunals Service would break the relationship (described as 'indefensible') that previously existed whereby certain tribunals received administrative support from the government department whose decisions were being challenged;
- **Coherence:** all of the existing tribunals were to be brought together under the umbrella of the Tribunals Service;
- **Consistency of appeals:** there would also be a single appellate tribunal, with a subsequent appeal to the Court of Appeal.

Sir Andrew's report received widespread support. A. W. Bradley, in 'The Tribunals Maze' [2002] PL 200, for example, commented that:

> one of the great advantages of the new comprehensive structure . . . is that it would prevent a new maze of tribunals growing up in future. Inevitably, as new legislation affecting the powers of government over individuals is needed in the future, there will be a need for rights of appeal to be created against official decisions made under the new powers.

The government accepted Sir Andrew's recommendations and in April 2006 the Tribunals Service was established to provide administrative support for several, but not yet all, of the country's biggest tribunals. At a stroke, a large number of tribunals became independent of the government departments whose decisions they reviewed. Five years later, in April 2011, the Tribunals Service was amalgamated with HM Courts Service, creating the HM Courts & Tribunals Service, which provides administrative support for the country's courts and most, but still not all, of its tribunals. For more information, visit the HM Courts & Tribunals Service website: **www.gov.uk/government/organisations/hm-courts-and-tribunals-service**.

17.3.2 The First-tier and Upper Tribunals

The establishment of the Tribunals Service was by no means the end of the reform of the tribunal system. The problem of the 'hotch-potch' appeals procedures had still to be addressed. The Tribunals, Courts and Enforcement Act 2007 was passed

Table 17.1 Chambers within the First-tier Tribunal

Chamber	Jurisdiction
General Regulatory Chamber	This carries out the functions of a variety of now abolished separate tribunals, such as the Charity Tribunal, the Consumer Credit Appeals Tribunal, the Gambling Appeals Tribunal, the Immigration Services Tribunal, and the Information Tribunal, among others.
Social Entitlement Chamber	This has taken over the functions of the Asylum Support Tribunal, the Criminal Injuries Compensation Appeals Panel, and the Social Security & Child Support Appeals Tribunal.
Health, Education & Social Care Chamber	This has replaced the Care Standards Tribunal, the Mental Health Review Tribunal, and the Special Educational Needs & Disability Tribunal, among others.
Property Chamber	This has taken over the functions of the Adjudicator to the Land Registry, the Agricultural Land Tribunal, and the Residential Property Tribunal.
War Pensions & Armed Forces Compensation Chamber	
Tax Chamber	This carries out the functions of what used to be the VAT & Duties Tribunal and the General and Special Commissioners of Income Tax. Since the Parliamentary Standards Act 2009, it also deals with appeals against decisions of the Compliance Officer involving MPs' expenses.
Immigration & Asylum Chamber	This replaces the Asylum & Immigration Tribunal.

in order to achieve this. The Act created two new 'generic' tribunals, the First-tier Tribunal (FTT) and the Upper Tribunal (UT), which came into existence in November 2008. The functions and personnel of dozens of pre-existing tribunals were transferred to the new 'generic' tribunals, with the consequent abolition of those pre-existing tribunals. The FTT is presently subdivided into seven 'chambers', as shown in Table 17.1.

Section 11 of the 2007 Act provides that appeals (on points of law) from the FTT will be heard by the UT. The UT is subdivided into four chambers, as shown in Table 17.2.

Section 13 of the 2007 Act provides that appeals (on points of law) from the UT will go to the Court of Appeal. There is also the possibility of taking a case to the High Court in order to seek judicial review of a tribunal decision. This is not provided for in the 2007 Act but, in *Cart and Another v Upper Tribunal* [2011] UKSC 28, [2012] 1 AC 663, the Supreme Court held that judicial review was available. However, this possibility will only be available in cases where there is an 'important point of principle or practice' or some other 'compelling reason' for the case to be reviewed

Table 17.2 Chambers within the Upper Tribunal

Chamber	Jurisdiction
Administrative Appeals Chamber	This body deals with appeals from the General Regulatory Chamber, the Social Entitlement Chamber, the Health, Education & Social Care Chamber, and the War Pensions & Armed Forces Compensation Chamber of the FTT.
Tax and Chancery Chamber	This body hears appeals from the Tax Chamber of the FTT.
Lands Chamber	This body hears appeals from the Property Chamber of the FTT.
Immigration & Asylum Chamber	This hears appeals from its namesake in the FTT.

(per Lord Phillips in *Cart*). These conditions are designed to be restrictive and, if anything, subsequent case law has narrowed them. In *PR v Home Secretary* [2011] EWCA Civ 988, [2012] 1 WLR 73, Carnwath LJ in the Court of Appeal explained that 'compelling' meant '*legally* compelling, rather than compelling, perhaps, from a political or emotional point of view, although such considerations may exceptionally add weight to the legal arguments' (emphasis in the original).

It was deemed necessary to provide the High Court with the power to judicially review tribunal decisions because 'there is a real risk that the exclusion of judicial review will lead to the fossilisation of bad law' (per Lord Dyson in *Cart*). However, it was simultaneously deemed necessary to restrict the availability of judicial review, for several reasons, including:

- **Legal certainty:** the desirability of ensuring that, in most cases at least, tribunal decisions were final, without the possibility of disputes being prolonged by contesting those decisions in the courts.
- **Cost:** the need to ensure that resources were not needlessly expended in litigating cases through the courts which had already been decided at tribunal level.
- **Specialisation and mutual respect:** the recognition that the Upper Tribunal, in particular, is staffed by subject specialists who are experts in what are often complex areas of law such as social security and immigration, whereas the High Court is a court of general jurisdiction.
- **High Court workload:** the need to avoid overburdening the High Court with judicial review cases.

As already noted, not all of the pre-existing tribunals have been transferred to the 'generic' First-tier and Upper Tribunals. For example, ETs and the EAT have not (yet) been transferred because of the nature of the cases that come before them, which involve one party against another, unlike most of the other tribunals, which involve citizens challenging decisions made by government departments. Some of the more noteworthy tribunals which (for the time being at least) remain outside of the First-tier/Upper Tribunals structure include:

- The Competition Appeal Tribunal (**www.catribunal.org.uk/**). This is described on its website as 'a specialist judicial body with cross-disciplinary expertise in law, economics, business and accountancy which hears and decides cases involving competition or economic regulatory issues'. Appeals are heard by the Court of Appeal.
- The Employment Tribunal (ET) (**www.gov.uk/employment-tribunals**). According to its website, 'You can make a claim to an employment tribunal if you think someone has treated you unlawfully, for example your employer, a potential employer or a trade union. Unlawful treatment can include unfair dismissal, discrimination and unfair deductions from your pay.' Appeals are heard by the EAT.
- The Employment Appeal Tribunal (EAT) (**www.gov.uk/courts-tribunals/employment-appeal-tribunal**). The EAT website states that it is 'responsible for handling appeals against decisions made by the Employment Tribunal where a legal mistake may have been made in the case'. Appeals are heard by the Court of Appeal.
- The Investigatory Powers Tribunal (**www.ipt-uk.com/**). Its website states that the IPT 'provides a right of redress for anyone who believes they have been a victim of unlawful action by a public authority using covert investigation techniques. The tribunal [will] also consider complaints about any conduct by or on behalf of the UK intelligence community, MI5, SIS and GCHQ, as well as claims alleging the infringement of human rights by those agencies.' Originally, there were no appeals available against determinations by the IPT (other than taking a case to the European Court of Human Rights in Strasbourg), but s.242 of the Investigatory Powers Act 2016 introduced a right of appeal on points of law to the Court of Appeal.
- The Special Immigration Appeals Commission (SIAC). The SIAC allows people to 'challenge a decision taken on national security grounds' to refuse them entry into the UK, to refuse or remove British citizenship, or to deport them from the UK. Appeals are heard by the Court of Appeal.

Diagram 17.1 shows a summary of the tribunal structure in England and Wales.

17.4 Membership of tribunals

Membership of tribunals varies. Some, such as the FTT (Gambling) and the Lands Chamber of the UT, usually sit with a judge sitting alone. However, many tribunals sit with a panel of three people: a judge who acts as the chairperson and two non-legally

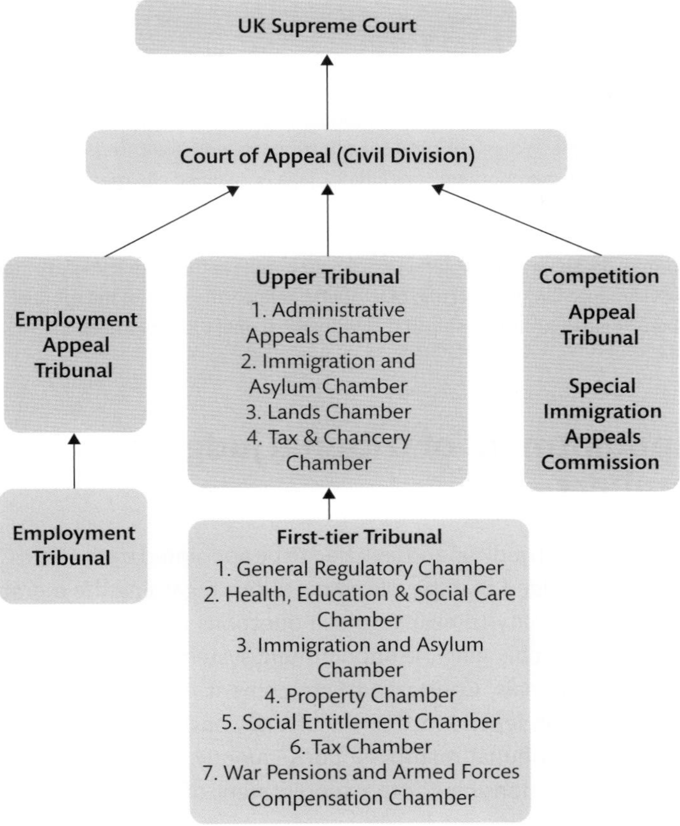

Diagram 17.1 Summary of the tribunal structure in England and Wales

qualified (lay) members, sometimes known as 'wing members'. The reason why some tribunals have wing members differs according to the tribunals concerned.

Some tribunals' wing members are chosen for their expertise in a particular subject matter. For example, medically qualified people sit in cases before the Gender Recognition Panel. People experienced in data protection matters sit as wing members on the FTT (Information Rights). Wing members of other tribunals are chosen for their representative qualities. For example, the lay members of the ET have experience representing employees' or employers' interests. The FTT (Mental Health) has both types of wing member: a medically qualified member (usually an experienced consultant psychiatrist) who provides expertise and a lay member who represents the wider community (in practice, these members are experienced mental health specialists without necessarily being medically qualified, for example probation officers, occupational therapists, or psychologists).

Thinking points

What roles do the lay members of tribunals perform?

It is important to note the composition of tribunals. Many include both legally qualified people and lay people. When looking at specific tribunals, note the composition of the tribunal and how the members are appointed. A legally qualified chairperson for a tribunal is considered to be essential for resolving any points of law that may arise. Many tribunals deal with specialist fields of activity, such as immigration, mental health, or tax, whereas other tribunals deal with the problems of ordinary people in their capacities as employees or benefit claimants. Lay membership of a tribunal reflects the work of the tribunal. Choose three tribunals with lay membership and identify the role of their lay members.

17.5 Appointment of tribunal judges and lay members

Tribunal members (both judicial and lay) used to be appointed by the Lord Chancellor. It has been acknowledged that this raised questions regarding the members' independence and impartiality (similar to those questions involving the judiciary that have led to Parliament changing the appointment system of judges: see Chapter 8). Section 1 of the Tribunals, Courts and Enforcement Act 2007 provides that the guarantee of judicial independence in s.3 of the Constitutional Reform Act 2005 also applies to most tribunal members. Consequently, the Judicial Appointments Commission is now responsible for the appointment of most (but not all) tribunal members.

17.6 Access to the employment tribunal system: the *Unison* case

From their inception as industrial tribunals in the 1960s and continuing until July 2013 (by which time they had been renamed as Employment Tribunals), no fees were payable for employees (or ex-employees) bringing a case to enforce their statutory workplace rights (for example, the right to non-discrimination on grounds of age, disability sex, race, and religion; protection against unfair or wrongful dismissal; rights of pregnant workers, etc.). Many of these rights are conferred on workers by Act of Parliament, for example, the Equality Act 2010. Many more are derived from EU law, such as the Pregnant Workers' Directive 92/85 and the Working Time Directive 2003/88.

However, in January 2011, the Coalition government published a report entitled *Resolving Workplace Disputes: A Consultation*, in which it announced its intention to introduce fee-charging into employment tribunals (ETs) and the Employment Appeal Tribunal (EAT). Charging fees was considered desirable by the government for three reasons:

1. Fees would help to transfer some of the cost burden from general taxpayers to those who use the tribunal system.
2. Fees could incentivise earlier settlements.
3. Fees could disincentivise unreasonable behaviour, such as pursuing 'weak' or 'vexatious' claims.

After consultation, detailed proposals were published in a consultation paper issued in December 2011 by the Ministry of Justice, entitled *Charging Fees in the Employment Tribunals and the Employment Appeal Tribunal.* This proposed two fee systems, and the one which was eventually adopted based the fee on the subject matter of the claim and on the number of claimants. It was proposed that an 'issue fee' should be paid at the time of lodging the claim, and that a further 'hearing fee' should be paid in advance of a final hearing. The paper reiterated the point from the earlier report that the main purpose of introducing fees was to transfer part of the cost burden from the taxpayer to the users of ETs and the EAT. However, the paper acknowledged that fees must not prevent claims from being brought by making it unaffordable for those with limited means. A key component of the new policy would be a fee remission system, with the poorest claimants qualifying for full remission of the fees and other claimants entitled—albeit at the Lord Chancellor's discretion, and in exceptional circumstances—to remission of their fees. The other issues taken into account were the importance of having a fee structure which was simple to understand and administer, and the importance of encouraging parties to think more carefully about alternative options before making a claim.

In April 2013, the Employment Tribunals and the Employment Appeal Tribunal Fees Order 2013 was laid before Parliament by the Lord Chancellor under powers conferred on him by s.42(1) of the Tribunals, Courts and Enforcement Act 2007. The Order was subject to the affirmative resolution procedure but was duly passed by both Houses of Parliament and came into force in July 2013. It divided claims into two types, A and B, with the former being (typically) relatively simple cases and the latter being (typically) cases which were more complex factually and legally. The fees for bringing a type A claim in an ET would be £390, comprising an issue fee of £160 and a hearing fee of £230. For a type B claim in the ET the fees would be £1,200, comprising an issue fee of £250 and a hearing fee of £950. In the EAT, fees of £1,600 were payable, again in two stages: an issue fee of £400 and a hearing fee of £1,200.

In June 2013 (that is, after the Order had been laid before Parliament but before it had been brought into force), the trade union Unison sought judicial review of the Order in the High Court. They argued that the fees interfered unjustifiably with the right of access to justice under both the common law and EU law, and (indirectly) discriminated unlawfully against women and other protected groups who typically brought type B claims, which attracted higher fees. The High Court dismissed the claim (twice—the first time on the basis that the challenge was premature, and later on the merits). The Court of Appeal dismissed Unison's appeal, holding that the imposition of a fee would not constitute an interference with the right of effective access to a tribunal unless it made it impossible in practice to access the tribunal. Unison appealed again, to the Supreme Court.

In July 2017, the Supreme Court—comprising seven judges, in recognition of the importance of the issues—unanimously allowed Unison's appeal, holding that the 2013 Order was unlawful, under both domestic and EU law (*Unison v Lord Chancellor* [2017] UKSC 51, [2017] 3 WLR 409). Giving the main judgment, Lord Reed (with whom Lord Neuberger, Lord Mance, Lord Kerr, Lord Wilson, and Lord Hughes agreed) said that the 'constitutional right of access to the courts was inherent in the rule of law'. He explained that the role of the courts was to ensure that the law was applied and enforced, and 'in order for the courts to perform that role, people must in principle have unimpeded access to them'. That right of access was valuable to society as a whole, not just to the particular individuals involved. It had long been recognised. Moreover, 'impediments to the right of access to the courts can constitute a serious hindrance even if they do not make access completely impossible'. Furthermore, 'any hindrance or impediment by the executive' to that right 'requires clear authorisation by Parliament'.

Image 17.1 Unison celebrating victory outside the Supreme Court

Source: Andrew Aitchison/Getty Images

Lord Reed said that the 2013 Order 'will be *ultra vires* if there is a real risk that persons will effectively be prevented from having access to justice'. Here, statistical evidence was crucial. This showed that, since the introduction of the Order in July 2013, there had been a 66–70 per cent reduction in the number of claims brought in employment tribunals. Lord Reed said that the fall in the number of claims since the introduction of the fees had been 'dramatic and persistent'; it was 'so sharp, so substantial, and so sustained as to warrant the conclusion that a significant number of people who would otherwise have brought claims have found the fees to be unaffordable'. Persons whose employment rights had been breached, or who believed them to have been breached, were often under a 'practical compulsion' to apply to a tribunal for redress (given the lack of alternatives). That 'practical compulsion' made the fall in the number of claims indicative of something more than 'a change in consumer behaviour'. He said (emphasis added):

> The question whether fees effectively prevent access to justice must be decided according to the likely impact of the fees on behaviour in the real world. Fees must therefore be affordable not in a *theoretical* sense, but in the sense that they can *reasonably be afforded*. Where households on low to middle incomes can only afford fees by sacrificing the ordinary and reasonable expenditure required to maintain what would generally be regarded as an acceptable standard of living, the fees cannot be regarded as affordable.

Lord Reed said that the Court could not be 'deflected' from that conclusion by the Lord Chancellor's discretionary power of remission. The statutory scheme of remission was 'of very restricted scope', and the effects of the Order had occurred 'notwithstanding the existence of that scheme'. Furthermore, it was not only where fees were unaffordable that they could prevent access to justice. They could equally have that effect if they rendered it 'futile or irrational' to bring a claim, for example where the reward sought was not financial, such as in claims to enforce the right to regular work breaks or to written particulars of employment. If the financial award was for a modest amount, 'no sensible person will pursue the claim unless he can be virtually certain that he will succeed in his claim, that the award will include the reimbursement of the fees, and that the award will be satisfied in full'.

In practice, said Lord Reed, the Order had had a 'particularly deterrent effect on the bringing of claims of low monetary value'. The Order 'effectively prevents access to justice, and is therefore unlawful'. This was the case at common law. The Order was also unlawful in the sense that it infringed the rule that specific statutory rights are not to be 'cut down' by subordinate legislation passed under a different Act. Moreover, many of the rights asserted before ETs were rights contained in EU law. It followed that the Order imposed limitations on the exercise of EU-derived rights. Here, Lord Reed concluded by saying that the Order was unlawful under EU law as well:

> Given the conclusion that the fees imposed by the Fees Order are in practice unaffordable by some people, and that they are so high as in practice to prevent even people

> who can afford them from pursuing claims for small amounts and non-monetary claims, it follows that the Fees Order imposes limitations on the exercise of EU rights which are disproportionate, and that it is therefore unlawful under EU law.

Baroness Hale agreed with Lord Reed but delivered her own judgment. She added that the 2013 Order was indirectly discriminatory, within the meaning of s.19 of the Equality Act 2010, because type B claims, for which higher fees were payable, were more likely to be brought by women. She held that charging higher fees for type B claims had not been shown to be a proportionate means of achieving the stated aims of the fees regime.

After the Supreme Court judgment, the then justice minister Dominic Raab said that the government would cease taking fees for employment tribunals 'immediately' and begin the process of reimbursing claimants a sum of about £32m in fees paid since July 2013. Raab said: 'The tricky, the difficult, the fluid balancing act that we've got is we want to make sure there's proper access to justice, we want to make sure frivolous or spurious claims don't clog up the tribunal and at the same time we've got to make sure we've got the right way to fund it.'

Thinking points

Was the Supreme Court right in *Unison*? Is there a 'right way' to fund employment tribunals?

What do you think of the Supreme Court's ruling in *Unison*? Do you agree with Baroness Hale that charging higher fees for discrimination cases is itself discrimination (against women)? What do you think would be 'the right way' to fund employment tribunals?

17.7 Supervising the tribunal system

Until quite recently, a body called the Council on Tribunals had the task of supervising the constitution and working of tribunals in the UK. However, the Council was described as conspicuously lacking in powers and suffered from a lack of resources. Consequently, ss.44 and 45 of the Tribunals, Courts and Enforcement Act 2007 replaced the Council with a new body called the Administrative Justice and Tribunals Council (AJTC), which had a broader remit over the whole of the administrative justice system. Under the 2007 Act, the functions of the Council were: to keep the administrative justice system under review; to consider ways to make the system accessible, fair, and efficient; and to make proposals for research into the system. In 2013, the AJTC was replaced by the Administrative Justice Forum (AJF) which was itself replaced in 2017 by the Administrative Justice Council (AJC). Despite the various name changes, the role of the AJC is very similar to that of the AJTC.

17.8 Legalism in tribunals

Tribunals are subject to precedents established by the courts or by appellate tribunals. This has attracted criticism. Over the years the ET (previously known as the Industrial Tribunal) in particular has been accused of over-reliance on precedent, leading to rigidity of decision-making. According to Judge McKee QC ('Legalism in Industrial Tribunals' (1989) ILJ 110):

> Legalism can be defined generally as an inflexible adherence to strict legal formalities and, more particularly, as an undue and an unnecessary reliance on legal authority . . . There is no place for 'legalism' in Industrial Tribunals. All those involved working in these tribunals must be on their guard to prevent it. 'Legalism' properly so called, is contrary to the principles on which Industrial Tribunals were set up.

Similarly, R. Munday ('Tribunal Lore: Legalism and the Industrial Tribunals' (1981) 10 ILJ 146) has written that 'legalism' refers to the 'unnecessary, narrow-minded formalism' with which the layman associates lawyers. He said that tribunals should 'continue to dispense with the flummery and much of the procedural and evidential paraphernalia of the law courts' but he did acknowledge that, in some respects, tribunals do closely resemble courts.

In *Clay Cross (Quarry Services) Ltd v Fletcher* [1978] 1 WLR 1429, after argument lasting two and a half days during which a wide selection of Court of Appeal, EAT, European Court of Justice, and various American authorities were cited, Lawton LJ remarked:

> I found all these complications disturbing. Parliament intended that Industrial Tribunals should provide a quick and cheap remedy for what it had decided were injustices in the employment sphere. The procedure was to be such that both employers and employees should present their cases without having to go to lawyers for help. Within a few years, 'legalism' has started to take over. It must be driven back if possible.

Lord Denning, in *Walls Meat Co. Ltd v Khan* (1979) 1 IRLR 499, said: 'If we are not careful, we shall find the Industrial Tribunal bent down under the weight of the law books or, what is worse, asleep under them. Let principles be reported, but not particular instances.'

On the other hand, reliance on precedent means that tribunal decisions are more predictable, which brings with it the advantage of legal certainty. The competing values of flexibility versus certainty were considered by Sir John Waite, president of the EAT from 1983 to 1985 ('Lawyers and Laymen as Judges in Industry' (1986) 15 ILJ 32):

> A single-minded pursuit of the Franks/Donovan objectives of informality, speed, cheapness and accessibility is bound sooner or later to come into conflict with the aim of certainty. A voice moved wholly by the spirit of Franks and Donovan would say . . . leave the tribunals to apply their own definition of fairness according to the notions of

> industrial practice, which it is their unique duty to interpret and apply. The guardian of certainty would be heard to reply that such a course would leave the tribunals navigating in an uncharted sea where they would be at serious risk of collision with each other.

(The reference to 'Franks' is to the Franks Committee Report on Tribunals (1957) and that to 'Donovan' is to the Royal Commission Report on Trade Unions and Employers' Associations (1968), known as the Donovan Report.)

Thinking point

Is 'legalism' inevitable in tribunals?

Judicial processes must be operated according to rules, and 'legalism' in tribunals will occur due to the need for the involvement of lawyers, especially in complex areas of law, such as employment law. Is it inevitable that tribunals will suffer from 'legalism'?

Summary

- Tribunals are effectively specialist courts dealing in single issues, for example immigration, housing, social security, and tax.
- In 2008, the tribunal system in the UK was thoroughly restructured under the Tribunals, Courts and Enforcement Act 2007. Most tribunals have now been relocated to one of the seven chambers in the First-tier Tribunal (FTT) or one of the four chambers in the Upper Tribunal (UT), although some (such as employment tribunals and the Employment Appeal Tribunal (EAT)) remain outside of that structure.
- Decisions of the FTT can be appealed on points of law to the UT and decisions of the UT can be appealed to the Court of Appeal; tribunal decisions can (in limited circumstances) be subject to judicial review in the High Court, following *Cart and Another* (2011).
- The 2013 introduction of fees for accessing employment tribunals and the EAT (which were previously free) caused a dramatic drop in the number of claims being brought. The fees were held to be unlawful by the Supreme Court in *Unison* (2017).

Questions

1. What is a tribunal?
2. What is a 'lay' tribunal member? Give an example.
3. Why have some tribunals been kept outside of the new First-tier/Upper Tribunal structure?
4. What did the Supreme Court decide in *Cart* (2011)?
5. In the context of tribunals, what is 'legalism', and is it necessarily a bad thing?

Sample question and outline answer

Question

The existence of tribunals is essential to the proper administration of justice in England and Wales. The courts could not perform this function alone. Discuss.

Outline answer

Begin your answer by explaining the similarities and differences between courts and tribunals. Explain that both offer a means of resolving legal disputes, but whereas the courts typically have a wide-ranging jurisdiction over a variety of legal disputes, tribunals tend to be more specialised. Explain that this can only be a generalisation given the creation of the specialised Family Court in 2014. Give some examples of highly specialised tribunals, such as the SIAC and the War Pensions & Armed Forces Compensation Chamber of the FTT.

Explain that whereas courts are exclusively staffed by legally qualified judges, one of the distinctive features of at least some tribunals is the presence of 'lay' members (sitting alongside a legally qualified chairperson) to provide expertise, such as psychiatrists in the Mental Health Chamber of the FTT.

Describe the other features that tribunals enjoy: refer, for example, to the Franks Committee Report on Tribunals' description of the defining qualities of tribunals as 'cheapness, accessibility, freedom from technicality, expedition and expert knowledge of their particular subject'.

Explain that courts would not be able to cope with the sheer volume of cases, with tribunals handling a far greater volume of case law than the County Court and High Court combined.

Explain that there is a system of appeals to ensure consistency, with most tribunal decisions being susceptible to appeal, either to another tribunal or to the Court of Appeal. Observe that, in addition to appeals, tribunals' decisions are, at least in principle, susceptible to judicial review following the decision of the Supreme Court in *Cart* (2011). Note that some tribunals' decisions are however not susceptible to appeal, such as those of the Investigatory Powers Tribunal.

Explain that the system of tribunal adjudication in England and Wales has undergone profound reform in the last fifteen years or so, with the establishment of the Tribunals Service (now the Courts & Tribunals Service) and the passage of the Tribunals, Courts and Enforcement Act 2007, which re-organised the majority of tribunals into the First-tier and Upper Tribunal structure.

Discuss the merits of these reforms, such as enhanced coherence in terms of procedures, greater consistency of appeals, better administrative support for tribunals and their users, and greater independence from government.

Reach a conclusion.

Further reading

- ***Doyle, B.*** *'Alternative Dispute Resolution: The Employment Tribunal'* (2015) 81 Arbitration 20

  Examines the interrelationship between ETs and various forms of ADR, including conciliation and mediation, as means of resolving employment disputes.

- ***Elliott, M.*** and ***Thomas, R.*** *'Tribunal Justice and Proportionate Dispute Resolution'* (2012) 71 CLJ 297

  Examines the relationship between tribunals and courts following the Tribunals, Courts and Enforcement Act 2007 and the Supreme Court's ruling in *Cart and Another* (2011).

- ***Jacobs, E.*** *'Something Old, Something New: The New Tribunal System'* (2009) 38 ILJ 417

  Examines the changes to the tribunal system under the Tribunals, Courts and Enforcement Act 2007.

- ***Partington, M.*** *'Tribunals Reform: Achievements, Disappointments and Prospects'* (2019) 1 Tribunals—available at **https://www.judiciary.uk/wp-content/uploads/2018/03/TJ-1-of-2019-15-April.pdf**

  Provides an excellent overview of the changes to tribunals over the last twenty years, starting with the Leggatt Report in 2001 and continuing via the creation of the Tribunals Service, the Upper and the First-tier Tribunals, the replacement of the Council of Tribunals with the AJTC and now the AJC, and the landmark *Unison* case in the UK Supreme Court in 2017.

- ***Ryder, E.*** *'The Modernisation of Tribunals 2018'*—available at **https://www.judiciary.uk/wp-content/uploads/2019/01/6.5332_JO_Modernisation-of-Tribunals-2018-Report_v3.pdf**

  In which Sir Ernest Ryder, the Senior President of Tribunals, describes an ongoing '£1 billion modernisation programme' for tribunals that 'will simplify language and process, streamline and expedite procedures, removing unnecessary complexity, duplication, error and waste and put the user in the driving seat', to be achieved through a combination of judicial training and investment in digital technology.

Online resources

You should now attempt the supporting self-test questions and end-of-chapter questions available at: **www.oup.com/he/wilson-rutherford4e**

Chapter 18

Criminal and civil appeals

Learning objectives

By the end of this chapter you should:

- understand how decisions of magistrates' courts may be appealed or reviewed;
- understand the ways in which decisions of the Crown Court may be appealed or reviewed;
- be aware of the test applied by the Court of Appeal (Criminal Division) to determine an appeal against conviction;
- understand the role of the Criminal Cases Review Commission (CCRC);
- be aware of the mechanisms for appealing or reviewing decisions in civil proceedings;
- know the composition and powers of the various appellate courts;
- appreciate the nature of the various civil and criminal appellate processes.

Talking point

In October 2013, Alexander Blackman (also known as 'Marine A') was convicted of murdering an Iraqi insurgent and sentenced to life imprisonment. Blackman and his squad were on patrol when they located the insurgent, who had been seriously wounded by helicopter fire. Blackman shot him at point blank range. The killing came to light after video footage of the incident was discovered. His appeal against conviction was dismissed by the Court of Appeal in April 2014. A public petition called for Blackman's release and a national newspaper campaigned for a fresh trial, alleging that a 'shameful injustice' had been done.

In this chapter we will explore the grounds upon which a person can appeal in both civil and criminal cases. The usual rule in a criminal case is that a convicted person has only one opportunity to appeal. However, the Criminal Cases Review Commission (CCRC) has the power to refer a case back to the Court of Appeal if there is new evidence, or a new legal argument, that means there is a real possibility that the conviction will be quashed.

The CCRC carried out an investigation and found fresh evidence that Blackman was suffering from a mental disorder at the time of the killing. They referred the case back to the Court of Appeal and, in April 2017, Blackman's murder conviction was quashed and substituted with a conviction for manslaughter by reason of diminished responsibility. Blackman had by then served three and a half years in prison, and received a sentence that resulted in his immediate release.

As you read this chapter, you will learn about the different tests that civil and criminal courts must apply when deciding appeals, including the test the Court of Appeal used when quashing Blackman's murder conviction.

Before you start, consider the following questions:

- Do you think the restrictions on rights of appeal are fair and reasonable?
- Why do you think a convicted person in a criminal case has only one opportunity to appeal?

Introduction

A party to criminal or civil proceedings who is unsuccessful may wish to challenge the court's decision. This chapter is concerned with the various mechanisms by which the decisions of courts may be appealed or reviewed. It will also consider the nature, composition, and powers of the appellate courts and the procedures involved in bringing appeals before those courts.

As was seen in Chapter 2, the appeal court system in England and Wales is hierarchical. Where a decision of a court has been challenged on appeal or by way of judicial review, a party who is dissatisfied with the outcome of the appeal or review may sometimes be able to appeal to the next court in the hierarchy against the decision of the appellate court itself.

18.1 Criminal appeals

As was seen in Chapter 13, there are two criminal ***courts of first instance***, namely the magistrates' court and the Crown Court. The avenues of appeal from each will be considered separately.

Court of first instance
A court of first instance is a court in which a case is first tried.

A number of factors need to be considered in studying the appeals process. In relation to criminal appeals, you should consider the following points as you read this section:

- the decision that is the subject of the appeal or review may be a decision of fact or a decision of law;
- not all avenues of appeal are available to both the prosecution and the defence;
- the decision that the appellant wishes to challenge may relate to a conviction, or sentence, or both;
- some avenues of appeal or review require the appellant to obtain leave (that is, permission) to appeal.

18.1.1 Appeals from magistrates' courts

The decisions of magistrates' courts can be appealed to the Crown Court (see 18.1.2) or to the High Court by way of case stated (see 18.1.3). Alternatively, application may be made to the High Court for judicial review of a decision of a magistrates' court (see 18.1.4). Diagram 18.1 sets out the routes of appeal from a magistrates' court. The most appropriate avenue of appeal will depend upon whether the appellant wishes to challenge a decision of fact or a decision of law.

18.1.2 Appeals to the Crown Court from magistrates' courts

Under s.108 of the Magistrates' Courts Act 1980, a defendant who pleaded *guilty* may appeal to the Crown Court against sentence. A defendant who pleaded *not guilty* and was convicted after trial may appeal against either conviction, or sentence, or both.

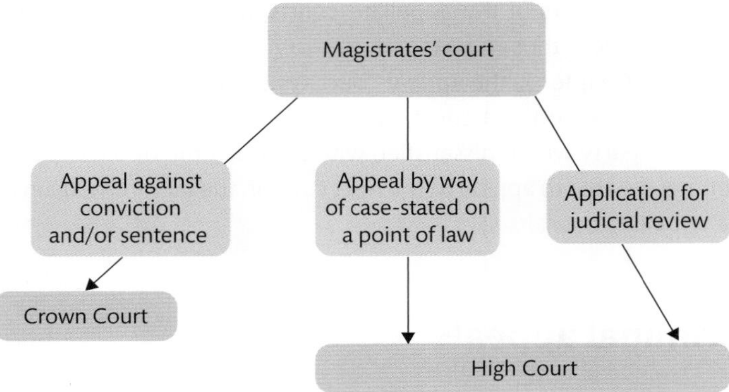

Diagram 18.1 Routes of appeal from magistrates' courts

Thinking point

Why are there limitations on the right to appeal following a guilty plea?

A person who pleaded guilty may only appeal against conviction in limited circumstances, for example if their plea was equivocal (that is, ambiguous) or if it was made under duress. Why do you think this is? If there was a general right of appeal against conviction following a guilty plea, is there a risk that there would be too many appeals for the courts to cope with? It was said in *R v Durham Quarter Sessions, ex parte Virgo* [1952] 2 QB 1 that '[i]f everybody who pleaded guilty and found that the sentence was one which he did not like could appeal . . . against his conviction there would be no end to it'.

A defendant must give notice of appeal to the Crown Court no more than twenty-one days after sentence, although the court may extend this period (CrimPR 34.2).

The Crown Court in its appellate capacity usually consists of a judge plus two lay magistrates. An appeal against conviction takes the form of a complete rehearing of the case. Any witnesses who testified at trial will need to do so again and the Crown Court will consider the evidence afresh. This is, therefore, the most appropriate avenue of appeal for a defendant who is dissatisfied with a magistrates' court's decisions of fact.

Under s.48 of the Senior Courts Act 1981, the powers of the Crown Court on appeal include the power to confirm, reverse, or vary all or part of the magistrates' court's decision, or to remit the matter to the magistrates' court with the Crown Court's opinion (that is, send the case back to the magistrates' court). In relation to an appeal against conviction, the Crown Court will usually either allow the appeal and quash the conviction or dismiss the appeal and affirm the conviction of the lower court.

When considering an appeal against sentence, the Crown Court's role is to determine the appropriate sentence for the relevant offence. In making this decision, the

Crown Court should disregard the sentence that was passed by the magistrates' court. In relation to an appeal against sentence (and also following an unsuccessful appeal against conviction), the Crown Court has the power to impose any punishment that would have been available to the magistrates' court, whether more or less severe than that imposed by the magistrates' court.

Thinking point

Is it fair that the Crown Court can increase an appellant's sentence?

The power to impose a more severe sentence means that a defendant who appeals to the Crown Court risks having their sentence increased. Is this unfair to defendants? Or is it necessary for the Crown Court to have the power to impose harsher punishment on appeal in order to deter frivolous appeals?

The prosecution does not have the right to appeal to the Crown Court against either conviction or sentence. This prevents a person who has been acquitted from having to face a second trial of the same case in another court.

18.1.3 Appeals by way of case stated from magistrates' courts to the High Court

Under s.111 of the Magistrates' Courts Act 1980, a party to proceedings before a magistrates' court who asserts that the magistrates (or district judge) made an error of law or exceeded their jurisdiction may appeal to the High Court 'by way of ***case stated***'. The aggrieved party must apply to the relevant magistrates' court within twenty-one days after the decision appealed against, asking the magistrates to state a case for the opinion of the High Court. When a defendant applies to the magistrates to state a case, their right to appeal to the Crown Court comes to an end.

Case stated
A case stated is a document in which the court states its findings of fact, summarises the parties' arguments, and sets out its decision and the question(s) on which the opinion of the High Court is sought (CrimPR 35.3).

If the magistrates consider that an application to state a case is frivolous, they may refuse to state a case. 'Frivolous' means that the application is futile, misconceived, hopeless, or academic. The applicant may then apply to the High Court for a mandatory order requiring the magistrates to state a case. If the magistrates refuse to comply with such an order, they may personally be required to pay the costs of further applications to the High Court (*R v Huntingdon Magistrates' Court, ex parte Percy, The Times*, 4 March 1994).

Key point

An appeal by way of case stated may be brought by either the prosecution or the defence. This means that the prosecution is entitled to appeal decisions of law made by magistrates' courts, but not decisions of fact.

An appeal by way of case stated will be heard in the Queen's Bench Division of the High Court, by a tribunal consisting of at least two High Court judges of the Division. An appeal by way of case stated is not a rehearing and no evidence will be called. Rather, the appeal will be decided following legal argument by the parties. The High Court has the power to reverse, affirm, or amend the magistrates' court's decision or may remit the matter to the magistrates' court with the opinion of the High Court (s.28A Senior Courts Act 1981).

18.1.4 Applications for judicial review of decisions made by magistrates' courts

Alternatively, a party who wishes to challenge a decision made by a magistrates' court may apply to the High Court for judicial review of the decision. As with appeals by way of case stated, this avenue is available to both prosecution and defence. An application for judicial review requires the permission of the High Court (see s.31 of the Senior Courts Act 1981 and CPR 54.4).

Judicial review is a review of the way in which the court made its decision. It will be appropriate where, for example, a party asserts that there has been procedural impropriety, unfairness, or bias (*Council of Civil Service Unions v Minister for the Civil Service* [1985] AC 374). The High Court will normally refuse permission to appeal, or refuse to grant a remedy, if it considers the conduct complained about made no difference to the outcome of the case (Senior Courts Act 1981 s.31, as amended by the Criminal Justice and Courts Act 2015).

Where the case stated procedure is available (for example, where the challenge is based upon an error of law or excess of jurisdiction), an appeal by way of case stated, rather than an application for judicial review, will be the appropriate route by which to challenge a decision made by a magistrates' court (see *R v Morpeth Ward Justices, ex parte Ward* [1992] 95 Cr App R 215). Judicial review should not be used as a means of avoiding the twenty-one-day time limit for applying to state a case (*Westminster City Council v Owadally and Khan* [2017] EWHC 1092 (Admin)).

18.1.5 Bail: appeals from magistrates' courts

If a person is in custody following conviction by a magistrates' court for an offence, the magistrates' court may grant bail if notice of appeal has been given to the Crown Court or if the appellant has applied to the magistrates or district judge to state a case (Magistrates' Courts Act 1980 s.113). Alternatively, if the defendant appeals to the Crown Court, the Crown Court may grant the defendant bail (under s.81(1)(b) of the Senior Courts Act 1981). The High Court may grant bail in the context of appeals by way of case stated or applications for judicial review (Criminal Justice Act 1948 s.37 and Criminal Justice Act 1967 s.22).

For further information about trial on indictment see 13.1.

18.1.6 Appeals from the Crown Court

An appeal from the Crown Court relating to trial on indictment lies to the Criminal Division of the Court of Appeal (Senior Courts Act 1981 s.53).

Under s.55 of the Senior Courts Act 1981, the Court of Appeal will normally consist of three judges when hearing an appeal against conviction (although, exceptionally, it may consist of an odd number exceeding three). When hearing an appeal against sentence, the Court of Appeal may consist of two judges but will normally consist of three. In either case, the judges in question will usually be Lords Justices of Appeal or more senior judges (such as the Lord Chief Justice). High Court judges and circuit judges may also sit in the Court of Appeal, although a court may not include more than one circuit judge.

Appeal against conviction

Following trial on indictment, a defendant may appeal against conviction to the Court of Appeal either if the Court of Appeal gives leave to appeal or if the trial judge certifies that the case is fit for appeal (Criminal Appeal Act 1968 s.1). In accordance with s.18 of the Criminal Appeal Act 1968 and CrimPR 39, a notice of appeal must be served no more than twenty-eight days after the conviction, although the Court of Appeal may extend this time limit.

Applications for leave to appeal against conviction are made in writing and go before a single judge of the Court of Appeal, who makes a decision based on the papers. If the single judge does not grant leave to appeal, the appellant is entitled to renew their application for leave to appeal before a fully constituted court

Image 18.1: The Royal Courts of Justice in London is home to both the High Court and the Court of Appeal of England and Wales.

Source: Alexandre Rotenberg/Shutterstock

(Criminal Appeal Act 1968 s.31). Table 18.1 shows the numbers and results of applications for leave to appeal against conviction that were lodged from 1999 to 2018.

Unlike a defendant who is convicted in the magistrates' court, a defendant who is convicted following a trial on indictment does not have an automatic right of appeal against conviction. In particular, a defendant who is convicted on indictment cannot appeal simply because they disagree with the verdict of the jury.

 **Key point**

An appellant will only be granted leave to appeal against conviction if there are arguable grounds upon which the Court of Appeal may conclude that the conviction is unsafe.

Prior to its amendment by the Criminal Appeal Act 1995, s.2(1) of the 1968 Act provided that the Court of Appeal should allow an appeal if it thought:

(a) that the conviction was unsafe or unsatisfactory;

(b) that the judgment of the court of trial should be set aside on the ground of a wrong decision of any question of law; or

(c) that there was a material irregularity in the course of the trial.

However, even if any of these conditions was made out, s.2 provided that the Court could dismiss the appeal if satisfied that no miscarriage of justice had occurred. This was known as 'the proviso'.

In its 1993 Report, the Royal Commission on Criminal Justice (the Runciman Commission) criticised the wording of s.2, stating that it was confusing. In relation to the first condition upon which an appeal could be allowed, the Commission observed that the Court of Appeal rarely distinguished between convictions that were 'unsafe' and those that were 'unsatisfactory'. The Commission queried whether the latter term was necessary. The Commission also pointed out that if either s.2(1)(b) or s.2(1)(c) was satisfied, this would mean that the conviction was unsafe or unsatisfactory. Thus, even where paragraphs (b) or (c) were applicable, the Court of Appeal tended to rely upon paragraph (a). The Commission recommended replacing the complex wording of s.2 with a simple test, namely 'whether the conviction is or may be unsafe'. The Commission added that the proviso (which provided that the Court could dismiss an appeal if satisfied there had been no miscarriage of justice) was redundant: 'if no miscarriage of justice has occurred, the proviso is unnecessary, since the conviction need not then be regarded as unsafe.'

The Criminal Appeal Act 1995 amended s.2 of the 1968 Act so that the Court of Appeal must now allow an appeal against conviction if it thinks the conviction is unsafe. There is, therefore, now a single test for quashing a conviction.

Table 18.1 Applications for leave to appeal against conviction to the Court of Appeal (Criminal Division)

	Applications received	Applications considered by single judge		Applications renewed	Applications to renew granted by Full Court
		Granted	Refused		
1999	2,104	480	1,402	637	123
2000	2,068	508	1,351	551	144
2001	1,943	438	1,145	422	150
2002	1,914	405	1,334	457	140
2003	1,787	472	1,213	561	138
2004	1,782	348	1,187	545	144
2005	1,661	360	1,111	557	141
2006	1,596	291	843	481	137
2007	1,508	288	881	520	125
2008	1,588	212	774	400	146
2009	1,435	275	958	477	117
2010	1,488	242	773	370	148
2011	1,535	221	868	425	167
2012	1,697	252	1,029	495	110
2013	1,554	168	904	437	94
2014	1,419	153	881	442	136
2015	1,517	196	1,202	556	70
2016	1,368	67	686	321	73
2017	1,264	79	712	358	62
2018	1,191	84	692	318	74

A conviction may be unsafe because of an error or procedural irregularity at trial, for example, where the trial judge:

- misdirected the jury;
- failed to give the jury an important direction, such as a direction concerning the relevance of a defendant's previous convictions (see 13.11.2);
- admitted inadmissible evidence; or
- excluded admissible evidence.

There has been considerable debate as to whether the Court of Appeal ought to have the power to quash a conviction in the absence of any error of law or procedural flaw in the court below. Should the Court of Appeal be able to allow an appeal if it has a 'lurking doubt' about the safety of the conviction?

Example

In *R v Cooper* [1969] 1 QB 267, the appellant had been convicted of assault occasioning actual bodily harm. He contended that his identity had been mistaken for that of another man to whom he bore a striking resemblance. On appeal, no criticism was made of the trial judge and the appellant accepted that his trial had been fair. The Court of Appeal underlined that it would be 'very reluctant indeed to intervene' in a case where all of the relevant issues were put before the jury and the jury was properly instructed by the trial judge. The Court nevertheless allowed the appeal, acknowledging:

> In cases of this kind the court must in the end ask itself a subjective question, whether we are content to let the matter stand as it is, or whether there is not some *lurking doubt* in our minds which makes us wonder whether an injustice has been done. This is a reaction which may not be based strictly on the evidence as such; it is a reaction which can be produced by the general feel of the case as the court experiences it. (emphasis added)

Subsequent cases revealed a lack of enthusiasm on the part of the Court of Appeal for the subjective, instinctual approach suggested in *Cooper*. Indeed, in 1993 the Runciman Commission criticised the Court of Appeal's general reluctance to consider whether juries had reached the wrong decisions. The Commission observed that most appeals that were allowed involved errors at trial, such as a mistake by the trial judge when summing up the case. In its Report, the Commission concluded: 'We are all of the opinion that the Court of Appeal should be readier to overturn jury verdicts than it has shown itself to be in the past' (p.162). However, although the phrase 'lurking doubt' continued to be used, it is only in the rarest of cases that appeals have been allowed on this ground alone. In *R v Pope* [2012] EWCA Crim 2241, the Court of Appeal held:

> It can . . . only be in the most exceptional circumstances that a conviction will be quashed on this ground [of lurking doubt] alone, and even more exceptional if the attention of the court is confined to a re-examination of the material before the jury.

Critical debate

Professor L. H. Leigh, a former law lecturer and former CCRC Commissioner, has argued that it is not appropriate for the Court of Appeal to take an instinctual approach and allow an appeal on the ground that their Lordships have a general feeling of unease, or lurking doubt, about the safety of the conviction. In 'Lurking Doubt and the Safety of Convictions' [2006] Crim LR 809, Leigh explained that 'to set aside a verdict upon which a jury could properly arrive where there is no apparent flaw in the case strikes at the heart of the constitutional division of functions between judge and jury'. Do you agree that the ability of the Court of

Appeal to quash a conviction where it has a 'lurking doubt' as to the guilt of an appellant usurps the function of the jury?

In *R v Pope* (noted earlier), the appellant was convicted of murder. On appeal, his barrister submitted that there was a lurking doubt about the safety of the appellant's conviction because the jury could not have excluded the possibility that the victim had been murdered by her husband. The Court of Appeal dismissed the appeal, saying that 'the application of the "lurking doubt" concept requires reasoned analysis of the evidence or the trial process, or both, which leads to the inexorable conclusion that the conviction is unsafe'. More recently, the Court of Appeal has criticised the use of the term 'lurking doubt', suggesting that 'it represents an invitation to [the Court of Appeal] to substitute its view for that of the jury. The question . . . is whether . . . the convictions are unsafe' (*R v Fanning* [2016] 2 Cr App R 19). To what extent do you think this approach restricts the use of lurking doubt as a ground of appeal?

In addition to the grounds already discussed, an appeal may be based on new evidence. Under s.23 of the 1968 Act, the Court of Appeal may receive 'fresh evidence' (that is, evidence that was not available at the original trial) where this is in the interests of justice. In deciding whether to hear fresh evidence, s.23(2) of the 1968 Act provides that the Court must take the following factors into account:

(a) whether the evidence appears to the Court to be capable of belief;
(b) whether it appears to the Court that the evidence may afford any ground for allowing the appeal;
(c) whether the evidence would have been admissible in the proceedings from which the appeal lies on an issue which is the subject of the appeal; and
(d) whether there is a reasonable explanation for the failure to adduce the evidence in those proceedings.

Again, the appeal must be allowed if the conviction is unsafe in light of the new evidence. In *R v Pendleton* [2001] UKHL 66, the House of Lords ruled that, in a case of any difficulty, 'it will usually be wise for the Court of Appeal . . . to test their own provisional view by asking whether the evidence, if given at the trial, might reasonably have affected the decision of the trial jury to convict'. This is sometimes referred to as the 'jury impact test'.

Where the Court of Appeal allows an appeal against conviction and quashes the appellant's conviction, it may order a retrial if it appears the interests of justice so require (see s.7 of the 1968 Act).

Appeal against sentence

Under ss.9 and 10 of the 1968 Act, a defendant may appeal against sentence to the Court of Appeal, both where sentenced by the Crown Court following trial on indictment and where sentenced following committal for sentence. In accordance with s.11 of the 1968 Act, a defendant may only appeal against sentence to the Court of Appeal if either the Court of Appeal gives leave or the sentencing judge certifies that the case is fit for appeal. An appeal notice must be served no more than twenty-eight days after sentence being passed. As in the case of appeals against conviction, written applications for leave to appeal are determined by a single judge of the Court of Appeal. Again, if the single judge refuses leave to appeal, an appellant may renew their application before the full court. Table 18.2 shows the numbers and results of applications for leave to appeal against sentence that were lodged from 1999 to 2018.

Section 11 of the 1968 Act empowers the Court of Appeal to quash the sentence and to pass any sentence that the Crown Court could have imposed. However, the Court of Appeal cannot increase the appellant's sentence.

Table 18.2 Applications for leave to appeal against sentence to the Court of Appeal (Criminal Division)

	Applications received	Applications considered by single judge		Applications renewed	Applications to renew granted by Full Court
		Granted	Refused		
1999	6,170	1,743	4,095	1,072	306
2000	5,672	1,597	3,892	932	291
2001	5,497	1,551	3,475	759	240
2002	5,804	1,695	3,876	825	252
2003	5,664	1,736	3,582	878	338
2004	5,809	1,740	3,634	890	283
2005	5,178	1,541	3,092	824	326
2006	5,082	1,261	2,503	831	425
2007	5,087	1,363	2,763	845	519
2008	5,422	1,204	2,468	670	663
2009	5,443	1,298	2,948	763	429
2010	5,454	1,184	2,608	667	500
2011	5,623	1,063	2,454	607	425
2012	5,644	1,289	3,093	768	388
2013	4,997	986	2,805	813	338
2014	4,660	907	2,528	685	333
2015	4,444	1,092	3,140	816	293
2016	3,980	708	1,862	517	280
2017	3,798	640	1,897	492	231
2018	3,589	581	1,737	513	257

Thinking point

Should the Court of Appeal be able to increase an appellant's sentence?

The Crown Court, in its appellate capacity, has the power to increase an appellant's sentence if appropriate. Should the Court of Appeal have similar powers? Note that the Court of Appeal has the power to direct that any time served in custody by the appellant between the date of sentence and the date of appeal should not count towards their sentence (see s.29 of the 1968 Act). This means that, where an appeal is dismissed, the appellant can effectively be ordered to start serving their sentence afresh from the date of their appeal, regardless of how long they have spent in prison since originally being sentenced. It is this power that helps to deter frivolous appeals.

18.1.7 **Miscarriages of justice and the CCRC**

There is no single agreed definition of the term 'miscarriage of justice'.

Example

Under s.133 of the Criminal Justice Act 1988, compensation is available to a defendant whose conviction is reversed on the ground that a newly discovered fact shows beyond reasonable doubt that there has been a miscarriage of justice. In *R (Adams) v Secretary of State for Justice; In re MacDermott; In re McCartney* [2011] UKSC 18, the three appellants challenged decisions that they were not entitled to compensation following the quashing of their convictions for murder. Lord Phillips observed that the phrase 'miscarriage of justice' is capable of having a number of different meanings but the following four categories of case 'provided a useful framework for discussion':

> (1) Where . . . fresh evidence shows clearly that the defendant is innocent of the crime of which he has been convicted. (2) Where . . . fresh evidence is such that, had it been available at the time of the trial, no reasonable jury could properly have convicted the defendant. (3) Where . . . fresh evidence renders the conviction unsafe in that, had it been available at the time of the trial, a reasonable jury might or might not have convicted the defendant. (4) Where something has gone seriously wrong in the investigation of the offence or the conduct of the trial, resulting in the conviction of someone who should not have been convicted.

There can be no doubt that miscarriages of justice occur for all of the reasons identified in *R (Adams) v Secretary of State for Justice; In re MacDermott; In re McCartney* [2011] UKSC 18. High-profile miscarriages of justice include the cases of the 'Guildford Four' and the 'Birmingham Six'. The eventual release of the appellants in these two cases fuelled concerns about the potential for defendants to be wrongly convicted. As a result, a Royal Commission on Criminal Justice (the Runciman Commission) was established in 1991. The Commission recommended that an independent body should be set up to examine potential miscarriages of justice and to refer matters to the Court of Appeal where appropriate. Consequently, the CCRC was established in 1997.

The CCRC is an independent public body. Its principal role is to review or investigate cases in which an appeal to the Court of Appeal against conviction or sentence has been unsuccessful, or where leave to appeal was refused. Under the Criminal Appeal Act 1995, the CCRC may refer a conviction or sentence of a defendant back to the Court of Appeal if there is a real possibility that the conviction or sentence would not be upheld if the reference were made (Criminal Appeal Act 1995 s.13). Thus, for example, where fresh evidence is discovered, the CCRC may cause a case to return to the Court of Appeal several years after the defendant's original appeal to the Court of Appeal was unsuccessful. Similarly, where a defendant was originally convicted and sentenced by a magistrates' court, the CCRC may refer the conviction or sentence back to the Crown Court.

Between April 1997 (when the CCRC began its work) and August 2019, the CCRC received a total of 25,497 applications. By the end of August 2019, the CCRC had referred just 667 cases to the Court of Appeal.

Although under 3 per cent of applications to the CCRC result in a referral to the Court of Appeal, the CCRC's success rate appears to be relatively high, as 441 of the 657 appellants whose cases *were* referred had their appeals allowed. Investigative journalist Bob Woffinden, who has written extensively about miscarriage of justice cases, contends that these statistics create a misleading impression. In a newspaper article entitled 'The Criminal Cases Review Commission has failed' (*The Guardian*, 30 November 2010, available at **www.theguardian.co.uk/commentisfree/libertycentral/2010/nov/30/criminal-cases-review-commission-failed**), Woffinden explained that some of the cases referred were appeals against sentence. Any reduction in sentence, even a minor one, is an appeal that has been allowed. In relation to appeals against conviction, the fact that an appeal has been allowed may not mean that the appellant has been absolved of liability altogether, as sometimes the Court of Appeal substitutes a conviction for an alternative offence, such as manslaughter for murder. Woffinden also pointed out that a number of the CCRC's successes involve relatively minor convictions, including dishonestly obtaining a telecommunication service, allowing a dog to be dangerously out of control in a public place, failing to comply with a notice requiring proper maintenance of land under the Town and Country Planning Act, and keeping a disorderly house. Although the CCRC was set up in response to miscarriages of justice in major cases, it has referred very few serious cases to the Court of Appeal. The case of Alexander Blackman, discussed in the Talking Point at the start of this chapter, is an example of a recent referral in a serious case. In 2014, the House of Commons Justice Select Committee held an inquiry into the CCRC. The Committee's Report can be found at **www.publications.parliament.uk/pa/cm201415/cmselect/cmjust/850/850.pdf**. One of the main issues considered by the inquiry was the test that is applied by the CCRC in deciding whether to refer cases to the Court of Appeal.

Thinking point

What test should the CCRC apply in deciding whether to refer a case?

The CCRC will only refer a case to the Court of Appeal if it thinks there is a 'real possibility' that the appeal will be allowed. This means that the CCRC must focus on what the Court of Appeal will think, rather than on whether a miscarriage of justice may have occurred. What test do you think the CCRC should use to decide whether to refer a case? Some possible alternatives to the 'real possibility' test are set out in the Justice Committee's Report on the CCRC (*Twelfth Report of Session 2014–15*, HC850) at para. 14.

The Justice Committee concluded that the test should not be changed at present, as it would be a waste of resources for the CCRC to refer cases in which there is less than a real possibility of success. However, at para. 27 of their Report, the Committee recommended that consideration be given to expanding the grounds upon which the Court of Appeal can allow an appeal. The Committee expressed particular concern about the Court of Appeal's reluctance to allow appeals in 'lurking doubt' cases (see earlier at 18.1.6). Michael Gove, then Justice Secretary, subsequently rejected this proposal, stating 'there is insufficient evidence that the Court of Appeal's current approach has a deleterious effect on those who have suffered miscarriages of justice.' (See **https://www.parliament.uk/documents/commons-committees/Justice/correspondence/15-09-30-Michael-Gove-to-Chair-on-FOI-Court-of-Appeal-Joint-Enterprise%20.pdf**.)

At para. 20 of their Report, the Committee also recommended that the CCRC should be less cautious in its approach to the 'real possibility' test. The suggestion is that the CCRC should be less concerned with its success rate and should err on the side of referring cases where it is possible that a miscarriage of justice has occurred.

In addition to criticisms that the CCRC refers too few cases to the Court of Appeal, its limited resources mean that it can take many months, or even years, for it to evaluate cases and make a decision about referral. In the case of Alexander Blackman, discussed in the Talking Point at the start of this chapter, the appellant's solicitors lodged an application to the CCRC in December 2015. The CCRC's decision to refer his case to the Court of Appeal was made a year later. Some applicants to the CCRC have endured even longer delays than this. Representatives of Colin Norris, a former nurse who is currently serving life imprisonment for the murder of four elderly women and the attempted murder of a fifth woman, state that they lodged an application to the CCRC on 20 October 2011 on the basis that fresh scientific evidence casts doubt on the safety of Norris' conviction. To date the CCRC has still not made a decision as to whether to refer his case to the Court of Appeal.

The Justice Committee noted that the CCRC had seen significant cuts to its budget, alongside an increased workload. However, at para. 35 of its Report, the Committee made clear that 'the current level of delays is unacceptable' and recommended that the CCRC be granted additional funding. In their book based on a four-year empirical study of decision-making at the CCRC, Professor Carolyn Hoyle and Mai Sato analysed the balance between efficiency and thoroughness in case reviews (*Reasons to Doubt: Wrongful Convictions and the Criminal Cases Review Commission*, OUP 2019).

Thinking point

Striking the right balance between efficiency and thoroughness

Does a shift towards prioritising efficiency to cope with resource constraints increase the risk that applications by innocent defendants will be too quickly rejected?

In 2019, the Ministry of Justice carried out a 'tailored review' of the CCRC, which did not propose any increase to the CCRC's income. Instead the review suggested cutting the CCRC's workload by removing the requirement to review summary cases (cases dealt with in magistrates' courts) or cases involving appeals against sentence only.

18.1.8 Bail: appeals from the Crown Court

The Court of Appeal possesses the power to grant bail pending appeal (under s.19 of the 1968 Act). Alternatively, the Crown Court may grant bail where the Crown Court has certified that a case is fit for appeal (Senior Courts Act 1981 s.81(1)(f)).

18.1.9 Attorney General's references

So far, we have only considered the rights of the defence to appeal from the Crown Court against sentence or conviction. In certain circumstances, the prosecution may have a right of appeal from decisions of the Crown Court in criminal cases. For example, where a defendant is tried on indictment and is acquitted, the Attorney General may refer a point of law that arose in the case to the Court of Appeal in order to obtain the opinion of the Court (see s.36 of the Criminal Justice Act 1972 and CrimPR 41). No matter how the Court of Appeal rules, the defendant's acquittal will not be affected.

Thinking point

Are certainty and finality important to the criminal process?

This means that even if the Court of Appeal agrees that a point of law was wrongly decided in the defendant's favour (and against the prosecution), the defendant cannot be retried for the offence. Why do you think this is? How important is it to have certainty and finality in criminal proceedings?

If the Attorney General considers that a sentence passed by the Crown Court was unduly lenient, he or she may refer the case to the Court of Appeal under s.36 of the Criminal Justice Act 1988. The Court of Appeal may quash the sentence and pass any appropriate sentence that the Crown Court had the power to pass. An Attorney General's reference may only be made in relation to an indictable only offence or to certain specified either way offences.

Moreover, under Part 9 of the Criminal Justice Act 2003, the prosecution is now entitled to appeal against 'terminating rulings' made by the trial judge in the context of trial on indictment. A terminating ruling is a ruling that has the effect of bringing the prosecution to an end, such as a ruling that the defendant has no case to answer (see 13.9.2). The Court of Appeal may confirm, reverse, or vary the trial judge's decision. The result may be that the proceedings resume, or a retrial takes place, or the defendant is acquitted.

If further provisions of Part 9 of the Criminal Justice Act 2003 are brought into force, the prosecution will also be entitled to appeal to the Court of Appeal against certain 'evidentiary rulings', that is, rulings relating to the admissibility or exclusion of prosecution evidence.

18.1.10 Appeals by way of case stated from Crown Court decisions

In accordance with s.28 of the Senior Courts Act 1981, a party wishing to challenge a decision of the Crown Court that does not relate to trial on indictment may appeal by way of case stated. Thus, the case stated procedure described at 18.1.3 may be used to challenge a decision made by the Crown Court upon an appeal from a magistrates' court. This route of appeal will be available if the Crown Court has made an error of law or exceeded its jurisdiction.

18.1.11 Applications for judicial review of decisions of the Crown Court

Alternatively, decisions of the Crown Court that do not relate to trial on indictment may be challenged by way of application for judicial review (Senior Courts Act 1981 s.29). For examples of the grounds upon which such a challenge may be based see 18.1.4.

18.1.12 Appeals to the Supreme Court

Appeal from the Court of Appeal (Criminal Division)

Under s.33 of the Criminal Appeal Act 1968, the defence or the prosecution may appeal from the Court of Appeal to the Supreme Court, but the leave of the Court of Appeal or the Supreme Court is required. Leave will not be granted unless the Court of Appeal certifies that a point of law of general public importance is involved, and then only if it appears to the Court of Appeal or the Supreme Court that the point of law is one that should be considered by the Supreme Court.

For further information about the Supreme Court see 2.5.8.

An application for leave to appeal to the Supreme Court should usually be made either orally immediately after the Court of Appeal gives its decision and reasons, or no more than twenty-eight days after the date on which the Court of Appeal gives its reasons for the decision that is the subject of the appeal (see s.34 of the 1968 Act and CrimPR 43).

When hearing an appeal, the Supreme Court must consist of an uneven number of (at least three) Justices of the Supreme Court (Constitutional Reform Act 2005 s.42). In disposing of an appeal, the Supreme Court may exercise any of the powers of the Court of Appeal or may remit the case to the Court of Appeal (Criminal Appeal Act 1968 s.35). The Court of Appeal may grant bail where a person appeals, or applies for leave to appeal, to the Supreme Court (Criminal Appeal Act 1968 s.36).

Appeal from the High Court

Under s.1 of the Administration of Justice Act 1960, there is also a right of appeal from decisions of the High Court in 'any criminal cause or matter' to the Supreme Court. This right of appeal is available to the prosecution or the defence. It is subject to leave and certification requirements which equate to those considered in the preceding paragraph in relation to appeals from the Court of Appeal to the Supreme Court.

18.2 **Civil appeals**

Subject to certain limited exceptions (such as committal orders, by which a person in contempt of court may be committed to prison), a party who wishes to appeal from a decision of a County Court or High Court judge will require permission to do so (CPR 52.3). Permission will only be given where the court considers either the appeal would have a real prospect of success or there is some other compelling reason for hearing the appeal (CPR 52.6).

An appeal in a civil case may relate to the final decision of the court, such as a judgment given at the conclusion of a trial. Alternatively, the appeal may be against a decision taken before trial, such as a decision about case management (for example, decisions relating to disclosure, directions about the trial timetable, or security for costs). When the court is deciding whether to grant permission to appeal against a case management decision, CPR 52A PD provides that the court is entitled to consider whether:

- the issue is sufficiently significant to justify the costs of the appeal;
- the procedural consequences of appealing, such as losing the trial date, outweigh the significance of the decision the party wishes to appeal; and
- it would be more convenient to determine the issue at the trial or after the trial.

These criteria are designed to restrict the number of appeals against case management decisions in order to save time and expense.

18.2.1 **Permission to appeal**

CPR 52.3(2)(a) provides that a party may apply for permission to appeal to the court that made the decision that is to be the subject of the appeal. Such an application should be made at the hearing at which the decision to be appealed was made. If the court refuses permission to appeal, application may be made to the appeal court. Alternatively, an application for permission to appeal may be made directly to the appeal court by way of an appeal notice (CPR 52.3(2)(b)).

Thinking point

Why does an appellant in a civil case require permission to appeal?

Is it fair that a party to civil proceedings should require permission to appeal? What purpose does the requirement of permission serve? Is it necessary to have this process to filter out hopeless appeals?

Where a party applies to the appeal court for permission to appeal, CPR 52.12 requires the party to file an appellant's notice either within twenty-one days after the date of the decision which is to be appealed or within such period as the lower court directs.

The appeal court may vary the time limits for filing appeal notices (CPR 3.1(2)(a)) and may permit appeal notices to be amended (CPR 52.17). Where there is a compelling reason to do so, it may even strike out all or part of an appeal notice and may fully or partially set aside permission to appeal (CPR 52.18). An application for permission to appeal will be decided without a hearing. However, if the application is made to the County Court or the High Court and permission to appeal is refused, the applicant may ask the court to reconsider the decision at a hearing (CPR 52.4). If the application is totally without merit and the judge who refused permission to appeal was a judge of the High Court, a Designated Civil Judge, or a Specialist Circuit Judge, the judge may make an order preventing the decision from being reconsidered at a hearing (CPR 52.4(3)). Where the application is made to the Court of Appeal, a hearing cannot take place unless a judge decides that the application can only be determined fairly at an oral hearing (CPR 52.5).

18.2.2 **The nature and consequences of a civil appeal**

Normally, in accordance with CPR 52.21, an appeal will take the form of a review of the decision made by the court below, although appeal courts possess discretion to order a rehearing if it is in the interests of justice to do so. Indeed, in certain, limited circumstances, an appeal court may be required to hold a rehearing. The appeal court will not normally receive fresh evidence or evidence that was not before the court below, but does have discretion to receive such evidence.

An appeal will be allowed where the decision of the court below was wrong or was unjust in consequence of serious procedural or other irregularity. The appeal court may: affirm, set aside, or vary the order or judgment of the court below; refer a claim or issue back to the lower court for determination there; order a new trial or hearing; order the payment of interest; and/or make a costs order (CPR 52.20).

18.2.3 **Avenues of appeal**

Ignoring the possibility of a leapfrog appeal (see 18.2.5), the main avenues of appeal are usually as follows (see Access to Justice Act 1999 (Destination of Appeals) Order 2016 (SI 2016/917)):

- from a decision of a district judge in the County Court to a Circuit Judge in the County Court;
- from a decision of a Circuit Judge in the County Court to the High Court;
- from a decision of a Master, Registrar, or district judge of the High Court to a single judge of the High Court;
- from a decision of a High Court judge to the Court of Appeal.

An appeal from a decision of the County Court or High Court, which is itself a decision on appeal, can only be made to the Court of Appeal.

It should be noted that appeal routes are different in the context of insolvency proceedings and family proceedings. For further information, see CPR 52A PD.

18.2.4 **Composition of the Court of Appeal (Civil Division)**

In accordance with s.2 of the Senior Courts Act 1981, the judges who sit in the Civil Division of the Court of Appeal are Lords Justices of Appeal (or Lady Justices of Appeal) plus certain other senior judges (such as the Master of the Rolls, who is the president of the Court of Appeal's Civil Division). Section 54 of the Senior Courts Act 1981 provides that the Civil Division of the Court of Appeal is duly constituted if it consists of one or more judges. However, while applications for permission to appeal are normally dealt with by a single Lord Justice, a court which hears a full appeal usually consists of three Lords Justices.

18.2.5 **Leapfrog appeals in civil courts**

Under s.57 of the Access to Justice Act 1999 and CPR 52.23, an appeal that would normally be heard in the County Court or in the High Court may be transferred to the Court of Appeal where it raises an important point of principle or practice, or where there is some other compelling reason for the Court of Appeal to hear the case. Such a transfer may be ordered by the court which made the decision to which the appeal relates, or by the court from which permission to appeal is sought, or by the Master of the Rolls. This is known as a 'leapfrog' appeal. However, the Court of Appeal or the Master of the Rolls may subsequently remit the appeal back to the original appeal court.

Another form of leapfrog appeal is an appeal from the High Court to the Supreme Court. In accordance with ss.12 and 13 of the Administration of Justice Act 1969, a High Court judge may certify that a case involves a point of law of general public importance and:

- the point of law wholly or mainly relates to statutory construction;
- the point of law is one in relation to which the judge is bound by a previous decision of the Court of Appeal or the Supreme Court;
- the appeal raises issues of national importance;
- the result of the appeal is so significant that it justifies being heard by the Supreme Court; or
- the benefit of earlier consideration by the Supreme Court outweighs the benefit of consideration by the Court of Appeal.

The Supreme Court may then grant leave to appeal directly to the Supreme Court.

18.2.6 'Second appeals' to the Court of Appeal and appeals to the Supreme Court

In addition to the appellate routes outlined previously, 'second appeals' are possible in civil cases (see Diagram 18.2). A 'second appeal' is an appeal to the Court of Appeal following an initial appeal to a County Court or to the High Court. A 'second appeal' is possible only with the permission of the Court of Appeal. In accordance with s.55 of the Access to Justice Act 1999 and CPR 52.7, such permission should only be given where an appeal has a real prospect of success and either: (a) it raises an important point of principle or practice; or (b) there is some other compelling reason for the Court of Appeal to hear it. A second appeal may only be made to the Court of Appeal;

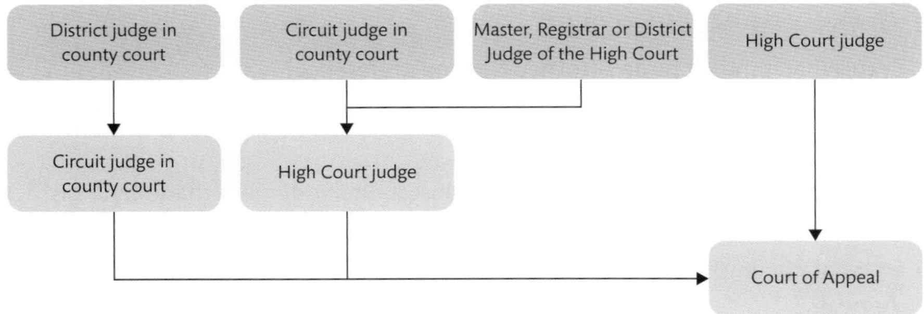

Diagram 18.2 Usual routes of appeal in civil cases

thus, neither the County Court nor the High Court may hear a second appeal (see art. 6 of the Access to Justice Act (Destination of Appeals) Order 2016 (SI 2016/917)).

A party may appeal against a decision of the Court of Appeal to the Supreme Court. In accordance with s.40 of the Constitutional Reform Act 2005, the leave of the Court of Appeal or that of the Supreme Court is required.

Summary

- From magistrates' courts, a defendant may appeal to the Crown Court or the High Court, or may apply to the High Court for judicial review.
- From the Crown Court, appeal normally lies to the Court of Appeal. However, certain Crown Court decisions may be appealed to the High Court or may be subject to judicial review by the High Court.
- When a defendant appeals against conviction following a Crown Court trial, the Court of Appeal will only allow the appeal if it deems the conviction to be 'unsafe'.
- The CCRC may refer cases to appellate courts.
- The Attorney General may refer a point of law to the Court of Appeal on behalf of the prosecution.
- The route of appeal in civil proceedings depends upon the nature of the decision to be appealed, the type of judge who made it, and the court in which it was made.
- Following an initial appeal to a County Court or the High Court, a 'second appeal' to the Court of Appeal may be possible in a civil case.

Questions

1 To which court(s) could a defendant appeal if convicted following summary trial and to which court(s) could a defendant appeal following trial on indictment?

2 (a)What is the role of the CCRC?

(b)What is meant by an Attorney General's reference?

3 What are the differences between an appeal by way of case stated and judicial review?

4 To which court may a party appeal against a final judgment made by a district judge in the County Court?

5 In what circumstances may a party to civil proceedings appeal to the Court of Appeal?

6 What powers do the different appellate courts possess in both criminal and civil proceedings?

Sample question and outline answer

Question

'The time has now come to acknowledge that [the Criminal Cases Review Commission] was an experiment that failed': Bob Woffinden, *The Guardian*, 30 November 2010.

Critically discuss the role of the CCRC and its effectiveness in rectifying miscarriages of justice.

Outline answer

Your introduction should identify any key terms and set out the issues to be addressed. In the context of this question, you should recognise the importance of the term 'miscarriages of justice' and explain that you will discuss whether the CCRC has been an effective mechanism for addressing such cases. Your answer should address the following issues.

First, outline what the term 'miscarriage of justice' means. There is no agreed definition of the term but Lord Phillips suggested four categories of case in which a miscarriage of justice could be said to have occurred (*R (Adams) v Secretary of State for Justice; In re MacDermott; In re McCartney* (2011)). The first three of these relate to cases in which fresh evidence is discovered. The fourth category refers to cases in which there was a serious flaw in the conduct of the investigation or trial.

You should provide some background information by discussing why the CCRC was set up. Refer to the high-profile wrongful convictions that finally persuaded the establishment that an independent body was needed to examine such cases and refer them back to the Court of Appeal where appropriate.

Before you can analyse the CCRC's performance, you need to outline the legal test that the CCRC must apply. The CCRC will refer a case if there is a 'real possibility' that the conviction would not be upheld by the Court of Appeal (Criminal Appeal Act 1995 s.13).

You can now discuss whether the CCRC is 'effective' or whether it is an 'experiment that failed'. Refer to the CCRC's own statistics, which indicate that a high proportion of cases that are referred result in successful appeals. Discuss whether these statistics are misleading. Given the number of applications that the CCRC has received, very few cases have been referred to the Court of Appeal. Reasons for this may include scarce resources resulting in significant delays. Discuss the recommendations of the Justice Committee in this regard.

The 'real possibility' test has also been criticised as it prevents the CCRC from forming a view itself as to whether a conviction ought to be overturned. Rather, the CCRC must consider what the Court of Appeal will do. This may be a particular problem given that appeals are only likely to be successful where there was an identifiable error or procedural irregularity, or where there is fresh evidence. One reason why applications to the CCRC rarely result in referral back to the Court of Appeal is that any mistakes of fact or law, or procedural flaws, will usually have been identified and dealt with at the applicant's original appeal. There is no real possibility of success before the Court of Appeal where an issue has already been considered. As the Runciman Commission observed, the Court of Appeal is reluctant to simply consider whether a jury made the wrong decision. The fairly recent case of *R v Pope* (2012) places further restrictions on the Court of Appeal's ability to allow an appeal solely on the ground of a lurking doubt about the safety of the conviction. The Justice Committee suggested consideration should be given to expanding the grounds upon which the Court of Appeal may allow an appeal against conviction.

In conclusion, you should state whether you agree that the CCRC is 'an experiment that failed'. Summarise the main issues that you have identified, including the lack of resources to enable the CCRC to investigate cases more expeditiously and the difficulties with the legal framework within which the CCRC must operate.

Further reading

Your wider reading should develop your understanding of the court hierarchy and grounds of appeal in both the civil and criminal justice systems. Focus on some of the controversial concepts found in the appeal system, such as 'lurking doubt', 'fresh evidence', and 'miscarriage of justice'.

- ***Blaxland, H.*** *'Sappers and Underminers: Fresh Evidence Revisited'* [2017] Crim LR 537

  Explains and critically analyses the jury impact test in light of recent case law.

- ***Elks, L.*** *'Righting Miscarriages of Justice? Ten Years of the Criminal Cases Review Commission'* (JUSTICE 2008)

  One of the first CCRC Commissioners analyses cases referred to the Court of Appeal by the CCRC and explains how miscarriages of justice are dealt with.

- ***Hoyle, C.*** *and* ***Sato, M.*** *Reasons to Doubt: Wrongful Convictions and the Criminal Cases Review Commission* (OUP 2019)

  Based on a four-year empirical study of decision-making at the CCRC, this book explores how the CCRC contributes to remedying miscarriages of justice. In addition to exploring the law on appeals, the authors discuss the practicalities of decision-making in the context of austerity and swingeing cuts to legal aid.

- ***Leigh, L.H.*** *'Lurking Doubt and the Safety of Convictions'* [2006] Crim LR 809

  Discusses the extent to which the Court of Appeal has allowed appeals against conviction solely on the ground of lurking doubt.

- *Report of the Royal Commission on Criminal Justice. (Cm 2263), Ch 10,* **www.official-documents.gov.uk/document/cm22/2263/2263.pdf**

  Explains the law prior to the Criminal Appeal Act 1995 and recommends that an independent body should be set up to rectify miscarriages of justice.

- *Report of the Justice Committee on the CCRC, Twelfth Report of Session 2014–15.* HC 850, **www.publications.parliament.uk/pa/cm201415/cmselect/cmjust/850/850.pdf**

  Discusses the work and effectiveness of the CCRC and whether it has fulfilled the expectations of the Royal Commission on Criminal Justice.

- ***Sjolin, C.*** *'Prosecution Appeals and References - Not Enough of a Good Thing?'* [2019] Crim LR 934

  Explains prosecution rights to appeal or refer cases to appellate courts. Analyses the exercise of these rights using statistics from 2006–2017.

- ***Taylor, P.*** *'R v Pope—Case Comment'* [2013] Crim LR 421

  Discusses whether the judgment in *R v Pope* unnecessarily restricts the concept of 'lurking doubt'.

- ***Woffinden, B.*** *'The Criminal Cases Review Commission has failed', The Guardian*, 30 November 2010, **www.guardian.co.uk/commentisfree/libertycentral/2010/nov/30/criminal-cases-review-commission-failed**

  Sets out criticisms of the CCRC and explains why the CCRC's published statistics are misleading.

- ***Zander, M.*** *'The Justice Select Committee's Report on the CCRC—Where do we go from here?'* [2015] Crim LR 473

  Summarises the key points raised by the Justice Committee's inquiry into the CCRC.

Online resources

You should now attempt the supporting self-test questions and end-of-chapter questions available at: **www.oup.com/he/wilson-rutherford4e**

Index

D

L

R

S